The Century's Midnight

Dissenting European and American Writers in the Era of the Second World War

Clive Bush

Peter Lang Oxford

First published in 2010 by

Peter Lang Ltd
International Academic Publishers
Evenlode Court, Main Road, Long Hanborough, Witney
Oxfordshire OX29 8SZ
United Kingdom

www.peterlang.com

A catalogue record for this book is available from the British Library

ISBN 978-1-906165-25-3

COVER ILLUSTRATION:
Jackson Pollock, *War* (1947), The Metropolitan Museum of Art, New York.
Gift of Lee Krasner Pollock, in memory of Jackson Pollock, 1982.
Image © The Metropolitan Museum of Art (1982.147.25).

Printed in the United Kingdom
by the MPG Books Group

For Edward C. Gallafent

Contents

Acknowledgements

It goes without saying that none of those mentioned below are responsible for the judgements and opinions expressed in this book.

A book of this nature is indebted to many people, and I apologize in advance to any whose names I will have inadvertently missed out. The many people who have helped me with permissions will be acknowledged in a separate section.

Various sabbatical leaves and fellowships have expedited the making of this book. I was in receipt of a Beinecke Fellowship in 1995, and visiting fellowships in the American Studies Department at Yale in 1999 and 2004. I am grateful to members of the English and American Studies Departments at King's College London for study leave in 1999 and 2004, and I gratefully acknowledge an AHRB award in 2004. My thanks also to the members of the Intellectual History Group, pioneered and supported by Richard King and Michael O'Brien, meeting twice a year, at Cambridge and the Universities of Sussex, Leicester, and Nottingham among others.

At King's College, London, I am indebted to the English Department, and to the staff and graduate students of the former American Studies Department. Among many graduate students over the years, I would like to mention Lacy Rumsey and Pedro Garcia-Caro who provided special help with this book. Elsewhere in Europe and for enduring friendship and intellectual support I must thank Enikő Bollobás who has energetically represented American culture in the best possible way at Eőtvős University in Budapest and who, on visits to Budapest, has been kindness itself. Ika and Gyula Kodolányi, formerly at the National Gallery and also at the English Department at Eőtvős, have remained staunch friends also over many years, and represent the best of central European artistic intelligence and humanistic learning. Gyula Kodolányi was a founder member of the Hungarian Democratic forum in 1987 and is a considerable poet. I thank him for our many conversations. On this side of the Atlantic, I am finally here indebted to my friend Patricia Kücklemann for introducing me to Arabic musical culture and literature, and whose energy and exuberant interests in matters artistic, political and cultural have provided the needed inspiration for the later stages of this book.

My first American debt is to Muriel Rukeyser, 'your Jewish mother', as she called herself when she became a close friend in the early 1970s, helping me not only through a very difficult period of my life but responding with enthusiasm to my first book, *The Dream of Reason*. Not only was the range of her intellectual work extraordinary, and her radical politics faithful to the end, but her best poetry had a rare capacity to touch the heart as well as the mind. It was she who introduced me to Lewis Mumford in 1973. I spent a memorable September day with him in 1973, only to return to my post at the University of Warwick, bitterly regretting I was unable to take up his offer to stay and talk for a week. There was plenty to talk about. He was intrigued and surprised that this very young Englishman knew something about his circle: Waldo Frank, Alfred Stieglitz, Georgia O'Keefe, Dorothy Norman, Hart Crane among dozens of others, had even read right through *Camera Work*, and had a passionate interest in the history of technology and architecture. My writing was to take me in many other and different directions, but this book must have started its journey at that point.

For any British scholar, the great American libraries and their always welcoming and enabling staff set a world standard in care for the researcher, and in library expertise. Their collections are unparalleled anywhere else in the world. At Yale, staff at Archives and Manuscripts in the Sterling Memorial Library have been unfailingly courteous and helpful, and at Beinecke where I have worked on and off for thirty-five years, the staff are a scholar's dream. From the time of Donald Gallup onwards it has been a pleasure to work there. Like many others I have been indebted to the knowledge, courtesy and good humour of Steve Jones. I would, however, mention in particular many kindnesses from, and conversations with, Patricia Willis who retired in 2008. Hundreds of scholars must be in her debt and it is a great privilege to be among them. One learns more in five minutes conversation with Patricia Willis, than in a month scouring catalogues. In the Special Collections, Van Pelt Library at the University of Pennsylvania, I would particularly like to thank John Pollack, and also Dan Traister whose personal kindness made my research there an absolute pleasure and whose passion for books has remained a permanent inspiration. The Manuscript Reading Room of the Library of Congress is again outstanding. A spirit of open democratic access and assistance is the general tone notwithstanding the priceless nature of the materials. In my time spent going through the Rukeyser papers, Frederick Bauman embodied that general tone to perfection.

I have also experienced much hospitality and general help during the course of this book. At the University of Pennsylvania which has a special programme at King's College, London, I am grateful for many different types of assistance from Loretta Williams, Al Filreis, Bob Perlman, Wendy Steiner, and I am especially in debt to Magreta da Grazia who in the summer of 2000, lent me her house (and piano). In Washington I am very grateful to Steve Want (and Merlin) for a wonderfully enjoyable stay during my research at the Library of Congress.

In Connecticut, long friendships endure with Joel Pfister and with Laura Manuelidis, erstwhile pupil of Muriel Rukeyser, poet and scientist. My friendship with Alan and Betty Trachtenberg goes back thirty-five years and more. Without Alan's support and encouragement of my work, I might well have faltered. I cannot thank him enough.

From 1995 to 2003 I had the enormous privilege of staying, at various times and for varying lengths of time, with my equally long-term friend Alison Richard and her husband Bob Dewar and daughters, Bessie and Charlotte, not to mention the late Hattie Williams, at the 'Provostry'. This book simply could not have been written without their generosity, hospitality, love and kindness and which was unfailing before, during and after, a major, near-fatal critical illness.

I must also thank my brother, Malcolm Bush, erstwhile head of the Woodstock Foundation in Chicago, now at the University of Chicago. For a lifetime Malcolm has kept his idealistic brother's political feet on the ground. I am grateful to his sophisticated, humanistic intelligence and above all his sense of humour. Much has been shared in the best fraternal way in the course of writing this book.

Finally this book is dedicated to Edward Gallafent whose friendship of many years has been the rarest of privileges in a wicked world.

PERMISSIONS

I wish to thank: the late Victor Kibalchich for permission to quote from the unpublished writings of Victor Serge; Santiago Vidal Kibalchich for a letter of Laurette Orfilo; William Rukeyser for the unpublished writings of Muriel Rukeyser; Robert Wojtowicz for the unpublished writings of Lewis Mumford; the estate of Michael Gold for unpublished writings of Michael Gold; and Elizabeth Sifton for the unpublished letters of Reinhold Niebhur. Quotations from letters of Hannah Arendt to Dwight Macdonald are reprinted by permission of Georges Borchardt, Inc., on behalf of the Estate of Hannah Arendt. The Yale Committee on Literary Property, which represents the Marsden Hartley Estate, has authorized quotations from Marsden Hartley's letters. Yale University library has authorized text from a letter of Dwight Macdonald. I wish to acknowledge Pollinger Ltd and the Estate of Frieda Lawrence Ravagli for permission to quote from D.H. Lawrence's unpublished correspondence. Unpublished writing by Henry Miller has been reproduced with permission of Curtis Brown Group Ltd, London, on behalf of the Estate of Henry Miller. Citations from the letters of Eric Mottram are printed with the permission of the Eric Mottram Collection, King's College, London. Quotations from letters of Anaïs Nin have been used with permission of the Anaïs Nin Trust. Citations from the unpublished letters of

Dorothy Norman have been authorized by the Center for Creative Photography, University of Arizona. Quotations from the letters of George Orwell (© George Orwell) are authorized by Bill Hamilton as the literary executor of the Estate of the late Sonia Brownell Orwell and Secker & Warburg Ltd. Citations from Eleanor Roosevelt's correspondence are in the public domain. Copyright in the unpublished writings of Frances G. Wickes held in the Library of Congress has been dedicated to the public. Unpublished material by William Carlos Williams is from The Previously Unpublished Material, © 2008 by Paul H. Williams and the Estate of William Eric Williams, used by permission of New Directions Publishing Corp. I have been unable to trace concerned literary executors for Ivy Litvinov and Michael Fraenkel.

Without repeating life in imagination you can never be fully alive: 'lack of imagination' prevents people from 'existing'. 'Be loyal to the story.' As one of her [Isak Dinesen's] storytellers admonishes the young, 'be eternally and unswervingly loyal to the story,' means no less than, Be loyal to life, don't create fiction but accept what life is giving you, show yourself worthy of whatever it may be by recollecting and pondering over it, thus repeating it in imagination; this is the way to remain alive. And to live in the sense of being fully alive had early been and remained to the end her only aim and desire. 'My life, I will not let you go except you bless me, but then I will let you go.' The reward of storytelling is to be able to let go: 'When the storyteller is loyal [...] to the story, there, in the end, silence will speak. Where the story has been betrayed, silence is but emptiness. But we, the faithful, when we have spoken our last word, will hear the voice of silence.'

Hannah Arendt

Introduction: Lighting the Circle

> Vous tendez une allumette à votre lampe et ce qui s'allume n'éclaire pas. C'est loin, très loin de vous, que le cercle illumine.
>
> — RENÉ CHAR[1]

> Do you not see how necessary a World of Pains and Troubles is to School an Intelligence and make it a Soul?
>
> — JOHN KEATS[2]

Opening the Field

This book is about time, memory and writing. It ranges from the poet to the historian, from the writer of fiction to the cultural commentator. It touches not only the ambiguous clarity of the cool prose of the historian, but also the metaphorically rich indirection of the poet. Our sense of time stretches from the indifferent eternity of the cosmos to the calendars of the powerful and the superstition of the horoscope. It involves the terror of mortality and forgetfulness, the strangely intimate eternity of love, the trans-temporal permanence of ethical value, the *longue durée* of the biologist and geologist, the eschatological fictions and rituals of religious faith, and the haunting of involuntary memory in the psychologically distressed. Memory and its sense of time involves not only the past but answers to present need and to our hopes for the future. There can be no sense of the past without a sense of the future and both are linked to a present that is as fleeting as it is ungraspable.

Memory can be denied, traduced and rejected, as well as provide a sustaining richness for that reciprocity and recognition of the self as honestly acknowledging its own life in that finite and concrete moment of historical time in which, contingently, it finds itself. It can be fought over, betrayed and lied about, as well as imaginatively evoked and loved. From ideology to religion and psychology, from a representation of the past in the epic and historical narrative to the most intimate of human arguments, a story is required: 'but you said this, what do you mean by it?' The recalled story ranges in its implications from the political to the personal, from the public to the private. Time and story are signalled in the fossil, the archaeological fragment, architecture: the very marks, industrial and agricultural, of human activity on the landscape itself.

In the great mystery of writing itself, the inscribed trace offers a world for critical thought, and articulates that world in a variety of forms: the intimate diary, the historical account, every genre of narrative from the folk tale to the fictional and poetic masterpiece. A tale of memory and time even haunts the activity of the scientist, who daily needs to test, supersede and challenge what has gone before. An almost eschatological faith is needed that the truth will emerge. Even here, where the art of forgetting may play an equally important role, perhaps at its most imaginative, a sense of the scientific past may help reframe abstract questions that have persisted for centuries. It is writing that extends and enriches in so many complex ways the story of our human sense of presence in the world itself. Many commentators from old and new philosophers, to the historian, poet and artist will assist the story offered in this book, a story which is in fact a web of many stories. It will show ways in which a small number of very determined, sensitive and gifted men and women responded to a terrible moment of human history in ways that may remind us of the best of human strength and imaginative possibilities of cooperation in the worst of times.

In more specific terms the story told here addresses a tumultuous historical period in Europe, the United States and far beyond, roughly from the end of the 1930s through to the end of the 1940s. It will not, however, relate familiar stories of battles, military technological advance, ideologies in conflict, nor narrate simply of those who survived and those who did not, who won and who lost. Nor will it focus on those legitimating narratives of coercion and action offered by radio, films, newspapers or 'documentary' descriptions. In this book we shall not specifically address the well-known images of the Japanese emperor surrendering, of the detritus around Hitler's bunker, of the bodies in the concentration camp, of the dancing in Trafalgar Square, nor catch a glimpse of Churchill's cigar, nor watch the battle around Stalingrad, the opening guns at El Alamein and Guadalcanal, nor contemplate again that photograph of the victorious leaders at Yalta in all its slyness and ambiguity. Here there will be no visual recall of American women in munitions factories, no 'Rosie the riveter', no heroic communist gathering in the harvest, no miraculous stories of escape, nor shots of rollered-up hair, nylons, flowered broad-lapelled dresses, lindy-hopping couples in or out of uniform, nor serried ranks of soldiers listening to Vera Lynn.

All these visual iconographic moments can be starting points for more profound investigations but perhaps they are almost too familiar. The sense of life this book uncovers will emerge in contradistinction to the world offered by endlessly run black-and-white films and documentaries, some now retrieved almost uncannily in colour as if that sped time forward to our own day or we back to it, almost authenticating 'greater' immediacy and 'more' relevance. This is certainly not to say the impact of visual culture will be ignored, this story by implication is juxtaposed with it. However, with one very important exception, this book will not address those images whose implied narratives haunt the 'history' television programme and the apparently self-validating black-and-white documentary, all of which seem to offer a period transparency coeval with truth itself. Their ubiquitous wallpaper-like presence haunts our contemporary lives like retro furniture, antiques shows and programmes recalling television 'decades'. On a Memorial Day weekend I once sat in a crowded waiting area in Philadelphia Airport with Orwellian television screens endlessly rerunning black-and-white Second World War combat newsreel. No one took the slightest notice of them as grandparents (veterans included) complained about delays and young parents concentrated on keeping their babies and children in reasonable order. The stories of time and the ways in which we are presented with them are a problem that contemporary commercial practice seems to betray at every turn.

If the judgement about the ubiquity of these images seems exaggerated, in the *Radio Times*, a British television and radio guide, in this specific week of writing, without any special commemorative Second World War event, the National Geographic, UKTV History and History channels sent out roughly one hundred programmes dedicated to the Second World War, that is, on average fourteen per day. There were eleven ordinary programmes dealing with some aspect of the war, and it would have been possible during the week to see around a dozen Second World War films.[3] Of course even within the list of iconic events, endlessly reinforced by these programmes that rarely investigate the longer history or the causes behind what is essentially assumed to be a 'naïve' record of fateful contingent incidents, there would be a place for other events: a counter iconography and different images. Hospitals for the insane or permanently crippled thirty years after the war might be shown or perhaps documentaries of the 1944–5 famines in Bengal and Vietnam that claimed four million un-remarked lives in the chaos of the collapsing European empires. Memory is political in its endless recreation or obliteration of events that determine precisely what is permitted to be remembered by the dominant ideological power. Current awareness of the respective twentieth-century holocausts of the Armenians and Jews is a classic case in point. Who now remembers the fate of the Spanish refugees in France in the Second World War? Much as the lives of ordinary people in wartime are continually investigated, recorded, broadcast or written up, they stay detached from the fuller political story, remaining empathetic instances of isolated biography, stumbling inarticulacies which cannot but powerfully move us while distancing the deep questions. What slow- and fast-moving patterns of economics, geography, politics, cultural memory, biology, and social and anthropological shapes bear on any individual story?

Why should we not, as Paul Fussell has done, call it all 'wartime' and treat it as a fundamentally gambling narrative of fate, irony, 'human nature', military luck, superstition and fateful drifts of technological development? We might then employ a witty yet profoundly cynical *Catch-22*-style humour against the high and mighty, the bumbling generals, the incompetent conscienceless politicians and the scavenging black-marketeers, accompanied by a refined melancholy, delicately relieved by the nicer sort of British literature, self-reflecting poetic lyricism, and be grateful to all the mothers who sent socks?[4] Life as we all know is 'unfair'. 'As the universal thump is passed round', declared Melville's Ishmael in *Moby-Dick*, all hands should rub each other's shoulder-blades and be content'[5]

This view of the world at war has the considerable advantage of its pragmatic, ultimately sardonic and self-reflexive ironic vision, directed to keeping the spirits up; a practical resource for ordinary individual survival. As such it is far from negligible. Because, however, it is finally a satiric mode, it is necessarily conservative. It assumes that success and survival are paramount. It does not touch the meaning of genuine personal sacrifice and courage, it does not investigate specific cause and responsibility, the relation of belief to engagement (the one rarely endorses the other) nor does it invite a pre-history nor imagine a future. Neither past nor future appear in its relentless present of ethical irony. Here the hero's actions have one point, to expose the intrinsic sentimentality of any ethical position and to stake a claim that these actions can only be validated by pure success in a world in which the capitalist entrepreneur's invisibility and irresponsibility have replaced the hero's glory.

Fussell's satiric mode, with its genuine sense of anguish and melancholy (that 'gloom' of the Tory satirist) inflects the very structure and meaning of the history he offers. His common-sense worldly seriousness is as relentless as Joseph Heller's famous *Catch-22*. This book, however, will look for generic modes of truth beyond that of either satire or black humour. In a counter, or perhaps more generously a parallel, critical movement, this book will be about the very 'soul' of the person under duress, as revealed and communicated in writing – that deeper experience of the inner life suffered as a result of external circumstances – and will oppose a too-swift characterization of internal and external reality and the relation between them. At the heart of the problem is an unresolvable mystery. As Jean-Paul Sartre wrote: 'Simply put there is an outside on the inside, an outside that is perpetually regrasped. It is this relationship of outside and inside that makes the event escape each and every one of us.'[6]

In the towering mid-*nineteenth*-century masterpiece *Moby-Dick*, it is Melville's wandering sailor-narrator, Ishmael, the ironically placed doyen of the ordinary working man whose naïve common sense invites satiric distance, who is finally seen to be part of a much more complex story. His experience of the Fussellian 'universal thump' is set in the more problematic world of the novel itself whose rehearsal and comparison of many existential interpretive discourses and narratives of human power-relations open up a profound and tragic sense of the human being and the world, a richer and more engaging view that invites the seriousness of mourning, contemplation, and a quest for intelligibility against a nihilism of pure survival and fate. Melville's great work is a cry of rage against the compulsory truth of 'wartime'. Like us he lived in and reflected upon a time of ideological melt-down, industrial and technological hazard, the brutal treatment of workers and capital's indifference to locality in its relentless mixing of traditions, religions and ethnicities in its search for a cheap workforce and its destruction of nature by remote and invisible investment. It was also a time of the 'failure' of the grand political and religious narratives and of a new awareness of human inessentiality in a dehumanized universe operating in cosmic indifferent time. Fussell's influential populist conservative thesis raises none of those issues and his argument will be looked at later and his idea of 'fate' examined rather more sharply. Perhaps indeed we are more preoccupied with survival than mourning.[7] This book nonetheless will turn that priority on its head, for mourning (not necessarily overwhelming and passive) fundamentally engages a story of the past, memory, telling and speaking to others, while defining a future, a thought-through presence-in-absence that must shape our lives. In more senses than one, there seems to be no time for the past.

In any case the past is not ever, as G.K. Chesterton once wittily remarked, what it used to be, a sentiment vigorously endorsed in rather different tones and terms by that other 'Catholic' thinker Simone Weil. In her book *The Need for Roots* which has, along with several other works to be addressed shortly, profoundly influenced this study, Weil recognized that 'history' is 'a tissue of base and cruel acts in the midst of which a few drops of purity sparkle at long intervals.'[8] History is of course mainly written by the victors, and much of the rest of humanity is ignored, hence: 'We must love the past which is inarticulate, anonymous, which has vanished.'[9]

Against this more difficult and strenuous narrative, is ranged a very active 'evil': the political and social enforcement of mediocre memory:

> The transmission of spurious greatness down the centuries is not peculiar to history. It is a general law, and governs equally well, for example, literature and the other arts. There is a certain domination of literary talent over the centuries which corresponds to the domination of political talent in space; they are forms of domination of a like kind, equally temporal, equally attached to the realm of matter and force, equally base. They can, furthermore, form the subject of sale or exchange in the open market.[10]

In populist culture, not to mention the overstocked academic 'market' that now dominates nearly all serious production and reception, there is a fundamental suspicion of what used to be called the value judgement: the basic notion that some things are worth more attention than others. It is not necessary to sign up to all of Weil's often sweeping and sometimes blindly wrong judgements to see the usefulness of the above words in countering that spurious anti-elitism, often carrying with it a kind of absolutist endorsement of the contemporary moment. For Weil the past had to be 'grown', and, to continue the conceit, weeded out, to discover the flower that blushed unseen. A creative memory of the past, fearless of fashion, was for her a condition of the 'human soul' itself, a phrase that of course had little meaning in the secular therapeutic or Marxist vision. Her argument ultimately comes down to a question of the perception of time and narrative and how the latter delivers an account of the former in the human heart itself.

For Weil the need for the past was primary. Memory was a condition of the human itself. Telling the story of the past, however, is not easy. From the right the past is always threatened by conservatives who tend to think that they know exactly what it is. This is a past that never changes. It becomes an exemplary point, the forward movement from which is always downwards. For the left, it must be rearranged in terms of a narrative closure that characterizes a collective future on the basis of a fundamental rupture with the past.[11]

So this book is in many ways about the inner lives of people compelled under pressure to make sense of their often-strenuous political engagement in the external world when every ideological security was in doubt, and where that world was falling apart. The 'forgotten' voices are highly educated (by various routes), though not necessarily *a priori* privileged, and they are sensitive people who almost instinctively think outside received wisdom. They have in common a certain integrity that rises above prejudice of nation, class, economic inheritance and dogma. Many of them were more or less in touch with, or apprised of, each other. To that extent this book provides some surprising biographical connections. They come from diverse countries: Poland, Russia, England, France, Croatia, Italy, Spain, Germany, India, the United States and Mexico. Effectively it was the political events of the 1930s that threw them together as a 'global' group, loosely co-existing like flotsam and jetsam in a whirlpool during and after the storm. They were in communication with each other by 'war-time' Atlantic shipping, flying boats, and the proto-McLuhanesque world of the postal service, radio and telegrams. Writing, for them, was not a logo-centric illusion but a means of action and a quest for intelligibility at the political, social and personal levels. What they wrote rehearsed a sense of themselves in worlds whose meanings engaged politics, science, technology, literature, art, philosophy, religion and metaphysics.

In addition to the five main individuals examined here (Victor Serge, Dwight Macdonald, Dorothy Norman, Lewis Mumford and Muriel Rukeyser), two further thinkers in particular have influenced the following pages. The first is the late French philosopher Paul Ricoeur, especially his magisterial work *Time and Narrative*. The second is Hannah Arendt, along with her circle, but while it is her thoughts on narrative and time that have been highlighted, these cannot simply be connected with her general views on politics. Ricoeur's general approach and insights have been foundational, though I have chosen not to follow the French analytical style, preferring a less philosophically oriented and more discursive mode of critical and cultural analysis whose terminus and justification is finally the risk of personal judgement in the closely read text.

Until pointed out by a colleague and friend, I had not realized consciously that four of the five selected figures were Jewish. On reflection this is not surprising, given my own roots in dissenting Protestantism. Primo Levi in his novel *If Not Now, When?*, a retrospective story of the Russian, Polish and Jewish partisans trapped behind enemy lines during the Second World War, noted that the 'Ukrainian Baptists, despised and persecuted by both Germans and Russians ... had good relations with the Jews.'[12] 'Jewish' is of course, like 'Baptist' no *a priori* guide either to truth or political authenticity, especially given the current manic and violent nationalism of both these groups in Israel and America. Nonetheless, at their best and in better times (one thinks of Rosa Luxemburg or Martin Luther King), they have historically offered a common radical tradition of seriousness and intellectual engagement, not to mention resistance to the excesses of political power. As the radical Freudian writer Norman O. Brown once said in an introduction to his work *Life Against Death*, summing up the mid-century's ideological chaos and the defeats of the liberal thought of the 1930s and 1940s:

> Inheriting from the Protestant tradition a conscience which insisted that intellectual work should be directed towards the relief of man's estate, I, like so many of my generation, lived through the superannuation of the political categories which informed liberal thought and activities in the 1930s. Those of us who are temperamentally incapable of embracing the politics of sin, cynicism, and despair have been compelled to re-examine the class assumptions about the nature of politics and about the political character of human nature.[13]

The best of radical Jewish thought as this book demonstrates is very close to the invocation of a legacy outlined here. All the writers examined in this book are part of that historical 're-examination'.

In terms of the general critical approach, the narrative worlds of the writers under consideration contribute traditions of thought and analysis that can be reread heuristically both for their own work and for the work of others. For example the book will engage with novelists and journalists such as the English George Orwell, the Italian Ignazio Silone and the Russian Boris Pilniak, together with the Croatian-Italian autobiographical writer and journalist Anton Ciliga, among many others. These occupy a minor but significant role alongside the writers and editors under major review: Serge, Macdonald, Norman, Mumford and Rukeyser. Their work invites insights outside formal analytic discourse but remains of inestimable critical value. Two questions hence arise. What are the further parameters of the field proposed here and why have these people been selected? Second, what kind of 'cultural history' is offered and on what critical basis?

First and foremost, these are dissenting voices of varying political sophistication and insight. Their political ideologies range from the Polish-Russian ex-Bolshevik Victor Serge, via the American and disillusioned Trotskyite Dwight Macdonald, to the American radical conservative Lewis Mumford, the liberal centrist Rooseveltian democrat Dorothy Norman, and finally to the more left-leaning but non-Marxist Muriel Rukeyser. Second, they are all people displaced intellectually, and in Serge's case geographically, by the early twentieth century's cataclysms that shook the world from Russia to Germany, Italy and Spain, which terminated, albeit temporarily, in the Second World War. Third, they remain related to but occupy a critical position outside the then main parameters of current ideological contention: Marxism, fascism and capitalism. Nonetheless, their thought and actions are of great significance in offering a clear-eyed, politically sophisticated and ethically sensitive response to a world in ideological and political chaos, a world in which the major countries of Europe, and later Japan, experienced autocratic barbarity on a scale not witnessed before, even in the wars of religion from the Crusades to those in sixteenth- and seventeenth-century Europe, in the wars of succession, in the Napoleonic wars or in even in the First World War. The writers in this work are crucial for current memory, notwithstanding the fact that their public visibility in their own time varied from the considerable (Mumford) to the virtually non-existent (Serge, Rukeyser).

One way or another nearly all of them knew of, or were in touch with each other across divisions of language, nation, theoretical political position, and class. They formed a loosely knit transnational intelligentsia with many lateral connections with other refugees, both well-known (Brecht, for example) and obscure. For many who come under attention in this book were stateless refugees with prices on their heads who had the luck to fall in with old-fashioned democratic Americans minded to assist them in spite of a far-right-wing State Department that had cancelled the admission to America of German Jewish refugees in 1941. All of them had been sympathetic to early twentieth-century socialist movements, were strongly anti-imperialist and sceptical of unfettered free-market capitalism. They were initially buoyed up by the hope of the 1917 Russian revolution but were rapidly, and long before most, disillusioned, honestly preferring the truth about Stalin to lying for the sake of loyalty to a violently betrayed cause.

A fourth shared characteristic was their internationalism: an internationalism framed neither by the grand narrative of the dictatorship of the proletariat nor by the consumerist heaven of a world in which the benefits of life had 'trickled down' equitably to the entire world by the natural working out of the 'market'. It was an internationalism forced into action by the contingent events of the mid-century, but prepared for by independent intelligence based on certain shared historic traditions of political practice, cultural legacy, and theory. Any dogmatic edge that might have initially structured any of their thinking post-1917–18 was taken off by their commitment to the more complex world of literature, intelligent religious practice, sophisticated journalism and the arts. The grand political narrative was accompanied, softened, repudiated, or occasionally reinforced by a deep concern for the nature of the person outside conventional politics and political dogma, left or right.

Theirs was the complex vision of the world offered by the serious writer who could variously draw on whatever insights might be usable from Marxism, Christianity, or post-Weberian theoretical analyses of a social-democratic kind. It was also a vision in which the inner life of the person, intelligent analysis of traditions of politics and ethics, and the freedom of the multiply oriented active individual life were radical testing sites for assessing the nature and direction of historical patterns of power and political practice in the external world. For all of these thinkers, despite frequent accusations of exactly this, it was not a simple passage from disillusioned politics to a generalized ethics. The practice of politics remained the final reason for ethics and ethical practice the final judge of politics.

The evidence of the following pages will demonstrate once and for all that their dissenting voices within the historical parameters and opportunities offered to them did not represent a withdrawal from the real world. Many of the people in the pages of Macdonald's and Norman's journals (*politics* and *TWICE A YEAR*, which are the subjects of parts two and three of this book) had been tortured or imprisoned by power regimes of left and right, or racially abused for their beliefs, the colour of their skin or for their refusal to accept autocratic practices from the deep South of America to the Soviet Union, Nazi Germany, Fascist Spain and Imperial British India. Their lives and works offer hope and encouragement to the equally internationally violent twenty-first century, where no ideology seems plausible and barbaric evangelical power in the 'Muslim' and 'Christian' worlds is on the increase, to the despair of the apparently powerless genuine Muslims and Christians. Unscrupulous polarization by entrenched power always precedes actual war.

At the current time, unthinking nationalist populism again seems unstoppable. Until Barack Obama recently ushered in a new and fragile hope, this populism was aided and abetted by a United States whose leaders seemed completely contemptuous of international treaties and hostile to the United Nations and whose use of international law was unscrupulously selective in the United States' own interests, whose militaristic brutality in the name of 'democracy' was a scandal. With Russia also 're-Stalinizing', the lives and works of the people in this book are worth recalling. They provide a remarkable example of how to live without disillusionment, neurotic apathy and cynical fatalism, of how to remain active, creative, politically responsible and un-self-pitying in the scarcity of any believable organized official politics, long destroyed by the white noise of 'post-modern' hyper-reality. Necessarily a highly selective group, all of the people under discussion here have multiple links with greater or lesser-known people of the period. The arguments here, though they engage with individual biography, generalized intellectual history, straight history, fiction, poetry and analyses of historical cultural and intellectual shifts, not to mention contemporary critical theory, are framed somewhat differently from those generally offered by these familiar generic practices.

The selection of topics has in part been generated by the discovery of internal links in the process of research. The overall picture given here claims neither to be comprehensive nor definitive, nor does it attempt to cover its period in any complete or representative way. It aims to illuminate by a sharp and deep focus particular moments of dissent from received literary and political practice and to favour no national perspective. The writers were often in touch with each other, and when possible supported each other, renewing and attempting to think through the best of the thought of the past in relation to their contemporary moment. In more social-political terms, these people anticipate the world of non-profit organizations and NGOs, Amnesty International, aid organizations and the work of radical lawyers, but they were essentially writers and many were much more directly and generally politically engaged than these contemporary organizations are permitted to be. In addition, every subject under review in this book had to cope with an Orwellian collapse of the traditions of reliable critical discourse, whether Marxist or capitalist, as they affected the writing of history and literature. Since they were creative writers and not for the most part political philosophers, the discourses examined are synthetic, inclusive and variously descriptive rather than analytic as such.

In some senses, to borrow a phrase, it is a complex fate to be an Englishman, a 'European', in the early twenty-first century, writing about the relationship between 'America' and 'Europe' in the middle of the previous century and especially at the present time. Some of the implications of that position will be taken up again in the text. The words 'America' and 'Europe' are in inverted commas because what follows will show that in all countries there is a spectrum of national definition that runs from the patriotism that Dr Johnson famously called 'the last refuge of a scoundrel' to a sense of a country in a creative narrative memory of local pride, that involves an ongoing fight for real democratic practice within its own traditions, that demonstrates an inclusive and generous perspective towards those who live outside its boundaries and that is finally respectful of the cultures and beliefs of others. It is exemplary practices of the latter in all their complexity that form the subject of this book. The stories offered are of ways in which people fought crisis with political intelligence, ethical probity, courage, a care for and recognition of others, and last but not least, bold, practical help that ignored all statist boundaries and divisions. The aim of the book is to create new memories from old, to take seriously Weil's insight that the past has to be fought for and lifted above that level of mediocrity with which it is inevitably presented.

The first section of this book deals with the case of Victor Serge, novelist and journalist, Polish-Jewish refugee, ex-Bolshevik and finally ex-Trotskyite. He fled revolutions turned sour in the early part of the twentieth century, saw fascism triumph in Spain, was hunted by Nazis through France and miraculously escaped finally to Cárdenas's Mexico, leaving behind him a record of inestimable value of the turmoil of the first half of the twentieth century, of the small people of decency and articulate intelligence crushed first by Stalin, then Franco and finally by Hitler. His novels, written under impossible conditions take us far beyond pure documentary. He worked to a degree in new narrative and symbolic modes, fully aware of the possibilities of fictional modernism whether practised by an André Gide or a John Dos Passos. His autobiography *Memoirs of a Revolutionary*, unpublished in his lifetime, is still one of the unsung masterpieces of the twentieth century. The writing is a great work of mourning and testimony, and it is offered here because of his extraordinary correspondence with the American libertarian thinker, journalist and editor Dwight Macdonald and his wife Nancy Macdonald who created, in New York, a supportive international community of European refugee writers and American dissenters in a moment of global war. Serge's own work created a memory that touched on the long history of pre-revolutionary Russia, a world that was not only generated by the Marxist tradition, but by other writers and beliefs, from the Old Believers to Pushkin, Herzen, Bakunin, the utopian dreamer Chernyshevsky and all that the brilliant Italian scholar Franco Venturi has written of in his work of creative scholarship that itself reads like Russian novel: *Roots of Revolution: A History of the Populist and Socialist Movements in 19th Century Russia* (1952; translated into English in 1960). In the creative moments that all too briefly followed 1917, these traditions were present in the writings of Pilniak and many other novelists and poets, often friends of Serge, who were to perish under Stalin.

The next two sections deal with two journals and the narrative worlds they created. They will be treated holistically, in spite of being obviously multi-voiced and multi-authored. The first is Macdonald's *politics*. The conjuncture of many writers and refugees in that journal was an exchange of different worlds, cemented by clear-eyed political intelligence and ethical probity. The emphasis here is on its international, mainly European, correspondents. It is not intended simply to review the narrative of the international connections, which has already been done elsewhere, but to use that narrative to create a further one by looking at selected writing of some of those correspondents that an alert reader of the paper in the 1940s might have been directed towards; in other words to explore the world of further texts that the journal opened up. To read Ciliga or Silone at that time was a valuable American experience, a practical demonstration of America's foundation in multiple cultures, together with its best traditions of openness and unprejudiced inclusiveness. It offered, for an American, a sense that there were achievements and memories that would outlast the crisis, and remind people of a Europe that had resisted Stalin, Hitler and Franco, while not forgetting that the resistance had been difficult and had often failed even with the best of people, including Silone himself. For there is a sense in which the Macdonalds were creating an international textual world of intelligent resistance and hope within the boundaries of the only major country that was not (after Pearl Harbor) seriously depleted by the actual war itself. From a European perspective, to recall these Americans selflessly and energetically devoting all their skills and natural flair for organization in seemingly intractable circumstances, tirelessly assisting at ground level so many desperate Europeans, still has the power to move the spirit half a century on.

So, too, with Dorothy Norman's journal, *TWICE A YEAR*, examined in the third section of the book. While the achievement of *politics* is beginning to be recognized, a deafening silence still surrounds this remarkable journal, one of the finest in mid-twentieth-century American culture. Norman is not perhaps 'left' enough for those who would normally seek her out and perhaps also she is too embarrassingly upper-class. She certainly had no obvious roots in a left tradition. Yet her journal published many of the figures also published in *politics*, including Muriel Rukeyser, Richard Wright, Jean-Paul Sartre and Simone de Beauvoir. Her own aim was to celebrate the new American liberal-radical culture that had grown up around the famous American photographer Alfred Stieglitz and his circle in the early twentieth century. Polemical as they were about a newly independent American culture, they saw themselves as part of and heirs to that remarkable flowering of European science and art in the later years of the nineteenth century and early years of the twentieth century up to 1914: the world of the post-impressionists, the new architecture, the new music, the new science and the new push for enfranchising working people. Consequently, and even paradoxically, they embraced that tradition, searching for new syntheses and inspiration for their American art. Norman herself opposed British imperialism in India, published records of American labour negotiations, provided information about the founding of the United Nations and the Bretton Woods Agreement, kept as sharp a watch as Macdonald on civil liberties and insisted that art and politics demanded the same intelligence, fearlessness and commitment. She was also a fine photographer.

TWICE A YEAR, therefore, will be read here in a similar fashion to *politics*. It will be examined both for its own content and as an index to some of the other works of the writers that it published. These include selected writings by, for example, Henry Miller, Ignazio Silone and the autobiographical memories of the Pandit daughters in exile from war and British imperialism in India, who were in part cared for in their exile by Norman and other American well wishers. Again, as with the previous two sections, the international nature of the *TWICE A YEAR* world will be emphasized, as well as Norman's insistence on creating a new past for Americans themselves by reprinting new translations from Proust, the modernist writer most concerned with memory, time and narrative. She also aimed to bring back to attention the very best of American radical thought by republishing essays by Randolph Bourne.

The fourth section of the book deals again with a single figure: Lewis Mumford. Mumford was a close friend of Norman and Stieglitz, and the greatest of twentieth-century American cultural historians. He is vital to the argument of this book for two reasons: the first is, against popular American instinct, he insisted upon the continuity and the necessity of a renewable past as a vital guide to the present and future. Second he was widely aware of international politics, a rarity in the traditionally inward-looking and isolationist America of the early twentieth century. Mumford is a well-known figure; his many works on American art and architecture, technology, the history of the city and his interests in early twentieth-century regional development have received much commentary and deservedly much praise. The approach taken here is a little different. The section concentrates on the Lewis Mumford of the 1930s and 1940s, on his actual political work and on perhaps the least-read of his work, *The Condition of Man* (1944), which came out to respectful rather than enthusiastic reviews. In it Mumford densely reviewed, from the ancient world onwards, the entire European cultural and social past. As the war ended it was a multiple and generous gesture that offered mourning, a reassessment of strength and a linking of the best of the past through the present to a promise of the future. It was a tribute to the strength of European culture at the moment of its greatest depletion and crisis, an invitation to Americans to look at it again, and to share it as intimately linked, in all its complexity with the deep roots of their own culture. This has never been a popular stance in the United States. Cultural apologists from the late eighteenth century onwards have always stressed the need to 'free' themselves from 'Europe' and promote themselves by absolute difference. 'Eurocentrism', as a current American academic term of cultural negativity, is the latest twist in this two-hundred-year-old tale and will be examined later. It is now, rather ironically, the name the Americans give to American racism and to American class and colour prejudice.

The last figure is Muriel Rukeyser, a friend of the Mumfords and of Dorothy Norman. She was widely known in the late 1930s and early 1940s for her political activism as a journalist and as a poet. Currently she is receiving increasing attention mainly by critics on the left who write on her early work and political activity in the 1930s. The aim here is to extend that picture into the 1940s and show that while her direct political activism continued in various forms for the rest of her life, her poetry cannot fully be understood entirely within a 1930s

American leftist tradition. While loyally writing, like the African-American novelist Richard Wright, up to and including the very early 1940s, for the widely read communist publication *New Masses*, it was clear from what she actually wrote in her articles and reviews for that paper, she was already in strong dissent from communist literary orthodoxy. Her fleeting experience in Catalonia at the outbreak of the civil war in Spain pushed her rapidly towards an Orwellian position on the effects of Stalinist activity in that war.

It is her sense of the past, her sense of the importance of the story that marks her out for attention here. Like all the other writers in this book, she reflected deeply on the nature of the way the past is remembered. The two biographies that she wrote are both of scientific figures: one at the beginning of the scientific revolution, Thomas Hariot who accompanied Raleigh to the New World; the other, the Yale mathematician Willard Gibbs who lived in the late nineteenth century.[14] Neither were, or are, household names yet both, as they emerge from their buried lives in her narrative, become indispensable keys to the modern world.[15] The focus here, however, is on her series of poems entitled *Elegies*, written from the late 1930s to the late 1940s. These will partly be examined within the terms of her own poetics that show poetry's own deployment of ways that deal with the human experience of time in relation to the inner and outer life, and with the private and public spheres.

These are the broad parameters of the themes and content of the book that follows. A few words, however, must be said about the way in which the subject will be approached with its overarching theme of writing, time and memory.

Stories of Time

The nature of the story of time has been most abstractly analysed in Paul Ricoeur's *Time and Narrative*.[16] Nonetheless it ends with a moving and less than analytically inflected reading of Proust's *À la recherche du temps perdu*. The following narrative owes much to his work but prefers a less abstract critical discourse. In the spirit of that work, however, 'plot' is assumed to be a profoundly human activity that stretches from the borders of logic to metaphysics. For all the analytical complexity, 'plots' operate in a very practical field of the agent and suffering victim. They begin a dialogue between the time-bound nature of inner and outer experience in history itself. It is this dialogue that the book seeks to illustrate and analyse.

Within the 'structural identity' of the narrative function itself is, also, the human experience as such. The very way in which we tell the story of the tragedy of the human condition becomes a 'poetic solution to the paradox of time'.[17] Meditating on the 'external' analysis of plots in Aristotle, and the 'internal' world of St Augustine's *Confessions*, and influenced by Heidegger's magnum opus *Being and Time* (which deals so profoundly with the experience of time in relation to anguish), Ricoeur makes the story crucial to our deeply personal and subjective sense of being in the world. The story, with its ability to engage with and transcend the formal methodologies of psychology, sociology, and purely historical or anthropological discourse, as well as analytic thought and the formal moves of social and political analysis, becomes the very heart of human experience. In a move which will be crucial when reading Muriel Rukeyser, Ricoeur argued, for example, that 'Poetic texts speak of a world, even though they may not do so in a descriptive fashion.'[18] That world is 'the whole set of references opened up by every sort of description or poetic text I have read, interpreted and loved'.[19] But Ricoeur does not abandon us to some sort of never-never land of the imagination. Reviewing many authorities, Ricoeur insisted that 'fictive time is never quite cut off from lived time, the time of memory and of action'.[20] His aim is to push life and literature towards an almost unbearable intimacy. At its most intense, life is profoundly delivered in art, even while the intervention of a clearly irrecoverable past and our experience of death will never let us forget that absolute disjuncture that haunts the pairing. Ricoeur is at his best with Proust. The experience of time lost and regained are to be understood together in the French master's fictional world, for it is not time that is at stake but truth.[21] Literature becomes a way of regaining the lost impression of memory itself, a revision that itself, in Proust's words, brings the 'joy of rediscovering what is real'.[22] Art goes beyond history by the very nature of its eternal present, yet history too approaches art in this respect, in its remembrance of the dead.[23]

Proust's *À la recherche du temps perdu*, recalled by Dorothy Norman to American attention, leaves us less with a sense of the terror of loss and dissolution, than with an experience of the world it creates: a narrated world offered for slow, imaginative reading, a world of people in failure and anguish, voluntary and involuntary cruelty and manipulation. It is unsparing in its depiction of carelessness and selfishness, of the cruel contradictions of its historical, class and societal moment. These moments are inflected both by great historical events and, in gender terms, by wayward manipulations of desire. A surprising warmth is generated towards even the worst of others, for their helplessness is exposed as a version of ourselves. Furthermore the work lingers. No one expressed that feeling better than Conrad on Henry James:

> One is never set at rest by Mr. Henry James's novels. His books end as an episode in life ends. You remain with the sense of the life still going on; and even the subtle presence of the dead is felt in that silence that comes upon the artist-creation when the last word has been read. It is eminently satisfying, but it is not final.[24]

What follows then will be an investigation of many of the issues raised here. What is the nature of the past and the nature of narrative? What are the political ethics of narrative and the imaginative possibilities of narrative in a generic range from prose to poetry? How is it possible, thinking along these lines, to give a different sense of criticism not only of the formal moves of writing itself but of the historical moment with which it is linked?

Perhaps, however, the most vital question concerns the threatened loss of all pasts. The writers in this book had experienced within living memory not only terrible wars and technological disaster but a fading memory of the last moments of Victorian optimism that sustained creativity in all branches of knowledge and social and political thought in the first decade of the twentieth century. The sense of a better future and the possibility of new beginnings after the dead weight of late Victorian manners and art had been reflected in the new science, the modernist movements in art, the political fight for women's suffrage and better conditions and a new political role for the working class.

By the mid-twentieth century and in relation to art at least, Lewis Mumford was sounding a warning note about the relentless present of what today is called postmodernism: that horizontal ubiquitous present in which the past becomes a junk shop of kitsch for instant consumption, marketed less for democratic access and enlightenment than for profit: an abstract numbers game in promotion and reception and detached from any qualitative value whether of intrinsic worth, local custom and place, or relevant personal and collective memory:

> it is not the dead past that threatens to choke life now, but rather the hyperactive present, our danger springs not from a surfeit of traditional forms, many of which were effete and meaningless, as was true in both the religion and art of the recent centuries; our difficulty rises rather from a plethora of undigested and often indigestible novelty, produced by the revolutionary forces that are at work, without brake or impedance, in our society. The danger to the artist today is not that he will worship the past and copy the empty forms handed down from the past; the danger springs rather from an unwillingness to realize how poor and illiterate and misguided a generation is when it makes its own limited experience the whole criterion on the possibilities of life; for the experience of a single lifetime is not sufficient in which to take the dimensions and potentialities of human life as a whole.[25]

As for writing that past, it is, for all the writers examined in this book, an imaginative act that creates memory itself. Hence Conrad:

> Action in its essence, the creative art of a writer of fiction may be compared to rescue work carried out in darkness against cross gusts of wind swaying the action of a great multitude. It is rescue work, this snatching of vanishing phases of turbulence, disguised in fair words, out of the active obscurity into a light where the struggling forms may be seen, seized upon, endowed with the only possible form of permanence in this world of relative values – the permanence of memory.[26]

Hannah Arendt, having lived through another war, doubted the solidity of any memory, but nonetheless called for imaginative narrative. What is important for this work is the need she saw for both the historian and the poet:

> as long as the meaning of the events remains alive – and this meaning can persist for very long periods of time –'mastering of the past' can take the form of ever-recurrent narration. The poet in a very general sense and the historian in a very special sense have the task of setting this proves of narration in motion and of involving us in it. And we who for the most part are neither poets nor historians are familiar with the nature of this process from our own experience of life, for we too have the need to recall the significant events in our own lives by relating them to ourselves and others. *Thus we are constantly preparing the way for 'poetry,' in the broadest sense, as a human potentiality; we are, so to speak, constantly expecting it to erupt in some human being.*[27]

This relation of poet and historian in the final section of this book will finally be seen from the perspective of a poet, Muriel Rukeyser, who had thought very seriously about the problematic offered here. With the collapse of the religious eschatological narratives, the disappearance of the human and animal astronomical systems, the myths of origin of earlier societies, the sense of the utter irrelevance of the human subject in 'scientific' perception in the times of evolution, geology, and astronomy, the human story seemed to shrink into insignificance. The *locus classicus* of putting human history in its insignificant place was Darwin:

> The whole history of the world, as at present known, although of a length quite incomprehensible by us will hereafter be recognised as a mere fragment of time, compared with the ages which have elapsed since the first creature, the progenitor of innumerable extinct and living descendants, was created.[28]

Pascal, however, would have replied that 'all bodies, the firmament, the stars, the earth and its kingdoms are not worth the least of minds, for it knows them all and itself too, while bodies know nothing'.[29]

Quite how we know the history of the world is, however, another matter. For it is possible to be alert or mesmerized or merely fascinated. A good example of the latter is nowhere more comically captured than in Patrick Leigh Fermor's *A Time of Gifts*, the autobiographical story of a young man's journey from Rotterdam to Budapest on foot in 1933, a fateful year in which the very fact of walking and encounter gave perhaps a last sense of an ancient middle Europe about to disappear forever. On that journey, itself recollected in tranquility some time after the event, Leigh Fermor told of encountering a polymath historian attempting to master time, both politically and in terms of movement across physical geography:

> His pencil leaped feverishly into action. The Huns put forth their own arrows of migration and began coiling sinuously about the paper till Mitteleuropa and the Balkans were alive with demons' tails. 'Chaos! The Visigoths take shelter south of the lower Danube, and defeat the Emperor Valens at Adrianople *here!*' – he twisted the lead on the paper – 'in 476. Then – in only a couple of decades' – a great loop of pencil swept round the tip of the Adriatic and descended a swiftly-outlined Italy – 'we get Alaric! Rome is captured! The empire splits in two' – the pace of his delivery reminded me of a sports commentator – 'and the West totters on for half a century or so. But the Visigoths are heading westwards,' an arrow curved to the left and looped into France, which rapidly took shape, followed by the Iberian peninsula. 'Go West, young Goth!' he murmured as his pencil threw off Visigothic kingdoms across France and Spain.[30]

Here the feverish pencil gives a feverish history. The fascination with time, historical appearance and disappearance is comically presented. Time is felt as distance, exoticism and speed. But there is a gentle satire on such vast knowledge set at the disposal of a 'sports commentator'. In the end it is only a catalogue of transient events whose explanation collapses into a movement mounted on the back of a galloping vitalist metaphysic. The tone of this book, it is hoped, will show that the choice between the sports commentator of history and the historian has never been more urgent.

In contrast Albert Schweitzer once noted that 'the real truth of that which here meets us as history we experience within ourselves'. To reconcile new with old thought was very difficult and he commented 'We have not yet arrived at any reconciliation between history and modern thought – only between half-way history and half-way thought.'[31] All the writers and editors offered for commentary in the following pages were deeply conscious of the truth of these words. They were most articulate about the history as experienced within themselves, a history felt above all emotionally and on the pulses. In his short piece 'Adieu à Gramsci', Victor Serge wrote:

> The poverty of words! How could anyone sketch out his portrait before a freshly-filled grave? How to speak that which we have lost, that which remains for us that must not be lost – when death extinguishes so much soul, grandeur, and faithfulness behind bared windows. Even the power of feeling itself reduces you to a kind of impotence – adieu, comrade, adieu.[32]

But the word 'adieu' spoken so powerfully at a moment of absolute loss and by such a one as Serge, lingers, a-presence-in-absence, to our own day, creating an emotive memory without which no serious scholarship and no serious political activity can continue to flourish. The work of mourning will be an important aspect not only of Serge's writing but of his political vision.

When the writers under review in this book spoke of the nature of narrative, time and history, they also invoked an ethics. The perspective this book offers on their stories has been to a degree influenced by Sartre's unfinished *Notebooks for an Ethics*, with its thesis that somehow we need Pascal as well as Marx, or at least the apparently opposed dimensions of human experience they investigated. This is meant as guiding principle of approach, not as an attempt to reconcile these two world-views or to endorse their respective ideologies in any literal way. There are things to be learnt negatively and positively from Pascal's sense of temporality fallen outside time and Marx's projection of the absolute into a future to come. In criticizing both it seems essential to recover a different temporality for ethics and a different ethics for temporality. Sartre managed to turn Pascal's wager into a human project. In fiction and poetry, as opposed to theology or political theory, the configuration of the interior world of the psyche and the exterior world of historical event, chance and fate will be seen to have many complex moves within different generic frameworks and many different ways of interpreting the private and public spheres.

What remains important is that the ceaseless movement between future, past and present remains acknowledged, otherwise each moment loses its human definition in pure abstraction.[33] For the writer is indebted to the past and it is this strange sense of debt 'which makes the master of plots into a servant of the memory of men [and women] of the past'.[34] It is hoped that this final ethical judgement that we owe the past our apprenticeship and devotion will become clear in the course of this study. It was again Conrad who insisted on the historical truth of fiction:

> Fiction is history, human history, or it is nothing. But is also more than that; it stands on firmer ground, being based on the reality of forms and the observation of social phenomena, whereas history is based on documents, and the reading of print and handwriting – on second-hand impression. Thus fiction is nearer truth. But let that pass. A historian may be an artist too, and a novelist is a historian, the preserver, the keeper, the expounder, of human experience.[35]

The historian would demure at the faint praise and challenge the 'but let that pass', nonetheless Conrad's polemic is about a different kind of historical truth, that of the felt quality of life undergone by people in history. History is suffered in its inherited structures, whether creeping at snail's pace in the grand epochs, in economic cycle or in the slow time of religious thought and practice, in law and family pattern, or more swiftly in the shape of political events. In suffering the interweaving patterns of history the person is in danger, and needs many means of survival. When Serge, for example, described the onset of the 'post-modern' world, his attitude contains a directly ethical appeal:

> We are in an age of States, of machines, of masses, delivered up to this triple power that from one moment to another hems us in, crushes us, crushes us en masse [...] We must calmly refuse the abdications of thought, the fratricidal madness, the global plots of those who profit from catastrophe. To take this firm decision, while it is hardly sufficient to save us from the guns, at least disengages us from complicity with the lords of war.[36]

Narrating a past for the present and future is as much a part of that disengagement now as then. Sartre's contemporary, the French resistance fighter and poet René Char, warned that the task was hardly going to be simple:

> We will be quick to forget. We will quit throwing out rubbish, cutting away and healing. We will suppose that the dead in their graves have nuts in their pockets, and that one day the tree, fortuitously, will sprout.[37]

The catastrophic effects of that assumption were given chilling expression by Orwell in *Nineteen Eighty-Four*: 'Do you realize that the past, starting from yesterday has been actually abolished? [...] Nothing exists except an endless present in which the Party is always right.'[38]

Finally it was Muriel Rukeyser who declared that the sense of history did not operate as 'a series of past events but as a world of ideas that one carries in the present' and forms 'a structure of resonance that one finds in a poem, a figure of time, as Valéry says a poem is [...]'.[39] Rukeyser would have agreed strongly with Hannah Arendt in her incomparable essay on Isak Dinesen where she cites Dinesen to the effect that the very dignity of the experience of human life consists in repeating life in the imagination: 'Without repeating life in imagination you can never be fully alive: "lack of imagination" prevents people from "existing". As one of her story tellers admonishes the young, '"be eternally and unswervingly loyal to the story" means no less than be loyal to life, don't create fiction but accept what life is giving you, show yourself worthy of whatever it may be by recollecting and pondering over it, thus repeating it in imagination; this is the way to remain alive.'[40] This repetition in the imagination is the site where the external and internal worlds meet. That meeting emerges in writing itself and hence becomes a means of articulating the sense of the world of the self in the contingent circumstances of history. This ability to articulate simultaneously a sense of the 'soul' in 'history', the subjective and the external experience together, is particularly true of all the writers and commentators in this book, and perhaps no one exemplified it better than Victor Serge, who is the subject of the first section.

1

'It is Dead and it is Not Dead': Time and Testimony in Victor Serge[1]

The unconsumed stern was the last to sink; but the paint had gone, had cracked, had peeled off, and there were no letters, there was no word, no stubborn device that was like her soul to flash at the rising sun her creed and her name.

— JOSEPH CONRAD[2]

Images were first made to conjure up the appearances of something that was absent. Gradually it became evident that an image could outlast what it represented; it then showed how something or somebody had once looked – and thus by implication how the subject had once been seen by other people. Later still the specific vision of the image-maker was also recognized as part of the record. An image became a record of how X had seen Y. This was the result of an increasing consciousness of individuality, accompanying an increasing awareness of history.

— JOHN BERGER[3]

Since History cannot save the sufferings of the children of Oradour, even if it has a direction, it does not have a meaning. Always the illusion of *one* history. But not just the Anabaptists at their stake are not saved by the dictatorship of the proletariat: brought back to life, they would condemn it as impious. Thus History is lost without recuperation. It is not necessary to seek an ethical collectivity to save History but to realize ethics.

— JEAN-PAUL SARTRE[4]

In the attic of some Moscow house or in a barn on some country estate that has escaped burning, he will find a table, a three-leaved mirror, a sofa – dating back to Catherine, Paul, or Alexander – and for months on end he will worry away at it in his cellar, smoking, thinking, measuring with his eyes to bring back life to dead things.

— BORIS PILNIAK[5]

I

Writing and Refuge

That writing 'conjures images' is a thought that takes us back to those historical times when the mark of writing made meaning a kind of physical presence. In Foucault's words it belonged to the order of things.[6] Modernist poets such as Ezra Pound and T.S. Eliot attempted to give some echo of that in their early 'imagist' work. But a quasi-visual or sensory image can also both condense a narrative and work within it. An image might, in a longer prose narrative, become a reference point, a moment of stillness within the sense of time that the story itself offered. Indeed among modernist prose writers such as Henry James, Marcel Proust, Virginia Woolf, James Joyce and William Faulkner, meditations on 'the image in time' offered a haunting presence in the longer story: the golden bowl in James, the madeleine and the mother's kiss in Proust, the lighthouse in Woolf, the carved graffiti in a lecture room in Joyce, the muddy drawers in Faulkner, to cite only some of the more famous examples.[7] As is well known, among modernist writers Bergson's philosophy of psychological time played a major role in recovering a human time of psychological intensities and memory from the crudely translated linear time of Newtonian science.

Victor Serge, the subject of this chapter, attended Bergson's lectures in Paris in the 1900s. However John Berger's final sentence, cited above, moves us to the largest human narrative framework of all and invites a speculation on both the historical emergence in time of individuality as such and on how X sees Y within the seeming indifference of the historical process. How does anyone look at someone else, what traces of a vanished world does any object extend into the present, what is history, and what language or discourse can make sense of it all?

The quotation from Sartre also given above provides a major clue. Throughout all readings and recoveries of historical events the impulse towards an ethics that transcends temporary considerations continues, even though every concrete historical moment must be realized in a culturally specific way. What Sartre does not say is that an imaginative contemporary 'translation' of history, that is a poetic reading of both 'heresies' (Anabaptism and Marxism) directed to current needs might yield vital clues for solving contemporary problems. The 'impiety' of Marxists, for example, might interrupt a dialectical drama in which good is indistinguishably mingled with evil. The 'piety' of the Anabaptists might well do the same. The radicalism, the impulse to democracy and renewed theological and ethical life of the Anabaptists, it might be judged, sits uneasily with their apolitical withdrawal from the world. As for history itself, it is thought and written by us from clues rescued from an absolute void or absence. Sartre was right. There is no way history will, as such, rescue us since it is we ourselves who must reclaim it.

Victor Serge (Victor Lvovich Kibalchich) lived an extraordinary life. Its main external parameters can be quickly sketched out. Born in 1890 to a family of revolutionaries who fled Russia after the assassination of Alexander II, at the age of eighteen he was a photographer's apprentice and lived for a short period in an anarchist utopian community in the Ardennes. In Paris before the war he edited the French anarchist newspaper *Anarchie*. In 1912 he was implicated in the trial of the anarchist outlaws known as the Bonnot gang. While abhorring their methods he refused to inform against them and spent the next five years in a French jail. In 1917, after release he went to Spain where he was involved in the abortive syndicalist uprising. It was there that he wrote his first article under his pen-name Victor Serge.[8]

On his way back to join the revolution in Russia he was again detained in France. In 1919, however he arrived in Petrograd at the height of the civil war, working with Zinoviev organizing the Communist International. He became a close friend of Trotsky. During the next few years he participated in the Comintern Congresses, worked for Comintern as a secret agent and editor of *Imprehor* in Berlin and Vienna, returning in the mid-1920s to fight for the 'left opposition', eventually falling foul of Stalin and being expelled from the Communist Party in 1928. During the next five years, barred from political activity, he became a novelist, publishing work in French. In 1933 he was arrested and deported to Orenburg in Central Asia. Under pressure from French intellectuals, including André Malraux and André Gide, he was released, but he was then deprived of Soviet citizenship and his manuscripts confiscated. He was finally expelled from the Soviet Union. His first wife went mad under the pressures and his children were murdered by Stalinist agents. As an anarchist journalist in Brussels he supported the POUM in the Spanish Civil War, was endlessly slandered in the Communist Press, wrote a book on the counter-revolution in the Soviet Union and campaigned against the Soviet Trials. He finally quarrelled with the ever-rigid Trotsky, but continued to revere his memory after the assassination.

When the Nazis invaded Belgium he fled to France; when they invaded France, he fled to the 'free' zone ending up in Marseille at the house of the Surrealists. Here he encountered the American rescue mission and began his long correspondence with the Macdonalds, finally leaving France with Claude Lévi-Strauss and André Breton on *Le Capitaine-Lemerle*. After his flight from France he was pursued by Stalinist agents in Mexico and harrassed by party-line communists. He wrote his last novel and memoirs 'for the desk drawer' since publication was impossible. He also wrote an unfinished book on Mexican antiquities; he was as alert to the landscape of his exile as he had been in the trans-Caucuses. That is the exterior life, but it is a fraction of the story. Socrates said that the unreflected life was not worth living and if any life was reflected upon it was Serge's. Serge's writing is both testimony and testament. A record of the worst of times, it is also the work of an indomitable spirit.

This section is about memory, time, writing and perhaps startlingly for such an initiating trio, politics. All four are touched on in the following extract about the 'recovery' of the past, by the gifted and 'forgotten' Russian writer Boris Pilniak, a close friend of Victor Serge and ultimately a victim of Stalin's purges. In this passage a Soviet archaeologist, sent to excavate Scythian burial mounds at Uvek in the Siberian Steppes finds himself 'entangled' in time and history. The passage begins with a narrative ghost-like voice tracing visual signs of ancient Scythian 'gold, bonework and stones':

> [...] a saddle, embossed with gold, bonework and stones, and the skin had become mummy-like. In the stone vaults it was deathly, there was no longer a smell of anything, and every time it was necessary to enter them, thoughts became precise and peaceful, and sorrow entered the world. The summit of Uvek, stony, had grown bald, wormwood had grown on it like a silver, dusty stubble, it gave off a bitter smell. – The centuries teach just as the stars do, and Baudek knew the joy of grief. The archeologist Baudek's concepts were entangled with the centuries. A thing always says more not about life, but about art, and a way of life is already art. Baudek, measured life by art, like any artist. And from the centuries and revolution Baudek and Gleb Ordinin wanted to follow these members of the sects who lived in farmsteads in the steppes. And bitter on Uvek was the smell of wormwood.[9]

This highly poetic prose condenses, while laying out, many narrative times: the mute present of the post-revolution archaeologist, conscious of a cataclysmic political and social upheaval in which the customs of an ancient aristocratic oligarchy with its sanctifying ideological reason has been overturned; a present in which the study of ancient cultures whose ideological remoteness from the space and time of the revolution and technological modernity becomes suddenly fascinating as a gone world. The ancient world itself suggests that *longue durée* of pre-capitalist history, whose psychological appeal is now figured in the anthropological impertinence of the 'untouched', almost as a return of the repressed unconscious. For the writer not to be entangled with 'centuries' is not an option. Yet the absence of the centuries is unwritten and so represents, *pace* Herodotus, whose writings tell us most of what we know about these ancient peoples, an essentially 'lost time' whose mark is death itself. Finally, revealed in that extraordinary sentence, 'The centuries teach just as the stars do, and Baudek knew the joy of grief', is a powerful metaphysical paradox of likeness in which an indifferent eternity underwrites a human sense of time and mixes wonder with tragedy in the depths of the human soul. Yet Pilniak's 'nostalgia' was shot through with an ironic commentary on the emerging Stalinist state. In his story 'Mahogany', for example, cited at beginning of this section, the 'real communists' are Leninists and Trotskyites, not Stalinists.[10]

This fictive moment and the questions it throws up announce the problematic of cultural self-awareness and the layering of temporality in any archaeological exercise including that of scholarship itself. Hence it was that one day, reading through the 'European' correspondents of Dwight Macdonald in the Sterling Memorial library at Yale, and discovering his correspondence with Victor Serge, it became only too obvious to me that the experience itself involved multiple temporalities. It was a good place to think about the historical nature of things, and of time and narrative. Under huge mock gothic windows, built by out-of-work Italian stone-masons during the American depression, this architectural space itself is a reaction to a threatening modernity. In its compellingly energetic eclecticism, it is a place which, to my English and European eyes, held traces of the Victorian medieval revival and the nostalgias of 'robber barons' (with educational consciences) who oddly thought that learning was exclusively 'European'. The Sterling Memorial Library is a wealthy and privileged space of multiple times: the Middle Ages; the Victorian era; the 1930s; the virtual postmodernist present with the researchers' lap-tops; the timeless and the silent economic flow of the Yale Corporation's billions. Here, the severe but helpful guardians of the tracings of the past, brought to my desk, folder by folder, letters of an extraordinary and desperate story. In that atmosphere, the research itself was becoming shaped by an insistent sense of displacements in space and time, personal as well as scholarly, colouring the very experience of what could be discovered, seen, noticed and written.

The letters were mostly airmail letters, addressed by Victor Serge to 'Chers amis' (Nancy and Dwight Macdonald), a phrase which became so insistently repetitive in its series, that it took on the aura of a title, a mark of address which turned the vocative into a vocation which underlay the very possibility of the meaning of significant existence itself. For the correspondents were never destined to meet. The letters were the friendship, its most authentic existence. The art, in Pilniak's terms, was the life. Single-spaced type crammed the fading blue paper, the ribbon of the typewriter sometimes so weak that the print was hardly readable, although in a sense everything here was readable, the fragile paper, the date stamp, the place of posting, the occasional photograph in the more conventional envelope, the telegram, and the postcard. Sixty years disappeared in the sleepy, over-heated silence of winter afternoons. There was passion, desperation, the sense of a world at war, the death of millions and above all the powerful presence of man who was a refugee, whose fate presaged millions of our own time, a man without a country, hunted, pursued in the wake of the terrible failure of the biggest revolution against tyranny since 1789, the Soviet 'Thermidor' passing into an industrial war on the Eastern Front between two totalitarian powers, with unimaginable loss of human life and unimaginable human suffering. These grand narratives signalled all too vividly their absence and presence in the date, the postmark and the fading type and that always-uneasy withdrawal from the world that marks writing and scholarship. That withdrawal had nothing to do with the familiar anti-intellectual image of the ivory tower, rather it came from the insistent haunting presence of the excluded and terrible world of the black New Haven poor, their soup kitchens less than half a mile from my desk, as the past presence of the war overwhelmed and haunted a reading which was to recover a story of one man's 'entanglements' with time.

Serge came into contact with the American libertarian thinker and ex-Trotskyite Dwight Macdonald and his wife Nancy Macdonald in the early 1940s, during what he called 'the battle of the visas'.[11] I have described their extraordinary epistolatory correspondence and friendship elsewhere.[12] It had all the drama and emotional force characteristic of those excellent people who today maintain correspondences and fight legal battles for prisoners of conscience or those awaiting judicial execution. To summarize briefly: after many twists and turns Serge, who fled to France during the Nazi invasion of Belgium, found himself with his wife, Laurette Séjourné, and his two children, Jeaninne and Vladimir Kibalchich, in Marseille, at the *surréaliste* refugee house he renamed 'Espervisa'. Macdonald hounded the State Department for exit-visas for the family to find refuge in the United States. They were finally refused the visas on the grounds that this active anti-Stalinist had once been a Bolshevik.

Serge and his family, after extraordinary adventures and cliff-hangers that the correspondence with the Macdonalds reveal in all their detail, were ultimately to find refuge in Cárdenas's Mexico.[13] The entire drama was to involve a large number of ethically principled Americans in and around the Emergency Rescue Committee in New York, a number of other organizations, and some individuals working on their own account. Their frontman in Marseilles was the extraordinary Harvard preppie, Varian Fry, who was eventually to help some two thousand people to escape.[14] The backup team, included, in various capacities, not only the Macdonalds, but also Freda Kirchway, Reinhold Niebuhr, Mildred Adams, John Dewey, Sidney Hook, Margaret Marshall, Meyer Schapiro, Max Eastman. In France, canny and strategic Americans helping out under the very noses of the Nazis included Miriam Davenport Ebel, Dr Bohn (less useful) of the American Federation of Labor, and Hiram Bingham the American Vice-Consul not to mention the unlikely Chicago heiress and socialite Mary-Jayne Gold.

Most noteworthy in his correspondence with the Macdonalds for our purposes is the fact that Serge spoke of writing his memoirs, an autobiographical work which he hoped would be 'the faithful mirror of our struggles'.[15] What that mirror will show, from the perspective of its single human life, is a world changing towards a new 'totalitarian' state of affairs in which bureaucratic tyranny, endless surveillance of citizens and contempt for the rule of law became the rule. It was to become a world in which old socialist, communist or bourgeois democratic capitalist enlightenment ideals become the propaganda tools of invisible and unassailable power which had little interest in either socialism or social democratic capitalism. Ultimately invisible means of coercion will increasingly assist the effectiveness of the visible means of power. The model of semi-permanent war was to prepare the destruction of and to show the fragility of the hard-won but precarious social democracies of the more favoured countries of Europe and the United States. Serge's attempt to obtain a visa condensed, in a single, graspable and infinitely human moment, all the larger forces at work.

Nothing better illustrates these developments than an issue that has become even more contentious in the contemporary world. It is the whole question of the stateless person. In Serge's time it was a result of a world at war, in our own time it remains that also, but it is aggravated by disparities of national wealth and compounded by the desperation of the economic migrant and even climate change. Serge's "battle of the visas" prefigures the problems of our own time. His metaphorical phrase was designed to illustrate how the document and visible sign occupied a space between authority and suppliant with every agency concealed. Prison and freedom, life and death may depend on the exchange. In the end the moment is about the authenticity of stories and their reception, the difficult relation between fiction and history. Narrative and narrativity are fundamentally and politically involved in this drama of identity and power. It was the aftermath of the Smith Act and the activities of the Dies committee, fore-runners of the McCarthy Cold War terror in America, that constituted part of the actual political force behind this individual story. One example from the extensive Serge–Macdonald correspondence will suffice here. It shows the difficulties his wife Laurette Séjourné encountered in attempting to leave France and rejoin her husband. She confronted the American State Department authorities in the Embassy in Marseille. In a most touching letter to Nancy and Dwight Macdonald, Séjourné spoke of her hesitancy in writing to them, feeling inadequate at the side of the famous Serge. Nonetheless she described her interview with the visa bureaucrats in some detail; how she prepared herself thoroughly by reading up on the procedures, recalling rumours of other reported failed encounters with some degree of panic.

In the waiting room there was a motley crowd: Austrian Jews, Germans and hardly anyone who had their papers in complete order. The atmosphere grew more tense and desperate as time went on and silence fell as each individual wondered if they would be the next to be called. Laurette read the American travel brochures in the waiting room and she recalled in her letter:

> I was transported far from these trembling and beaten people, dreaming of those marvelous places which are so evocative when I read the history of the magnificent pioneers who had made America. And I felt strong, I found striking arguments for everything the consul might ask me, and the great question: why do you want to come to the United States, a question everyone dreads. I would reply, speaking to him of a country which perhaps he loved less than me [...]

> So the hours went by and they called me in. A few steps and I was in the presence of an unjust, terrible and all powerful male. All at once I would have wanted to explain to him that I was not frightened of him, and that he would quickly find himself put down if he reckoned to talk to me as he talked to the others [...]
>
> After a preliminary skirmish, he stood in front of me and in a brutal accusatory tone, said, 'can you swear that if you had an accident, and accident in which perhaps both your legs were cut off, that you could guarantee that this Mr. [G.L.K.] Morris [her sponsor[16]] would look after you to the end of your life? And on this subject he talks to me for a long time, in a way that made me appreciate his imagination, of the accidents that could happen to me in a town like New York.

Having managed to reduce her to a considerable state of distress, he suddenly asked her if she had any children. She mentioned Vlady, who was eight years old. The consul suddenly smiled and granted her the visa. Outside she was overwhelmed by the other supplicants and suddenly feared what America might mean. She recalls that the struggle for existence was fierce in America and adds to the Macdonalds, 'I am so happy to come and I can't wait to see you, you, who in no way match the image I have of America.' She concludes that she's sorry she hasn't a photograph of herself that she can send. She mentions that she is quite short and believes that American women are rather tall: 'I wonder how I'll get on, barely five feet tall in a country where all the women are so big.'[17]

The letter is a mixture of art and passion. As a former *monteuse*, who had worked with Jean Renoir, she knows how to splice her cuts: the pan around the waiting room, the selection of an agonized face, the close up of the travel brochures, the fade to a dream sequence, the inter-cut shots of the clock, perhaps a low camera angle for the 'terrible' male, high medium shot for her crumbled figure, and her reappearance Ford-like at the door of the waiting room, the camera pulling back as she descends into the crowd, perhaps all with a faintly *noir* lighting. The point to be made here is a serious one, however, for as Oscar Wilde said, life imitates art. The interior life of the suppliant refugee's agony needs the complexity of the offered *mise-en-scène* to combat the reification of the human figure under the gaze of power. In a later letter to the Macdonalds who had sent him a copy of Laurette's letter, Serge comments that he found in it her very voice and gesture and the whole atmosphere of the American consulate. He further comments on his wife's character, saying that her short stature seems to aid a natural inferiority complex but that at the same time she was someone of strong moral character ('*une grande force morale*') with an inexhaustible capacity for fighting and suffering ('*une profonde capacité de lutter – et de souffrir*').[18] It is most moving that Laurette separated the Macdonalds as Americans from the type of personality she imagined to be produced by the individualist competitiveness of American capitalist ideology; such a vision would have been reinforced by the atmosphere of the American Consulate in Marseille.

If this seems a harsh judgment then the evidence of Miriam Davenport Ebel, also a worker on behalf of refugees in France, is pertinent:

> A strong odor of xenophobia and anti-Semitism permeated the premises. I was learning fast. The business of my government was business; American interests overseas were economic interests. Americans with jobs or investments overseas had no passport problems; those with moral obligations or family ties were a nuisance, their pleas worthless irrelevancies.[19]

She also noted dryly that the Consulate had no portrait of Roosevelt displayed, a fact perhaps not very surprising given the efforts of the First Lady on behalf of the refugees. It was with the connivance of this American Embassy that Varian Fry himself would be expelled from Marseille in August 1941.[20] He had already been arrested and imprisoned with the support of the American embassy on a trumped up charge of the theft of 'an official envelope from the Ministry of Foreign Affairs'.[21] Two long letters between Serge and Nancy Macdonald outline the plight of refugees in both general and particular ways. Serge speaks of the growing hostility towards refugees in the United States and begs for asylum for anti-Nazi refugees. Again with enormous perspicacity Serge writes, 'The asylum question for political refugees is intimately bound up with the fate of tomorrow's Europe.'[22]

Aside from politics, Serge's letters to Dwight Macdonald also reveal some of his own thoughts on narrative. The context, it has to be remembered, is the obligatory demand for social realism in Stalinist Russia. In a most instructive letter to Dwight Macdonald, just after arriving in Mexico, Serge spoke of his own preferred narrative mode:

> I consider the contemporary novel, in general as no longer valid either in form or substance; it says almost nothing new about man and society because, from Balzac to Proust and Dostoyevski, it is exhausted, just like the world which it mirrors. I want therefore another novel and I'm working at it out of necessity, because this form is the only one which allows us to express some essential things which completely escape theoretical explanation (theory is always an algebra, it always eliminates the vital substance – or a large part of that substance, it only addresses itself to the intellect which in us is a relatively superficial element, superficial like the light which exposes things.) My novels are exclusively about atmosphere which only exists in harmony and in accord with the whole because it is like that in reality. [23]

Serge's radical rebellion against Stalinist social realism in particular and against the misuse of prescriptive theory in general aligns him with others of his time such as Richard Wright in America. 'Atmosphere' becomes at once a mark of dissent and an offer of a different way. The immediate 'atmosphere' of Marseille, for example, illustrates a kind of enforced *suspension* of ordinary reality, an inertia in the relation of past present and future: between memory, experience and expectation clearly induced by the enforcement of political stasis by tyranny. Serge goes on:

> Marseille, flushed and carefree with its crowded bars, its alleys in the old port festooned with whores, its old bourgeois streets with lattice-windows, its lifeless wharves and its brilliant seascapes, is first and foremost a 'Red City', but its exact shade is Off-Red, Dirty-Red or Racket-Red, so to speak. The Vichy regime has sacked the Socialist city council and the key man in the new administration is Sabiani, a real gangster from Doirot's party. The man in the street knows what's what pretty well: 'Nothing one can do while the Nazi occupation lasts. After that, we settle matters with the bastards. That'll be it – a gay time and some faces bashed in.'[24]

At the same time there is irony. The expectation of action, to borrow Marxist terms, is a pseudo-praxis without revision of consciousness. Pure violence invites pure revenge. The ideological gangster replaces the economic gangster. In 1943 the Nazis, their populist puritanical gaze designating old Marseille as sexually and politically threatening, will evacuate the inhabitants and raze it to the ground. With such a challenge to authority, 'atmosphere' is clearly more than an aesthetic supplement.

There is another sense of time in Serge's *Memoirs* that has a longer extension. It is a time which begins in 1917, and which continues the history of the radical socialists and artists fragmented and hounded across Europe by Stalin and Hitler. The fortunate ones were those rescued by Varian Fry's American Relief Committee. But for them, Serge says, 'a goodly number of refugees would have had no reasonable course open to them but to jump into the sea from the height of the transporter-bridge, a certain enough method.'[25] Then there is the short time-span of the Vichy government and its betrayals, spatially indicated from the renaming of the streets in the attempt to wipe-out historical memory of even a longer duration: from Rousseau to Pierre Curie. The 'atmosphere' also includes the practice of 'anti-Semitism' whose history is thousands of years old and which in this moment becomes both exemplary and contingent. There is also a time-frame that outlines the ineptitude of bourgeois Western propaganda, reeling from the economic crisis of the First World War and 1929 and inadequately confronting the lurid dynamism of National Socialism over the dying embers of revolutionary Marxism and Social Democracy. It might be noted that the American rescue operation was initiated and supported by liberal Christians (Reinhold Niebuhr) and ex-Marxist humanist atheists (the Macdonalds). Finally there is in the *Memoirs* a personal diary-time that shifts from the past tense of reconstituted 'fictional' narrative to a pure present induced by the vehemence of a psychological present of almost Bergsonian intensity: 'Our very existence *is* hanging from slender threads which may break at any moment'.[26]

Serge, as teller of the tale, impersonally connects and disconnects from his own narrative and fictionalizes his encountered milieu across complex intentionalities. Thus he calls the château of the surrealists '*Espère-visa*', renaming the desperate present as a possibility of freedom. The act of writing itself is a shown as a resource: 'I wrote some pages of a novel, not, however, from any love of literature. For this age must be witnessed; the witness passes, but his testimony manages to endure – and life still goes on.'[27] The very downgrading of the 'author' in relation to the tale has the opposite effect: for the offer of impersonal testimony both calls for judgement, and poses as truth. For it is about the 'atmosphere' of Vichy. The boundary between life and art in terms of time is deliberately confused. The dash linking and separating the last phrase cited above, opens up the disjuncture between narrative and life itself, a disjuncture which indicates a despair that this testimony is not only disembodied because it cannot yet be heard, but because the witnesses are dead. The compulsions to write go beyond the love of writing but it is writing itself that endures in its paradoxical form of simultaneous life and death. Serge manages to suggest that this is not theory, but a disjuncture tied intimately to a moment of precise historical confusion and despair: the writer is reduced to witness through denial of participation, and in that witness asserts a continuity with time in what can only be an imagined reception. The despair of and hope for completion in reception become part of the tale.

In order to understand fully Serge's story, whether as revealed in the letters to Dwight Macdonald or in the slightly less desperate reflections of his *Memoirs of a Revolutionary*, the politics of American twentieth-century history need to be taken into account: the 1918 immigration act; the Dies Act; the Alien Registration Act; and the hurried legislation against the refugee in 1941. These need to be grasped in all their brutality. At the cultural and psychological levels, recalling these historical moments illustrates the 'fear of invasion' that has always haunted the American psyche, the dark side of the less-than-innocent presumption of individual inviolability within the American dream itself.[28] In order to be understood at the legal and political levels a longer history is required: the captivity narrative and the colonial experience; the nativism of the 1840s; the anti-immigrant legislation first proposed by the trades unions after the Civil War; the closing of the frontier in 1890; the Haymarket riots of 1886; the first red-scares; the events of 1919; the endemic isolationist foreign policy throughout most of American history. Serge's experience requires a detailed sense of the politics and representations of immigrant history and the law, and of the culturally determined economic, social and class assumptions and practices which guarantee authentic human status.

In technological terms, the narrative presages the virtual global world of the telegram, modern postal systems, electronic money transfer and modern transport. Fry describes how, at the end of a long day in Marseille, he would take his cable down a rat-infested alley to the little police station, get the cable stamped (no one could read a word of English), show a passport to validate the name and then go over to the post office:

> The night window was a small opening in a temporary wooden partition in a room which looked as though it was being rebuilt after a bombing. We would pull a bell like an old-fashioned doorbell and the little window would open and we would push the telegram through. All we could see of the post-office clerk was his hairy hands as he filled his thin scratchy pen with violet ink, counted the words, calculated the charge and made out the receipt.[29]

Here, the global and provincial worlds collide linguistically, technologically and politically. As in Henry James's short story 'In the Cage', what the operator of the communications system might or might not know becomes a crucial question. Culturally we see the emergence of a world of the apparent arbitrariness of Kafkaesque bureaucracy, Sartrean terror, Pynchonesque sign and the edgy black humour of the Burroughsian inter-zone of arbitrary authority, as this moment in Burroughs's fiction shows:

> The agent looks at my passport and sneers.
>
> 'Is this something of your own invention? ...' There is a girl behind me in line holding an American passport. I point out that my passport is the same. He snatches her passport and looks at it. Then he slaps both passports down on the table and turns to his assistant.
>
> 'Destroy these documents.'[30]

Serge's aim was to create a 'faithful mirror of our struggles'. That seems to offer events in their simplicity but 'struggle' covers a range of things that go beyond the pictorial image. It assumes events and reactions in contradiction and dissonance and hence opens a space for judgement. In fact Serge's account valorizes the 'witness', and indeed his memories are characteristically full of the short biographical sketches of the dead who have perished in the struggle. Serge is the witness as obituarist and the brief narratives, vividly characterized and modelled to a degree on Dos Passos's similarly condensed lives in his trilogy *U.S.A.* (1930–6), have the strangely disconcerting atmosphere of the brief life, where the narrative delay of fateful chronological insistence is so short as to create an almost hallucinatory temporality which is filled with anguish.[31] At the same time there is the contrast of Serge as witness himself, inviting juridical judgment over many pages and whose miraculously preserved life, or delayed death, is almost fictional in its capacity for being spared.

It is this hovering between two roles of witness and sufferer (this happened – to me) that gives autobiography its unique position between history and literature. Serge's role as witness does not offer pure data, assuming that ever to be possible. He is impassioned, the seeing is informed by the whole range of values his dissenting Marxism offers. It contains an ethics: 'It is necessary to conclude against the existence of fatality, and for the immense power of man and for personal responsibility', and to condemn 'systems which concentrate maddening power in a few hands, force a selection of perverted elements, destroy even an imperfect check upon power by the average man, and paralyze the public conscience'.[32] Serge does not enclose 'literature within a world of its own and break off the subversive point it turns against the moral and social orders'.[33] The ethical judgment directed against fatality also understands that narrative comes to an end with its affective pathos. In Serge's case it is deflected by an appeal: 'May the passion, the experience and even the faults of my fighting generation have some small power to illumine the way forward!'[34] In the semi-fictional time of the autobiography, and especially this one, dozens of witness have already given their stories through the obituary narratives. Is it possible to read them as evidence and judgment simultaneously? Absolutely, despite the fact that the evidence is prejudged and then re-judged or, in literary terms, reconfigured. As history it is judged against other accounts and as a fiction in terms of the ordering of incidents and of its rhetorical procedures. Neither of these is pure, and narrative understanding governs both. Historical explanation and narrative understanding are given in each other.

Autobiography also demands that we judge the self behind the mask: that self, written in relation to things and events. As a figure in his own story Serge presents himself in the most classic of modes, as Job, the one 'escaped alone to tell thee'.[35] Yet this *auteur of himself* sees himself as part of a greater design: a revolutionary at a moment of the fragmentation of ideology itself, of a very real betrayal, yet retaining a faith that the moment of chaos will also be productive of new meaning. His relation to the lives of those only recently completed is one of restless knowledge, passionate witnessing, celebration and mourning. But through the narrative trope of Job, what Serge gives us is a Hebraic narrative of what Ricoeur called the 'suffering just'. [36] The aim is to show that faith in history has a meaning accessible to the person: to tell a story whose significance is beyond the structure of a proposed historical rationality. In the recall of a moment whose present is as fleeting as it is uncertain, a truly human meaning is delivered in a story that binds listener and speaker, writer and reader. In Ricoeur's words, 'history is a form of knowledge only through the relation it establishes between the lived experience of people of other times and today's historian […] the initiative in history does not belong to the document but to the question posed by the historian.' [37]

With both the individual and the event *hors de combat* in structuralist and post-structuralist times, the autobiography and letters would seem scarcely to be worthy of attention. Yet the personally experienced event and the letter are never merely fascinating for the first has to be described by someone to exist and the other is expressed by an identifiable individual in his/her own voice: a voice that calls to others. As narratives or potential narratives they are already partly pre-formed, the one by the passing of the irreducible moment, the other by the signing, the form of discourse, the date and the act of closure. Were it not for this, narratives about the refugee would be swallowed up in formal chronological population movements at one end of the scale or become merely exemplary of a universalist ethics of the Other at the other end. The questions asked by the historian or literary critic are both different and similar. But in both cases they depend on ethical questions arising from the way 'people' in all their constructed differences might behave or act together.

In the historian's case there is the need to realize that all evidence is coded and that questions are ideologically shaped. For example it could be asked: what were the forces were that shaped the necessity for the Dies Committee? What, in terms of ideology and those 'stories' of ideological worlds in conflict, mediated and constructed the play of power? Yet in more personal terms, even if the story turns out to be typical of a carefully framed question, something unique will escape the anticipated result in a life suffered as a negotiation of inert structures. Ultimately it is the intelligence of our imagination that must serve the curiosity of human beings investigating human beings. For the literary critic, less queasy about the significance of the individual life, evasion might lie in the temptation to concentrate on the identifiable rhetorics of the narrative, a too simple thematics, and to suggest a fatality of operations which designates the moment as typical in a taxonomy of hierarchized genres. In short, truth is often surplus to anticipated results and strange as well as recognizable.

It is Ricoeur's concept of 'temporal moves' within narrative which are useful for this study. The most important factor in approaching issues of time and story in Serge is that these 'moves' mediate a field of discourse that thematically include his activist politics, his anarcho-syndicalist ideological positions, his strong belief in ethics and his openness to non-Marxist discourses about the world, including those of religion and psychology. These concerns also mediate his attempts to stay balanced at a time when almost every ideological position seemed inauthentic in a war in which only survival and victory were the issues. It was a period of history when technological and economic power-drives might use, simplify and corrupt any ideological practice: scientific, capitalist, Marxist or Christian. It was, in addition, a world in which a pope mumbled ethical generalities while Jews were despatched to the camps, in which Stalin executed all the founding fathers of a communist revolution, in which a liberal American president, with the connivance of the British, developed fire-bombing strategies and atomic weapons to the point where the absolute obliteration of the civilian population of an entire city was felt to be strategically and morally acceptable.

In approaching the intransigence of the problem of meaning, no single discourse can claim precedence: political, psychological, sociological, ethical, economic, technological or anthropological. The interpretations of testimony and political judgement need help from every quarter. Furthermore, how is it possible to interpret an absolute sense of failure and of human disaster without recourse to an atemporal declaration of the ubiquity of tragedy, a divine plan, a blind indifferent and inhuman Nature or by manipulating some founding event in a chronology which translates a fictional cosmic authority into fate? What is signalled here is the use of the view of fate that inevitably authorizes and permits unchecked revenges, foists a cynical millenialist narrative on its victims and, worst of all, promotes a sense of the worthlessness and meaninglessness of the human project itself. The temptations of the stoic, the nihilist, the cynic, the pragmatist and the utilitarian armed with all-too-probable statistics and touting the 'art of the possible' become stronger when all principle is characterized as sentimental, impracticable or *a priori* doomed by 'the lessons of history'. The person, lost in what Allen Ginsberg called 'the animal soup of time' is offered only models of contentless survivalist heroics.

In a generally fine book, one critic, familiar with the testimonies of the Holocaust rightly points out the inadequacy of the heroic narrative that involves what he calls the 'suitable accolades' that do not honour the 'painful complexities of the victims' narratives.'[38] No one doubts the necessity for courage and positivity. Stories of heroic survival can become oppressive, giving inadequate descriptions of what is undergone and suffered. The state of the soul is ignored, as the results of technique dominate all meaning. One wonders what comfort such narratives give to the dying or to the permanently psychologically or physically damaged, for there are severe limits to a relentless positivity which obliterates both the reality of the moment, the patient's own sense of the past and future, and the selfless compassion of ordinary kindness and love where no future is possible and which mediates as best it can the technocratic and managerial hell of modern medicine in the contemporary experience of dying.

The novelist James Baldwin once wrote of the 'unnerving cheerfulness' of the medical profession and the 'awful knowledge' the cheerfulness hides.[39] What is less convincing is: 'The raw material of oral Holocaust narratives, in content and manner of presentation, resists the organizing impulse of moral theory and art.'[40] But how do we know it to be the 'worst' and 'beyond', if that organizing impulse is not resisting in turn? And further if the worst realism numbs us into silence, nonetheless the very silence cries out. Finding a form for the speaking of anguish tests the highest forms of human imagination, but it is not *a priori* defeated. That thought gives nihilism too dogmatic a role. Any experience cannot be communicated or thought about outside narrative itself, including silent gesture. There is in fact an art of memory that engages all the parameters of narrative temporality, that is to say, it shows how the past leaks into the present, and this in turn offers a horizon of future expectation. There are also human events to which the only response is silence, but such silence is more expressive than words. It is expressive of powerlessness and rejected love, as Cordelia knew in *King Lear*.

Writing the Heretical Self in History

The subtleties of Serge's 'temporal moves' in his narratives become readily apparent. They supplement and express themes he negotiated purely as a result of philosophical speculation and ideological critique. Richard Greeman has pointed out that Serge's writing is deeply involved in the problem of evil.[41] That problem forms one pole of a highly tensioned polarity between itself and a Marxist ideology that ignored personal ethics and the interior life. Marxism, like capitalism, psychology and the social sciences, had no word for evil. In Europe the word itself was discredited with secular post-Nietzschean thought, and with the decreasing authority of Christian theological discourse and religious belief. With their disappearance went most of the intelligibility of literature from ancient times as well as what was most valuable in the greatest theological, ethical and religious writing. Nonetheless, as a novelist, polemicist, poet, political journalist and autobiographer, Serge's work is tensely strung between the problem of evil, almost atemporal in its fundamentally existentialist orientation, and a Marxism grounded in a particular view of its own historic privilege, its own narrative of history and its millennialist grand narrative. In order to examine this nexus of issues I propose first to examine Serge's own theoretical writing in relation to politics, ethics and literature (and to illustrate the way these diverse issues converge in moments in the *Memoirs* in relation to the big questions of time, memory and narrative), and then to complete that analysis by looking at the novels of the 1930s.

There are continuities and consistencies in Serge's writing from the early period onwards. The 'anarcho-syndicialist' of the late nineteenth and early part of the twentieth century was preoccupied with holding together a number of incompatible and contradictory positions of ethical commitment and praxis: direct action versus cooperation and organization; revolutionary spontaneity versus revolutionary discipline; freedom to criticize versus party loyalty; obedience to the cause versus distrust of all authority; anti-bourgeois thinking and behaviour versus respect for the lives of others with different values and cultural practices; a commitment to the absolutely contemporary direct action versus a passionate concern for historical culture, art and literature. Such were the problems mulled over by Victor Serge and his young contemporaries, and his very early writing clearly demonstrates his concern with the possibility (or impossibility) of being an ethical revolutionary. More than the positivist Marxist the anarchist was alive to contingency, the unpredictable, the sense that a proposed course of action might well be robbed of its best-intentioned results. How to retain an ethical view of the world when ethical actions, for example, might lead to unethical consequences was something Marxists, like many other ideologues, capitalists included, had difficulty with in their rigid views of the 'logic' of history or the market. Dialectical thinking should have encompassed this difficulty with its Heraclitean view of the ceaseless transformations of time, but in practice it rarely did.

Serge's early writing in *L'Anarchie* and his enthusiastic but contradictory responses to the first years of the revolution itself give many clues to the parameters of his thinking. As well as the grand narrative of human history, Serge was concerned, like the ancient Greeks and Marcus Aurelius, with the well-lived life of a man – '*Être un homme, simplement*' (and we must add woman): a solid sort of beast, he joked, with good muscles, well built, with powerful instincts, directed by a well-developed intelligence, equipped with extensive knowledge, endowed with sensitive feeling, combining strength with delicacy, able to be both reasonable and daring, proud and ethical, openly proud of himself and generous at the same time.[42] This was not an essentialist definition. The irony is patent. It was a definition that opened a sense of the person as a nexus of possibilities for good and for ill.

In his later 'snapshots' or portraits of individual lives, the contingent detail of the person within the reversals of historical fate would rescue the very nature of the self from abstract numerousness. Marxists were not concerned with such matters. For them personal ethics were still infected by an outmoded religious discourse, which was seen mostly to drew a veil of sentiment over the activities of the hypocritical bourgeoisie. However, unlike most Marxists, Serge did take religion seriously. The French anthropologist Claude Lévi-Strauss, escaping with André Breton and Serge from Marseille, in 1941, somewhat intimidated by this old friend of Lenin, noted that he did not look very much like a revolutionary: 'the clean-shaven, delicate-featured face, the clear voice accompanied by a stilted and wary manner, had an almost asexual quality, which I was later to find among Buddhist monks along the Burmese frontier [...]'.[43] For a Marxist of Serge's type, Russian history itself, with its late Christianized Slavic populations and with its many folk traditions capable of resisting Eastern Orthodoxy or of integrating to make syntheses between Christianity and pagan traditions, was to be of prime historical importance. In Russia, as much as in the United States, new prophets and new religions seemed to find a fertile breeding ground. The survival, production and destruction of new faiths and beliefs in relation to inherited religious and social practices could not but have provided an anarchist of Serge's intelligence with compelling historical material for political analysis.

Serge's moment in history was also ripe for investigating the disappearance of ways of life before industrialization and modernity. At the end of the nineteenth century, all over the world European and American anthropologists, ethnologists, musicians, painters, cultural historians, linguists and historians of religions were complementing imperial conquest with a study of those historic forms of life and culture it was set to destroy. From Boas to Bartók, from Picasso to Frazer, the intellectuals, writers and artists got to work on the cultures of imperial conquest. Serge, as will be shown, never lost an intense interest in the early religious forms of ancient cultures. Many others were paradoxically figured, however historically specific, as a strangely timeless area of universalist human psychological truth and in that sense were often used as a powerful tool of resistance to a Whig view of history. The ethical self was as much a problem for Serge, therefore, as an analysis of capitalism. How to find self-discipline and maintain a sense of vision in a world of confidence men, careerists and profiteers? This was the first directly personal question Serge put to himself. It was easier to sell out than to conquer fear in oneself, to take what one desired or, even in one precise example (attractive to those traumatized by the 'text-bite' style of contemporary literature teaching), get stuck into long and 'difficult' books.[44] Resistance to any easy option was a fundamental core of Serge's ethics. Difficulty resisted the demagogue in any life activity, from politics to scholarship.

The present also owed the past a debt in spite of the fact that too often the vital ideas of the past had become the propaganda of the present. The once radical discourses accompanying the Enlightenment or the Russian revolution had been reduced to formulaic incantations. To go back to Serge, in an early article from 1911:

> We have heard them these famous words that hide the most terrifying emptiness. Why did they live, why did they die, those who went to mass graves for Justice, Law, Righteousness, or a human future?[45]

This article finished rather conventionally by advocating 'being' and acting, rather than being merely intellectually seduced by the lure of words and theories in ivory tower-like isolation. But the questions posed here were ones that were to haunt the rest of his writing and were to involve Serge in the political act of testimony, of translating the past through story into a vivid and containing present and with imagination and compelling political honesty.

In another early article, 'Reflections on Morality', Serge spoke of religion in an age of atheism, noting that if Marxism demanded the sacrifice of the personal good for others, Christianity had demanded no less. If Christians forlornly accepted the idea of being a slave (and here Serge shows that he is perfectly aware of Nietzsche), nonetheless Christian morality had one advantage over an atheist ethics.[46] The true Christian never gave in and never surrendered her or his soul. The uncrushable soul of the Christian was her or his greatest strength. Here Serge, as Mumford was to do, called attention to the passive resistance of the Christian to society's conventions and games of power. Such concerns are threaded throughout Serge's life of writing. In an article written in 1941 he described how Stalin had destroyed the cathedrals and forbidden Christian feasts, substituting grotesque cavalcades organized by 'L'Association (gouvernementale) des Sans Dieu'.[47] Nonetheless Christianity survived, as in Revolutionary France, along with the pagan customs. Poor people would offer passers-by a little Christmas tree hidden under their coats, noted Serge. He was alert to the radicalism and political critiques offered by the best of the Christian tradition. He valued, along with Lewis Mumford, the teachings and traditions of the European Huguenots and Protestant non-conformists, which produced Christians who, Serge dryly commented, were quite unlike contemporary French Catholic bourgeois citizens who paid lip service to exterior social forms and venerated icons.

On the other side of the coin, Serge also doubted the possibility of a scientific ethics as much he doubted a 'scientific' Marxism. He also put a question mark over the possibility of any simple form of common morality, given differences of historic cultures, beyond the desire for life itself. In an almost Blakean vision, he believed that morality is that which leads to a release of energy and exuberance, and preserves the basic Enlightenment freedoms. Finding one's way among so many inherited conventions, manners, social coercions, inherited deadness and personal psychological damage was, Serge thought, a serious journey in the dark for any single life. Morality for Serge, like woman's nature for Simone de Beauvoir, was always to be found out in its practice.[48]

The anarcho-syndicalist was fundamentally engaged with ethics. Serge's sense of the unfree person had political consequences in terms of the Marxist millennialist vision of the worker's state. It was not the contemporary proletariat who would inherit the earth, they were neither less nor more sympathetic than their bourgeois masters. The Hegelian master–slave relation had to be broken, or transformed first. Serge was also sophisticated enough to realize that this relation was not simply an economic one. It was a big mistake to argue that the complexities of social life and habit depended on economics alone. In a Weberian moment, Serge argued that the production of social life depended on all relations between people, as well as on symbolic practices.[49] The link between religion, ethics, psychology and politics would occupy Serge all his life. It attracted him significantly to André Gide, whose work had wrestled with the relation between Catholicism and Marxism.

In that respect Serge's brief but late correspondence with the Abbé Ignace Lepp of the Seminaire Universitaire de Lyon, a pupil of Teillard de Chardin, is instructive. The Abbé, popular with radical Catholics in the 1960s, wrote widely distributed books on the working class, existentialism, Christian approaches to Marxism, psychoanalysis, atheism, death and love. He was hardly a conventional friend for a revolutionary but their warm correspondence has the Abbé at one point saying that, dogmatism apart, Serge seemed to him much more authentically closer to Christianity than most of those who professed the faith.[50]

Serge noted too the historic contribution of the Jewish and Christian traditions to Socialist thought. From the Hebrew prophets to the early Christians, the Vaudois, the Hussites in Bohemia, the '*pauvres de Lyon*' and the seventeenth-century English Protestant sects, Serge, like Mumford, took the long view of 'heretical' radical resistance to overweening power and the cruelty of entrenched absolute authority. In choosing the long time-frame, Serge not only brought back to life a usable past but articulated a radical 'socialist' Jewish–Protestant tradition still very much alive in the period during which he was being hounded from Europe to America. In Switzerland that tradition of scholarship and radical action was still signalled by Karl Barth who was combining a somewhat intransigent spirituality (theology itself being a self-sufficient discourse of truth without justification from other discourses) with total active opposition to the Nazis, which for all its perceived later inflexibilities was needed at one of the darkest moments of human history.[51]

Serge, however, also acknowledged that religion had become an instrument in the class war and that historical study had seriously undermined its more literal claims to truth. At the same time he seemed also to see it as a mediating praxis and discourse between the raw biological givens of human life and psychological consciousness itself. He was particularly curious about its relationship with the new psychology: the memory of infant love and fear of the oedipal relation as a discursive narrative projected onto a metaphysically indifferent nature. The thought of Christian redemption becomes a means of maintaining equilibrium in a terrifying world. Nonetheless, for Serge, organized world religions with their founding figures (Abraham, Jesus, Mohammed) and with their intransigently hierarchical social and state formations developing special castes and organizing power, were also indubitably a means of exploiting both existential terror and material misery.[52] His final word on religion is simply to break down the atheist–materialist and religious divide as part of his broader critique of the dissociation of rational and affective life. It was wrong simply to oppose religious faith to a combative atheism, for the roots of belief themselves lay in the human unconscious and the human sense of the unknowable mystery of life over and above the teachings of a historically compromised church.[53]

In the last years of his life, Serge was again wrestling with the relation between politics, psychology and religion. Serge's interests in both behavioural and ego-psychology extended through his massive reading (it was extraordinary how he found the time to do it): Wilhelm Wundt, Josef Breuer, William James, Freud, Pavlov, Jung, Alfred Adler, Wolfgang Koehler and Erich Fromm. Citing Marx's

18th Brumaire and the 'traumatic' sense of the past as a nightmare from which the living 'psychologically' struggle to awaken, he both invoked and critiqued Marx's view of a virtually Cartesian dualism, between mind and world in the base-superstructure model, arguing from Marx's more sympathetic position of the wholeness of the person, that the psychological and material worlds cannot be seen apart. Human activity as such forms an indivisible whole, '*un ensemble indivisible*', in which instincts of conservation and reproduction are directed by the brain. There is no binary division and mental activity is not simply voluntary. Marxism had to take on board what the new sciences of psychology had discovered from pre-natal formations right through to the foundational role of the libido.

Serge clearly felt, along with many commentators since, that Marx's work might be enriched, not diminished by such discoveries. Serge's last writings continue his interest in the psychology of power, a subject that from his anarchist beginnings had always marked him off from the positivist Marxist. What was it that caused the Holocaust? Certainly not pure economics. Irrational fears, inherited anxieties, the unscrupulous technicians of mass psychological manipulation and fear itself motivated totalitarian reaction as much as economics. The cult of leaders was of ancient historical, and certainly pre-capitalist, origin. To characterize Freud simply as a bourgeois, idealist, and metaphysical reactionary, as the left did in mid-century, was to distort the facts.[54] In fact there is a direct link between Serge and the radical psychologists. An extensive set of notes written sometime after the 1942 translation of Wilhelm Reich's *Function of the Orgasm*, shows Serge astonishingly well up with that brilliant but wayward pupil of Freud and Marx. It would not be an implausible speculation to state that it was owing to the poor mental state of his first wife that Serge was so passionately interested in mental illness. Most of the five folded pages of notes on Reich in the Serge papers excerpt passages and it is hardly surprising that Serge copied out Reich's most famous sentences: 'Love, work and knowledge are the well-springs of our life. They should also govern it.'[55]

Serge was not, however, uncritical. He questions the appeal to 'nature', the vitalism, of Reich's almost Rousseau-esque conception of the orgasm and his somewhat utopian hope of spontaneous regulation. He doubts too the quantitative reduction of some of the analysis, and he questions the nineteenth-century ethnological story of freedom from the patriarchal impulse before the establishment of the patriarchal order, just as he regrets the narrowing of the field of repression to infant sexuality and adolescent sexuality within the authoritarian family. The history of repression is to be found in the entire field of the history of culture – '*il s'agit de tout l'histoire de la culture*' – including material conditions.[56] Rightly Serge will not let go of either the best Marxist nor the best Freudian insights, and it is of course the novelist rather than the historian or theorist who will dramatize that multiply dramatic and unpredictable field of human interactions in relation to necessity that in turn produces a surplus of meaning in relation to any theoretical analysis.

His sympathy with Reich's 'that which is alive is in itself reasonable', which he underlines in his notes is complemented with a Gramscian echo in: '*Bon. Optimisme d'action*.'[57] Hence Serge's most faithful contemporary advocate and critic in the English-speaking world alongside Richard Greeman, Bill Marshall, is right to emphasize Serge's view of the self as self-willed and self-defining. His characterization of the work as a positive anthropology needs setting alongside Serge's search for a further, 'higher significance' initiated by 'historical consciousness'. This is found in art and in the all-encompassing field of narrative itself that creatively imitates life in a corresponding movement. Here Serge, and there is a touch of creative Stoicism in Serge's view of the world, to a degree follows what modern commentators such as Badiou, rephrasing Spinoza in his discussion of Deleuze, calls 'the grace of the All': 'For what is, is the grace of the All.' Unlike Deleuze's, however, Serge's 'cheerfulness' was never indifferent.[58]

It should be evident from these preliminary observations that Serge cannot be simply approached along traditional political theoretical lines. Marshall's sensitive and accurate description of Serge's 'political itinerary' show the fractures at every point: his sympathy with the ideas and practices of those outside the party, a doubt of the efficacy of revolution, his refusal to adhere to the strict 'logic' of Marxist Leninism, his lack of belief in dialectically progressive historical reason.[59] Here is a 'Bolshevik' who maintained good relations with the Mensheviks, who agonized over the use of terror and the 'temporary' violent measures during the first years of the Russian revolution, who could not accept an American capitalism that had sent Sacco and Vazetti to the electric chair and who had watched conditions in Germany deteriorate after the failure of socialism there with the deaths of Rosa Luxemburg and Karl Liebknecht. He was a theoretician of some breadth. He analysed global developments in article after article. He prophesied the Cold War, the politics of uneven global development, the nationalist anti-imperial struggles of decolonialization, and foresaw the importance of Mao. Last, but not least, he foresaw the re-emergence of the Muslim world.

These global changes are not reducible to purely economic causes. They were for Serge also ideological in the sense ideologies may be defined against the narrow Napoleonic view (where your enemy is an *idéologue*) as definable fields of beliefs and cultural practices both inherited and proposed. So, for example, the various 'isms' and other collective practices might be both negatively and positively evaluated. Social democracy developed a bourgeois mentality but its fidelity to democracy and humanist values was admirable. Bolshevism was dogged by statism and intolerance but it released energy and a sense of active organization. Stalinism was characterized by corruption and a total absence of scruples, but it had an extraordinary capacity for mass direction and mass technical development – Serge never got quite as far as 'small is beautiful'.[60] Like

Mumford, Serge hoped for great things from an enlightened trade union movement in a system of devolved power. It was never realized. While the movement's organizing historical activity with its genuine concern for working people, its idealism and its capacity to criticize the state were admirable, argued Serge, it remained politically passive, splitting skilled and unskilled workers. Furthermore it was often anti-intellectual and not politically efficient enough.

Like a number of other commentators of the period, Serge recognized two universal tendencies irrespective of pure theory: the emergence of bureaucratic forms of power and a totalitarian impulse implicit in technological development. The latter allowed the mechanization not only of means of production but also of what commentators such as Jacques Ellul and Lewis Mumford were to characterize as mechanical orders of mind. These would produce new views of the person and systems of power. The predations of the latter would be concealed under marketed claims of truth to technique, as if the truth of technique were truth itself. In short, the technological revolution (itself driven by capitalism) would further drive a social revolution along with the development of global corporate power. Along with James Burnham (whom Serge otherwise loathed), Dwight Macdonald and Trotsky in his later writings, Serge believed that a kind of 'bureaucratic collectivism' would characterize new forms of political power. Certainly Serge foresaw the working class as such largely losing any kind of homogeneity amenable to radical organization, and the middle class splitting between highly paid middle-class technicians who would tend to view everything in terms of technique and a gradually impoverished remainder. One thing, however, was clear: the old lines of oppositional thought were dead for ever. An extraordinary confusion of ideology, belief, and practices was the legacy of the years from 1917 through to 1933 and then to 1945. What perhaps Serge did not articulate so clearly was the imminent loss of the socialist intellectual tradition, the tradition in which he himself had been nurtured.

For Serge's was a generation in which liberals and radicals had investigated the limits of Bentham and Carlyle and examined the romantic protest against mechanization in both the English and German traditions. In the social devastation of the industrial revolution they had argued passionately about solutions: utilitarian, religious, economic and political. They had read the works of the *encyclopédistes*, they had been inspired by Rousseau. They had discussed the roles of the Jacobins and the inevitability or not of Thermidor, the modern world that emerged with Napoleon and the industrial revolution. They knew the traditions of the Calvinist revolution in Europe, the Protestant political thinkers of the English Civil War, the Victorian non-conformist liberal reformers. They understood the contribution of utopian thinkers to early socialist thought; they had read Blanqui's *Société des Saisons*.

The 'rights of man' and the limits of natural law were for this generation issues of burning concern. They had read about movements to improve factory conditions. They knew about Robert Owen and the Comte de Saint-Simon. They read Charles Dickens and in Britain sang the hymns of Charles Wesley. They remembered the Chartists, they shook their heads over the political quietism of Proudhon and his conservative view of women and the family, but they remembered that property was theft. In continental Europe, they had discussed the relation between Catholicism and socialism, contrasting the passivity of the Irish in the potato famine in 1845–7 with the Spanish Catholic peasantry flocking to anarchism in the 1870s. In the Marxist tradition they discussed the usefulness of the metaphysical thinking of the German philosophical tradition and its relationship to the development of a scientific socialism. They wondered just how scientific socialism could in fact be. They developed grand narratives of human progress and development, shifting around taxonomies of whole eras of human history. They argued the difference between Fichte and Schelling. They debated whether a philosophical indictment of civilization could be made into critique of capitalism and, indeed, vice versa.

The Enlightenment thinkers had looked back to the lost harmony of the Middle Ages; Marx and his contemporaries had looked to the Greeks. Both options were available and their merits could be discussed. They discussed the philosophical nature of necessity and historical logic, a tradition that was to extend far into the twentieth century in the writings of Jean-Paul Sartre, but had begun with Vico and had continued with Spinoza.[61] In Russia the followers of Herzen fought it out with the followers of Chernyshevsky. Kropotkin turned the reactionary simplifications drawn by sociological adaptations of Darwinian theory on their heads, and Plekhanov shifted all their thoughts from a critical utopia of Slavic peasantry to the newly industrialized working classes. In Paris Bakunin's anarcho-communism found uncertain support in Proudhon's work. In London, the British found their own path to socialism through positivist approaches to Marx, pragmatic local activity and spontaneous organization. There, the Labour Party theoreticians, insofar as they had theories, took a humanized Comtism via Fabianism into the refined circles of Bloomsbury and in the Hampstead Public Library the labour theory of value and the theory of surplus value were hotly discussed by the literary cognoscenti.

In Spain the anarchists developed their own traditions out of Bakunin, Kropotkin and others, and (this is important for understanding Serge) the 'religious character of anarchism as a doctrine and a morality [suited] an uprooted peasantry which had lost its land and its traditional way of life and got nothing worth-while in return.'[62] Yet that 'religious' character as we have seen was not some sentimental reversion to metaphysics as it seemed in the atheist gaze of the Marxist, rather it opened the way to connecting Marxism with discourses relating to *la vie intérieure* and to the psychology of the person. It is this multiple leftist tradition, ranging in Serge's time from an intransigent Marxist-Leninism to a too-accommodating social democracy, that was to be a casualty of Stalinism, the Second World War, the Cold War and the global domination of American economic and cultural power.

In addition to narratives of grand theory, Serge and others like him knew in detail the history of what they called the 'struggle'. They were intensely historically aware, and had studied and analysed the years between 1789 and 1795 in France, all of Europe in 1830 and in 1848, and the brief years of the Chartists and the Paris Commune. These moments became loci of a grand narrative of progressive socialist history which gathered the past in terms of ideas, and in terms of theories and practices from the Greeks to the present time, in ways which kept the horizon of the socialist future as part of its essential narrative vision. Furthermore they had what appeared to disappear forever with the explosion of the atomic bomb in 1945. They had a hope, not always necessarily millennialist, that justice and a fairer world (inspired by that great bourgeois Victorian optimism which held up to 1914) were within human reach. Collectivist in theory and sometimes in practice, they turned the ego-psychology of romantic heroic individualism into the selfless, often self-abnegating collectivist psychology of impersonal devotion to the cause. How many Bolsheviks went to the Stalinist firing squad believing in their personal sacrifice to 'temporary' reaction (or did they?) in order to save the greater cause of the revolution itself?

The sense of history that Serge put into play drew on the fading legacies of nineteenth-century historical narrative, with its chronologies and eras. A different, non-linear sense of time that Hannah Arendt discovers in Karl Jaspers is worth recalling here. Jaspers's temporality is spatial, she argued, because it remains in reference to the world rather than to any discrete existing space, and it is hence diametrically opposed to that particularly nineteenth-century conjuncture of ideology and chronology, which promised, one should add particularly for the Marxist view of history, a secure guide to the past. Without it, in the chaos of the twentieth century, there was left only a sense of helplessness:

> In this predicament, with the whole relation of modern man to his past at stake, Jaspers converted the succession in time into a spatial juxtaposition, so that nearness and distance depend no longer on the centuries which separate us from a philosopher, but exclusively on the freely chosen point from which we enter this realm of the spirit, which will endure and expand as long as there are men on earth.[63]

Serge was not without a sense of chronology, but his sense of history also profoundly illustrated an imaginative ability to enter a freely chosen point against all orthodox chronologies as a way of celebrating the human spirit. In Serge this sense of the time of the world is in conflict with the fossilizing time of Marxist historiography. Put most simply, the *humanitas* of the former will shadow and interact with the utopian expectation of the latter. In Arendt's terms, Serge attempts to enter the spirit of the unfamiliar culture to make himself freely at home there. As for his own moment, his last quarrels with his expatriate contemporaries are a result in part of his abandonment of a Marxist narrative of history in favour of the person and a greater openness to the changing times of the world, together with their unpredictable and more various sense of what that past actually was.

Serge wrote historical notes towards defining the psychology of the twentieth-century person. In a last holograph, sometimes difficult to read, Serge made notes for an article to be called 'The Writer's Conscience'. In these darkest of times, Serge began, he had seen men give up their lives for the writer's freedom of conscience. The destruction of that freedom had taken on the proportions of a nightmare. In the totalitarian atmosphere Serge, in Orwellian mood, speaks of the threat of love and the genuine religious spirit as more dangerous to tyrannies than at first appears. In poetry and prose they threatened that 'scientific' prose whose 'realism' was the imperative of state discourse. One remembers Orwell whose magnificent parody in *Nineteen Eighty-Four* has Winston claiming that 'The Revolution will be complete when the language is perfect.'[64]

In that sense literature, poetry or prose, expressive of the interior life ('*la littérature de la vie intérieure*') is directed against 'scientific' social realism, and has a powerful revolutionary function in that it recreates the possibility of what Serge called living profoundly ('*vivre profondement*'). Like William Faulkner in his Nobel Prize speech, Serge brought back the large ethical words: vision, integrity, fidelity, truth, probity, intelligence and intransigence. Serge spoke in a charged atmosphere for he was aware of the suicides of Stefan Zweig, Ernst Toller, Walter Hasenclever and Walter Benjamin and the murders of Federico García Lorca and Boris Pilniak, just a few of those who had paid for writing truthful literature in totalitarian Europe. Of the Russian poets who shared similar fates he listed Pavel Vassiliev, Nicholaï Alexeivitch Kliouev, Pierre Orechine, Alexander Ganin and Prince Sviatopolk-Mirsky. Elsewhere he spoke of Osip Mandelstam and Margarita Hilguer, who had written in a nineteenth-century style, a style that in itself became a revolutionary act in a culture of Stalinist social realism.[65] Later, in the *Memoirs* Serge would write portraits of the Russian poets Nikolai Stepanovich Gumilev, Sergei Yesenin ('thirty years old, at his peak of glory, eight times married [...] he was our greatest poet'[66]), Vladimir Mayakovsky, ('earning a great deal of money publishing official poetry'[67]), Ilya Ehrenburg, Andrei Bely and Alexander Blok.

In terms of prose Serge looked at selected European masters in relation to the ideological foundations of their fictive worlds, but unlike for Lukács, the valorization is without a demand for realism, merely for the most appropriate mode in relation to historical truth. Hence Balzac's world is articulated by money and capital, Hugo's by the contradictions of the Empire, Flaubert's by an interior truth produced by a the formal aesthetics of quasi-psychological documentation, Zola's by his dissenting idealism in the context of the Dreyfus

Affair, Dostoevsky's by political reaction, Christianity and the soul's interior struggle. Tolstoy writes the drama of both the interior life and the external life of the state equally, in opposition to political censorship, absolutism and the Orthodox Church. Gide writes his own time by an aesthetic approach to plot disjuncture, incorporating a dissenting view of both Christianity and Marxism, not to mention homophobia.

Bill Marshall has noted in detail Serge's important debt to Gide. It was Serge who openly appealed to Gide as he was about to set off on his celebrated visit to Russia, on grounds of the Stalinist Terror with its conformist literary imperatives and the disappearance of poets and writers such as Mandelstam. Serge helped Gide with the manuscript of *Retour de l'USSR* and Gide himself, sympathetic to the left oppositionists in the Soviet Union, met Léon Blum to assist Trotsky's transit from Norway through France on his way to Mexico. Serge never condemned Gide as a bourgeois decadent writer.

The acceptance of analyses opaque to Marxist criticism was revolutionary in itself, just as any submission of art to orthodoxy is always counter-revolutionary. Marshall notes the humanist Marxist emphasis on consciousness and, borrowing the word from the new existentialist writers such as André Malraux, personal authenticity.[68] In French, however, *conscience* means both consciousness and conscience, and the latter, in Serge's case, needs to be placed on equal footing with the Marxist imperative of raising consciousness. Serge noted, with the emphasis on the former rather than on the latter, though both meanings would be appropriate: '*L'état totalitaire réduit la conscience à un rôle technique, subordonné*' ('The totalitarian state reduces conscience [consciousness] to a subordinate technical role').[69] But it was not only Marxist humanism that was the source of Gide's *conscience*. Critics have noted that Gide's 'autobiographical discourse is steeped in a kind of secular Protestantism'.[70]

Memoirs of a Revolutionary

We come now to Serge's own autobiography. It begins in fin-de-siècle Russia, with Serge himself born into a milieu of intellectual Russian anarchists ('On the walls of our humble and makeshift lodgings there were always the portraits of men who had been hanged.'[71]) It is a journey that ends in Cárdenas's Mexico during the Second World War. The portraits of the hanged men on the wall might seem a moment of curiously black-humoured nostalgia, but it is also a key to the psychology of Serge's writing career (the elegiac rewriting of the historical trace), just as the 'criminal' description he gives of himself as a small boy wrecking his mother's clothes and his father's scientific notes, spilling ink, rushing off to bed in grief thinking of Lear leaning on Cordelia and climbing trees 'as if evil never existed',[72] alerts us to the fact that this future 'Marxist' will be profoundly engaged with psychology and ethics, the unfathomable problem of historical contingency, and the continuous pull of the world away from a too-absorbing interior life.

A first survey of the text reveals one of the most extraordinary life histories of any century. No writer of a picaresque story could quite so plausibly, nor with such suspension of disbelief, ensure the sheer survival of its hero. Unlike Thackeray's George Osborne, this hero should have been killed off not just in the middle of the story, but in the first paragraph of the first chapter.

> For my part, I have undergone a little over ten years of various forms of captivity, agitated in seven countries, and written twenty books. I own nothing. On several occasions a press with a vast circulation has hurled filth at me because I spoke the truth. Behind us lies a victorious revolution gone astray, several abortive attempts at revolution, and massacres in so great number as to inspire a certain dizziness. And to think that it is not over yet. Let me be done with this digression; those were the only roads possible for us. I have more confidence in mankind and in the future than ever before.[73]

It is difficult to give a sense of the unquenchable faith and the compelling need to bear witness, to make and investigate history as a gift to human beings yet to be born. Socialism for Serge gave meaning to life as Christianity had done for believers. In its name everything could be suffered and endured. But its paradise was this-worldly, including the sense of a this-worldly future. That sense of the future still, to a degree, bore traces of a Victorian sense of progress. What is less difficult to understand is the need to write the twenty books. It was not an either–or; it was not faith and praxis versus writing, even though Serge presented the writing as a survivalist occupation in compulsory default of available political activity. What it offered was a past of the relation of the agent and witness to history and hence provided a kind of testimony: a story providing memory, evidence and inviting judgement. It was a story of political vision at a moment of political failure, in which contingency everywhere interrupted propaganda. Its honesty inevitably sought new means of analysis.

Serge's autobiography also feels like a cross between a saint's life, *The Pilgrim's Progress* in reverse, and Ben Jonson's *Bartholomew Fair*. Here are accounts of every man (and they are largely men) in his humour, counterbalanced by both a mystical and quasi-Protestant mingling of emotional and ethical judgement. The ethics were personal. A man did not betray his friends even if they were idiots. Serge, when arbitrarily arrested, refused, like the mythical English public school boy, to 'sneak' on the early twentieth-century anarchist terrorist Bonnot Gang whose tactics he abhorred. Commenting on his subsequent first five years of prison in France, which led him to what he astonishingly called 'the enriching experience of cell life',[74] he remarked, 'I understood, and ever since have always missed, the old Christian custom of retreats which men spent in monasteries, meditating face to face with themselves and with God, in other words with the vast living solitude of the universe. It will be good if that custom can be revived.'[75] Putting saints in jail has ever been the despair of the state and its judiciary. For Serge this was typical of his ability to invent another interpretation, a positive renegotiating of a crippling fact or experience, an ability which enabled him to survive whereas others did not. In prison, twenty-five miles from the Marne, Serge lived out the Great War in the 'rumour of war', in a prison which boasted its own considerable mortality rate.

Throughout the text of the autobiography there is a sense of the arresting detail of a life lived significantly in history. Buying guns from the Finns in 1919, Serge exchanged 'whole casefuls of beautiful 500 rouble notes, watery in appearance, with the image of Catherine the Great and the signature of a bank-director as dead as his bank, his social order and the Empress Catherine'.[76] When Trotsky arrived for the defence of Petrograd and the troops sang in the amphitheatre of the old Imperial Duma, Serge noted: 'I reflected that the psalms sung by Cromwell's Roundheads before their decisive battles must have sounded not different a tone.'[77]

Fragmentary narratives turn into historical and political parables. When Serge was off to a 'French' commune in 1920 to live the utopian good life on an abandoned estate north of Petrograd with French communists, Hungarian prisoners-of-war, his father-in-law and a Tolstoyan doctor, the latter needed to open the neck of his blouse to show a golden cross to an obdurate peasant woman and to declare 'We're Christians too, little sister', in order to stop the peasants from burning the house down and stealing everything within sight.[78] The actual event and its symbolic and ideological significance are virtually indistinguishable in this rueful critique of the utopian impulse.

Contemporary criticism is obsessed with the fatalistic nature of the fractured subject and deploys its exquisitely complex psychological and cultural discourses with a certain relentlessness. Few take it into a political critique, hamstrung as they are by the partial explanations of the politics of identity. With Sartre no longer read and Brecht neither read nor seen in a world of televised real-life dramas endlessly critiqued in jargonized language by the globalized academic commissars of 'popular' culture, few remember the old political theatre of the subject in social and economic circumstance. Travelling illegally into Berlin in 1922 Serge 'fractures his own ego-subject' by giving us a unique and comic historical sense of the atmosphere of the early Weimar Republic:

> Without any difficulty, I bought from the Berlin *Polizeipräsidium*, at the price of ten dollars and a few cigars, a genuine residence permit which, moreover, transformed me from a Belgian into a Pole. Soon I had to change my nationality again, this time

> into a Lithuanian, since the cafés in Berlin were plastered with notices saying: 'no Poles served here.'[79]

Having to dodge surveillance in Berlin, in the early years of the revolution, Serge recounts how he was

> successively Siegfried and Gottlieb; in town I was Dr. Albert, on my papers Viktor Klein and, in my journeys to Russia, Alexei Berlovsky, a former Russian prisoner-of-war in Germany. Victor Serge date-lined his articles (which were reprinted as far away as China) from Kiev, a city to which, as it happened, I had never been.[80]

The insouciant humour of an essentially anarchic spirit was part of an *élan vital* that characterizes all of Serge's writing and is valuable today as a critique of those who exploit xenophobic fears of the ever-threatening immigrant stranger who is at once everywhere and nowhere and in infinite disguise because he or she is officially invisible and unable to speak.

Reversing the current slogans, for Serge, the political was personal, or at least so the original faith required. Nowhere is the 'religious' faith of the revolutionary better expressed than in the moment following the death of Lenin when there was an ominous sense of the gathering clouds of counter-revolution:

> Events continued to overwhelm us. Even where they took place at a distance I find it hard to separate them from my personal memories. All we lived for was activity integrated into history; we were interchangeable; we could immediately see the repercussions of affairs in Russia upon affairs in Germany and the Balkans; we felt linked without comrades who, in pursuit of the same ends as we, perished or else scored some success at the other end of Europe. None of us had, in the bourgeois sense of the word, any personal existence: we changed our names, our posting and our work at the Party's need; we had just enough to live on without real material discomfort, and we were not interested in making money, or following a career, or producing a literary heritage, of leaving a name behind us; we were interested solely in the difficult business of reaching Socialism.[81]

The key issue here can be simplified by engaging with problems of temporality. Socialism is a millennialist goal with its strangely paradoxical sense of infinite time in no real moment. For Serge, events are confusion, generalized and characterized by intensity, so the sense of the present becomes psychological rather than discrete and chronological. Space too is similarly generalized and distance is shrunk in the recognition of a politically homogenous activity, not under the eye of God but of 'History' itself. For the rest the only recourse is to religious language, that renunciation of self, in order to find it in again in the collective body of the group. Even the adopting of different pseudonyms, though tactical, puts the party before self. The world's goods are renounced: money, success, fame. The supreme paradox is that materialist socialism is not of this world, but of a world to come.

Yet such a declaration cannot simply be taken on the terms here offered. It has an even more important role as a tactical proposition in Serge's narrative. It is at once a point of faith, of implausibility, of self-mockery, of irony. This is because what immediately follows in the text recounts the slaughter of the Estonian Communists, of Poles in Cracow and of Russians in Georgia. The next paragraph begins in fact with 'At 5.15 a.m. on 1 December 1924, Estonian Communists, following the orders of the E.C.C.I.,[82] attacked the public buildings of Tallinn with the objective of seizing power.'[83] The precisely temporally and spatially located contingent event sparks off not a universality of predictable praxis, but a narrative of rebellion against rising Bolshevik totalitarianism.

How do the self-abnegating life of the socialist and the pragmatic betrayals fit together in the ongoing narrative? Serge in fact never theorizes the juxtaposition. What is left is an ominous sense of a reaffirmation of faith in danger, and a sense of a larger game being played. With the ethical outrage at the betrayal of faith, however, is an anarchist's best sense of the corruption of power. Serge articulates this in ways which, reading it at the beginning of the third millennium, seem uncannily familiar:

> [...] could Red Russia, as a great Power, agree that two little countries like Georgia and Azerbaijan, prone to hostile influences and bound to become a hunting-ground of foreign powers, should keep their petroleum, manganese and strategic roads all to themselves?[84]

This moment, therefore, recalls the past faith of the revolution, now five years old, articulates a present which seriously betrays it in the brutal pragmatism of the Zinoviev appointment, and suggests an explanation in which the future of capitalism, State or Private, will further betray the revolution. Furthermore, our contemporary reading recognizes a continuity of human history at the personal, political and economic levels. Again it is a kind of parable of the defeat of the common interest in favour of self-interest. The key words 'as a great Power' are ambiguous here: they represent a longing to maintain the power of a revolutionary great power against capitalist power, while at the same time questioning the right of any great power over the democratic sovereignty of small nations.

Against power politics was commonality of interest. The reverse side of the power of economic interest is the picture given in Serge's rather world-weary description of the mafia-like actuality behind the dream of Balkan Federation (1920–39):

> Around the great conception of Balkan Federation there swarmed hordes of secret agents, impresarios of irredentism, pedlars of the influential word, night-walking politicians engaged in six intrigues at a time; and all these smart gentlemen, with their over-gaudy neckties, sought to harness the unbridled energy of the *Comitajis* and sell it to and fro to any buyer. There was the Italian wing, the Bulgarian wing, the Yugoslav wing, two Greek tendencies, one monarchist and one republican, ideologies, personal cliques, and vendettas. We knew the cafés in which the revolvers of any given group lay in wait [...] [85]

What Serge builds up here is the impossibility of authentic engagement without democracy, without principle, without conviction and without faith. As the revolution degenerated into totalitarian rule, those who would sell it out descended into individual competitiveness. They are vividly characterized as 'pedlars of the influential word', all with their 'gaudy neckties' and 'smartness'. It is a critical dystopian model for any contemporary competitive bureaucracy: academic, political, legal or medical. Against these people (men and women who 'get themselves about', careerists, fifth columnists and institutional climbers with well-advertised slender achievements), Serge posed a left-wing Carlylean description of 'worthy men',[86] a multiple portraiture of inevitably 'hanged men'. Part of the pleasure in reading Serge is his black Pynchonesque sense of the totalitarian character-type and the perpetual irony of the historically contingent moment within the system, but it comes without Pynchon's (albeit comic) folksy fatalisms, heritage-style simplifications of history (merry Brits rolling cheeses down hills in Gloucestershire), and too-ready and perhaps too-clever dismemberment of the conscious agent.[87] Satire is only one of Serge's modes.

From 1926 onwards Serge describes himself as out of the party. Off the committees but well-informed and aware of the collapse of radicalism of the revolution, he finds himself increasingly isolated, eventually being arrested as the war against the peasants and the liquidation of the *kulaks* begin to take its terrible toll. Serge's polemical self-directive not to be embittered by the misfortunes of individuals is belied in a mounting sense of outrage as his portraits of the 'disappeared' begin to multiply. It is as if what cannot be acknowledged to fail politically (that is, a vision of a collective transcendence of individual interests) is reaffirmed by a kind of hagiography of exemplary men. However, whereas the saint is traditionally 'signed' and scarce, Serge's multiple portraits of resistance suggest a widespread stubbornness borne out by the sheer numbers of ordinary communist men and women, both highly differentiated and highly specific, whom Stalin needed to murder. Such interpretations are reinforced by those small Tolstoyan transcendent moments that disrupt the almost fatalistic narrative of defeat and that Serge often employs to take the edge off the monstrous banality of the process of the trials. Transferred to the House of Arrest, and in the company of a plain-clothed police officer, 'clean shaven and open-faced', he is given a moment or two to 'lean for a while on the embankment overlooking the dark waters of the Neva'.[88] 'The air from the open sea is bracing', says Serge, 'I always find this river so charged with turbulent power that I am stirred by it as though by some Russian song.'[89]

In recognizing the plain-clothed policeman as a human being and, to an inevitably small degree, as generous, Serge saves himself the anguish of the isolation of the assumption of universal political psychosis and predictable human behaviour. The frankly romantic moment of the contemplation of river and sea is perhaps less an ironic contrast to the forthcoming imprisonment and deportation than it is a moment of 'retreat' from the world, in which the 'blind' universe of nature becomes a friend, a steadying psychological moment of enlargement of vision that Serge will carry with him through the interrogations. The analogy of the Russian song recalls an older folk Russia, whose art now becomes a resource of the soul itself and implicitly questions the values of present tyranny in the longer context of achieved human value, anticipating also, therefore, the historical mortality of this ultimately finite period of Terror.

Exiled in 1933 to Orenburg, with its relentless extreme summers and winters, Serge noted the devastated Kirghiz people, the motley crowds of famished thieves and scroungers from far-flung Turkestan and Pamir. He stepped aside from his grand narrative to notice particulars like a latter-day Beat writer of the 1950s: 'A weird Turkmenian in a turban divined the future by throwing goats' vertebrae upon engravings from an erotic book in French published at Amsterdam in Voltaire's time.'[90] This moment like a 'found poem' articulates the compulsory 'globalization' of the devouring Soviet empire. Its postmodern pastiche of signifiers articulates the merely fascinating. It retains, however, an authentic melancholy derived from the displacements of time, culture and meaning. The thrown bones of the goat in the image are a classical–Christian sexualized *memento mori*, as a Muslim becomes the prophet, while Serge notes Voltaire to recall a more sceptical and long-gone Enlightenment. Yet, more fundamentally, there is pure annihilation of meaning here; the collaged images make sense only as an collaged advertisement makes sense. The real meaning lies in a confidence trick where an already designated future becomes a source of present profit.

In a world turned upside down, all normal connections are broken. Serge was living on the 'income of a well-paid technician',[91] an income derived from post office fiscal compensation paid out for his manuscripts and letters that had gone astray, that is, that had been seized by Stalinist agents: a wonderfully ironic combination of abstract exchange values and state capitalist theft which the compulsory state-buying system authorizes to the profit of its victim. What comes across throughout the book is Serge's ability to live wherever he happens to be: his instinct for adaptation, his humour, his complete lack of self-pity. This is not to say his emotions are not engaged. Leaving Orenberg, with its little knot of exiled comrades and its ancient folk traditions, Serge is devastated:

'I was severing attachments of a unique quality. I should have liked to have those dear faces, that I would never see again, imprinted on my brain, and those landscapes of white countryside, and even some image of our great Russian misery, lived out by this brave, gritty, patient people [...] I should have been content to remain there – even if it were in some little Mongol fishing village inside the Arctic Circle.'[92]

This hugely patriotic, romantic love of the Russian landscape and his comrades is celebrated in enforced renunciation. Two things are hence affirmed. Ordinary life in personal terms has become like living in constant war-time, so there is a curious sense in which the ordinariness of life with its rites of passage, its births and deaths, its family and local connections is not an option. It is hard to tell in Serge's writings whether his virtually ego-less relationship to ordinary life was the decision of the writer, the revolutionary or compelled by the turmoil of the post-revolutionary era. Sometimes the rallying call to collective destiny sounds like a slightly tired mantra, yet Serge's observations were always individual: the 'people's palace' of the Moscow underground, he noted on his return to Moscow, lacked a place in its marbled halls for a tired working woman to sit down.[93] That Nietzschean ability to relinquish the past, at least in terms of personal life and possessions, as Serge was chased from the Soviet Union to Belgium to France to Mexico, forms a crucial part of Serge's exuberance, at once intoxicating and desperate. Fleeing south from Paris in 1940, he remarks: 'our flight is accompanied by a sense of release bordering at times on gaiety'.[94] He has enough self-reflexive irony also to offer the understatement of his life: 'It is true that I am used to it.'[95]

It is also true, as the letter from Serge to Macdonald during the flight to Mexico shows, that the separation at key moments from the women of his second family, his wife Laurette and their daughter Jeannine, was far from exuberant.[96] So in a sense these observations are part of a subject he deliberately constructs in the *Memoirs*, not *the* self but a complex revolutionary self, an ideal self invaded and torn by historical pattern and contingency, a self, in his terms, bearing his own unique 'sense of history'. It is a self not easily recognizable today where personal 'revelation' is cast within the genre of the confession, that always-aggressive attempt to dominate others, and within the predictable image of the 'personality', which is essentially part of a commercial transaction. Part of Serge's exuberance was caused by an ironic sense of helplessness: 'nothing in fact was possible [in France] any more: certainly not a revolution, with this working class gorged on fresh Camembert, pleasant wine, and ancient ideas which had become mere words – a working class, moreover, ringed on all sides by Nazi Germany, Fascist Italy, Franco Spain, and insular, Conservative Great Britain.'[97] The French bourgeoisie were also unlikely to resist, those with vaguely anarchist convictions and with châteaux in the Dordogne or Gironde were distinctly unhelpful to the family on the flight south in 1940. As always it was the poor who helped the poor. Once again Serge readjusts: 'A man can sleep, and sleep well in a stinking over-priced hotel next to the slaughter-house as we did. He can cook his meals in a school and work in cafés; for the Age of Waiting has begun [...]'.[98]

Serge's last paragraphs are almost the most moving in the book. In the catastrophe of war he realizes 'no ideology has stood before the shock'.[99] Paradoxically it is the tyrannies that have broken the mould of history itself. But using an appropriate apocalyptic rhetoric of historical chaos and a phoenix-like prophecy of an utterly different world, Serge closes with a kind of prayer and invocation and it has all the power of an authentic testimony of a life simultaneously lived, reflected upon and perhaps above all written. Surely that rhetorical plea, cited earlier, was there in the testimony offered: 'May the passion, the experience and even the faults of my fighting generation have some small power to illumine the way forward!'[100] These closing words of the *Memoirs*, in which the past and present are prophesied simultaneously and in conjunction, were written in February 1943 and never published in his lifetime.

Politics and Ideology

No examination of Serge's work can ignore the political and ideological issues. Serge was to bring that more holistic sense of the world offered in great literature, to an increasingly dogmatic Marxism. Throughout the *Memoirs*, in terms of praxis and theory, Serge stresses the failure of Marxist-Leninism to move from a monolithic dogma to a more multiply engaged and more flexible ideology. He insists, often humorously, on a pluralistic experience of free political discussion over political correctness, recalling days on the Left Bank, for example, where 'syndicalist-royalist' doctrines invoking Nietzsche, Georges Sorel, 'the social myth', the communal Guilds of the Middle Ages and national sentiment confronted those absolute vegetarians ('no wine or coffee, tea or infusions') who felt that those who 'ate otherwise' were insufficiently 'evolved'.[101]

Authority always fears laughter, and Serge's almost Jamesian insistence on the psychology of any compulsive activity is always a powerful satirical weapon. Vignettes like this are scattered throughout the text. In the Russian group in Paris he noted 'only one Bolshevik, the chemical engineer Krauterkraft, whose constant antagonist I was, since he advocated a merciless dictatorship, suppression of Press freedom, authoritarian revolution and education on Marxist lines. (Later on he refused to leave for Russia.)'[102] This ironic vignette has an ethical thickness of course: the contrast between the absolutism of demagogic theory and a total absence of democratic or even human practice. There's more than lurking humour in the selection of name and incident: *Krauterkraft*, for example, means 'cabbage power' with a hint of Prussian rather than Russian absolutism.

Serge's 'strong leanings towards heresy'[103] were to stand him in good stead. They were to lead him away, with considerable personal sadness, from Trotsky's 'rigid ideas, with their schematism and voluntarism',[104] and they account for his sympathy with Martov, the Menshevik leader who predicted to Serge that free cooperation with the Bolsheviks would not be possible.[105] Yet at the same time Serge knew the weaknesses of the social democrats who had not understood that the world had moved on since 1848, with the rise of industrialization and a relatively homogeneous industrial proletariat.

As Trotsky, in practical terms Serge did not see the peasantry as simply 'counter-revolutionary'. In 1920 he opposed requisitioning and economic centralization. Nonetheless it is important to realize that Serge stood with the revolution even to the extent of not going to see the dying Kropotkin because he did not want to get into awkward exchange with the man who constantly complained to Lenin about Bolshevik intolerance and the nationalization of the book trade.[106] Serge's ideological position in the *Memoirs* differs from that in his work written closer to the revolution because he responds more freely and honestly to Stalin's rise, the war against the peasants, the trials, his own expulsion from the Soviet Union, and the outbreak of the Second World War. In some ways, *Memoirs*, more flexible in its judgements, reconnects ideologically with the very early writings. In *Year One of the Russian Revolution* (1930), for example, Serge is keen to present the 'historical necessity' of the Bolshevik cause and largely suppresses his anarcho-syndicalist past, following the Marxist-Leninist line. The book describes the condition of the Russian worker before the revolution, Lenin's decisiveness is emphasized, the Bolshevik seizure of power is unambiguously praised and the diction is redolent with phrases such as 'scientific analysis of the historical process' and the 'logic of history'. In addition Lenin is made the supreme iconic hero and the communists are seen as reluctant to suppress civil liberties. The gains of the eight-hour day, warm clothing for the army, the abolition of class hierarchy, civil marriage, secular education, the right to divorce and fair legal codes are all highlighted.

The very real encircling threat to the Soviet state is properly emphasized. Serge was aware that in the crisis faced by the fledgling Soviet Union, ideological positions had to be both simplified and sometimes abandoned in the face of pure necessity. From 1917 onwards a terrible famine threatened and the Western Allies and Germany were poised to intervene at every point. In turn, the famine was posed to create anarchy, the Czechoslovaks threatened the trans-Siberian railway, the Japanese were in Vladivostok, the British and French were at Murmansk and the Germans were at Pskov and Minsk as well as all over the Ukraine. The Cossacks were in the South Urals and the Soviet state itself was effectively reduced to 'the Grand Duchy of Moscow, just as in the fifteenth century'.[107] It was at this point that press censorship was introduced and the Bolsheviks, expropriating land, finance and peasant capital, began the nationalization of large-scale industry.

Serge is also harsh in his judgement of the anarchists. As Peter Sedgwick points out in his introduction to *Year One of the Russian Revolution*, Serge does not make the usual Trotskyite case (nor the Rosa Luxemburg and Menshevik case) against the authoritarian ideological bias of Lenin's thought.[108] In a sense *Year One of the Russian Revolution* can be explained ideologically by Serge's position in 1925–8. During this period he was a secret agent for the Comintern in Berlin and Vienna; he was not expelled from the Communist Party until 1928 when he finished the work. In 1930, when the book appeared, he was still three years away from his arrest.

Even so, there are, in the last chapter, entitled 'War Communism', a few hidden cracks in this somewhat simplistic ideological picture. Lenin's intransigence is attributed entirely to the needs of the time but it is nonetheless seen as too brutal. The food problem is prophesied as being partly resolved in 1921 with a return to a free market and an establishment of tax in kind. That was not an innocent remark in 1930 with the first stage of the disastrous collectivization of the peasants well under way. The emphasis on local ingenuity, improvisation and a certain amount of accommodation of the petit bourgeoisie and skilled bourgeoisie, for example, would have seemed positively anarchic and dangerously subversive by 1930, as would a reminder of the right of the Mensheviks to go on publishing their journals and tolerance towards 'bourgeois' writers. This narrative of the Bolshevik drama, of transforming simple intelligent honesty under dire necessity, had some plausibility in 1919 but there are, even so, several ominous sentences a few pages from the end of the book:

> The party's old democratic customs now give way to a more authoritarian centralization. This is necessitated by the demands of the struggle and by the influx of new members *who have neither a Marxist training nor the personal quality of the pre-1917 militants*: the 'old guard' of Bolshevism is justly determined to preserve its own political hegemony.[109]

Within six or seven years of the publication of *Year One of the Russian Revolution* they would all be slaughtered; terrorized lackeys, careerists, opportunist bureaucrats and fundamentalist courtiers would take their place in what Serge was one of the first to call a totalitarian system. Equally, Serge's account of poets rallying to the cause and prose writers seriously demurring was the last time he would be so simplistic. Ideologically, the rest of Serge's life would be spent recovering from these all-too-loyal and blindly hopeful ideological judgements. For Serge there was the tragedy of a gigantic ethical failure, a failure to live up to that visionary sense of history shared by selfless disciples who moved in implacable obedience in relation to it: 'The highest praise that can be bestowed on him [the communist] is to say that he "has no private life", that his life has fused totally with history.'[110]

The doctrine was hardly new: 'And everyone that hath forsaken houses, or brethren, or sisters, or father or mother, or wife, or children, or lands, for my name's sake, shall receive an hundred fold and shall inherit everlasting life.'[111] But in communism it was secularized and the 'sense of history' failed the vision of paradise. The glory of the Idea in History lacked even Hegel's Lutheran God. Its weakness was that it took no account of other forms of the experience of time: the intensity of the interior or private life, the mystery of existence itself and, above all, human weakness, all of which Christianity so richly addresses and, as Nietzsche noted, so powerfully exploits. Like Christianity, Marxism required everybody to be a saint, but there was no saving grace, no doctrine of forgiveness, no radical sense of evil, no realism that 'many are called but few chosen'. The dictatorship of the proletariat, like capitalism, promised no rest for the wicked (that is anyone who refused to work all the hours that were), but proposed none either for the weary.[112] In the Heraclitean flux, and in the Hegelian dialectic there was no sign of a beginning no promise of an end. As it emerged, the doctrine was abstract, impersonal and ruthless. In the end, the absence of a socialist democratic party to which allegiance might freely be given while retaining freedom of thought, and which might temper the practice of power (for the state was clearly not going to wither away), was the greatest tragedy of all.

Returning to the *Memoirs*, a few moments show the gap between 1930 and 1940 in Serge's ideological positions. In the early 1940s, he can freely tell of the rigging of the voting in one of the Petrograd districts by Lenin and Zinoviev in 1920, approve of Kropotkin's protests to Lenin over the implicit censorship of nationalizing the book trade,[113] reveal an 'emergent totalitarianism'[114] and question ideologically the 'totalitarian' demands of a Marxism bewilderingly 'simultaneously democratic and authoritarian'.[115] Lenin, though still admired, is now shown warts and all: 'He has Bogdanov, his old friend comrade, jailed because this outstanding intellectual confronts him with embarrassing objections.'[116] Gone too is Serge's disparagement of the Mensheviks: '[Lenin] outlaws the Mensheviks because these "petty-bourgeois" Socialists are guilty of errors which happen to be awkward.'[117] 'Petty-bourgeois' is hence exposed as a simplistic convenient slogan demonstrating how a once-analytical terminology has become a propaganda of oppression. Within the first few years after the 1917 revolution, Lenin reneged on his sympathy for the anarchist Makhno and he promised the churches freedom but slandered religion by half-quoting Marx on the opium of the people.[118] Serge can now, with his fledgling but growing concept of 'totalitarianism', and unlike his Marxist friends, show the similarities between fascism and Stalinism 'in matters of repression and mass-manipulation through propaganda'.[119] Like Orwell, Serge saw the language of Marxist analysis harden into totalitarian slogans as ideology itself switched from a creative philosophical discourse into a kind of inert theology: '*le sabir de l'agit-prop*'. 'Agitprop-Pigin'[120] is Serge's version of 'newspeak'.

In purely ideological terms, Serge sees Trotsky's analysis of the failure of the German revolution in terms of the crisis of revolutionary leadership as insufficient. He had not taken into account an already bureaucratized Comintern and the scepticism of both the social democrat with a stake in the system and the German worker who had seen in the Russian revolution only famine, terror and a suppression of freedom.[121] Where Serge ideologically stood with Trotsky was on his opposition to excessive industrialization (in spite of its achievements), forcible collectivization, the development of bureaucratic totalitarianism and the worship of gigantism and force. In any case, ideology was never a supra-analytical or an ethically motivated given. It had constantly to be renewed and especially that 'authoritarian, intolerant tradition of turn-of-the-century Russian Marxism'.[122]

With supreme irony, Serge recalled, 'for use against Trotsky himself, a sentence of astounding vision which he had written, in 1914, I think: "Bolshevism may very well be an excellent instrument for the conquest of power, but after that it will reveal its counter-revolutionary aspects."'[123] Serge's already-cited conclusion that 'no doctrine has stood before the shock'[124] of the events he has witnessed should, however, not be seen as either pessimistic or fatalistic. The point is that no ideology or doctrine is authentic unless renewed in historically aware, imaginative, ethical practice in a complex vision of the always-unpredictable concrete moments of history itself. In honestly reflective thinking, the effect of the contingent is to reveal as well as challenge the structural assumption in any area, however much chance is built into the system. It is a measure of Serge's greatness that he acknowledges: 'Moulded themselves by a defunct world, the best and most clear-sighted of us have often been revealed, in the tempests of the age, as more than half blind.'[125]

Religion and Ethics

The Bolshevik ideology was for Serge a 'vision confined to the realms of pure theory'.[126] Those who attracted Serge among the intelligentsia were independent thinkers who thought synthetically across a number of discourses, men like Rozanov 'in whom there had been something of Nietzsche, Tolstoy, and Freud, all subsumed in a carnal Christianity which was perpetually at war with itself'.[127] It is already clear in considering Serge's views on religion and ethics that they were bound up both with psychology and with the large existential questions. This was a Marxist who could value, as has been shown, the restorative contemplation of a Christian retreat. But it was accompanied by an ethic of engagement and of collective action. In Spain in the closing years of the First World War, like Simone Weil in London during the Second World War, Serge found it difficult to assume the ordinary life of the peace-time citizen.[128] As with the right-wing

Dostoevsky, imprisonment and first-hand experience of the death sentence, left him with a life-long revulsion towards capital punishment and the entire penal system. His deep and practical involvement in revolutionary struggles had shown him what the great poets like Blake had always understood: that 'the best and the worst live side by side, and sometimes mingle – and that what is worst comes through the corruption of what is best'.[129]

Prison had taught Serge the reality of that inverse mirror of the power structures of normative legality at least as well if not better than an Althusser or a Foucault. He also knew that the most surprising people could detach themselves from their structurally fatalistic behaviour under the gaze of power. The Finnish soldiers escorting Serge and his companions to the Soviet Border in 1919 'ignored their instructions and started to be pleasant to the children'.[130] He equally knew that a looting working-class crowd in starving Berlin had the capacity to limit the stolen food to three cans each and that similarly people in a shoe shop came out empty handed if the right size was not available.[131]

For Serge there was no ethics without an understanding of need. He glossed the Marxist (and incidentally capitalist in this instance) language of necessity in the Soviet Union when it spoke of the 'insufficient production of commodities', by quoting the poet Tyutchev, 'no corner of you is untouched by Christ the slave'.[132] Relating to the slavery of necessity is not a simple ethical matter, any more than as Sartre once said the question of freedom is suspended for the sick.[133] In addition for Serge, as for Sartre, 'there is no abstract ethics, there is only an ethics in a situation and therefore it is concrete'.[134] Like Sartre, Serge believed that the denial of history in ethical judgement (Pascal) and the affirmation of it (Marx) are both right.[135] He shares Sartre's view therefore, that 'at the heart of History, each historical being is at the same time ahistorical'.[136]

Sartre's rich though disordered and unfinished *Notebooks on Ethics* will be used again in this argument. Here they are useful in flushing out certain contradictions in Serge's thinking. More complex issues of temporality are often absent from Serge's rhetorical appeals to collectivity and the future. These do indeed produce that 'terrible impersonality', which was a kind of legitimation by high abstraction of the operations of power in concrete situations. Serge can waver between the abstract and concrete universal as an object of the ethical demand by suppressing the question of time. Simultaneously, however, he negotiates quite successfully Sartre's Christian 'eternal with man as inessential' (actually sub-Christian since such a view ignores the Incarnation), less so the Marxist-Leninist view of the future absolute with the present as inessential.[137] Even so, the whole historical character and drift of Serge's writings attempts to give a transcendental narrative of temporality which stretches self-reflexively and indissolubly between past, present and future, as articulated in the magic of fiction, autobiography, the verbal portrait, the testament and the parable. Glossing St Augustine's famous assertion, Sartre also articulates much of Serge when he states 'There would be no ethics if man was not a question in his being.'[138] For both men, the historical fact is a situation, to be reflected upon in and through narrative. (They would of course fundamentally disagree about the nature of poetry, but that is a question that will be taken up elsewhere.)

Both accept that ethics can therefore only be realized in a concrete situation but whereas Sartre precedes today's humanist thinkers by declaring that God has fallen into time, thereby depriving 'humanity' of the eternal absolute and infinite existence in God, Serge retains a distinctly religious, even mystical view of ethical action and history. 'Modern historical myths', says Sartre, 'tend to consider man as inessential in relation to the total endurance of time'.[139] In this respect Serge's account in the *Memoirs* of the suicide of Adolph Joffe, who killed himself on 16 November 1927, having written a letter, a last testament, to Trotsky, is instructive. Serge describes himself entering Joffe's office with its picture of Lenin where 'the old revolutionary had written the last pages – wonderful pages expressing his convictions':

> He slept, his hands placed together, his forehead bare, his greying beart neatly combed. His eyelids were tinged with blue, his lips dark. In the small black-edged hole in his temple, someone had stuffed a plug of cotton wool. Forty-seven years – prisons, the revolt of the fleet in 1905, Siberia, escapes, exile, Congresses, Brest-Litovsk, the German Revolution, the Chinese Revolution, embassies, Tokyo, Vienna [...] Nearby, in a little room full of children's toys, Maria Mikhailovna Joffe, her face dry and burning, talked to some of the comrades in a low voice.[140]

Joffe's written testament argued that the political man had a duty to depart at the right time, when he can be no longer useful to the cause served. Human life was without meaning 'except insofar as it exists in the service of something infinite – which for us is humanity; since anything else is limited, to work for the sake of anything else is devoid of meaning'.[141] He writes that his death is a protest against those who have traduced the principles of the party, the immediate concrete example being the expulsion of Trotsky and Zinoviev from the Central Committee.

All this is relatively uncomplicated in terms of Sartrean ethics. Suicide is an example of bad faith and the self-imposed death is the ultimate denial of truth for the self since death removes the self from the world. There is always freedom and choice in the worst state of unfreedom. Even sickness is no excuse for bad faith even though Serge might argue 'the path of agitation was closed to Joffe because of his sickness.'[142] Joffe has fallen for the illusion of eternal humanity, a pure historical myth and ethically has committed himself to the chimera of historical myth: a surpassing 'which conserves and saves, whereas it saves nothing whatsoever'.[143] Serge's comments – 'the man who wrote these lines, prepared to seal them with his own blood, here touches on heights of faith where neither reason nor unreason counts any longer; there has been no better expression of the revolutionary's communion with all mankind in all ages'[144] – have merely the inauthenticity of an expostulation of gratitude in prayer.

I have argued the toughest case against Serge's implied evaluation, only because one can use Sartre against Sartre here. By Sartre's own admission there is Pascal as well as Marx. Authenticity requires that one be in and out of history at the same time. Serge (the Jew) leans towards Pascal and Sartre (of Protestant intellectual heritage in Catholic France) towards Marx. Sartre too quickly dismisses the 'myth' of history as he will superficially, probably under the influence of Carnap, dismiss poetry as prayer. Joffe in fact makes an existential choice; he decides by his suicide to leave history as protest against a concrete historical situation that has refused him the possibility of serving others during the formation of a totalitarian state. The retreat into private life was for such a man both a disgrace and a betrayal of the fact that he is connected with others in common humanity, as the totalitarian state abstracts the people it controls, also by the denial of commonality. The gaze of the autocrat never recognizes herself or himself in another. The other is reduced to a thing.

Serge describes Joffe as asleep with his hands folded. The folded hands are pure inactivity of the meaningless corpse. The 'sleep' is pure sentimental illusion. Or is it? Brought up by his father as an atheist humanist, Serge remarked he had been given no religious instruction: 'through books, I came across the word "soul"; it was a revelation to me. That lifeless body that had been bundled away in a coffin could not be everything.'[145] It is not a minor point, nor an intellectually inauthentic reversion to an outmoded discourse, to say that for Serge his writing was an attempt to recover both his own soul and the souls of others. Serge weaves the magic of narrative in creating this iconographic and certainly hagiographic moment of a human 'soul'. The reality is not the corpse, but Serge's story about it. At its most simple the story is the 'soul'. He does not analyse the suicide note except to say it is 'beyond reason and unreason'. In a sense it offers the mysticism of the revolutionary saint's communion with the infinite and the drama of the eternal Pascalian man outside history, but nonetheless somehow incarnates a profound view of the self's relation to history itself. The leap of faith is just that, but there is no illusion in Serge that this is a salvationary surpassing. Sartre's error is to assume too quickly that the one produces the other: 'For what is seen is dead and it is not dead.'[146] And does not Serge, the artist, choose 'to create imaginarily the real world' as one for whom 'perception is already unreal creation'?[147]

This is so because of the parable-like story Serge gives to this fictional death mask. Everything has an added meaning. The office death shows a death in harness, a death which rejects the private space and realizes itself in public. The portrait of Lenin, that incarnation of the spirit of the old Bolsheviks, themselves now in process of liquidation (or is it martyrdom?), is linked with the finite portrait of the body: two portraits within a portrait, the servant forsaken but held under the iconic gaze of the founding father. The 'wonderful pages' are the last testament of faith, the word as imperishable continuity (the GPU had tried to seize the pages but failed), against the frozen but time-threatened moment of the corpse with its distinctly non-transcendental and soon-to-vanish details of neatly combed greying beard, blue-tinged eyelids and dark lips, the bullet hole plugged with cotton wool.

This 'personal' narrative of 'impersonal' historical events undergone allows the contingent, unpredictable events of history to be humanized, that is reclaimed for time, and made significant by a passionate and imaginative retelling. Here, again, one can turn Sartre against himself. Joffe's life record is of someone who has given himself to the contingent and taken up his responsibilities towards it.[148] His tragedy is, however, not the Sartrean one of the impossibility of remaining free in unfreedom, but choosing his own death on his own terms before the state chooses for him. In that sense he robs the state of the meaning of the ceremonies of false accusation and the humiliations of prison, torture, confession and summary execution: the meanings and acts for which the state wants to use his death. The room full of children's toys and the bereaved wife talking, like Lear's Cordelia, 'in a low voice' to comrades might seem a touch sentimental, almost Victorian (women are mostly, though not always, seen as softening adjuncts or de-sexed betrayers in Serge's male revolutionary world) in terms of filling out this portrait of a 'good' death, but it is also an icon of continuing life, presaging a 'future' for 'humanity'. Serge does not deal with the abandonment of wife and child, at worst because it never occurs to him for she is among comrades, at best because there is no question but that Joffe was, in any event, a proscribed man; his future in any case would have been cut off.

In this narrative, humanity is not a surpassing nor a substitute God, but is represented by one who has chosen, against the purely utilitarian notion of survival as the highest good (a notion, as Arendt once said, essentially linked to the ethics of the gambler), to reclaim his own death, to substitute his own time, the 'right time', for the time of nature and for the time of tyranny. In a reciprocal act of comradeship and love, Serge takes the void of the given life and recreates it in the narrative. Here history and nature, standing outside the person, are seen as both undertaken and undergone by a suffering human being. Joffe has chosen to end his life and reclaims a world for those who remember. His biographical forty-seven years among the contingent, un-chosen and implacable events of history, including the Brest–Litovsk treaty, are seized on together to be recreated as a narrative of personal and impersonal time in an ultimately poetic conjuncture. The issue of temporality in the portrait as testament and as elegy will be returned to, together with the nature of the autobiography in relation to the same issues, but here it is sufficient to note the link between ethics and problems of temporality both in a narrative and in a historical moment.

Religion itself Serge sees in ruins, but the ruins form a contrast with the present and offer an implied critique of Stalin's vision of modernity. The past becomes a silent accuser. For example, while in exile at Orenburg Serge noted that 'the rubble of the dynamited cathedral formed an islet of quaint little rocks in the middle of one of the squares'.[149] The white church on the hill, which was associated with the pre-socialist Pugachev rebellion of 1774 against the colonialist politics of Catherine the Great (famously the setting for Pushkin's extraordinary short story 'A Captain's Daughter'), had also been destroyed. Communists had ironically destroyed their own pre-revolutionary history. By 1933 synagogues had been closed or destroyed. With no kosher butchers the Jews were refusing to eat meat. The mosques, representing the largest groups, had not been damaged for fear of an Islamic uprising but the best had been converted into a Kirghiz high school. Christian churches were used as goods warehouses, or they would have been had there been any goods. Orenburg was now essentially a military camp, with barracks and military schools, technical schools, a couple of factories and a small concentration camp. At the height of the purges (1933–6), the new élite were the airmen with wives who had money. Forced labour brigades tramped through the town. Deracinated and demoralized Kirghiz ethnic tribes rotted in the ruins of churches, dying, and stealing to survive. Stalinist state capitalism in its absolute destruction of traditional ways of life and other beliefs is shown by Serge as offering nothing to the human 'soul' or to human dignity. In comparison Serge notes that in Paris in the late 1930s, the best of the left-wing Catholics of the review *Esprit* simply loathed lying: 'in their simple teaching of "reverence for the human person" I felt immediately at one with them'.[150] What teaching, said Serge, 'could be more wholesome in an age in which civilization itself is cracking like rocks in a volcanic eruption?'[151]

Along with ideological confusion, there emerged a new category of the oppressed alongside the mass of the poor, alternately exploited and cast adrift. Serge's experience of continuous exile made him acutely aware of it. In contrast with the nineteenth century, it was a twentieth-century phenomenon. It was the rise of the stateless refugee. Propelled by the collapse of the Austro-Hungarian Empire in 1917, the 'displaced person' of 1918 onwards became the 'refugee' of the post-Second World War period. In the twenty-first century, with so-called globalization, the refugee dominates political, economic and ethical discussion, under new names such as 'economic migrant', or 'immigrant'. In the endless propaganda against the collectively demonized, and at the farthest end of definition, the refugee becomes an 'alien' or 'terrorist'.

For Serge, typically, it showed the historic re-emergence of ancient tyranny in a contemporary form:

> I have witnessed the birth of the enormous category of 'stateless persons', that is, of those men to whom tyrants refuse even a nationality. As far as the right to live is

> concerned, the plight of these men without a county, (who are in truth those who are most attached to their own countries and to the country of mankind) can be compared only to that of the 'unacknowledged man' of the Middle Ages who, since he had no lord or sovereign, had no rights and no protection either, and whose very name became a kind of insult.[152]

Equally typically (in a dialectical shift, describing himself as Russian, French, European and Eurasian), Serge affirms the birth of the human being who is 'stranger to no land' despite the law.[153] The 'stranger to no land' and the 'unacknowledged man' were two sides of a political drama of human recognition, always in motion and dependent on deep psychological constructions of irrationality and terror. Again, that contrary operation of the historical and non-historical person which Sartre articulated as a short-hand contradiction between Marx and Pascal can be seen. The one is in the world and its sign is historical injustice, the other is ahistorical and has its foundation in empathy and compassion. Arendt would reject compassion, as a form of contentless psychological reflex in which the other becomes a mere object of pity, in favour of justice which needs articulacy and will, but the truth is that without compassion and empathy it is hard to find a motivation for justice.[154]

The 'unacknowledged man' of the Middle Ages, without lord or master, whose very name is taken from him, is hence seen by Serge as atemporally analogous with the contemporary 'stateless person'. Given the injunction against atemporal analogy in historical practice, is it possible to make this judgement stick? It is, because Pascal is right. Ethical and unethical behaviour can be judged in history because we are both inside and outside history itself. That is why for Serge a stateless person like him might value a feeling of statelessness, in the sense of being able to be at home in every land, 'a stranger to no land'.[155] Perhaps only the saint, a child of God rather than man, could feel that way. Serge was a child of a revolution whose best faith was the fight for the whole person, free from the tyranny of masters and wastage of abstract capitalism's 'relations of production'. That fight for the whole person transcended, in this historical moment, the local movement and 'need for roots' in the sense that Simone Weil was to use the phrase. Serge's sheer openness to all the variations of human culture came with a remarkable curiosity towards everything that was different from himself. There was nothing so interesting as something he did not know. To be interested in 'man' was also to be vitally engaged in the particular ethnic and cultural detail. Heaven and hell were on earth and best studied there. To be exiled to the Urals was an opportunity to study the history and native cultures of the Urals and to find a home there.

Serge is hence essentially right when he talks about 'the unity of the world and of mankind'.[156] Such language is embarrassing to much contemporary thought. The thought of 'unity' is taboo in every liberal institution of education where difference is preached from gender to ethnicity with a sometimes paralysing 'unity' of consensual confidence. Few realize, though radical anthropologists having being doing it for some time, that difference is perceived by a sense of oneself as the ground from which difference is judged, and it may be a true or false ground, involving a true or false play in an ongoing theatre of difference in which self and other are at once constantly robbed of intended meaning and given unanticipated meaning. There is equally, therefore, a dogmatism of the proposed 'other'. Few realize that once difference is minutely established, anthropologically, psychologically and culturally, that this represents only a first awareness of the self at the beginning of the task of reciprocal encounter.

That task is at once simple and difficult. It is to behave as if there might be a 'unity' of man- and womankind. Potential mutuality is a horizon against which likeness, difference and the judgement of the same and other must be considered. Such a horizon can be glimpsed poetically in religious insights of the world's unity of peoples, and in some of the great metaphysical narratives of science. In chaos theory the most cited example of 'unity' claims that the beat of the butterfly's wings may produce a tempest halfway round the world.[157] Unity is, less tendentiously, always possible in courageous and honest relations between peoples. In the last analysis the other is ourselves.

So ethics, in its grand narrative and temporal judgements, emerging only in the historical moment and through action and reflection in the concrete nature of that moment, was for Serge at the heart of democratic politics. Hence this section on ethics must end with such a moment. During the Spanish Civil War, campaigning for persecuted socialist comrades in peril equally from the Stalinist communist machine and the Loyalists, Serge commented on the disinformation and autocracy of the Soviet-led communists: 'only in minority parties and among isolated individuals did conscience still burn'.[158] Significantly he quotes Rossi, an editor of the journal *Le Populaire*, 'The conscience of the masses – my friend, it doesn't exist!'[159] For Serge, the list of those who did not lie and were not compromised was tiny but their names were worth inscribing in the text. Serge notes the fact that the British Independent Labour Party, for example, produced the indomitable Fenner Brockway, son of a Christian missionary in India (whom I saw at the age of ninety-five addressing a rain- and wind-swept anti-nuclear rally in Hyde Park in the 1980s, passionately declaring his hopes for the future). But there were others in Britain (Maxton, MacGovern and MacNair), in Holland there was Sneevliet's revolutionary socialist party and in France there was the revolutionary left in the Socialist Party (Marceau Pivert, Collinet, Edouard Serre and Paul Schmierer).

It was George Orwell, of course, in *Homage to Catalonia* (1938) who had most clearly intuited and (partly) seen what was going on in Spain. His parallel account is useful, for Serge was deeply involved with the Catalan Spanish anarchists. For Orwell the anarchists in Catalonia were the only time he ever saw a real working class in control of a situation. In spite of their utter inefficiency (Orwell's own section at one point didn't even know how to load a modern rifle) he was struck by their 'essential decency'.[160] At the same time he noted that 'in practice the democratic "revolutionary" type of discipline is more reliable than might be expected'.[161] In spite of his initial reaction to the acrimonious fractiousness of the left, described somewhat Etonianly as 'tiresome', Orwell challenged the reductive binary representation of the opposition to Franco, from the right as blood-sodden Bolsheviks and from the left as gentlemanly Republicans quelling a military revolt.

Orwell sketched in detail the Soviet shifting of the Spanish resistance from home-grown anarchists to born-again communists and, like Serge, came independently to the conclusion that the communists were an anti-revolutionary force. While he also distrusted the purism of the POUM, who seemed unaware that there was a war to be won at all costs, and while he was initially more sympathetic to the better organized communists, Orwell came to realize that the POUM 'were almost blameless compared with their adversaries'[162] and that the severity of the Stalinist propaganda against them meant that eight to ten thousand Spanish working men in the front lines with hundreds of international helpers were denounced by the communists as 'Fascists' at a time when the anti-Franco forces needed everyone they could lay their hands on. Orwell in fact came to doubt that the communist war policy 'made for victory'[163] and he was most trenchant in his criticism of the British left and the British press, not to mention the continental left and their press, who blindly accepted the communist version of events. Why it is important to read Orwell now, alongside Serge, is precisely to remember the ability of these rare voices to speak the truth against the ubiquitous lying of the masters of propaganda in and throughout any historical moment. In terms of the strategic struggles of the Spanish Civil War, these moments are virtually irrelevant to the historian, but in terms of what must be remembered, they are vital.[164]

No one described better than Orwell the Spanish loss of faith in resistance to fascism and the re-establishment of 'normality' on his second visit to Barcelona. The middle classes had previously lain low, even wearing working-class clothes. Then 'make-over' replaced renewal.

> The revolutionary forms of speech were dropping out of use. Strangers seldom addressed you as *tú* and *camarada* nowadays; it was usually *señor* and *usted*. *Buenos Días* was beginning to replace *salud*. The waiters were back in their boiled shirts and the shop-walkers were cringing in the familiar manner. My wife and I went into a hosiery shop on the Ramblas to buy some stockings. The shopman bowed and rubbed his hands as they do not do even in England nowadays [...] In a furtive indirect way the practice of tipping was coming back.[165]

But like the tiny minority of members of the British Independent Labour Party, and their fewer descendents, Orwell had glimpsed something else:

> One had been in a community where hope was more normal than apathy or cynicism, where the word 'comrade' stood for comradeship and not, as in most countries, for humbug. One had breathed the air of equality. I am well aware that it is now the fashion to deny that Socialism has anything to do with equality. In every country in the world a huge tribe of party-hacks and sleek little professors are busy 'proving' that Socialism means no more than a planned state-capitalism with the grab-motive left intact. But fortunately there also exists a vision of Socialism quite different from this. The thing that attracts ordinary men to Socialism and makes them willing to risk their skins for it, the 'mystique' of Socialism, the idea of equality; to the vast majority of people Socialism means a classless society, or it means nothing at all.[166]

Dwight Macdonald suggested that Serge send his *Memoirs* to Orwell to ask for his help in getting them published in the face of intransigent American publishing houses who, during the war, would not have their Soviet ally attacked at any cost but Serge refused, believing with many socialists at the time that *Animal Farm* was fatalistically pessimistic in its seemingly seamless cyclical narrative of rising and falling power.

It was sadly a lost opportunity. Orwell's useful letter to Macdonald about *Animal Farm* would surely have complicated Serge's view. Orwell, in turn, might well have been extremely helpful to Serge. Orwell had previously written to Macdonald to say that he had thought of having a word with T.S. Eliot at Faber about Serge, but he added that in spite of Eliot's anti-Stalinism, he 'doesn't like fighting against public opinion for the sake of some left faction he feels no sympathy for'.[167] Orwell was surely right: one cannot imagine Eliot publishing Serge. In fact, in *Animal Farm*, Orwell argued to Macdonald that the kind of revolution he was satirizing was of a specific kind, it was not a diatribe against organized resistance to tyranny as such, but it was against Bolshevism and above all against Stalinism: 'I meant *that kind* of revolution (violent conspiratorial revolution, led by unconsciously power-hungry people) can only lead to a change of masters.'[168] Like Serge he believed a leadership unchecked by the masses was an invitation to tyranny, oppression and autocratic rule. The two men also both believed that that the seeds of autocracy were there with Lenin and the Bolsheviks, and had not somehow emerged with the failure of Trotskyite opposition after 1926.

II

'I Began to Write a Story': The Novels

The second section of this study of Serge will leave the *Memoirs*, and rehearse some of these issues not simply in terms of critical analysis but in terms of how the 'ensemble' of the text mediates multiple issues. More specifically, it will show how the patterns of narrativity throw a different light on things that have so far been approached in more abstract terms. Before moving on to specific examples of the way Serge writes a story, it will be useful to consider the many clues as to his own choice of literary practice scattered about his published and unpublished writings.

It has already been noted that Serge wanted to go beyond the traditions signalled by Balzac, Dostoevsky and Proust, and that his 'atmosphere' was designed to move through and beyond the demands of social realism: 'My novels are exclusively about atmosphere which only exists in harmony and in accord with the whole because it is like that in reality.' 'Uneven, certainly', noted Serge to Macdonald in relation to his novel *The Case of Comrade Tulayev*, 'but above all it's a novel of atmosphere and constructed like a fresco'.[1] The simile should be taken seriously. The technique that requires the quick gesture of definition, before the living movement hardens forever, touches the rhythms and patterns of Serge's prose in a way, perhaps, that more deliberate and considered writing could not. In the same letter there is an even more revealing moment when he replies to criticism from Macdonald:

> The episode in miniature, which seems inadequate to you, is enormously important for me which should be obvious. Kostia [the ostensible main character] is barely sketched in, but that was my intention, he's more of a component of the whole [element] than a person.[2]

What Serge is suggesting here is his allegiance to that construction of the person within a range of constraints: social, economic, psychological and cultural. In that sense, his narrative retains a certain fatalism of agency and representativeness derived from the expressionist drama of his youth, but in practice it is in fact neither purely class-determined, nor oriented to mass movement definition. Serge's debts to Expressionism should not be ignored. His moving note on the death of Ernst Toller was not simply motivated by his identification with a man hunted from exile to exile whose truthfulness made him a Bolshevik for the bourgeois, a Trotskyite for the Stalinists and a petit bourgeois for the Trotskyites.[3] In any case, the episode in miniature embraced not only small subsections of the longer plot but the Sergean portrait.

In terms of narrative and temporality, the miniature episode which is at the heart of Serge's prose has several further important aspects. There is the narrow focus on the contingent event. In *The Case of Comrade Tulayev*, this takes the form of an adaptation of the Gidean *acte gratuit*, creating a classic foundational crime whose solution is not along the binary rationalist/intuitional route of the detective story, but hovers between the expectation of it and its denial in an undercover psychological narrative that articulates a personal sense of political and religious oppression. In the same way Lafcado's 'unmotivated' crime in Gide's *Cellars of the Vatican* is given psychological justification by a clear suggestion of the aristocratic desperation of the Nietzschean *isolato* and of a man haunted by estrangement from his father. The miniature episode also has a contradictory effect of isolation (in its contingent character) from any grand narrative while becoming exemplary in the non-linear time of ethical judgement. Each episode can be complete and self-sufficient, performing its own discrete closures and linked only by 'atmosphere' to other miniature episodes. That atmosphere, the atmosphere of the ubiquitous Stalinist Terror, thus links the episodes without needing ordinary causality. Part of the atmosphere of Terror is to suspend rational, legal and psychological sequence in any case. The peculiar sense of the brief encounter with, at another level, the brief life, will give Serge's work an extraordinary capacity to articulate modernity's fragile sense of the self without letting go of that more generalizing 'atmosphere' whose meaning is ultimately and recognizably political. The cumulative effect gives the operation of narrativity within Serge's stories a uniquely compelling sense of temporality, both at the level of the plot and in the thematics of his fictive world.

To take the tradition of French literature first, Serge admired what surrealism had revealed about the psychology of creativity but he had doubts about some of the quick archetypal answers it supplied, stemming as it did from literary Parisian bohemia.[4] If surrealism had brought back perhaps too obviously a set of iconic Freudian truths to show a world reacting in disbelief and incomprehension to the First World War, Serge's 'atmosphere' could suggest something more subtle. Serge knew that 'atmosphere' was somehow always in the service of something. His judgement sometimes swings one way, then another. In conservative terms he admired Saint-Exupéry's *Terre des hommes*. He felt that the exhilaration of flight, of man and plane was '*un hymne à la Technique*', and had transformed the way we looked at the earth, although its power had to a degree enslaved the makers of the machine. In socialist terms, while complaining that social realist Henry Poulaille's novel *Pain Quotidien* (1934) was full of virtuous women who supplied household needs while stifling their misfortunes and male workers who talked of strikes and succumbed to industrial accidents, he felt that something had been communicated, in spite of evident literary and political clumsiness, of the real condition of working people.[5] He had elsewhere described Henry Poulaille as the ultimate proletarian writer, distrustful of theories, using no subtlety of characterization and passing no reflection on the workers' role in the capitalist relations of production, indifferent to the radical chic of the Parisian cafés, never seeming to rework his prose or feel the need for polishing a sentence, but as having nonetheless having found a way of writing which had its own truth in rough dialogue and action articulating a world that no one else had spoken of and to.[6] (It might be noted, in passing, that it was the subtitle of Poulaille's *Le Pain Quotidien: Les Damnés de la Terre* that Fanon took as the title of his much more famous work.) When it came to the orthodox French communist writer Louis Aragon, Serge was much more severe. Aragon's Committee for Spanish Culture had never faced up to or acknowledged the disappearance of his Catalan friend Andrés Nin at the hand of the Stalinists. They had accompanied the disappearance with a barrage of lies and calumnies. Aragon was also to be severely criticized in Macdonald's *politics*.

Serge was, however, steeped in French culture, in the poetry of Mallarmé and in the novels of Proust. There is, for example, a vivid late piece of writing during Serge's period in Mexico showing the influence of both alongside other European masters, when he describes the *bricolage*-like effect of the interior of the Museum of Guadalajara. Serge (and the paragraph is strongly reminiscent of Walter Benjamin) describes its warehousing of the crazy yet living objects of the Mexican past that index its histories of crime and bestiality: snuff-boxes, miniatures of ugly women with beautiful breasts, water clocks, canes, mother-of-pearl fans, old banknotes, feathers and gilded paper. Somehow in the museum no object relates to another without a Mallarméan sense of detemporalized cultural parataxis. Serge also mentions that a Hoffmann or even a Kafka might also be needed to organize the means of telling what had been visually juxtaposed.

Serge's description of the useless debris of time in the museum creates a kind of dislodging vertigo of absolute strangeness and nostalgia, like an exotic version of the shop in which Henry James's protagonists bought the Golden Bowl. But as Benjamin said of the collector of books – the museum is first and foremost a collection – the acquisition of an old book is its rebirth: 'this is the child-like element which in a collector mingles with the element of old age'.[7] It offers thus a sense of time regained. Serge thought, he said, of a 'Mexican Proust'.[8] If Proust, he continued, had analysed the complexity of the ultra-refined society of a certain type of Parisian life, where its love affairs were as knowingly and sophisticatedly futile as its gossip, here in Mexico the instincts surpass those who only know a kind of pure existence. Mexican psychology, he went on, depended on the arid mountain close to the city, a knife in the hands, anger or laughter, elemental passion without complications, faith which drives you mad and guarantees pardon, where lust is a fire, love is violent and death not bourgeois, but near and dark, the whole whirling in some *danse macabre* of Dürer's. Here, too, are the sadistic instruments of transposed Catholic self-flagellation and torture.

In spite of a certain cultural conditioning of Serge's own gaze here, should we judge this picture as purely a tourist's perception of the Mexican exotic? More generously, perhaps, it bears the marks of a first visual encounter with a new civilization. Serge, however, does incorporate in his analysis the fact that the objects are in a museum. The objects are already marked by being collected. They are in indifferent relation with each other and formally detached from narrative, yet bearing a first significance in primitive designation as 'national'. They are dead and not dead in the time-bound, yet timeless space of the museum. Their placing, frozen in intentionality and time is nonetheless subject to a shifting contemporary gaze. Their temporality is hence *attributed by* Serge and he gives some clues as to what informs his looking.

Serge's point of reference is the European fin de siècle. Encountering the *déraciné* peasant proletariat of Mexico, he thinks of Picasso's *The Absinthe Drinker*, which he remembers seeing in Moscow. The culture is viewed from the multiple perspectives of Beardsley's aestheticism and Zola's naturalism, the urban proletariat and its underworld classes with its complementary bohemia for whom he finds a perspective in Toulouse-Lautrec and Verlaine. As for writers like Carlos Fuentes now, Paris supplied the cultural and philosophical touchstones. Far from his beloved Europe in 1945, Serge revives the perspectives of the great modernist artists and writers of the turn of the century to assist with his analysis of the transplanted European Catholic imperial society in conflict and in dialogue with the defeated indigenous people of Mexico. The objects are at once both national (political) and universal (ethical) signifiers of a real history.

Naturalism and aestheticism, the exposed, almost biological, reason of historical fatality and the detached forms of art contend for position here. The frank sexual and violent reality of, say, Zola's *La Terre* superimposes itself on Mexico. The poor struggled against the rich in Mexico also and unofficial forms of religion contended with the organized religion of powerful interests. A solidarity with the poor, and their modes of resistance, saves and tempers the exoticist gaze. The old believers in seventeenth-century Slavonic culture both adapted and resisted the Russian Orthodox Church with their crypto-democratic forms of worship and a locally organized priesthood, which, as with the Puritans in seventeenth-century England, 'in large measure helped the development of dissident thought [*inakomyslie*] in Russian Christianity'?[9] The general parallels were clear.

Serge also gave many clues to his fictional and historical techniques in the *Memoirs* themselves. In the Soviet Union, 'we have on our hands', says Serge, 'a literature that is conformist and corrupt'.[10] Serge's own account of his writing of history is worth setting out. It was his love of history, Serge affirms, that led him to his first book, *Year One of the Russian Revolution*, but he felt dissatisfied with it. He does not mention that one of the reasons for his dissatisfaction with it is its Leninist ideological orthodoxy. Slightly disingenuously the reason he does give is that historical discourse itself 'does not allow enough scope for showing men as they really live, dismantling their inner workings and penetrating deep into their souls.'[11] He continues, 'a certain degree of light can only be cast on history, I am convinced, by literary creation which is free and is interested, which is to say devoid of any market preoccupations.'[12] There is such a thing as 'free' historical writing also. Here Serge equates historical discourse with the ideologically loaded idea of social realism that paradoxically denies the truth of 'men as they really live.' The sense of needing to include in any description (to keep the romantic terminology) the depths of the human soul, is, however, key. The needs of the soul for this dangerously placed ex-Bolshevik were primary.

Serge's writing engages both historical and literary discourse, or at the very least gives some sense of one in the other. Because of the focus on the inner life, the novels, for example, are not traditional 'historical novels' because, again to use Sartre's shorthand, Serge viewed Marxist historical process from the point of view of Pascal. For Serge, literature written for the pleasure of writing (even by rich people) or writing to earn a living and a name is passable, the rest are 'suppliers to the book trade'.[13] For himself: 'my conception of writing was and is that it needs a mightier justification: as a means of expressing to men what most of them live inwardly without being able to express, as a means of communion, a testimony to the vast flow of life through us, whose essential aspects we must try to fix for the benefit of those who will come after us. In this respect, I belonged to the tradition of Russian writing.'[14]

This very important statement can be broken down into three main points. For Serge, first Russian literature gave a crucial sense of the inner life in turmoil; second, it was concerned with that inner life's relation with the 'outside' whether in history or nature; and third, Russian literature always posed the question of ethics. In the testimonies of the characters, the speech of the witnesses, the two discourses of history and fiction begin to come uneasily together in a dialogue of souls at the heart of the human drama. The inward life for Serge, however, was not inner personality or subjectivity, even though that might structure a perspective on the event. Any individual life, including his own, was only significant in connection with or varying with the collective life ('*en fonction de la vie collective*').[15] Even solitude was a sense of others *in absentia*. So, invariably, in the novels which are about prison, failed revolutions, cities under siege or life in a totalitarian world, the characters show the degree of freedom with which it is possible to respond to personal and public unfreedom. Individual survival in history and in nature will have a deep ethical, psychological and political meaning.

The question of testimony (*le témoinage*) is complex. It passes from the witness who offers it to the one who receives it and engages with it in a further argument. A fiction or an autobiography adopting the mode of testimony hence engages witness and judge at the same time, offering a narrative which has been encoded in a rhetoric of persuasion. Testimony also appears as proof, so testimony offers a play of finality in ambiguous relation to an ongoing argument. It equally oscillates ambiguously between confession and profession (in its oldest meanings, in the language of the Old Testament, for example, it has the authority of profession, as in the 'testimony' of Mosaic Law). Among all these possibilities, however, is the idea of the public space. No testimony is private. French definitions of the term stress the speaking of what is seen in the service of truth, the writer who bears witness to her or his times. *Le Petit Robert* cites Michelet in relation to historical evidence: '*J'entends, par ce mot histoire rien autre chose que les actes du temps, les témoinages sérieux*.'[16] The sense of the translation is as follows: 'I understand by this word history nothing but the acts of time, serious testimonies'. At the end of the *Memoirs*, Serge added a specific and general temporal inflection to the public need for 'serious testimony': 'For this age must be witnessed; the witness passes, but his testimony manages to endure – and life still goes on.'[17] Like Benjamin, Serge sets writing above life yet in life. However briefly writing endures, it is necessarily longer than the single life. Writing history compels an attempt to make meaning beyond biological fatality and counters the indifference of cosmic time in its lingering.

As for the politics of the writer, Serge was clear: 'Poets and novelists are not political beings because they are not essentially rational.'[18] Political intelligence and action, for Serge, needs idealism tamed by pragmatism and rationality and should have strictly defined social ends. This is close to the Trotskyite position (the artist must be free of ideological compulsion) and has the merit of its half-truth. Writers under Stalin were certainly 'political' beings in that they threatened the state enough to be arrested and executed. The degree of irony in Serge's statements here must not be underestimated. For Serge, the artist is much closer to the unconscious, to intuition, to dealing with the 'lyrical inner life' and lives in uncertainty as to results.[19] Dostoevsky, Gorky and Balzac 'brought to life, all lovingly [are] criminals whom the Political Man would shoot most unlovingly'.[20] Serge adds, more soberly, however, that the totalitarian state, controlling writers by 'strict ideology and absolute conformism, succeeded only in killing the creative faculty within them'.[21]

Serge leaves the obvious inference unsaid, that the writer who refuses to write according to the dictates of the totalitarian state becomes notwithstanding, a political being. Turning to the writers who write for the state, Serge argues that Mayakovsky's suicide was at least in part due to the fact that he had become 'the most requested writer of hack journalism'.[22] His last poem wrote of the 'petrified crap of the present'.[23] 'He became so official', said Serge, 'that I never met him again'.[24] Serge knew what he was talking about. The official books were printed in tens of thousands and translated into foreign languages. Serge describes the atmosphere as one of 'sickening absurdity' and 'fanatical obedience'.[25]

Serge's own political escape was assisted by publicity at the International Congress of Writers for the Defence of Culture, held in Paris in June 1935. Aragon and Ehrenburg were effectively the Stalinist spokesmen but Serge had friends present in Gide, Malraux, Magdeleine Paz, Charles Plisnier and Poulaille. Roger Shattuck has written about the Congress in detail, noting the complexity of different political agendas and its polarised positions. He pointed out its Stalinist organizational manipulation by Aragon and Ehrenburg, its socialist realism (which by this stage demanded a dictatorship of proletarian literature,[26] and the vigorous defence of Serge by Poulaille, Paz and Gaetano Salvemini, an Italian historian and Socialist deputy exiled by Mussolini, as well as Gide's rather vacillating commitment at that point to the cause. It was a later crucial intervention by Romain Rolland that actually saved Serge.[27] Recent work has indicated that the Congress was not quite as stage-managed by the communists as originally thought for there was a not inconsiderable amount of prior organization against Stalinist orthodoxy.[28]

There were certain practical constraints on Serge's work. His own time for writing was invariably disrupted as he was hounded around Central Asia, Europe and across the Atlantic. He had to write in short concentrated bursts and whole manuscripts were lost. This meant that writing long and complex plots, revisable at leisure, was not an option. Hence one powerful structural aspect of his works, by necessity and design, is the brief elegiac portrait. The Serge portrait, together with what has already been identified as the short parable-like narrative, has significant implications for the narrativity and temporality of his plots. In *Memoirs of a Revolutionary* it was in the context of discussing the representation of the person in the collective life, rather than the person in private life (the French bourgeois family for example) that Serge admitted that, from *Men in Prison* to *Conquered City*, he had been influenced by the American writer John Dos Passos.[29] Since it was not his 'literary impressionism' which interested Serge, it is safe to infer that it was Dos Passos's new view of the person in relation to the collectivity that is the key issue. Nothing could have been more ironic than thus to equate the condition of the person in Stalinist Russia with the fate of the person in the United States of America.

Aside from the crucial fact of the shared technique of the brief biographical portrait (principally in Dos Passos's *U.S.A.*), the two writers seem hardly comparable with each other. The ideological connection, with Dos Passos in his short-lived socialist phase, weakens the moment the analysis drops below a certain level of generality. Here Jean-Paul Sartre's short essay on Dos Passos's *1919*, the middle section of the trilogy *U.S.A.*, serves as a useful starting point.[30] Sartre had been to the United States for the first time in 1945 and, like Simone de Beauvoir, had recorded many of his impressions in essays and letters. In 1939 de Beauvoir had written to Sartre about both William Faulkner and Dos Passos in the context of bad faith (that pretence that you are not free in your relation with others) while discussing Sartre's lover Kos (Olga Bost):

> There's a way of being watchful in your casualness, of letting yourself go in controlled way, of becoming less adjusted without loss of awareness, which works people up in their relations with themselves: false relations with themselves, transposed into social ones. It's a kind of bad art – with as much bad faith as that of Faulkner or Dos Passos – and which creates ambiguous objects. [31]

It was that transposition of the personal relation into a purely social one (so that the person watched themselves doing things and judged others' reactions) that fascinated Sartre about Dos Passos's characters who were indeed 'ambiguous objects'. Sartre noted that he reports 'all his characters' utterances to us in the style of a statement to the press'.[32] In a dazzling series of analytic sentences of which only a few are presented here, he wrote 'It is as if there were a Platonic heaven of words and commonplaces to which we all go to find words suitable to a given situation. There is a heaven of gestures, too.'[33] Every gesture is a public demonstration 'performed to a humming accompaniment of flattery'.[34] One might add that that American flattery is generally a report on what others think of you which is used in order to stifle your own response. It is endemic in American academic life. It is one behavioural aspect of totalitarian conformity in an age of anxiety. In that sense it was common in both bureaucratic Stalinist Russia and in the individualistically competitive commercial world of the United States.

Sartre hones in here on something which strikes every European visitor to the United States: that commercialized easy socialized language of a country where you are expected to praise others in order to be praised yourself. Everybody seems to be looking at themselves doing something under the eyes of others. The interior dialogue of Stephen Crane's famous *Red Badge of Courage* is the classic example in American literature. No thought or gesture is possible without the imagined looking or judgement of others. The fact that it is a terrified soldier under orders in battle appropriately symbolizes the deep roots of the psychosis. The self, to re-appropriate a phrase of Sartre's, is 'the fine appearance of nothingness'.

Dos Passos's drama of insincerities needs first of all the establishment of the resigned self. Since this process is never seamless the Dos Passos character is never in or out of him- or herself but somehow both at once, like an endless social gathering in a hotel lobby where you can be neither truly private nor truly public. Imagine, says Sartre, you see your best friend and express to him your passionate hatred of war. In a brilliant Gallic parody of the style, Sartre wrote the following:

> And they ordered two beers and said that war was hateful. Paul declared he would rather do anything than fight and John said he agreed with him and both got excited and said they were glad they agreed. On his way home, Paul decided to see John more often.[35]

The question here is: are you experiencing *la vie intérieure* or an omniscient narrative of truthful behaviour to which all interior lives sign up? There is no larger context, no reasons why they should either drink beer or hate war – the two experiences being reduced to the same level of value. There is no suggestion that Paul might fancy John. It has that quality of all soap opera, the assumption that the real is a conversation faithfully reported and that all that remains is 'the unpleasant impression of an indeterminacy of detail' without any law governing its appearance.[36]

It is precisely this that creates the sense of absurd and persistent illusion in Dos Passos's world. Politically it is a populist and anti-intellectual view of the world. Simplicities govern it: luck, celebrities, contingencies (that is, pure events), paranoid uneasiness about 'them' (the big guys) and 'us' (the little guys), proverbial truths about unfaithful classy women on the make and regular good guys down on their luck, the swinging upwardly mobile bourgeoisie, the flash lives of reporters, diplomats and glitzy hangers-on at international conferences, rags-to-riches technocratic heroes and plutocrats of unimaginable power who will get their comeuppance because they have messy private lives and die just like anyone else. We 'recognize' ourselves immediately in this world without having to think. The 'camera eye' and the newspaper tell it 'like it is'. What is missing is precisely what lies behind the show: the structures of power in the property-defending police, the deep historical psychology of racism, the politics of the oil barons, the ideology of puritan individualism, some analysis of right-wing newspapers in the service of their paymasters who create and maintain the belief systems which lead to poverty and the violence of consumer paradises. There needs to be, above all, some analysis of all the historical and political roots and practices of technocratic modernity as capitalism withers away local loyalty and family.

Since Serge insists on the 'collective life' and, like Dos Passos, the individual character's relationship to it, it is instructive to establish Dos Passos's practice as a point of comparison with Serge's, both in detail and at the level of what is essentially a metaphysics and politics of grand narrative reason. In fact, the observations offered here are from the later part of Sartre's essay on Dos Passos. The first part is concerned with narrativity and hence with questions of time. Sartre argued that Dos Passos's time was neither fictional nor narrative: 'it is rather, if you like, historical time'.[37] He noted that everything is told as if someone is remembering. The event does not actually touch us, standing as it does between fact and law: 'in Dos Passos, the things that happen are named first, and then the dice are cast, as they are in our memories'.[38] The result of this is that 'past things retain a flavour of the present; they still remain, in their exile, what they once were, inexplicable tumults of colour, sound and passion'.[39] Things join by a quality of pure addition.

In fact, what we have is an illusion of historical time, an illusion of instantly recognizable ordinariness whose authentic reality, as Marshall McLuhan said of newspapers, is the dateline. What McLuhan did not say is that it is therefore without historical narrativity. No past leaks into the present and no present is addressed to a future. No one, said Mencken, puts down a newspaper without a feeling of disappointment. This is because events are encoded in formalities of the same, paradoxically they are achronological, and are generally addressed to anxiety and robbed of closure. The new not only becomes the same, but in the passing of one day, perhaps even by late in the same day, irrelevant and no longer truthful. Truth is the appearance of fresh contingency guaranteed by the fatality of pure appearance, pure parataxis, pure juxtaposition. Replacing reflection, ironic cynical stoicism enshrines natural process: 'bankruptcies, warloans, starvation, lice, cholera and typus: good growing weather for the House of Morgan.'[40]

It is the same with the shrunken biographies that litter Dos Passos's texts in the form of a newspaper obituary. Here lies the closest generic connection with Serge. The obituary differs from the biography in its relative brevity. In the reading a life shrinks to a few minutes. Dos Passos's public lives tend to be about three or four printed pages, thus giving the illusion of biography. Their style recaptures that of a *Who's Who* entry, essential facts for recognition in some never-never club-land. Dos Passos's portrait of Paxton Hibben for example, shows in telegraphic summary how a young man with prospects moves from a good Mid-western family to progressivist politics with Teddy Roosevelt, to red baiting by alumni at Princeton and finally to a list of official awards. Events move through Hibben, he is constructed in and through pure event, there is no sense he could ever have done anything different. We are told he's an old-fashioned American who believed in the New World but who by inference is disillusioned at every step as America goes into a phase of extreme chauvinist nationalism and depression. At no point is he allowed an interior life. As diplomat and journalist he is described in pure passivity responding to the luck of a position in space and time assigned to him by others, experiencing the effects of power but allowed only to represent not execute it.

Yet in fact Hibben's biography of Henry Ward Beecher (1927) links him with the literary historical movement which attacked the genteel tradition in the tradition of Mencken, and he was a founder member of *New Masses* with Dos Passos himself. In short there's plenty to think about here (not least the rise of the tabloid press empires and their opposition to it) and to reflect on. Hibben must have made some serious choices as to his life, given his class position, and there is evidence of real commitment as a public intellectual and real scholarship. As a figure of impotent pure radical chic in Dos Passos's portrait none of this can be suggested. There is no indication as to whether he preferred 'riding home from the islands with the Grand Duke's mistress' to sympathizing with the attack on the Winter Palace, or to editing *New Masses*.

Serge's narrativity in relation to both the person and temporality in the brief portrait could not be more different. The first thing to notice is that Serge engages with historical time rather than with Dos Passos's universalist time of naturalist, statistical fate. What would appear to be superficially a similar indifference to the person is contradicted by a founding assumption that the collectivity is valuable, indeed that the person can only be seen in a reciprocal relation to it. Further there is a clear ethical distinction, and hence some freedom of choice, between those who align themselves with that reciprocity and those who do not. There are as many fifth columnists, bureaucratic careerists, totalitarian and plutocratic monsters, abject victims and drop-outs in Serge's work as there are in that of Dos Passos, but they are evaluated as such in contrast with others who are not. In Dos Passos no person can have a deep relationship with any other. It is hardly possible to make any ethical judgement beyond saying 'life is unfair', which is already an ethic of irresponsibility and resignation and courts the danger of bad faith. Nor is there any sense that any but the powerful can exercise control over events; even the powerful are but puppets functioning in some greater but anonymous design.

However, both writers are good at the single-line brushstroke, condensing narrative into an almost poetic sentence. Here is Dos Passos in *U.S.A.* on J.P. Morgan: 'in the last year of his life he went up the Nile on a dahabeeyah and spent a long time staring at the great columns of the Temple of Karnak'.[41] We already know who J.P. Morgan is and are aware of his monopolistic wealth, his instinct for power here falling short of the historical accomplishments of the permanent residents of the Valley of the Kings, and confronted by a record of historical time which approaches the cosmic as near as any historical time can. The irony is patent. The long (and envious) time J.P. Morgan spends contemplating the temple will not resolve the issue nor guarantee him the same immortality. It will not disclose any sort of human evaluation of the experience, whether in hubris or in anguish. It is simply another event added to the events of his life. He will not be remembered as long as the Pharaohs and his deep silence shows, comically, that he is certainly troubled by that.

Here, by contrast, is Serge at his closest to Dos Passos:

> Guilbeaux's whole life was a perfect example of the failure who, despite all his efforts, skirts the edge of success without ever managing to achieve it. He wrote cacophonous poetry, kept a card-index full of gossip about his comrades, and plagued the cheka with confidential notes. He wore green shirts and pea-green ties with greenish suits; everything about him, including his crooked face and his eyes, seemed to have touch of mould. (He died in Paris, about 1938, by then an anti-Semite, having published two books proving Mussolini to be the only true successor of Lenin.)[42]

The death is similarly noted with the surviving books. The difference is that we are told, with some wit and in a larger context containing a judgement, as to what the books are about. The life is theorized as 'an example' and however crude the taxonomy it attempts to explain a certain type of behaviour which is more than either purely reactive to or purely determined by events. The informer is at once passive and active in relation to his fate, but there are political and psychological hints as to why he is representative of a human 'type'. He is not a pre-established celebrity of a newspaper report, but a figure anonymous to history who has been personally encountered and figures in the memory of the author. The details offered, while hardly attractive, show him to be much more than an add-on statistic to the human race. He is a type, a cowardly lackey to a system, but also a particular distinguishable man in this place and in this time.

The temporal extension of this little narrative is from the adult encounter to death. The God-like authority of announcing the birth is taken away (Sartre once said we cannot be realists because we have not lived through our birth as we will not realize the interrupted dialogue which is our death), de-sacralizing and making mortal the offered type while modifying the purity of the obituary's narrative obligation to show the dates of birth and death.[43] This is someone who lived rather than was born, who qualitatively bowed out of history rather than was biologically erased. That defiant placing of history above biology, of course, depends on witness and testimony. One wonders when reading Dos Passos if anybody human is actually noticing the lives of the characters, they so often seem to be moving silently, unobserved, as in an anonymous bad dream. They are just out there. The resulting radical loneliness of the American, let loose in her/his own country as if it were a space of eternity, is familiar in American literature from *Moby-Dick* to the Beat writers and beyond. In addition, Serge's wit is far from Dos Passos's world-weary yet confident seriousness that is embedded in a nihilism which hovers between a cynicism with ironic limits and a fatalism that has no human cause.

A brief look at temporality and characterization in Serge's fiction before finally returning to the *Memoirs* will focus some of these issues more clearly. Is it possible to distinguish between the 'sense of history' offered in the letters, the autobiography and the novel in purely generic terms? The group of novels *Men in Prison* (1931), *Birth of our Power* (1932) and *Conquered City* (1932) were written because Serge had officially been expelled from participating publicly in the historical process itself. He could not publish in the Soviet Union so the manuscripts went to France. In 1933 Serge was arrested and deported to Orenburg. The first point then is that Serge writes in default of acting. Nonetheless, in the Sartrean sense, this writing is in any case a political act, for it is a committed literature and its terms, its very generic modes are also political. Put most simply, writing against the banality of social realism was challenging the capacity of the state to describe reality in its own terms. More than that, even Serge knew, with Benjamin, that 'only that historian will have the gift of forming the spark of hope in the past who is firmly convinced that *even the dead* will not be safe from the enemy if he wins.'[44] Serge also knew, as Orwell knew, that the first task of any authoritarian power is to obliterate the past.

> 'What shall it be this time?' he said, still with the same faint suggestion of irony. 'To the confusion of the Thought Police? To the death of Big Brother? To Humanity? To the future?'
>
> 'To the past', said Winston.[45]

Benjamin's famous theses on the philosophy of history coincide closely with Serge's own philosophy of history, from the recovery of personal time as a kind of redemption, to that Husserlian sense of extension in which past, present and future are neither discrete nor chronological entities: 'our coming was expected on earth. Like every generation that preceded us, we have been endowed with a weak Messianic power, a power to which the past has a claim.'[46] In Aron's words, 'free to choose, mankind has a history because it is in search of a destiny.'[47] For both Serge and Benjamin it was tradition itself that was in danger, it needed to be rescued from 'a conformism that [was] about to overpower it.'[48] As Serge wrote, Stalin was preparing to kill off the revolution of 1917 and murder all its leaders. Citing Nietzsche, Benjamin added 'We need history, but not the way a spoiled loafer in the garden of knowledge needs it.' [49] History was an imaginative seizing of the past for present political needs, 'a unique experience with the past'.[50] In forming that 'constellation' of his own time with the past 'he establishes a conception of the present as the "time of the now" which is shot through with chips of Messianic time'.[51] The essay might have been written as a commentary on Serge. For both, to articulate the past was, in Benjamin's words, 'to seize hold of a memory as it flashes up at moments of danger'.[52]

In the 'historical novels' and in the *Memoirs* Serge did just that. The novels were themselves a defiance of the moment of danger. They brandished the unacceptable story, 'that secret agreement between past and present', in the face of those who thought they had *the* story.[53] As Benjamin regretted the European social democrats' erasure from history of August Blanqui, '*l'enfermé*' as he was known, Serge attacked the living erasure of ordinary men from history in *Men in Prison*. It was to be at one and the same time a personal and public testimony, a history, a fictional autobiography and a novel.

Serge's dedication of *Men in Prison* to his son and his declaration that 'everything in this book is fictional and everything is true' have to be taken seriously. How do we approach this? One way might be by taking up Ricoeur's distinction between the narrative character of history and narrative history. What Serge's fiction will demonstrate is the former not the latter:

> Indeed the inserting of history into action and into life, its capacity for refiguring time, brings into play the question of truth in history. The question is inseparable

> from what I call the interweaving reference between history's claim to truth and that of fiction.[54]

But what the fiction will not do is attempt to rival or reproduce the temporalities of possible historical discourse: chronologies of ideological and power shifts, legal time, geological time, ideological narratives, ethnological and social patterns of long duration, the slow moving anthropological and economic shifts, or even biography and political events. Instead it will give a fictional sense, and actually more than a fictional sense for it will cross the line with poetry, of an historical moment lived through and in defiance of chronological destiny, legally imposed (as in prison) or fatally submitted to (as in biological time). To abandon chronology is already to challenge the judiciary's sentence of time.

The passing of five years (the duration of Serge's sentence for his refusal to collaborate with the police over the Bonnot affair) is absent in *Men in Prison*. But time is a psychological presence characterized in and through the experience of radical unfreedom. It is not simply a Bergsonian response to pure emotional intensity but to an identifiable deprivation of ordinary time and space interpreted by the emotions both in their involuntary presence and submission to human will and choice. This is made clear in the differences between the characters' response to prison. *Men in Prison* already redirects the autobiographical impulse to egotism by claiming a narrative of the self only in and through others. The convenient use of the first person singular, Serge wrote to Panaït Istrati, is misleading: 'I don't want to write memoirs. This book is not about me, but about men.'[55] Truth will vary according to Serge between the 'photographic' observation of things seen but noting that sometimes it 'differs in every respect'.[56] There are, therefore, as many modes of standing outside time as recording being in it (the illusion of fictional time in which the present of history appears as present) in this strangely fictional autobiography.

For the prisoner, the founding moment of a new time is the arrest, in which 'all present time [...] is fading away':[57]

> The contrast between this vacant, empty prison time and the intense rhythms of normal life is so violent that it will take a long and painful period of adaptation to slow down the pulse of life, to deaden the will, to stifle, blot out, obliterate every unsettling image from my mind [...] My inner life pursues its feverish course in a silence void of time.[58]

Judicial, and therefore political, time is therefore experienced as the brutality of pure chronology. It obliterates the variable times of the world in pure number. Interiorized in the prisoner it produces solipsistic madness. Narrative itself will become the first defence against the terror of assigned time. All narrative from Scheherazade (the narrator of *One Thousand and One Nights*) onwards is produced under sentence of death, here literally so: 'On the second day [...] I began to write a story.'[59] At the heart of the book is a meditation on time itself:

> I think of the mystery of time's passage. There are minutes and hours which have no end: the eternity of the instant. There are many empty hours: the vacuity of time. There are endless days; and weeks which pass without leaving the least memory behind them as if they had never been. I cannot distinguish the years that are behind me. Time passes within us. Our actions fill it. It is a river: steep banks, a straight path, colorless waves. The void is its source, and it flows into the void. Time could not exist outside of my thought. It is whatever I make it. The instant which I fill with light is priceless, like a ray of light forms a star which shines for eternity through the space it illuminates. The empty hours and days which I yield to dead things have no more existence than shadows. My very dream is the surest reality.[60]

It does not take much imagination to see how the social realists would have reacted to such a passage. But the intensity of this inner experience so described is a way of making something of the void assigned to *l'homme enfermé*. Serge knew, as Arendt paraphrases Isak Dinesen, that 'without repeating life in the imagination you can never be fully alive.'[61] Here, Serge takes a time thrust on him by others and twists its neck. In this remarkable passage, thought struggles with terror in a double movement, a movement in which chronological time is turned upside down: moments are eternities, time is emptied in vacuity, the connection between time and memory is broken, recognizable segments of time lose their meaning, twenty-four hours is neither day nor night nor a seventh of a week. By an act of will, thinking gives words to the chaos, a moment of light defeats Chronos and old night. For Serge the story and the poem are a practical defence against political despair and simplistic religious mysticism, the twin perils for human beings at the end of their tether.

In Serge's work it is the poem that gives meaning to the limits of human experience. To be sure, the fictional narrative in this work negotiates with familiar tropes: the descent into hell in which the survivor re-emerges to tell the tale. But the rhetoric of emplotment, as Hayden White long ago reminded us, involves an ideological choice. Serge hurls his story of the dark night of the soul against the French positivistic 'correction' facility (Santé prison) which architecturally embodies a manic totalitarian dream of absolute security and absolute surveillance. Hence, decades before Foucault, Serge noted of his own prison: 'From the center of the hub a single man can keep his eye on the whole prison without difficulty, and his glance can ferret into the most remote corners.'[62] So perfect is the building that the only thing to do with it is to destroy it. In his insistence on the foundational experience of time and narrative as rescuing the human psyche from both history and chronology Serge reclaims a different universality, a universality that has been lost in the Stalinist universality of the totalitarian uninspired lecturing for the Soviets on the nineteenth-century treatment of the Russian working class as he had been doing genealogical research for the former *nouveaux-riches* in Imperial Russia before 1917, is giving a lecture to the Soviet Poor People's Committee on the execution of Dr Millière during the period of the Paris Commune. After the lecture he is confronted by 'the man from Onega', a worker who comes up to him and speaks to him about the death of the martyred Communard, Millière, and who then in a 'parallel' story recalls his own part in the 1917 revolution with pride:

> 'On the road I had read Arnould's pamphlet, *The Dead of the Commune*. I was thinking of Millière. And I avenged Millière, citizen! It was a beautiful day in my life, and I haven't had many. Point by point, I avenged him. I shot the richest landowner in the area, on the steps of the church, just like that – I don't remember his name, and I don't give a damn!'
>
> After a short silence he added:
>
> 'But I was the one who shouted, "Long live humanity"'
>
> 'You know,' said the archivist, 'basically Millière wasn't a real Communard. He was only a bourgeois republican.'
>
> 'It's all the same to me,' said the man who had come back from Onega.[80]

This moment is quintessential Serge. It is of course a parable, plausible as reportage but thickened by the questions posed in Serge's arrangement and selection of the incidents. The questions are: what is history, what is the nature of the historical sense and how does the interpretation of the past intermesh with and guide present conduct? Is an ethical judgement of the historical event even possible?

To get the full measure of Serge's irony a few details are necessary. Arthur Arnould, anarchist and journalist, the author of the pamphlet that the 'man from Onega' has read, had been a French member of the First International. A friend of Bakunin who was exiled to Switzerland, he was an archivist, writer and teacher during the Paris Commune. Later drawn to esoteric religions, he had been active in opposing the totalitarian tendencies of the Commune's Committee of Public Safety.[81] Millière's death was one of the many brutal executions of the counter-revolutionary aftermath of the Commune. A deputy, not a member of the Commune, he had sought only conciliation, but his articles against Jules Favre, a high official of the Third Republic who had been thoroughly duped by Bismarck, had been enough for the vengeance of the reaction. He had to be forced to his knees to be executed and his last cry, 'Long Live Humanity', became one of the great historical memories of the history of the Commune.

Just these few facts, virtually forgotten in our own times, form the basis for Serge's fictional-historical parable. Irony and reversal are the key tropes here because this story of 'the man from Onega' with its nameless 'revolutionary' and nameless 'richest landowner' shot on the steps of the Church, satirizes the new indifferent gods but people who will do anything to keep a grip on their ever-threatened power or their place in a totalitarian bureaucratic hierarchy. Stalin himself will never experience retribution. The temporality of tragedy needs a metaphysic of Greek cyclic time to work, and the fatal flaw is not quite the same as Serge's redeployment of Gide's *acte gratuit*.

In *The Case of Comrade Tulayev*, the main figure, Kostia, shoots Tulayev, the high party official, without premeditation and almost without any specific ideological or political reason. The event is not logically connected with anything that follows, there is for example, no detective plot, although there is detective action, an ironic sub-plot demonstrating the mania of the controlling state. However Serge will show how the consequences of a violent *acte gratuit* in a totalitarian society articulate the absolutism and illogic of political tyranny in its paranoid fear of insecurity. Kostia is not the high figure of tragedy doomed by the gods. All we know about him is that he acts on impulse. In the opening scene he buys a miniature of a woman rather than a pair of shoes he had set out to buy: '"I'll take it," Kostia said, to his own surprise.' Even at the end of the book, completely free of pursuit and consequences, he cannot confess his crime to his wife in a straightforward manner:

> [if I had] killed a man, ages ago or a few days or a few months ago, on a night of unbelievable snow, without knowing him, without a thought of killing him, without having wanted to, but voluntarily just the same, with my eyes wide open, my hand steady, because he was doing evil in the name of ideas that are right, because I was full of the sufferings of others, because, without knowing it, I had pronounced judgement in a few seconds – I for many others, I who am unknown, for others who are unknown and nameless, for all who have no names, no will, no luck, not even my rag of a conscience, Maria, what would you say to me?[83]

Maria tells him to keep his nerves under control, to stop telling her his bad dreams and to kiss her. A moment later she adds, 'I know how much harm is done involuntarily when the struggle is desperate. Just the same we're going forward aren't we?'[84] I think that the final question can only be the crowning irony in Serge's fiction, just as the thickness of Maria's emotional self-deception arises from her fear of the truth here and interpenetrates with the political 'answer'. Serge's optimism of the will was unconquerable, but his pessimism of the intellect again and again told him that this historical struggle was going backward. Again, Kostia's fledgling conscience is the only retribution. His wife responds in denial, remonstrance and by changing the subject. What dignity of meaning can this question and answer suggest in the ubiquitous absence of any justice at all? Certainly the response of the very Sergian Maria (a sort of Dostoevskian Sonia) leaves all the questions unanswered and, as for the question 'we're going forward aren't we?', it is left unanswered in both Pascalian and Marxist terms.

Just 'how much harm' is also a key unanswered issue, as well as the degree to which Kostia mimics the oppressor in arbitrary violence.

Unpremeditated, individual, involuntary violence, the text argues, is better than the collective cold-blooded violence of the state, but then it is extremely hard to inscribe that within the millenialist temporality of 'struggle' with any sense of authentic meaning, that is to say how much it contributes to any 'forward' movement. The suggestion is that it does not. At what point in the future will violence be seen to be justified? The famous Mao verdict on the meaning of the French revolution ('too early to tell') is hardly helpful to present judgement or decision, though it clearly encourages millennial dreamers. Even in personal and affective terms, one might imagine a further novel in which Kostia, in old age, is driven mad by the need to keep the crime hidden. The absence of cause and effect which Serge's closure reaffirms, at once speaks the truth of the disjuncture between intention and result, while ironically mimicking the arbitrary nature of absolute power.

Are long time-frames more truthful than short ones? Who decides, and with what authority, when, so to speak, the time is up? That question of temporality which Serge raises in Kostia's reply also mirrors in reverse the issue of an authentic justification proposed as a future. Curiously, Kostia offers a series of times when he might have done it. Ironically, while illustrating the nervousness with which he 'reveals' the possibility of murder he seems to raise the question of whether the statute of limitation applies to murder.

The profoundest irony for Serge here is that this implausible 'innocent', with his colt revolver representing the modernity of American technocratic violence, and his representativeness as *l'homme moyen sensuel* of the 'masses' is less reprehensible than the apparatchiks of the Soviet state. The further irony is that in the ordinary world, the human fascination about the long-ago crime is a compulsive issue, from the myth of Adam's fall and the murder of Abel, to the New Testament declaration about the sins of the fathers, to modernity and the plays of Ibsen. The past is defined in the immediacy of psychological presence. The issue here is: did Kostia do it in Marxist time or in Pascalian time? And is murder better in the one than the other? Any legal judgement would have insisted on a reconstruction in chronological time just as the sentence would have involved a chronological prophecy. The clearest point that Serge makes is about the arbitrariness and ambiguity of judgement, legal, ethical and political, in the authoritarian state in which the relation of master and slave forms an unbroken circle. The issue is also clearly raised of the degree to which a Nietzschean obliteration of history is sometimes necessary.

The latter question is raised in negative form in a remarkable passage at the heart of the book in the portrait of Ryzhik, a member of the old guard of Bolsheviks. He will die through neglect in prison, against the wishes of the authorities and that 'neglect' will implicate in turn the careerist interrogator

Zvyeryeva, a Sergean *femme fatale*, whose sadism and bureaucratic hunger for power within the system is, in Reichian terms, surrealistically and psychologically characterized by showing her masturbating on a bed with a tilting mirror having fantasies of young girls being brutally raped. Serge begins his portrait of Ryzhik by showing the state's difficulties in implicating this Trotskyite will-o'-the-wisp who seems to bear a charmed life (rather like Serge's own): 'what could one think of an engine driver who had escaped unscathed from thirty telescoped carriages'.[85] Authority cannot deal with the contingent and unpredictable. Serge begins with a parody of the temporality of the secret police dossier, that authoritarian but strictly chronological litany of the suspect's life:

> member of the Party since 1906, deported to the Lena in 1914, returned from Siberia in April 1917; had several conversations with Lenin immediately after the conference of April '17; member of the Petrograd Committee during the Civil War, defended the workers' opposition before the Petrograd committee in '20, but did not vote for it ... expelled from the Party in '27, arrested in '29, deported to Siberia, in July, '29[86]

In such a temporally atomized list, historical time is reduced to the pure succession of event. Causal, ethical, ideological, personal and political significance is lost in the panoramic sweep of the paranoid police gaze which homogenizes that already abstract chronological time as events characterizing the 'criminal'. Serge piles irony on irony as he shows Rizhik abandoned in a kind of solipsistic timelessness in the Siberian desert where hunter-gatherers still wonder at the invention of the clock:

> Another envied treasure was his clock, which people sometimes came from the neighbouring houses to see. When a Nyenets hunter crossed those plains, the people explained to him that there was a man living among them who was being punished, and that he owned a machine that made time, a machine that sang all by itself, without ever stopping, sang for invisible time. And in fact the obstinate nibbling of the clock devoured a silence as of eternity. Ryzhik loved it, having lived almost a year without it, in pure time, pure motionless madness, earlier than creation.[87]

Thus Serge offers another parable of the historical temporality. The clock, the story tells us, had been sent as a present to Ryzhik by the last survivors of the revolution's old guard, whose time is 'past', and who are now being systematically exterminated by Stalin. The irony is that in 'doing time', the exile has been deprived of that vital sense of the past and historical connection with it necessary to sanity. In or out of prison capitalist–industrial time is punishment. The gift of the clock returns the sense of time but in meaningless chronology thus mirroring the extensions of judicial time (the 'stretch') and offering only another illusion of time:

> That it gained an hour in twenty-four when he forgot to hang his penknife on the weight that made it run, was really of no importance. But Ryzhik and Pakhomov never tired of their joke. In consisted in one of them asking the other: 'What time is it?' 'Four ...' 'With or without the penknife?' 'With the clog', Ryzhik once answered very seriously, for he had been reading last month's *Pravda*. Bearing their half century of master-less servitude, Ryzhik's host and his wife – he stroking his rough beard, she with her hands clasped in her sleeves – had come to look at the wonder and they had spoken in its presence, saying only one word, but a profound word, risen from the depths of their souls (and how had they come to know that word?):
>
> 'Beautiful,' he said, shaking his head.
>
> 'Beautiful,' his wife repeated.
>
> 'When the two hands are here,' Ryzhik explained to them, 'in the daytime it means that it's noon, at night it means that it's midnight.'
>
> 'By God's grace,' said the man.
>
> 'By God's grace,' said the woman.
>
> They crossed themselves and left, shuffling awkwardly, like a pair of penguins.[88]

The historical sense that involves a consciousness of the meaning of time, is highly varied in this ironic and comic episode. The time of the person and the time of the political world bear no relation to each other, any more than the peasant time of the seasons bears any relation to industrial time. Even mechanical time, working theoretically correctly, is without significance. It is ironic that the penknife becomes abstract weight in a world of arbitrary mathematical signifiers. Its 'use value' is obliterated through its use as pure weight pulled by gravity in the creation of arbitrary numbers of no use to anyone.

Lewis Mumford once speculated that the canonical hours were introduced in the monasteries as a refuge from the chaos of the disintegrating Roman Empire. Here abstract orderly time embodies the chaos of the Soviet Empire. For Mumford the clock was not merely a 'means of keeping track of the hours, but of synchronizing the actions of men'.[89] Detached from the world of men the exiles, however, do not even experience a mechanical relation with others. Mumford also noted, and it is of pointed relevance to this passage, that 'only yesterday, in the midst of the industrializations of Soviet Russia, did a society come into existence to further the carrying of watches there, and to propagandize the benefits of punctuality.'[90] If the first cheap watch had been produced in Geneva and then in mid-nineteenth-century America, the Soviet cheap watch Serge notes just before this passage, 'was procurable for ten roubles in city co-operatives'.[91] 'When', said Mumford (recalling the French expression *se coucher avec les poules*), 'one thinks of the day as an abstract span of time, one does not go to bed with the chickens.'[92] Indeed the 'scientific' numerical orders of Stalinist prophetic historical time 'clog' that experience of time, all that is left is the 'how long' as Heidegger put it, 'until then'.[93] Statistically drunk capitalism, Marx observed, asked 'no questions about the length of life of labour-power'.[94] Neither did statistically drunk Stalinism.

The peasants, however, are entranced by the skill of clockwork as yet ignorant of the power it will come to have over their lives. Certainly they still go to bed with the chickens. In terms of the psychology of temporality itself, theirs is an irrecoverable time, unreal, an uncanny sign of something already doomed. What will vanish is personal time itself when the length of life of the person in relation to labour power now becomes irrelevant: 'Once time has been defined as clock time then there is no hope of ever arriving at its original meaning again.'[95] At the same time Serge notes that their capacity for wonder shows the pure attraction of the object almost as an exaltation before a future they will not experience. There are literally disappearing from perceived time for their future in Serge's narrative irony no longer exists. In a sense prisoner and peasant share the same fate. For different reasons they are robbed of human time.

It was just such a sense of the clock and time that Serge must have picked up from his friend Boris Pilniak's extraordinary novel *The Naked Year* (1922), the temporal implications of the title barely indicating its surreal juxtaposing of times, eras and epochs in the shaky chaotic present of the post-revolutionary historical moment in Russia. The narrative context of the following quotation is the moment where an aristocrat is forced to leave his estate under the watchful new Communist 'chairman':

> Just then the clock struck three quarters – the clock was the work of Kuvaldin, an eighteenth century craftsman, it used to be in the Kremlin palace in Moscow, then journeyed with the Vadkosky princes through the Causcasus – how many times had it gone 'tick-tock' to take away two centuries.[96]

Serge hence illustrated the boundary between the pre-capitalist and capitalist eras in terms of the experience of time. In the first, nature is linked with human time in the rhythms of the sun and earth as well as through the church calendar, articulated by religious memory in the saints' days. It is well known, for example, that in medieval Europe people had more time off by virtue of the length of the winter day, and in respect of sacred and secular feast days, than in any modern capitalist country. As for the capitalist era, 'in time-keeping, in trading, in fighting men [it] counted numbers; and finally, as the habit grew, only numbers counted'.[97]

When Serge's character Ryzhik connected the spatial abstraction of the moving hands with cosmic time, the peasants' religious expostulation 'by God's Grace' showed them accurately intuiting the hubris of connecting a number system, based on infinity, with an eternity, represented by a mechanical icon more coercive than the ones before which they habitually knelt. As mechanical time conquered all, 'eternity ceased gradually to serve as the measure and focus of human actions.'[98] Just as they intuited what might be beautiful, the 'ignorant' peasants, waddling like 'penguins', intuit the absence of a human distinction between the finite and infinite in the capitalist process itself, and a loss of a discourse in which the sense of that 'eternity' which Ricoeur has said, shadows our experience of the finite, might be articulated. Serge had a special fondness for the villages of the trans-Caucuses, victims of an earlier Russian imperialism: 'here the Middle Ages are preserved right to the beginning of our century, they have still not disappeared. Here Russia is a stranger one distrusts as an imperial master.'[99] That, as today's suffering people of Chechnya know, did not alter with a change of masters.

The historical sense of experience of times in and out of joint is most patent in the title of Serge's novel *S'il est minuit dans le siècle* (1939), a stunningly elegant and compressed title (which for English readers cannot but recall the paradoxical proposition of Donne's 'Tis the yeare's midnight, and it is the day's').[100] Whether Serge knew the poem or not cannot be known though Gide almost certainly would have known it. In Serge's title, solar time and the arbitrary decimalization 'century' just beyond the limits of the average human life, juxtapose to provide a richly haunting sense of lostness, bewilderment, and fatality. Yet the ambiguity of the French 'si', meaning if or when, offers the shadow of the conditional within the inevitable, between despair and a call to resistance in the question 'What is to be done?' It also hints at an injunction framed in a speculative if-then proposition 'if this is what you must do, when?'

Just before his death Serge wrote a response to the new 'existentialist' writers of France. It was not a complex piece but an indicative one. He put the phenomenon in various frames rather than writing about it philosophically. The first is the twentieth-century history of seemingly continuous and accelerating human atrocity: two world wars, Stalinist purges, Nazi concentration camps, British and American saturation bombing and America's development and use of atomic weapons. He connects the existentialist's primary proposition that 'we' are inessential in the face of the nature with the anguish of contemporary history. Paradoxically he shows how the metaphysical proposition and the affective historical judgment are somewhat artificially allied. The world escapes our despair. The loss of all hope, said Sartre, citing Heidegger's *Being and Time*, 'does not deprive human reality of its possibilities, it is a way of being towards those possibilities'.[101]

Serge contrasts the two wars and French writers responding to them. Romain Rolland, Barbusse, Duhamel and Léon Werth still had the resources of the European humanist tradition and the immediate intellectual ferment of the Russian revolution from Marx to Trotsky. The French writers of 1945 have no such resource, European civilization was in disgrace, the socialist revolution had been betrayed and the intellectuals had fallen back on Kierkegaard, 'the philosopher of anguish'. Serge had obviously not read Sartre's *Search for a Method*, published in the same year as *S'il est minuit dans le siècle*. Had he done so, he would almost certainly have been more sympathetic to Sartre's position where, in a discussion of Marxism and existentialism, the French writer cited Kierkegaard as placing the 'irreducibility and the specificity of what is lived' against the seamless ideal structure of Hegel's system.[102] In a sense the argument foreshadows that of the *Ethics* in the dual appeal to Pascal and Marx.

Serge describes the Sartrean person as 'dizzyingly free' ('*vertigineusement libre*') and as 'irreducibly indeterminate' ('*un centre d'indétermination irréductible*'). For Serge, this flies in the face of all modern psychology. Serge is responding to what Ricoeur, commenting on Kierkegaard and Plotinus, called the seduction of anguish.[103] The soul can appear hemmed in by a vertiginous (the same word is used) sense of being surrounded by exteriority. Serge also comments on Camus's 'Myth of Sisiphus', where the person is subject to pessimism without remedy, save in the recognition of the unique value of the individual life which becomes the very principle of life itself. Further, while acknowledging that Bataille is certainly not an existentialist (he was on the contrary critical of much of Sartre's position), he accuses him of a kind of parallel nihilism quoting '*Le ciel est vide, l'homme ne sait rien*.' Serge saw the French anthropologist and author of *Literature and Evil* as lacking even the iconoclastic and creative faith in the self of a Nietzsche.

Typically then, Serge has a historical view of modern pessimism, which he traces back to the nineteenth-century reaction to the industrial and scientific revolutions. Given the events of 1939–45, these attitudes he conceded were perfectly understandable but nonetheless unsustainable. For Serge neither the self nor the cosmos were 'empty', they were full of the glory, if not of God, then of the very stuff of human history and human wonder. Unlike Sartre and Camus, Serge had lived the agonies of the biggest historical failure of the only major modern revolution undertaken in the name of the oppressed, and as an active participant. Throwing himself into a project in order to convince himself he existed in a semi-hostile relation to others was hardly needed. It was mutual aid and solidarity that historical pattern revealed as the meaning of human life, even if his novels had shown that to be only minimally possible at the time of the twentieth century's most catastrophic global wars. To what extent, he asked, were these new French writers actually dealing with, for example, the scandalous plight of the Spanish refugees in France at that very moment. Serge would not live long enough to see Sartre more directly politically active but his comments were not without some justification in 1946.

Serge seems to have had an instinctive faith in the connectedness of the world and human beings. There was an *a priori* meaningfulness, if not in order or design, then in the shifting and moving patterns of history which were made and given meaning by human beings themselves. So here, he felt the propositions of the new French writers were emotional reactions, with their own validity to be sure, rather than convincing as such. It is easy to see why Serge's great love of the world and endless scientific and historical curiosity about nature and human affairs would make him unsympathetic to the tone of the French writers. There was more than a touch of the progressive optimism of the nineteenth century that clung to him to the end. His Marxism scented the old metaphysical agonies produced in the wake of the French post-Enlightenment atheist but, quite unlike a Marxist, he affirmed again and again how religious and ethical writers might be a source of nourishment. The writers he cites in support are Marcus Aurelius, Pascal and Spinoza. Above all it was that long time-scale of human historical experience suggested by these writers that sustained Serge's sense of himself in history. For him, the Nazi occupation of France was not the first brutal and tyrannical imperialism in human history. To derive the indifference of the universe from it was not an option, as he dryly commented: 'All philosophers enthused by the Great Contemporary Walking Wounded of the Universe are probably, in all reasonable expectation, transitory.' There were things to act for. He possessed an almost childlike delight in the latest books on science and psychology and an old-fashioned Renaissance eagerness about knowledge itself. Like Marcus Aurelius, he had a poised ability to keep in and out of the game.

Midnight in the Century (1939), the final novel to be considered here, fictionalizes Serge's own experience of exile in trans-Caucasia and the experience of the Siberian exile of the Bolshevik and Trotskyite old guard. It illustrates vividly Serge's unique combination of mourning, testimony and sense of tragedy, and authentic affirmation of the self in connection with history in complex ways. At one moment, two of the central characters discover a proscribed book by Trotsky in a pile of junk sold by an old peasant woman. One recalls Lukács dumping German books and works by Bukharin and Trotsky into the Moscow river during the 1940s.[104] The time in the novel, however, is the mid-1930s. A book by Trotsky, on the junk heap of history, is at once mourned yet remains minimally present:

> But of what matter now the rhythm of that bygone language, the precision and ardour of that thought, bound to events in order to force them, ceaselessly invoking history in order to make it? The old text lives because it expresses a fidelity, a necessity. It is necessary that someone not betray [...] The essential thing is to remain true.[105]

The moment may have failed but the present value of the book is as a witness directed forwards to the future and recoverable in this present moment, less like a message in bottle thrown from a ship-wrecked vessel than as a truth of its time yet to be discovered and re-imagined.

History, however, can be 'read' in any Sergean descriptive passage. The very landscape is a book open to deciphering. In a remarkable passage describing

Chernoe, the trans-Caucases town that is the setting of the story, Serge sets out a miniature parable of its history. Its name means 'Black-town' and Serge plays the 'atmosphere' of 'blackness' as a shadow behind every movement of its history. Blackness is of course the colour most associated with anarchism. Its origins are various. In France the black flag was used in a demonstration by the unemployed in 1883, a year later it was used in Chicago. It was widely adopted by anarchist groups throughout Europe in the 1880s and at the funeral of Kropotkin in 1921. The *Chicago Alarm* called it 'the fearful symbol of hunger, misery and death' and Murray Bookchin, a contemporary American anarchist, has called it the 'symbol of the workers' misery and [an] expression of their anger and bitterness'. Certainly it seemed to capture the nihilism of the 1890s: 'so black is negation, is anger, is outrage, is mourning, is beauty, is hope, is the fostering and sheltering of new forms of human life and relationship on and with this earth.'[106]

Chernoe's story, that is to say, the history of blackness, begins, with geological time turning its outcrops of black rock into a naturalist image of history itself, the earth's revolutions paralleling that of human society. Nature 'tells a story about the town'.[107] Serge's slightly heightened language invests the narrative voice with that of the story-teller, almost bardic in its willing suspension of disbelief. Certainly it is prophetic, for the founder of the town is a religious dissenter, heretical and anarchist in spirit, Seraphim Bezzemelny (Seraphim Lack-Land) who also seizes on the blackness of the geological outcrops to cry, like Isaiah whose lips were touched by the Seraphim with a burning coal, 'On these black stones we will build our house.'[108] Serge combines Jewish and Christian mythology, to create a mythical founding event for a chronology. Like Christ before Herod, and in the Garden of Gethsemane, the Heresiarch confronts the Patriarch, crying 'remove not this cup from me'.[109] In this folk-like tale of the origin of a town, the new Patriarch then calls Lack-Land to the Kremlin for forgiveness but he refuses to stop denouncing the abuses of the official faith. In prison 'he could hear the bells of the false faith ringing. But he needed only to close his eyes to see the pacifying Holy Face.'[110] Serge adds 'they sometimes tell the story of his life, with many other details, on long winter evenings'.[111]

Reverting to the fictional present, Serge notes these tales inspire 'Tikhon, the disabled pensioner, who fought through the whole Ural campaign under Blüchner in 1918.'[112] Then again Serge lengthens the time frame: 'Between Seraphim and Tikhon two centuries empty of history passed over Chernoe, Black-Town, Black-Waters',[113] and he continued:

> The Zyrians besieged the town at the beginning of the XVIII Century. They shot reed arrows tipped with fish-bones. (but maybe they weren't Zyrians). The town burned down every thirty years more or less, so that the generations have succeeded each other there from one fire to the next and all improvements are connected with great calamities. The Revolution happened all by itself.[114]

Serge's 'blackness' in this, the bleakest of his novels, is about the inessentiality of the person, swept along by the forces of history itself. The little parable of origin can be literally refigured in the relation of Trotsky and Stalin, but its general meaning is broader than simple political allegory. The play of temporalities embraces several time-frames. There is geological time, always melancholy and outside human feeling, and the immediacy of the ineluctable landscape impinging on the daily life of the people – the Black River, for example, sweeping the odd child away in its whirlpools: 'they find the little bodies three kilometres downstream on a sandbar where they seem to be sleeping desperately, washing and bruised in an unreal blue light'.[115]

A past and present permanence of fatality, almost cyclic, haunts the people. In the immediate Revolutionary present, one Lebedkin, a political deportee, still stuck with classics of Victorian liberalism in his reading, after telegrams from Moscow, finds himself mayor. No one has any connection with the revolution but historical time bound to shifts in power has taken another fateful turn. Lebedkin, like a second Lack-Land, meditates on a black rock overlooking the river, haunted by mystical thoughts of Russia. He is shown to be more concerned about exile from the warmth of a woman left behind him and that haunts his memory. He is found dead in the market place having been murdered by a counter-revolutionary or a Stalinist agent: 'His brains were spread over the dandelions, but his *pince-nez* glasses, their frame mended with a black thread, were still perched on the bride of his nose.'[116] He will have a street named after him, a text which will outrun that personal time.

Serge had noted earlier in the novel: 'the great storm, centuries in preparation, began with total simplicity. Where are the actors of those bygone days and who remembers them? Each year's thaw renews the earth.'[117] There is no real comfort in this 'eternal' renewal of nature as such. In spite of its naturalist vehemence, however, it serves several functions, stretching from underlining of nature's indifference to the human story as such, to ironically proposing a parallel in a cycle of renewal and destruction, sometimes offering hope in the impartiality of its renewal and sometimes despair in the impartiality of its destruction. This is an indifferent present of genuinely tragic poetic force, a type of temporality that will be returned to in Simone Weil's commentary on the *Iliad*, to be examined in the next section. There is also a Pascalian present in the political allegory. Allegory is where one story is explained and thickened by an unspoken, known and parallel story. This allows Serge to make ethical judgements which are outside historical time since the two stories may connect across time, as Dante's fourteenth-century hell articulates the times of both Roman and Christian history. Hence Tikhon and Lack-Land can be compared as types of ethical integrity, here with a touch of irony because Tikhon has no historical fame, that is to say he is without a story in official remembrance. Narrativized time has everything to do with political power.

Pure renewal for Serge, as we shall see that it is for Mumford, is useless without memory and story. To that extent, the pure Nietzschean fire of the continually burned over town, and the drowning of the children, empties two centuries of history in the ironic time-condensing gaze of the author. T.S. Eliot's death by fire and water in *The Waste Land* similarly structured an essentially religious landscape of earthly hell in the stasis of the Christian view of a permanently 'fallen' world whose resolution would be outside time. The lurid blue light of the child's dead body is just that, a haunting without a story. In spite of the bleakness, unlike Eliot, Serge never leaves either time or history. The blackness of the old anarchist symbol offered a renewal through a simultaneous recognition of both the ahistorical patterns of human misery and those who have challenged it historically by intervening. Remembrance creates a world of story alongside fate which includes a different and human version of the past, present and future, giving it a finiteness which offers meaning to the fatality of history and death. The indifferent cycles of revolution itself are never the same in their reappearance in history. Greeman's afterword to the novel cannot be bettered here: 'They illuminate a past which is the origin of our present and tell us that the future may yet be a new beginning. As Rosa Luxemburg said, "Every revolution is doomed to failure except the last one."'[118]

Serge's world is supremely accomplished in a narrativity that crosses, and is revealed in, both the fictional and autobiographical modes. What connects them is a writing which shifts beyond the surface of chronology and linear narrative in modes of parable, self-revelation, fictional narrative and discursive discourses, which pose and enact large questions about the nature of time and memory and which contribute towards what Serge called 'the sense of history'. That sense of history was a moving space of judgement which included ethical and ideological issues and in which behaviour and practice were perceived in a dialectical relationship with the contingent event, collective practices, ideological expectation and ideological demand. Nowhere is the question of the use and abuse of power far from the surface of the discussion.

Like Proust, whom, as a Marxist, he uncharacteristically defended, Serge's own works are tales about time. The question of truth immediately presents itself. Here Ricoeur's meditations on time and memory again become relevant. How did Serge attempt to recapture lost time: 'the meaning of an earlier life, itself wholly fictive?'[119] One needs to combine Ricoeur and Sartre in order to relate in new ways the Deleuzian distinction between the exposition of memory and the apprenticeship to signs (for example the social world and art) and which for Serge includes the archaeological traces of ancient civilizations, pre-capitalist ethnic ways of life, the behaviour of people moving from a fledgling communist to a totalitarian state and the conjunction of urban and wilderness landscape.

Surely, as for Proust, Serge's apprenticeship to signs involved a form of 'interminable wandering', with its 'sudden illumination that retrospectively transforms the entire narrative into the invisible history of a vocation'.[120] Ricoeur famously attacked the Marxist reading of Proust which tied a promotion of the psychological to the deterioration of a metaphysics, and anecdote to a philosophical knowledge forged elsewhere. The solution, grounded in the narrative composition itself, that Ricoeur offers, is no longer then 'how the philosophy of a lost unity could have degenerated into a quest for lost time but how the search for lost time, taken as the founding matrix of the work, accomplishes, through strictly narrative means, the recovery of the Romantic problematic of lost unity'.[121]

We have seen some of those narrative means in operation. There is always at least a double narrative voice, 'the thoughts of the narrator accompany the hero's lived experience and shed light on it'.[122] This is precisely what Serge did with flair and a searing conscientiousness. The lost unity for Serge will not be that of the psychological self as such, though it includes it, but that of a historical unity of the person broken up by capitalist disintegration (division of labour, the class system, the atomization of the person as a result of capitalist productive forces), which is however not located in pre-capitalist time though to a degree it may be minimally signalled there (God's grace is figuratively a higher truth than the culture of the clock), but in the precarious promise of the first years of the revolution in which the 'future of the past' in Serge's retrospective gaze is already threatened.

The early revolution becomes at once a site of nostalgia already surpassed, a theme of closure, a fictive possibility and, most paradoxically of all, a symbolic space of hope outside the process of history itself. For the premise of Serge's autobiographical fiction assumes 'a future in the past' simply because the Pascalian judgement is timeless: 'the mysterious eternity that circulates between the present and the past'.[123] It is also the very premise of historical writing itself in its demand for a present judgement within its telling of the story. The past makes demands on the historical impulse, calling as it were to its own future in the very activity of the fictive-historian. Certainly the relation between the happy moments, and the not so much invisible but denied history of a vocation is at the core of Serge's work. In Serge, however, it is the unhappy moments, a history of multiple separations accompanied with all the signs of death, that he attempts to decipher successfully within a narrative of an unwilling shift of vocations from revolutionary to writer, a narrative which interweaves with the other narrative of the (named and judged) Soviet *Thermidor*. As with Proust, the fiction dramatizes the tragedy of separations but, unlike Proust, for Serge there is no consistently familiar space to trigger memory. Sartre said that both Pascalian and Marxist time are needed. Ricoeur noted that recognition is the 'mark of the extra-temporal on lost time'.[124]

In his view, that recognition was less the imperfect visual haunting of the ruins of time than a recognition in new historical moments of atemporal patterns of psychology and behaviour that the work of narrative and ethics offered.

> Finally, it is the impression regained, which reconciles life and literature. Indeed, inasmuch as life is the figure of the way of time lost, and literature the way of the extra-temporal, we have the right to say that time regained expresses the recovery of life in the work of art.[125]

For Serge the impression regained was less a drive to a recovery of the unity of the self, or a vivid insight 'that eternity was in love with the productions of time', than a work of mourning and celebration in the strange generic form of the fictional obituary.

One might almost reverse Ricoeur's proposition and say that equally for Serge there is a recovery of art in the work of life. In Serge a quasi-public voice confronts the private life of the person, in Proust a quasi-private voice confronts public life. Both voices are artful fictions, both writers articulate from both ends of the public–private spectrum the terror and tragedy of the human condition with a pitiless clarity that banishes sentiment yet which is accompanied by a great love. For Serge, that lost time of youthful hope and revolution foundering in internal and external wars of unimaginable death and terror was recovered in the long view of history, in an ultimately poetic configuration of narrative temporalities, with a sense of wonder that did indeed reclaim the indifference of cosmic time and the inessentiality of the self for a meaningful sense of life. In what Edward Thompson called 'those magnificent last scenes in the church' in William Morris's *A Dream of John Ball*, Morris's fictional fourteenth-century priest John Ball surveys the dead from the day's battle, and with friend and foe lying beside him, sums up the entire spirit of Serge's work in celebrated but always relevant words:

> I pondered [...] how men fight and lose the battle, and the thing that they fought for comes about in spite of their defeat, and when it comes turns out not to be what they meant, and other men have to fight for what they meant under another name.[126]

2

Posts of the Good: Dwight Macdonald's *politics*

So when Appleby-Smythe finds my attack on the profit motive 'amazing', and says that our job is not to abandon it but to retain it and harness it to the public good – he does not even mean for a few decades, he means permanently – I am confirmed in my view that marxists generally, and most ex-marxists as well, understand very little about ethics.

— VICTOR GOLLANCZ[1]

Still as a slave before his Lord
The ocean hath no blast

— SAMUEL TAYLOR COLERIDGE[2]

I

Wartime: Bridges and Not-Bridges

It was Dwight Macdonald, the American journalist, moralist, libertarian and public intellectual who, as Victor Serge noted in his *Memoirs of a Revolutionary*, at the moment of his family's supreme danger in war-time Marseille had grasped 'his hand in the dark'.[3] Serge himself was to publish in Macdonald's journal *politics*. The journal and its devotion to covering international affairs, is the first of two major (yet still virtually unrecognized) achievements of American literature and culture during the 1940s and will be examined in this and the next part of the book. That clasp of the hand will be a guiding image in the discussion. In this respect, the focus will differ from some American commentators. For both Macdonald and Dorothy Norman of *TWICE A YEAR*, the clasp of the hand was extended far beyond America itself. What will be celebrated here are moments of American sympathy with the non-American, the foreigner, the stranger: an American imaginative reaching-out to other cultures, in recognition of their otherness, and with a selfless generosity that the world of the twenty-first century finds difficult to imagine of the America of the present moment.

Macdonald's journal *politics* and Norman's *TWICE A YEAR* invalidate Paul Fussell's claim that America could produce nothing like Cyril Connolly's *Horizon*, which appeared in Britain in the 1940s. The British journal, according to Fussell, demonstrated 'the unlikelihood if not the impossibility of, of a phenomenon like *Horizon* appearing in the wartime U.S.A.'.[4] In fact, *politics* and *TWICE A YEAR* at the very least rivalled, and to a degree surpassed, the scope of *Horizon* in their international range. They were at least as good and often more adventurous in their coverage of diverse intellectual life and in the qualitative commentary on literature and art. Ironically and clearly unbeknownst to Fussell, the three journals had a number of contributors in common. *TWICE A YEAR* advertised *Horizon* in its back pages. It could, the advertisement noted, be bought at the New York Gotham Book Store. It is clear that the journals were generous to each other.

In general Fussell treats war as a natural event, lacking real intelligibility and to which the only human response is a tragic weariness and satiric stoicism. The tone of his book *Wartime* (1989) is humorously bitter. It is a powerful position because the claim of absurdity seems to pre-empt all challenges to his very articulate point of view and no one brings it off as well, or as brutally, as Fussell. There is no reply to an absolute scepticism except pure faith in the role of the well-informed imagination, in courage, and, in the darkest times, an unquenchable and positive love of the world. While Fussell's position usefully scours out sentimentality, it also therefore has the limits of its nihilism. In his view, every soldier fights unwillingly because he is simply indifferent to or unconscious of anything that might be valuable or worth saving except his own skin – intelligibility is only for the powerful (who, in any case, are not to be trusted, could not care less and are in any case largely out of control). This seemingly incontestable view was most directly fictionalized in Joseph Heller's *Catch-22* of 1961. Its fatalism and 'apolitical' cynicism, wittily portrayed, made it an instant bestseller. In black humour, of course, wit disguises unendurable emotions, people suffer history like biological fate and there is no intelligibility in any case. The absurd rules without challenge even though, as Camus long ago remarked in order to know what is absurd, there also has to be idea of what is not. Fussell's perspective, generalized to cover all human life (and the premise is generality), is treacherously quietist. It despairs of change and sanctifies the pragmatic.

Fussell is, of course, not innocent of ideology. He promotes a kind of populism which offers the truth of the world in the generalized sentimentalized GI Joe of the cartoons and right-wing tabloids. The book is dedicated to his mother who sent him socks. This soldier figure is then marketed as the Whitmanian 'democratic average', the man who knows what's what. Not a whisper of historical, ideological or political debate enters the censored silences of Fussell's view of the world that depends on the satirist's common-sense *reductio ad absurdum* of 'behavioural' 'understanding'. War*time* (my emphasis) is dehistoricized in terms of its ethical tone, though the facts are all there (the first British tanks were useless and so forth). History becomes aestheticized as a particular local and time-specific 'colour' in the general condition. War is pure suffering in a fatalistic 'climate'. It is a world elsewhere, something that truly great commentators, such as Tocqueville on the American way of war, never entertained for moment. The Pascalian ethical judgement outside time, which at its best such a view invokes, is flawed by a too-repetitive response. In *Nineteen Eighty-Four*, George Orwell presented the Fussell viewpoint ironically:

> 'When I was a young man, mild beer – wallop, we used to call it – was fourpence a pint. That was before the war, of course.'
>
> 'Which war was that?' said Winston.
>
> 'It's all wars,' said the old man vaguely.[5]

Orwell uses the ethical judgement to point up the loss of meaning in a specific totalitarian system. In Fussell's universal 'war-time', his chosen literature can only exhibit an impoverished nostalgia and a purely negative irony: 'it's all wars'. More specifically it is a world elsewhere which exhibits an irrecoverable past – in this instance the limited view points of British upper-class war poets and writers, the selective 'Bloomsbury' adored by East Coast-educated Americans. In such a world an Evelyn Waugh can rank higher than a Tolstoy, as witty life-hating despair ranks higher than courageous hope in a deeply imaginative life-enhancing vision. Orwell caught the mood perfectly; the example offered above has the critical intelligence to politicize this 'eternal' condition and distance its pathos.

Returning to *politics*, Macdonald (Exeter and Yale) was every bit the 'class' equal of Connolly (Eton and Balliol College, Oxford). Like Connolly, who published Pasternak, Eluard, Blok and Muriel Rukeyser, he vigorously sought out international writers, and writers in danger. A three-way comparison between Connolly, Macdonald and Norman, which is not attempted here, would reveal much richness and difference of cultural tone, and political nuance in the three ensembles. All three had writers they published in common. Nonetheless all three provided a home in exile for those needing to find a necessary point of stability and sanity, a home of temporary refuge in a world of chaos, and, in spite of the displacements and radical alienations of war, moved to promote a transnational, more humanistic, and ultimately more connected and continuous view of the world.

The aim here is to try and discover the shape and nature of the cultural ensembles offered by the two American journals, while giving some idea of what it feels like now to read both their transplanted and home-grown contributors. At selected points the materials the two editors offer will be reread in order both to invoke a vanished reception and to offer critically once more the distinctly non-canonical radicalism of the original, albeit now historical, selection. What views of the world did the journals prompt, what unknown writers' worlds did they present and introduce to their American audiences? The international literary and journalistic encounters offered bridges between diverse and dissimilar cultures and the resultant discourses can be read in many ways. Present are the usual serious journal's various generic forms: historical narratives, journalist's reports, poetry, political commentary, art, literary and film criticism, book reviews and the personal story. This section looks at *politics*, a journal that offered a bridge between cultures and worlds at moment of world crisis.

An ex-Trotskyite and life-long libertarian anarchist thinker, Dwight Macdonald broke with *Partisan Review* in 1943, and went on to edit (largely with his wife's money) the journal *politics*, which ran from 1944 to 1948. It thus covered the emergence of the post-war world from the late years of the Second World War to the beginnings of the Cold War. While Japan must not be forgotten, never had Americans (and to a degree against national instinct) been so focused upon and involved in European affairs. In this section we shall see how the complex fate of a few Americans met in a brief moment the complex fate of a few Europeans. The terms, of course, are relatively narrow. Many of the people involved were highly educated, articulate and were in various degrees politically radical or liberal. They were the kind of people Varian Fry had gone out to rescue in Marseille. They were the people we remember today as representing some of the finest achievements of twentieth-century art, literature and philosophical and historical thinking. Many have been forgotten. Some, such as Victor Serge and Anton Ciliga, only haunt the fringes of memory, at least in the Anglo-American world.

Nonetheless, the thrust of Macdonald's journal was also egalitarian. Letters from ordinary American soldiers (who showed themselves to be a lot more than 'GI Joes') and sympathetic reports of oppressed European groups – from the women of Berlin as the Russian army entered to the Spanish exiles in Vichy France – were all covered in the paper. Macdonald's circle, despite State Department hostility (as has been shown in the case of Serge), stretched out their hands to all sorts and conditions of beleaguered Europeans. The transatlantic bridge here, in this moment, was unquestionably solid and no European, even at this distance in time, can write about it without emotion and an extraordinary sense of gratitude.

A nationalist cultural tone can touch even contemporary American left and liberal commentaries on Macdonald's *politics*. About halfway through Gregory Sumner's very thoughtful and well-researched book on the *politics* circle (a work to which this chapter is heavily indebted), there is, for a 'European', a rather amusing moment when he invokes the commentaries of two other fine American scholars, Richard King and Christopher Lasch, to the effect that Macdonald's *politics* was much too 'Eurocentric', adding that American radicals have 'too often turned abroad for sustenance'.[6] This is precisely the charge that the Book of the Month Club and Dorothy Canfield Fisher famously laid against the black novelist Richard Wright's *Black Boy* in the same period. Could not Wright say anything nice and positive about white Americans and white American culture, Canfield Fisher had plaintively asked him. The answer was to be a categorical no. The embattled Canfield Fisher, negotiating with the Book of the Month Club judges, wrote to Wright:

> Was it only in Russian, and British or French fiction that you found anything to give you tidings from afar that there were human brothers of yours on the globe who had any ideals?[7]

Wright replied that even the American writers that had influenced him the most were rebels who had depended on European writers: Mencken on Nietzsche; Dreiser on Spencer and Marx; Anderson on Chekhov. He found, he went on, 'richer springs' elsewhere: 'the Carnegie Corporation had to import a Swedish Scientist, Gunnar Myrdal, to write the first honest and objective analysis of the negro in our society [...] personally, I have had to depend mainly upon outside influences for my view of myself and others in America.'[8]

The spirit of this book is that in certain situations it may be necessary to rely on the elsewhere. International scholarship should always endorse that outward-looking movement, even sometimes to the extent of abandoning its own limitations and certainly its chauvinist centrism. The supreme paradox is that 'Eurocentrism' is produced by Americocentrism. An abandonment of its most naïve parameters might be a worthier national gesture. There is never for the scholar, or perhaps we should say a genuine intellectual, the option of endorsing or attempting to privilege the nationalist perspective. The naïve competitive comparison is futile at best.[9]

With all these caveats, cultural and intellectual, about bridges and Eurocentrism (and I am aware that the term currently has a somewhat different use), it is instructive to take a more empirical and careful look at the content of *politics*. The inescapable conclusion can only be that *politics* was by no means even mildly 'Eurocentric' in many of its most important aspects. From the beginning there is a huge emphasis on detailed dissenting American political activity: the dubious dealings of the communists in the New Jersey labour movement; the well-known trial of the Trotskyites in New Jersey in 1944; the political experience of African-American activists in the unions and elsewhere; trade union activity of any ethnic stripe; the effects of American capitalism and foreign policy in Mexico, Bolivia, Columbia, Costa Rica, Cuba and Brazil; the Harlem race riots of 1943; American racism in the armed services; Henry Wallace's bid for the presidency; the Dumbarton Oaks conference; race prejudice in the AFL, CIO and UAW; and the manic and reductive Americanism of Hoover at the FBI. Macdonald's

American correspondents and contributors included Daniel Aaron, Lionel Abel, James Agee, Sherwood Anderson, Daniel Bell, William F. Buckley, Dorothy Day, John Dos Passos, T.S. Eliot, Waldo Frank, Nathan Glazer, Paul Goodman, Irving Howe, Jane Jacobs, Alfred Kazin, Irving Kirstol, Melvin Lasky, Mary McCarthy, Norman Mailer, Ezra Pound, Philip Rahv, Kenneth Rexroth, David Riesman, Delmore Schwartz, Diana and Lionel Trilling, and Edmund Wilson.

Macdonald's journal also reprinted passages of Melville's novel *Redburn* to recall a literary tradition of American protest writing, here, in a spirit of international solidarity against the conditions of the people of Liverpool in the mid-nineteenth century. Macdonald himself reviewed Alice Tyler's *Freedom's Ferment* (1944), an absorbing and beautifully written book which outlines that uniquely pervasive American communitarian radicalism of the restless 1830s and 1840s, those historic roots of 'beloved community'. Macdonald was particularly fond of the writers of what the Harvard critic F.O. Matthiessen was currently calling 'The American Renaissance': the 'classic' American writers of the mid-nineteenth century. Macdonald's letter to Simone de Beauvoir advising her on what to read in American literature, recommends Hawthorne's dystopian novel of 1852, *The Blithedale Romance*, and added 'it's a personal favorite of mine among Hawthorne's writings. I think you will enjoy it. The first half, about Brook Farm, gives a wonderful sense of the atmosphere of the best period of our history between 1800 and 1860'.[10]

Alice Tyler's book was part of a new passion for the American past, which writers like Lewis Mumford, Van Wyck Brooks, Muriel Rukeyser, Constance Rourke and a good number of others were then showing for the first time and which would inspire the generation of the 1960s and beyond in a particular tradition of American art and radicalism. Macdonald brought to the fore new American writers and social commentators such as Paul Goodman, James Agee, Robert Duncan, Mary McCarthy, Daniel Bell, C. Wright Mills and Jackson Mac Low. Even a Canadian, Marshall McLuhan, prophet of the hyper-real electronic world, had his moment in *politics*. In the journal's pages, Irving Kristol praised Saul Bellow's *Dangling Man* as 'our best war novel', George S. Schuyler reviewed Gunnar Myrdal's *An American Dilemma* and Wilfred H. Kerr reviewed Richard Wright's *Black Boy*. Felix Giovanni reviewed the famous *Kinsey Report* and Irving Howe reviewed that great mid-century classic *Let Us Now Praise Famous Men* by James Agee. Macdonald himself commented extensively on Henry Luce's 'frankly chauvinist' editorial, 'The American Century' and Wallace's slightly more subtle version of the same thing at the *New Republic*. Sumner properly acknowledges Macdonald's support of the then embattled Ezra Pound for the Bolinger Prize. Macdonald had been dazzled by the sheer dynamic range and quality of Pound's actual poetry in spite of his politics.

The conclusion is inescapable that notwithstanding Macdonald's generally melancholy views about the decline of American culture and his nostalgia for the period of the New England Golden Age, his instincts thankfully subverted his prejudices. Though in some respects the picture was partial – it mainly showed an appreciation of a thriving cultural, political and literary East Coast America – Macdonald, given his background, was not particularly in tune with more experimental writing of the post-Great War kind: William Faulkner, Gertrude Stein, William Carlos Williams, Hart Crane, the painterly generation of Stieglitz and the young Rukeyser, to name but a few. But Robert Duncan appears (and was to mature into one of the finest twentieth-century American poets), though Charles Olson does not; Pound is acknowledged though Zukofsky and the Objectivists are not. Sumner rounds off his book with a stirring quotation from that well-known American writer, Albert Camus, on the pressing need for a nationally transcendent humanism.

It is also, however, important to note those moments when bridges are precariously constructed or are incapable of being built. Not to acknowledge the treachery of a too-hastily built bridge (perhaps we should recall Milton's use of the word 'pontifical') or a bridge in the wrong place is to fail to recognize the ongoing dialectical process of constructing bridges.[11] Two examples illustrate the dangers. In September 1945 Macdonald wrote a reply to a Frenchman who had written praising *politics* as demonstrating that the spirit of high free intellectual inquiry was not dead in America and stating that this was a relief after talking to American soldiers who were completely indifferent not only to French problems but to politics in general – they seemed only interested in football. Macdonald laconically replied that *Time* and *The Saturday Review* were much more representative of the quality of American intellectual life than *politics*, adding:

> Furthermore, many if not most of the contributors to *politics* are refugees, so that the magazine is kind of transplanted spore of European culture growing in an environment that is physically and politically more favorable to Europe than that of modern Europe. What this latter atmosphere has been like is movingly suggested in still another European reaction to the magazine, as reported by a soldier-friend stationed in Heidelberg: 'I visited old Prof. Karl Jaspers here at the university. I had previously given him the issues of your magazine featuring the Weber controversy and your own 'Responsibility of Peoples.' He was delighted at the opportunity of reading critical and clashing articles, excited to a twinkle (really) at the spirit of independent discussion. 'How long has it been! …' Marianne Weber, Max Weber's widow, was visiting and she borrowed the issues […][12]

The Europe here lacks 'Europe' as much as America lacks it. The Europe needed was a Europe temporarily rescued from a Europe in ruins, and it was needed by both America and Europe, that is to say, a revival of a tradition of the best kind of humanism, which had been crushed by forces for which it had been unprepared. Reciprocally, Europe undoubtedly also needed Macdonald's 'America'.

The second example bearing a dose of realism about 'bridges' and rescue is nowhere better articulated than in Simone de Beauvoir's letter to Jean-Paul Sartre of February 1947. De Beauvoir was in severe culture shock after confronting the editors at *Partisan Review* and other New York intellectuals. The letter deserves to be quoted at length:

> For 6 hours I argued in English, alone against them all, passionately. I was battling with Greenberg, Phillips, Rahv, and a tall, pretentious young man who says we have no right to dabble in philosophy because we don't know Russell. We discussed politics and they simply turned my stomach. Abel and Chiaromonte had already disappointed me, with the total emptiness of their thinking: but they're nice and I like them. Whereas this lot, with their so-called cultural internationalism and freedom of spirit, are pure American imperialists. They attacked me about Merleau-Ponty and came out with two real gems: 'it wasn't Stalin who fed you, but UNRA', and 'Stalingrad?' 'Of no importance!' 'We're the ones that won the war for you.' For them, dollars count far more than all the blood shed by others. We went at it hammer and tongs. I felt like quitting the table – and at any rate left all the steak on my plate. They were very upset, because personally they were congratulating me on my success and feting me. They served me up the argument of the firing-squad victim of course. They don't give a shit about anything, except *Partisan Review:* they'd send the whole world up in flames to ensure the survival of their worthless rag. I'll never give another article to that filthy outfit [...] I've been pretty disgusted these past two days. With the people from *Politics* and *Partisan Review*; with publishers and magazine editors; and with that purely commercial way of inspecting your brain, as if it were a dancer's legs. They talk about existentialism as they would about a worm-powder, and they award marks: Camus so many, Sartre so many – My God in the end I was quite scared [...] What is everything we write for them? A product that's consumed in six months. As I don't think there's any more to be hoped for from the 'other side', it's discouraging – for I don't have any impression of hope here.[13]

The great French writer was in political culture shock. (An academic cash-nexus has now unfortunately become the norm in English and American universities, with citation-counting machines and quantitative assessments. Only a degree of happily ubiquitous irony and resilience on a personal level saves the little that is left of value.) De Beauvoir recovered in the company of Richard Wright, temporarily in the United States, before his final return to France. He took her to hear some gospel singing in Harlem and despite being a determined denizen of the adult world she even melted so far as to play with Wright's daughter and to buy her a present. In many respects, nonetheless, de Beauvoir was charmed and fascinated by America and its difference, as only an open-minded and brilliant *grande-dame* from the Écoles could possibly have been. She even came to feel, as she travelled across America, like a transplanted New Yorker. But her sharp appraisal of certain American politically dim and chronically chauvinist intellectuals in this instance drove a necessary critical wedge between the two cultures. If the bridge was not to be a ten-lane highway there was, perhaps beginning with her friendship with Richard Wright, the possibility of a rope thrown across a chasm.

War and International Ideological Chaos

Gregory Sumner's book on Macdonald and the *politics* circle, together with the chapter on *politics* in *A Rebel in Defense of Tradition: The Life and Politics of Dwight Macdonald* by Michael Wreszin, are the best possible introductions one could have to the subject. Sumner's plea is cogent for 'a fresh hearing of the debate'[14] and furthermore his political argument that Macdonald offered in *politics* a communitarian alternative to 'Marxian socialism' and 'cold war liberalism' is persuasively argued. Sumner tackles the general parameters of the *politics* phenomenon with a deft historian's skill. In the historical context of the devastation of war and European refugee operations in which, as we have seen, Nancy and Dwight Macdonald were particularly engaged, he accurately notes, perhaps with the above caveats, that 'the best metaphor for the magazine [...] is that of a bridge: a bridge between radical generations, between 'Old' Left and 'New', and between Europe and America.'[15]

The journal embraced Victor Serge, for example, precisely because of its international perspective. It informed American readers of the plight of the Spanish refuges and the non-aligned left of the POUM. It was well aware of the butchery of Marxist socialism under Stalin, and of the details of fascism in Europe. Sumner effectively outlines the importance of the contacts between the magazine and its European correspondents, who were dissident leftists: figures such as Hannah Arendt (from the Frankfurt School), Andrea Caffi, Albert Camus, Nicola Chiaromonte, Anton Ciliga, George Orwell, Niccolò Tucci, Simone Weil and the English anarchist George Woodcock. Their vision enriched 'politics as a vehicle to publicize and encourage possibilities for radical change [...] developing, both at home and abroad, as the war moved to its climactic stages'.[16] British, French, Italian, Greek, Soviet, Japanese and American postwar politics were covered from a complex non-aligned leftist position, rare in any country and unique in the United States. Altogether it was probably the greatest achievement of dissenting journalism ever accomplished on such a consistent scale in a country, which had produced, and still produces, many great dissenting writer-journalists from Stephen Crane and the muck-raking journalists of the Teddy Roosevelt era to Martha Gellhorn, Norman Mailer and Noam Chomsky.

The position in France, for example, was covered in detail by Lewis Coser who spoke of the growing cult of de Gaulle, the doctrinaire Moscow-directed

Communist Party and its journal *L'Humanité* (incidentally a particular *bête noire* of Victor Serge) and the rather unsurprising inability of a heterogeneous resistance movement, briefly united against a common enemy, to turn that resistance into an effective radical politics. Coser provided the readers of *politics* good coverage, though his ideological panjandrum that 'a society in turmoil is receptive to revolutionary ideas' seemed not yet to have learned the lessons of 1933.[17] Coser's hope, also, that the new British Labour Party would provide a radical alternative to communist socialism showed how little he knew of the history of the formation of that particular party, and of the core conservatism of the British people (with here and there a remaining touch of Victorian liberalism and local activism), nor could he have been aware of the heavy reactionary hand of the United States upon the Labour Party (now the right-of-centre New Labour Party and on the extreme right in terms of foreign policy) from 1945 to the present day.

Nonetheless, Coser anticipated new forms of totalitarian control and was alive to class divisions within the resistance, to the more-than-lingering spirit of French nationalism and to the virtual practical impossibility of socialist and libertarian renewal in an exhausted Europe which craved only peace, food, shelter and a return to the comfort of the most conservative forms of living. Sumner rightly notes that the broad-brush approach to an analysis of mass mechanical homogenization also had a touch of arrogance and that, practically, the overall situation was not dissimilar in post-1989 Eastern Europe. Andrea Caffi, an important European correspondent who is generally agreed to have been the most acute political analyst of the journal,[18] added a more critical note to the analysis of the French situation that anticipated, as did Macdonald himself, a more cultural and psychological analysis of the emerging 'totalitarian' world of the post-imperial era.

In Europe this type of emerging analysis is associated, in the immediately succeeding period, with the names of Arendt, Horkheimer, Benjamin, Adorno, Marcuse and Habermas in Germany; Foucault, Lyotard, Baudrillard and others in France. In the United States and Canada the names of C. Wright Mills, James Burnham, William H. Whyte, Daniel Boorstin, Vance Packard, Betty Friedan and Marshall McLuhan come to mind among others. These commentators did not share the same ideological positions and were not even concerned with the same things, but they responded critically to the new postwar world order. Their analyses, anticipated to some degree by Orwell and others, focused on the media-driven political pacifications of the populace within the normative practices of modernity, the atomization of the individual under capitalism, the rise of mass culture and consumerism and, later, the only-apparently de-historicizing and de-hierarchizing world of postmodernity. Caffi, for example, connected centralizing forces with 'the habits of automism, of *zusammenmarschieren*, of responding to slogans that as imperative as they are trivial, habits which the cinema, the radio, the newspaper headlines, the rationalization of work and pleasure, the tyranny of schedules, have spread and developed to a maximum point'.[19]

Back in the United States and from 1946 onwards Macdonald focused on dissenting local 'revolutionary pacifists' and made sure that the 12,000 conscientious objectors in 'Civilian Public Service' were not forgotten.[20] As for many in our own time, working outside established institutions of power seemed the only possible option. Certainly it was something Macdonald wished to foster. Here, his links with British anarcho-pacifists such as George Woodcock and with farm cooperatives were important. In his book, Sumner does not mention the fact that Macdonald was also in touch with Kenneth Rexroth and, through him by association, the Californian traditions of anarcho-syndicalism, for example groups that formed around the Fine Arts Camp at Waldport, founded by the poet William Everson and the book designer Adrian Wilson, and from which the Interplayers Theater also grew. This literary and cultural legacy was to be very important, fostering poets such as Rexroth himself and Kenneth Patchen, writers such as Henry Miller and the radical KPFA radio in Berkeley, and prefigured the Beat movement in the 1960s with Alan Watts lecturing on Zen Buddhism and poetry readings by Brother Antonius (William Everson), William Stafford, Lawrence Ferlinghetti and Allen Ginsberg. Obscure though these 1940s beginnings were, they were a thin line which became nationally prominent and, above all, politically significant, as part of 1960s opposition to the war in Vietnam. The importance of the small dissident group for a continuing legacy of resistance was as crucial then as it is now. In painting, the work of Morris Graves and Mark Tobey (the friend of the great English potter Bernard Leach) marked new directions in American art.[21]

That Macdonald did not pursue some of these options for correspondents and copy when suggested by Rexroth is almost certainly owing to his very strong atheist convictions and his somewhat conservative artistic tastes. [22] To that degree he was insensitive to the religious left of Dorothy Day of the *Catholic Worker* and others.[23] Rexroth had noted it in his usual trenchant way in 1945:

> I wonder. Are you still in that strange half-lit world where people take out their watches and dare the Deity to turn on the lightning? How about Catholic revolutionaries? Dorothy Day, or one of her people, might do a number on that tradition, which of course is tremendously important right now, and a wholesome antidote to the NeoThomist late analism of MM Eliot, Gilson, Maritain et Cie [...][24]

Yet, even if the point is taken, the radicalism which derived from Marx's sense of the horror of religious exploitation and hypocrisy still has to be taken on board, not something the average American commentator is keen to do: 'Christian socialism is but the holy water with which the priest consecrates the heart-burnings of the aristocrat' wrote Marx in the *Communist Manifesto*.[25] Unfair though this is in true instances of unimpeachable Christian-socialist belief (such as that of Reinhold Niebuhr, though he approved of the atomic bomb – and of Dorothy Day), it was more than a half-truth in a country whose individualist Christian ethics shamefully neglected the old, the poor, the sick and those whose skin was not white. As for Christianity itself, its authoritarian use of repressive sexuality had been analysed in countless novels and other art forms in most western cultures since the 1880s. In psychological terms, the sheer anguish caused in the poor religious households by patriarchal manipulations of Christian ideological practice was a particular American concern for writers such as Dreiser and Sinclair Lewis. Black writers such as Wright and Baldwin gave searing accounts of interiorized race violence within the family, coded in psycho-religious language.

In pursuing the contexts for Macdonald's atheism, it might be noted that Marx had not been wrong to see the church, in many of its bourgeois manifestations and political practices, as fully supportive of the class oppression of working people, not to mention its historical role in oppressive wars. At best, a bowl of soup was handed out after an obligatory hymn and prayer. The practices of Niebuhr and his friends, however, in relation to European refugees, were unimpeachable.[26] The traditions of genuine Christian charity are an unsung palliative narrative in the obvious cruelties of human behaviour throughout history. The contradictions of an all-too-earthly church cannot, however, be minimized, perhaps especially now in contemporary America, given the rise of the religious right. As Marx wryly remarked, 'original sin is at work everywhere'[27] (and not least, perhaps, in the prayer meetings of war-mongering presidents).

Marx's satire on the practices of the church had, ironically, the religious radicalism of the Jesus who chased the money-changers out of the temple. The right hand of virtue and the left hand of exploitation have too seldom connected in history. In a famous passage in the 1844 manuscripts, noting the avarice and intemperance of the profit-driven owners of the means of production, not to mention the blandishments of commercial advertising, Marx exposed the psychological drives of capitalist hypocrisy: 'No eunuch flatters his despot more basely or uses more despicable means to stimulate his dulled capacity for pleasure [...] than does the industrial eunuch [...] in order to sneak for himself a few pieces of silver, in order to charm the golden birds out of the pockets of his dear neighbours in Christ.'[28] On greed, wealth, commercial manipulation and opportunism, there is not a great deal to distinguish Marx from Jesus. Even this recall of a few textual moments gives some historical context for Macdonald's atheism in the last generation to have read Marx and (one sometimes wonders) the New Testament seriously.

From the opposite ideological direction in the 1930s and 1940s it is also worth remembering that Simone Weil herself would declare that no true Christian could remain within the current church. With the pope turning a blind eye to the deportation of the Jews it was not an implausible suggestion. It would have taken a lot of Albert Schweitzers, Dorothy Days, Reinhold Niebuhrs and Quaker conscientious objectors to persuade radicals of the 1940s generation to believe in a Christian God. The resurrection of these historical debates gives some context to Macdonald's difficulties in trying to find any principled ground to recreate a believable ethics, particularly in a traditionally 'religious' America. If Macdonald threw out the Christian baby with the pseudo-Christian bathwater, it seemed to him a lesser error at a time when Christian soldiers were marching off to war.

Other American issues in *politics* included the fight against racism. Gunnar Myrdal's *An American Dilemma* was welcomed by the journal.[29] Macdonald's more positive intellectual touch-stones in *politics* can be seen in his reconstruction of a usable past in the series he called 'Ancestors'. Sumner reviews his 'alternative reading list': Tolstoy, Weber, Godwin, Tocqueville, Proudhon, Herzen and Tucholsky. He notes it was vague, general and fell short of a programme for action.[30] This criticism is, perhaps, a little severe. There is a distinction to be made between 'raising consciousness', which is brought about by being thoroughly politically informed and educated and reading books that might assist the formation and critique of a strategic programme of action. As the English labour historian E.P. Thompson used to say to students who claimed that direct action was superior to the life of the mind: 'There's always an excuse for not reading books.' A reading of Franco Venturi's *Roots of Revolution* (1960) would quickly show quite precise historical examples of the relation between reading, writing and the proven political action of some of the authors on Macdonald's list. Sartre's dictum that a committed writing is also an action is probably worth remembering. As Muriel Rukeyser wrote in her early poem 'The Lynchings of Jesus': 'Bruno, Copernicus, Shelley, Karl Marx: you/makers of victory for us: how long?'[31]

With Marxism compromised by Stalin, and in an America where red scares were part of an old and ongoing history, it is also difficult to see what kind of 'programme' with what kind of mass base Macdonald could have proposed. He was perhaps rightly criticized by the left for abandoning organized leftist local action, Trotskyite or otherwise. He was extremely socially organized, however, when it came to getting packages to starving Europeans in 1945. He knew, however, that given the extreme conservatism of American political practice, and the minimal impact of any type of socialist thought on that culture, that a fantasy of any Bolshevik-style revolutionary activity was precisely a fantasy. With only the traditions of communitarian anarchism, and a few figures such as Henry David Thoreau, Randolph Bourne and John Dewey, there was never, in the immediate future, going to be a radical movement in America inspired by purely American theory.

Macdonald was simply looking for some means to sustain himself and a few others in what Arendt called 'dark times'. In other words, in a time of great despair he looked for a personal ethics and for reasons to keep on living. His aim was to provide a bridge from times of lesser evil and greater insight in order to keep some sort of critical tradition alive. He did not believe in teleological superstitions with their varying temporalities, whether eternal life, the spirit of history, the victory of the proletariat or the technological and free market solution. Macdonald was in a sense trying to revise a prolegomena for a politics and Sumner rightly points out that he found in Tolstoy a scepticism about the power and ideology of science (he might also have found this in Henry Adams), the work ethic and the violent abstractions of life promoted by capitalism paradoxically destroying any kind of individualism, and in Weber a useful critique of centralization and bureaucracy. Sumner is critical of Macdonald's advocacy of Godwin's localism and his critique of large systems but there is an argument on both sides here. Gigantism, whether urban, corporate or state, all too often leads to forms of oppression that need challenging as the urban historian Mike Davis has shown.[32] Sumner's comments also neglect the historical context in which Godwin's discourse emerged. The utopian strain in the Enlightenment philosophers was not only a heavenly city but offered a particular critical utopian perspective on a particular historical moment. However flawed, the Enlightenment philosophers inspired generations of those who wished to crack the congealed ice of normative living and totalitarian political practices.

Tocqueville's critique of the emerging mass democratic society is also highlighted in Sumner's commentary on Macdonald's selections of Tolstoy. Here, the key criticisms invoke that competitiveness which destroys community, individualism, and the growth of a 'power elite'. As for Proudhon (whom Chiaromonte brought to Macdonald's attention), he too, for Macdonald, joins this basic outline of an anti-statist, anti-bureaucratic tradition. To be sure, it is very vague. Its merit, however, is that it still depends on some faith in ordinary people. Sumner notes just how difficult this position is to sustain in terms of a certain historical scepticism by recalling Chiaromonte's reaction to the hypnotic behaviour of the masses' embracing of the First World War. Faith in 'ordinary people' and a sense of 'immanent justice' seem to fail at such moment.[33] To argue on the other side, it is precisely here that these 'morally universalist' grand political concepts fail the test of a more complex historical narrative, and where explanations from economics and psychology, not to mention the cultural systems which mediate power, are needed. Nonetheless, in any historical situation the 'socially constructed individual', to use the dreadful current jargon, is mercifully still unpredictable, and 'ordinariness' cannot be assumed in any class of society. By essentializing ordinariness Chiaromonte's view of democratic theory was, in my view, superficial. Ordinariness was not equatable with an extra-historical principle, and hence with 'immanent justice'. Marxists made the same mistake about the proletariat. What was Macdonald actually abandoning in his historically understandable shift from dialectical materialism to an analytic anarchist and quasi-universalist ethics?

To illustrate this point more fully it is instructive to look at the letters from the Californian poet Kenneth Rexroth to Macdonald. Rexroth continually hounded Macdonald on the politics of *politics*, producing both considerable heat and considerable light. Self-taught, a Catholic and widely read in socialist literature, Rexroth was fully informed about both the traditions of socialist and dissenting literature from the beginning of the modern era and virtually every American dissenting political group since the time of the Wobblies. He had been in touch with Macdonald since 1939 when he had taken an isolationist view of the coming conflict, choosing, quite irresponsibly, like so many on the left, not to distinguish between rival imperialisms, whether Russian, German, Italian, British or French. With satiric probing, he nonetheless dissected the weaknesses of many of Macdonald's positions, accusing him of being one of the 'sleepwalkers of liberalism'[34] and worrying that the isolation of 'the few irreconcilable revolutionists, Marxists, syndicalist or anarchist [... was] going to be suicidal' (c.1939).

Like any good anarcho-syndicalist of the period, Rexroth was up to date and knowledgeable. He saw through the pseudo-Marxist-Stalinist facade of the Russian 1930s long before Macdonald. He was certainly helped in this by his acute and honest evaluation (like that of Victor Serge) of the culture produced by Stalinist Russia, especially literature with its cult of social realism. Unlike Macdonald, he vigorously defended the new art of the post-Dada era:

> Do you think the paintings of Mondriaan have nothing to do with the struggle for a world of organic social relationships? If you do, you are nothing but an inverted Stalinist. Do you think the loud, vulgar, slick paintings of Rockwell Kent are only accidentally associated with Rockwell Kent the militant political parvenu? Do you think the 'very modern' academicism of Kenneth Hayes Miller et al that today litters Post Office walls under the aegis of the Nude Eel has nothing to do with the demagogic meliorism that masks the inexorable processes of capitalist decay in America? Mike Gold, author of the sentimental dishonesty of 'The Girl by the River', is also author of the sentimental dishonesty of critical merde-ism of every species of sentimental political jingoism? (c.1939)

The polemic against the art of the three hypostacized practices of capitalism, Rooseveltian progressivism and Stalinism has, within its exaggerations, a refreshing bluntness of critique. As will be shown later, Rexroth, like Muriel Rukeyser, insisted that imaginative thought might serve at the centre of democratic truth. In more strictly political terms, Rexroth chided Macdonald over his belief in Trotsky's 'Fourth International' ('a little too damned immaculate for me'). Where the two men coincided was in their support for pacifists and conscientious objectors and other resisters to the war.

Rexroth's anarcho-syndicalism meant he opposed both Stalin's centralizing five-year plans and, less happily, Roosevelt's New Deal, whose disposition to centralize state activity, he argued, could only lead to 'a militarized society run by an upper caste which holds power thru direct exercise of terror'. (In fact, this was to come from the corporate world rather than the state.) He similarly spotted the authoritarian tendencies in Marx and much preferred Kropotkin's less teleologically driven sense of a world of mutual aid. For better or worse, he said to Macdonald, 'I'll stay in my old position, somewhere between [Alexander] Berkman and Rosa [Luxemburg]' (c.1939). In 1945, however, he wrote to Macdonald saying how moved he was on his article on the atomic bomb and added: 'The Manhattan Project's headquarters was on Morningside Heights. The symbol of America is the pseudo-will of John Dewey's nursery school ethic. Carefully systematized irresponsibility, with lots of nice vitamins, minerals and roughage in the Frigidaire for the kiddies' lunch.' Like Macdonald he believed, therefore, that the 'ethical level of action must be raised to a plane of the most acute sensibility'.[35]

But Macdonald did not publish Rexroth nor the people he suggested, and the poet retaliated by pointing to the lugubrious moralism that often lay at the heart of Paul Goodman's sincere but dreary prose: 'when I have figured out what Paul G is talking about it turns out to be "Wreck the system by not paying your carfare," or something equally deep.'[36] Macdonald loved nonetheless what he called Rexroth's 'electronic style', noting that 'we seem to agree and disagree in a very complicated way.'[37] These exchanges give a very concrete sense of the actual historical moment; they are more instructive perhaps than any attempt at an ideological summary. Rexroth was most valuable in being a perpetual, if sometimes wayward and inconsistent, gadfly to Macdonald's jettisoning of a more rigorous philosophical, political and economic critique. Rexroth, for example, objected strongly to the Chiaromonte-inspired resurrection of Proudhon as a relevant, somewhat de-historicized, political theorist: 'It does absolutely no good to go back and restate the notion of a libertarian movement of 100 years ago as if nothing had ever happened.'[38] Marx, he reminded Macdonald, had stated the case against Proudhon with 'great clarity'.

Here Rexroth is referring to Marx's once-famous polemic against Proudhon in *The Poverty of Philosophy* (1847), which had directly taken on Proudhon's *The Philosophy of Poverty* (1847). Marx had criticized Proudhon's economic analysis as too metaphysical and bound to discrete antinomies (socialism/political economy; use value/exchange value) that had a kind of autonomous metaphysical status. He saw Proudhon as ignorant both of the historical power hierarchies in different modes of economic exchange and of the complex, dialectical, but above all historical, concreteness of the operations of productive relations. So Rexroth warned of the dangers of justice as a kind of 'rhetorical conviction'. There is, he reminds Macdonald, only 'class justice'.[39] He added that, in terms of metaphysical grand narrative, Kropotkin's 'biological principle – historically demonstrable – verifiable in the lives of races and individuals – Mutual Aid – [ought to be substituted] for the shaky foundation of Proudhon's system.'[40] Behind Proudhon's theory of contract lay an abstract enlightenment principle of rights and duties, a kind of sentimental glossing over the realism of Marxian property relations. In other words, Proudhon had ignored both class and the operations of power.

It was a familiar argument but it was also one that went to the heart of the matter. Rexroth also attacked the abstractions within simplified and positivist Marxism itself (its overt scientism, its prophetic teleologies) and argued that human relations could never be reduced to statistical equations of value reified in the process of productive relations. Rexroth's advice on what to read gives a sense of what other lines of political dissent *politics* touched upon briefly but did not foreground. In November 1946 Rexroth accused *politics* of 'softening up'. He was responding with some coolness to Quaker conscientious objectors appearing in the pages of *politics* and reminding Macdonald of the nitty-gritty and contentious nature of political debate in difficult times. 'Look', he said to Macdonald, 'make it a rule – no fucking cocoaswilling Quakers in politics. If you only knew what most C.O.s. think of them [...]'.[41]

I shall return to Rexroth, whose language, always happily immoderate and sometimes simply silly, cheers any scholarly day in the archives. He gives a rare sense of the liveliness of the atmosphere that was produced in and around Macdonald's enterprise. He also raises a question mark, or at least fires a warning shot, over the political direction of *politics* after the war: that is, Macdonald's attempt to build 'New Roads' for future political theory and activism. Sumner argues that the three most important voices at the core of the enterprise were Macdonald himself, Nicola Chiaromonte and Andrea Caffi, one part American to two parts European. Nonetheless, this doubtless practical simplification for the purposes of clear argument to a degree leaves out everything else that was going on in the journal itself. The glory of *politics* was that it allowed debates for and against itself with total impartiality as to nation and often, to a generous degree, political ideology. It presented for democratic acceptance or rejection, strident voices capable of equally attacking and supporting many different ideological and practical positions, with greater or lesser analytic skill.

Macdonald's essay 'The Root is Man' was the key document and it appeared in two parts in *politics*, in May and June 1946. The very title is of course deliberately transnational. Its force at the time derived from its quasi-confessional style, whose theme was a dramatic personal break from 'Marxism' by someone who was known to have built a career in journalism by offering social and cultural critiques heavily influenced by Marxism. In the ideologically charged atmosphere of New York in 1946 the essay was something of a *succès de scandale*. Commentators tend to summarize it by saying that it shows a shift from a political vision to an ethical one. That view seems to me difficult because it compares like with unlike and evades the even more difficult question of whether the one is intrinsically bound up the other.

Macdonald began, politically, with Trotsky. The reason was not simply tactical. He took up an article of 1939 called 'The USSR in War'[42] in which Trotsky had proposed two contradictory routes for the development of the Soviet Union. The first (in which he said firmly believed) was a second proletarian revolution in which the Stalinist bureaucracy would be overthrown, thus the matter of whether the bureaucracy was a 'class' development or a parasitic growth on the workers' state would be clear. The second was a failure of proletariat leadership to achieve this end in which case there would simply be a new exploiting class from the 'Bonapartist fascist bureaucracy'.[43] As to the first proposition, Trotsky's 'belief' was purely irrational and to a degree it completely blinded him to the realities of Stalin's grip on power. Macdonald was quick to point out that it simply had not happened, nor was it likely to. But Trotsky's second point was more prescient and much more interesting. If, Macdonald noted, he was wrong and the proletarian revolution failed a second time, then 'the socialist programme based on the contradictions of capitalist society' would be seen purely as a Utopian project of the worse kind. In that case 'a new minimum programme would be required' in order to protect the 'slaves of the totalitarian bureaucratic society'.[44] A more accurate description of what is needed for the contemporary debt-ridden victims of so-called globalization in the face of corporate politics and the inhuman strategies of the World Bank would be hard to find.

There is a sense, then, in which Macdonald, facing the hard facts, takes up Trotsky's 'minimum programme'. In so doing he acknowledges that the Marxist and Soviet theory of self-destructive internal capitalist contradiction, with its concomitant guarantee of socialist emergence, has failed: 'Let us face the fact that Trotsky's deadline is here and that his revolution is not'.[45] Like Hannah Arendt, who spoke eloquently of the 'rule of nobody', Macdonald focuses on the new 'totalitarianism' and (the buzz-word of that historical moment) 'bureaucracy': what he himself, borrowing the term from Ciliga, called 'bureaucratic collectivism'.[46] At the same time, he acknowledged that French existential thought was moving along similar lines and he rejected more simplistic critics and apologists of 'bureaucracy' such as James Burnham. Confessing he is not a sophisticated political philosopher, Macdonald appears to swing right over, figuratively, to the side of Pascal. There is a pressing need to be outside history, for 'non-historical' values.[47]

Macdonald's critique, therefore, remains essentially a useful negative one. Like Henry Adams and Lewis Mumford before him, he directed his attack against Marxist scientism as a flawed universalist metaphysic. He attacked the propagandist misuse of socialist and conservative theories in Nazi and Stalinist propaganda. He disputed any political meliorist or progressivist teleology and, like Niebuhr, reassessed the importance of tragedy as a radical perspective on the human condition. Like Niebuhr and Weil, he attempted to wrest these concepts from right-wing discourse though he differs from them, in that he also wishes, for all the reasons outlined above, to prise them from any hint of a religious discourse in order to refurbish them for a more secular critique.

Macdonald's 'philosophical' mistake was to place Pascal against Marx. In other words, the fact that 'war and the preparation of war has become the normal mode of existence of great nations'[48] tends, by the use of the words 'normal' and 'existence', to place that war and preparation for it outside history. The decision to step outside history is itself paradoxically a historical decision which responds here, in despair, to a specific historical moment. The danger is that 'war' can become an exemplum of a universalist original sin rather than a specific responsibility of particular people at particular times. Of course, the judgement of truth or falsehood must take the Pascalian disinterested stance but the universal judgement must also engage with something historically concrete before it can register as a judgement. Tocqueville once said that war reveals the precise historical character of the state.[49] Not to understand this is to dissociate tragedy from the specific moments of history, which, however seemingly universal in character, or contingent and unpredictable in terms of the generalized operations of chance, can lead to fatalism and disengagement.

Niebuhr and Macdonald spoke of 'tragedy' and the sin of pride, but rarely about Aristotelian catharsis or, more precisely, about the rituals of state and kingship that historically embodied it. The Marxists were not altogether wrong to reject too broad a brush in the painting of 'tragic' truth. Macdonald in fact did step back into history in many of his examples. He compared Marxist universalist truth with the conditions in Germany after the First World War. Not to account for the bitterness, discouragement and reactionary politics of the working class in any given situation was, he said, to substitute wilful blindness for recognizing both failure and the inadequacy of the articulating theory. Looking at the world as he saw it, nationalism seemed everywhere on the increase, the state controlled the economy according to its own war-like interests and the one-dimensional world of scientific and technological activity (with its abstract goal of 'full production', supposedly in the service of human needs) was everywhere thwarting them. The socialist and capitalist states are hence dedicated to the same ends by different means. 'It is', said Macdonald, 'becoming increasingly difficult to distinguish the "right" from the "left" wing.'

Any party in power, and here he cites the British Labour Party in 1945, behaves very little differently from its predecessors. The Australian labour government with 'all but 3 of the 19 cabinet members former Trade union officials' was, he noted, completely racist with regard to the Aborigines. He noted, too, the autocracy in Peron's 'third way' in Argentina as well as the undemocratic opposition which supported the Argentinean right, viz. the US State Department 'and *The Nation*'.[50] Macdonald, in practice, is examining both the complex factual dynamics of a historical situation and making an ethical judgement about political lying.

Macdonald's essay reflects its historical moment. It is not so much about the 'end of ideology' but the inadequacy of then-current ideologies in a world devastated by the war and the betrayals of pure force. Macdonald, like Mumford, charted some of the contradictions of ideology and practice in the run-up to the war: the centralized war-like nature of the totalitarian state–Stalinist fighting force; the collusive pacifism of the 1930s Tory British and right-wing French, the eventual resistance of the British and French left; and after 1945 the desire of the European right for a 'soft peace' and that of the European left for a 'hard' one. With the mass rape carried out by Soviet soldiers in Berlin in 1945 and the United States liquidating by atomic fission hundreds of thousands of non-combatant Japanese civilians, never had Humpty Dumpty's words seemed more relevant:

> 'When I use a word,' Humpty Dumpty said, in a rather scornful tone, 'it means just what I choose it to mean, neither more nor less.'
>
> 'The question is,' said Alice, 'whether you can make words mean so many different things.'
>
> 'The question is,' said Humpty Dumpty, 'which is to be master – that's all.'[51]

The historic breakdown of speech in relation to action is eloquently expressed in Lewis Carroll's story. It does not, however, tell the whole truth. It has the limits of a merely satirical truth from an Oxford don at the height of the British Empire. This extreme case of the demonstration of power invites a cynicism about all speech. Humpty Dumpty's absolute rejection of speech is no more truthful as a general proposition, than Macbeth's soliloquy expressing the temporally repetitious futility of a series of nihilistic 'tomorrows' and 'yesterdays' that had only 'lighted fools to dusty death'.[52] Eloquent egg-heads talking to little girls have a certain fragility about them as do all operations of absolute power, which ultimately all the king's horses and all the king's men have the historic problem of not being able to maintain in perpetuity, as fate turns its wheel.

Returning to Macdonald, the hard question is: was there no principle, even in the betrayals on all sides and with state propaganda machines fully geared up in all countries, worth fighting for during the Second World War? Macdonald's answer would be a somewhat tentative embracing of the time-honoured arguments of pacifism. In spite of all the complexities and difficulties that this involved and given Macdonald's later involvement in the non-violent Vietnam resistance movement one cannot impugn his personal decision.[53] There is, however, something lacking when the preservation of human life is absolutely paramount. It is not only that the argument that every soldier who dies does so in vain is hard to explain to a survivor of Auschwitz, but that a life sacrificed on behalf of others both acknowledges a debt to the memory of a particular collective past, valued more highly than the individual life, and also indicates a faith in a particularly imagined future, which the same individual will not experience. In the end, the stories of the dead are at least as important as the mere fact of biological survival. This is why the United States where popular philosophy, as opposed to assumed Christian convictions, designates mere survival and individual material success as the highest goods, is in a poor position to understand the Muslim world.

Simone Weil, whose argument is partially being followed here, used the Christian model of redemptive sacrifice but even without that central myth ('the defence of the country as an imitation of Christ's passion realized on a national scale') the argument still stands.[54] Her argument, that the obligation to others in defence of genuinely free and genuinely imagined historical roots turned towards a proposed future legitimizes the soldier in combat, is hard to disprove. Her defence, equally, of conscientious objectors as needed saints who aspire to an unattainable perfection is also both just and tolerant. For those of us less persuaded by Christianity, or for that matter by Islam, the 'transcendent' death, nonetheless, does become deeply and humanly significant in terms of the story for remembrance it courageously and imaginatively offers. The story assists in bringing memory through writing itself, with narrative judgement and understanding, to transcend dread, political and personal fate, and the indifferent contingency of biological fate. To that degree, there is such a thing as the memory of transcendent sacrifice that leaks from the past to the future and it can be reliant neither on the universalist symbolism of the hanged god nor on the promise of secular or sacred paradise, both of which can deny the value of mortal time in an absolutism of contentless continuity and extra-temporal redemption. In the finite expressions and drama of human anguish the matter is more complicated.

Macdonald, however, while rejecting Marx's grand historical narrative and his scienticism, also re-reads Marx as a moralist. Hence, in a more complex view than leftist commentators have sometimes allowed him, he also promotes Marx in certain directions. He approves Marx's vision in *The Gotha Programme* (1875) of the free individual and 'production by freely associated men'.[55] He generally also approved Marx's critique of Hegel and statism and correctly noted that Marx's utopian vision of the fully active and variously occupied individual was prior to his definition of collective social means. However, Macdonald's attack on progress (in Marxism and capitalism) suffers from the same problems as his use of the concept of tragedy. Macdonald's sense of fatality about the rise of the corporate state, bureaucracy and the permanent war economy seemed to suggest that the radicalism of the Hegelian negation of the negation was no longer possible. The image is of a linear descent into the abyss where all change is decay. There is an inescapable upper-class melancholy here. Since Macdonald hoped to produce an ethical argument out of Marx, one might reasonably ask about the role of hope, the autocracy of fatalism and his ruling out of the contingent and its radical role in refreshing thinking. Here Macdonald's critics were on target. However, as an argument against sentimental optimism (especially in America), as a dirge for the various radicalisms that the years 1917–19 destroyed in the United States, as a polemic against the rhetoric of the teleological assumptions of communist propaganda, it worked well enough. When the atomic bomb was exploded, noted Macdonald, the unionized proletariat reacted with 'patriotic cheers'.[56] The rest of Macdonald's attack in 'The Root of Man' is reserved for a critique of the planned economy, whether the state capitalism of the Soviets or the war economy of Nazi Germany, which did away with even the illusion of free contract in the exchange process of capitalist productive relations. The social democratic 'mixed economy' was not much of an issue at this time, though it would be highly developed in the Scandinavian countries and in Germany after the war.

'The Root of Man' pursued political and ethical arguments relentlessly. Following the Trotskyite Ciliga's analysis in his 'remarkable book', *The Russian Enigma* (trans. 1940, orig. 1938), but now arguing against Trotsky, Macdonald saw no new predictably dialectical Marxist 'antagonism' between a recuperating bourgeoisie and Stalin. Absolute power was absolute power and terror was terror. In 1946, given Soviet sacrifices, it was still difficult to criticize the Soviet Union. But thanks to Ciliga, not to mention Serge, Macdonald knew exactly what had transpired in the 'Thermidor' of the Russian revolution. His final judgement was to a degree simplistic but instinctively on target. Struggling to find words for the new political realities he anticipated Arendt's 'totalitarianism' in Ciliga's notion of 'bureaucratic collectivization'.

For Macdonald, socialist theorists also failed through being too preoccupied with a simplistic view of class struggle to work out a theory of war. Macdonald's thoughts, in their analysis of the fatalistic anonymity of technical and military production, unchecked by political process, here anticipate Eisenhower's remarkable farewell address of 1961, in which the Republican president warned that public policy would become the captive of a scientific-technological elite, in which government contracts would become 'virtually a substitute for intellectual curiosity' and warned against a world in which the 'military industrial complex' would affect every aspect of American life, 'economic, political, even spiritual'. With uncanny prescience, Eisenhower also warned that the 'potential for the disastrous rise of misplaced power exists and will persist'. After Eisenhower ironically it was two Democratic presidents who would be the next to pursue disastrous wars. War and the war economy were to transcend traditional party claims to ethical behaviour and Macdonald in the last phase of his active life had ample proof of the effect of permanent war on American life.

In 1946 he had rightly accused Marx of superficiality, even indifference, to the nature of war. Marx's millennialist time-frames were not sympathetic to suffering in war. Unlike workers on the factory floor, workers in war were somehow part of a more abstract historical scheme. The Franco-Prussian war simply gave the proletariat practice in arms for a future revolution.[57] As for the 'productive' nature of 'crisis', the atheist Macdonald waxed biblical against Engels's view of the productive opportunity provided by the first World War for the proletariat and added, in relation to the same hope provided by the Second World War: 'Nerves twisted by saturation bombing raids, feelings numbed by massacre and suffering, vigour sapped by too little food for too many years – out of these thistles we must not expect figs.'[58]

Recalling Simone Weil's 'Words and War', published in the previous issue of *politics* to 'The Root of Man', Macdonald noted that capitalist power to go to war was in order to continue the means of war: 'oil fields, strategic bases, friendly smaller nations' (a proposition that rings especially true today) rather than for classic Marxist reasons.[59] As for economic crisis, Macdonald argued, citing Keynes and others, that capitalists were getting rather good at managing capitalism in order to avoid crises like that of 1929, at least for rich countries. The full production of war-time, he noted, paradoxically increases recruitment for trade unions compared to times of recession.

The following month, Macdonald published the second part of the article. Following in the steps of Henry Adams and Lewis Mumford, he attacked the idea of extending scientific objectivity (even assuming that it ever existed in its pure form) into all areas of human life. In a later book, Mumford was to sum up the problem, the problem of what T.S. Eliot succinctly called the 'dissociation of sensibility':

> Once indeed scientists decided to exclude theology, politics, ethics, and current events from the sphere of their discussions, they were welcomed by the heads of state. In return – and this remains one of the black marks against strict scientific orthodoxy with its deliberate indifference of moral and political concerns – scientists habitually remained silent about public affairs and were outwardly if not ostentatiously 'loyal.' Thus their mental isolation made them predestined cogs in the new megamachine.[60]

Macdonald is particularly acute on the numbing effect of this disengagement in contemporary horror. The quantitative rise in the technological means of mass murder and cruelty had the qualitative effect of indifference to ethics. Brecht wrote in his journal in 1941: 'the old armies compete like distaffs against the spinning jenny, valour loses out to good driving, indefatigability to punctuality, stamina to diligence, strategy has turned into surgery, an enemy country is "opened up" after it has been anaesthetized, then it is swabbed down, disinfected, sewn up etc. all with the greatest of ease.'[61] Brecht was perhaps more acute about human psychology than Macdonald; he noted with approval soldiers in a train switching over from the news programmes to the music programmes.[62] That request for 'numbing' should not too quickly be equated with political or ethical indifference. There is a limited amount of horror and propaganda anyone can stomach in any given day. The numbing, however, was not creative. Elsewhere Brecht noted: 'you can hear rousing music on the radio here 100 times a day, jingles encouraging the purchase of coca cola. It's enough to make you call for *l'art pour l'art* in desperation.'[63]

Propaganda, technique, the concealed madness of impersonal scientific technological process, mass manipulation and the extension of a quasi-scientific pseudo-objectivity into every assessment of human behaviour were, for Macdonald, as for many others of his time, as least as much key areas for analytic attention as class war, dialectical materialism or dubious Marxist historical reason. For example, against Rousseau's monolithic 'human nature' Macdonald placed the anthropologist Ruth Benedict's relativistic 'human natures', although he unwittingly threw out the question of the ethical human being's relation to history as he did so. The Marxist J.T. Farrell's haphazard attempt to link evolution and human nature, Macdonald dismissed by noting that human nature is more likely to be deformed by millennia of exploitation and more 'adapted' to servility than freedom. If, added Macdonald, the Marxes and Deweys of this world really thought that there might be scientific explanations of human behaviour, that very fact was more likely to lead to total control than to freedom.[64]

Like Henry Adams, Macdonald objected to the grand narrative of any sanctioning metaphysic, whether it was God's purpose, evolutionary science adapted to sociological ends or the unconscious posing as the endlessly postponed revelatory truth in the discourse between analyst and patient. Whereas for Adams, such mandarin explanations were used ironically to explain an almost Weberian location of power in a society, for Macdonald they were more closely allied to an all-explanatory mystical dogmatism that ignored the nitty-gritty of actual existence, rather like Marx's view of Hegel. At the same time he defended the atemporality of ethical teaching against the simplicity of an overly embracing metaphysics. Just as Weil might draw an ethical judgement across centuries (Descartes, for example, defends his work from rivals by omitting links in his account of geometric equations and is thus less praiseworthy when compared with disinterested thinkers such as Pythagoras or Plato), so Macdonald asserts the continuing validity of Tolstoy or Lao-Tse for a 'residue which is not historically relative'.[65] The key point to understand here is not that Macdonald embraced Tolstoy's Christianity (he did not) but that he saw there were lessons to be learnt from Tolstoy that transcended a relativistic view of history.

So it was 'values' that Macdonald wished to reintroduce into the wasteland produced by a purely 'scientific' view of the world. If Mumford was to lament the rejection of theology, metaphysics and philosophy, Macdonald, thinking against himself, tried to fill the gap with some of his immediate contemporaries in psychology, anthropology and social analysis. While he himself disputed the usefulness of any scientific model in ethics, he noted that there were at least two kinds of science (that today are called 'soft' and 'hard' science) and that soft science might have some answers. In the second part of his article he drew a line from the French *encyclopédistes* who 'looked to biology, psychology, anthropology' and noted that Wilhelm Reich and Paul Goodman were their contemporary successors.[66] Reich, of course, opened up the question of whether Freud might be used alongside Marx to produce a theory of human behaviour which would combine, or at least address together, human sexuality and 'scientific Marxism': the eternal person of Freud and the historical person of Marx. Goodman, on the other hand, though he embraced Reich, was very much a rationalist who was to dislike the Beat generation, but he is the key American communitarian anarchist thinker of the mid-century. The conjuncture of these two thinkers in *politics* is an important trans-Atlantic bridge which deserves further exploration.

Macdonald selects three Marxist 'texts' with which, sermon-like, to continue his argument. All three illustrate the relation of time to politics and ethical judgment. First, Macdonald cites Engels's *Ludwig Feuerbach and the End of Classical German Philosophy*: 'all successive historical situations are only transitory stages in the endless course of development of human society from the lower to the higher'.[67] Second, Marx from *Capital*: 'all human acts, movements relations [...] must first deal with human nature in general, and then with human nature as modified in each historical epoch'.[68] And finally, Marx from the *Communist Manifesto, Part II* (1845): 'but Communism abolishes all eternal truths [...] it therefore acts in contradiction to all past historical experience'.[69] In each case Macdonald presses the case for a temporal vision that includes an imaginative reciprocity between time and eternity, consciousness and biological indifference and some sort of Braudelian *longue durée*. Against an ultimately indifferent Heraclitean flux, he places an ethics of the temporal; against the break instituted by Marx between nature and human nature he places a Kropotkin-like sense of conscious cooperation with an ecologically interdependent nature; and against absolute historical rupture he places the vitality of a re-imagined past and narrative continuity.

Macdonald turned a more imaginative and unpredictable sense of truth, together with a sense of a revivified sense of the story's continuity with the past, against the abstract Marxist revolutionary break with the past, and against Stalinist neo-Marxist positivism. He further makes the perfectly sophisticated point (for a philosophical *naïf*) that you cannot tell a lower from a higher evolutionary development if you do not have some idealist comparative standard to know the difference. The second point from the second quotation is implied in the first. Marx needed the general (a totalizing process) as a framework for a potential dialectics in which the particular moment could only be manifest within that general movement, and vice versa. Marx wished to replace human nature with a nature that is only manifest in concrete historical processes, hence he says in the third quotation that that nature can be totally lost, indeed should be lost, in the movement of contraries. The contradiction here is that something recognizable as prior in the negation of the negation is always retained, though transformed. The pure revolutionary break is hard to fit in any simple terms into a dialectical movement, and even harder in the inner psychological life of the soul. For Macdonald, the temporality of any choice is directed at once both to the past and to the future. In practical terms, as George Santayana once noted: 'Those who cannot remember the past are condemned to repeat it.'[70]

As for the past, Macdonald pondered the nature of the Victorian century of progress when so many writers and poets, unlike Victorian social theorists and economists, attacked the industrializing world and its rising bourgeoisie as barbaric. For Macdonald, like Henry Adams before him, Tocqueville is a dissenting conservative voice to whom attention must be paid in relation to any assumption about progress. To Macdonald, 'the process of history in a word, appears now to be a more complex and tragic matter than it appeared to the socialist and anarchist thinkers, who were, after all, children of their age, not of ours.'[71] Macdonald uses the notion of the finitude of time within temporal argument to distinguish present from the past and, like Marx, insists on the contingency of the newness of experience, though here the argument is slightly muddied with a Spenglerian sense of decline. Indeed, Arnold Toynbee and Oswald Spengler are cited a little later in the argument.[72] Toynbee's large cultural-religious frames and Spengler's fatalistic pessimism inform to a degree Macdonald's metaphysics of historical process. They are, of course, just as biased towards what he had called 'the metaphysics of Progress' but within Macdonald's mode of lugubrious satiric irony, and as a response to the shock of Hiroshima, they also work locally as part of a countervailing rhetoric of tragic persuasion.

More than ideological argument, it was art that provided the ground for complex and enlightened insights into the human condition. Macdonald posed the question of art's relevance in terms of temporality by citing Marx: '[is] the *Iliad* at all compatible with the printing press and the steam press'?[73] In some respects it was also an old American question that went back to the early years of American culture when democratic, progressive science and technology were felt to be preferable over elitist, aristocratic and reactionary European art and literature. Macdonald shows skilfully how Marx's argument slid imperceptibly from one temporal system to another. Marx had the problem, within a progressivist time-frame, of explaining why Greek sculpture had never been equalled. He never does explain this because he has no extra-temporal criteria for why he thought it was 'highest' in the first place. Instead he slips into a historical explanation of why such work was possible then but not now, thus suspending the question of how it fits into any need for contemporary attention beyond pure fascination. Marx's simplistic and very non-dialectical view that 'myth' was superseded by the 'reality' of 'automatic machinery and railways'.[74] courts a fantastic temporal positivism of Comte-like banality, which in the early years of the nineteenth century also bedevilled the American popular imagination. The judgement is analogous though not equal to Marx's treatment of religion. As Lewis Mumford was to note, nearly forty years later, to assume science and technology were free from 'metaphysics' was a delusion.[75] Marx, as Macdonald states, was still bothered with this conclusion, since he clearly enjoyed looking at Greek sculpture. The 'solution', in classic Victorian manner, was to place the authenticity of the Greek experience into an essentially nostalgic time-frame of the 'childhood of the race'.[76] There was, states Macdonald, with perhaps too temperate a judgement, no way for him else 'to escape acknowledging that there are supra-historical values in art'.[77] For Macdonald this was an 'appalling' judgement, one of philistine sentimentality.[78]

Searching for a theory of ethics and political action, it was the eternal question of 'what is to be done?' that haunted Macdonald. He felt that mass representative democracy was crude and self-corrupting and that existing institutions of protest from the unions to the Communist Party were equally corrupt and self-serving. The degree of pragmatism that was needed to belong to either was unacceptable. Macdonald in fact had no answers except in the development of small-scale resistance and pressure groups. E.P. Thompson complained in a late interview that his greatest sorrow was that there was no party with a broad-based platform to which he could subscribe, that is, a party with a wide organization for that very human need of rootedness and solidarity which encourages activism.[79]

Both Thompson and Macdonald stood between worlds. They had grown up under the shadow of the Russian revolution, they lived to see a complete fragmentation of all forces that could oppose or even begin to tame the environmental devastation and human cruelty of unbridled market-driven global capitalism. Facing up to the new reality in a sense was one of Macdonald's few options. Rescuing the fragmented insights of past radicalisms for the beginnings of a new critique was one of the others. He adapted Lukács's use of 'reification' and cited *The German Ideology* on the way a person is claimed by the structuring of class interests and class antagonism so that human behaviour is alienated from itself, in order to build a new critique of that American quantitative, bureaucratic, corporate, mass systems reality which had emerged after the war. Some twenty years later this complex of issues would emerge in the English-speaking world as anticipating certain critiques of the Frankfurt School and the political, technological, bureaucratic and personal world it analysed would be satirized by writers such as Thomas Pynchon, Norman Mailer and Don DeLillo.

Insofar as he had a coherent answer, Macdonald followed in 'that subterranean tradition of organic and decentralist economics whose major spokesmen include Prince Kropotkin, Gustave Landauer, Tolstoy, William Morris, Gandhi, Lewis Mumford, [...] Alex Comfort, Paul Goodman, and Murray Bookchin.'[80] This tradition has often been commented upon as the major radical tradition available to American liberals, given the historic failure to organize political parties in seriously capitalist-limiting platforms within the national framework. It has not perhaps been noted enough that the American disposition towards, and ideology of the small 'beloved community', is so powerful and so tenacious, because of America's ever expanding military industrial complex, appalling record on the environment, suburban sprawl, violence towards the urban poor, aggressive consumption of global resources (with a foreign policy to match), racism, gun culture, hypocritical religiosity and traffic-choked ugly cities.

In America in the 1940s, this home-grown communitarian tradition was ferociously attacked by the Stalinist-dominated sections of the American left. Chiaromonte was vilified in one particularly hostile Greenwich Village basement evening discussion attended by J.T. Farrell, Mary McCarthy, Meyer Schapiro, William Phillips, Philip Rahv, Hannah Arendt, Niccolò Tucci and the Macdonalds. Communists like Farrell rained down the street-corner leaflets of their reality principles on the *partie de campagne* of the communitarian bohemian utopians, accusing them of frivolous psychiatry, moral absolutism, unempirical blathering, a lack of detailed organization on the factory floors and disengagement from the American working class, the only 'scientific' basis for the coming salvation of the as-yet-to-be-attained American 'socialist' Jerusalem.[81] As Rexroth, particularly responding to Farrell, wrote to Macdonald in 1946: 'Whatever gave you the idea they were Marxists?'[82] From the 1930s onwards Stalinist Marxists had particularly attacked liberals and social democrats, and indeed anyone who did not follow the hypostacized mantras of a debased largely positivist Marxist theory together with an acceptance of an even more ruthless post-Bolshevik autocratic power. A favourite term of abuse was 'social fascist'.[83]

However, it may well be that in the end the growing protest of somewhat uninformed and incoherent young people today against 'global capitalism' may find this small group 'anarchist', 'ethical' and 'international' tradition immensely valuable as a way of locating themselves within a usable past, however defeated in historically measurable terms. For Macdonald it was the 'old I.W.W.' (Industrial Workers of the World) who preserved the spirit of internationalism better than the stage-managed bureaucratic junketings of the Stalinist Internationals. Ethics were at the core of Macdonald's socialism, any dissent was a personal decision and, on however tiny a stage, it was valuable. The order of the day was to be pacifism, non-violent activism, anti-pragmatic thinking, emotionally sensitive co-operation with others, small supportive communities, a theory of limits and decorum for behaviour and a refusal of irrationally compulsive materialism (sex and shopping), parading as liberated behaviour.

It was to endorse the Greek rather than the Roman, Kroptkin rather than Marx, a certain humility in relation to nature and natural process; it called for a personal quasi-Thoreauvian dissent outside a reality not dominated by the compulsive blandishments of mass media and commercial brainwashing. These values seemed to belong to radical, traditional religious thought rather than to the materialist, class and economic analyses of Marxism. They combined what seemed impossible utopian ideas with hopeful small-scale practical solutions. This radicalism, as for Marx (though not for many Marxists), had a theory of the person at its core. Macdonald was the first to acknowledge that the person in daily life was a 'mixture of chivalry and cynicism' but that the messy individual had nonetheless a need to resist the increasingly all-powerful oligarchy of the 'military industrial complex' in whatever way possible.

Did Macdonald therefore sell his Marxist soul for a mess of moralism? There is a sense in which he had little choice. Given the re-enslavement by Stalin of the Russian poor (and the not so poor), not to mention his termination of the likelihood of any form of Soviet democratic socialism, together with the hopes, the disappointments and horrors of the first half of the twentieth century, some *point d'appui* had to be found. This inevitably undermined increasingly oversimplified and dogmatic thinking. A rethinking of the tradition, a clarification of the historical situation, a reassessment of the lessons of history and a recourse to some clear-sighted ethics was not a bad place to begin. It had the merit of inviting a transnational and trans-ideological analysis. Macdonald exposed the Marxist historical prophetic narrative, Marxist economic statism, Stalinist totalitarian and technological gigantism and Marxism's arrogant scientism with its scant treatment of other social critiques of power structures whether in anthropological, gendered, cultural or psychological terms. That particular Marxist soul, judged Macdonald, was not worth defending.

The failure and descent into reaction of the Soviet revolution, however, was a wake-up call and a signal to pick up the considerable remaining contributions of Marxism to radical thought: its view of the primacy of the person and its insights into the contradictions of capitalist exchange relations that always disadvantaged individuals who were compelled to sell their labour in an unequal power contract. Revised, it still had things to say about class, human and material wastage, about the compulsive fetishisms within materialism itself and much about capitalism: its faith in natural trickle-down; the banal metaphysics of its all-seeing market; its cosmopolitan indifference to local need and small-scale manufacturing; its quantitative undoing of qualitative value; its preference for reactionary paradigms of personal behaviour bolstered by travesties of Christian doctrine; its gigantic appetite for material resources anywhere in the world accessed at any environmental and political price; its view of state 'order' as legitimate only if friendly to its profiteering; and, ironically, its Soviet-like disposition to global gigantism and monopolistic power.

Michael Wreszin's summary of the ideological impact and substance of *politics* is still the most reasoned and discriminating. He distinguished between Chiaromonte's somewhat puritanical take on political activity and Macdonald's more bohemian proclivities and one may add, by extension, his need to combine psychology with economic and political theory. He correctly points to the fact that, whatever else *politics* was or stood for, it considerably extended the parameters of both political discourse and debate. Macdonald brought in non-academic gadflies such as C. Wright Mills (who suggested the journal's name); Paul Goodman; one of the most important gender and communitarian analysts of the time; Daniel Bell, about whom Macdonald later had serious reservations; and old American Trotskyites such as Melvin Lasky and Harold Orlansky.[84]

The most positive sense of the contribution made by *politics* to political and social theory can be seen in Sumner's generous reading of the idea of 'sociability', which he first locates in the Russian-Italian intellectual and active opponent of fascism Andrea Caffi. His few pages of commentary on Caffi and *politics* create a convenient departure point for this section's concentration on the 'Europe' that appeared in *politics*. Caffi was, as Sumner says, 'a voice from an earlier generation, a definer of ways for radicals to 'move against the grain of a murderous "History"'.[85] These opening statements signal the relation of narrative times in conflict: personal time, historical time and ethical atemporality with its shadow of the fatality of eternity. Sumner does not pursue these possibilities for analysis; his direction lies elsewhere. He summarizes Caffi's criticism of Marxist authoritarianism, its fascination with violence, its narratives of historical reason and its views of revolutionary apocalypse. There was a need for what Gino Bianco later called 'thinking outside politics' and, following Caffi's teacher George Simmel, a need for 'sociability' which resisted market pressure, state power and other institutional forms of instrumental logic.[86] Caffi made the judgement that the word 'civilization' in any meaningful sense had been destroyed by the mid-twentieth century. A letter to Macdonald, published in *politics*, stated 'For the time being there is no solution, one can only wait for some unpredictable turn of the historical tide.'[87] It will be shown that that statement was not a call for inaction but a recognition of a serious still-contemporary truth, particularly in relation to the experience of Caffi's own life.

Sumner points to Caffi's choice of a tradition of resistance: Plato's model cities; the monasteries; early Christian dissenting sects; More's 'Utopia'; peasant free cities and cantons of the Middle Ages; communal experiments of Quakers and Anabaptists; early socialists; particularly those crypto-socialists favoured by anarchist thinkers such as Owen and Proudhon. Part of that list is encountered again in Mumford's *The Condition of Man* (see pp. 374–5) and the whole question of choosing a 'tradition' through a profound understanding of the past reappears again in Muriel Rukeyser (see pp. 441–2). Here, Sumner summarizes:

> The most exciting aspect of Caffi's ideas, preliminary as they may have been in the 1940s, is that although they jettisoned the Enlightenment project of mastery and its supporting metanarrative of historical rationality, they kept alive its vision of a universally shared culture. Unlike other 'postmodern' formulations that celebrate

> essentialist differences, identity politics, or the recovery of various populist traditions, 'free sociability' – potentially, at least-implies a decentered but inclusive sphere of intimate and voluntary association, transcending (though not effacing) the boundaries of class, race, ethnicity, gender, and geography.[88]

Sumner speaks with passion to the cultural prejudices (a certain depoliticized emphasis on gender and ethnicity) of the American academy in the early years of the twenty-first century and makes a powerful plea for grass-roots activism taking place outside the official politics that has ceased to be believable. In beginning a new 'utopian' genealogy, a past for the future, Sumner looks to Martin Luther King, Václav Havel, Gyorgy Konrád.

To turn, however, from theory to practice and to creative records of that practice in narrative is at this point crucial. The concern should be with the experience of ideology and political behaviour within the framework of temporality and the human story. The past never becomes more important than when the present is chaos and the future unimaginable. In that sense, the Europeans in Macdonald's *politics* had stories to tell. This section will look at European writers associated with *politics* who crucially had something to say about time and narrative, and hence about ethics and politics. Macdonald's European list included Arendt, de Beauvoir, Cáffi (whom Wreszin thought the most important), Camus, Chiaromonte, Ciliga, André Delacourt, a zany satirist somewhat contorted in prose style called Niccolò Tucci, Sartre, Serge, Weil, and George Woodcock, the noted British anarchist. Macdonald was also in correspondence with Europeans such as W.H. Auden, George Orwell, Bertrand Russell, Stephen Spender and Trotsky. Though several of these will be touched on in the following discussion, the focus is on Arendt, Weil, Ciliga and the French existentialist writers Sartre, de Beauvoir and Camus, with a postscript on Bataille.

Hannah Arendt: Navigating Time

It seems to have been Daniel Bell who introduced Macdonald to Arendt. In July 1944 Bell enclosed in a letter to Macdonald 'a remarkable piece' ('The Jew and the Pariah') by Arendt, which had appeared in *Jewish Social Studies*, and suggested that he might like her as a contributor to *politics*.[89] Arendt's letters to Macdonald from 1945 onwards spoke of the old left's respect for Weber in relation to his non-servility, his civil courage and his fighting spirit. She also expressed her admiration for Macdonald's attack on the dropping of the atomic bomb in his recent article in *politics*. She spoke freely, too, of the fate of the Jews under Hitler. It was not so much the material dispossession as the destruction of what she called the 'valid names', the bonds between them, moral dignity, that very self-consciousness that united a people. Probing deeper than most, she mourned the destruction of 'inner' freedom under what she was soon to call 'totalitarianism'. The consequences of that were a paralysis of action and responsibility.[90]

Arendt clearly felt that she could speak passionately and openly to Macdonald of the need for new individual risk-taking, the need to refuse despair, cynicism and nihilism in the face of what had been revealed in Germany. A year later she wrote to the Houghton Mifflin Fellowship Committee that Macdonald's long essay 'The Root of Man' showed a resistance to contemporary orthodoxy. It had all the qualities of intellectual fearlessness, she wrote, and, by rejecting his ideological positions of the 1930s, Macdonald was concerned to build a modern humanism in the face of emergent bureaucracies and the atomic bomb. Arendt continued to write to him during his depressed and inactive years in the early 1950s, pleading with him to come back to political journalism.[91] That 'humanism' is the subject of her later letters to him during the 1960s where she vigorously defended the European humanistic tradition from the charge that somehow it was the 'root of Nazism'. It was, she said, simply unprepared for it. The real danger to 'humanism' as Arendt saw it was the possibility of 'humanism' itself becoming irrelevant.[92]

In 1945, however, Arendt was able to confess to Macdonald not only her own sense of despair but her sense, too, that no loss was irretrievable. Here especially she emphasized the *longue durée*:

> [that] fundament of history, first for us a thousand years of German history, the history of Western humanity, finally history of all mankind. Open as man for man, we may go down to the depth of these fundaments, to the nearest and most remote memories.[93]

The nearest and most remote memories: this was the range, the one thing necessary, and the writer's skill was to be tested in a narrative of a juxtaposition of the temporally distant and the temporally close up. Here, paradoxically, the Pascalian stance outside of history recovers a freedom for choosing a recoverable story. Arendt's temporality also had an ethical dimension. The sense of responsibility was to an active recovery of the past, present and future as the one leaked into the other. 'For Christ's sake', she wrote to the depressed and inactive Macdonald in 1951, begging him to come back to journalism, 'this is no century for having a good time', though this plea was then affectionately softened enough to suggest that you could do something and have a good time.[94] It was 'men in dark times', those of the century's midnight, to whom Arendt was to give most of her attention. Those dark times were to be confronted in a complex view of temporality.

The following review of Arendt will provide a further contribution to the theme of time and narrative that threads through this book: a supplement to the framework already provided by Ricoeur. Arendt's re-reading of Greek political thought (*The Human Condition*, 1958) was to challenge Marxist historical reason, not least in terms of its temporality. A re-reading of Greek definitions of the public and private spheres was to provide the basis for a powerful critique of modernity. A further analysis of contemporary shifts of political power (*The Origins of Totalitarianism*, 1958) was to place anti-Semitism in different cultural time frames, those of the nationally distinct, slow-moving social customs, congealed memories and practices of the historical state.

As for Jewish people, their slow hypostacization of custom and memory, the retreat to inner experience and the bourgeois retreat to an atemporal view of 'art', as a superior place to be, left them outside the time-frames of political policy and historic responsibility: 'Jews became people with whom one hoped to while away some time.'[95] Art became part of that 'whiling away', rather than that serious standing aside to gather insight and energy to re-launch oneself into the world with a more engaged wisdom. As the critics have noted, Arendt turned Heidegger's repetition into Augustine's 'imitation', defined as the foundation of a free choice out of the world, and followed it by a return to community in which new beginnings ('natality') and 'foundation' can break out of the hermeneutical trap (the circularity of the thoughtlessness which comes from meaninglessness and dispersion of thought).[96]

For the Jews there was a kind of retreat to the social time within the heavily promoted exclusiveness of the family's boundaries and a retreat to comfortable styles of psychological behaviour which were reinforced in contemporary America by the need to be ethically distinctive. 'Jewishness', in its essentialist atemporality, provided a model for every other group with an inward-looking identity retreating with a sense of political helplessness from a terrifying political world. For an Austrian Jew of the late nineteenth century this identity was what Arendt called 'fictitious'. As such, it involved a narrative, a story which placed the person in a fictitious and legitimating history. Ethically it implied a story: this is how I came to be the sort of person I am and these are my resulting freedoms. I can do this but not that. Here, Sartrean 'bad faith' normally has a field day, and humour and irony become not only the Nietzschean death of the real emotion but the death of a real possibility of engagement in the political process.[97] As is well known, the analysis of the historical moments reviewed by Arendt were not very popular among those of small courage and large prejudices about their sense of personal time in history and their over-determined sense of historical destiny or fate. However, Arendt's exposure of the temporality of narratives, especially concerning race, religion and gender, are fundamental to an understanding of this and any other time of history.

In the more strictly political realm, Arendt charted the slow historical victory of the realm of the social over the political. The argument (in *The Human Condition*) is well known, but what is emphasized here are those views of temporality and narrative with which she engaged. Arendt began with the dissociation of sensibility of the scientific revolution and, in an argument familiar to critical philosophy since Hegel, challenged the right of the abstract calculations of the scientific world and the progressivist, utopian drive to mastery within it, to speak for all of human life. Science occupied an 'Archimedean standpoint [...] outside the earth'.[98] Tradition, the normal expression of 'speech and thought', earth-boundedness and tragedy are given short shrift in this world of science.

Arendt's opening scientific time-frame is from the seventeenth century to the atomic bomb (Mumford's was to be much longer). She then, in a kind of philosophico-historical gesture, dismisses it as the subject for the book. But of course it lies as a shadowy context for an apparently more quasi-'Pascalian' argument about the 'origins' of a 'condition'. The brilliance of the work is its Victorian search for origins as a paradoxically atemporal speculation about consciousness, like the early ethnologists who erased the 'primitive' from history, then brought it back as psychology (the childhood of the race), finally combining it with a moral speculation about the large existential questions about meaning, the self and others, death, birth and eternity.

As Scheherazade held off death by telling a different story for one thousand and one nights, so Arendt held to the power of narrative as a response to mortality itself:

> The mortality of men lies in the fact that individual life, with a recognizable life-story from birth to death, rises out of biological life. This individual life is distinguished from all other things by the rectilinear course of its movement, which, so to speak, cuts through the circular movement of biological life. This is mortality: to move along a rectilinear line in a universe where everything, if it moves at all, moves in a cyclical order.[99]

At the same time, Arendt compellingly outlines the historic rise in the contemplation of the 'eternal' in sharp distinction from 'immortality', which it was to suppress in the Christian era, from its speechless form in classical antiquity to its Christian death-like capacity to denigrate the human experience of the actual world. The resulting impoverishment of the sense of the process of time and the significance of even the importance of history becomes clear.

In the contemporary world of an engineered propaganda of universal terror on the one side and actual terrorist activity on the other, the former banishes all stories in favour of propaganda's monolithic tale and the latter displays the sheer arbitrariness of execution in revenge and obliterates all connection between violence and recognition of a universal human story. The executioners take on the mantle of an 'eternal' God outside history. Here all story disappears in the broken connections between law and action, personal activity and consequence, fate and responsibility, thought and action and, above all, in mutual lateral connections between people. The powerful with huge military resources and the impotent with explosives and stones are in collusion to banish human complexity and difference in their claims to tell the story of human life. They depend on and need each other.

Crucially in Arendt's argument, which to a degree is being followed here, there is no chance of that absolute requirement for a story: a beginning. That slightly clumsy word 'natality', rather than 'mortality', is foundational to her political thought.[100] For Arendt, 'the new always happens against the overwhelming odds of statistical laws and their probability, which for all practical, everyday purposes amounts to certainty; the new therefore always appears in the guise of a miracle.'[101] Human beings are born not to die but to begin. In Arendt's radical re-reading of the Christian nativity, the killing of children prevents the potentially dangerous radicalization of beginning in every birth of a child.[102] Similarly the loss of the 'immortal' is a loss of continuity, the sense that something might be preserved for the future. The poor quality of contemporary admiration for philosophy and poetry falls short of that admiration which constitutes 'a space in which things are saved from destruction by time'.[103] So Arendt pitted a political definition of temporality, narrativity and the life of the mind itself against 'dark times'. It was a revised view of narrative and time which raised a call for immortality against the eternal, a temporality inflected by birth not by death and for a meaningful story freely exchanged without fear between people. Creative memory was needed against the banality of a continually promoted 'realistic' present of the masses, against the silence, loneliness, atomization and reification of the person suffering totalitarian grand narratives of impersonal destiny and disembodied terror.

Arendt noted the ancient cultural birth of temporality in her own grand narrative: she creates an originating moment for a chronology of humanness. For her it began in human consciousness between the fifth and second centuries BC, in the rise of the great world religions and civilizations. It was coeval with the growth of thinking and reflection itself:

> It was a time when mankind first discovered the human condition on earth, so that from then on the mere chronological sequence of events could become a story and the stories be worked into a history, a significant object of reflection and understanding. The historical axis of mankind then is 'an era around the middle of the last millennium B.C., for which everything that preceded it would appear to have been a preparation, and to which everything subsequent actually, and often in clear consciousness, relates back [...]'.[104]

Having cited her mentor Karl Jaspers, Arendt goes on to suggest, via this recognition, a foundational unity of human beings. It involves both a large time-scale and a multitude of small ones which nonetheless relate to it: the historic unrepeatable birth of a moment of humanness in the triumph of story over chronology, of meaning and significance over indifferent biological and cosmic process. This transcendent principle is human unity to which only the diversity of human stories can give credence. Jasper's view of the present as a suspense between a no-longer and not-yet was designed politically to keep beginnings open in a world that appeared to have ended and seemed doomed. It asserted intelligibility against Kantian 'melancholy haphazardness' and the Hegelian world spirit's 'ruse of reason'.[105] Jaspers's existentialist temporality had a direct political inflexion, which is always latent in any view of temporality, as indeed it is in every story told to another: 'Compared with Kant, Jaspers's concept of mankind and world citizenship is historical; compared with Hegel, it is political.'[106]

Some of Arendt's most cogent thoughts on temporality occur in her essay on Isak Dinesen, the Danish author of *Seven Gothic Tales* and *Out of Africa*. They give a less abstract description of temporality with its gift of the active and imaginative life that mediates with intelligibility the indifference of biological survival. Dinesen, as Arendt pointed out, loved mottos. The Latin tag *navigare necesse est, vivere non necesse est* was foundational for both of them. [107] Arendt substituted the model of the act of writing for the 'being' of the writer to illustrate one way of being significantly alive:

> Without repeating life in imagination you can never be fully alive, 'lack of imagination' prevents people from 'existing'. 'Be loyal to the story,' as one of her storytellers admonishes the young, 'be eternally and unswervingly loyal to the story,' means no less than, Be loyal to life, don't create fiction but accept what life is giving you, show yourself worthy of whatever it may be by recollecting and pondering over it, thus repeating it in imagination; this is the way to remain alive.[108]

This moment of the philosopher's tribute to the story-teller, is worthy of Proust or Henry James at their most incisive and indeed equally captures the spirit of their art as well. It extends to a greater depth Wilde's 'life imitates art' and displaces 'fiction' from its commonly perceived place as standing in pure contradiction to 'life'. At the same time, for Arendt, it extends to everyone. In another place she wrote: 'there is nothing in the ordinary life of man that cannot become food for thought'.[109]

The story is a rich way, therefore, of showing how its 'historic present' is poised between the no-longer and the not-yet. Furthermore, it reanimates the past in the act of reading. That an effort has to be made is not in doubt. Arendt cites the French poet René Char's *Feuillets d'Hypnos*. Here, her capacity to quote well rivals that of Benjamin: '*Notre héritage n'est précédé d'aucun testament*' ('Our inheritance comes to us by no will-and-testament').[110] That is to say it has to be both looked for, found and imagined at the same time. The past in that sense cannot be taken for granted. It is the no-longer that must be brought back into narrative intelligibility. This sense of 'choosing' the past is also crucial in the work of Muriel Rukeyser.

At the personal level of lived experience, Arendt also pointed out that time varies. A year for a child is longer than a year for an adult. Unlike the adult the child lives in the world without calculating the 'years left', more aware of the 'objective' time of the unvarying year.[111] Arendt's drive, like Mumford's, is against the mechanization of the world picture. Indeed, the self and the world's offered chronologies become a neurosis that dominates and oppresses the thought of oneself and oneself in thought. A sense of matter and spirit is the complement of such linearity. Science relies on the sameness of our inner organs, just as psychoanalysis relies on a certain similarity of phenomena ultimately predictable in all. Weil, too, spoke of the 'monotonous sameness and pervasive ugliness' of these perspectives, generalized to embrace all experience. She, too, defended the power of the story to restore complexity and unpredictability to the human sense of the self and the world. Narrative is unable to be a science because it acknowledges the difference between inside and outside the body. [112]

Ultimately, this transformatory power of narrative adding meaning to the world lies in metaphor itself. Arendt explains that this is poetic rather than philosophical in origin. This is the crucial point and it is also is why this book, which examines time and narrative seemingly most relevant to prose and fiction, will end in poetry as such. Arendt cites Ezra Pound's 'little known' (*sic*) edition of Fenellosa's *Chinese Character*: 'Metaphor is the very foundation of poetry'; without it 'there would have been no bridge whereby to cross from the minor truth of the seen to the major truth of the unseen.'[113] For Kafka, Arendt recalls, in his collection of aphorisms entitled 'HE', 'the battle ground [the contested present] [...] is the metaphor for man's home on earth [...] an extended Now on which he spends his life.'[114]

> Man lives in this in between, and what he calls the present is a life-long fight against the dead weight of the past, driving him forward with hope, and the fear of a future (whose only certainty is death), driving him backward to 'the quiet of the past' with nostalgia for and remembrance of the only reality he can be sure of.[115]

This sense of time has nothing, of course, to do with chronology. Somewhere in the connotative penumbra of such a statement must be the power of Old Testament poetic narrative. One might take as an example the story of the prophet Elijah where, after political failure and abandonment, he is forced back into the political world from which he has fled in terror by a power which wholly depends on the exquisitely human image of the divine: 'And after the earthquake a fire; but the Lord was not in the fire: and after the fire, a still small voice.'[116] The persistence of that transcendent human voice, however, does not for Arendt push towards quietism. For her, Kafka jumped out of the world altogether. What is needed, as she poetically rather than logically writes, is 'the quiet in the center of a storm which, though totally unlike the storm, still belongs to it':

> In this gap between past and future, we find our place in time when we think, that is, when we are sufficiently removed from past and future to be relied on to find out their meaning, to assume the position of 'umpire,' of arbiter and judge over the manifold, never-ending affairs of human existence in the world, never arriving at a final solution to their riddles, but ready with ever new answers to the question of what it may all be about.[117]

However 'timeless' that ongoing arbitration, to a degree withdrawn from the world, the statement certainly reflects Arendt's experience of war and exile during the 1940s, an exile in which her friend Walter Benjamin and many others had been victims of 'storm', 'earthquake' and 'fire'. Her emphasis on 'beginnings' is rooted in an ethical courage to start again and not be tempted by nostalgia or self-pity. These are, however, beginnings that, in a reflex gesture, acknowledge a past both to be acknowledged and to be re-imagined. Indeed, beginning is in a sense re-imagining by searching not simply for a 'usable' past (a phrase risking a purely instrumental vision) but one that inspires, reveals and sustains at the same time. To a degree the past is authentic only by re-imagining it. Narrative at once throws the self into the world while simultaneously placing it at an imaginative and critical distance. It relates and does not relate (in both senses of the word 'relate') to a world which replaces the given or the givenness of too apparent absence. As for Weil, the loss of narrative, the loss also of the past itself in narrative, in philosophy or in poetry, or indeed even in the history of science itself, is that loss of a sense of continuity and memory which finally deprives the world of meaning, and that significance which enables human beings to continue as human beings rather than as biological survivors.

It is not surprising that Arendt would write for *politics* and form a firm friendship with Macdonald. Her revision of Marx would be much more sophisticated and philosophically acute than his. However, her sense of ethics, her valuing of the discourse of the interior life that Augustinian Christianity had introduced to Western consciousness, combined with an awareness of critical utopian political models derived from Athenian democracy, gave her thought a rich and flexible basis for criticism. Her pitting of the reflective intelligence against a world subjected to state terror by methods of mass persuasion, whether directly political, psychological or purely materialist and economy-driven in terms of its promoted realities, together with her insistence on the human story in all its wayward complexity, made her contributions a sustaining strength in the bridge thrown by *politics* across the Atlantic.

Anton Ciliga: Russia and the Story of Time

It was precisely that conjuncture of the importance of the 'poetic' placing together of interior and exterior narratives that prompted Arendt to quote from another European contributor to *politics* in her second major contribution to political philosophy, *The Origins of Totalitarianism.* At one point in her discussions of 'totalitarianism', she was particularly concerned with the nature of blanket consent, the surrender of will within the closed group where total loyalty by virtue of an original power-elite privilege is unbreakable, even when the group decides to kill you. Here she cites Anton Ciliga on the well-known phenomenon of the Bolshevik Old Guard and members of the Cheka passively surrendering to execution during the late 1920s and 1930s. But it was not just the elite. She points out how ordinary prisoners in the GPU prison of Leningrad who had been condemned to death allowed themselves to be taken to execution 'without a word, without a cry of revolt against the government that put them to death'.[118]

She cites Ciliga again when analysing the inevitable move to reaction of revolutionary groups who seize power in the name of a single clichéd quasi-utopian vision of history: the victory of the proletariat or making the world safe for democracy. For those genuinely engaged in the respective visions, for whom the utopia vision corresponds critically, even imaginatively to the conditions of the existing world, the disappointments can only be of the bitterest. For the world grows worse to the extent that they succeed in organizing their aim politically. Quoting Ciliga's words, Arendt noted: 'the repression of socialists and anarchists had grown in severity in the same ratio as the country became pacified'.[119]

Referring to Ciliga a final time, Arendt documented a moment of that shift from reflective ideologically aware praxis to pure power play. 'During the peasant revolts of the twenties in Russia, Voroshilov allegedly refused the support of the Red Army; this led to the introduction of special divisions of the GPU for punitive expeditions.'[120] The replacement of an army (with its memories, its traditions, here especially its revolutionary successes and above all its responsibility to visible political power) with a special secret police force marks a decisive shift, a translation of 'the ostensibly foreign policy of the totalitarian state into the potentially domestic business of the totalitarian movement'.[121] The point insisted upon here is not simply the alliance of organized violence with power, but the erasure of all political dialogue and a living story of the past. In Russia's case it was of course Victor Serge who so magnificently restored the lost stories.

Who, then, was Anton Ciliga? He gets relatively little notice in contemporary commentaries.[122] Nevertheless, excerpts from his *Dix ans au pays du mensonge déconcertant* (1938, often known by the title *Le grand mensonge* and translated into rather accommodating English as *The Russian Enigma* in 1940[123]), from which Arendt made her citations, first appeared in *politics* together with four chapters of Victor Serge's *Memoirs* and pieces by the Czech dissident Josep Gutman (writing as Peter Mayer).[124] Macdonald wrote to Serge in 1941 that he had just read *The Russian Enigma* and also expressed his surprise that such books could appear in England in wartime.[125] Serge replied that the book's general perspective appeared accurate but that Ciliga's historical judgements were a bit naïve and idealistic. This was true. Ciliga ended his book by predicting that Stalin would be too compromised by his revolutionary past and predicted possible coups by the new army elite which had sprung up after the execution of the generals. Ciliga, however, was not to know that the Second World War would delay that possibility, even had it been plausible in the first place. Ironically, Macdonald's letter was written just a week before the opening of the Eastern Front.

Macdonald talked about Ciliga again seven years later, in his correspondence with Camus:

> Finally, I have seen Ciliga. He is a nice man, but tired, of course. It is the pity of all these old fighters. They have had a life of hardships, action and suffering which really had only one meaning; the eventual triumph of their ideas, so that they cold at least feel they had not wasted their time. But they have sacrificed a lot of things to their aim, one of them being complexity of outlook a full sense (I don't mean enjoyment) of life. Defeated as they are, they find themselves with very little intellectual resources, cannot even change their ideas a great deal, only refuse to prostitute them, which is of course a great achievement. Ciliga is an intelligent man, but simple-minded. He is writing something on 'Lenin and Gandhi', which is of course a good subject and shows the kind of preoccupations that has gotten hold of him [*sic*]. I shall see him again.[126]

There was a limited sense in which Serge and Macdonald were right. There is a tenacity of Marxist vision in the book and a rhetorical admiration of industrial gigantism, which is to a degree more than 'naive'. In spite of the fact that Ciliga could criticize the elite apolitical technicians enjoying special conditions when in jail (just as Thorstein Veblen in America noted their high-salaried political quiescence), his admiration for the awakening of Soviet power is real. He appeared not to have been fully aware of the terrible irony of his statement: 'A new America, immense and cruel like its elder, was being born on one-sixth of the land surface of the earth.'[127]

Macdonald nonetheless was wrong to infer that Ciliga was simple-minded and that the book had not offered a sufficient complexity of vision. One senses that Arendt, on the other hand, had understood just where the strengths and indeed the honesty of the book lay. It was in the story, in the detail and in the effect on psychology of incipient totalitarianism on people clinging to the last shreds of political hope. It was in the complexity, not to mention courage, of the narrative it offered, at the time it did. The tiny fragmented moments of narrative, not dissimilar to the way a narrative accumulates evidence in Victor Serge's episodic accounts, pile up to an indictment offered beyond ideological simplicity, or even indeed to Ciliga's own clinging to a Marxist-inflected and prophetic socialist vision of the future.

Le grand mensonge opens with a simple Pascalian judgement. Everyone in Russia lies. It is a lie that frames a particular historical narrative offered to the world. Far from old tyranny being extirpated by the revolution, a new tyranny is concealed in what has emerged: 'Modern Russia shows its originality in the fact that this new edition of the past is bedecked with the brightest colours, the most advanced theories, the most modern slogans and the most daring dream visions.'[128] Modernity conceals old tyranny. Unlike Mumford, Ciliga will never abandon the idea of progress nor a certain naïve faith in technological development, but his faithfulness as witness will often contradict, by narrative inference, the naïveté of the general position. His aim is to report rather than to judge as such, though inevitably the reporting is moved by an implied judgement, one that is derived less from a need of ideological justification than from a precariously willing suspension of disbelief.

He places himself at the outset as an idealistic child of the Bolshevik revolution. As a Yugoslav Bolshevik activist and with all possibility of revolution extinguished in Western Europe, he accepted an offer in the mid-1920s to go to the Soviet Union to study the politics and people. Sympathetic to the left opposition he quickly got into trouble and was eventually arrested and exiled to Siberia where, like Serge, he was miraculously released (largely by claiming an original Italian citizenship – his birthplace in Yugoslavia had been colonized by the Italians) just before the very worst days of Stalin's terror. His account runs parallel in some respects to Serge's, though there are important divergences, politically and also in terms of things noticed and spoken of.

Ciliga was articulate about the credibility gap between propaganda and the actual state of affairs. Jacques Ellul spoke of the limits of propaganda in an appendix to his powerful book against the corrosive trans-ideological effects on democracy of the technique of propaganda.[129] First propaganda comes up against powerful pre-existing attitudes, second it has to adapt to the fundamental representations of national memory and history, third there is always the invalidating stubbornness of actual facts and events, and finally there is a need to make it unrelentingly continuous and consistent. It is, therefore, exhausting and difficult for those who attempt to maintain it and victory is, as for the torturer, never secure. There are other factors too. It can only operate effectively within a closed group in which the individual feels isolated from dialogue with others but is induced to need general communion with them. Orwell's hero of *Nineteen Eighty-Four* captures this characteristic perfectly. Then there is always the danger of the 'foreign' perspective and comparison. Propaganda is hard to export because it has to be tailored to the initiating country's memory and psychology.[130] This fact alone leads the argument back to questions of temporality. What memory survived and how would the stories add up in relation to the 'official version?' Like any other ideology or even religion, Marxism had a narrative of the past, a view of the present and a vision of the future. The leaking of one into the other mediated by historical contingency could only with difficulty produce the simple tale required by propaganda.

Ciliga's account more than exemplifies these aspects of propaganda during the period of his 'visit'. To begin with he was from the 'outside' even though the close kinship between the Yugoslav and Russian languages made communication easy. The Yugoslav left had a different historical and cultural experience, whatever the homogenizing discourse of history that the increasingly post-Bolshevik world offered. Those Yugoslavs who had been before on the same journey to the Soviet Union had already begun to return with their stories:

> These comrades, some openly, others secretly, began to tell the most terrifying tales of the state of the manual workers in the factories [...] Their lot was indeed worse, for in the [capitalist countries], the workers can protest in the Press and at meetings.[131]

Here, foreign experience combines with stubborn fact to undercut the almost metaphysical dimension of the story of the Stalinist future as endlessly progressive. Whatever technology was doing, the only human progress seemed to be backward as 'pre-existing attitudes', here bourgeois ones, seemed to flourish as citizens cynically adapted to new routes of personal survival and careerism. Party members were apparently the worst:[132]

> In his efforts to succeed, each man gave evidence of a totally unscrupulous capacity for adaptation and a shameless aptitude for the flattery of those in power. It was written in every gesture, on every face, in every eye. It was expressed in every act, in every speech, in the coarse revolutionary phraseology.[133]

Ciliga's critique is based on betraying signs of gesture and speech which construct a kind of psychological and behavioural theatre that undercuts the official story. The signs are read as evidence for an alternative story, a kind of Orwellian return, not at the level of ideology, indeed ideology only points up the difference, but a return to a kind of psychological and ethical truth of the ways in which people behave well or badly under the conditions of overweening power and terror. At the level of ethical behaviour the observation is, formally, ironic, measuring the distance between belief and act.

Ciliga gives endless examples of these formal 'ironies': better pay for Party members working at similar jobs to non-members; peasant workers denied the same rights as industrial workers in terms of pensions, holidays, social insurance, eight-hour days and holidays; rich men unpunished for speculating in the famine of 1921; the queues of the poor for food and basic commodities; men of poor origin, now powerful, abandoning their working-class wives for middle- or upper-class younger women; the thriving prostitution provision for the upper echelons of the Party. Of the latter Ciliga dryly commented:

> It is very reminiscent of what takes place in bourgeois society, where pretty girls marry rich old men. Socialists have always denounced this form of prostitution called marriage. And the analogy goes further. One day I had occasion to read a letter of the young wife of a very prominent People's Commissar to her lover, a student. It reminded me of the old cabinet ministers of Europe and the cheerful lovers kept by their wives. Nature, even in Soviet Russia, has her own back.[134]

What we have here is Ciliga's own little 'Balzacian' story. One hardly knows whether Ciliga approves or disapproves. Two ethical standards are applied. The socialist disapproval is clear if somewhat routine in tone, but 'nature' with its 'cheerful lovers' is rather approved of and much more emotionally engaging. The joint result is a distinctly bourgeois irony with its standard comic subplot, but the ensemble nonetheless illustrates with further irony the gap between ideology and practice.

Beyond this, however, is an approval of the power of the contingent to interrupt the secure world of totalitarian order, even if it is regularized in the genre of the comic sexual sub-plot, that is, to a degree made safe in a customary discourse of personal and historic memory. The phrases 'very reminiscent' and 'it reminded me of' call up the power of one story to refer to another. The 'story' depends on a metaphysical grand narrative of stoic cycle. A trans-temporal stability in the inferred repetition of the story's challenge to inhuman order (nature brings in its revenges) is of course a mode of satire that needs the regularity of its oppositions over time to appeal to an ultimately ahistorical common sense or, read more positively, to a unvarying Pascalian ethics outside history. Ciliga also cites moments when these kinds of incidents threatened to overwhelm the smooth façade of official order. Wives of GPU officials were known to prostitute themselves in secret to eke out the incomes of their husbands. Such behaviour, Ciliga suggests, seemed to thrive in the new Soviet society.[135]

Ciliga also objected to the new cult of the leader. It was profoundly opposed to the spirit of socialism and, if more tenuously, Bolshevik communism. Ciliga commented:

> It was not some over-zealous provincial bureaucrat, it was Stalin himself who was propagating his own cult within the precincts of the Committee. This fact alone is more significant than all the arguments on the true situation of party and country.[136]

But it is the cycle of absolute power of Orwell's *Animal Farm* that forms the central question of Ciliga's book:

> Neither the fact that the new order had ousted the bourgeoisie and the landowners in favour of bureaucrat and intellectual, nor the fact that it had supplanted the cults of Christ, Czar, and private property by those of Marx and Lenin, Soviet rule and State property-ownership, was really enough to make it palatable. There was undoubtedly an element of the incredible in this question: how was it possible that the great effort of 1917 towards emancipation should have ended in a new slavery, whilst preserving the 1917 slogans.[137]

Ciliga had the honesty to realize that a good deal of the theoretical apparatus of Marxism had to be rethought. It was necessary 'to look for an explanation, a new theory, and not to deny the facts in order to preserve the vanished theory'.[138]

As with Serge it is the haunting stories that are the most valuable part of Ciliga's book. They are stories of oppression in which the normal process of law is set aside under the totalitarian authority of State bureaucracy. The case of Zaune, a Latvian barrister, is a good example. Having distinguished himself in the Red Army during the revolution he eventually settled in Moscow as a barrister, specializing in cases where peasants were robbed of cattle during collectivization. Given the statutes of Soviet law, he won every case. He was therefore arrested under the pretence that this would facilitate his repatriation to Latvia but he was held first at Tver where he witnessed numerous executions of the peasants and then in Leningrad. Ciliga ends the story by noting that he is on hunger strike demanding to be repatriated, occasionally catching a glimpse of his wife who is imprisoned with their two daughters.[139] So the testimony of ruined lives and ideals drifts in and out of the narrative, with or without closure, in an atmosphere where there is no logic except that of arbitrary power, the torture of delayed judgements and the endless suspending of promised action; there is no common-sense connection between cause and effect or act and consequence. Here we have a narrative presentation of what Orwell, cited earlier (see p. 20), called the silence of an 'endless present'.

By contrast, the trans-Urals prison of Verkhne-Uralsk to which Ciliga was ultimately sent was comparatively free. The community, isolated within the walls that politically neutralized them, was free of bureaucratic harassment and Orwellian thought-police. Ciliga was struck by the fact that 'in the immensity of silence-stricken Russia the two or three small islands of liberty where men still had the right to think and speak freely' were the prisons.[140] Here, though the food was inadequate and monotonous (six slices of white bread in three years), Ciliga had the privilege of the foreign communist prisoner of being able to obtain adequate clothes and footwear. Two hours a day outside enabled the prisoners to walk, hold meetings, play tennis, football or *gorodki* (Russian ninepins) and in the summer they were allowed to grow flowers or vegetables.

There was also a considerable library with works in Russian, German, French and English. Books on sociology, politics and history were donated by incoming and released prisoners and the prison authorities occasionally even bought books. Ciliga himself was able to read André Gide's *Voyage au Congo* and B. Traven's *The Cotton Pickers*, both of which had been recently published. Gide is well known, but it is worth noting that Traven had an internationalist anarchist career as committed and sparkling as Serge's. Like Serge, he fled to Mexico where he eventually died. These days he is perhaps best known for the magnificent film adaptation of his novel *The Treasure of the Sierra Madre* by John Huston in 1948, starring Humphrey Bogart, Tim Holt and Walter Huston. However, *Der Wobbly* (or *Les cueilleurs de coton* in French) is the novel Ciliga refers to. It had already sold millions of copies in the non-Anglo-American world before it was translated into English eight years later. His description of the book as '*Coton*' presumably means that Ciliga read it in French.

The prison then was 'home'. This 'post of the good', with its sense of solidarity and the life of the mind, in a real sense saved these 'foreign intellectuals', serving much the same function as the small community of Serge's Marseille with its assorted artists and writers: 'it is no exaggeration to say that the political isolator of Verkhne-Uralsk, with its 250 political prisoners, constituted a veritable university of social and political sciences – the only independent university in the U.S.S.R.'[141] Finally, Ciliga was briefly interned in Irutsk, in an even better equipped prison which dealt with prisoners convicted under civil law and where 'Terror itself had ceased to impress.'[142] Ciliga charted remorselessly the progress of the totalitarian bureaucracy: its chief weapons of threats and psychological terror creating conditions in which rumour and paranoia were the principal methods of control.

The point about bureaucratic terror was its need to live in a timeless world. Jacques Ellul, speaking of Pierre Mendès-France in the de-colonializing world of the mid-twentieth century, highlighted the need to create a silence about the past: 'there was complete silence on past policies in Indochina, past events in Morocco that had led to events in Tunisia, and agreements on Indian banks signed by the preceding government.'[143] In Serge-like mood, Ciliga notes 'The execution of the men of the Leftwing Opposition or even of Yagoda, chief of the GPU, might be considered as the liquidation of the past, the removal of phantoms.'[144]

Ciliga's small narratives deal with the issue in various ways. One is the familiar device of slowing down time in an offered pastoral vision, the induration of the Wordsworthian shepherd. Such a narrative move involves running an ironic parallel of human time with cosmic time to show the vanity of human folly. Its tone is always ethical, as it suspends the movement of history:

> Towards the right the valley was broader. A few hills appeared between the road and the mountains. On the nearest one we perceived the ruins of an old castle, and we climbed towards in the glory of the rising sun. Shrubs had invaded the relics of feudal grandeur; there, where armed men used to drill, a flock of sheep was grazing.

> An old Georgian shepherd told us the legends of the land. He had been a shepherd before the revolution and had remained one since. In his eyes the world had never changed. He told the ancient legends with the same ceremoniousness as ever, perhaps with more, for he was grown old.[145]

The tone recalls Biblical wisdom literature: 'And moreover I saw under the sun the place of judgement'.[146] The broad recall of history, the rise and fall of power, the pastoral cycle replacing the epic, the romantic ruin and the shepherd himself, a cross between a 'survival' and 'survivor', retaining his local habitation and his name forms a vivid contrast with the bright new world of the homogenous proletarian worker with his heroic production quotas. The Georgian shepherd speaks, above all, the ancient stories. In the personal time he inhabits, the old ceremonies are threatened for they and he are growing old together. That poetic temporal conjuncture, the closure of a social *longue durée* and the closing of the individual life, creates a poetic synthesis in which one is not sure whether one is seeing the dead living or the living dead, for the tone is radically nostalgic: that is, the presence of the distant is somehow magically close by. For Ciliga, as for Victor Serge, the Caucasian world had a deep enchantment. It betokened a world beyond 'Europe'. It was also a pre-modernist past: exotic, distant, where the peasant bore a unique name in a specific locality with a particular folklore and music, distinguishing costume and crafts, genuine oral traditions and stories. It was a world still inflected with nomadism, transition, and cultural space-time interactions with a further East as far as China and a South-East that touched and embraced the Islamic world and India.

At a social level, Ciliga observed the Russian religious groups, the sectarian Russians, living in 'modest plenty'. The longevity and tenacity of religious life encouraged a resistance to the Soviet state, which outlived its existence. Baptists, many of whom who have lost their old radical integrity under pressure from mindless right-wing American evangelicalism, now flourish in the new Russia. But even the Molokans (milk drinkers) still cling on in small groups, divided between Russia and America, 150 communities having re-appeared in Russia since the fall of the Soviet Union. The Molokans had originally resisted tsarist-dominated Russian Orthodoxy as 'Spiritual Christian' Russian peasants in the early seventeenth century and, like Protestants in general, they were Bible-centred.[147] Russia, of course, has a long history of local resistance to orthodoxy in religion and state. What is emphasized here, however, is the radicalism of the preservation of a continuing past in a regime which rules by its insistence on an absolutist present. The religious groups preserved a holding operation within an inhuman totalitarian state where 'progress' or 'modernization' became a core concept of propaganda. Modernization revealed itself, in Mumford's words, 'as a perverse fantasy, born of ignorance or indifference to the phenomenon of life.

"Leaving the past behind" is the equivalent of leaving life behind – and with this, any desirable or durable future.'[148]

However, it is also important to remember that the Russian religious groups had often nourished within themselves seeds of a democratic community resistant to the pressures of centralized power. Tight-knit, hard-working and resilient, Russia's 'Old Believers' of the sixteenth and seventeenth centuries in Siberia had roots in a pagan Russian past. Their elders, like the radical seventeenth-century Protestants of the English Revolution:

> [...] were consistent advocates of the separation of church and state, each to be independent of the other. 'The prince has no right to consult with monks', or with 'those who have died' to the world, yet neither should the church have to obey the world; the shepherds should not 'be frightened of power' they should calmly stand for the truth, since 'holiness is greater than Tsardom', and the secular ruler is not the judge in religious matters. Faith is the personal affair of each person's conscience, and therefore a secular power has no right to persecute religious convictions.[149]

Later in *The Russian Enigma*, Ciliga gives a short account of the struggle between the church and state under Stalin. Here indeed was a classic Orwellian cycle of truth and absolute power repeating itself within a new historical situation. If the Old Believers had struggled against the tsars and the Russian Orthodox church, so the twentieth-century sects struggled against both the right wing of the Orthodox church and Stalin. Naturally the latter two formed an alliance, with the Orthodox service including a prayer for the 'secular' Soviet government.[150] Ciliga remarked ironically on the parallel struggle within the Communist Party. Speaking of the famously collusive Metropolitan Sergius (Ivan Stragorodsky), Ciliga remarked dryly: 'While on the Soviet stage, the comedy of the struggle against all religion was still being played, Stalin was entering into relations with the orthodox religion behind the scenes.'[151] Ciliga knew that the bishops' rebellion against Metropolitan Sergius was immensely significant, creating a new wave of martyrs and driving a wide range of church activity under-ground. He described the priests he met in prison, their varying theological positions rather like the political prisoners' varying ideological allegiances. Ciliga was clearly fascinated by all shade of opinion in the prison: Trotskyites (left and right), Decists, Zinovievists, Miasnkikov's 'workers' groups', revolutionary socialists, Armenian socialists, Maximaliksts, Mensheviks, Georgian social democrats, anarchists and even Zionists. 'The reader will exclaim', noted Ciliga, 'that twenty groups and sub-groups for two hundred prisoners seems ridiculous.' Drawn from all over Russia to Trans-Caucasian exile, they constituted what he called 'an illegal parliament'.[152]

Honest and openly expressed ideological difference always threatens the demagogue. Failure to remain different is one familiar result of any totalitarian system.

It is for many too psychologically strenuous a task, as indeed Orwell's Winston in *Nineteen Eighty-Four* found out. For those who did fail, Ciliga observed:

> A foreigner can hardly understand the attitude of the victims themselves. In no way did they put themselves up as champions of a political cause, less even as adversaries of the system. On the contrary, they thought only of being taken back again into society, such as it was, or finding work, of earning money, and of deserving their liberation. This tendency led to the following paradox: the workmen and the peasants remained on the lower rungs, whereas the members of the so-called 'abolished' or 'hostile' classes received favourable treatment, enjoyed privileges and mixed with the representatives of authority.[153]

Ciliga's critique of Marxism did not run to economics. It was offered as social, psychological and ethical judgements. His book offered clear evidence that the Soviet Union had drifted away from anything resembling a socialist vision. Free ideological discussion had degenerated to threats and intimidation. The workers' lot was worse than in capitalist countries and the peremptory boldness of Stalin had consolidated power through secret organization, mass propagandistic appeal and the cult of the leader. Quoting Goethe's 'All theory is hoary, but the tree of life is green', Ciliga spoke of the consequences of an hypostacized Marxist theory that was more and more out of touch with reality and reduced to the slogans of propaganda.[154] He also doubted the historical linearity of positivist Marxist prediction and closure. This meant in practice the reduction of 'progress' to technological development.

Given that Britain's industrial revolution was the model, this devotion to mass industrialization was taken for granted. Lewis Mumford's 'paleotechnic' civilization not only seemed an act of unstoppable fatality but was enthusiastically embraced. Was it this, or (given his Italian background) some futurist dream of industrial gigantism that led Ciliga, in the context of his approval of Stalin's agrarian policy, to declare that the 'industrialization of European and Asiatic Russia' was 'of fundamental importance to the historic progress of the Asiatic continent; for the economic, social and political revolution that is ripening throughout Asia'?[155] Elsewhere, however, he rejected this idea: 'If one were to judge merely by the number of factories, America would long since have been a socialist country. Socialism is not a factory but a system of human interrelationships […] The interrelationships in Russia are not of a socialist nature.'[156] The contradictions here are not resolvable, and need reformulating along Mumfordian lines, that is, a radical question as to exactly what the grand narrative of 'historic progress' is needs to be asked. Technological gigantism and industrial power are not necessarily the *sine qua non* of a 'great' civilization. They might indeed be its undoing. This particular contradiction was endemic in Russian liberal and radical theory right through the nineteenth century. Isaiah Berlin once noted, for example, that 'Chernyshevsky's writings contain statements both in favour of and against the desirability of large-scale industry.'[157]

But Ciliga was clear enough about the new technological elites. The construction of the road across virgin forest from the Pacific to the Arctic, 'the last word in American technique', is criticized in terms of the conditions of workers who 'died like flies', the high salaries of the chief engineers, and the new technocratic class who 'did not mix with the "middle layers" consisting of small officials and other convicts; as to the humble workers of peasant stock, whether free or prisoner, they had no contact with their superiors.'[158] The technical personnel (the IRT) formed one of the three main strands of power that Ciliga identified in Russia. The other two were the communist bureaucracy and the church.[159] Althusser would doubtless have seen all three as an unholy trinity of the ideological state apparatus.

Mercifully, Ciliga's text enjoys the advantage of presenting a complex discourse. He was critical of both Lenin and Trotsky. Lenin he attacked ironically, and not without humour, in the name of scientism: 'I find proof that you yourself have subjectively accepted the regime you were objectively bringing into being.'[160] As for Trotskyites, they did not criticize the emerging Stalinist dictatorship strongly enough: 'they were slightly more polite and human, that is all'.[161] Ciliga had been irked by Trotsky's refusal to assert that the new Soviet state was not a workers' state. He found tedious the tendentious purity of a clichéd projective historical narrative that the 'Soviet Union has not entered into the socialist phase as the Stalinist group teaches it, but only into the first phase of an evolution towards Socialism.'[162] As the English eighteenth-century satirist Alexander Pope famously remarked: 'Man never is, but always to be blest.'

There remain textual questions of genre, narrative perspective and its discourse of temporality. These frame and orientate the issues as much as ideological negotiations, and in the end their meaning does move beyond merely aesthetic considerations. Ciliga, like Daniel Defoe and Henry Adams, was writing a quasi autobiographical journal. Unlike Defoe the plague smacked more of Camus-like allegory than physical disease but, like Adams in his *Mont Saint Michel and Chartres*, the pose of the 'tourist' was ironically embraced. If the tourist from Yugoslavia set out to admire and returned to mourn, here was a possible epic temporal drama of Russia being drawn from the murky historical nightmare of 'backwardness' into the clarity of a society more 'modern' than any that yet existed. Like the American revolution of 1776 it would show that the future worked, a future however that could not be negotiated and was entertained beyond the shadow of a doubt.

To an extent Ciliga did admire. He was entranced by the exotic vastness of it all:

> A new style was making its appearance. 'The passion for destruction is a creative passion' were the words of an 1918 inscription on the Nikolskaya Gate. That inscription was soon to vanish along with the gate it adorned and the wall of Kitai-Goruod.

> The town was overflowing with vitality. The Five Year Plan was drawing near. One may criticize Moscow as much as one likes, one may lament the discrepancy that exists between the reality and the ideal, between promises and their realization, but one cannot deny the energy that inspires it and which makes itself everywhere felt.[163]

The peasants were initially enthusiastic: here was a chance for the destitute and poor to receive an education. The women of the Caucuses were feeling their power as women in a public world for the first time; the pride and dignity of the workers in Leningrad was beyond doubt.[164]

The extent of the admiration, however, was eventually to accent a terrible disillusion as the tourist descended through the various circles of hell. The tourist arrived to have a first conversation with a cab-driver who thought that the smartly dressed foreigner must have come from America.[165] His first conversation was hence with a man who praised the conditions of workers in America. Cab-drivers, who generally drive the comparatively rich and endlessly boast of celebrity passengers, are notoriously conservative but it was not a good start. Ciliga felt the 'drabness' of Russia on the pulses. The first woman he met who had taken an active part in the October revolution condemned the Soviet regime lock, stock and barrel.[166] A coachman in a Caucasian frontier town informed him that all the peasants were being persecuted in the name of the rich kulaks. Ciliga was self-critical enough to understand the temptations of impressionism. He also was very aware of the privilege of his own position, that of the revolutionary foreigner. Like Serge, he was a 'tourist' without a country. The exiled Yugoslavs, who included many Trotskyites as Ciliga tells it, criticized the collusiveness of communists in Yugoslavia to find themselves immediately *personae non gratae* in the Soviet regime, in conflict with the Comintern.

Ciliga's narrative voice became then, in shifting political circumstances beyond his control, one of a man without a country. It was a voice of exile, of someone without hope of return, to an extent a virtual refugee, moved from prison to prison, one forced to make a life in the present without the richness of a past or an immediate hope of a future. He did indeed find himself condemned to an Orwellian present. However, if the past was dead and the future unimaginable, he had the comrades of exile, a wandering band, largely of men who gave their survival the thickness of comradeship, intellectual thought and therefore significant meaning. He also had the advantage also of being young and up for adventure.

As a 'tourist', Ciliga found strangely that there was no real interest in foreign communist movements among Communist Party members in Russia. Ironically, especially given western paranoia, 'such a spirit [of internationalism] would not be tolerated.'[167] The reasons were obvious. If the workers of the world had united, individual comparisons of conditions and actual successes would have threatened every demagogic ruler the world over. No political leader likes foreign comparisons at any level. Keeping news relentlessly local or, at worst, national is the instinctive aim of any 'Ministry of Truth'. 'Socialism in one country' was the Soviet version of the phenomenon.

Russia itself was a problem in time. It was usually articulated in terms of a comparison with Europe: Russia had somehow 'missed' the Enlightenment and the Industrial Revolution. Like Napoleon's China, it 'slumbered' in relation to 'history'. In its place was 'Russia', celebrated by the poets as a unique spiritual space-time that transcended both ideology and the sufferings of despotic rule. Nineteenth-century Russian writers had focused closely on the phenomenon in both private and public terms. Indeed they had almost created it. There was something unique about Russia. It was not European. It was close to the earth, its peasant tradition encompassing an eternal, passionate, fertile, generous and ultimately mystic identity. As the exiled Ciliga climbed the slopes of Urals he wrote: 'Here neither men nor things showed the least sign of change. It was neither Asia nor Europe, it was simply Russia.'[168] Even the Orthodox church had to accommodate the ancient rituals and fierce sense of independence from the sects who claimed a profounder spirituality. In the myth created, the most enlightened rulers would be close to the farmlands and forests and attempt, patriarchally, to look after their serfs, even to share their lives.

In Tolstoy's *War and Peace*, Pierre, back from the historic encounter with cosmopolitan Europe at war and together with his wife Natasha, is settled finally into a deliberate nationalist isolation, exhibiting Tolstoy's distrust of the demagogic power of ubiquitous printed communication and the soullessness of natural science. Somewhat comically for contemporary readers, Natasha, unlike those French women who unreasonably seem to want to remain attractive throughout their lives, lets her figure go, abandons her 'feminine witchery' and her singing – music temptingly exported also by the French – and settles into a romantic individual icon of Mother Russia, immured in family values and a spreading waistline, a strong defence against the corruptions of foreign feminism and European modernity.[169] In Russia there was the same resistance to the inevitability of European industrial modernity, which is ironic now given the terrible ecological devastation created by big industry, inherited from Stalin's industrial push in the 1930s through to the Cold War. The nineteenth-century rhetoric of 'time lag' and 'modernizing' surely might not have meant catching up along the same lines. In historical terms the peasant *obshchina* had traditionally provided a resistance to the militarized and bureaucratized aristocracy. That resistance was ultimately broken, first by industrialization and then by Stalin.

In historical and cultural terms, the Slavic, utopian religious, local church-oriented (rather than strictly Orthodox and national) communal nexus of the village became a kind of Pascalian ethical site outside history, a tradition first given discursive reality by August Freiherr von Haxthausen, a German baron, but politicized as a critical utopia by Alexander Herzen. The tradition persisted, in cultural terms, from Tolstoy to Pasternak right down to the films of Andrei Tarkovsky. As late as 1981, Elem Klimov's extraordinary film adaptation of a story by Valentin Rasputin, *Farewell to Matyora*, provided a terrible and moving requiem for that nineteenth-century village dream under the ecological apocalypse of mindless technological gigantism. Herzen, Nikolai Chernyshevsky and even Marx had hoped that Russian development would bypass, in a more pastoral and organic way, the murderous and obscene conditions of the British Industrial Revolution with its utter disregard of working people and the natural environment.[170] The 'time-lag' could be read as backwardness needing radical revision or as a good conserving backwardness. It was a point of origin in a kind of Russian manifest destiny. 'Time lag' was a utopia to be moved towards, a golden age to be preserved against all progressiveness, and a scientific opportunity in the reason of history. The temporality (here looking forward, looking backward and looking to a universalist, paradoxically extra-historical time frame) within the narrative could therefore shift according to the requirements of a discourse produced in and offered to, any actual historical moment.

Ciliga more than reflects these considerations in his narrative. In seeking 'the final end' of all these dynamic forces,[171] his position hovers between a view of temporality inflected with the impersonal fate of Marxist productive relations, as well as doubts as to the ethical intelligibility of temporal purpose, since 'end' is at once goal, closure and meaning: 'the winter of 1927–28 marked the end of a stage in Soviet development; life itself as it were, drew some conclusions from the preceding evolution […] These conclusions had nothing cheerful about them.'[172] Winter is symbolically, even poetically, identified as a recidivist 'turning point' in a chronology of stages. Marxists were as obsessed with stages and redefining chronology as the Jacobins were before them, or indeed any bureaucratic administrator with a prophetic cast of mind. Evolution, approved in its Darwinist form by Marx as 'scientific', again stands outside human temporality but the cosmic time of its story sits uneasily with the frailty of human time. And irony is what Ciliga has in mind as the discourse of scientific evolution applied to human affairs spirals downwards to an increasingly terrorized society in which the food supply has faltered to the point of famine.

In place of progress, Ciliga offered a narrative of degeneration. He blamed the West for needing a narrative of progressive Marxist imperialism. Nothing, he asserts, could have been further from the truth:

> Even when their agents transmit revolutionary slogans to Communist Parties, they take precautions so that these slogans may remain matters of pure phraseology and never be put into practice. As for the hundreds and thousands of foreigners who go to visit Soviet Russia, they come back from it disappointed, demoralized and incapable of action. The Russian revolution in itself degenerating, drags the international revolutionary movement, to which at one time it had given so lively an impetus, down with it.[173]

Above all, this degeneration showed itself in the way the identity of the past and its discursive narrative itself was controlled. At the communist university in Leningrad, Ciliga noted, the history syllabus was altered every year, 'and historical facts and appreciations were biased with increasing insolence'.[174] Ciliga noted the shift in favour from the 'Extremists' to the 'Jacobins' as the Soviet Union descended into its own 'Thermidor'.[175] Even more comic was the yearly alteration of the *History of the Formation and Development of the Comintern*, one interpretation insouciantly contradicting another.[176]

With change and decay seemingly unstoppable, Ciliga, though less carefully than Serge, revalued the narrative use of stillness and cycle. Negative stillness was incarcerated in Lenin's mausoleum – still a site of contested iconography and duration:

> The mausoleum had been built in the style of the royal tombs of ancient Persia. It was the incarnation of the ideas of eternity and autocracy. There had been no reply made to the protests of the Left-wing architects against this reactionary style.[177]

Narratives of eternity, necessarily beyond time, and ancient despotism, the autocratic past of early civilized power, hence together characterize the psycho-pathological nature of Stalinist power and challenge, through a narrative of ethics as the eternal return, the crippling rhetoric of quasi-Marxist progressiveness. Lewis Mumford, in a late work, spoke of the return of the cult of divine kingship in the twentieth century: 'with the new dictatorships in Russia, Turkey, Italy, Germany and China since 1918, the once-banished cult of divine kingship was resurrected and made more effective by the new technologies for mass control'. He added: 'but the end product of this fraudulent inflation is a mummy: a corpse preserved in the Egyptian fashion, placed in a tomb for public worship. Even Lenin, who according to his widow "wanted no memorials to him," could not escape this ignoble deification.'[178]

There remains the question of personal time. There is a touching moment in Ciliga's sequel to *Le grand mensonge*. It is a tiny story of a woman that has echoes of Strindberg's *Miss Julie*. A young *bourgeoise* from the old regime becomes fascinated by the emergent male power-brokers of the Bolshevik revolution: 'with all the ardour of eighteen years, [she] was enchanted by the new rulers and their ideology'.[179] She marries but then, becoming tired of her first communist husband and his ideology, she marries a non-party specialist. He is now away in the north and she takes a proletarian captain up from the ranks as a lover. Both are thirty years old:

> There is something feverish in her passion, something of anguish. She is tired of life and of the Revolution. She clings to life still, it is true, but she is no longer sure of the future.
>
> With him it is quite otherwise. His rise is steady and continuous. For him she is a real prize; a social, cultural and physical conquest. Behind him and before him on life's road, he see nothing but victories [...] It is the middle of the day, but they close the shutters; they are not at home to the rest of the world. They live recklessly, for themselves alone.[180]

Here, the couple live history in different ways on a different trajectory of emotional temporality. Several time-schemes cross: the confidence of young beauty moves towards instability for the woman of thirty, paralleling the hope and then the betrayal of the revolution. Here, time is characterized as fate, impartial and almost cosmic in its Heraclitean restlessness. The contrast of futures is also pertinent. Differently gendered needs and a return to a traditional psychology of prize and capture come up against the woman's sexual attraction, like Miss Julie, for a rising class power. The power of Eros here translates itself into malign desperation. First and further erotic encounters are class nuanced and fascinating, denying an equal exchange that might lead to real comradeship in a world of contradictions. There is something here outside historical meaning, in the depths of the psyche. There is a fear that lurks at the heart of sexual happiness that does not escape an uneasy sense of temporality, loss or even a disappointment of fulfilment in comparison with previous need. In the adjustment of memory there is never complete satisfaction with what would have made for happiness at the moment of having nothing.[181]

Ciliga's narrative moment does not even have the tragic intelligibility of Hemingway's 'separate peace' in *Farewell to Arms*. Rather, in Ciliga, history's contradictions structure the desperation of a passion in which the lovers' isolation becomes a manic isolation. It reinforces Ciliga's perception and promotion of the 'inevitability' of an ironic Balzacian conservatism (but without the wit) in private life when the public sphere is a mass of lies. Its only outcome can be petty tragedy as the inertia of the old gendered expectations of melodrama take over. The failure of the public sphere is paralleled in the failure of private life. The experience of Ciliga's lovers, to adapt Marcuse's memorable phrase for use here, becomes 'euphoria in unhappiness'.[182] As real people live through real history, narratives of ideological certainty and the 'revolutionary' social theatre of desire crumble simultaneously.

And what of the author himself? Narrative closure is indicated in two ways. First, there is the romantic injunction to tell the tale in retrospect. One hundred comrades see Ciliga off on the first river trip to Krasnoyarsk, authorizing him, as the one escaped from Hell, to speak the truth. Here the narrative will partly pass into fable, that is, into ahistorical proverbial time. Yet it is not quite the last word, for Ciliga ends on a more personal temporal note: 'I left behind me the hardest years, yet the richest in experience and emotion, of my life.'[183] This distancing, the perspective from a different and very personal space and time creates nostalgia, that rich emotion where the unique individual memory links the present into its vanished past and is haunted by it. At its best, involuntary memory and deliberate memory are brought together in strange ways in the telling of the story. Ciliga's experience of failure is different from the woman already haunted by ageing. His narrated experience rests somewhere between the old captain and the young boy of Conrad's *Youth*, somewhere between a Miranda, anticipating a brave new world, and an ageing Prospero. Nonetheless, as the greatest political failure of the twentieth century passed into the unforgiving light of common day, Ciliga's story held in its traces a historical vitality and a refusal to countenance despair in the face of a very great betrayal. Even if it is occasionally crude and some of the judgements are naive, this narrative record with its narrative complexity and its unsparing ethical and political insights goes some way to refuting Macdonald's claim that the final truth of this defeated revolutionary was tragic weariness.

II

Simone Weil and the Time of the Soul

It was Nicola Chiaromonte, according to Sumner, who was among the first of Macdonald and his circle to criticize Marxism in terms of its inattention to the problem of ethics, the tenuousness of its narrative of historical reason, the chimera of the dictatorship of the proletariat, the banality of its scheme of progress, and its lack of a human sense of contingent existence and fate. He had offered a first analysis in *politics* in 1946. In the 1947 issue of *politics*, he extended the argument in a development of the idea of justice. Injustice, as Sumner correctly observes, was another term for dehumanization: a consequence of the 'petrifactive' qualities that Simone Weil had identified in the abuse of 'force'.[1] In 1933, as a twenty-four-year-old teachers' union delegate attending an action committee against war and fascism, Weil asked for information on the whereabouts of Victor Serge. She was immediately viciously attacked by the Stalinists. In the same year, on Christmas Eve, her parents put up Trotsky and his wife overnight so he could have a small conference with sympathizers. The French government had banned any meetings as a condition of his asylum. Soon Simone was arguing passionately with Trotsky. It turned into a major row. Trotsky's wife, who was listening in the room next door, remarked 'This child is holding her own with Trotsky!'[2]

Having beaten Simone de Beauvoir into second place in the *agrégation*, Simone Weil became one of a handful of truly outstanding thinkers of the twentieth century in politics, philosophy, theology and matters relating to the philosophical aesthetics of literary and artistic practice. She was also an outstanding teacher. Whether it was possible to agree with her or not, for she was as exasperating as she was dazzling, she was a scourge of lazy thinking and habitual thought. Her very dogmatism had the advantage of intuitive insights few could match and her disposition to Pascalian aphorism hinted at wisdom, albeit with a French toss of the head, rather than professionalized argument. Marxists and Catholics alike came under her scrutiny and both were found wanting. While she yearned to embrace the best truths of the Christian and socialist alike, her intellectual scrupulousness insisted on a tragic distance from the shallow opportunism, the hypocrisy and betrayals of organized church, state and party.

It was, of course, the ever-alert Macdonald who introduced her to the readers of *politics*. Her essay on the *Iliad*, 'The Iliad, or, the Poem of Force', translated into English by Mary McCarthy, produced an extraordinary reaction among the American readers of *politics*.[3] Demand for it was so heavy that it was reprinted and obtainable as a separate offprint. Even today suddenly to come across it for the first time and read it in the November 1945 issue of *politics* is to feel its power like a physical shock. Two months later, in the January issue, which had outlined the horrors of the mass rape of Berlin women by Russian soldiers, Macdonald wrote that it had raised a great deal of interest, adding: 'A great many people seem to share my own view that, in spite of the superficial remoteness of the theme, Simone Weil's article, besides being a profound interpretation of a great work of art, is also one of the most important political articles to appear in many years and relates directly to the present historical crisis we are living through.'[4] It is all the more strange, therefore, that a recent biographer in English wrote that 'it is the only essay [that she wrote] that is not of a social or political nature'.[5] That judgement, as we shall see, is entirely untrue. That poetry is neither social nor political is, however, a familiar theme. Whether on the right or left of the political spectrum, poetry is rarely thought to have any relevance to history and politics. Macdonald's view was correct, however. This poem was fundamentally political, though he somewhat wearily added that the Marxists would put such a claim down to the growing 'religiosity' of *politics*.[6]

In fact, part of the reason for the essay's power is that it contains, in an almost poetically compressed space, almost the whole range of Weil's thought from the political to the ethical, to the metaphysical. Her central concept of 'force' was to embrace (at the very least) the Marxist concept of reification, the Christian concept of affliction centred on the crucifixion (the abandonment of the Son by the Father), the concepts of the project, contingency and inessentiality of the Existentialists and Kantian ethical concepts of ends rather than means in defining the relations between human subjects. The result was a trans-disciplinary response to a poem that suggested that to lose any one of these different areas of human knowledge, in responding to the way the poem helped to understand the catastrophic effects of the ideological and political failures of human civilization between 1933 and 1945 would amount to political, ethical and spiritual lying. In it, the insights of both Pascal and Marx would became different sides of the same coin.

For it was precisely the political nature of 'force' that Weil had identified as a result of her experience of French working-class life. For her it was the worker's 'soul' rather than the body that, in submitting to force, was the greatest casualty of the industrial system. Positivistic secularizing Marxists, and humanists had ruled out, of course, the very possibility of discussing the human 'soul': it was merely a bourgeois individualistic red herring, a metaphysical nonsense. In redeploying the term, Weil showed that what was at stake was human dignity, choice and an authentic sense of selfhood and participation in historic and cultural activity. In a sense, she made central that whole view of the person that Marx had identified as divided and distorted by the experience of capitalist productive relations. Challenged by an engineering executive in 1936 that her view of working-class life was too dark and over generalized, she wrote that while she may have overreacted as a middle-class young woman to the shock of the rigours of factory work, it was precisely that distance between the middle- and lower-class work experience that enabled her to judge the damage:

> In the University, I had rights, dignity and a responsibility to stand up for. What do I have to defend as a woman worker in a factory when every day I must give up every kind of right at the very moment I glance at the clock.[7]

She spoke no less eloquently than Mumford had of this '*chronométrage fantaisiste*' (capricious timekeeping)[8] at the heart of the condition of slavery. The loss of self was absolute. She quotes Mimi, a young working-class woman, labouring in a sweatshop for eleven francs a day: 'They think we're machines [...] other people are there to think for us.' Exactly the sentiments of the American Frederick Taylor, noted Weil.[9] In her lectures on philosophy, Weil said that choosing to act in time gave time a semblance of eternity. By implication, the worker is robbed of this action and its accompanying enriching experience and is tempted to submit to time, that is to seek refuge from time in entertainment or drunkenness.[10] Like Marx, Weil distinguished sharply between work and labour. The difference in the experience of time was at the heart of the distinction.

Such insights on the nature of time had dominated her famous essay on factory work. Here she tried to plumb the depths of the degradation of the factory worker's radical unfreedom in detail. The first detail again was the time-clock which rendered the 'flow of time [...] as something pitiless, leaving no room for the play of chance.'[11] As for Mumford, it was the first effect on the human soul of that mechanization of the world picture. Today a tiny minority of favoured workers are endowed with 'flexi-time'. When the worker rebels and quits his job, Weil noted he will 'ask for his time'.[12] Power is about controlling time. Should the worker retire aged sixty-seven because we as a species are living longer? Pay and therefore power is regulated by the hour and the year. No qualitative judgement is allowed. Drunk with the quasi-youthful exoticism of power, a statesman or stateswoman clings desperately to the job at the age of eighty. The working drudge welcomes relief from the drudgery at any age. The worker's time, hence, literally belongs to someone else: 'From the moment one is clocked in to the time one is clocked out, one must be ready at any instant to take an order, like an inert object that anyone may move about at will.'[13] Any exercise of freedom outside that framework is put down with brute force, erasing any thought directed to a future: 'Thus, thought draws back from a future', in stupefaction.[14] The emotional experience of other categories of time, 'the week' for example, is similarly affected. At one point Weil exclaims 'And Sunday evenings!'[15] Sartre's incomparable description of Sunday afternoon in a small working-class town (Le Havre) in a chapter in *Nausea* comes to mind. Its final sentence sums up a day begun in its directed freedoms and ending in anticipation of the workers' bleakest of immediate futures: Monday morning. 'Behind me, in the town, in the big straight streets lit by the cold light of the street lamps, a tremendous social event was dying: it was the end of Sunday!'[16]

Speed of process within the dragging of time in work and in the fleeting time of leisure, the anxiety of not working fast enough, monotony, a reduced grudging comradeship directed by the statistical success of the product, isolation within competitive judgement; all these states of the workers' soul are outlined by Weil with forensic accuracy. She hence supplements Marx's analysis of the alienation of the worker from the ends of production. For Weil, as for Marx, the intelligibility of the industrial process is granted only to the owners of the means of production. A reversal of human value takes place: 'Society must be corrupted to its very core when workingmen can feel at home in a plant only during a strike, and utter aliens during working hours.'[17]

This is the effect of the operation of 'force' within the industrial system. Social, economic and political reforms are but sops to the system unless there is 'a radically changed awareness of the passing of time while working'.[18] For Weil 'time and rhythm constitute the most important factor of the whole problem of work'.[19] Her argument, worth quoting at length given the central topic of temporality in this book, has a metaphysical and religious dimension as she ponders, by implication, the great Jewish creation myth of Genesis.

> This world into which we are cast *does* exist; we are truly flesh and blood; we have been thrown out of eternity; and we are indeed obliged to journey painfully through time, minute in and minute out. This travail is our lot, and the monotony of work is but one of the forms that it assumes. But it remains not the less true that our thought was intended to master time, and this vocation, for such it is, must be kept inviolate in every man. The absolutely uniform and at the same time varied and continually surprising succession of our days and season are exactly conformable to our misery and our grandeur. Everything that is in some degree beautiful and good reproduces in some way this mixture of uniformity and variety; everything that does not is bad and degrading [...] What happens in a factory is that uniformity and variety are mingled all right, but the mixture is scarcely that achieved by the sun and the stars, to pursue our cosmic instance. For the sun and the stars, time is filled beforehand with a framework of ordered and limited variety having regular recurrences. This framework may lodge an infinite variety of events that are absolutely unforeseeable and partially innocent of order. The Futurity of one working in a factory, on the other hand, is empty because of its absolute unforeseeableness, and deader than the past because of the identity of the moments which succeed one another like the ticking of the clock.[20]

In her essay on the *Iliad* Weil noted that the suppliants before the sword in the *Iliad* were in precisely the same position: 'unfortunate creatures who have become things for the rest of their lives'.[21] In short, they are robbed of their futures, of the possibilities of the unforeseen and chance itself and reduced to present of the linear monotony of quantitative time. As with the existentialists, the 'project', that anticipation of acting produced by foresight, the heart of being human, is here denied. In her essay on factory work, Weil had insisted that 'throwing the future open to working men in the sense of making it possible for them to envisage it'[22] articulates the fundamental role of the ancient virtue of hope in human consciousness itself.

The connection between political theory and the poem is sealed in the following statement from another essay:

> Thus there is in the very essence of power, a fundamental contradiction that prevents it from ever existing in the true sense of the word; those who are called the masters, ceaselessly compelled to reinforce their power for fear of seeing it snatched away from them, are for ever seeking a dominion essentially impossible to attain;

> beautiful illustrations of this search are offered by the infernal torments in Greek mythology.[23]

War was the most naked theatre of force. While attacking the assumption of the prestige of war from Proudhon to Engels, that is, in terms of its calculation of interest for the proletariat, Weil noted the difference between this and the later communist assumption that all wars are imperialist in character and can only defeat the working class. In addition, 'the formulations of the great theoreticians of socialism on the impossibility of condemning war as such were completely forgotten'.[24] The coming war, noted Weil, will not be a war between two imperialist powers but between two political regimes.

In her earlier essay for *politics*, 'Reflections on War', Weil had noted: 'war constitutes a clearly determined species of violence, the mechanism of which we must study before we can form any opinion'.[25] While she emphasized the need for specific analysis, she noted that modern war had generalized and abstracted the meaning of war via technological advance and a capacity for the centralization of power. It was led by men who did not fight, and allowed the state apparatus to mobilize against 'all men old enough to bear arms'.[26] That is, without risk to themselves, she dryly noted, they send them to their deaths. The further need is for internal as much as external security. Each man feels the force of state power over his destiny assisted by a religion of state, however ideologically legitimated. This was the central insight of the essay on the *Iliad*. She cited Robespierre: 'The condition of war settles for the State all other cares; one is quits with the people as soon as one gives it a war.'[27]

Weil originally wrote 'L'Iliade, ou le poème de la force' for *Les Cahiers du Sud* while in Marseille (like Serge, with whose work she was acquainted) at the end of 1940 and the beginning of 1941. It was in this essay, under the name of Émile Novis, that Weil distilled the entire range of her thoughts on ethics, politics, philosophy, religion and metaphysics into a single piece of commentary that rose to the rhythmic intensity and intellectual compression of poetry. Macdonald's selection of this essay bears witness to his genius as an editor and to the young Mary McCarthy's skill in translation. Like Macdonald's essay on the atomic bomb, it reached the notice of, and was publicized by *Time*. It was reprinted as a separate pamphlet available to the readers of *politics* and many subsequent commentators have thought it her finest essay. The date of its appearance at the end of the war spoke uniquely and with appalling ethical relevance to, a world in physical and psychological ruin. Weil's selection and political and ethical judgement of the poem can be contrasted with its virtual censorship in the American Armed Services Editions issued by the Council on Books in Wartime. Fussell makes the point that they reprinted the *Odyssey* but not the *Iliad*.[28] In a sense, then, and with almost too neat an immediate political relevance, *politics* delivered a powerful counter judgement, and broke the censorship.

The essay can be considered in three interlinking ways: in its powerful analysis, via critical philosophy (principally Hegel), of 'force': a static almost atemporal concept; second, in relation to this book's major theme, as an analysis of temporality which will involve a politics of human narrative; third, in relation to the extension of Greek thought into Christian thought about the nature and practicability of a human ethics. Beginning with critical philosophy, one of the central concepts of the essay is the notion of externality. For Weil, violence is external to the participants who even seem, in a sense, innocent of it, that is, they are innocent of its meaning. The very fact of birth means each one is destined to suffer violence. Further, 'violence obliterates anybody who feels its touch. It comes to seem just as external to its employer as to its victim'.[29] Further, 'the conquered brings misfortune to the conqueror, and vice versa'.[30]

Weil seems in many parts of her essay almost to be paraphrasing classic moments of Hegel's famous section 'Lordship and Bondage' in *The Phenomenology of Mind*. It seems almost as if she had the book propped up in front of her. It was here that Hegel analysed the dialectical play of self-consciousness between its own consciousness and other consciousnesses as a play of forces, a flux of 'inherent necessity'.[31] During this movement, the self confronts itself as 'an independent object' while simultaneously the reciprocal action of the other also senses 'a pure abstraction of existence for self.' The self in a moment of insight realizes that it is not 'tied up with life'. In this realization, or one might even say ensuing panic, of participating in a process which is only half-willed, the self 'must aim at the destruction and death of the other'.[32] The 'struggle' is unavoidable, a fact, as Weil says, of birth. However, in Hegel's words this trial by death also contains within itself two tragic results: the first is that it cancels the truth projected in its very promotion; the second is that it also destroys the certainty of the self. This latter point is fundamentally assumed throughout Weil's essay.

Taking the argument about consciousness and existence into the ethical and political domain, Hegel famously showed how these two interdependent moments vividly articulated the relation between lord and bondsman or, as it is sometimes translated, master and slave. Each continually cancels the other's otherness, while recognizing themselves as each other only in a life-and-death struggle. Weil agreed with Hegel that the master can recognize himself in the slave who, as a slave, is inessential thus cheating the master of anything worth having power over. The slave, in his inessentiality, cancels his relation to any kind of natural existence. Both place themselves outside any positive relation to natural existence since each must aim at the death of the other.[33]

Weil, as an essentially Platonic French writer, finds 'a geometric strictness' in the operations of violent power, which exhibits, nonetheless, by the sheer absence of limits, an external and equilibrating operation of force over human beings. Weil uses expressions such as 'pure momentum' and speaks of retribution as 'geometrical rigor'.[34] There is here an absolute power, incapable of moderation and the human spirit is bowed beneath what it encounters. Destiny shows no favours either to the powerful or those they oppress. In short, in violence no one wins. The radicalism of this argument makes a distinction between suffering and affliction. Affliction is the deeper experience, just as death is less a trauma than life-in-death. Weil begins at the beginning with the murdered human body: a thing without value, a thing in itself without immortality. In sheer absence the victor has nothing to triumph over, no relation to the thing that opposed him. The intoxication of force, the wantonness of the conqueror, as the victim is crushed, is a hallucination. It is only an almost impossible and rare generosity that can break this circle of mutual destruction.

What concerns Weil more, however, is the idea of those effectively living death. Their oppressors rely on 'that ability to turn a human being into a thing while he is still alive'.[35] As Priam clutches Achilles' knees he is already dead in a ruthless denial of his presence: 'In their presence, people move about as if they were not there; they, on their side, running the risk of being reduced to nothing in a single instant, imitate nothingness in their own persons.'[36] She speaks of those who without dying 'have become things for the rest of their lives [...] a compromise between thing and corpse.'[37] In his famous essay on civil disobedience, Thoreau once defined the nature of the soldier in not dissimilar terms, as 'a man laid out alive and standing'.[38]

These are trans-historical and trans-ideological moments of ethical judgement that articulate the silence of the slave, the statistical anonymity of the holocaust victim, the patient whose physiological symptom is the only thing recognized in the gaze of the scientist, doctor or nurse, people of other faiths and nations before the religious or chauvinist fanatic, the migrant worker or refugee in an immigration office, the slave, the hostage before an executioner, the tortured before the torturer, those reduced to bare subsistence, or dying of hunger, and anyone held illegally without charges or trial. Weil insists on that nadir of horror in the repetitions and permanence of historical practices of overweening power. The final secret of war is not between powerful opposing strategists (unlike for Marxists and capitalists, issues of temporality and history occupy for Weil an important but ultimately lesser, that is pragmatic, level of truth): 'battles are fought and decided by men [...] who have undergone a transformation, who have dropped either to the level of inert matter, which is pure passivity, or to the level of blind force, which is pure momentum. Herein lies the last secret of war [...]'.[39]

For Weil, pacifists and conscientious objectors were needed saints, but in recognizing and acknowledging them, she also recognized their rarity. That rarity, the exception that proved the rule of an ineradicable atemporal ugliness and violence, also suggested, somewhat paradoxically, the foundational temporalities of human history and behaviour. Against the millennial vision of progress and peace whether Marxist or capitalist, she placed the permanence of human 'death drawn out the length of a life' for the mass of the earth's peoples, and then investigated that condition precisely in terms of a denied temporality for both the oppressor and the oppressed. The victor of the moment, a Hector or Achilles, 'forgets to treat victory as a transitory thing'.[40] The future has been ignored in a hallucinatory present. For the victim the relationship between death and the future is reciprocally different:

> For other men death appears as a limit set in advance on the future; for the soldier death *is* the future, the future his profession assigns him. Yet the idea of man having death for a future is abhorrent to nature.[41]

Here Weil acknowledges, as the existentialists did in somewhat different terms, that fundamental human need to imagine the future as a freely chosen project. This present is a nightmare without past or future where the mind passes continually through the spectre of death itself.

Turning to the human experience of history, Weil, like Ricoeur, insists on the connection, linkage and leakage between the traces of the absent past reconstructed in generous and informed memory living through the 'having been' and imagining the 'not-yet'. It is precisely in the context of an argument about temporality that the constituents of Weil's grand narrative of the requirements for the soul emerge. The condition of the slave or bond-servant is characterized by that loss of inner life in which the human subject remembers the past, makes choices in the present and imagines a future. This 'loss of the whole inner life' is the fundamental condition of slavery: 'curses, feelings of rebellion, comparisons, reflections on the future and the past, are obliterated from the mind of the captive; and memory itself barely lingers on'.[42]

Nor is it simply an abstract view of memory. Weil specifies the contents of historical memory in very diverse ways and not always as a resource. At its most extreme, memory can become unbearable and paralysing, involving the human subject in acute trauma. In the *Iliad*, death far from home and loved ones occurs again and again. Distance in time and space characterizes an unbearable nostalgia, a violent rupture from the paradox of a living past which is 'present' but not at hand. Again, this is true for both victor and vanquished. Suffering has to be perpetuated because it blots out that reflection on the past that becomes unendurable: 'Troy and Helen are in reality mere sources of blood and tears; to master them is to master frightful memories'.[43] The cure is another round of destruction to alleviate a despair in which silence is as powerful a weapon as the sword. Nietzsche was only half right to observe that the aristocrat has no memory. Half right because the refusal points to a further truth in which a brutal denial of memory is shown to result from panic in the soul.

One small moment in the essay is of crucial importance in this respect. It is where Weil notes the image of the fountain at the gates of Troy. As Hector runs past it to attempt to save his life it signals, for Weil, a 'poignant nostalgia':

> Close by there stood the great stone tanks.
> Handsomely built, where silk-gleaming garments
> Were washed clean by Troy's lovely daughters and housewives
> In the old days of peace, long ago, when the Greeks had not come.
> Past these did they run their race, pursued and pursuer.[44]

Here stone tanks indicate the peaceful life of the city with its long memories enshrined in its very architecture and civic amenities ('handsomely built'). As Lewis Mumford and Patrick Geddes knew, one reads the past in the present in the landscape of a city and that past is what gives city and citizens the very essence of human existence itself. It is precisely for this reason that Weil asserts: 'The whole of the *Iliad* lies under the shadow of the greatest calamity the human race can experience – the destruction of a city.'[45] Coventry, Dresden, Hiroshima and, in our own time, Grozny and al-Fallujah bear witness to the capacity of all national powers, irrespective of ideology or declared aim, to commit this grossest and most unforgivable of political acts.

Here in the discussion of the *Iliad*, therefore, Weil touches her great theme of the necessity of the past or, in her terms, 'roots'. Conquest is nearly always an evil because it involves uprootedness.[46] This literal 'alienation' is, however experienced in many other ways. She noted that United States was formed by a massive historical uprootedness and that it might become a very dangerous country as its power increased. Certainly its inability to recognize other ways of belief and forms of life as human, as well as its tendency to smash up other peoples' ancient and long-established cultures to give them the benefits of Coca Cola and 'democracy', may well at least in part be a result of this unique historical fact of settlement, though this abuse of imperial power and indifference to others is hardly unique to the United States. The nation merely, in this respect, joins a dreary historical list.

Certainly, however, the following admonition seems of particular relevance to American popular consciousness, what Gertrude Stein once mocked in her great work *The Making of Americans* as 'beginning again'. As Weil wrote in *The Need for Roots*:

> It would be useless to turn one's back on the past in order simply to concentrate on the future. It is a dangerous illusion to believe that such a thing is even possible. The opposition of future to past or past to future is absurd. The future brings us nothing, gives us nothing; it is we who in order to build it have to give it everything, our very life. But to be able to give, one has to possess; and we posses no other life, not other

> living sap, than the treasures stored up from the past and digested, assimilated and created afresh by us. Of all the human soul's needs, none is more vital than this one of the past. [...] The destruction of the past is perhaps the greatest of all crimes.[47]

Long before Eisenhower's famous speech about the 'military-industrial complex', Weil identified the nature of war with capitalist production itself. Trapped inside a double oppression of the factory and the army, the worker becomes as much a thing as Priam before Achilles, knowing 'the sensation of no longer existing, accompanied by a sort of inner vertigo'.[48] Again, time comes into it, the time that Mumford so clearly identified with the machine: 'There is a certain relation to time which suits inert matter, and another sort of relation which suits thinking beings. It is a mistake to confuse the two.'[49] The result of that confusion is to reduce the worker to something less than human: 'To be free and sovereign, as a thinking being, for one hour or two, and a slave for the rest of the day, is such an agonizing spiritual quartering that it is almost impossible not to renounce, so as to escape it, the highest forms of thought.'[50]

Weil uncovered the deep structure of the exploitation of working people, not in the materialist terms of positivist Marxism, nor indeed as the mass abstract tool of historical productive forces, but more in the spirit of Marx's earlier insights that the individual human subject in the exercise of her or his powers begins in freedom, and in multiple directions at precisely the point where necessity ends. For equal with hunger was destitution of mind. Her solution was to radicalize traditional right-wing positions. Against the 'Protestant' call to sacrifice and devotion she placed the 'Catholic' principle of obedience as a liberating principle. She translated the concept of original sin into the ubiquity of the universal and unalterable operation of force. Here we reach the limits of Weil's thoughts. Her God has cut himself off, ethically speaking, from the world. It is the world of Plotinus where God can look down but man cannot look up: 'between me and him is the thickness of the universe – and that of the cross is added to it.'[51] Her call is for sainthood in a world where it cannot be effective. An endlessly limited action against radical evil clears away all sentimentality about the prospect for change, but it hardly motivates it. For Weil, unless the self permanently realizes its loneliness, it will never see straight. There is little comfort here to be found in human solidarity and ordinariness which probably prompted Kenneth Rexroth's outburst in a letter to Macdonald, picked up by a recent biographer, to the effect that Weil should get baptized, obey the ten commandments, go to Mass, put some meat on her bones and get a husband.[52]

That thread of irritation, whether in exactly these terms or not, must be common to many readers of Weil. There is her dogmatism and over-hasty judgements about literature. In her conversation, by all accounts, these might have been deliberately provocative gestures to engage in the fierce exchanges she loved: an almost courteous cue for opposition. She seemed to have missed the warmth within Proust's pitiless irony, the radically altered world that the surrealists honestly confronted, the integrity of the torments of Gide and the morality of his depiction of amorality. Her valorization of goodness as truth, essentially in specific types of art, is as dubious as is her too ready and certainly too hasty denunciation of decadence in the writers of modernity. She declared it hard to believe anyone could be evil, for example, 'who thirsted for Gregorian chanting'.[53] Many find this quite possible, a fact which has little to do with the glories of Gregorian chant.

Weil saw the faults of democracy more than the necessity of its imperfect virtues. Ultimately, in spite of her love of poetry and the classics, she distrusted language as much as Plato distrusted music. The highest truth was wordless. Her Platonic view of the world afforded her greatest insights but it also had its limits. There was a final irresolvable contradiction between her powerful plea for roots, being 'at home' in the world and her mystical conviction that 'appearance chains being down'.[54] Between chastity and faithful marriage there was no compromise, no room for a generosity towards human error, nor indeed complexity. And while the marvellous insight that friendship needed distance is an ethical insight of enormous value, and while she wrote movingly on its supreme value per se, to compare it simply with the compassion called forth by affliction was too quick a judgement. Distance is only one powerful strand of the truth of reciprocity in the always multiple-layered experiences of that foundational human experience. [55] There is something darkly and passionately masochistic in Weil's reverence for affliction even when it is accepted that it is the most powerful truth of the human world and of human consciousness itself. Her Platonism also needed, in religious terms, for the world to be abandoned by God even though, paradoxically, beauty for her indicated the incarnation.

Rexroth, in spite of his patriarchal judgements, also knew Weil's value. After all, here was a woman who wrote in *Gravity and Grace*, almost echoing the evaluation of Pound in *The ABC of Reading*: 'Poetry: *impossible* pain and joy. A poignant touch, nostalgia. Such is Provençal and English poetry. A joy which by reason of its unmixed purity hurts, a pain which by reason of its unmixed purity brings peace.'[56] So moved had he been by her work that in an earlier letter to Macdonald he had given a quite different sense of her impact on him. In January 1946, he commented on the *Iliad* essay that it was 'very very good'.[57] When she died, he emotionally wrote again to Macdonald:

> I owe to Simone Weil what rehabilitation of my moral integrity I have been able to manage. And she was only thirty-four? My God, she must have written that essay sometime in her twenty-sixth year![58] I feel as though I had killed her. And of course – ultimately – metaphysically – I did kill her. Every time a person acts beneath the fullness of his humanity, he commits murder.[59]

Extravagant though the response was, it reciprocated the sense of responsibility that lay at the heart of Weil's work, and to which, thanks to Macdonald, American readers of *politics* had access to for the first time. It was finally predicated on her profoundest insight in her conclusion to the *Iliad* essay, that whoever does not know that necessity and fate are common to all, the very fact compelling love of and justice towards those whom chance appears to have separated by an abyss, will be incapable of human love. Sadly, she noted, such insights were as rare as a true description of misfortune and anguish itself.[60]

politics and the Existentialists

The last great European writers Macdonald introduced to American readers were the so-called 'existentialists'. Since Macdonald's publication of Weil's essay in 1945, the world had settled into an uneasy peace. The exploding of the atomic bomb seemed, to sensitive and thoughtful people, to have cut off a human future and produced a torment of the soul, at least the equivalent to the silent physical suffering of millions, which of course continued, always radically unpublicized and pushed out of sight by the powerful immediately after any war. Memories of lost homelands, children, husbands, wives and lovers, the irreparably psychologically damaged and physically incapacitated will always remain, with the defeated, outside history unless that memory can be manipulated, often as right-wing political capital.

It was the merit of *politics* not to flinch from that task and here Macdonald was ably assisted by the vision of the existentialist writers. Americans in general dubbed the existentialists 'too gloomy' and at best were to prefer the gentler Camus to the more politically aggressive Sartre. The second point will be taken up later, but first of all it is important to note that the acknowledgement of misfortune was something Americans were, officially at least, not good at. To be gloomy was to be un-American. It upset the powerful. It was something to which pessimistic Europeans and unsmiling 'niggers' were prone.

Gloominess had its temporal inflection of course: Europeans dwelt on the past, Americans on the future. In *politics* by contrast, between the issues that contained Weil's essay and Macdonald's introduction of the new French writers to the American public, some of the shocking events of the war and its aftermath were unsparingly covered: the mass rape of the women of Berlin and the plundering of luxury capitalist goods by Soviet soldiers in an absolute frenzy of revenge for almost four years of terrible suffering; boys in Naples pimping their female relatives for British soldiers; American officers flying to North Africa and prioritizing transport of cans of paint for their clubhouses while, owing to their inattention, American infantry died in their thousands; American backing of the Japanese collaborationists in the Philippine parliament and judiciary;

American collaboration with Soriano (who helped fund Franco and headed the local Falangist club); General MacArthur imposing a censorship on news; American soldiers accusing British soldiers of being 'nigger-lovers' and their general hostility and contempt; Churchill's incitement of an ideological war against Russia and his brutal crushing of Greek left opposition; the 'ambiguity' of the British Labour Party over the fast-fading British Empire; the continual failure of agricultural business interests in America to release food to starving Europe; Soviet mistreatment of prisoners and deportation of Germans; the assignment of 'steerage' to Jewish immigrants to the United States when their relatives had paid passage far above the cost of 'steerage'; Jim Crow behaviour in the American Seafarers International Union and Sailors Union of the Pacific; the British Labour government clamping down, imprisoning and deporting trade unionists from Cyprus to Singapore; the exposure of the notorious Soviet scientist Trofim Lysenko, a geneticist who claimed he could make four harvests a year; the continued harsh treatment of conscientious objectors after the war; the moves towards Apartheid in South Africa; the Treaty of Potsdam, which Macdonald described as 'this hysterical project of Carthaginian vengeance'; the colonial arrogance of the British officer class in defeated Germany; the antics of Herbert Hoover as America moved to Cold War; the shocking treatment of the mentally ill in United States medical institutions.

'Gloomy' would seem a relatively mild response to even a small proportion of this rare uncensored news. Even so, *politics* missed some of the worst tragedies: for example, two million Bengali and two million Vietnamese citizens dying of famine owing to the incompetence of the British and French in the dying days of their respective empires. Nevertheless, Macdonald printed all the news that was not fit to print, and it is to his absolute credit that he did so, even at the risk of being 'gloomy'. On the more reflective scale of things, not the least of Macdonald's achievements was to bring knowledge of misfortune, and uncensored descriptions and analyses of it, into an aggressively optimistic society. A protagonist in James Baldwin's *Tell Me How Long the Train's Been Gone*, speaks of the 'unnerving cheerfulness' of the medical profession: 'one does not dare speculate upon what awful knowledge the cheerfulness hides'.[61] One might with equal justification contemplate the unnerving cheerfulness of the American Dream.

It was hardly surprising, perhaps, that it was intellectuals living in defeated France who attempted to think and analyse misfortune in more profound terms than others, and in that analysis found wanting the apparently happy certainties of Stalinist communism and American capitalist individualism. Given the orientation of the European critical philosophical tradition (Hegel, Kierkegaard, Heidegger, Jaspers, Sartre himself, to cite some major names), which placed a response to the anguish of the human condition at the centre of philosophy, any denial in 1945 of (in Muriel Rukeyser's words) 'the inner frenzy and the outer doom' in individual and historical experience respectively, would have seemed dishonest. The pervasive, deafening and ubiquitous charge by Americans against the existentialists was that they were simply 'pessimistic'. This charge involved grotesque simplification, blindness, anti-intellectualism, intellectual laziness, fantastic historical denials, a failure to recognize the existence of abuses of power and a refusal of a fate common to all in the mutuality and reciprocity of human historical existence. For Americans, the vision of the existentialist was too much a mirror of the war, time had moved on (all by itself) and Husserl's no-longer was irrelevant to the not-yet.

In 1945, somewhat to the chagrin of American and British thinkers, whose logical positivist tradition held virtually unchallenged sway in their own countries, these 'existentialist' philosophers from France were beginning to write some extraordinary works which would dominate the life of the mind for the next two decades. It should be noted that a second wave from France, including Lévi-Strauss, Derrida, Foucault and half a dozen others would eventually dominate the humanities departments of the Anglo-Saxon academy, especially 'cultural studies'. Given the home-grown tradition of both pragmatism and logical positivism, and general ignorance of German, French and traditions of idealistic philosophy, the encounter would produce some curious results among largely monoglot Anglo-American academics, as historians scurried to their pragmatic and positivistic corners and literary theorists to a heady world of reified abstraction.

The seeds were all there in 1945. A very useful recent book on the reception of Sartre in America outlines some of the difficulties of getting across this particular transatlantic bridge, at least from east to west, with any idea intact.[62] It provides a useful retrospective context for the November 1945 issue of *politics*. There was, for example, an initial difficulty of the 'vogue' of Sartre in an increasingly publicity-conscious and nationalist academy. Lacking adequate translations, quite unlike the luckier Camus who wrote novels for example, few American philosophers had the means of grappling with the work at first hand. Analytic philosophy, as already mentioned, was another barrier. The pre-reflective ego as primary consciousness could not be assimilated within its framework of thought. In the pragmatic tradition, attempts would be made to link William James and Sartre.[63]

Sartre's philosophy was also felt to be 'impure', the cardinal sin of the always categorizing academy. Mixing up literature and psychology with philosophy was like bringing the question of ethics into Marxist dialectical materialism. Not until the generation of Ricoeur was a philosopher likely to agree in a hurry that a literary text might reveal philosophical truths of a nature that might equal or even outshine formal philosophical thinking. There was no training, no experience, nor inclination for a richly synthetic text. Anything that mixed up genres and subject boundaries, that introduced colloquial gestures, referred to immediate events as an indication of contemporary relevance, or, heaven forbid, ventured humour, was simply 'literary', or worse, 'poetic'. Sartre was as fiercely opposed as

Mumford to reductive academic specialization and he stands almost unique to this day, the unsung heroic foe of a debilitating and meretricious 'seriousness'.

Sartre was known to be a militant atheist and as someone (much assisted by the nineteenth-century tradition of the European novel) who hated the banalities, the self-satisfied consciousness and hypocrisies of certain types of middle-class existence, his thought, emphasizing negativity and alienation, simply puzzled the well-fed and insular communities of the American city, the American suburb and the American suburban campus. In any case, to recognize officially the anguish and difficulty even for the well-fed, at the heart of all daily existence was simply un-American. Both atheism and an acknowledgement of anguish were therefore hardly factors that would endear him to Americans. His later links with Marxist traditions ran up against the suppression of socialist thought and action, endemic in America following the Haymarket riots of 1885, the reaction of 1919 and, most pertinently post-1947, the prejudices of the Cold War and McCarthyism.

Husserl's (along with Heidegger's) reappraisal of the tradition of ontological thinking after Nietzsche's powerful demolition of it in the nineteenth century, had led Sartre to reformulate appearance as a disclosure of being, but the French thinker's insistence on the immediacy of concrete experience (in all its complexity including 'bourgeois' existence) and his clear literary sense of the contingent led him to value the explanation more as an untidy description than as something approaching an *a priori* theory. In the reception of Sartre, the status of metaphysics itself was to be a thorny question. From Heidegger Sartre had also reintroduced the whole question of temporality, turning anguish into an occasion for choice and the future project. For this book's investigation of narrativity, Ann Fulton's summary is crucial: 'Sartre adopted Heidegger's view that the individual's past was not a compendium of completed events; the meaning of the individual's past was continually reinterpreted to determine its relevance for future projects.'[64] And that went for class experience as well.

Sartre, along with the other existentialists, emphasized the temporalized concreteness of history itself. In American popular consciousness, the past was not something that needed reappraisal. It was completed and over. Psychologically, at any rate for Americans, the American revolution had revealed the Great Design with its eternally lingering eighteenth-century atemporality. It was the more primitive Europeans who looked to the past, indeed they were the 'past', which the revolution had simply superseded. It was equivalent to temporal racism. Americans knew that the future was theirs and that it was going to work. To investigate the past as something that might be relevant to this future seemed pointless. It unsatisfactorily re-opened a satisfactory completion of history as such. Such a point of view, of course, was very useful to those who wished to preserve the *status quo*. The Latin tag *in statu quo ante* or *nunc* elides the possibility that the present might be different from the past, a move which paradoxically confers immobility on the future by assigning it *a priori* a non-reflection on the past. A proverbial immobility inflects this kind of nationalist consciousness. *Plus ça change, plus c'est la même chose.*

By transforming Husserl's no-longer, and not-yet into an occasion for reflective thinking, Sartre insisted on a re-creative knowledge of history itself. The danger of this was that the American past, as an American past, might be found wanting. For Sartre, an individual's place in history could only be recognized by a reflective participation in it. Along with his parallel re-reading of Hegel, Sartre opened up a means of recognizing both the historicity of reason and a real possibility of investigating undisclosed rationalities as descriptions of history itself.

It was thirteen years before Sartre's *L'Être et le néant* was translated into English in 1956. On average it was fifteen years before each of Sartre's works was translated. There were exceptions to this general poverty of reception. Philip Rice, the chair of the philosophy department at Kenyon College, in an article published in the *Kenyon Review* in 1950 wrote: 'the French philosophers have at least been seeking wisdom, whereas our own younger men have been seeking merely clarity'.[65] And there were others, as Ann Fulton has shown. Americans were, notwithstanding, particularly receptive to Sartre's emphasis on the individual and the nature of choice in his philosophy. Although the word about the existentialist writers had been out since 1945, the August edition of *politics* in 1947, gave most of its readers their first chance of reading some very distinguished French thinkers. I will read here the ensemble of what was offered to them, by concentrating briefly on articles by the five of the most famous names: Simone de Beauvoir, Georges Bataille (not an existentialist thinker as such), Albert Camus, Maurice Merleau-Ponty and Sartre himself.

To take them in the order of their appearance in the journal, de Beauvoir ('An Eye for an Eye') wrote on the collapse of certain tenets of the liberal consensus in which the strongest and most violent personal and political emotions had been ruled out of court, and further on the nature of vengeance and punishment. Camus ('Neither Victims Nor Executioners') wrote on the nature of fear, the situation of Europe wedged between America and Russia, the intransigence of ideological conviction, certain aspects of Marxism, eschatological narrative, power and the reality of war. Bataille ('On Hiroshima') asked the difficult question of why this gigantic shift in the human condition had made so little general impact and offered a radical critique of John Hershey's famous narrative on the bombing of Hiroshima (see also pp. 190–6). Sartre ('Materialism and Revolution'), in by far the longest piece, analysed the philosophical limits of materialism, Marxist positivism, scientism and the nature of certitude. Taking tentative steps towards a revised Marxism, Sartre used the concept of class relations to undercut the confidence of liberal progressivism. Finally, Merleau-Ponty also spoke of the question of Marxist scientism and re-read Marx to suggest that he had possessed a far more complex view of the human condition than was currently being offered by Stalinist apologists.

While clearly all these writers went on to develop further, and in different directions, the essays in *politics* contained a rich core of their thinking. Any American reading these articles attentively would have found much to think about, by inference and indirection, not only on the immediate condition of the world in 1947 and the haunting aftermath of 1933–45, but on the Russian and American conditions, the fragility of the beliefs and narratives offered in support of those conditions, all of which was of enormous relevance on the threshold of the Cold War. While it would take years for a full appreciation of this extraordinary moment in French intellectual history to penetrate America and then never more than partially, nonetheless Macdonald's enterprising editorship provided more than an introduction for those willing to read and learn.

Different though positions, methodologies and approaches were, there were certain themes that swirled through all four essays. They can be briefly summarized: the nature of human barbarity, its psychology and theatre; questions of state terror and its effects; the nature of law in a world where state murder had been legitimate for over a decade and a half; questions of ethics and morality where every boundary had been exceeded together with its effect on human psychology and customary practices of limits; legitimations of state involving an unreflective faith whether left or right of the political spectrum; pleas for the unmasking of an overwhelming social belief in scientific rationalism; Hegel's 'fetishism of merchandise'; and the limits of philosophy. While clearly engaging with the Marxist-inflected tradition of European critical thinking, it is clear from this brief summary that all four were implicitly reintroducing questions that Marxist ideological simplifications and intransigence had deliberately and consistently ignored.

De Beauvoir spoke of a loss of innocence. Before the war 'the language of vengeance and expiation had no meaning for us'.[66] New emotions emerged through the Resistance, the pure joy of vengeance against the occupying powers, against the butchers of Oradour-sur-Glane and Buchenwald. But with the ending of the war people lacked the means of sufficient hatred. When virtually an entire nation has colluded, many, she argued, will escape their crimes. A certain lassitude and exhaustion sets in, the desire for vengeance atrophies. In this context, de Beauvoir posed the question of punishment. Older words once rejected (doubtless as bourgeois moralizing) – vengeance, justice, pardon and charity – suddenly reappear with new relevance. All have felt the need of vengeance, but how does it take shape and are there distinctions to be made? The killing of wartime, she continued, is abstract but even strategically useless killing has the secondary effectiveness of terror. Punishment can also be renounced for strategic ends. If you need a stable Italy and Germany, you simply cannot time waste energy in hunting down every fascist and every Nazi. There is a distinction between the vengeance directed against the person and the totality of a people. Beauvoir suggested that the lynching of snipers in Paris, summary executions of national guardsmen and SS jailors, and the shaving of the heads of women who had been lovers of Nazi soldiers answered to a need that transcended the reasonable, the practical and the strategic. It is a 'metaphysical demand'.[67] It must be grasped in its 'true spontaneity', in its attempt to wipe the fact of scandal or 'true evil' from the world.[68] Echoing Simone Weil, de Beauvoir sees it as a kind of impartiality of fate against those who have reduced others to objects: 'the degradation of a man into a thing'.[69] Later she called it the 'tragic ambiguity of the human situation'.[70] A woman who had a German lover might be the victim of sexual jealousy as well as being punished for giving legitimacy to a foreign power which has reduced her own nation to a powerless object.

Like Weil, de Beauvoir knew that there were limits to revenge, even when spontaneous. The victim must know that he has been made a victim. Herein lies a further difficulty: what degree of pain is necessary? Death removes the victim from reach, torture can overshoot the mark when suffering blots out all consciousness of anything else. What de Beauvoir calls casting a spell over the enemy's freedom, the calculation of despair, is practically very difficult. All felt defrauded by Hitler's death, for example. Close to Weil, de Beauvoir argued that only rarely can the butcher's required self-laceration be adequately realized and satisfactorily prolonged. Further private vengeance becomes suspect as soon as the avenger becomes judge. The circle of violence remains just that: a circle. But it is not clear if abstract justice can encompass the complexity of the theatre of judgement. So contemporary society replaces vengeance with sanctions and gives birth to the idea of impersonal social justice, that is, an abstract justice that upholds a community's values. In terms of temporality, the future becomes more favoured than the past, in spite of the inexpugnability of the crime from memory.

French intellectuals had, for example, been divided over the trail and execution of Robert Brasillach, the editor of François Coty's right-wing anti-Semitic newspaper *Je Suis Partout*. Camus signed the petition that François Mauriac (the Catholic resistance fighter) had sent to de Gaulle asking for clemency because he was opposed to the death penalty. Sartre and de Beauvoir refused, arguing writers were not immune against taking responsibility for their acts. With the memory still fresh de Beauvoir nonetheless observed that he bore himself with dignity at the trial: 'We wanted the death of the editor of *Je Suis Partout*, not the death of this man who was completely absorbed in dying well.'[71] Hence Brasillach places himself beyond reach of vengeance in his absorption with and performance of his own death. Camus certainly had the finer instinct here in his rejection of the death penalty *tout court*. We were aiming 'confusedly', admitted de Beauvoir, at the impossible.[72]

Occasionally, the horror that emerged at the trials overwhelmed everybody. In a further twist on the human sense of temporality the past was 'so real and so near that the torturers could not escape it'.[73] Such cases however were rare. In a sense the death always intervened. Two temporalities here conflicted, the temporality of social myth and ritual inflected with ethical value and a man's death: 'a real and concrete event', not the accomplishment of a rite. 'The more the trial takes on the aspect of a ceremonial, the more scandalous it seems that it can end in real shedding of blood.' For de Beauvoir, lawyers, judges, the public and the speeches of counsels were played out under the fanfares of a comedy drama: 'only the accused belonged to this world of flesh in which bullets kill'.[74]

These irreconcilable universes seem to cancel the linkage between crime and punishment, something of which non-judicial vengeance could never be accused. As will be shown later, this argument is close to Mumford's insights into the murder of Mussolini, praising it in the same terms as de Beauvoir when she used the word 'spontaneity'. She revealed, however, a disquiet within that spontaneity of which Mumford would be innocent. De Beauvoir, working out of the philosophical tradition described earlier on, appealed to a general sense of human anguish in which the absolute division between good and evil, for those who do not deceive themselves, is rarely very simple. Was it with real purity of will that the Nazis committed the crimes they committed? She cited Socrates: 'Nobody is bad voluntarily.' The lack of the purity of volition, however, is acknowledged. In describing its tragic implications she comes close to the teachings of the New Testament: 'which one of us will dare to say I am better than that man there'.[75] Further, she argued, no error expresses the whole nature of the man who commits it.

De Beauvoir does consider the implications of the Christian position. The ubiquitous nature of evil prompts the urgency of charity. She finally acknowledges that 'there is a great deal of truth in this point of view'.[76] In more secular terms, not all impossible situations are freely chosen, there are the realities of psychological and social damage, the past can be redeemed by changed behaviour. There remains however, as for Weil, the question of the unforgivable sin. In the words of the classic American writer Nathaniel Hawthorne, it is to have 'violated in cold blood the sanctity of the human heart'.[77] In de Beauvoir's terms it is 'when a man deliberately sets about to debase man into a thing, he lets loose a scandal on earth which nothing can make amends for'.[78] The Christian believing in the supreme judge can elect for charity and has the option of forgiveness. It 'is ruled out for people who profess a human morality and human values'.[79]

Finally de Beauvoir emphasizes the existential ethics of choice and freedom. To understand is not to excuse; to see complexity and life in all its concrete wholeness is also to note that choices have been made. Brasillach, in choosing to die nobly and without remorse, chose again a solidarity with his past. Such an act also renewed the need for punishment, closing the temporal gap between crime and court appearance. There remained the issue of who is to punish. De Beauvoir dismissed the argument from objectivity, 'the worst part of the Kantian heritage'.[80] Here, objective justice reduces men and women to abstract symbols, representatives of abstract crime, under universal law. It commits the same crime of cold-bloodedness that it is punishing. Yet, equally, summary vengeance invites the 'freedom' of tyranny. Punishment therefore always involves a defeat but to punish is also to demand freedom. Men are free to choose evil or good, by the use made of freedom itself. In that sense, to punish is to desire the good.

In acknowledging the tragedy, confusion and contradictions inherent in the notion of punishment, de Beauvoir knows that she cannot, short of Christian forgiveness, resolve the issue. For her, to hate the sin and love the sinner is impossible, the full responsibility for action has to be that of the human being acting on her or his own responsibility. If it is not, the sentimentalities of abstraction, false objectivity and extra-worldly legitimation can authorize the very wickedness it seeks to extirpate in the never fully analysable messy theatre of human life. The essay is remarkable for its combination of possible arguments: the Weilian sense of fate, force and the reduction of a person to a thing; the complex reciprocities indicated in rethinking the old Hegelian master–slave relationship; the recall of Christian and Socratic ethics; the doubt of Kantian ethical objectivity; the insistence on human responsibility; the exposure of the crude and imprecise ceremonials of the courts; the refusal to recommend absolutely any type of punishment or to see the issues in easily resolvable terms; and finally the analysis of the concrete historical events of the Nuremburg trials in their immediate historical moment. Its only weakness is that, unlike the article by Camus, it failed to address the issue of capital punishment.

The contribution from Camus dealt with the question of terror. In a broad sense he was also dealing with what de Beauvoir called 'new emotions'. He highlighted the psychological fear that produces denial and inertia. After the horrific experience of war he asked: 'who can deny that we live in a state of terror?'[81] Academicians and politicians are always proclaiming new 'eras' for their own critical and political narratives, but Camus's sense of something new in the postwar 'era' had a ring of truth. Who can deny, he asked, that we live in a state of terror now that man has been completely submerged in 'History'? 'History' is no longer part of a human being's nature, the depths of its violence and cruelty have produced a radical alienation. The relative truth of small things has, Camus argued, been devalued by the messianic confidence of powerful men, whether in machines or ideas, which reduces populations to silence and destroys any context in which reflection itself is possible. Less abstractly, Camus noted that in that precise historical moment, Europeans were strung impossibly between the Soviet Union and the United States and radically doubted that socialism had been achieved in the one or liberal democracy in the other. They had no home on earth and no place in 'history'. The desolation of mind, guilt and sense of displacement for sensitive Europeans would last for decades. For the state of consciousness produced by the machine and the dogmatism of non-negotiable quasi-religious political faith signalled a world in which 'murder is legitimate and where human life is considered trifling.'[82]

Hence, in a self-reflexive gesture, Camus confronted his previous pre-war pacifism. Nothing was permissible that demanded a human life. Accused of utopianism, Camus had defended himself by asking whether his accusers could actually imagine other people's deaths. Anticipating some effects of the hyper-realities of the post-modern world, Camus noted 'we make love by telephone, we work not on matter but on machines, and we kill and are killed by proxy. We gain in cleanliness, but lose in understanding.'[83] Like so many others examined here, Camus attacked the eschatological narratives of communism and capitalism. For both, the notion of progress (identical faiths in technology for example) and the happy ending were demanding too high a price.

The use of violence, so cavalierly theorized by the communists, argued Camus, had led them to precisely the position where they might find themselves in a position of doubt, a 'revolutionary' emotion whose victims were contemptuously characterized in a previous age by Louis de Saint-Just: 'They recoiled in the face of horrors.'[84] Any vacillation in faith produces an inflexible either-or. An absolute adherence to the Marxist narrative of history finally places the communists in the position of Saint-Just, a less than absolute adherence collapses socialist intelligibility and praxis just as precisely. It will be necessary, observed Camus, 'to choose a less costly Utopia.'[85]

Story-teller that he was, Camus doubted the narratives. The revolutionary break, the violent seizure of power in the face of overwhelming state technological power is a romantic illusion: '1789 and 1917 are still historic dates, but they are no longer historic examples.'[86] The domino theory of revolutions is merely 'a totting up of miracles.'[87] He argued more concretely that a socialist revolution in France would knock out American credits and ruin the country. A right-wing coup might expose France to Russia. World revolution was simply too dangerous. With uncanny prescience for our own time, Camus noted that every 'future revolution would be a foreign revolution [which] would begin with a military occupation [...] or what comes to the same thing, the blackmail threat of one: [a revolution] that would become significant only when the occupying power has conquered the rest of the world.'[88]

Camus pleaded for an ethical and ideological relativism and accompanied this with a further plea for a more universalist tolerance. 'As a Frenchman and still more as a Mediterranean', Camus found the idea of living under Soviet or American hegemony 'repellent.'[89] Nonetheless, he has to refuse this sentimental argument. Nationalism is to be feared as much as ideological hegemony. His ultimate call for a world parliament was based on a rising fear (amply justified in hindsight) that a clash of 'civilizations' might follow the break-up of the colonial empires. Certainly this plea for a genuinely democratic world order was made in full knowledge that the power-structure of the United Nations, then coming into being, was radically undemocratic in terms of a fair representation of nations. Similarly, at home, Camus observed that entrenched political positions on the left and on the right had not prevented the French conniving in the annexation 'without a referendum of Briga and Tenda' (districts on the French–Italian border, which were given to France as 'war reparations' in 1947), thus destroying any credibility in international democracy. So Camus called for an international peace movement, a reconsideration of political values 'from the ground up'.

The difficulty of a call for this type of ethical thinking and political behaviour (accusations of the 'moral high-ground' and 'utopian sentimentality' flow easily from left and right) is understood more plausibly in the context of Camus's articulate doubting of the narratives of 'political realism' from any member of any power structure or nation intent on undemocratically maintaining the *status quo* or pursuing selfish nationalist interests at the expense of others. Camus joined Mumford in his call for a greater human meaning to be given to everyday life, and a return to ethics. Pascal must radically redefine Marx:

> It is true we cannot escape 'History', since we are in it up to our necks. But one may propose to fight within History to preserve from History that part of man which is not its proper province.[90]

Here Camus seems to suggest a new separation of the public and private worlds, which new forms of terror and an over-burdened memory of horror had coalesced in every household. The strongest part of Camus's argument is a radical doubt of necessary evil which was to be universalist in character.

It is not surprising that Americans took Camus to their hearts, if not, unfortunately, as a guide to their foreign policy. He was certainly easier to understand than Sartre, and his more ethical approach sat more easily with a country where most people went to church regularly. He also wrote novels, which, however philosophically complex, did not require an education in philosophy to be read. Sartre, as we have seen, was in a different position, and his 'Materialism and Revolution' by its very title would not have even seemed relevant to anything except 'the enemy' in a country embarking on the Cold War. In France there was still a large communist party loyal to the Soviet Union, Labour was in power in Britain, and Germany and Italy had important communist and social democratic traditions. These countries had political histories in which socialism, in its many forms, was part of a widespread national practice and memory, from various forms of social democracy to communism itself. In Europe the subject was a concrete issue, in the United States it had, with some exceptions, never been a plausible aspect of political discussion, except as part of an all-too-easily exploitable binary narrative of political good and evil, which depended on the paranoia and psycho-pathological fears of an increasingly penetrative mass media.

Sartre, however, in his essay in *politics*, appeared to start simply: 'the young people today are ill at ease', but the subsequent arguments certainly would need some knowledge of Hegelian critical philosophy, Kantian ethics, the rough outlines of theories of dialectical materialism and the history and philosophy of science. Even so, the main subject matter for a persistent reader should have been reasonably accessible. Sartre wrote with a deft touch. The mixing of subjects philosophical, political and scientific was also likely to appeal to the generally intelligent American reader, even if it was anathema to the academic specialist. If access to Sartre was to be limited, what is remarkable about this contribution is how much of the essential parameters of his thinking it revealed.

Like de Beauvoir, Sartre initially emphasized the affective consequences of the war among the young. If the European bourgeoisie are being eliminated – in retrospect a somewhat premature assessment – the traditional period of the young middle class for experiment and 'having a fling' has gone with them. Sartre's students are hurling themselves at a young age into marriage and starting a family before completing their studies. Hence they have abandoned their own explorative subjectivity in the greater imperative of trying to recover a believable and authentic world in more private terms. The reaction seems visceral. Ideologically, however, they are sea, unable to believe in either materialism or idealism: they do not see how material could engender material and it is all too apparent that idealism functions as a myth in the hands of the ruling class. This interesting shift was to end in the 1960s and then reappeared in the materialistic 1980s. (In the twenty-first century, rearing children seems to have been abandoned altogether for the sake of a life-long consumerist 'fling', largely driven by the expense of rearing children in a 'libertarian' capitalist society and by that society's promotion of a goods-oriented authentic 'life-style' over life itself.)

So Sartre begins a reassessment of Marxist 'scientific-materialism' from the standpoint of an older teacher, burdened by the memory of occupation and war and now confronting a different generation. Time and contingency lurk behind every sentence and add urgency to the analysis. Sartre takes apart the secret metaphysics of positivist materialist Marxists. How, asks Sartre, can you reduce spirit to matter without recourse to metaphysics? This is Sartre at his incisive best:

> When the materialist claims to be *certain* of his principles, his assurance can come only through *a priori* intuition and reasoning, in other words, through those very speculations which he condemns. I now understand that materialism is a metaphysics disguised as positivism; but it is a metaphysics that destroys itself, for, by undermining metaphysics as a matter of principle, it deprives its own statements of all foundation.[91]

Sartre reveals the psychology of materialism in philosophical terms. It is the certainty and the assurance of the blinkered thinker that he attacks. Even the disciples of Comte did not go so far, they confined their positivism to human experience without generalizing it in universalist terms while steering clear of questions about the existence of God.

The progressive stance of the materialist, placing the human being beyond subjectivity, turns humans into objects and invents an objective eye in order to see them. Everything real becomes rational. Sartre mocked the fantastic optimism of the position and asked, as pure products of the universe, where our agency and organizing activity registers itself and exactly how it operates. Equipped with a post-Heideggerian critical ontology, Sartre demolished the crude Marxist positivists with ease. Tackling the more complex issue of dialectical materialism, Sartre focused on the question of implied narrativity and time within dialectical movement: 'I know that the mainspring of this immense movement is the attraction exerted by the future on the present and by the whole, even when it does not yet exist, on its parts.'[92] The problem for the materialists is that matter is inert (and best understood in quantitative terms) unless subjected to immaterial force, and that the totality, the totalizing movement, is not merely materialist. Quantity in fact 'is the opposite of dialectical unity'.[93] In fact, Sartre argues (against Hegel), the movement of the world in its externality is never dialectical. In later work he posed the 'scholastical totality' against the 'totalizing investigation', which is an extension of the same thrust of the argument here.[94]

In *Search for a Method*, some fifteen years later, Sartre complained of the tedious vacillation in Marxist historical explanation, that is, a narrative which swung between eschatological certainties (goals) and a kind of fatality of mechanical diffusion, a 'diffusion of a physical movement across an inert milieu'.[95] The absolutism involved in the identification of those goals through formal elimination 'reflects the bureaucratic practice of unifying everything.'[96] Today the same tendency is to be found in capitalist apologists whose (certainly tedious) explanation offers the market as an objective diffusion of physical movement across an inert milieu, vacillating with the eschatological certainty of endless limited self-corrections and guaranteed by a metaphysic of a grand spirit of overall equilibrium: a balance that, God-like, mediates uncertainly and contradiction.

Sartre's whipping boy for these thoughts in 1945 was Engels in *Dialectics of Nature*. Sartre doubted that there could be a dialectics of nature as such. He gives a short narrative of the history of science in terms of its play with intentionality, internality and externality. Following Hegel, he insists on the externality of nature. The problem then becomes that of the 'internality' of the human subject submitted to nature and history. 'Is it not evident', asks Sartre, 'that by the very idea of the synthesis, life cannot be reduced to matter, nor the human consciousness to life?'[97]

Finally a true narrative in its synthetic unpredictability cannot be an object of science. The 'jam tomorrow' of Marxism's ultimately determinist historiography circles endlessly in upon itself, 'floating between being and nothingness'.[98]

The Stalinist falls back on pure faith: argument and criticism become moments of weakness in a predefined action whose end is known: 'kneel down and you will believe, said Pascal. The materialist recommendation is very similar.'[99] That there is a profound relationship between the situation of oppressed class and the materialist expression of the situation cannot give materialism the status of a philosophy as such. Sartre went on to expose the materialistic dogmatism that ran the risk of legitimating the revolutionary under the sign of the natural. Only a thorough understanding of the unpredictable shifting of class relations and its rituals could justify the revolutionary's actions. The domain of the sacred (a delusional hallucination for Sartre) might be equally expressed in the upper-class rituals of relentless entertainment or in the sacrificial gesture of revolutionaries who redouble their efforts having lost sight of their aims. The risk was that a society attentive to means would be replaced by society only justifying itself by ruthlessly attained ends.

Value, argued Sartre, in that classic existentialist move by which he introduced ethics into a discourse of Husserlian temporality, is 'the appeal of that which is not yet'.[100] The way out of the materialist's dilemma is to accept the contingency of existence, to throw oneself into the world, to realize that any human order can be transcended, that value is socially based and conservative, but subject to reinvention which can be anticipated as being checked by contingency, but not prophesied. Any revolutionary philosophy must therefore be a philosophy of transcendence. If not, it risks a certain anti-intellectualism, a descent into the non-reflective pragmatism of the act where faith is underwritten only by unthinking discipline. Hence it also means that the revolutionary is subject to nature and history in all its particularity and harshness: '*this* body, *this* family, and perhaps *this* race'.[101] Sartre insists on the freedom to act in subjectivity which recognizes the full multiplicity of the situation, by throwing oneself towards a future which will disclose itself in endlessly transcendent and unpredictable pluralities in which human responsibility emerges within a human narrative of a concrete worldly tension between the no longer and not yet.

While Sartre's words were addressed largely to the much battered historical narratives and souls of European Marxists struggling for life as the chill of another Russian communist winter swept in from the east, the analysis, insofar as it addressed materialism as such, was not without relevance at the theoretical level to Americans. While they may have welcomed, and did welcome, the emphasis on psychology, individual ethics and plurality, the attack on the class structure and the rituals of the middle classes must have produced an uneasy feeling. Good comfortable middle-class living, as a materialist utopia, was not a goal of life generally envisaged by French intellectuals (whether from a devout Weil or an atheist Sartre) while one person on earth starved. The redeployment of Husserlian historical linkages within a redefined temporality including an appeal to a future project framed without dogmatism in full critical knowledge of the past, also by implication challenged the certainties of the American Dream: its desire to obliterate the past; its future orientation in popular psychology as a temporal legitimation of nationalist supremacy; its envisaged materialist and individualist utopia; and its quasi-metaphysical, that is idealistic, foundational myths of national origin that gave America a permanent right to express its essence as democratic.

Sartre was to refine these arguments in what was possibly his most remarkable book. In a long footnote in *Search for a Method* Sartre mocked the Hungarian Marxist critic Lukács's accusation against the existentialists as those who had placed consciousness before existence. Sartre reclaimed both existence and consciousness as concrete 'moments' in the flux of history, moments which endlessly acted upon each other, a theatre or drama of historical situations in which dissolving and re-emergence of certainties as to subjectivity or existence are part of the very nature of the human condition. If, however, the Americans liked the reclaiming of subjectivity implicit in Sartre's argument, they would have been wrong to assume that its strictly local moments in praxis redefined a recovered agency as a naive individualism. Knowing was, to keep the technical language, being situated in the world. The subject consciously decides to participate or not but participation is the condition under which a man or woman is revealed to herself or himself as a subject. Degrees of subjectivity, in freedom and unfreedom, in relation to a theory of the formation of different types of human groups, that is, from the perspective of collective, totalizing activities would receive further analysis in his magisterial *Critique of Dialectical Reason*, which appeared in 1960.[102]

Merleau-Ponty's essay for *politics*, 'Marxism and Philosophy', was shorter, less abstract and characterized by a gracefulness in argument that is evident in most of his work. Like Sartre, he argued powerfully against Marxist scientism, and also described it as an inherent contradiction within Marxist thought itself. The notion of an essentially unstable 'totality' in Marxist thought (ultimately deriving from Hegel and even Heraclitus) contradicted the certainties and atemporality of what he calls the worship of science along with its unassailable methodology.[103] For Merleau-Ponty, the false objectivities were, in an important sense, another aspect of Weil's outrage against the reduction of men to things. In more Marxist terms, it is another expression of alienation.

However, Merleau-Ponty also proposed to read Marx in a more complex way. Complexity always defeats demagogues and those Merleau-Ponty had in mind were again the positivist Marxists sustained by Stalinist dogma. He recalled, for example, Marx's precise words on religion. Like everyone else, he would have been aware that most Marxists only knew Marx's phrase about the 'opium of the people'. Acknowledging that it is possible to find in Marx's works arguments of a positivist and simplifying kind, he nonetheless argued that the notion that religion literally means nothing is much more ascribable to Voltaire than to Marx.

He quoted the whole context of the famous phrase from Marx's *Contribution to the Critique of Hegel's Philosophy of Law*:

> Religion is the general logic in a popular form, its spiritual point of honor, its enthusiasm, its moral sanction, its solemn complement, is general cause for consolation and justification. It is the fantastic realization of the human essence, because the human essence has no true reality [...] Religion is [...] the soul of a world without heart, and the spirit of a period without spirit.[104]

At the very least, Merleau-Ponty argued, Marx wanted to find the human significance of religion and to 'treat it as the symbolic expression of the social and human drama'.[105] In many respects socialism had a hard act to follow. Religion, whatever its derelictions, was the first to help human beings to think beyond nature, to challenge secular power and to think and indeed reflect Marx's own desire for a 'reign of freedom'.[106] Religion was not 'hollow'; it was grounded in human relations. Good religious practice in history, though undeniably rare, had always promoted a first awareness that 'man is not a thing'.[107] While state-controlled religion, especially at its borders with other religions, had helped engender and legitimate appalling historic cruelty and violence, it had also sought at its best to soften and palliate the very conditions it had often helped to generate.

Merleau-Ponty continued, arguing that Marx understood the reciprocity between general and particular existence and that he understood the dangers of hypostacizing 'society' as such. Like Sartre, he emphasized the concrete nature of human inter-subjectivity. Materialism (and he takes up Sartre's critique of its contradictions from a slightly different direction) cannot be considered as an all-embracing phenomenon but only as integral to a system of human existence.[108] Merleau-Ponty attempted to straddle the divide between inner and outer existence by a recall of the affective nature of human life. He spoke of the 'inner conviction' of human activity in relation to the external world, of 'sensitivity and suffering' as part of the intelligibility of human existence, of the 'cultural atmosphere' in which nature becomes human.[109] For Marx at his best, Merleau-Ponty explained, 'economics and ideology [were] inherently connected in the totality of history as matter and form in a work of art or any perceived object'.[110] For Merleau-Ponty, Marx anticipated the phenomenological concept of the human object. The connection between ideology and economy remains subjective in a phenomenology of a cultural world. Defending the importance of Hegel's thought (he is only abstract not untruthful), Merleau-Ponty argued powerfully for a pluralism of partial existences and ideologies, together with a more modest role for the philosopher: a full realization that by no means can the thinker escape the imperatives of being caught in a particular and radically unfinished time in its full complexity and, responsible like others, 'with a future to build'.[111]

Hiroshima: Georges Bataille and John Hersey

Bataille's essay has been left to conclude this section because he is not connected philosophically with the other French writers appearing in that volume of *politics* and because he was the only one of them to comment directly on an American text. In a sense he is a useful anti-existentialist thinker. His comments in his *politics* essay on John Hersey's famous account of the dropping of the Hiroshima bomb for *The New Yorker* (31 August 1946) signal a powerful dissent from the piece that had led to huge sales for the magazine. Macdonald's *politics* had already shown distaste for the Hersey article by publishing Mary McCarthy's review. in which she had declared as that to have done the atomic bomb justice, Mr Hersey 'would have had to interview the dead', implying that he had failed to grasp the totality of the event's nihilism.

The late twentieth-century collection of essays *Hiroshima's Shadow* edited by Kai Bird and Lawrence Lifshultz (which usefully reprints pieces by McCarthy, Macdonald and Mumford) was published in 1998, prompted by the cancellation of the 1995 Smithsonian exhibition on the dropping of the bomb, after pressure from the American Legion and others. This volume demonstrates that the ethical issues around the bomb are as alive as ever.[112] Commenting on the situation in Japan and the United States immediately after the event, James Cameron noted:

> It is a fact that in the years after the bomb everyone behaved in the most extraordinary way, on both sides. For five years the American censorship forbade almost any public discussion of the thing, even Japanese research into its physical effects was stifled; it was as though already a great load of guilt was settling over everyone which could be exorcized only by repression – the Americans by bans and censorship, the Japanese by wild reversions to normality.[113]

Sensitivity to the issue in the United States obviously lasted more than five years. The disgraceful cancellation of the 1995 exhibition that questioned the morality and strategic legitimacy of the American decision to drop the bomb has robbed the younger generation of a vital piece of history. It signalled an accelerating drift in American 'spin' (or organized lying) that less than a decade later was to rob the United States of all credibility as to any of its motives and action in almost every country of the world. As with many ideological empires before it, America's global credibility was to diminish with the increase of its military might. The tragedy is all the greater, given the extraordinary quality of the thought and actions of the Americans that this book seeks to represent as the best of 'America'.

This landmark 1940s event, the dropping of the Hiroshima and Nagasaki bombs, opens a debate of the utmost seriousness. The reactions to it are conducive to an absolute polarization. Between the 'religious' declarations of Paul Fussell's 'thank God for the atomic bomb' and Robert Oppenheimer's recall of the Bhagavadgita, 'I am become Death the Destroyer of Worlds', there is not, and can never be, any reconciliation. Both statements, however, simultaneously conceal and reveal the truth about the issue. The appeal to God or to apocalyptic reason accurately suggests the intransigence of a moment of historical contradiction, which captures that operation of indifferent historical fate and in which decisions are robbed of envisaged consequences. At the same time, it muddies real issues of human agency and responsibility in a universalist causal metaphysics. The issues are as alive now as they were in 1945. The cancellation of the exhibition and the furore that accompanied it show that narrative understanding, as a foundational act in creating a human world, throws history itself forwards as a poetic theatre of conflicting agents, linking the having-been with the no-longer and the not-yet, in a living debate. Hersey's famous account of the dropping of the bomb accurately embodied the contradictions of popular modes of understanding that from the start muddied the waters in American thinking about the event itself.

Bataille began his article in *politics* by offering the cynical world of 'wisdom'. In Hersey's account, he argued, the chronological world is characterized as an indifferent theatre of statistical operations in which fate and tragedy escape intention and desire equally. Human fate has a heart of darkness. Fear haunts the liberal intellectual as well as the indifferent masses. 'Sheepish dread [...] swaddled in curiosity' becomes the fate of the masses, a willed and helpless frivolity numbs the senses. But does this blind wisdom of the masses, who simply go on living, confound the prophetic moral anguish of one such as Camus? Brecht observed soldiers in a train going to New York in 1943 who switched off the radio whenever a news bulletin came on. Theirs was a truly serious and moral gesture against a calculated 'seriousness' that was going to kill many of their number.[114] Bataille was surely right 'that we have been too quick to believe that the moral resources of man are not equal to even a truly insane experience'.[115]

Civilization, noted Bataille, is no longer synonymous with an aristocracy maintaining order. But then neither is there a language in which the apocalyptic anxieties of the modern era, faced with the statistical immensity of the atomic bomb, can provoke any kind of countervailing emotion or action: 'the leaders of the smallest and weakest parties evoke some echoes, but one does not even see *born* the movement that would meet the deep anxiety of the modern world with acts as well as with phrases'.[116] Bataille, rejecting the universal implications of the bomb because they are limited by statistics and a view of cosmic technological fate, sees the immediate guilt as unique to the British and Americans. Hence he re-politicizes the issue. By rejecting the universal (insisting on 'Anglo-Saxon' responsibility) Bataille returns us to political distinctions, if somewhat exclusively juridical, in terms of responsibility.

The issue then becomes: to what extent is a different type of the universal relevance of the fact of the bomb plausible to the French who by luck were absolved from this particular game? Here the crucial issue of the narrative comes into play, together with its disposals of time. Hersey's style of 'factual' reporting, noted Bataille, was virtually unknown in France. What Bataille means by American factual reporting is event-oriented description, that is, the event detached from considerations of narrative understanding arrived at by the linkages of time in the Husserlian sense. Ethics are suspended without 'horizon' and without any meaning conferred through narrative links with either the immediate or distanced past. Truman, argued Bataille, had at least the honesty to note that 'Hiroshima' introduced a new turn of history. By a comparison with a preceding state of affairs, something had changed.

When Hersey elicits information from his interviewees, only an immediate emotional or animal reaction is possible, since intelligibility in relation to the event is not possible to survivors in the immediate aftermath. This presents then, 'the perspective of the animal, walled-in, deprived, by an error, of passage into the future through the understanding of an event that significantly affected the destiny of man'.[117] However, this contrasts with the perspective of the perpetrators who have undertaken the project in cold blood. This takes the event out of the domain of natural disaster and death (which is there, unlike the bomb's surplus death, as a condition for renewing life) and confers on it human meaning.

For Bataille, the cumulative effect of the narrative is to show that hope and reflection are but brief illuminations in a pervasive animal daze. In fact, the emotions are so numbed, the scale of the event so monstrous, that an appeal as a political or human gesture fails. These are emotions without 'appeal' to others. Hence they are unavailable to those who wish to organize strategies to prevent a recurrence of the horror. The man-made disaster aligns itself in scale with natural disaster. Horror is everywhere the same. Evil, as Arendt famously declared, is banal; it has the banality of natural process observed by a neutral panoptic eye. What is needed is a more sovereign sensibility to counter a liberal sentimentality.

> The stand point of the *sovereign sensibility* which has nothing in common with sentimentality or even with pity, – since these are equivocal – seems to me to have been perfectly expressed by Malraux when he said to the communists: 'at this moment what do you do about the man run over by a train?' Malraux was wrong to confront the communists with this difficulty since they frankly subordinate emotion to reason. But the objection would be valid if addressed to those who think that they act in obedience to their feelings.[118]

Bataille brilliantly detached Hiroshima from its uniqueness as catastrophe, to relocate it as integral with the anguish of human existence itself. It is the failure to recognize this that promotes 'an idealistic reverie' and denies the depth of anguish, assuming that certain ideological moves and practices can somehow contain it in a practical activity. America, somehow, never fails to promote its own version of practical activity and future security over the need to acknowledge the fullness and complexity of life itself. Bataille here, as in his other books, sees a profoundly ritualistic and liberating force in the ecstasy of the worst, that of standing by horror (in both the possible English meanings of 'standing by'): committed recognition and the detachment of the finally lonely witness of suffering. In that sense he notes that Hersey's description is better than the mythological action of the Crucifixion and the Buddhist contemplation of the 'bone-heap': it is a horror of mythic proportions paradoxically fixed within the parameters of the immediate reality of the human world.

Hersey's article was a success not least because it retained the darkly religious power of apocalyptic narrative, to a degree mythologized outside time. It focused on the day but not the *year* that would have linked it to other days. *The New Yorker* gave it the context of an exceptional *week*. It hence placed it in the domain of the sacred by banishing Mammon from its pages for one issue: the cartoons and advertising were offered on the altar of virtuous sacrifice ('time from laughter' as the *New York Times* declared) and the commercial lambs went for one week to a higher altar of truth to have their throats cut. The space of the word was in this holy moment re-sanctified. The high sales had all the character of an American revivalist meeting. They came to Hersey (the son of Chinese missionaries) as they came to Jesus, in full submission to the ecstasy of the worst. The scales fell from their eyes. They wept. Hersey even became a 'real' martyr. Henry R. Luce, the media mogul, who felt 'America' had been given a ticket to rejoin ordinary sinning nations and thus be judged guilty like any other nation, made sure that Hersey never worked for *Time* magazine again.

Bataille put a different question mark over the entire phenomenon of Hersey's report that went beyond technique or detail or right-wing reception. There was an unidentifiable 'surge of activity', transcending the event, in the theatre of Hiroshima that constituted its mass appeal and of which Hersey's report was quite unconscious.[119] Bataille thus added an important dimension of implied catharsis, tragic darkness and 'deeper' knowledge, that came from a life-long analysis of Sadean ecstatic rituals, whether located in the domain of 'primitive' rites or in the habitual theatres of military and civil physical humiliations. However, it too ran the risk of the alignment of the historic event with natural disaster being explained by universalist and transcendent vitalist structures and behaviours (rituals), thus producing too seamless an argument from nature or psycho-biology, an argument which was both static and circular at the same time. Living, violent cultural practices are not without agents capable of choosing, modifying, rejecting and resisting: culturally fatal secret psychological expressions of the denied terrors of biological contingency and annihilation. It is open to question whether the human being loses all credibility here by the sheer profundity of the experience. The dark love of endless suffering and obscenity can never be violent enough, never close enough to death itself.[120] The romantic journey of 'going under', of the voyage to the heart of darkness, the Christian 'losing yourself to find yourself', the closeness of sexuality and death in Western representation, the return bearing prophetic insight are all powerful narratives for indeed they are religious and psychological tropes. They relate to the deep structures of the representations of power and act as legitimating narratives of the sources of power. But they are not *a priori* truthful narratives in and for themselves, nor are they automatically productive of a world whose truth seems to be guaranteed by darkness, as Melville knew in his dramatization of the demonic character of Captain Ahab in his masterpiece *Moby-Dick*. Bataille's best insight comes when, like Blake, he shows the contiguity of good and evil: the longing for good is passionately desired because of the overwhelming nature of misfortune and evil.[121]

It is possible to take a harder look at Hersey's narrative produced by the 'ecstasy' of the event. Its matter-of-factness receives its power from a contrastive horror between reporting style and content. Nowhere, however, is the desire for the good acknowledged. In fact, few ethical judgements are made at all. Much is left to natural assumption and this is not quite good enough. The weaknesses are there in a narrative whose concealments, as in all popular writing, run the risk of flattering 'bad faith': that inauthentic legitimation of evil in which the subject declares he or she is not 'free to act'. The clues are there in the structure of the narrative itself. The viewpoint is Olympian, God-like, as indifferent as Nietzsche's aristocrat to historical fact and memory: the secret making of the bomb, Robert McNamara's total destruction policies in Japan and imperial Japanese aggression. It is also indifferent to the future by situating the event as purely 'natural' and isolated from a history that will continue in and through it. The event-oriented disposition of the mosaically distributed stories of the newspaper presents truth without truthfulness. Hersey did not even have the excuse of the deadline for the daily copy, he had a year to write it. Here Bataille was on target. The narrative technique of American reporting depended on the illusion of realism authenticated by a date and time. It was McLuhan who remarked on the phenomenon of reading a newspaper that one suddenly discovers is a day old and immediately ceasing to read it. The *prima facie* reality of the event disappears with the discovery of the past. Like Dos Passos, Hersey transfers this reality to the novel, whose primary terrain had previously been precisely that of memory, the interior life with its haunting past and the future insofar as it suspended death.

In Hersey's account there is no palpable anger towards Americans and no sense that as an American he has any emotional or political involvement in what is presented. There is no ambiguity about the politics of technological 'achievement', indeed at one point an overweening nationalist bombast articulates his sense of universal wonder, and there is no criticism of the relation of unrestrained (capitalist) technological development to a human world and human ethics. The issues of disproportionate strategic force and the previous destruction of 60 per cent of all major Japanese cities are not raised and not a single American is named. This is all the more surprising given that at least a year passed between the event and its publication. In terms of time, the praxis of journalistic immediate comment on an event that is only just 'no longer' is to a degree retrospectively reconstructed. This is journalism as historic illusion. Like the 'heritage' reconstruction of the 'Blitz experience' in London museums, the aim is to make you feel you were really there. Bataille-like ecstasy, the shock of standing beside yourself overwhelmed with horror, is the effect desired. The assumption is that if you were really there you would understand more than those who were not there and much more than any detached ivory tower historian. The whole sorry set of assumptions depends on a spurious notion that the spectator can become a reflective witness by the sheer force of the event.

In Hersey's account, simply because of the scale of the bomb's ontological vehemence, there is not even the sense of a judicial process where different witnesses give different verdicts. There is only the pure facticity of divergent luck, the thrill of horror such as the man on the cliff experiences when he sees another man drowning at sea. What we have, in short, is a horror movie, articulated by cuts and flashbacks, which place the spectator in and out of the diversely non-causal narrative games in perfect safety. The flashback (too obviously filmic though quite original in this odd genre of less than immediate 'journalism'), playing with Aristotelian beginnings, middles and ends, is part of Hersey's plot and reinforces a relentless theme of fatalistic linear time. The narrative conventions of 'reporting' are unambiguously backed by a metaphysic of unmediated mimesis that takes 'social realism' to an absolute level. As Brecht said of Shakespeare's history plays, all we get is 'the illumination of established facts'.[122] Here, the light is lurid indeed.

Commenting on Hanns Eisler's sense of danger when 'putting technological objects into circulation' and on popular culture unconnected with personal social function (the ubiquitous rousing music on the radio, jingles advertising Coca Cola), Brecht, as has already been noted, observed: 'It's enough to make you call for *l'art pour l'art* in desperation.'[123] The same applies here and to a degree it parallels Rexroth's claim in a letter to Macdonald, that it was the culture of consumer goods (its soul-numbing pragmatic materialism) that produced the bomb.[124] It produces a mindset in which the Japanese as victims are somehow caught in the drift of market forces. All values are exchange values and can be abstractly measured by statistics: distance from blast, degree of burns, likelihood of death and so forth. To a degree, Hersey does realize this, if clumsily, when his priest-character, recalling his 'occidental' experience of 'oriental' silence, speaks the unspeakable:

> To Father Kleinsorge, an Occidental, the silence in the grove by the river, where hundreds of gruesomely wounded suffered together, was one of the most dreadful

> and awesome phenomena of his whole experience. The hurt ones were quiet; no one wept, much less screamed in pain; no one complained, none of the many who died did so noisily; not even the children cried; very few people even spoke. And when Father Kleinsorge gave water to some whose faces had been almost blotted out by flash burns, they took their share and then raised themselves a little and to him, in thanks.[125]

This 'oriental' silent suffering is of course risks a grossly simplified movement from fact to meaning. Kleinsorge, it is suggested, needs the human sound of suffering in order to not to be alienated from what visually presents itself. The civil politeness of the gesture of thanks is ambiguously a mark of cultural distinction (in both senses) surviving in extremis and an obscene instance of obeisance to the 'occidental' mission-man being thanked by the suffering for the imperial superiority of his Christ-like role. They may die horribly but they manage to tug their forelocks. In spite of Hersey's moments of truth, the monstrous hypocrisy of the assumptions behind the double power of American technology and the Bible is vividly illustrated.

These assumptions of the Japanese as children to be saved or converted from primitive to civilized ways of thought reaches its nadir in the following passage:

> Those victims who were able to worry at all about what had happened thought of it and discussed it in more primitive, childish terms – gasoline sprinkled form an airplane, maybe, or some combustible gas, or a big cluster of incendiaries, or the work of parachutists; but, even if they had known the truth most of them were too busy or too weary or too badly hurt to care that they were the objects of the *first great experiment in the use of atomic power, which (as the voices from the short wave shouted) no country except the United States, with its industrial know-how, its willingness to throw two billion gold dollars into an important wartime gamble, could possibly have developed.*[126]

One longs for a greater degree of irony. Suffering makes the Japanese only indifferent to the fact of American technical and capitalist power, indifferent to the experts in military-industrial risk and indifferent to 'important' gambling. Two billion dollars shimmer with nationalist pride. Hersey lacks any sense of what we shall see as Mumford's sense of historical nemesis and dehumanized scientific practice.

Japanese cultural practices are referred to only in passing. The Japanese garden of Asano Park 'with their quiet pools and arching bridges [...] very Japanese, normal, secure', a 'heritage' indictor in a pure Hollywood gesture, is engulfed in flames as the fire spreads. The concentration on Western Christians further obliterates the distinctiveness of the Japanese other. The narrative ends in death. The only victim who stands up for Japanese culture as such is a retired shipping company official, Mr Tanaka, who in fact hates Christians for attacking Japanese culture. He gets his nationalist come-uppance as Hersey arranges his incidents. In a moralistic cautionary tale, Tanaka who is 'selfish and cruel' and accuses the nice Methodist minister of being an American spy, winds up dying, 'willing to be comforted by any religion' while the minister reads to him from the Bible:

> For a thousand years in Thy sight are but as yesterday when it is past, and as a watch in the night. Thou carriest the children of men away as with a flood, they are as a sleep; in the morning they are like grass which groweth up.[127]

This re-contextualizing of the famous words from Psalm 90 at this point has a curious effect. Let us suspend disbelief and assume that the text and the incident are true. It confirms the cautionary tale of the sinner consumed by vanity and then confronted by the power of God, but it also (unaware of the obscenity of an American technologically induced dark night of the soul) collates the bomb with the operations of divine cosmic time. The beauty of the King James Version of the psalm, which also senses the regeneration of nature is de-emphasized by context here, with its inevitable emphasis on a remote extra-temporal vision. One wonders quite what comfort the wicked Mr Tanaka received from the essential stoicism of 'We live our years as a tale that is told', which demoted human narrative to fictional stoic evanescence. One begins to understand Mary McCarthy's fury with Hersey's account.

The cast of characters is oddly expressionist. They are defined by role: a clerk, a doctor, a poor widow, a German Jesuit priest, a young surgeon, a Methodist minister (albeit educated at Emory, with 'excellent English', dressing in American clothes, with many American friends). In class terms they are all professionals with one representative of the traditional poor and one lower-middle-class white female clerical worker. There is no representative of Japanese religion, no Japanese worker, no Japanese boss and no Japanese middle-class businessman. Most of the other Japanese appear as 'mass', crowds, heaps of dying, anonymous exiles of the dying without differentiation in this medieval portrait of hell. Japanese customs are referred to as if they are something to be aware of like a business brochure, orienting a few key points of cultural information. It might be said that Hersey could only interview those survivors who could speak English, but that is not thematized in the text which hence by omission claims representative wholeness. He also had a whole year to find translators if he had been so minded. The focus on the fate of Christians somehow elides the fact that a Christian nation was responsible for the horror. The style is a combination of Dos Passos-like representation of time and character, with, occasionally, a hipsterish side crack as if from someone perpetually propped on a bar uttering solemnities from an all-seeing slightly drunken eye. Thus Hersey says of his representative men and women, with a slow all-knowing drawl: 'now each knows that in the act of survival he lived a dozen lives and saw more death than he ever thought he would see. At the time, none of them knew anything.'[128] One might imagine a solemn Hollywood orchestra (playing 'Nearer my God to Thee'?) reinforcing the atmosphere. The knowing of the other is simply reduced to a visceral and inarticulate intuition of mortality.

Sartre captured the phenomenon perfectly in his commentary on Dos Passos: 'The facts are clearly outlined; they are ready for *thinking about*. But Dos Passos never thinks them':

> Like our real memories it is a jumble of miniatures and frescoes. There is relief enough, but it is cunning scattered at random [...] Each event is irreducible, a gleaming and solitary *thing* that does not flow from anything else, but suddenly arises to join other things. For Dos Passos, narrating means adding [...] We suddenly find ourselves inside a horrible memory whose every recollection makes us uneasy, a bewildering memory that is no longer that of either the characters or the author. It seems like a chorus that remembers, a sententious chorus that is accessory to the deed. [129]

Hersey's simultaneously partial narratives and reconstructed flashbacks are derived from Dos Passos. Hersey's hugely popular report plugged into the most basic of human experiences: a fascination with inevitable horror so universally immediate that the vicarious nature of it, shattered any normal check between fantasy and reality. The vicarious passes into the real with a resultant thrill. The question arises: to what degree does any hugely successful bestseller reinforce Sartre's sententious and collusive chorus?

His filmic techniques were also clear, for example the establishment of the location: 'a fan-shaped city, lying mostly on the six islands formed by the seven estuarial rivers that branch out form the Ota River'.[130] Japan becomes an American geography seen from a commanding aerial perspective where space is more important than time. There is not a shred of Japanese political history in the entire account. What we have instead is quasi-cultural anthropology: 'the house consisted of a wooden frame and wooden walls supporting a heavy tile roof'.[131] A good suburban mother might encourage her five-year-old to draw them from the *National Geographic* and repeat proudly to adoring relatives that the little one said they 'looked like a cool cave full of fat cushions'.[132]

But a good B-movie needs melodrama. The fate of woman and children touch the heart without too much insistence: 'She heard a child cry, "Mother help me!" And saw her youngest – Myeko, the five-year old – buried up to her breast and unable to move.'[133] Hersey is secured against the accusation of sensationalism by facts whose horror takes it almost beyond the margins of the human ability to respond. Yet what emotion to drive an ethics is being elicited here? It is the same with the vignette, for the narrative proceeds through vignettes. Take, for example, the twenty-year-old mother refusing to be parted from her dead baby girl. It is not political shame, but the obliterating all-purpose emotional and even sentimental trope of the mother and child in danger, shamelessly used to take our minds off responsibility and into the vicariously experienced instant.

The vivid 'illustration' increases the horror by the same brevity of human contact characteristic of the urban crowd which, from the days of Edgar Allan Poe in narrative terms, has signalled human alienation. The people of Hiroshima are all briefly noticed beggars. Again and again physical symptoms of radiation sickness are detailed. Hersey reproduces Dr Sasaki's medical notes, oddly enough written in German, on the clerk Miss Saski's symptoms. One wonders what happened to medical confidentiality in this exhibition of the report on her invaded body. On the spiritual side of things, however, she is tended by the Jesuit priest, who justifies the dropping of the bomb by Christian Americans to her by arguing generally on the fallen state of the world. With this 'Jesuitical' elision of responsibility, it seems she converts to Catholicism and gets better, though she remains a cripple: an endorsement at once of American righteousness and a reminder of original sin.

In his concluding paragraphs Hersey notes that the Japanese felt a hatred for Americans that nothing could erase. Nothing in the text thematizes the observation. Its obviousness is so patent that paradoxically it disappears from sight. The only ethical reflection in the entire piece is put in the hands of the Jesuit priest who, with the other German Jesuit priests and 'as foreigners [...] could be expected to take a relatively detached view'.[134] In short the issue of the bomb, in ethical terms, is avoided. Children looking for their mothers constitute the vignette of closure: 'but Kikuk's mother was wounded and Murakami's mother, alas was dead.'[135]

Sometimes the characterization is almost comic. Dr Fuiji, a *bon viveur*, passes his evenings 'drinking whiskey with friends, always sensibly and for the sake of conversation.'[136] Is this the Methodist missionary's son who knows the shadow cast by prohibition in Middle America? This man is risqué but safe, thus addressing both sides of the debate under the appeal of moderation. Father Kleinsorge's mission is much described and he is there to ensure that Christian narrative is part of the plot which universalizes the event as natural tragedy. Hersey gives both Japanese and English versions of the appeal to the Almighty: 'Shu Jesusu, awaremi tamai! Our Lord Jesus, have pity on us!'[137] The symmetry of the two languages is exact, it makes cultures one under the sign of the cross, and nothing, remarkably, is lost in the act of translation: a neat accolade for the missionary translators.

The exactness of time and the exactness of statistics is everywhere apparent. Americans, said Gertrude Stein, needed to know the exact number of everything. The surgeon's hospital is 1,650 yards from the centre of the blast. This is of course a retrospective assessment from the scientists, here presented as fictionalized knowledge of immediate space. A fascination with exact numbers is always a feature of a reported catastrophe and Hersey obliges: 'of 1,780 nurses, 1,654 were dead [...] only six doctors out of thirty were able to function'.[138] He is also obsessed with the time people got up, for this moment of time becomes an originating fatal event to establish the narrative of a day in relation to the moment when final destiny strikes. A spurious God-like causality is implied, decorating the writer with omnipotence.

Chronological time confronts an implied cosmic time. It is like a repeated close-up of a clock: the female clerk gets up at three o'clock, Father Kleinsorge at six and the surgeon wakes half an hour earlier than usual as we move slowly towards 8.02am. Besides acting as an originating event to found individual narratives, the times of rising have thematic consequences because the temporal and spatial locations would determine the survival or not of the citizens of Hiroshima. Like Hitchcock's stranger on the train, being the wrong person in the wrong place at the wrong time addresses itself to a psychopathology of fear in the audience rather than to anything that might be narrativized about the external world. The fact of approaching fatal time is fictionalized in terms of retrospective knowledge. Hersey reconstructs himself as God who 'knoweth the hour' but here the auteur-god blasphemously reveals it to his bewitched audience, who become enchanted by the forbidden knowledge. Survivors are thrilled to know the hour of these deaths.

Future time as nemesis becomes an illustration of general fear, fate and contingency, ruling out human agency and any sense of the interior life of the victims. Survival is pure luck or 'providential interference', which is the way Father Kleinsorge apparently saw it.[139] However, getting up at the wrong time is not the substantive cause of their deaths, even though 'realism' suggests it is. The cause among countless causes belonged to Japanese imperial brutality and American technological brutality in creating a show for the Soviets in order to forewarn them that they would not be the major players in the ensuing peace.[140] Bataille's article, together with Mary McCarthy's, would at least have given the readers of *politics* a certain scepticism about Hersey's account, one year after the event. That Hersey's 'Hiroshima' moved people could not be doubted and to a degree it did, with Hollywoodesque narrative technical flair. It did 'illustrate the facts' but whether it helped the Americans and the collusive British to understand exactly what they had done is quite another matter.

Macdonald's own *politics* article on the bomb in September 1945 was one of his finest. He was one of the first to point out the devastating effects of radio-activity, noting that the bombs were designed as explosives not as 'gas' bombs. After the official military attack was 'over' and after peace was declared the war operation of killing continued in the deaths from radio-activity. His anguished sarcasm about the 'most magnificent scientific experiment in history' was powerful. His analogies for the closeness of good and evil were also powerful: 'A century of effort has failed to separate the Good of capitalism (more production) from the Evil (exploitation, wars, cultural barbarism)'. Further, said Macdonald, there is only one answer to Dostoevsky's Grand Inquisitor: 'if all mankind could realize eternal and complete happiness by torturing to death a single child, would this act be morally justified?' Hence all the arguments of the authorities on this basis alone (and we now know many of them to have been lies), for Macdonald, stood condemned.[141]

Macdonald, an astute film critic, also noted that the fears of the power of scientific discovery were old ones: 'From Frankenstein's laboratory to Maidanek [...] is not a long journey.'[142] The rational and the scientific were now 'chilling our blood'.[143] The 'normality' of ordinary good American activity claimed by Truman in its production simply showed how 'inhuman our normal life has become.' (259) Noting that even though only the handful of people ever knew what was going on, nonetheless when they did, neither the corporate world nor the labour unions showed any sign of remorse about a 'good job well done'.

Macdonald re-invoked the old Greek sin of *hubris* (arrogance) to characterize the triumphalism of what appeared to be the entire American nation. In practical terms it seemed that anyone in the academy could be bought, and if not bought, seized and held whether in the Soviet Union or in the United States. Macdonald held the scientists themselves responsible. The only hope lay in the few men who said no: 'These scientists reacted as whole men not as specialists or partisans. Today the tendency is to think of peoples as responsible and individuals irresponsible. The reversal of both these conceptions is the first condition of escaping the present decline to barbarism.'[144] Certainly it seemed, to a few in the generation of the 1940s, to betoken a first step towards barbarism. Macdonald drew the lessons in an era where the historical experience of unparalleled and appalling violence stemming from a kind of mass psychosis had seriously weakened both Marxist and social-democratic assumptions that an intelligent and well-educated human society might be able to resist well-organized demagoguery.

In the next section the question of the atomic bomb and the shock it produced on sensitive Americans will open another chapter in an argument on the political problem of ethics and politics and their relation to the narrativization of time and memory. Dorothy Norman's *TWICE A YEAR*, from a different ideological and cultural perspective, was to parallel and supplement Dwight and Nancy Macdonalds' extraordinary critical achievement in the short but outstanding life of *politics*.

3

'My Dear Plutocratic but Lovely Friend': Dorothy Norman and *TWICE A YEAR*[1]

Aristotle calls memory 'the scribe of the mind.' When all else is taken away the mists of memory still remain. None can take away the joy we have had in reading lovely books, or listening to great music and poetry. Nor can the love bestowed on us by those whom we love fade even when the loved ones are far away or have passed into the shadow of death [...] Were it not so, human nature could hardly bear the weight of sorrow.

— RANJIT S. PANDIT[2]

I am convinced that there are many layers of history and that the final reading will be delayed until the gift of seeing past and future as one is restored to us.

— HENRY MILLER[3]

I

Faustian Visions: An 'American' Beginning

In 1945, just after the news from Hiroshima and Nagasaki had come through, Alfred Stieglitz, the ailing founding father of American photography and friend and companion of Dorothy Norman, was reading a page of cartoons. The cartoonist had capitalized on the first use of the atomic bomb by drawing a cigarette 'that's *atomized* for your protection', together with a sexy figure of the curvaceous 'Beautiful Beatrice La Bump', described as being 'known to her press agent as "The Proton"'. Scrawled over the top of the page (now in a miscellaneous file in the Stieglitz Papers at Yale University), written in the shaky hand of a man near to death are the words: 'Is there any place for our kind of thinking in the world of below?'

The moment has extraordinary pathos, and raises questions which at least appear even more difficult to answer today, in a world that fears authentic seriousness. For then the implied ethical judgement was clear: the eroticization and sexist humour of the newly discovered power underlying the Hiroshima bomb went beyond a joke. 'Our kind of thinking' was a world apart and tragically defeated in an America that had lost her soul. In such a moment the 'joke' had commercially and collusively placed itself beyond the bounds of all civilized decency. The cartoon's 'bad taste' depicted a staggering ignorance and brutal miscomprehension of the founding event it relied on. 'Must then Christ perish in torment in every age', asked Shaw's Saint Joan, 'to save those that have no imagination?'[4] The burning flesh of Japanese civilian non-combatants was the concealed narrative behind the media wise-crack of Beatrice La Bump: a synthetic conceit, doubtless temporally post-modern, of sixteenth-century *femme fatale*, a 'sexy' French woman, striptease artist and atomic particle.

Perhaps, on the other hand, Stieglitz should not have been surprised or shocked. Had he fled the modern world in horror? Bombing crews after all painted pin-ups on the noses of planes that firebombed foreign cities; 'forces sweethearts' in various stages of deshabille bestrewed the quarters of every military barracks, feeding the masturbatory fantasies of cripplingly bored men in the prime of youth, under the threat of death, and far from their wives and lovers. Erotic fantasy and fetishistic technology, as the 1950s and 1960s satirists, and the postmodern novelists never tired of reminding their readers, were wedded together forever. Prostitutes, as from time immemorial, followed the armies and thronged the ports. Was not Stieglitz over-reacting to the 'real world' of popular culture and 'ordinary blokes' with a touch of elitist, precious, middle-class morality? Had he not realized that where life was cheap so too were sex and erotic experience and that you took what you could get? Should he not have given a Fussellian shrug of the shoulders and written it down to the 'realism' of 'the way things are'?

The poet William Carlos Williams had indeed reacted to a certain apparently exclusivist strain of high art 'seriousness' in Stieglitz's approach to culture and ethics. He had initially responded warmly to Dorothy Norman, the woman who followed the painter Georgia O'Keeffe in Stieglitz's life and whose journal *TWICE A YEAR* is the subject of this chapter. In May 1941 Williams wrote to Norman, however, that the reason he had not visited Stieglitz's gallery in New York was because, as much as he admired him, he seemed to be 'dramatizing his death too much', and there was a kind of view of art as a sort of high sacredness which was putting people off: 'Much too Old Testament for me'.[5] The remarks caused an immediate breach between the two correspondents. Williams, a highly secular doctor who had perhaps seen too much death, had had a moment of irritation. A week later, Norman rejected one of Williams's short stories. The next letter is five years later, after Stieglitz had died and a special commemorative issue of *TWICE*

A YEAR was being prepared for press. Williams, again sympathetic, nonetheless pursued his theme. He is curious to see what people will say about 'the great man', adding 'they should have burnt him on a funeral barge in the East River'.[6] His own invited memorial for that occasion ('What of Alfred Stieglitz?') was again rejected by Norman. She explained that while she did not expect absolute praise from everybody about Stieglitz, nonetheless what Williams has written might be open to misunderstanding.[7] It was a fairly feeble response, though relations between Norman and Williams resumed a warm cordiality later in the year and, at his request, Norman sent a copy of *TWICE A YEAR*, with a personal note to Ezra Pound when he was incarcerated at St Elizabeth's Hospital in Pennsylvania. In the late 1950s, Norman, hearing of Williams's poor health and troubled state of mind, sent him a kind message of support.

These small moments of human relations and difference of judgement open some serious questions. Williams had, in fact, by no means written a totally hostile piece about Stieglitz (although Stieglitz is spelt 'Steiglitz' all the way through the typescript). It begins critically enough, objecting to the abstractions of his ethical and aesthetic philosophizing and to a kind of exclusivist world of high art. He felt that Stieglitz was the 'master' of his entourage of artists, virtually locking up the pictures far from the madding crowd. His gallery prevented a more diverse reception for the paintings; you had to enter his world on his terms or stay out. Again it was the 'aura of holiness' that the paediatrician from working-class Paterson, New Jersey, objected to, together with his 'pretence of poverty', even though he acknowledges that Stieglitz would have starved if necessary to promote his cause. The poet's point was: why bother to compete with the recalcitrant Museum of Modern Art? Was it 'Jewish' intransigence and a need for battle? At this point, however, Williams insouciantly turned his own argument on its head. There was a real sense, he insisted, in which Stieglitz wanted to beat the dollar-sodden art market at its own game. The 'big money' boys dictating art fashion were a real enemy and Stieglitz was to be admired for 'fighting them down to the wire'. Stieglitz *was* finally all right, he concluded, 'as an intelligence, as a profound prophet of real values as opposed to murderous falsity of cash over everything else, as a pioneer photographer, as a friend, as a lover of peace, and as a fighter'.[8]

Was it a difference of a generational, even a national, style? Stieglitz had deep roots in European romanticism, a fact which heavily conditioned his view of the artist as prophet and seer, necessarily distinguished from the crowd. As for Williams, from Sir Thomas Browne (whose '*credo quia impossibile*' seemed a little over insistent) onwards, perhaps a majority of doctors have been at least ambiguous about the nature of the sacred. For Stieglitz, however, the work of the artist was to a degree 'sacred'. But it was not just art. As with William Morris, John Ruskin and the Arts and Crafts Movement, what was at stake was a sense of worth and dignity in all the activities of human life: 'Whether it is scrubbing a floor or painting a picture – only the best work of which man is capable will finally satisfy him [...] only work born of a sacred feeling.'[9]

Stieglitz grew up in the late nineteenth-century world of Ibsen and Strindberg, the great English and Scottish pictorial photographers and the post-impressionism of Rodin and Cézanne. Out of these diverse strains he fought to encourage an American art by redeploying as well as acknowledging its European roots and parallel influences. The internationalism of the romantic and enlightenment ideals as well as the generalized and now tabooed 'man' of humanist discourse, to a degree modified the need to express those now less criticized but equally essentializing 'romanticisms' of nationalist and ethnic identity, and nationalist production, from which today's cultural politics of identity are themselves not absolutely immune.

William Carlos Williams too, however, had also been engrossed in European culture; in Breughel, Bach, Wagner and the 'unicorn' tapestries given by Rockefeller to the Cloisters Museum, a museum described by Mumford as morally facing down the vertical canyons of Mammon at the other end of Manhattan. Unlike Mumford, Williams took the tapestries together with the fractured cultural world of the working-class immigrant, spurning the ancient and medieval utopias of Pound and Eliot as pure atemporal refuges that fled modernity, yet still insisting on this ancient art's relevance as a 'critical-utopian' critique of an American life viewed from the perspective of modernity and Paterson, New Jersey. However, no less than for Stieglitz, Pound or Eliot, the seriousness of great art for Williams was non-negotiable. Was the difference in 'seriousness' an inflection, a matter of temperament rather than ideology? And was not Williams, too, somewhat over-reacting? Mrs Williams had, after all, taken her husband to task for writing like that to Norman when Stieglitz was seriously ill.[10] The last word must surely be Robert Lowell's in 'For the Union Dead':

> There are no statues for the last war here; on Boylston Street, a commercial photograph shows Hiroshima boiling over a Mosler Safe, the 'Rock of Ages' that survived the blast.[11]

Sometimes it seems we have need of our patricians.

The argument thus comes full circle. The either-ors are in the end dogmatic. Not to acknowledge the crass callousness of the cartoons or Lowell's commercial picture of the Mosler safe was just as much a blindness as to create a holy martyrdom of the artist out of a misconceived romanticism that reinforced the relentless, liberal, middle-class need for suicidal, critically ill or irrational images of the isolated, abandoned creative soul: that bourgeois class revenge for the genuine artist's refusal of the cash nexus as a foundation of primary human activity. For, in spite of contemporary 'democratic' prejudice, where the genius is a male hormonal problem and insouciantly 'master'-minded by the agentless metaphysics of 'cultural construction', there is more than a little to be saved from the romantic vision. The alienation of the serious artist was a fact of life rather than a chosen hauteur; struggle, effort and the choice of art before life was part of that struggle rather than an evasion. The facts persist that some things are very much better than others and that real quality is mostly served in very small quantities. Henry Miller, always alert to the barrenness of modernity's relentless banality summed up the issue succinctly in a letter to Dorothy Norman in 1940: 'it's as though he [Stieglitz] functioned as an axis and pole star both: he talks from far out in space, from some super-dimension, which paradoxically enough situates him nearer to the heart of things than those who are swimming in the stew.'[12]

There are distinctions to be made between snobbery, publicity-seeking and honest judgement, between collective action on behalf of the poor and the excluded and the narcissistic verbal polishing of politically correct attitudes and finally, above all, between price and value. Between God and Mammon there was an inflexible contradiction. In a world where all had won and all had prizes, perhaps not to join the race in the first place was a serious and authentic option in spite of the temptations. Cutting oneself off was even, perhaps, necessary. Withdrawal was not escape, but the very *point d'appui* of an enabling distance. Hannah Arendt's lament for the loss of the distinction between the private and public space, articulated a few years later, was another way of tackling and extending the issue. The world of commerce and mass marketing occupied a social space in which public and private disappeared in a turmoil of anxiety about the price and success of the advertized product which now, given that desire is equally marketed, seems seamlessly independent of even the old constraints of the market.

There is no more startling juxtaposition of the world offered by the artist and the 'real' world than two contiguous photographs in volume VII of *TWICE A YEAR*. The shock on first turning the page is on a par with a first reading of Weil's essay on the *Iliad* in *politics*. The first photograph (see fig. 1) is of the mushroom-cloud of the Nagasaki atomic bomb, an aerial view provided by the War Department; the second (see fig. 2) is one of Stieglitz's pictures of clouds, one of his 'Equivalents'. On the broadest view of the juxtaposition Stieglitz's question returns with force: 'Is there any place for our kind of thinking in the world of below?' The contrast is first and foremost 'romantic'; the division between the results of human activity is absolute. It reflects a comment made by Stieglitz about his favourite work of literature, Goethe's *Faust*. I am not interested, he said, in Faust, 'I am interested in Marguerite and the Devil', that is, the relation between innocence and evil.[13] Yet the absence of Faust is a fault, for it is the arrogance and cruelty of the temptations of power that are dramatized in detail through Goethe's protagonist. Is it possible or even desirable to find a sense of social and political meaning in Stieglitz's pronouncements? Put another way, to what degree is he offering art as a site of critical utopia rather than a collusive evasion? That Stieglitz habitually used a universalist figure of the human subject as 'man' is not in doubt, though it is sometimes humorously inflected: 'I never much thought of myself as a Jew or any other particular thing, but I'm beginning to feel that it must be the Jew in me that is after all the key to my impossible make-up.'[14]

Fig. 1: American Air Force photograph from *TWICE A YEAR*.

Of course there are dangers in a universalist humanist rhetoric. It was to a large degree exposed in Waldo Frank's accurate but overly brutal assessment of Dorothy Norman's own writing: 'The language is upper-middle class New York abstract jargon.'[15] Frank's often acerbic and aggressive tone to Stieglitz (stemming largely from class anger) was frequently met equably and generously. Nonetheless Frank's point is not without its accuracies. For example, Norman's little book of poems, *Dualities*, printed on beautiful paper and dedicated to Stieglitz and the spirit of 'An American Place', is virtually unreadable. Its quasi-religious generalities are vulnerable to infinite parody, perhaps in the mode of Gilbert and Sullivan's *Patience*, with its lofty, breathless, arty, urban upper-class 'spirituality'. It is Stieglitz but without his deep European reading, humour, scepticism, Manichean sense of conflict or his very un-abstract confidence in the necessity of art. Norman's language is dangerously close to a combination of sub-thespian vacuity and banality.

Its sincerity is not, however, in doubt and the 'spirituality', lamentably expressed, is clearly genuine and must be acknowledged as such. As the young Proust said about bad music: 'Those arpeggios, too, or that "re-entry" of the theme have aroused in the soul of more than one lover or dreamer, an echo of the harmonies of paradise.'[16] Norman did quite genuinely aspire to the 'harmonies of paradise' in her poetry, but her real (indeed very remarkable and abundant) gifts lay elsewhere and were better served in other forms of art and action: in her photography, her international social and political engagement, her relentless encouragement of an American art and her strenuous and unremitting activity on behalf of the world's hungry, dispossessed and poor.

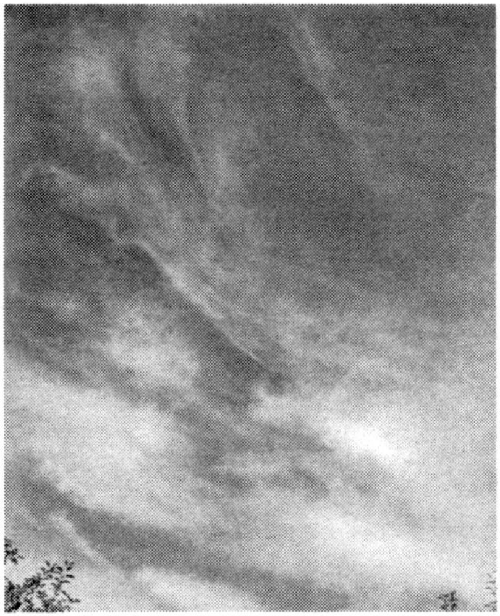

Fig. 2: Stieglitz's 'Equivalent' (1935).

Was then Stieglitz's cloud photograph a utopian antithesis to the photograph of the mushroom cloud of nuclear fission? Did the implied judgement too easily suggest that this moment of visionary pastoral was more important, for example, than the world of scientific materialism? Was there any kind of logical ground for the comparison, and how might the intuitive contrast, to a degree so obvious as well as striking, be described? What narratives were concealed in both and what did the juxtaposition imply about the nature of human temporality? What, to borrow terminology from Ezra Pound's poetics, did the images condense? Did *TWICE A YEAR* unrealistically throw the world of high aesthetic culture with its sense of 'eternal values' against historical scientific technological reality? These questions have to be answered in at least two ways and the very terms made more complex: first, in a more particular examination of the photographs themselves; second, and more broadly, in a detailed examination of the entire project of *TWICE A YEAR* as a quasi-text, both formally and ideologically.

The appearance of the two photographs in volume XIV–XV (Fall–Winter, 1946–7) has its own context. They are the last two in a visual sequence of illustrations that begin with a *drawing* by George Grosz, 'Our World' (1918), followed by a series of anti-fascist photomontages by John Heartfield, followed in turn by the American Air Force's official photograph of 'Nagasaki: Japan under Atomic Bomb Attack'. The sequence is completed by Stieglitz's 'Equivalent' of 1935. It would be relatively easy, though deceptively so, to construct an implied narrative through the arrangement of the incidents simply because they depend ultimately more on a poetic or metaphoric suggestiveness of meaning than on a figurative drama that might denote a historical sequence, though there are glimpses of a fragmented chronological story. In fact, it is a 'story' of the collective human soul in crisis, in which history becomes illustrative of that crisis rather than the other way round. Its implied ethics are therefore both in and out of history.

Grosz's lineally figured, spider-lined cartoon world needs the dateline 1918 to authenticate its vision of an earthly Bosch-like hell populated by the denizens of a capitalist-imperialist decadence who were responsible for the Great War's millions of deaths. It is a visually expressionist world of Reichean emotional plague: the be-hatted respectable and satisfied leaders of society are dependent on a sleazy

Fig. 3: George Grosz, 'Our World' (1918).

underworld of crooks, prostitutes, uniformed police, 'Jewish' business men, respectable housewives with lust in their hearts, burglars, drunks, homogenized working men, bored office workers and bureaucrats, tinted by the anonymous mass of the filthy tenements of the poor. The tiniest of trains weaves over a far viaduct, indicating at the horizon the anonymous world of the industrial city. Tenements rise higher than the sun, the tiniest of churches on the tiniest of hills with the tiniest of crosses, define a non-existent 'horizon', while a hill-walker with rucksack, pipe and knee breeches walks purposefully in no identifiable geographic space. Knives, parts of naked bodies, dogs, vases of flowers and lonely human beings emerge from broken lines and broken perspectives.

Heartfield's photomontages also show the political consequences of thwarted and manipulated erotic desire industrially reproduced, which in this case produce a manic rage for order. A old uniformed general stands ceremoniously to the right of one picture (see fig. 4) while in the top half of the frame are a row of skeletons standing to attention while, at the bottom uniformed men march in the opposite direction. An anti-Hitler election poster of 1932 shows the Führer from the waist up, his chest like an x-ray of a thorax, exposing a line of gold coins rising from the stomach to the throat as the face yells with open mouth. Another ('Pillars of Society') shows Chamberlain among other state leaders of the League of Nations against the detritus of a bomb site. In 'That's the Blessing of the Nazi Salute' (1936) Heartfield shows a black skeletal hand whose fingers

Fig. 4: John Heartfield, anti-fascist photo montage.

are sky-written in black vapour trails from five biplanes. To the right there are bombed-out buildings and to the left a line of corpses of young children. The pictures are an exact and terrible premonition of the war to come.

To a degree, then, the American Air Force photograph of the mushroom cloud continues the vapour trail but without trace of human beings or any suggestion of human activity. Its presence is anonymous. The title ('Nagasaki') is fundamentally ironic – there is no sign either of Nagasaki or of the destruction and the burning of human beings and their anguished and painful deaths. This is a 'detatched' scientific photograph, taken from high above the earth with no reference to author, script writer, director, cast, producer or fundraiser. It is the ultimate expression of the scientifically monumental, in Mumford's sense, celebrated as nature. Its undeclared meta-narrative is the destruction of a city. Its brilliant agents have kept, modestly, an objective distance. A dark column of man-made vapour rises from natural clouds while the bright head of the mushroom cloud lifts off from it like a reverse falling of a drop of water from a tap, and its crown is haloed, brilliant in the sunshine. The relation between light and dark is almost hallucinatory. The atomic cloud is an act of hubris, an intrusion into the order of things. Disorder masks itself, Faust-like, as the mastery of the invisible order of nature itself.

In contrast, Stieglitz's photograph declares its links with the earth: the leaves of trees are emerging from the bottom of the frame, a point of reference to the sentient biological world. The clouds are cirrus wisps that fan out in a suggestive arrested vertical movement with the subtlest gradations in light and shade. The disk of the sun is barely visible, veiling the power of life itself in a diffuse play of contraries. The gaze looks upwards, the cloud images are part of a world continuous between earth and air, the effect is to be lifted and still at the same time. The interiority of the human world and exteriority of the prospective world of nature, bracketed in this fraction of time, are held briefly in a moment of mutual recognition of the other's existence. Through the magic of art, the sky looks back at the eye looking towards it. Order becomes an object of wonder. It is personal and impersonal at the same time.

In the production of both images, the ends of science and technology are offered for questioning. Beyond the spontaneous, intuitive comparison just given, however, how did Stieglitz himself think of his 'Equivalents', and what kind of general discourse did he feel was appropriate to the act of creation in the photograph? In the discussion that follows, the statements made by Stieglitz and his friends about the purpose and nature of the pictures have been taken very seriously as a prolegomenon to a more complex criticism.

In 1925, a commentator who interviewed Stieglitz had noted that he said that those who called the 'Equivalents' 'cloud studies' knew neither the nature of clouds nor the nature of study, adding that he had studied under the great nineteenth-century German physicist Hermann von Helmholtz. However scientific Helmholtz's theme, Stieglitz had asserted, 'he gave himself'.[17] Stieglitz's biographer notes that the budding photographer had been a little out of his depth in Helmholtz's lectures, but nonetheless Stieglitz had clearly caught the spirit if not the abstruse details of Helmholtz's goal: his passionate personal quest for knowledge and a sense of an almost magical order in the world of nature.[18] Helmholtz's work, in simplified summary, indicates a certain *Zeitgeist* to which Stieglitz would certainly not have been immune.

Helmholtz, one of the greatest German physicists of the nineteenth century, was a key player in what was to become known as the 'classical' system in which the whole of nature was thought to be mathematically explainable in terms of the twin poles of 'atoms' and 'radiation'. The concept of 'energy' (force) itself might be all embracing as most famously expounded in Helmholtz's 1847 law of 'energy' conservation. Later in the century the corporeal and incorporeal world would be broken up again and radiant heat, light, magnetism, and electricity gathered under 'under the wings of a common theory of radiation and force-fields'.[19] The significance of Stieglitz's recall of Helmholtz lay in the photographer's view that art and science had a reciprocal vision of a 'unified' and mysteriously ordered world and that the personal and the collective endeavour were interdependent. This nature philosophy was commonplace in the Germanic world at the time and goes back to Goethe and beyond. Even the Swedish playwright Strindberg had made 'cloud photographs' on the basis of a somewhat monistic view of correspondences in nature encompassing both the animate and inanimate worlds.[20] Almost in the tradition of the alchemists, love of the world and the purity of the self should assist and guide an investigation of it. Further, there was a sense that the world was there to be deciphered, that its signifying surface referred to a more coherent invisible order. In a way, the 'force field' was a unifying metaphysic. It provided a set of magical signs, to be imagined and discovered simultaneously in the questions asked of an assumed but as yet invisible order in nature itself.

The project was therefore heavily underlined by faith. In the romantic view, and even further back to the Renaissance, the world of appearances was radically symbolic: 'And what if all of animated nature', asked the Platonizing Coleridge, 'be but organic harps diversely fram'd'.[21] A reproof of the implied pantheism is delivered at the end of the poem by the poet's wife because of the possibility of human hubris in a world deciphered entirely sufficiently by arrogant human beings.[22] Might not man become God with the key to secrets of nature exposed? In *Moby-Dick*, Captain Ahab muses on the decapitated head of the whale, as mysterious as the Sphinx, noting that it had 'seen enough to split the planets and make an infidel of Abraham' but that it could not speak. As the romantic vision of the world's mystical oneness with the self turned to nightmare, the fact that 'not the smallest atom stirs nor lives in matter, but has it cunning duplicate in mind', had yet to find its voice, let alone its ethical and metaphysical justification.[23]

For Stieglitz, however, the matter of hubris was not religious, but one that opened questions of the ethics of human intellectuality. To engage in an imaginative act of analysis and celebration of the natural world was less an invasion of the domain of God than an acknowledgement of the deepest manifestation of life in the act of recognizing it in its very emergence. Here the activity of the artist and the scientist might be seen as sharing common endeavours and common dangers. The wonder of the radiant fields of force shown in Stieglitz's photograph contrasted strongly with the destructive exploitation of the knowledge of atomic energy in the photograph released by the American Air Force.

Stieglitz wanted 'through clouds to put down my philosophy of life'.[24] He expressed that philosophy in many ways but in the following statement it was clearly one that was closely related to an almost Blakean play of contraries:

> I feel the duality of world forces forever at work. But it is when conflict hovers about a point – a focal point – and light is on the ascendancy, that I am moved.'[25]

The moment of movement to light, the stillness and attentiveness required to describe the unperceivable moment of change and the shifting reciprocities of the visible and invisible in science and art will all be taken up again in the last section on Muriel Rukeyser. These themes are in opposition to the driven, competitive, profit-oriented nature of the self and work under capitalist conditions, the world of power and its positivistic reliance on crude materiality and common sense. To a degree, Stieglitz's nature has a utopian premise: 'the clouds are there for everyone – no tax as yet upon them – free'.[26] Stieglitz loathed 'the professionalized American Scene' – 'what went on in the name of art and politics and religion'.[27] Not clouds – nor sky, wrote the African-American poet Jean Toomer to Stieglitz in early 1924, 'but life itself'.[28] That life, for Stieglitz, meant a life in which art was primary and above all available for everybody. Anyone who put art in museums, in private houses or who bought it had missed the point. The 'exhibition' itself he felt seriously put people off art. Those who accused him of exclusiveness had missed his radical utopian first principles. As for Marx, the primacy of exchange value killed the process of life together with the meaning of the product of labour itself.

Certainly Stieglitz's romantic and scientific sense of the world entered Toomer's own poetry with poems entitled, for example 'Worlds of Shadow-Planes and Solids Silently Moving'. It is the penetration of the mask of nature and the world, which nonetheless paradoxically registers itself on its surface that informs Stieglitz's post-romantic vision. In contrasting his work with his 'Parisian Contemporary', Eugène Atget, Mumford marked his distance from the Frenchman, who deliberately composed 'a documentary history of [...] [the city] after the fashion of Zola'.[29] For Mumford, Stieglitz touched the city only by implication: 'He extracts the minute particle of radium [*sic*], which accounts for the strong behaviour of the whole mass.'[30] Stieglitz's 'Equivalents' thus acknowledged that deep romantic intuition of dream and reverie, the interrelatedness of the diverse phenomena of the world, the work of the imagination in mathematics and poetry.

To the extent that 'Equivalent' indicates the possibility of finding similitude rather than difference, it is actually a poor word for the transformations of the metaphoric act in which Stieglitz was really engaged. His other title 'Songs of the Sky' in the group *Music – A Sequence of Ten Cloud Photographs* from the 1923 exhibition, which were a forerunner of the later 'Equivalents', were lyrically and more intuitively nearer the mark. However, it failed to indicate the modernity and highly self-conscious, and synthetic nature of the vision. As a young man in Germany, Stieglitz had not only studied engineering but had hovered around the periphery of the Liszt–Wagner circle, helping with productions of plays by Shakespeare, Calderón, Goethe, Lessing and Schiller, as well as operas such as *Tristan und Isolde* and *Carmen*. All his life, Stieglitz was an avid reader of literature.

In more familiar poetic terms, Wordsworth's most famous lyrical poem had invoked the fleeting movement of the cloud as part of an epistemological drama of creative reverie. It spoke quite literally of the 'bliss of solitude'. The photograph and the poem become tangible poetic traces in Gaston Bachelard's felicitous phrase about the nature of reveries: as 'coordinating liberties.'[31] The retreat into solitude is by no means inevitably evasion. 'I have been through a lot this summer', Stieglitz wrote to Marsden Hartley in 1923, that is 'why "Clouds" (really the Sun) & I became fast friends'.[32] In terms of the earth, Stieglitz thought one sun was better than a thousand suns. Ten years later Mumford wrote to Stieglitz of sinking into a chair after a hard day's writing and looking into the clouds: 'you are often with me in that quiet hour. Some of that sky goes everyday into what I write.'[33] And choosing the last photograph for *The Condition of Man*, published a year before the Hiroshima bomb, Mumford wrote again, speaking of how he needed a final plate 'to symbolize the life springing out of the dark world through which we move today. Only you have the photograph that would symbolize this, the Lake George skyline and clouds in America.'[34]

In short, there is a visionary theme in Stieglitz's work. It is a theme which haunts the modernist and post-Impressionist artists of Stieglitz's youth and middle age. Ralph Flint, in his article in *America and Alfred Stieglitz*, noted that Monet's own attempts to develop the possibilities of 'transforming the play of direct sunlight to canvas' had begun with a Turner exhibition in the National Gallery, London, in 1870.[35] In Marsden Hartley's voluminous letters to Stieglitz, he spoke of the revision of the philosophy of vision in Cézanne, Picasso, Kandinsky, Van Gogh, Gauguin, Braque and Gertrude Stein. He spoke, too, of Blake's mystical vision, of his pan-nationalism (the Blake of Kathleen Raine[36] rather than of Daniel Erdman[37]), of the influence of Kandinsky's 'On the Spiritual in Art' and of the turn of the century interest in mysticism of the *Blaue Reiter* and Stefan George circles who were influenced by Jakob Boehme, Meister Eckhart and the *Bhagavadgita*. This is the more mystical end of the world as 'signatures', and tellingly it is not until 1917 that Hartley finally writes to Stieglitz that he is outliving his mysticism.[38]

Yet the strain would persist from the early years of Stieglitz's *Camera Work*, to Dorothy Norman's involvement with Gandhi and his heirs and with Indian culture, politics and religion. It was fundamentally a strategy that argued a resistance to naïve realism and it proved useful in the fight against the Stalinist social realism that dominated the 1930s. Ethically it lamented the discrediting of the human 'soul' and with it a vision of universal brotherhood. Politically that 'soul' linked to all other souls could paradoxically be placed as a counterweight both to an aggressive capitalist individualism and the dangers of the positivist reductionism of scientific materialism. Pictorially, Stieglitz was of a generation that, as Charles Henry Caffin noted, saw Whistler as a 'bridge between Western and Oriental [*sic*] consciousness', though he added that he went a bit too far from the world, rather like the efforts of 'the anchorite to escape from the wickedness of the world'.[39]

In terms of intellectual history, the visionary claim was another thread in the modernist reaction against the mechanical and positivist frame of mind that had dominated much of the Victorian period. Stieglitz's photographic circle and post-impressionist painting shared a common purpose in doubting the given as reality. Hartley, painting in Maine, found in the 'Equivalents' a degree of calm: 'it is the sun and the incredible form of the light that does it'. He added later that when he looked at Stieglitz's 'Equivalents' he sensed that 'they look like I wish to feel and be – equable-continuous, tangible – ordered'.[40]

The manifestations of the human relation to worlds of invisible order were, then, radically different in the two photographs. If the world were simply in its mass and bulk, wrote the poet Hart Crane to Stieglitz, one would not need the 'chiaroscuro' of Stieglitz's photographs: 'But they are suspended on the invisible dimension whose vibrance has been denied the human eye at all times and saved in the intuition of ecstasy.'[41] But was that ecstasy revealing or entrapping? Stieglitz was scientifically trained and not antagonistic to science as such but to its ethics and its exclusiveness. Since the seventeenth century, it had officially ruled ethics out of consideration, reducing the complexity of human activity in relation to the world through its stance of neutral objectivity. It related to nature rather like the Plotinian God. This God was pantheistic and vitalistic, with an energy, like human desire, neutral for creation or destruction. When Oppenheimer famously quoted Shiva from the *Bhagavadgita* on the occasion of the Hiroshima bomb, 'I am become death, the destroyer of worlds', he at once brilliantly acknowledged the ethical lacuna in the scientific project between responding to the seductive beauty of discoverable order which motivates all scientists and the destructive carelessness of the Faustian quest.

Hart Crane's romantic view of science was also not without its problems. The 'new syntheses of vision', a phrase he uses in his letters to Stieglitz, risked the ambiguities of the exemplifying narrative of the exceptional person, artist or scientist: that traveller who had been to hell and had emerged with a prophetic vision. Alain Robbe-Grillet once called this emotion the 'sacred vertigo' and doubted its ethics. For the artist and scientist as well as (here) for the writer this traditional role consisted in:

> excavating nature [...] in finally unearthing some fragment of a disconcerting secret. The descender into Avernus would return triumphant messages describing the mysteries he had actually touched with his own hands. And this sacred vertigo the reader suffered then, far from causing him anguish or nausea, reassured him as to his power of domination over the world. [42]

From Mary Shelley's Frankenstein to Melville's Ahab and onwards, the 'sacred vertigo' has been well documented in literature. Was there a profound link between the sacred vertigo of the atomic bomb and the 'Equivalents'? Was the soaring vision of Stieglitz's cloud patterns somehow paradoxically linked to the vertiginous nightmare of the atomic cloud? Blake had known that good and evil were perilously close and that one could appear in the guise of the other. Did good and evil define themselves by inarticulate alterity? In which case what might ever be affirmed or denied? What here is the relationship between intuitive intellectual and emotional depth and suicidal or ecstatic height? To what degree are people trapped in their best endeavours? Flying back to New York in 1929, Stieglitz wrote to Mumford that the flight seemed to do something for him: 'to be alone near the sky – a pilot outside, I alone in the cabin [...] I couldn't read – not even Faust – which in a time of despair had always done for me what flying did this year [...] I have made a few Equivalents.'[43] To return to Stieglitz's question, what was the 'place' of the one in relation to the other?

These questions are far too difficult to be resolved logically. The answers can only be intuited in the deep contradictory movement at the heart of the metaphoric process itself. In Muriel Rukeyser's poetry these issues are crucial and to a degree her meditation on the worlds of art and science goes some way to setting out more clearly the terrain of the problem if not finally resolving it (see pp. 420–2). Did Stieglitz, as Mumford argued, in making the sky itself dominant in his photographs, unite 'his sense of the universal order' with the sense of the personality, as developed in the relation between men and women?[44] Were they redolent of that 'organic balance' that might be glimpsed at the heart of the play of contraries? This play of contraries is crucial to Stieglitz's art. It was the world he sought to realize between the black-and-white polarities of his photographic art. It was at once a very technical problem involving on the one hand the choice of subject and its location in relation to the lens, exposure, focus, depth of field, frame, plate, the chemistry of the development process and paper, and, on the other, a complex symbolic, existential and metaphysical issue.

The visual and human world, in portraiture and landscape, was played out in terms of the gradations of tone and shade between white and black, light and dark, life and death. The photographing of the world in black and white was a philosophical problem that had occupied Stieglitz from his student days with Hermann Wilhelm Vogel.[45] This fundamentally engaged the relation of white to black. It was not possible 'to conceive of black without white', for it was 'when conflict hovers about a point – a focal point – and light is on the ascendancy' that the human heart is moved.[46] That philosophy was most beautifully articulated by the twentieth-century English engraver Robin Tanner. A socialist in the Morris Arts and Crafts tradition, Tanner, in a commentary on Rembrandt's etchings, spoke of a dual light and dark world:

> human tragedy and ecstasy, the poignant beauty of the natural world and of the human head – and with all of them a celebration of light and darkness: sunlight, moonlight, and lamplight; dark shadows of night, and the depth of tone in clouds and foliage, drapery, architecture, and the earth itself.[47]

Stieglitz would have understood Tanner's attempt to create Blake's 'real and eternal world', where, as Tanner cited the English visionary poet Traherne, 'everything is at rest, free and immortal'.[48]

To cut the Gordian knot of this argument, it can be said that the Nagasaki photograph was only sentimentally significant. It offered only partial evidence of its own darkness. It was arrogant in its celebration of pure force, an icon of science and industrial organization in a time of war, made chillingly authentic and even grotesquely and expensively beautiful in the mass destruction of life itself.

It was in the first volume of *TWICE A YEAR*, that the young American poet Charles Olson published his essay 'Lear and Moby-Dick'. In it he took up the Blakean play of contraries. Writing of the worlds of Melville and Shakespeare, he offered a distinction, 'as old as Chaldea', emerging between the Faustian sensibility of the black art (he speculates that Melville derives the name Goetic from Goethe) as opposed to a neo-Platonic *theurgy*, a white magic 'in which, through self-purification and sacred rites, the aid of the divine was evoked'.[49] This poetic perception was fundamental to Stieglitz. In the issue of *Camera Work* devoted to Stieglitz in 1911, Sadakichi Hartman noted, in relation to modernism's preference for fluidity of form, that Blake had gone further than anyone else and cited Bergson on the vitalistic premise that subject and object were bound into a continuum that the artist uniquely was in a position to register.[50]

Structuring the Bergsonian crypto-unities, however, was for Olson, a much more Heraclitean flux: at once threatening and illuminating. Olson spoke of an almost Manichean world of duality articulating a contradiction between reason and truth, and evil: 'between black and white magic, the one of demons, the other of saints and angels, one evil, the other benevolent'.[51] The world of Ahab was, more than partly, the world of the atomic bomb, the world of Stieglitz's cloud songs that of the 'silence' of Cordelia or Enobarbus.[52] Rukeyser took up the world of Melville's 'contraries' in her *Elegies*, which are the subject of the last part of this book. There is here a common field of both intellectual intercourse and discourse. Stieglitz, Mumford and Rukeyser were closely aware of each other's work. Stieglitz had read every book by Mumford from *The Golden Day* onwards. On 7 July 1928, for example, he wrote to Mumford 'It is good to hear you are deep in & full of Melville.'[53]

Alfred Stieglitz and Ideology

Hence the poetic and political worlds were linked in the discourse that Norman was to inherit from Stieglitz for her journal. But ethics, ideology, the role of art and a practical politics were to weave in very contradictory terms throughout Norman's entire enterprise. In class terms, Stieglitz came from the high bourgeoisie. Photography was a very expensive pursuit. Stieglitz's note to Marie Bersault in 1917 about a cerebral haemorrhage of his mother's cook who had served the family for thirty-one years provokes, almost a century later, very contradictory reactions and lifts a curtain on women's lives at that time:

> She was the real backbone of Oaklawn – I don't know how my mother will manage without her – She belonged to the race that is dying out – Up every morning at 4.30 & worked until 9 p.m.
>
> That was her pleasure – Never a penny's worth wasted – a magnificent organizer – she is 67.[54]

There are many contradictions between Stieglitz's politics and his public and private value systems. He believed in the freedom and equality of women, even though he struggled when Georgia O'Keeffe went to New Mexico to pursue an independent career, a career that he had certainly fostered in its early stages. He was libertarian in sexual terms, recognizing that love and desire formed a complex dynamic. With D.H. Lawrence he hated the religious right's fear of and puritanical attitudes to the body and their use of sexuality for demagogic purposes, on one occasion agreeing with Lawrence to be posted *Lady Chatterley's Lover* to check the vigilance of US Customs and Excise. Lawrence characteristically replied to Stieglitz, 'they ought to censor eggs, as revealing the intimate relation of cock and hen'.[55] Many years later in 1954, Dorothy Brett would write to Dorothy Norman about Frieda Lawrence's troubles with the FBI over the 'moral turpitude' of Lawrence's paintings.[56] Stieglitz set this sexual libertarian tone for his circle. It later led Norman to publish Henry Miller. As Randolph Bourne so cogently observed: 'Every new generation, in fact, contrives to find some new way of being puritanical. Every new generation finds some new way of sacrifice.'[57]

In more public and political matters, Stieglitz (unlike Mumford) refused to condemn Germany in the First World War. His view that Western society was so rotten that it was inevitable and that no individual was to blame was rather like blaming the Holocaust on original sin. This level of generality seriously undermined the responsibility of a specific politics. Nonetheless, he sympathized with much in the labour movement and with the struggles of the ordinary worker. He entertained the German ambassador in 1916 but he also had visits from Russian revolutionaries and sympathized with the railway worker strikes of the same year.[58] He wrote to Marie Boursault in 1917 that he had just had an evening with Francis Picabia and a Russian revolutionary who had sung Russian folk and prison songs to them.[59] He had a radical belief in democracy and egalitarianism. His was a radical individualism, out of humour with the world of urban blight and shoddy commodities that modern industrial capitalism had made. Yet, a commitment to the modernist movement made him one of the great photographers of the city and the new abstract industrial-capitalist skyline of New York, that city of canyons and few horizons. He felt strongly that America not Europe was the better place for contemporary art. Like Mumford and Macdonald, he understood at once the horror and deep historical meaning of the atomic bomb.

In terms of politics, however, to the despair of Waldo Frank, Stieglitz refused to commit himself to the communist cause. In 1935 he wrote to Frank, 'I am sorry I disappoint you in not taking an "active" stand as far as Communism is concerned [...] in reality I am much more *active* in a revolutionary sense than most of the so-called Communists [...] So I am a man without labels and without party.'[60] That would hardly have gone down well, with the average party member or labour organizer, Stalinist or instinctive Jacobin but it did reflect Trotsky's notion that the artist must be independent of all parties. Politically, it was to the socialist and communist dissenters that Stieglitz felt most naturally drawn. The anarchist Adolf Wolff had written to him from prison in 1914 hoping that one day the spirit of Stieglitz's gallery '291' would wipe away the whole system of prisons and custodial sentencing.[61] Stieglitz published the letter in *Camera Work*.

Stieglitz was a friend of the Wobbly leader Big Bill Haywood and the anarcho-syndicalist Emma Goldman. To a degree, he was part of that radical New York scene of art and politics from the turn of the century up to 1919, where the playwright Eugene O'Neill, for example, was struggling between Nietzsche and Marx and where the world of Mabel Dodge Luhan coincided with the world of Eugene V. Debs and the Wobblies. In 1917, for example, Marsden Hartley wrote to Stieglitz from Paris that he was pleased that John Reed had liked his (Hartley's) poems.[62]

To revive a specifically American art therefore had to be described as a political need and it was in this spirit that Norman, who was to give much more thought than Stiegltiz to the political world, socialized Stieglitz's view of artistic freedom under the rubric of 'civil liberties'. There were perhaps other voices too from the American cultural past that encouraged this move. One important voice was undoubtedly the short-lived but highly significant *seven arts* journal, whose pacifism stopped its publication in 1917. However Randolph Bourne, Waldo Frank, Mumford's friend Van Wyck Brooks, John Dos Passos, Robert Frost and the music critic Paul Rosenfeld had all been associated with it. In his obituary of Paul Rosenfeld in 1946, Isidore Schneider wrote of the *seven arts* contributors in the communist *New Masses*, to remind its readers that they 'fought for the emancipation of women and for birth control, against the Puritan repression which was so often a pretext for political repression; and above all, they fought to set cultural values above the philistine and corrupted values of capitalism.'[63] His account tells the story of a continuing American radical criticism with links to its own past, and is important because *TWICE A YEAR* came out not only at a point at which faith in the Marxism of the Russian revolution was faltering as an opposing force, but also at a point where faith in American capitalism and its emerging imperial power was equally continuing to disturb the more politically conscious in terms of its social consequences. The agenda of *seven arts*, with its memories of Randolph Bourne and others made it one of the true precursors of *TWICE A YEAR*. The first issue of the latter would reprint Bourne's work.

Between Stalinism and decaying European imperialism, fascism and Nazism, crucial choices for an incipient neo-imperialist America lay ahead. There was a world order being produced where the state's power and the power of vast corporations with indirect means of mass persuasion seemed increasingly to curtail individual freedom and to threaten the basis of democracy itself. The significant writers of the early twentieth century in America had not spared the public the dystopian effects of the American Dream produced by the modern industrial state. From Theodore Dreiser's Sister Carrie at the mercy of the ultimately insufficient values of personal economic success, social-Darwinian survival and consumerist ideology, to Fitzgerald's *The Great Gatsby*, whose eponymous hero's capacity for romantic hope was based on gangsterism which mirrored the actions of the class in control, from Faulkner's poor Southern white playing the market at the end of an electric ticker-tape machine and castrating the unfit in the process, to Richard Wright's vivid account of African-American mid-Western urban life, a world was emerging in which American power was increasingly unevenly distributed, the victims more desperate, and the rich and powerful undeterred by democratic and legal controls both at home and abroad. Without significant political alternatives to an apparently national ideological consensus, 'civil liberties' and the rule of law were the last bastions of freedom in an increasingly polarized society. The war itself had accelerated a military-industrial complex with political, social and environmental consequences that no existing ideological analysis and political praxis seemed powerful or intelligent enough to comprehend, let alone control.

Stieglitz followed the twists and turns of American politics keenly. He read Marx alongside Proust and closely watched the rise of both Hitler and Roosevelt.[64] His major interests were of course not political but the legacies he left Norman and *TWICE A YEAR* included: an anarchist distrust of power and commitment to individual freedom; a sympathy with the struggles of the ordinary working man and woman; an instinctive dislike of the rich and powerful; a genuine loathing of materialist values; a commitment to women's freedom and independence with an attempt at least, despite a certain inevitable emotional anguish, to create a serious non-possessive sexual ethics; a wide-ranging international perspective on art and politics with a local loyalty to developing and encouraging the American arts; a conviction that only serious reading and an awareness of the past could be the basis for genuine innovation; and a sense that any serious artist had to be engaged with all the different aspects of the foregoing. These were balanced by his limitations: a lack of experience of the broader aspects of American society (he refused even to visit the South West to see O'Keeffe); a conservative distrust of the masses and lives that were increasingly dominated with forms of mass culture (he lacked Macdonald's and Orwell's aristocratic curiosity); a too pure distance from actual politics and the labour movement with its economic and class issues; a blanket distrust of many aspects of industrial modernity; and a somewhat wilful, personal prophetic manner. 'You just try arguing with him and see how far you get', exclaimed O'Keeffe, in a BBC documentary of 1979.

Dorothy Norman came into Stieglitz's life in the late 1920s, sending Georgia O'Keeffe into a temporary nervous breakdown but also forcing the American painter to discover her own path and values which were in the end liberating and conducive to enriching her art.[65] In fact it had been O'Keeffe's decision to live in New Mexico that had first put clear water between her and Stieglitz. They managed to remain friends, however, and she was there during his last illness. Norman's biography, unlike those of Stieglitz and O'Keeffe, has not yet been written, even in this age where the academic biography is king – it is currently a pressing need. Norman published her 'autobiography' in 1987.[66] It is a far from comprehensive personal account of her life and has significant lacunae. Nonetheless, it is certainly a work of art in its own right and will be examined again at the end of this chapter.

Norman was one of the most extraordinary American women of the twentieth century: a distinguished photographer in her own right, an art collector, editor of a journal that is one of the finest, still-unrecognized achievements of American twentieth-century culture, a sophisticated journalist, many years a columnist for the then-liberal *The New York Post*, a woman fully engaged behind the scenes at the highest level of international politics, an anti-imperialist, a friend of Indian independence, an intimate of the Nehru and Gandhi families, a student of Indian culture and religion, an active participant in aid and social assistance for a then frequently starving Indian sub-continent and a New York hostess with a range of contacts that would have been the envy of Madame de Staël. Her fight for civil liberties and social change involved actively supporting many libertarian and democratic societies: Americans for Democratic Action, the New York Urban League, the American Emergency Food Committee for India, the American Citizens' Committee for Economic Aid Abroad, the American Civil Liberties Union and the Planned Parenthood Association, among many others.

A wealthy woman from the upper echelons of American society, in *TWICE A YEAR* Norman attempted to provide a journal that would be engaged with art and politics, democratic ethics and their abuses, trades union politics, civil liberties, including ethnic, women's and children's issues, discussions of the New World Order emerging from the Bretton Woods Agreement and the rise of the United Nations in the context of Cold War. Like Dwight Macdonald, she provided a wartime, trans-Atlantic home for European writers. Much more than Macdonald Norman attempted to create and publicize an American radical tradition of letters and the visual arts. She was much more welcoming than the conservative Yale-educated Macdonald to form-breaking literary and visual art, but much less engaged with the faltering discourses of Marxism and the historical detail of Soviet, European and American politics. In a sense that was inevitable given the format, direction and focus. The weekly journal *politics* was closer to the broadsheet and tabloid newspaper whereas this twice-yearly arts and civil liberties publication in the format of a bound book but with subscribers like a journal gave reviewers and librarians some difficulty in terms of classification.

Dorothy Norman and TWICE A YEAR

It was money from Norman's husband, Edward A. Norman, that helped finance the project. The Normans' house, 124 East 70th Street, was built by William Lescaze and was a monument to American domestic modernist architecture of the period, transferring in a Stieglitz-like trans-Atlanticist gesture, the spare lines of high European modernism to American soil. Mumford liked Lescaze, praising his imaginative projects for renewal and renovation of waste sites and old brownstones in his famous 'Sky Line' articles for *The New Yorker*.[67] It is also noteworthy that Dorothy Norman corresponded with both Mary and William Lescaze about low-rent housing schemes in New York.[68] The denizens of this expensive Manhattan house, unlike most of their class, were seriously concerned with housing for the poor. Mary Lescaze was to be Norman's assistant editor on *TWICE A YEAR*. Edward Norman's commitment was at first absolute, in terms of time and money. Like Nancy Macdonald, his was the backseat but crucial role. Eventually though he took little interest in the project, feeling estranged from the world it opened up for his wife.[69]

Something of the genesis of the journal can be gleaned from Norman's correspondence with William Carlos Williams and Edward Dahlberg. Norman contacted Williams on 29 June 1937, saying she wanted to talk to him about the matter of a possible quarterly, one which would 'print and keep together material that really moves one beyond all isms and so-called platforms.'[70] The comment indicates a certain frustration with the congealing of ideological positions in New York journal publishing circles during the late 1930s. Williams wrote that he was too busy to be involved. The original notion was that Edward Dahlberg would be associate editor and that it would be called *American Quarterly*, the idea being to have a name that would avoid 'gimcrack propaganda' on the one hand and a 'cute foppish' title on the other. Dahlberg tried to rope Williams in by noting that the journal would be anti-statist, and that 'American writers from Melville to Bourne' would be given 'alms for oblivion'.[71] He wrote to Williams that he wanted it to be a *belles-lettres* magazine with a 'special Melville issue, a Randolph Bourne number and so on, but we want them sharply reinterpreted and re-felt'.[72] In the end though, Dahlberg was too absolute a pacifist to be useful.[73] Neglected writers, and past writers, as with *politics*, particularly would be revived to radicalize the tradition by seeking a usable past. Today this is known as canon breaking. Dahlberg asked in a postscript if Williams knew of anyone who might write something on the early anarchists: Benjamin Tucker, Joseph Warren, [Alexander] Berkman, Voltairine De Cleyre and so forth. Clearly the paper was not to have quite the *belles-lettres* image usually associated with conservative aesthetic withdrawal, and above all, quasi-philosophical questions of time, narrative and memory would offer defining parameters in the journal.

Norman also discussed the founding of the journal with Lewis Mumford. Her letters to him confirm that it was to be radically interdisciplinary, steer clear of the increasingly Stalinist communists (she was apprised of Richard Wright's difficulties with them), oriented towards good reproductions of photographs, reprinting out-of-print radical essays and literature and an attempt to re-politicize art but not in terms of social realism. It was also to reflect Mumford's holistic view of life and culture as exemplified in his recent book *The Culture of Cities* (1938).[74]

As for Dwight Macdonald, the dissenting independent 'socialist' would also play an important role. It was her husband's involvement in the Consumer's Cooperative Movement that encouraged Norman to embrace reformism, distrusting a Soviet Russia that 'for all its slogans' appeared 'cruel and repressive'. She added: 'We remain rebels, reformists at heart, but not revolutionaries.'[75] She even went on a pilgrimage with her husband to the English site of those classic dissenting communitarians of the early co-operative movement, the Rochdale weavers. Although perhaps too much culture-shocked by 'high tea', soggy Brussels sprouts and gloomy English rain, she was politically realistic enough to doubt that the cooperative movement would 'solve all the world's problems'.[76] On the feminist side of things, however, she oddly felt unable to understand O'Keeffe's refusal to be called Mrs Stieglitz.[77] Along with the dissenting politics went innovative poetry and she sympathized with breaking 'classic' forms in the Whitman tradition. She had experienced stifling conservatism in both politics and the arts at her wealthy in-laws: 'the correspondence between the Normans' reactionary political attitudes and their admiration for conservative works of art is as logical as it is disturbing.'[78]

Already a close friend of Charles Olson, Norman mentioned to Dahlberg that the poet, who came from Gloucester, Massachusetts, was using Williams's *In the American Grain* in his American literature course at Harvard.[79] In December 1937 Dahlberg wrote to Williams that they were considering calling the publication *TWICE A YEAR*. Williams suggested *three times a year* with a clover for a symbol, though he added somewhat facetiously that someone might mistake it for a shamrock.[80] Just nine months later, Norman wrote to Paul Rosenfeld that the first issue was going to press.[81] Norman's assiduity and energy had swept all before it. Her letters to her many correspondents show her almost invariably accurate criticism and sense of judgement and her hands-on fearlessness with some of the most distinguished writers, painters, photographers, political activists and refugees of the century. Henry Miller wrote to her in 1940: 'You are the most terrifically earnest, scrupulous, conscientious, persistent person I guess I ever met. How can you afford to give so much?'[82]

If Macdonald had turned to Proudhon and Herzen from the European socialist past, Norman sought out Thoreau and Randolph Bourne for an American radical tradition, along with writers such as Olson, Mumford, Rukeyser, Williams and Richard Wright, all of whom had a keen sense of the increasing historical depth of American culture and letters and held radical to liberal views. But at the same time, their vision of human history culture went far back in time, certainly beyond the nationalist founding temporalities that derived from 1620, 1630 or 1776. Olson, for example, who contributed essays to *TWICE A YEAR* on Melville and Dostoevsky, by far the most formally radical poet, developed a poetic exegetical narrative that stretched back to the pre-Socratics, and beyond that to the furthest reaches of geological time. Williams in 'Against the Weather' would review European art, Dante and Shakespeare in the spirit of Whitman in a desperate defence of art facing a conflicted political and ideological present. Rukeyser, in an essay for the journal called 'The Fear of Poetry' (which is foundational to the thought of this book and was eventually included in her defining work on poetics, *The Life of Poetry*, 1948), specifically highlighted the problem of the past and temporality.

Invoking the horror of war raging in Europe and calling on Americans to face up to the reality of the Nazi and fascist armies sweeping Europe, Rukeyser swiftly sketched the need for the present to find an 'unanticipated' past:

> We have our own tradition to retrace. So many times, when our scholars have talked of tradition, they have been thinking, 'Repeat! Repeat!' mourning some Golden Age to whose special knowledge they had felt admitted. But tradition is not repetition, that is blasphemy against tradition. Tradition is, rather, the search for the clue – to know oneself in one's own labyrinth, and be suddenly aware that by a thread, a subtle thread, by a thread only, could the center be reached. As it was, as it has been! But as it will not be again, except for indirection. Sheridan caught the phrase there: he warns us not to 'anticipate the past.' Kierkegaard speaks of the foreboding eye which looks behind so that it may see, by indirection what lies ahead.[83]

These sentences extended Pound's axiomatic 'make it new' into the larger field of political ethics, into the psychology of human dread and anguish, and into a more complex and personal sense of time as it re-invoked the depths of the past. In the second volume of the journal, it was no accident that Norman reprinted work by Proust as a Macdonald-style 'ancestor', with the first English translation of an early story, 'La mort de Baldassare Silvande, vicomte de Sylvania.' The translator, Emilie Amram, noted that the great themes of *À la recherche du temps perdu* were already present but that the unifying philosophical theme of time had not yet been established. It is, however, present enough in the final paragraph, as the dying *vicomte* recalls 'his Robinson Crusoe and the evenings in the garden when his sister sang.' The citations from Shakespeare that head each section make Pascalian ethical and atemporal signatures across that inevitable biological movement toward death, judgements that underwrite the elusive experiences of memory and time.[84] In the spaces between, Proust's profoundly human world emerges, a world that engages anguish, human indifference, cruelty, wayward passion and love with a warmth that is at once unsentimental and unsparing.

For the historian and the poet, the past was part of a present at once political and subjective. Nicholas Calas, writing in volume VII of *TWICE A YEAR* in 1941, noted that:

> The best description of the *Commune de Paris* is certainly not to be found in French text books which are written by the spiritual children of Thiers, the murderer of the Communards, but in the analysis made by a man who wanted to profit from the uprising of the Parisian works: Lenin. Likewise, it is not in a history of English literature that we shall learn very much about a poet such as Donne, but in the essays of a contemporary, whose conception of poetry was influenced by Donne's verse: T.S. Eliot.[85]

Calas had sub-headings in his article such as: 'The future is part of the past' and 'History is a conception of the future'. These journalistic quasi-proverbs pointed to profounder philosophical issues of temporality and writing.

TWICE A YEAR also invoked historical European traditions. In the main, nineteenth-century and modernist writers were reprinted, including works by Novalis, Heinrich Heine, Höderlin, George Sand, Flaubert, Tolstoy, George Bernard Shaw, Kafka, Proust, Arthur Schnitzler and Rilke. It is also worth noting that the first publication in English of aphorisms from Vico's *Scientia Nuova*, translated by Eliot Gianturco, appeared in the Fall–Winter 1940 edition. In a section called 'Revaluations' in same issue, contemporary writers reappraised earlier writers for the journal's readers. Olson wrote on Dostoevsky, Henry Miller on Balzac and others on Thomas Mann, Gide and Dante.

As with *politics*, the journal established a trans-Atlantic bridge with exiled European writers who had been under threat and whose legacy was thought essential for the cause of art and civil liberty in both Europe and America. These included Thomas Mann, Ignazio Silone, Albert Einstein, Arthur Koestler, G.A. Borgese, Ernst Toller, Carlo Rosselli, Hermann Kahler, Nicola Chiaromonte (Macdonald's close friend and correspondent), Erich Fried, Ernst Bloch, Edouard Roditi, Bodo Uhse, Klaus Mann, Harry Slochower, Oska Maria Graff and William Jay. Although Malraux had appeared in the first number in 1938 and Camus in

1946, Sartre, de Beauvoir and Brecht just made it into the last and tenth anniversary number of 1948. There were scholars from smaller European countries and beyond Europe itself: two of the most distinguished being Gunnar Myrdal, whose famous work *American Dilemma* came out in the era of *TWICE A YEAR*, and Ananda Coomaraswary, the Sri Lankan-born prolific scholar of oriental art, comparative religion and aesthetics, who had also been associated with William Morris and the Kelmscott Press in the English Cotswolds. Walter Gropius from the Bauhaus also wrote for the journal.

On the American side, as far as the writers were concerned, the American past and its continuing political and artistic tradition was represented by John Quincy Adams, Thoreau, Melville, Louis Sullivan, Randolph Bourne and Hart Crane; the present by Sherwood Anderson, e.e. cummings, Gertrude Stein, Charles Olson, Clifford Odets, Anaïs Nin, Theodore Dreiser, William Carlos Williams, William Saroyan, Muriel Rukeyser, Kenneth Patchen, Henry Miller, Waldo Frank and Richard Wright, as well as a number of younger and lesser-known writers. American critics included Lewis Mumford, Paul Rosenfeld, Jay Leyda, Henry Steele Commager, Harold Clurman, Brom Weber and Herbert J. Seligmann. Painters, architects and photographers were represented by Marsden Hartley, Georgia O'Keeffe, John Marin, William Lescaze, Alfred Stieglitz, Ansel Adams and Paul Strand; dance performers and composers by Agnes Enters, Charles Ives, Aaron Copland, William Schuman and Roy Harris.

Politics and Civil Liberties

Before asking what critical shapes of cultural multiplicity these names suggest, the third strand of the journal must now be considered. How did the journal position itself in relation to the tense political and social questions of the time? Could the legacy of Stieglitz's high humanism have any political relevance in a world torn apart by class, nationalism and mass-industrial technological war; a world that patently demonstrated the failure of more than one hundred years of diverse socialist and sometimes Christian-inspired progressive thought and the betrayals of Marx in Stalin's brutal autocracy. Shaky too were the philistine materialist goals of the American dream and the inequalities produced by increasingly right-wing American capitalism. Nazism and fascism were apparently triumphant over the ruins of an impotent social democratic consensus as the war embraced the last ghastly global aggression of the worst elements of a dying imperial and imperialist Europe.

The traditional socialist analysis had started with eschatological narrative tropes of class conflict and structural analyses of complex economic patterns called 'the relations of production' – large generalizing synchronic analyses of structure that had to be tested in historical revolutionary praxis from the ground upwards. It saw its natural constituency in the working class whose final victory only would abolish class division and collectivize the means of production. Dorothy Norman's 'bourgeois' journal, however, also took for granted that issues of race, gender and (to a degree) class were also crucial within a larger national and international context. But the term 'civil liberties' reintroduced the notion of individual freedom into the debate, as well as the freedom to act collectively. However it ignored more or less completely the whole question of what, in the nineteenth-century was called 'political economy'. A radical humanizing of the effects of capitalism was the aim of *TWICE A YEAR*, not its apocalyptic abolition nor indeed any specific economic analysis of its patterns.

It becomes clear quickly, however, that the 'redundant', 'enlightenment' values of the bourgeois revolutions of the late eighteenth and early nineteenth centuries took on a new life in *TWICE A YEAR*. They were, moreover, certainly more than coloured by the socialist debates of the 1930s, even if they spurned the collectivist sub-Marxist propaganda of the Stalinists and laid themselves open to the class scorn of men like Mike Gold, James T. Farrell and Earl Russell Browder, or even the class unease of William Carlos Williams. But the liberal tradition (as opposed to radical) of *TWICE A YEAR* showed that there was much to be admired in Norman's circle which had not, in fact, broken links with, though it eschewed the dogmatism of more orthodox leftist radicalism. After all, Silone, Sartre, de Beauvoir, Williams, Rukeyser and Wright wrote for both *politics* and *TWICE A YEAR* and Wright, Williams and Rukeyser for both the communist publication *New Masses* and *TWICE A YEAR*. Macdonald and Norman, who were not so very different in terms of class origins and privilege, also shared ethical and political values.

The radicalism showed itself in the relentless reporting of questions of 'civil liberty', from the civil internal effects of the war, to the trade union movement, and to the treatment of African Americans and women.[86] Dorothy Norman worked for the Emergency Rescue Committee and that fact alone links her with Macdonald, Reinhold Niebuhr and, at one point, even Victor Serge. In fact it is most moving that Serge wrote to Norman for the first time during the last few months of his life, saying that he didn't care whether she knew his work or not but that he profoundly admired *TWICE A YEAR*. He offered her some of his recent writings on Mexico, some memoirs of the tragic fate of his Russian writer friends and an essay on the present condition of the truly independent writer.[87] Had they ever met there would have been much to discuss, perhaps particularly international affairs and certainly the varied fate of the Litvinovs (the wartime Soviet ambassador and his wife), whom Norman had come to know well. There are also signs that the worlds of Macdonald and Norman occasionally crossed. Macdonald wrote to her, for example, about the anti-Jim Crow march in Washington in 1943.[88] They would have differed on the war, on contemporary art and perhaps on the nature of political discourse itself, but the concern for civil liberties would have brought them together as well as very similar views on certain key issues such as the atomic bomb.

Like Richard Wright, who busied himself with issues of African independence, both colonial and postcolonial, Norman was deeply involved in Indian independence and its aftermath and carried her radical activities far beyond the parameters of the United States. Her political positions and allegiances can probably be gauged from her friendships with Wright, Mumford, Rukeyser and, a little later, with Indian friends such as the Gandhis, the Nehrus, the Pandits and related members of the Congress party, rather than from the purely Euro-American legacy of Stieglitz. Civil Liberties for the first time were a global issue, as Norman explained to Mumford:

> What I am really trying to do with *TWICE A YEAR* is to bring together material that is out of print or generally unavailable and to relate such material to the evolving clarifications of our own day in such a way that a tradition will be freshly established and developed in which I really believe most deeply. Art in its highest sense is surely concerned with man's necessity to maintain integrity both as an individual or as a social being, in all realms of expression and experience. Civil Liberties are inevitably essential for precisely the same reason.[89]

For ten years, every issue of the journal had an extensive section focused on current political and social issues. What we witness in Norman's career is in fact an example of the internationalization of politics from the perspective of problems of an ethical and social nature, the birth of a transnational sense of responsibility, centred around questions of material resources, international law, and the treatment of prisoners, women and children. The internationalism fostered in war carried over into the peace. Norman's activity was a forerunner of the kind of work now handled by organizations such as Amnesty International, the World Social Forum and radical lawyers among hundreds of others.

In a world fraught with ideological conflict and uneven sovereign power and wealth, Norman worked, often against any plausible political hope and against that ever-present political 'realism', always defined by the powerful, calling for obedience to treaty and international law, international justice and individual dignity. It was not surprising that the founding of the United Nations should occupy so a large part of the later editions of the journals because in 1945 this event reflected a genuine hope for the future in a war-weary world, even though the Security Council, made up of the victors, became an *imperium in imperio* that began as a pragmatic motor for action but eventually led to an increasingly cavalier contempt for the wider world.

Lewis Mumford saw all the dangers besetting the United Nations, from the beginning. He felt that six or seven centres would be needed in order to show the rest of the world that the UN would not be dominated by America. It should embody an international university for study and be built on a human scale and slowly developed over some years reflecting many national styles.[90] From a somewhat utopian perspective, Mumford thought America had failed really to embrace the concept of world government that he felt was essential for controlling the spread of nuclear weapons. Mumford was among the first to call for UN inspection teams, whose findings have, in our own times, been arrogantly set aside by American and British administrations intent on war, now that other voices are becoming more powerful and more manifest. In more immediate terms he criticized the introduction of the veto and the ending of Lend Lease because it showed the international sidelining of many nations and selfish indifference to international recovery.[91] A decade later some of Mumford's worst fears were realized. 'What a dismal pall hangs over the U.N.', he wrote to Norman in 1960, during a tense moment in the Cold War where Eisenhower had boasted that America consistently violated Soviet air-space.[92] Mumford felt little hope that either Kennedy or Nixon would depart from the aggressive foreign policy of the Truman–Eisenhower era.[93] Events were to prove him right.

Mumford's ethical intransigence strikes a chord in the twenty-first century in which the United States, as now the sole super-power, pursues aggressive global policies in its own economic and material interests: policies that, with increasingly grave consequences, isolate it from the rest of the world. But as Norman's *TWICE A YEAR* and her voluminous correspondence showed, there were powerful countervailing currents present (and still are) in American life and culture. In public and in private the political discussion raised by Norman was sophisticated, nuanced and acute. Publicly, the journal's political analysis covered a wide spectrum.

In the United States, like Macdonald, Norman defended the rights of conscientious objectors and also attacked the Dies Committee. 'Despite the desirability of exposure of un-American activities', wrote one commentator, 'it seems perfectly obvious from the record that any committee under Congressman Dies is wholly incapable of giving the American pubic a fair inquiry or honest conclusions.'[94] From the Nativist riots of the 1840s to the Haymarket riots in late nineteenth-century Chicago, the deportations of 1919, Dies and the House Un-American Activities Committee, to Guantanamo Bay and the setting up of illegal 'courts' in other countries outside the Supreme Court's jurisdiction, there is throughout history a consistent paranoid and brutal reactionary thread in America's view of the threat from the stranger. As in most nations, Robespierre's advice on finding an enemy and a war to control the people, has often proved a more powerful influence than a desire for genuine civil liberty. In this the United States simply joins the rest of the world and, unexceptionally, history.

In *TWICE A YEAR* Herbert Seligmann exposed Nazi influence in the United States (that of Hamilton Fish among others), the Ku Klux Klan, the reactionary nature of the American Catholic hierarchy and so forth while the journal vigorously defended the right of all political parties to free speech. The journal attacked the passage in the House of Representatives of the three anti-alien bills at the beginning of the war with their now all-too-familiar advocacy of concentration camps, deportation of aliens and new classes of suspects for fingerprinting and exclusion. Norman's journal fought lock-outs, anti-union propaganda and censorship (for example the suppression of the film of Steinbeck's *Grapes of Wrath* in several States). It challenged the visa revocation of the British Labour MP John Strachey (then in a Marxist phase) and fought for the right of Jehovah's Witnesses not to salute the American flag. It reprinted sections from the Bill of Rights and its amendments. It printed the Senate hearings on the nomination of Felix Frankfurter to the Supreme Court. Frankfurter was Roosevelt's legal advisor and, until he blotted his copy-book in the McCarthy era, he was known as a liberal defender of civil liberties. *TWICE A YEAR* tracked Supreme Court decisions in the name of national security and national identity from 1937 onwards and, in the national emergency from 7 December 1941, it kept an eye on the same issues, now more urgent, throughout the war. The journal commented on the first use of the Smith Act (Alien Registration Act, June 1940) in the case of the Trotskyite Socialist Workers' Party prosecution in Minneapolis.

At the height of the war the journal preoccupied itself with the effects of the poll tax on the deprivation of African-Americans of their basic voting rights and on job discrimination and white primaries. Like *politics*, it vigorously defended African-Americans in a generally racist society. The black journalist Roi Ottley in Britain in 1944 wrote Norman a highly nuanced and sophisticated letter about racism, noting that the crude racism of America was relatively absent in Britain and how the British press has been concerned about segregation in the American armed services. He reported that the race riots in Philadelphia had been big news in Britain. Given racial oppression in America, he wrote, the British thought American views of the British in India hypocritical, especially as the race problem in America was creating anti-white feeling on a global scale. The British, he reported, were cynical about American support for Indian independence. They felt the United States just wanted the markets opened up for American business. He also noted that anti-American feeling in Britain was not helped by the swaggering airs of American soldiers. But he was happy to be in a country where ordinary people were much more tolerant, where he could go into good bars and restaurants unmolested. He was unhappy about a degree of anti-Semitism, but he felt that only in the British establishment and among the colonial officers and civil servants was there widespread colour prejudice.[95]

In the face of Pearl Harbor and newspapers printing the American flag in full colour, the journal ungraciously reminded its readers of the recent history of civil liberties and of the obviously foolish and head-in-the sand isolationism of the Hearst newspapers from June to December 1941. It further pointed out that the unions' opposition, left and neo-Nazi, had all been in cahoots against the war, and 'tactlessly' drew attention to the fact that the America First Committee had booed the names of Roosevelt and Churchill in mass rallies in Madison Square Garden. During the same period the State Department had closed the doors on European refugees, whether Jewish or Gentile. The journal noted that the Ku Klux Klan had been active again in Georgia, Florida, Tennessee, Colorado, Michigan, New Jersey and even New York, as well as in eighteen other states, 'selling bigotry as so much per shroud'.[96] The same article cited Morris Ernst's words that 'Hollywood is the sole remaining receptacle of cowardice in the fight against the censor in the American scene', noting that they refused to fight back when the Legion of Decency called Greta Garbo and S.N. Behrman 'corruptors of the youth of America' because of *Two-Faced Woman*, starring Garbo and Melvyn Douglas, 'debonair Hollywood trade unionist and anti-fascist'.[97] *TWICE A YEAR* sardonically reminded its readers that the filming of a nursing mother's breast and her child, the very icon of motherhood, at this time was considered unfit to be seen by decent people and to imperil the nation's core values at root.[98] Norman reprinted the legal papers surrounding Pan-American Films' *The Forgotten Village*, which in 1941 had been censored because it showed a woman in childbirth, and with exposed breasts.[99] The decision was later reversed in the state of New York. Like Macdonald's *politics*, the journal defended conscientious objectors and attacked racial discrimination in the armed services.

As for Europe, the journal speculated in the early issues on the Stalin–Hitler pact. It also reported on the 'Bertrand Russell case' when, in 1940, the English mathematician, philosopher and libertarian thinker was appointed to teach mathematics and philosophy for eighteen months in the College of the City of New York. Defending America against free-thinking, atheism and sexual immorality was an unholy alliance of fundamentalist Catholic, Protestant and Episcopalian clergy, right-wing organizations, Nazi sympathizers and Tammany Society office-holders. Liberal ministers, however, including members of the Yale and Harvard divinity schools and Rabbi B. Wise defended Russell, along with America's intellectual elite including Whitehead, Dewey, Einstein and libertarian activists such as Dorothy Thompson.[100] It is perhaps worth mentioning that Norman's friend, the pharmaceuticals multi-millionaire Dr Albert Barnes (of the Barnes Collection in Philadelphia) immediately offered Russell 8,000 dollars a year to lecture at the Barnes Foundation.[101] It was in the Barnes Foundation that Norman had first experienced a life-changing sense of contemporary art: 'Signs of something explosive – revolutionary – in the world outside [moved] onto my horizon.'[102]

In the Spring–Summer and Fall–Winter double-issue of 1943, Europe, and indeed the wider world of the conflict, for the first time took precedence. A somewhat bland statement from Chiang Kai-shek and a declaration of the strategy against the invading Nazis by Stalin were followed by much more politically incisive material on India which will be held over for closer consideration later. Koestler reported on news from 'Le Vernet', one of the notorious Vichy concentration camps for refugees from Franco's Spain in which he himself had been retained. The camp was north of the Pyrenees and housed various political refugees, Jews, communists and seven hundred men left over from the International Brigades. It was a clearing house for slave labour to Germany and North Africa but Koestler had news of a considerable resistance organized by the members of the old International Brigades within the camp. The latest report, however, was that disease had broken out, killing hundreds of prisoners. Koestler meditated on the fate of the men he knew, 'the salt of the earth'.[103] There were also articles on Italy and the possibility of finding a German underground for reconstruction.

TWICE A YEAR also investigated the totalitarian censorship and terror in Stalinist Russia, examining the way that the newly manufactured fundamentalist crypto-religion of 'Marxist-Leninism' censored freedom of thought, creativity in the arts and science and civil freedom in every activity of Soviet life. Echoing Serge, Max Nomad noted that 'the list of purged novelists playwrights and critics embraces most of those who were outstanding during the first decade of the Soviet Republic' and pointed out that Pilniak had alluded in one of his stories to the allegation that Stalin had played a direct role in the murder of the War Commissar Mikhail Frunze.[104] The journal also documented in detail the steps by which Hitler had risen to power and eventually published photographs of the appalling scenes in the German concentration camps. In the same issue in which the photograph of the Nagasaki bomb was published, Alfred Kazin wrote a brilliant and moving article on the struggle in Britain between the Army Bureau for Current Affairs and the Civil Defence Services over education in a weary, class-conscious, highly politically aware and heroic period of British history. Politics, he reported one soldier as saying, in a single sentence that broke the monolithic dumb cartoon soldier at a stroke, is what we live.[105]

In 1943 the young David Riesman, later to become famous for *The Lonely Crowd*, wrote a double-sectioned article on civil liberties in a time of crisis. The real difficulty in the United States, he noted, perhaps somewhat cavalierly as regards to date, began in the Great War. The Espionage Act of 1917, first tested in the Schenk case in the Supreme Court, created a new level of potential concern. It was in that case that the famous words 'clear and present danger' were used for the first time. As Riesman pointed out: 'When concerned with danger, the test neglects to weigh the values of what is endangered against the values of what is to be suppressed, and most significantly, the evil of suppression itself as a qualitative act.'[106] Riesman pointed out that in the case of the children of Jehovah's Witnesses refusing to salute the flag, the summing up was paradoxically fairer than the judgement delivered, the 'freedom to refuse obeisance, on religious grounds, to symbols of state power – was held of lesser value' and widely criticized.[107] Laissez-faire policy, though once revolutionary, Riesman argued, was now conservative. Neither the philosophy of natural rights nor constitutional legalism proved adequate.

Ominously, in the last issue of *TWICE A YEAR*, Norman reprinted the opening of the hearings before the House Un-American Activities Committee, together with Brom Weber's comment:

> They embody the pattern of cultural repression which has been dominant in recent decades in Europe and which may grow stronger here. The stupidity and callous disregard for legal procedure and individual rights revealed in the excerpts is unbelievably magnified in the full report. Seldom, except in previous Committee reports, has so vast a structure of personal spleen and legally-inviolable accusation been erected. Yet the greatest harm effected by the Committee has been the achievement of its primary aim, the successful intimidation of those who would ordinarily resent and combat its tactics.[108]

Compared with the Soviet Union, Nazism and fascism, the American experience of paranoid occupation with the total security state (marketed under threat of general terror) was to be relatively mild and of short duration, whatever the effect on the country's global image as a free society and its legacies to later resurgences of right-wing activism. The Cold War's effect on the poor nations of the world was quite another matter. The right-wing forces that produced it have remained strong, resurfacing on a number of occasions over the last half century. They are currently at a new height, and have remained a much more powerful and significant aspect of American life than is often acknowledged in liberal nationalist views of American history, politics and culture.

Norman's personal contacts kept her in close touch with the national and international political world at the practical, theoretical and ethical levels. The German painter Alo Altripp, on whom Norman had once written a piece for *Vogue*, kept her informed of conditions in East Berlin and of the migration of Germans to the West.[109] Harold Clurman of the Group Theatre, probably the greatest American theatre director and famously the producer of Clifford Odets's *Waiting for Lefty*, sent her a typescript of his Soviet diary and accounts of how he and Jay Leyda had responded not only to Soviet theatre but also to general conditions in the Soviet Union. They noted a strange sense of separation between the two.[110] V.L. Pandit, who is discussed below (see p. 245), also wrote to Norman about her sense of frustration as Indian ambassador in the Soviet Union in 1948, in relation to the start of the Cold War and American attitudes.[111] Louis Fischer, the wartime foreign correspondent and contributing editor of *The Nation*, shared with her his doubts about Walter Lippmann's abilities to see straight politically.[112] Waldo Frank discussed Spain, Italy and Germany with her and lamented that Bernstein had not broken with Mussolini until 1937.[113] The French journalist André Géraud, whose 1943 book *Gravediggers of France* was the first to examine the betrayals of the Pétain years, kept her informed about De Gaulle and the years immediately following the armistice. Ignazio Silone, whose famous trilogy is considered at the end of this section, and his wife Darima, who had a warm personal relationship with Norman, kept her up to date on Italy.

At a more theoretical level, Hannah Arendt herself, in a note suggesting meeting over lunch, congratulated Norman on publishing Camus's article 'The Human Crisis', which, translated by Lionel Abel, had appeared in the *TWICE A YEAR* of Fall–Winter 1946–7.[114] Camus had spoken of the desperate need in France, and by implication elsewhere, to find and re-imagine a living conception of the human being. He had pointed to a spiritual crisis left in the wake of the war, and to the breakdown of major traditional and contemporary ideologies, beliefs and practices. The war had shown how human beings had taken refuge in specialized, mechanical or bureaucratic tasks while remaining indifferent to common human concerns and the fact that the traditional practices of peace, which conferred dignity on human interaction and the crises of human life, had been completely abandoned. People had ceased to see each other as human beings: they were objects of history, passionless torturers and butchers of other human beings, reified pawns in complex abstract bureaucratic and paper systems.

Camus noted a more present and immediate problem: 'to come to America from France, I had to consume much paper in both countries [...] so much paper, in fact, that with it I should no doubt have been able to have enough copies of this lecture printed to be widely distributed here without having had to come'.[115] Between thinking nothing was true and abandoning oneself to historical fate, he argued that pure power was now dictating human action. Camus's further point was that this showed:

> [a] desperate universe in which each man [was] forced to live in the present – the very word Future evoking all his anxieties, – delivered to abstract powers, rendered destitute and stupid by a life lived in haste, separated form natural truth, intelligently ordered leisure and simple joys.[116]

Hence Camus accurately analysed the ethics of a view of imposed temporality in which the will to live towards the future was seriously endangered and the present was crushed to the extent that joy was impossible.

Camus called for an honest facing up to the facts of power, a certain ethical simplicity, a separation of emotion and the inner and private life from political practice and a pluralistic tolerance of the beliefs and practice of others. What was needed were 'communities of thought' to begin a dialogue across national boundaries. Not the least of the achievements of *TWICE A YEAR* was precisely the creation of such a community. Camus recalled the role of great literature in combating the nihilistic imperatives produced between scepticism and fatality: 'the Frenchmen of the Resistance whom I knew, and who read Montaigne in the trains transporting their propaganda tracts, proved that it was possible, at least among us, to understand the skeptics while at the same time having a concept of honor. And all of us consequently, by the mere fact of living, hoping, and struggling, were affirming something.'[117] It was an essay that scrutinized political action in terms of a revised ethics in order to face the shame of Europe and to appeal to the best wisdom of the United States. The sensitive American could not but have felt honoured in victory but was also warned of a general human tragedy in which America's own nationhood could have no special privilege, ethically or politically. The lines along which Camus was thinking had its echoes in the novels of Orwell and Silone and eventually in Arendt's powerful work *The Origins of Totalitarianism*.

Mumford's letters to Norman are just as penetrating in their insights and along not dissimilar lines. Mumford was close to Norman politically and his views on the United Nations as expressed in letters to Norman have already been noted. He sent her copies of his articles against the wartime conscription of young men, as well as expressing anxieties about his son in combat on the Italian front. He spoke freely to her of his opposition to the atomic bomb and of attempts to organize against it, and of his beliefs in a far greater degree of 'socialized planning' than America was currently prepared to countenance.[118] He sent her clippings of his *Saturday Review of Literature* article of 26 June 1948 ('Kindling for the Global Gehenna' – not, he said, his title) in which he spoke of his fears for a new totalitarian world, quoting the words of Henry Adams: 'morality would become police'. Like Macdonald, he feared the Wallace campaign of 1948 and wrote of his fears to Norman.[119] Later, during the McCarthy era, he wrote to her regretting that *TWICE A YEAR* no longer existed.[120]

Dorothy Norman: A Woman Among Women

In addition to Norman's involvement with politics and civil liberties, something needs to be said about her very important contacts with women and women's issues, and her work on behalf of children, both inside and outside strictly political frameworks. The list of her efforts and achievements not only in post-war Europe but in India and elsewhere where the condition and welfare of children was of serious concern, was also extensive and especially praiseworthy given so many calls on her time. Of course *TWICE A YEAR* was largely the effort of two women: Norman herself and Mary Lescaze.

Norman's contacts with creative and powerful women were of overwhelming importance in her life. They included Mary Beard (historian and founder of the first university course in feminism at Radcliffe),[121] Catherine Bauer (town planner, socialist and architect, a friend and lover of Mumford during his most creative period), Anaïs Nin (essayist, critic, diarist, companion of Henry Miller), Agnes

Enters (a now forgotten highly innovative and politicized American dancer of the 1920s and 1930s), Ivy Litvinov (originally English, but a highly placed Bolshevik and detective novelist, wife of the West's most famous Soviet ambassador of the Stalinist era, Maxim Litvinov), Eleanor Roosevelt (America's most distinguished first lady), V.L. Pandit (Indian ambassador to Washington and London and first female president of the United Nations General Assembly) and Indira Gandhi (the fourth prime minister of India). The friendships traceable in the correspondence throw a sharp and incisive light on the ways in which women of good will wrote and talked to each other across national, ideological, political, social and economic chasms, sometimes failing, for both good and bad reasons, but more often than not succeeding in maintaining a dialogue in the public interest. An occasional elusive glimpse can be caught of that undocumented influence of women both in and behind the scenes of high politics.

Apart from exchanging cheques for good causes, for example, there was clearly a warm relationship between Norman and Eleanor Roosevelt. Eleanor broadcast on behalf of food for India in 1951 at Norman's request, and her visit to India the following year was a resounding success. She was generally seen as a valuable face of American democratic integrity, compassion and humanity in a world that feared American power, distrusted its materialism, and its militarist Cold War violence. The two women's relations appeared to have had the odd difficulty during the fraught years of United States–Indian relations in the early 1950s, but they were soon back on course working together on discrimination in housing and on Adlai Stevenson's doomed presidential campaign of 1956. Eleanor Roosevelt's old-fashioned 1930s democratic integrity had made her suspicious about John F. Kennedy's cowardly neutrality during the McCarthy era but by this stage she was something of a lonely figure within the Democrat Party.[122] The two women were in correspondence over Norman's visit to India on behalf of international health legislation activities in 1959 and Norman also promised at this period to introduce Roosevelt to Indira Gandhi. In 1961 Eleanor Roosevelt invited Norman to lunch with Kwame Nkrumah, the Ghanaian president, adding 'I think we can both have a little influence on him which will perhaps be necessary.'[123] Later that year they went to the theatre together to see Genet's *The Blacks*.[124] Both at this time were working hard to set up a network for global famine relief.

Then there was Ivy Litvinov. In an article for *The Saturday Post* in 1958 entitled 'I Learn about the Communists', Eleanor Roosevelt wrote that she had learned a lot about the Russians over the years. In a clear attempt to plead for understanding and toleration during the Cold War, she noted that Maxim Litvinov, whose wife was English, had been the most skilful in getting along with Western diplomats and government officials during this period.[125] The English woman in question was Ivy Litvinov (*née* Low) whom Isaiah Berlin, reviewing Carswell's biography of her in 1983, described as

> a typically emancipated 'new woman' of her time, bold, headstrong, deliberately irreverent, *révoltée* and heterodox on principle, passionate, warm-hearted, observant, amusing, tactless, giving herself recklessly to people and to causes, not unlike her contemporary Rebecca West, but kind and neither obsessed nor egomaniacal. Her love was not politics but literature.'[126]

That last judgement may have been a little wishful thinking in the last years of the Cold War, for Norman's friendship and correspondence with her show both sides of this extraordinary woman, who had translated Russian literature alongside Constance Garnett and had been on friendly terms with D.H. Lawrence. Her favourite aunt and uncle had been Fabians and had known Shaw and Wells, as well as being advocates of Freud and stalwarts of the early British Labour Party.

Certainly a contradictory character, this 'Bolshevik' adored Jane Austen and wrote detective novels (surely a bourgeois art form) set in the Soviet Union. Her husband had the pragmatic skills and moral insensibility to stay close to Stalin and be a valuable ambassador for him abroad. Tracking Soviet foreign policy shifts, Victor Serge in a 1938 article for the Belgian newspaper *La Wallonie*, noted that Molotov temporarily replacing Litvinov in Stalin's entourage showed that it was totalitarian business as usual in the Soviet state.[127] Litvinov was dropped partly because he was hated by the Nazis – the fact that he was Jewish did not help – and Stalin was moving towards his infamous non-aggression treaty. Like the phoenix, thanks to his American and British experience and connections, Litvinov rose again from the ashes briefly after the opening of the Eastern front.[128]

Ivy Litvinov's letters to Norman initially show a dead straight Marxist-Leninist party line on art and life alike: 'so help me if I will read poetry that doesn't rhyme, yours or anyone else's'.[129] Like Waldo Frank she was damned if she would touch the domain of the aesthetic and what she saw as the 'truth equals beauty' philosophy of either Stieglitz or Norman. Strangely enough, given the divide in criticism at the time, she was a profound of admirer of Proust and took Norman to task for 'committing that sin against Proust' in an issue of *TWICE A YEAR* that Norman had sent her. This was almost certainly Norman's editorial comments on a translation by Louise Varèse of the twenty-three-year-old Proust's 'A Young Girl's Confession', a piece that Norman had described in her introduction somewhat breathlessly as illustrative of 'the basic need to fulfil oneself, to give love and to receive love', this being the greatest thing worth fighting for, something people needed to be reminded of in wartime.[130] One can only imagine the curl in Ivy Litvinov's lip as she read these lines in April 1943 with the victory at Stalingrad achieved only two months before.

In the same issue Norman had also printed work by children. Again, Ivy objected. She found all that juvenile stuff 'nauseating', typical of adolescents (a favourite phrase of condemnation) encouraged 'to express their beastly little selves', though she liked 'the little child's poem about death'. There was something in her direct style of language that recalled a typical D.H. Lawrence outburst. But she approved of one child's poem. It was by the six-year-old daughter of the working-class poet and civil rights activist John Beecher. In this instance she quite failed to notice that it did not rhyme. She also approved of Agnes Enters's story about an old down-and-out Hollywood star, doubtless because it was written in a social realist manner and illustrated the fickle values of capitalist America, though she confessed herself 'bored to tears' with 'her [personal] testament'.[131]

Stieglitz's theory of universal humanity was also given short shrift by Ivy. If the other was ultimately like oneself in the depths of human oneness, what happened when the other, he or she, simply wasn't? There was no point in kidding yourself that the other person 'felt' the same way. Who was not for was against, which ruled the 'other' out of court. A sort of British common sense, reinforcing the positivist Bolshevik's somewhat static take on the absoluteness of non-dialectical contradiction, swept mercilessly like a blazing sword through Stieglitz's and Norman's religion of humanity. Since the two women had obviously taken to each other, however, there were, inevitably, some odd problems. If I don't actually respond to you, argued Ivy relentlessly, wouldn't there be something false about your 'feeling' for me? Her intransigence, refreshing though it is in its demolition of some of the thespian fringes of Norman's thought, nonetheless had the equally severe limits of what Arendt was to call the dogmatism of the 'either-or'. Fortunately Ivy was also a passionate reader of literature and 'feeling' finally got the better of the day. Our correspondence has been simply 'adolescent', she wrote to Norman, but added 'you must have a ghastly inner power indeed, to draw me into such a one'.[132]

Perhaps it was Ivy's 'Englishness' that so objected to Norman's 'handing herself out'. Had Norman raised with her the issue of the Trotskyites, the disappearance of artists under Stalin? Much more likely is that it was simply Norman's vigorous defence of non-social-realist and abstract art. Whatever it was, there was something in the combined onslaught from Stieglitz and Norman that in conversation had made Ivy Litvinov feel, in her typically moderate language, that she was 'being raped'.[133] Slowly, however, a real relationship developed between the two women: they could agree on the treatment of African-Americans in the United States, on unequal social conditions and on the problems of adopting children. There were mutually acknowledged complexities in their views of art, education and their social effects. How was it possible to educate children, they mused, beyond producing nice suburban nonentities? Every time Litvinov watched the 'wild men' in Eugene O'Neill's *The Emperor Jones*, she argued, she feared for what culture postcolonial peoples would have when fully 'developed'. There's a real softening (one must remember that Ivy Litvinov originally came from a milieu dominated by the craft ruralism of Morris and Fabianism), when she admits to Norman that she'll never get used to 'radio commercials, technicolour, good works and war'. By contrast, she has somehow become reconciled to 'comic strips and street cars and other people playing billiards and city waste-lots'.[134] Her sensitivity to the cityscape surely also formed a common bond with Norman as the companion of Stieglitz and friend of Mary Lescaze and Lewis Mumford.

The detective novel that Litvinov had just republished in an American edition at the time she met Norman was called *Moscow Mystery*.[135] It had originally been published in 1930 by Heinemann in London, writer's block apparently having been overcome with sessions at a hypnotist. It was her third novel and the American publisher's blurb characterized it as 'the story of a city and its people'.[136] The story connected Norman and Litvinov through their interest in city children. It would be impressive if Litvinov had taken the detective novel into a more 'progressive' popular cultural form. The following reading shows, however, that it remains only as a sociological relic of an era, a generic transatlantic curiosity that reinforces the fact that literature can never be ideologically driven even by the most well-read of authors.

Ostensibly, the story showed the 'progressive' transformation of Moscow street children into Soviet citizens. However, in a preface written for the American reader, Litvinov compared the respective developments of New York and Moscow over the previous twenty-five years. She showed some sensitivity to the longevity of the spirit of the city. It was a compendium of more than historical continuity, to use Weil's terms, a vital soul dependent on the past and memory. She noted that her original publishers in England had reported that readers for the American market wanted less 'Spring over the Kremlin' and more 'murders' but she wrote that in 1943 her American readers might well prefer the reverse. In terms of a novel about Russia, heavily engaged on the Eastern front, positive, or perhaps one might say 'progressive' lyricism (as in the United States and England) took on a new lease of life in all popular art forms.

The spirit of the city, she noted in the American preface, remains. Hotdog stands may have been replaced by 'Hamburger Heavens' and the 'El' (the old New York elevated railway) gone forever, but New York is New York. Moscow, however, will never return to 'the legendary city of holy muddle', but one suspects a sneaking admiration for the 'glorious mixture of styles', from the Tartars onwards which make up the architecture of the Kremlin, in spite of Litvinov's obligatory note that the *art nouveau* mansions of the 1890s are inconvenient for nurseries. With the focus on children, the story is a paean to Stalinist progress and perfect for republishing as part of the war effort. Those who were young in *Moscow Mystery*, Litvinov explained, will have changed since 1930 but 'none has changed so much as Moscow's little boys', they have become the 'objects of a supreme salvage campaign'. One senses a nostalgia for a Dickensian plot (perhaps the Artful Dodger and his crew) when she characterizes the 'bad old days' in the 'old sprawling markets which once spread like bilge water over the road, cluttering the cramped sidewalks with the bodies and wares of vendors of hot pies, shoelaces, "butterbrod", and brassières, and making it easy for any active boy to lift a fountain pen from a breast pocket, snatch a purse, clutch at a fistful of bills from an incautiously opened pocketbook, of even slash a panel from the back of coat.'[137]

The plot has its fair share of 'correct' social realism: there are tsarist spies, a cityscape of obviously decadent ancient architecture and a detective who is a regular proletarian Soviet comrade, not a suave gentleman (a Holmes or a Poirot), as preferred by the imperialist English and French. The dentist Pavlov, the founding corpse of the narrative, obviously got what was coming to him (too many bourgeois conditioned reactions?) because of his 'Paris goods' on the mantelpiece: 'a waxed figurine of a dancing girl with a mauve chemise of real crepe de Chine and real silk stockings, rouging her slips with a real lipstick'.[138] With that on his mantelpiece, his life expectancy in the Soviet Union had to be short. The poor Pavlov is a little too obviously 'a banal *bon vivant*, a survival of the class that has gone under in Russia'.[139] Quite why he should have been ordinarily murdered rather than sent to Siberia or quietly shot in a cellar by the authorities is (with retrospective perspicacity) not really explained.

The heroine, an innocent street girl named Tamara (who had danced in the dentist's room for a pair of silk stockings – the latter item of irresponsible consumer values a sure sign of bourgeois danger throughout the book) manages to reject boys, take literacy courses, become interested in politics and is finally saved by reading Tolstoy. But there's quite a lot of the 1930s-style English public school 'plucky girl' about her too. Unlike her English prototype, however, she will, it is hinted, do something useful and perhaps give up ballet for the police force or the law. The high-point of unintentional comedy is in the chapter 'Tamara to the Rescue', with the following irresistible line from the heroine: '"But that's what I like about a life of crime," said Tamara earnestly, "it seems to purge you of all petty instincts."'[140]

There is the obligatory 'Artful Dodger' gang with boys, all with names such as 'Black Mug Peter', whose alibis are confirmed when they recognize a genuine song of the Volga boatman as opposed to Chaliapin, thus giving the little capitalist victims a nationalist instinct for folk-song on the basis of which they can be turned into potential Soviet citizens. The 'authentic' folk spirit (co-opted into a narrative of working-class cultural origins) triumphs over decadent bourgeois modernity at the moment (1930) when the peasant is about to be slaughtered, along with peasant culture, in Stalin's distinctly nonfictional world. There are also the inevitable White Russian villains. It is pure comedy when read today; the combination of *Scouting for Boys* and Marx makes it a true period piece, quite apart from the straight propaganda: 'The efforts of the State were by the year 1926 causing considerable depletion in the ranks of the flotsam and jetsam of Russian towns.'[141]

The language can fall into bathos as Litvinov writes in a stage cockney idiom, sadly lacking comedy. For example, the following comment is made by a manicurist: 'Of course you could have knocked me down with a feather when the girl came in and talked to me about it'.[142] Perhaps, however, the most unintentionally comic moment in this respect is the *dénouement* when, a bullet having just whizzed past the procurator's ear (the procurator is possibly modelled on Maxim Litvinov), all are saved thanks to 'plucky' Tamara:

> The procurator touched his neck just under his ear feelingly.
> 'Well Tamara, you're a brick,' he said.
> 'And so say all of us,' said Itkin with conviction.[143]

The Soviet revolution and the children's 'supreme salvage campaign' is saved in an Ealing Studios version of the English village hall, with the proletarian Soviet procurator as squire and Itkin as a jolly vicar. Perhaps Litvinov should have paid closer attention to the children's poems published in *TWICE A YEAR* and, indeed, poetry that did not rhyme. Happily, her short stories produced for *The New Yorker* and other papers in later life were of a somewhat higher order and her sketches show not inconsiderable skill in line drawings (she had had lessons from Grosz in America in 1943).

The Dorothy Norman–Ivy Litvinov exchanges are not mentioned in John Carswell's beautifully written biography of Ivy Litvinov: a scholarly gem whose rueful tone combines with a warm-hearted appreciation of this highly self-contradictory yet dazzlingly energetic figure. Hers was a life finally frustrated in its literary ambitions, all the more regrettable because it was one which, despite its vagaries, might in more disciplined hands have been set down as one of the most vivid women's autobiographies of the twentieth century. She might have been as much a witness to history as Victor Serge. While it is true that she was contemptuous of the regime under which she lived, however, neither she nor her husband opposed it. Both chose survival over truth. There were inevitable consequences both for the writing, and for the 'neutral' bureaucrat's career. In spite of her much emphasized, even hostile, 'indifference' to Soviet politics, the internal evidence of *Moscow Mystery* shows her to be ideologically and artistically under the heel of Stalinist realism, Soviet ideology and its literary requirements, firmly if not completely. On the conditions in the Soviet Union in the late 1930s she kept as silent as her husband.

The novel's condemnation of the 'Parisian' dentist fits ill with Litvinov's own later life of continual sexual adventure and affairs (including orgies), stemming from the 'free love' ideology of the late Victorian and Edwardian era, not to mention the 1920s. It was a period that included Strindberg, Ibsen, Edward Carpenter, Havelock Ellis, the Bloomsbury group, the Fabians, Isadora Duncan, Emma Goldman, Natalie Barney and George Bernard Shaw. Her views on the emergence of feminism, the beginnings of a more liberal attitude towards same-sex love and critiques of the bourgeois family, along with her friendships with the Meynells, D.H. Lawrence and Alexandra Kollontai, as well as her passion for Freud made her, within a certain circle, very much a child of her time. She adopted Kollontai's liberatory sexual views directed against bourgeois exclusiveness and possessiveness, though not the class and economic analyses that were their crucial context. Experiencing orgasm for the first time with a German doctor at the age of thirty-eight, Ivy Litvinov rapidly compensated for a life of conventional motherhood and monogamy.[144] In later life, wearying of men, she turned more and more to same-sex affairs, a proclivity she had had from the beginning. At times her reckless behaviour imperilled her precariously positioned husband and she was quite unforgiving of any mistress he turned to. Her views of sexual behaviour (she did not sleep with her husband after her first orgasm with the German doctor) may well have found a sympathetic ear in conversations with Norman, whose elderly but affectionately esteemed partner had similar views on sexual freedom and on the independence of women. Norman's letters also from time to time reveal passionate extramarital affairs.

Ivy Litvinov spoke with the slightly upper-class English accent of a bygone age, which perhaps accounts for the unintentionally comic dialogue analysed above. Her manner was patrician; Kremlin-privileged, she had enjoyed a life of servants and chauffeurs. She surreptitiously imported into the Soviet Union the English *Boy's Own Paper* for her children. Its class-toned dialogue would certainly have mirrored the accents and tone of *Moscow Mystery*. Her favourite English authors, Jane Austen and Anthony Trollope, guided her safely past the prose and narrative revolutions of Twain, Hemingway and Chandler, even though she read Edgar Wallace. She was apparently completely ignorant of all those writers whom Serge had admired before they went down to Stalin's henchmen. In the Soviet Union, to translate the classics was an eminently safe means of survival in an ideologically fraught and dangerous atmosphere. Ivy Litvinov was personally exiled, indeed frozen, in time as well as space.

Ivy Litvinov and Norman met at a moment of almost surrealist intensity for both Litvinovs. With the ferocious war on the Eastern Front at its height, the Litvinovs, now temporarily restored to favour, became supremely useful to Stalin in the ideologically divided alliance driven by the sheer force of war and historical necessity. For both Litvinovs, in retrospect, it was a final moment of Soviet privilege. Ivy Litvinov found herself an American celebrity: 'America with its swift burning enthusiasms and starry-eyed hustle in many ways suited Ivy's temperament better than any other country she had lived in.'[145] She wrote for women's magazines including *Vogue*, lunched with Eleanor Roosevelt, was fêted at the Warner Brother Studios and acted so freely in personal terms that Stalinist agents fumed. Maxim Litvinov could see the Cold War coming with Stalin's ambition to control the border states from Poland to Hungary, Czechoslovakia and Yugoslavia, and fell back on his instincts for 'collective security', the foreign policy he had so successfully pursued in the 1930s. It did not meet with Stalin's approval, and his brief resurrection was terminated before the onset of Cold War. After the war the Litvinovs miraculously managed to survive, perhaps simply because they were too well known in the West.

This transatlantic moment, therefore, is a fleeting story of a world in turmoil. Ideologically inflected, it defies ideological simplicity. Politically it shows a moment where everything is in flux. So many historical times are at play in this narrative: late imperial England and the Bolshevik present, the onset of European and American modernity in the arts, the congealed historical time of the decay of the Russian revolution in politics and art, the political emergence of the United States as the future global power and European self-destructiveness at the close of the imperial era. For Ivy Litvinov, the novels of Austen and Trollope perhaps became a refuge from a personal world of exile with its accelerating changes in time and space. At the personal level Norman and Litvinov found a momentary reciprocity, as women, across barriers of enormous artistic, political, national and cultural distance. As highly privileged women also, they perhaps indicated the rise of a new global international class. Its political influence and effectiveness was yet to be demonstrated.

At the opposite end of the ideological spectrum was Anaïs Nin, not the reluctant 'Bolshevik', in this case, but the perhaps the equally libertarian 'bohemian' and companion of Henry Miller. Norman published the first extracts from Nin's soon-to-be-voluminous diary in the first issue of *TWICE A YEAR* (Fall–Winter 1938) and then again in the Fall–Winter issue of 1941. This first extract would perhaps be the most celebrated moment of the diaries, which were not to be without their *longeurs*. Printed between three parables by Kafka and pieces by e.e. cummings and André Malraux, Nin described the birth of her stillborn baby in almost the same kind of emotional and physical detail that her companion Henry Miller had used to describe sex. It was most certainly a radical breakthrough for an intensely puritanical society in which Hollywood could not show the breast of a nursing mother. In feminist terms, Nin's reclaiming for herself the meaning of this terrible experience from the authoritarian presuppositions of the medical profession and chauvinist assumptions about women's feelings and intelligence alike was at once both imaginative and radical.

The story began with the announcement: 'The child', said the doctor, 'is dead', and ended with Nin forcing the medical team to show the 'little girl' to her: 'It has long eyelashes on its closed eyes, it is perfectly made and all glistening with the waters of the womb.'[146] In narrative terms, therefore, the brief story lifts the biological narrative into a narrative of the soul, instinct with tragedy, over half a dozen pages. She takes the story back from the medical, religious, 'puritanical' and bourgeois sentimental denials of the complex reality of the event. Nin redefined the objective narrative of contingent biological process (the medical perspective) and equally the sentimentality around childbirth by describing the hallucinations of pain, punctuated by a Proust-like unsparing recording of not only medical but trans-gendered indifference to the needs of the interior life of the soul:

> A curtain was parted, the voices still tripped over each other, falling fast like a waterfall, with sparks and hurting my ears. The table was rolling gently, rolling. The women were lying in the air. Heads. Heads hung where the enormous white bulbs of the lamps were hung. The Doctor was still walking, the lamps moved, the heads came near, very near, and the words came more slowly.
>
> They were laughing. One nurse was 'When I had my first child I was all ripped to pieces. I had to be sewn up again'.

Here too is the fury of a woman out of control of her own body, in the indifferent and careless hands and the routinized careless speech of hard-bitten women nurses, and confronted by the terror of the closeness of the death and sex in both nature and mind.

> The heat of my anger warms me, all the ice and pain are melted in the fury. I have an instinct that what he has done is unnecessary, that he has done it because he is in a rage, because the needles on the clock keep turning, the dawn is coming and the child does not come out, and I am losing strength, and the injections do not produce the spasm. The body – neither the nerves nor the muscles do anything to eject this child. Only my will and my strength. So now my fury frightens him and he stands away and waits.
>
> These legs I opened to joy, this honey that flowed out in the joy – now the legs are twisted with pain and the honey flows with the blood. The same pose and the same wetness of passion but this is dying and not loving.[147]

In her discussion of D.H. Lawrence, Simone de Beauvoir had spoken, at a deeper level, of the English novelist's difference from Henry de Montherlant, in that he was less concerned to define the special relations of woman and of man, preferring 'to restore both of them to verity of Life', not by exerting singularity but by fulfilling a generality that renounces ego, will and personal sovereignty in erotic experience. She cites Lawrence's description of the little statue of the woman in labour: 'A terrible face void, *abstracted almost into meaninglessness* by the weight of sensation beneath.'[148] It is the refusal to speak the horror of physiological helplessness in the face of pain and death that Nin protests against, as well as (in de Beauvoir's words) the projection onto women of the man's terror of 'carnal contingence'.[149]

In Nin's story the doctor's angry obsession with the clock is a displacement of that fear. This momentous event in personal interior time in relation to its correspondent biologically fatal time, is understood only in relation to the mechanical timetable of the clock. Looking fully at the dead child confronts that fear in both its horror and in its unexpected beauty. Both symbolize a distinctly non-medical grace that comes from the courage to acknowledge the heart of darkness in human life. Whatever the sense of anguish and loss, the vision will remain. The nurses do not want her to look at the dead child perhaps because of the terror that underwrites their own denials of the abyss in a too-ready pity for the mother. The denial of terror, now grown into habit, had perhaps long been shunted into the convenience of the lesser ethical domain of pragmatic and professionally approved judgement (what is known in management terms as 'best practice'), a judgement here that might have deprived the woman of a terrible but necessary experience of her own body in terms of her soul.

It is easy to see why Norman and Nin might find many things to share and also, given their strong personalities and intense sense of personal vision, why they might definitively quarrel. Their views on 'free love' and sexuality might well have coincided. Henry Miller, Nin's companion and friend, who is considered later (see pp. 264–74), was also published in *TWICE A YEAR*. The combination of sheer mental and physical vitality, sexual frankness, sexual vulnerability, mysticism, anarchism, wide reading and literary innovation that characterized both Miller and Nin would certainly have provided a ticket to Norman's circle. Certainly their verbal styles had much in common, that slightly breathy lyrical style of the upper-class bohemian world of the 1930s: 'the day began beautifully with Dorothy Norman of the *American Quarterly* [*sic*] accepting "Birth" Story and "Women in creation" essay, and saying she had great admiration for the purity of my work.'[150] So Nin wrote in her diary for November 1937. In the winter of 1939, she wrote a portrait of Norman:

> I met Dorothy Norman, who published my story 'Birth' in *Twice A Year*. Dark eyes and a smile that is not happy, serious, intelligent, strong. She took me to her small office in the Stieglitz Gallery. I met Alfred Stieglitz, the photographer, dressed like an old European artist, cape and soft hat, talking like a man accustomed to respect. Admired his photographs of New York, his sensitive approach and wisdom. 'Make me love New York,' I said as he took my hand to show me what he loved: a bridge's span like a spider web in strength shadows under the Elevated, a spire, a street.[151]

Later, Nin found Norman 'cold as a human being', objecting to her contrasting decadent Europe with 'healthy' America, a comparison that infuriated her.[152] There is nothing of that prejudice, however, anywhere in the pages of *TWICE A YEAR*. Nin found a certain harshness of surface in Norman's salon and she sensed the 'Negro' was a problem: a concept, not a person.[153] She detested the 'formal arctic climate' of Norman dinner parties, and shied away from the intense ideological discussions,[154] even finding her 'nationalistic and insular'. She sensed, like Henry Miller, the puritanical nationalism in America, even in artists and intellectuals, not to mention the cult of endless youth:

> They refuse to evolve, ripen, alter out of fear of death. They try to cheat time and remain young by standing still and remaining virgin. They think one remains young by not living, not loving, not erring, not giving or spending or wasting one's self. It's a kind of artificial preservation.[155]

Spending the weekend at the Normans' country resort she found a more open and emotional companionship with the actress, Louise Rainer who eventually broke with Norman and who, to Nin, seemed less puritanical, more 'European'. Meanwhile, Miller's letters from the West Coast enthused about John Cage and the emerging West Coast culture that was eventually to include the San Francisco Renaissance and the Beats, and poets such as Robert Duncan who increasingly dominates this volume of Nin's biography. It was to be a world of art and culture very different from Norman's. Nin's frustration with Norman was expressed in accusations of her indifference to pleasure, perhaps it was also a certain class propriety of manner: 'she lives by rigid conventions, protected by her wealth'.[156] One cannot imagine Norman, like Nin, gathering poets around and 'writing beautiful erotica'.[157] By the end of the third volume of the biography she is regretting being unable to break the 'artificial' friendship with Norman.[158]

There were of course difficulties with money at various times. Norman was generous but she had a lot of calls on her wealth. Doubtless Nin did react badly to a certain stuffiness in Norman's character, playing the banker with the liberal artistic and political worlds. But perhaps Norman had good reasons not to respond to Nin's insistent demand for generosity and personal affection; there is something irritatingly petulant in Nin's desire always to be at the centre of her own all-consuming universe. Whatever else *TWICE A YEAR* was, it was generous to the point of self-effacement of its editor, endlessly seeking out some of the greatest writers of the twentieth century and a more engaged political world than Nin ever had time for. Perhaps not making time for sitting around writing erotica because the Indian sub-continent was starving would exonerate a greater puritan than Norman. Was it too grudgingly that Nin also wrote that Norman was the only person (with the Cooneys, who were friends of Robert Duncan) 'who believes in my writing'?[159]

From the beginning Norman had responded enthusiastically to Nin's work. The early letters from Norman to Nin are undated but from the evidence of the date of the publication of 'Birth' and the encounter of November 1937 in the diary, it might possibly have been in the spring of 1938 that Norman read the diaries for the first time in manuscript and responded with open heart and soul: 'how alike we are', she wrote from Florida as she confided her difficulties with Stieglitz, having read of Nin's with Henry Miller. As she read the pages, she confided, she 'wept and wept'. It was their mutual difficulty of living with hugely talented men that had struck a chord: 'We are caged. Like two small filled-with-wonder birds' wrote Norman. The difficulty of communicating with men was another shared problem. She wrote her response to the surface meaning of their words was always negative and like those, however gendered, with the sense of impotence in the web of dominant discourse from time immemorial, she wrote, 'I suffered greatly at first from the inaccuracy which I felt contained a truth – until I got to disregard what they said and listened to the mystery behind them.'[160]

This initial, perhaps over intense, opening of hearts was short lived. Whatever happened (was it a cultural, class, financial or even a sexual brush off? Perhaps a combination of all these factors?), the relationship never recovered. In response, Nin wrote torrents of prose like a very hurt, rejected lover, even though she still praised Norman for admitting there are 'layers of life I can't penetrate – that I'm afraid of. And I'm ashamed of this fear', an admission she felt exonerated cowardice.[161] Norman had failed her, had no sympathy for her struggles, had not realized how deep her personal involvement was and so on. Something of the quarrel in class, money and personal terms, can be guessed at as Nin demands the carbon copies of her diaries back: 'Because of your children, the nature of your home, these volumes are out of place.' Certainly the disparity of wealth was an issue because Norman reminded Nin in 1942 that *TWICE A YEAR* did not pay for itself and that it was only through the generosity of her husband that it continued.[162] Nin wrote back that only those who have known poverty can understand the struggles of the artist and ordinary people who stick with each other in that poverty.

Whatever the specific pragmatic need, one feels it is to a degree less the facts of the case than a perverse effort in the just post-anti-capitalist 1930s to needle Norman at her most vulnerable points.[163] To accuse Norman of not understanding the diaries because she has never been poor is flying in the face of Norman's initial response and her decision to publish Nin. Norman explained again two years later that perhaps her failure to understand Nin's emotional and financial needs was due to her extraordinary busyness with *TWICE A YEAR* and the huge demands on her from many others. She added that she had not asked her for a loan but to be paid for her writing. There the correspondence stops.[164] There was doubtless failure on both sides, but these biographical moments illustrate unique difficulties in patronage with regard to radical publishing and go beyond gender considerations. As noted above, the relationship was seriously inflected with financial, ideological, class and perhaps even sexual anxieties. Nin felt she was calling Norman's bluff on the 'romantic' relation of the artist to the world. It was certainly more complicated than that.

A World of Women: Dorothy Norman and India

There were no such tensions in Norman's relations with Indian women. Her acquaintances were of a similar class and economic background, the modes of personal contact and propriety were more formal and, in any case, the focus was largely humanitarian and civil rights-oriented. Her Indian contacts and experiences were a major part of Norman's life at both the personal and political levels. It takes us appropriately and properly out of the strictly trans-Atlanticist focus of this book into that more 'global' world which is perhaps the most important historical legacy of the 1940s. No work on the 1940s can be unaware of the global historical shifts. So-called 'globalization', driven by the abstract economic relations of capitalist production, had been going on a very long time, (Marx had classically predicted its modern form at the end of the first volume of *Das Kapital*) and was in this historical moment comprehensively realized in global war. *TWICE A YEAR* was alert to that shift in many different ways.

As the Cold War was Atlanticist in character, Norman's experience of India was dominated by Atlanticist politics. Even so, her interest in India extended to its arts and religions. Lewis Mumford had written to her concerning these interests as early as 1931. He wrote about Raja Ran, 'a student of Geddes's glorified hostel at Montpellier', who had looked him out on Geddes's advice and whose philosophy struck him as 'being a combination of childishness and intellectual subtlety with which I am no longer immersed [...] a doctrine for sloughing off responsibility, because all that hurts or shocks is illusion.'[165] Norman would be rather more forgiving in relation to Indian religion and mysticism.[166]

In the last issue of *TWICE A YEAR* (1948) Norman had a section on India. She reprinted the South African field marshal J.C. Smuts's 'Speech on Return to Union of South Africa', V.L. Pandit's 'Speech at United Nations Plenary Session', a letter from Tolstoy to Gandhi of 1910, a 1920 essay by Gandhi on 'the doctrine of the sword' (originally published in *Young India*) and a record of a conversation with Gandhi by the American writer and journalist Louis Fischer who had published *A Week with Gandhi* in 1942. She had already published a series of prison letters between Gandhi and the Viceroy of India in 1943. The viceroy had spoken in the usual terms, drearily familiar, of holding the Congress Party responsible for 'terrorism' and the publication of the letters closed with an acerbic note from George Bernard Shaw who accused the British government of blundering stupidity and wondered why, given their moral crassness, they thought they were fighting Hitler: 'The King should release Gandhi unconditionally as act of grace unconnected with policy and apologize for the mental defectiveness of his cabinet.'[167] The same issue of *TWICE A YEAR* had also published the transcript of a radio debate on the subject of 'Would immediate freedom for India hasten or retard victory?'[168] In it the imperialist intransigence of Winston Churchill was clearly exposed and the British apologist (Lt Col. Stewart-Roddie), who in hindsight turned out to be right about Muslim–Hindu conflict, was not impressive on the crucial issue of sovereignty. Louis Fischer was particularly concise and to the point.[169]

Norman's friendship with Vijaya Lakshmi Pandit, the sister of Jawaharlal Nehru, reflected her long-standing interest in the cause of an independent India. The inclusion of material by J.C. Smuts on another area of the fast-fading British empire was owing to the fact that Pandit's speech and first activities at the United Nations, printed in *TWICE A YEAR*, took up the cause of the thousands of Indians in South Africa who were not being politically and socially included in a South Africa drifting fast towards Apartheid.[170] Norman was also a friend of the Nehru family more generally. In 1965, after the fashion of the documents she reprinted in *TWICE A YEAR*, she was to edit two volumes of Nehru's writings, speeches, journalism, court statements, press conferences, conversations and interviews.[171] She came to know Indira Gandhi, Nehru's daughter, a friendship that, though suspended in very critical silence during the years of the 'Emergency' of 1975–7 when Indira Gandhi's seizure of autocratic power threatened Indian democracy at root, nonetheless re-emerged afterwards and lasted until her assassination in 1984.

Vijaya Lakshmi Pandit was one of the most remarkable women of the twentieth century. Born 'with a silver spoon in her mouth' into India's highest caste and certainly its most powerful family, idleness and luxury were never an option. Her life and career reflect the turmoil of the mid-twentieth century. She lived through the experience of the dying imperial world as it rapidly moved into that post-imperial world whose promise of liberty was to be cruelly damaged by international debt and power politics. She engaged in international public service that ranged from mediating the destructive strategies of rival powers in the Cold War on behalf of non-aligned nations to bringing the teeming millions of China, Asia, Africa and South America to insular Western attention. She devoted her life to the cause of the dispossessed: women, children and the poor and starving of the world. She had been minister of health in the pre-independence legislative assembly but was jailed for resistance to the British. She was later Indian ambassador to the Soviet Union, the United States and Great Britain as well as to Ireland and Mexico. She was also the first female president of the General Assembly of the United Nations.[172]

The most fateful years of her life were 1944 and 1945, when she became a friend of Dorothy Norman. Fearing for her daughters' education in an India in the last throes of imperial disorder (she herself was jailed and the appalling conditions in an imperial jail killed her gentle scholarly husband, Ranjit Pandit, whose words are quoted at the beginning of this section), she sent her two eldest daughters Tara (now the writer Nayantara Sahgal) and Lekha to Wellesley College in the United States. They were never to see their father again. Ranjit Pandit died intestate and under Hindu law the widow was thrown on the mercy of her in-laws. Alone, on considerably reduced means after a bruising court case, she had to rebuild herself and her career.

In 1943 the two girls boarded a once-elegant Comte liner requisitioned by the American Navy as a troop carrier and, with seven hundred Polish refugees, set off for the America via Australia. The excitement and carefreeness of youth must have contrasted with the burdened mother in this Conradian moment: 'As for the submarine scare, it only added to the excitement of our first voyage [...] we were exhilarated at the thought of the adventure which lay ahead', remarks Sahgal in her extraordinarily engaging and vividly observed memoir *Prison and Chocolate Cake*.[173] The girls' impressions of the journey and of their new country gave them a sharp political and cultural shock. Deeply committed as highly educated, politically conscious young women, enthused with Gandhian ethical idealism and already experienced in active anti-imperialist resistance, they found themselves listening to horror stories from cynical American marines and the wounded from Guadalcanal. These young men of their own generation seemed to have come from a different planet. 'It was as if they had seen the worst and little was left which could affect them deeply again. Nothing in our experience had prepared us for such an approach to life.'[174] Among their first encounters with Americans was a meeting with a marine who said: 'We're fighting for apple pie *à la mode*, and don't let anyone tell you different.'[175] When one remembers that going to prison for the Pandits was an honour and a blessing and that the prisoners, like early Christians, saw themselves as 'pilgrims armed with song', in Sahgal's phrase, the contrast must have been absolute.[176] It had taken their class-privileged mother picketing shops selling English goods in 1930 for the girls to realize what the real world of Allahabad was like with its teeming poor.[177] As Sahgal remarkes: 'I do not know how well or ill prepared we were to meet the New World or, for that matter, any world outside our own.'[178]

Certainly their first reactions to Los Angeles combined intense curiosity with horror: 'it was as bright and shining as a new penny but its glitter, far from appealing to us, made us homesick for the more leisurely tempo of the Indian life we had known.'[179] Certainly, like any first time visitor to the United States, they experienced the utterly chauvinist insularity of the average American: 'We may as well get used to the idea', said Lekha, always practical, 'Nobody here has ever heard of India except ourselves.'[180] When her sister replied that they seemed to have heard of Egypt, the redoubtable Lekha replied that they had made a film about Cleopatra and 'Egypt had to be brought in once or twice.'[181] In New York, however, they began to recover. Not only did they drink in the cultural opportunities but they learnt 'to wash dishes, prepare our own breakfast, use a tin-opener and a vacuum cleaner'.[182] Soon they were turning themselves into WASP-like co-eds with skirts from Fifth Avenue stores and the 'sloppy joes' of college fashion. They never got used to the 'speed' of American life, however, sympathizing with the shop-girls and the tired feet of shoppers equally; the ritualistic leisurely barter of the East with the glittering textiles of Benares, in spite of the dirt, narrow streets and exterior dereliction, was a preferable experience to Fifth Avenue. Other contacts were more pleasurable. They had access to the radical and cultural elite. To be kissed backstage by Paul Robeson, still in his Othello robes, at the age of seventeen, was another, 'overwhelming experience' for Tara.[183] Equipped with a copy of Van Wyck Brook's *The Flowering of New England*, they arrived at Wellesley in saris 'among the casually clad throng of young women' and lacking all experience of lipstick, cigarettes and 'dates'.[184]

It was during the Wellesley years, which they thoroughly enjoyed, that they were most in touch with Dorothy Norman. In New York, the triplex apartment of the Lescaze house provoked an instant reaction:

> On entering the drawing room our voices dropped to hushed whispers and we tiptoed about on the thick carpet. We looked at more exquisite paintings, high stocks of the latest books on politics, poetry, sculpture and the theatre piled on every available table, shiny new magazines strewn all over the room in studied disarray, the glass bricks lining one wall and streamlined, clean-cut furniture. Here was a modernity of a kind we had encountered only in magazine illustrations of interior decoration [...] Dorothy's gracious house became home to us [...] To me, especially she became a close friend, as our conversations revealed that we shared many of the same tastes from chocolate milk shakes to metaphysics and modern poetry. I could talk to her on any subject and be assured of her quiet understanding. [...] It was an education meeting the many interesting men and women of New York's artistic and literary circle whom she continually entertained.[185]

Under her married name of Nayantara Sahgal, Tara has gone on to write many books, novels and memoirs and like Norman has found a career in political journalism, deeply engaged with civil liberties and feminist issues of the present day.[186] The Pandits' friendship with Norman was hardly foundational in their political and social commitments, but it must have certainly reinforced them and given them an international perspective as well as broadening their cultural horizons.

Norman also published two short stories by Tara's sister Lekha (Chandralekha Pandit), in the Fall–Winter 1945 issue of *TWICE A YEAR*. The stories are full of the bleakly moral and political passion of a twenty-year-old: one describes the interior thoughts of an impoverished woman who, fearing the future, kills her baby and is condemned to lifetime imprisonment; the other an incident where sons of rich merchants wantonly destroy the flowers in a public park ('What did they care for flowers? Their fathers had bigger and better gardens than this public park.'[187]), which are then gathered by a beggar girl to be given to her sick pregnant mother. They are social-realist fables, infused with Gandhian ethics, with an over-the-top romantic melodramatic edge. They are easy to smile at but are written with verve, displaying a radical political passion that is rare among the young of today's privileged elite.

Norman's feminist and civil liberties engagements, combined with her passion for art and literature, would create strong links with the Nehru and Pandit families. It was Gandhi of course who had insisted on absolute class and gender equality in India, even though his views of chastity within marriage met with more than a little scepticism among his more worldly and wealthy friends. Politics, however, were ever present. In 1945, Norman wrote to Vijaya Lakshmi Pandit, perhaps for information for one of her *New York Post* columns or perhaps as a direct demand for copy, asking her for precise reasons why the Congress Party had rejected the Cripps proposals, the Wavell offer and the new Labour government offer (all showing a British feet-dragging towards an inevitable Indian independence), adding that if she would like also to add something about her own attitudes to the Congress on freedom for other colonial peoples that this would be 'excellent'.[188]

Over the next three years or so Norman would correspond with Pandit and her American-exiled daughters, although her closest correspondent over the years was eventually to be Indira Gandhi. Pandit wrote to Norman, worrying over the increasing seriousness of the Cold War and her disillusionment in Moscow (not to mention her occupation with the various marriages of her daughters). Letters from Pandit's cousin Dr Krishna Lal Nehru to Norman show the difficulties tactless American communists and sympathizers such as Norman Thomas and James Burnham posed for the newly independent India as the foreign policy gulf between the United States and India in the Cold War deepened.[189] Norman also worked hard on Indian famine relief, health and women's issues, not neglecting to congratulate Vijaya Lakshmi Pandit on her ambassadorship to the United States in 1947.

Norman's relationship with Pandit's daughters, including a third daughter, Rita, remained close and their high spirits penetrate an equally high sense of political and social calling and seriousness: 'I must demonstrate the cocktail party with full actions when we meet', wrote Rita in 1946.[190] On her return to India, however, the gender freedom she enjoyed in America abruptly disappeared: 'An unmarried girl is criticized all the time. If I go out I'm engaged to my date – if I don't go out I have a lover in America whom I'm engaged to.' The letters show anxiety about the girls' sense of connection to their extraordinarily busy mother and on their return to India they poured their hearts out to Norman over the reverse culture shock: 'there is room only for the mature and serious minded who are ready and able to shoulder responsibility', wrote Tara in 1947. With Jawaharlal Nehru, their uncle, at the centre of things, they were concerned not only about the endless round of politics, but the strain on Nehru, worries over his safety and his utter loneliness in the position of leader. Rita's description of Gandhi's funeral and its effect on Nehru (she cites Shaw's 'it is dangerous to be too good') shows a thoughtfulness and seriousness beyond her years. Rita comforted Norman when her marriage broke up in 1953 and her mother kept Norman personally informed about Indian politics throughout the 1950s.[191]

TWICE A YEAR engaged with Indian culture and politics in a small but significant and wide-ranging way. Aside from Pandit's famous United Nations speech and her daughter's short stories, the journal published recorded conversations with Gandhi, responses to Gandhi and Indian politics from the journal *Young India* and Ananda K. Coomaraswamy's essay on 'ideal portraiture' in Indian, Buddhist Far Eastern and Christian art with its typically wide-ranging intellectual references, from Plato to Malinowsky. As early as 1941, Bhicoo Batlivala, an Indian barrister and specialist in women's education, wrote on the political and civil liberties situation in tense wartime India.[192] Certainly Coomaraswamy stimulated Norman's interest in both mysticism and Eastern religion. While she questioned his skirting around the issue of the politics of the pope in the prewar and wartime period, she remained deeply interested in the kind of range of writing he was involved in from Meister Ekhart and René Guenon to Hinduism and other forms of religious, symbolic and mythical expression.[193] These interests would later turn her to Zen Buddhism, though in an encounter with Suzuki, she felt she could not 'deny the rationalism of the West'.[194]

As for Batlivala, according to the contributor's notes in *TWICE A YEAR*, she was educated at Cheltenham Ladies' College, worked in the Inner Temple in London and been an advisor on legal matters to a London film company. Before returning to India she had undertaken a lecture tour in the United States on behalf of the Indian independence movement. Her article ended by citing Nehru: 'it would be a hollow mockery if we shouted for the freedom of a distant land and submitted to subjection ourselves'.[195] The Indian National Congress had condemned the Nazi and fascist regimes as early as 1936 but by 1941, when Batlivala wrote this, thousands of Indians were being imprisoned by the British as liberty was curtailed and 'legitimated' by the war emergency.

Although it strictly lies outside the time-frame of this book it is worth noting that Norman's major contact with Indian politics and relief work was via Indira Gandhi. It was a personal friendship that survived the 'Emergency' of 1975–7. Like Gandhi's aunt, V.L. Pandit, Norman's criticism of that emergency was unsparing and uncompromising. One can only imagine the personal disappointments. Most commentators agree that the two-year arrogation of absolute power was unnecessary. In consequence there is a gap of some four or five years in the published correspondence, resumed with a personal note on the death of Indira Gandhi's son, Sanjay Gandhi, in a plane crash in 1980. Indira Gandhi recovered some of her credibility and India the possibility of remaining a democratic country, when she called for elections, in which she was promptly defeated in 1977. She regained power in 1980 only to be assassinated by her Sikh bodyguard in 1983. What Norman must have thought of the less-than-exemplary political and commercial activities of the sons has to be left as a matter of conjecture. (Rajiv succeeded his mother as prime minister, only to be assassinated himself by Sri Lankan terrorists in 1991.)

Long before the Emergency, however, the two women had established a close relationship. Indira Gandhi could share her sense of loneliness, cultural as well as personal and political. Norman's formation of a broad-based citizens' committee to sponsor American food aid for India in the early 1950s had been much appreciated and in 1952 she lectured on Indo-American relations under the auspices of the State Department in India. They shared activities relating to women, children and health issues, and they shared too their disappointments in personal life. Given the almost total absorption of Indira Gandhi in politics, Norman managed occasionally to help supply her thwarted hunger for art and books. There were few people other than Norman with whom Indira Gandhi could share her responses to the films of Alain Resnais, to Dylan Thomas, Buckminster Fuller, Morris Graves and J.K. Galbraith. In almost the last moment of their correspondence, Indira Gandhi, for whom Mahatma Gandhi was one of the most powerful memories of her early life and the defining spirit of the struggle for independence, writes to Norman about Attenborough's film *Gandhi*, remarking that it was a pity no Indian film-maker had taken up the challenge and criticizing the 'super-star type of messiah' the film produced.[196] Like her father Nehru, Indira Gandhi needed 'a vibrant inner, intellectual world' and like him she sometimes seemed aloof and indifferent to others.[197]

What these small moments of Norman's involvement in *TWICE A YEAR*'s endorsement of India's anti-imperial struggle and its aftermath show is a model of principled internationalism (including undeviating support for the legal frameworks of the United Nations), a far from negligible spirit among informed and energetic women and practical aid to the dispossessed.

II

TWICE A YEAR and American Culture

Norman's journal, in terms of the arts if not entirely in terms of politics, had been founded on the wide-ranging innovative spirit of Alfred Stieglitz. Music, theatre, painting and photography all received at least some attention in the journal. Norman was in touch with Harold Clurman of the Group Theatre and Agnes Enters, a dancer who received major billing in the third volume of the journal (1939–40). Norman's own notes on dance forms emphasized their universal symbolism, their synthetic sense of dance history, their satire on and use of the conventions of dance, ancient and modern, Western and Eastern, their critique of social and gender history, their commentary on the psychological development of the child and adolescent and on political and religious culture – including by implication that of fascist Spain.

Given Stieglitz's love of music it is not surprising that *TWICE A YEAR* published a critical piece by Paul Rosenfeld on Edgard Varèse, with additional notes by Norman on *Espace*. Rosenfeld wrote that while composers such as Wagner and Stravinsky had intimations of the twentieth century's musical expression of the raw power of nature, Varèse's work had taken the process a stage further in its complete absence of the lyrical and 'atonal sky-scraping harmonies'. He stressed Varèse's connections with Apollinaire and Picabia. In the same issue that included Louise Varèse's translation of the early Proust story mentioned above (see pp. 220–1), Rosenfeld noted that *Amériques* was a 'signal to the Old World of the essence of the industrial giant of the North and almost a Swiftian caricature', while Norman remarked on the war-like industrial character of *Ionisation*: it is 'not music in the sense that it attempts to lull.'[1] Varèse was to write with a sense of shock to Norman over the deaths, close in time, of both Stieglitz and Rosenfeld.[2] Norman's correspondence also shows her in touch with Aaron Copland over his Pulitzer Prize in 1945.[3] Other correspondents kept her up to date in 1936 with the Federal Theatre Project's production of *Horse Eats Hat* (a translation and stage production of René Clair's 1927 movie *Le Chapeau de Paille d'Italie*), with music written by Paul Bowles who, of course, later turned to writing his novels about North Africa but who had studied in Paris with Copland. Orson Welles was the director.[4] She was also in touch with John Kirkpatrick, the scholar and promoter *par excellence* of the music of Charles Ives.[5]

In terms of the visual arts, the journal was active in painting and obviously in photography, given the legacy of Stieglitz. Perhaps something of the spirit of Norman's friend Albert Barnes seeped into *TWICE A YEAR*. The Barnes Foundation had artefacts from Egyptian and Greek times onwards, but was most famous for its collection of impressionist and post-impressionist paintings. With John Dewey as its first head, its educational spirit was progressivist and independent. Indeed Barnes's own employees at the A.C. Barnes Company stopped work daily for two hours to study philosophers such as William James and Dewey himself.[6] Norman was also very much in touch with Saul Steinberg, the Romanian cartoonist with a degree in architecture from the University of Milan, who emigrated to the United States in 1940 and took the cartoon itself to the very highest form of visual art, working famously for *The New Yorker*: 'a Swiftian tradition of satire', wrote one commentator.[7] The visual connections with Grosz whom Norman published in *TWICE A YEAR* are not difficult to see. Steinberg wrote to Norman of his fears for American influence in the world worrying that in a few hundred years the world, even India, would be like contemporary California.[8]

Norman herself edited and introduced the writings of John Marin, who had been part of Stieglitz's circle of painters and had exhibited at his gallery An American Place. Norman stressed the unique relationship between the two men, one of mutual aid and non-interference.[9] In the late 1950s she joined with William Carlos Williams and Duncan Phillips in a volume of tributes to Marin. Williams stressed the fact that though they were born with half a mile of each other they were never intimate but added: 'Would you expect more of our twin stem? We had business to do which we shared.' [10] The *TWICE A YEAR* Press had produced a similar memorial volume for Stieglitz in 1947 to which Marin himself had contributed (though Williams did not) and in which Norman had stressed the 'sacred' anti-materialistic basis of Stieglitz's view of art.[11]

TWICE A YEAR itself published Stieglitz's photographs and prose, and reproductions of work by Marin, Agnes Enters and Georgia O'Keeffe, as well as the visual European artists mentioned at the opening of this chapter, the sequence leading to the juxtaposition of Stieglitz's *Equivalent* next to the photograph of the atomic cloud over Nagasaki. In the Spring–Summer edition of 1940, Marsden Hartley had contributed three essays on Leonardo's *Mary with the Child* in the Pinakothek in Munich, on Memling in relation to Fra Angelico, Blake and Massaccio, and on Gaston Lachaise. The main visual emphasis, however, was on photography and in addition to Stieglitz there were photographs by Ansel Adams, Paul Strand, Edward Weston and Minor White among others, and in the final volume a fine set of photographs (portraits) by Norman herself. Architecture too, had its moment and the second volume included writings on architecture by Bernard Shaw, Louis H. Sullivan, William Lescaze (designer of the Norman house), Lewis Mumford and Walter Gropius. What cannot be emphasized enough is Norman's insistence on the relation between innovation and the long time-frame. The extension of the world of the artist back through time, the connection of the contemporary with the distant part as part of a renewable tradition was foundational to the project. Marsden's Hartley's own American work was realized on the basis of a knowledge that included artists as diverse as Memling, Fra Angelico, Leonardo and Blake as well as the revolutionary moment of modernism itself.

There was also a strongly nationalist thread to *TWICE A YEAR* that wove itself non-dogmatically in and through the generous presentation of work from Europe and elsewhere. *TWICE A YEAR* was founded after two decades of a new and more general realization that American art was no longer dependent on Europe. Paradoxically, the American revolution with its need to define itself in contradistinction to England and Europe produced a frame of mind in which a hostile 'other' was to be permanently necessary for self-definition. While appropriate as a dramatic trope (and fact) of origin, it seems these days entirely pointless, especially given the extraordinary achievements of American culture since the 1840s and 1850s. The robber barons of the *fin de siècle* are also partly to blame given that, as the maverick American economist Thorstein Veblen tirelessly pointed out, capitalism tends at worst to value art only in money terms and as imperial booty. A spurious 'European' classicism of taste was the result. Since the robber barons had imported 'Europe' to bolster their own prestige, it was natural that living American artists would resent 'Europe'. It was to the eternal credit of *TWICE A YEAR* that it avoided these simplicities. Its generous and imaginative internationalism was, and still is, too rare.

A new self-conscious pride in American art was the work of the 1920s and 1930s. The rediscovery of great writers such as Melville and Dickinson (though her recognition was slower) and New Deal support for American culture in many fields, from writers and painters to museums encouraging research in local history and crafts, added to the momentum. Among others, Mumford on American architecture, Constance Rourke on Audubon and the American comic tradition, Van Wyck Brooks on the cultural history of New England and F.O. Matthiessen on the 'American Renaissance' as well as Stieglitz himself, signalled a new confidence in the American arts. Though Henry James, Ezra Pound and T.S. Eliot had fled to Europe in horror, William Faulkner, F. Scott Fitzgerald, William Carlos Williams, Hart Crane and Muriel Rukeyser remained in the United States. *TWICE A YEAR* was very much part of this movement of new pride in American artistic achievement. Richard Wright was the exception that proved the rule, though he introduced a more sinister note and thought the unthinkable. Could the United States ever in the future become a place you might have to flee as the persecuted of Europe had done from the seventeenth century onwards?

TWICE A YEAR chose its past carefully. For its founding ethic it reprinted the writings of John Quincy Adams; for the doubt of that ethic, in a newly industrialized America, it reprinted Randolph Bourne. One suspects that Norman had spoken of Adams to Muriel Rukeyser, given that in Rukeyser's perhaps greatest prose work, *Willard Gibbs: American Genius* (1942), and in perhaps the best chapter of that work, she had described how the spurned, defeated and unwell Adams at the age of seventy-three had risen to defend, in the teeth of populist reaction, the slaves of the famous *Amistad* mutiny. The slaves had escaped from Havana by taking over the vessel and had wound up at Montauk Point at the tip of Long Island:

> Adams was not only passionately devoted to the cause under which the *Amistad* Africans were defended, he was committed to a future in which its justification would be taken for granted. He was concerned with the future – a future living in one's own time, whose origins are to seen in the flowing present, a future that must daily be found and helped clear. 'Besides anticipating by nearly a hundred years some of the most enlightened measures of conservation', say the Beards, 'Adams foresaw in a livid flash the doom of slavery in a social war.'[12]

This past in Rukeyser's terms is recalled precisely to note its contemporary dream of the future. That 'flowing present' ensures the Husserlian seepage between past, present and future. Finding the 'daily future' is precisely what, paradoxically, this recall of the past was designed to do, and it is in this spirit that Norman reprinted Adams in the context of a war generated by populist reaction in Germany and Italy. Selections from Adams's diary, then out of print, were reprinted in the 1943 and 1945 issues of *TWICE A YEAR*. The first selection appeared in an issue entitled 'Against the Spirit of Fascism', alongside contemporary commentators such as Koestler (who wrote on his time in a French concentration camp). The second selection was dedicated to Mumford's son (who had just been killed on the Italian front), as representative of all the young men killed in combat. That issue reprinted photographs of Nazi atrocities in Poland as well as a series of the founding documents of the United Nations.

Alfred Kazin's note to the first selection from the Adams diary recalled Van Wyck Brooks's comments on the work. He in turn had observed how Adams wrote 'with malice towards all and with charity for none, least of all himself'. Yet this frustrated idealist in his blackness and passionate integrity becomes an important 'ancestor' for Norman as for Rukeyser, a point of intransigent courage in the bleakness of 1943. The diary extracts, taken from 1784 to 1825, show the range of the man from his diplomatically withheld scorn of arrogant British officials to his passion for painting. For example, he records a visit to the Boydell Shakespeare Gallery, which he thought correctly held a mixture of good and bad things. One picture of *A Midsummer Night's Dream*, however, he condemned as 'nothing but the darkling errors of a sick man's dreams'. It was undoubtedly one of Fuseli's and clearly too much for a son of the Enlightenment. He disagreed with Alexander Pope's Catholic suspicion of Milton's *Paradise Lost*, a work for which his admiration increased on every reading. All justification of the ways of God to man, he remarked, in the spirit of his Puritan ancestors, 'should be established upon the assertion of free election in man'. For this a metaphysical argument was necessary including 'nice distinctions' (subtle clarifications), despite Pope's sarcasm. He perhaps correctly intuited Pope's drive for an apolitical aesthetics.[13] Adams's independent, certainly Puritan in the best sense, intransigence made him an unpopular member of the Senate and he noted in his diary:

> I see the impossibility of pursuing the dictates of my own conscience without sacrificing every prospect, not merely of advancement, but even of retaining that character and reputation I have enjoyed. Yet my choice is made, and, if I cannot hope to give satisfaction to my country, I am at least determined to have the approbation of my own reflections.[14]

Stieglitz might well have said the same, not to mention many of the contributors, European and American, to *TWICE A YEAR*.

Adams spoke of his conversations with Jefferson in 1803, which turned on the French revolution's swift surrender to the forces of reaction, and to the imperial absolutism of the Napoleonic era. Jefferson, he noted, had remarked 'how *contrary to all expectation* this great *bouleversement* had turned out. It seemed as if everything in that country for the last twelve or fifteen years had been a DREAM.'[15] The point would not have been lost on the readers of *TWICE A YEAR* in relation to the Russian revolution, especially with contributors such as Ignazio Silone and Arthur Koestler. This selection of diary entries, which was followed by another in the following volume, ended with Adams's critique of the design for the tympanum of the Capitol from which he advised that both the Roman Fasces and the cap of liberty should be removed. In terms of political psychology, the fascist and the Jacobin were not to be part of American life, nor were they to draw the ideological parameters of *TWICE A YEAR*.

In the second series of selections from the diary the issue of slavery dominates. Jefferson's real instinct for freeing the slaves and for liberty is one of the few unambiguous things Adams will grant this godless, 'epicurean' and pragmatically shifty slave-holder. Adams's animadversions against Emerson and the transcendentalists ought, perhaps, to be better known for their scepticism about radical, middle-class chic: 'Garrison and the non-resistant abolitionists, Brownson and the Marat Democrats, phrenology and animal magnetism, all come in, furnishing each some plausible rascality as an ingredient for the bubbling cauldron of religion and politics.'[16] For the devotee of classic nineteenth-century American literature, Henry James's *The Bostonians* seems to have received a first premonition here. (It is amusing to note that Norman, not without a transcendentalist strain or two herself, had a few utopian illusions somewhat shattered when she read Hawthorne's *The Blithedale Romance*: the same Hawthorne novel, as noted earlier, that Dwight Macdonald had recommended to Simone de Beauvoir.[17]) The readers of *TWICE A YEAR* could not have failed to have been moved by the Miltonic, indeed Shakespearean, rhetoric as from another age, that characterized the next diary entry of 1841, as Adams reflected on 'the case of the *Amistad* Africans':

> The world, the flesh, and all the devils in hell are arrayed against any man who now in this North American Union shall dare to join the standard of Almighty God to put down the African slave-trade; and what can I, upon the verge of my seventy-fourth birthday, with a shaking hand, a darkening eye, a drowsy brain, and with all my faculties dropping from me one by one, as the teeth are dropping from my head, what can I do for the cause of God and man, for the progress of human emancipation, for the suppression of the African slave trade? Yet my conscience presses me on; let me but die upon the breach.[18]

Kazin and Norman had chosen the extracts. For them it was clear that Adams's old relation to the universe had its merits in a historically racist North and South, a stance as relevant in the America of 1945 as in 1841.

The other American writer whom Norman wanted to put back into historical memory was Randolph Bourne. He had set the tone for the journal from the first issue. The essay 'War and the Intellectuals' was not a plea for intellectuals to adopt a passive stance in the coming war, rather it was to point out their accommodation at any time to power and the prevailing consensus. The essay was preceded by a series of Rilke's letters showing his change of mood from 1913 to 1919 in relation to German society and the war. A somewhat Wagnerian view of the 'ancient Knight's destiny upon a young man of today' and a description of an encounter with a Huzzar officer who admired his famous poem 'Christophe Cornet' rapidly darkened to a view of war, utterly soulless, and driven by the lies of the mass media and collusive cultural activity:

> How much hushing-up in the cities, how much dissipation of the worst sort, what hypocrisy in undistorted living along, supported by greedy literature and pitiable theatre and flattered by the irritating press, which surely is much at fault for this war and even more at fault for duplicity and lying and falsification making this monstrous event into a sickness, where it might have been allowed to be a pure frenzy.[19]

Whether or not 'pure frenzy' might be a good thing becomes a lesser issue than the corruption of human meaning. Here the possibility of living and dying with any kind of relation either to true feeling or authentic meaning is taken away. It was the same thought that Norman cleverly juxtaposed with Thoreau's address on John Brown later in the issue: 'It seems no man died in America before; for in order to die you must first have lived.' Newspapers, politicians, the great world of 'common sense' speak, 'as if a man's death were a failure, and his continued life, be it of whatever character, were a success.' For Thoreau, the conflation of 'life' with survival, is, (against populist tabloid common sense) contemptible, and beneath any level of human value.[20]

Hence *TWICE A YEAR* begins with an ethical doubt of secular militarist modernity and its biological positivism. For Rilke, Tolstoy and Cézanne ('those two powerful old men'), as well as Rodin, had 'uttered threats and warnings, like prophets of an ancient covenant'.[21] Norman had cited the Tolstoyan tradition of non-resistance in civil disobedience at the beginning of the volume, and Stieglitz of course had published reproductions of both Cézanne and Rodin in *Camera Work*. With the ethical and artistic parameters thus established, Norman reprinted Bourne's essay. In a foreword by James Oppenheim, the suspension of the old radical arts journal *seven arts* for pacifism in the Great War is brought to attention, as well as definitively establishing that journal's ancestral link with *TWICE A YEAR*. Above all, a model of transnational political ethics is offered, paradoxically with a certain national pride: 'We may rejoice that as England had her Bertrand Russell, France her Rolland and Barbusse, Germany her Liebknecht and Nicolai, so America had her Randolph Bourne.'[22]

Reading Bourne's 'War and the Intellectuals' today offers three temporal contexts for its reception. In 1919, it had some political bite as a critique of the United States, with 'its latent colonialism', rushing to join an imperialist war, though the more politically detailed Mumford, for example, would have disagreed to a degree about motives. In 1938 the essay would have been music to the 'pacifist' American left's ears, with its spurious refusal to fight anything but capitalism in the abstract. However, its real attack, and here it seems more important for our own times, is on the pragmatism (with a small p) of the liberal intellectual's refusal to challenge the status quo: 'The American university is a brisk and happy place these days. Simple, unquestioning action has superseded the knots of thought. The thinker dances with reality.'[23] The essay, from a purely pacifist standpoint, radically challenged the growth of a globalizing American myth:

> The task of making our own country detailedly fit for peace was abandoned in favor of a feverish concern for the management of the war, advice to the fighting governments on all matters, military, social and political, and a gradual working up of the conviction that we were ordained as a nation to lead all erring brothers towards the light of liberty and democracy.
>
> What shall we do with leaders who tell us that we go to war in moral spotlessness, or who make 'democracy' synonymous with a republican form of government?[24]

While the practical politics of that statement might be debated in either 1919 or 1938 and certainly with variable plausibility to the non-pacifist, the doubt of the justification of war in the interests of 'democracy' was a premonition of America's global neo-imperial role which was to accelerate after the war.[25] Its ethical incisiveness makes it of continuing relevance to the early twenty-first century. Opposition was always required, said Bourne, to 'any contemplated "liberal" world-order founded on military coalitions.'[26] To draw attention to Bourne was to draw attention to one of the fiercest critics of the corrupt nationalism latent in the American Dream, especially that offered by the narrowest of 'Anglo-Saxon' ideologies. Certainly *TWICE A YEAR* would make concrete Bourne's 'outward reaching wonder', not entirely towards some new definition of the American but to a genuinely transnational spirit involving all men and women of good will across the necessary singular identities of particular cultures.

Given hard-nosed Stalinist positivist Marxists on one side and Social Darwinist capitalists on the other, together with the greater activism and more pragmatic goals of the labour movements themselves, the joint voices of Adams and Bourne might seem too quiet in their attenuated puritanism and radical ethical pacifism. Of what real significance were their words in a world in which Trotsky, Rosa Luxemburg, Sacco and Vanzetti, not to mention millions of Soviet workers, were being slaughtered in the name of state order? This was a world in which fascism and Nazism ran rampant over most of Europe and in which incompetent dying British and French imperialism starved to death millions in India and Vietnam in 1944, even without the thousands who perished in the chaos which followed the collapse of their respective empires. Bourne admitted elsewhere that 'It is true that great social forces reck little of the writings of philosophers or of the thoughts of men.'[27] Nonetheless Bourne and Adams inspired Norman to debate furiously with arch-conservative members of anti-labour vigilante groups in defence of workers' interests, both in the journal and in radio broadcasts.[28] She had one encounter with New York City politics. It was a brief flirtation with the Liberal Party in the face of the apparently sold-out mayoral options of Republican and Democrat candidates but that ended with her realizing that the Democrat candidate, William O'Dwyer, had stood up to both the Christian Front and Tammany. A subsequent close relation with him enabled her to press various New York City causes on a personal level. O'Dwyer later became United States ambassador to Mexico, though scandals over his links with organized crime in 1950 were to dog him for the rest of his life.[29]

The persistently quiet voices of Adams and Bourne, however, were just sufficient to lay an ethical basis for other voices in *TWICE A YEAR*, to enable Norman and her co-workers to negotiate between ideologically fixed positions and to indicate a wider world, a more imaginative and profound sense of things outside what Bourne called 'the machinery of reality'.[30] Even liberalism needed its saints and in a world in which meaning itself seemed impossible, in which the God that failed was not only communist, any effort towards it took on the dimensions of a necessary heroic refusal of 'reality', without which the very nature of the human project was endangered.

The American writers published in *TWICE A YEAR* would claim meaning, like their European counterparts, beyond ideological reductionism, beyond pragmatism, beyond common sense and beyond state and social consensus. The writers reflected their times. Anaïs Nin has already been looked at, Rukeyser has been held over for the final section of the book. It is to Norman's credit that American poets figured so largely: Hart Crane, William Carlos Williams, William Saroyan, Marianne Moore, Charles Olson, Kenneth Patchen and e.e. cummings, as well as many other, then younger, now forgotten, names. Nor as has been shown, was children's poetry neglected.

Theodore Dreiser, Sherwood Anderson, Henry Miller, Anaïs Nin, Clifford Odets, Waldo Frank, Richard Wright and Gertrude Stein (whom Stieglitz had published in *Camera Work* before the First World War) were among the major American prose writers published by Norman. The ideological scope was broad. There was Dreiser, influenced by Mencken and turning social realism into psychological naturalism. There were Miller and Nin, peculiar varieties of American anarchist. There was Odets, a paid-up communist and then still famous for his play *Waiting for Lefty*. Finally, Stein was the boldest experimenter of them all, who nonetheless admired Mussolini and had written anti-New Deal essays in the 1930s.[31] *TWICE A YEAR* readers would also encounter prose from servicemen, reports from men such as Harlan Crippen, whose down-to-earth radicalism gave the lie to the absoluteness of the claim that every serviceman wallowed in know-nothing apolitical apathy. Distinguished critics such as Alfred Kazin and David Riesman made brief appearances, so too did the late Bartolomeo Vanzetti, part of whose diary was republished as a moving tribute to a man of poetic sensibility whose unjust judicial murder had cast doubt on the entire American justice system.

Henry Miller in Time and Eternity

The worlds these writers brought to *TWICE A YEAR* were therefore rich and various. To assess the range one only has to contrast the fictional worlds of Henry Miller and Richard Wright. Miller's radical individual anarchism, his refusal of all political alignment, paradoxically, was close to the pacifist core of Bourne's thinking and had the same limitations in its scepticism about collective action by imperfect people in a messy democratic system. War and the world were virtually synonymous, any organized connection that in the least assisted that reality was already a betrayal. For Miller you lived as best you could, took pleasure where you could, particularly underneath that middle-class self-advertised 'responsibility', too often a mode of collusion with powerful interests and (beneath its hypocritical puritanical code of sexuality) its frightened, neurotic and self-damaging codes of prudence. Its collective 'decencies' had, Miller argued, produced the world of the 'air conditioned nightmare' and nowhere more so than in the United States. The capitalist world enshrined individual risk and initiative, but built skyscraping cathedrals to insurance.

Miller is the American author selected here for analysis, partly to extend the largely East Coast focus of this book. Miller's projected autobiographical 'I', clothed with anarchist wit and scepticism, took the risks and showed a world beyond the suburbs where the shiny American Dream existed only in the billboards and magazine advertisements. Miller's world had all the strengths and limitations of libertarian satire. As with all satire, a deep melancholy lay at its core and *pace* the feminists, an even deeper sense of human, indeed male, vulnerability. The confidence of the expensively educated, of bankers, lawyers, university professors and financiers, of the generally respectable classes was absent from Miller's world in which ordinary people, in a way undreamed of by any socialist definitions of 'the masses', lived their messy and distinctly unromantic lives with quite un-raised consciousnesses, but with gut humour, shared survivalist skills, anguish, diverse sexual experience (revealed to the American public, in a very courageous though ludicrously 'scientific' set of mechanical categories and theories by Kinsey in 1948), and an utter disregard, voluntary and involuntary, for careers, official life and official wisdom. The communist and the capitalist officials, not to mention lawyers and the police, were simply part of an inhuman system of unprincipled careerists in bureaucratic systems to which anyone with modicum of decency would give a wide berth.

Miller's utopian common sense was very infectious and very funny. His work makes a good contrast with Orwell whose gloomy Etonian down-and-outness has its own searing accuracies. Orwell revealed the sheer dreariness and the dullness of the losers in the capitalist struggle in a Britain of industrialized workers living at subsistence levels during the final days of an arrogant aristocratic empire that they had financed with their broken bodies and spirits. Miller, on the other hand, mingled Ben Jonson's *Bartholomew Fair* with Rabelais to produce a world in which 'downstairs' had definitively the edge of life over 'upstairs' in a new 'imperial' space called the air-conditioned nightmare. Sex itself was pursued without lyricism, realizing only temporary though real peace, further to collapse in an exhaustion that might recall the classificatory and naturalist logic of Sade or Bataille, and with a surrealist intensity that suggested Ernst or Breton. In this world, personal loyalties of companionship were paramount; beyond their boundaries nothing else counted. Unlike the French masters, however, Miller's fictional world retained a real love of a desperate humanity, in which the least of people had a vividness and uniqueness of character that warmed the heart and a Byronic, even Thurberesque (though he appealed to a different class,) sense of the hypocrisies of the sex war.

His way with memory and narrative temporality, however, will be the chief focus of the following discussion. Miller's prose was further inflected by a visionary ecstatic 'religious' sense of the world in which, to borrow Allen Ginsberg's words, a poetic prose would attempt to trap 'the archangel of soul between two visual images', to join 'the elemental verbs and set the noun and dash of consciousness together jumping with sensation of Pater Ominipotens Aeterna Deus'.[32] It is a fair assumption that Norman would not have been immune to the more mystical and 'religiously' ecstatic aspects of Miller's prose. Miller noted to Norman in the early 1940s that *The Gospel of Sri Ramakrishna* had 'outweighed my whole American experience last year'.[33]

A large number of Miller's letters to Norman are undated, but the bulk of the correspondence seems to have been from the mid-1930s to 1943. Miller's *Tropics* were published in Paris in the 1930s but had, of course, to wait thirty years to be published in the United States. Norman would have been sympathetic to the sexual frankness of the texts and from a libertarian perspective would have supported any fight against censorship in an America defined by the right-wing banality of the Hayes Code. Miller's correspondence indicates that he was grateful to Norman simply for recognition: 'my time may lie further in the future than most writers'. He wrote to her of how much he owed Anaïs Nin, and vigorously pleaded the cause of the poet Kenneth Patchen whom Norman did publish in *TWICE A YEAR*.[34] For Miller, Patchen was an authentic writer against what he saw as the 'New York crowd', the 'gang of intellectuals' whom he thought sterile and ugly.[35]

He managed also to get some financial assistance to Patchen from Norman and suggested, in terms of his own work, that she might want to publish his essay on Proust and Joyce, something from *The Cosmological Eye* or *Black Spring* among other suggestions. Norman particularly liked *The Cosmological Eye*.[36] Rather like Rexroth with Macdonald, he suggested, to a degree unsuccessfully, writers of his own circle for *TWICE A YEAR*: Lawrence Durrell, David Gascoigne and Dylan Thomas. Miller declared himself intransigently and somewhat theatrically anti-American: a culture, he fumed, that wanted nothing but facts, that 'sends John Dewey to China'. With intransigent irony he declared himself particularly against American 'good' qualities.[37] Miller reminds us that the trans-Atlantic debate does not always have to be solemn. Nonetheless, as his advocacy of Blaise Cendrars showed, Miller both wanted and promoted the 'bridge' between European and American writers, mentioning for example that there were a lot of good translators in America. He particularly recommended Cendrars's *Une Nuit dans la Forêt*. He noted that the French writer had travelled extensively in America. In addition, Miller urged, Cendrars was an admirer of things American, as his book on Hollywood showed, and the Frenchman had very much supported and encouraged Miller's own work.[38] Miller was grateful for Norman's attention and seriousness, even though their views over D.H. Lawrence produced some testiness (Miller was critical). Norman, of course, reacted strongly to Miller's total cynicism about politics and defended her civil liberties commitments. Nonetheless, when the first issue of *TWICE A YEAR* came out, Miller wrote that just to have reprinted the piece from Thoreau would in itself have justified the entire enterprise.

Miller was thrilled to have had *Tropic of Cancer* (which he sent to Norman) published by the same publisher (Obelisk Press) as Céline. He enclosed for Norman a page of endorsements for the book, including one from William Carlos Williams who spoke of the *Tropic of Cancer*'s creative despair and of the final vision of the book: 'the quiet river, the fixedness of France – with the inevitable fling of the imagination toward an America which may or may not be the end of the world'. [39] Williams's words are worth recalling because they produce from the point of view of narrative temporality, an eschatological note as well as a trans-Atlantic exchange. That 'quiet river, the fixedness of France' would, however, in broad poetic terms, be even more sensed by Miller in a book on Greece that was available to Americans in 1941 and to the English in

1942. That book was *The Colossus of Maroussi*, chosen for analysis here because it is one of Miller's most perfectly achieved works. In early September 1939 Miller wrote to Norman to send first copies of *TWICE A YEAR* to the Greek poets George Katsimbalis and George Seferiades (pen name Seferis), adding that he was on his way to Corfu to live for a while with Lawrence Durrell.[40] Three years later in 1942 he wrote to Dorothy Norman that his 'Greek book' sold out its first edition in London in thirty days, in spite of having said only bad things about the English in the book, adding that he had not yet received a penny.[41]

TWICE A YEAR readers would have been introduced to Henry Miller in the 1940–1 issue, with his essay 'Balzac and his Double', which followed Charles Olson's on *Moby-Dick*. In this essay Miller, always an inspired and incisive writer about literature, had defined the nature of Balzac as revealed in two novels, *Seraphita* and *Louis Lambert*. In the latter, Miller described the hero, a child, starved of love, growing into a man committed to art through duty and work, taking to literature like a self-abnegating hermit in pursuit of an ecstatic vision: 'unlike the saints and mystics whom he revered, Balzac never returned from the desert. His immense production is simply a monologue, a wilderness of the soul's anguish in which the wanderer is lost.'[42] His vision that everything in the universe is possessed with life is backed by his reading, from Dante and Leibniz to Goethe, Schopenhauer and Spengler. That same vision, Miller argued, 'the total acceptance of every phase of life' realized in a Dante or Blake, escaped character and author alike.[43] It was the wisdom of the saint (Dostoevsky) over the fruitless struggle of the revolutionary (Tolstoy). Louis Lambert is lost because of a too absolute desire to communicate with the angels. The wisdom of the soul is subordinated to that of the head and the will. The only valid action occurs when the centre is at rest; all other action is vain. The frantic action of Balzac and his protagonist is one that ultimately produces and is reproduced by the air-conditioned nightmare. Selectively citing Lambert's 'lamentations' Miller drew the contours of the world of Balzac's nineteenth-century France:

> The poet's sensitive nerves are perpetually shocked, and what ought to be his glory becomes his torment; his imagination is his cruellest enemy; [...] Politics at the present time, place human forces in antagonism to neutralize each other, instead of combining them to promote their act to some definite end; [...] Man is still the same: might is still his only law, and success his only wisdom [...] governments pass away, as men do, without handing down any lessons and no system gives birth to a system better than that which preceded it [...][44]

Juxtaposing Balzac with Whitman's *Democratic Vistas* (1870), Miller goes for a transnational ethical narrative:

> Never was there, perhaps, more hollowness at heart than at present, and here in the United States. Genuine belief seems to have left us. The underlying principles of the United States are not honestly believed in [...] nor is humanity itself believed in [...] The spectacle is appalling. We live in an atmosphere of hypocrisy throughout [...]The depravity of the business classes of our country is not less than has been supposed, but infinitely greater. The official services of America, national state and municipal, in all their branches and departments, except the judiciary, are saturated in corruption, bribery, falsehood, mal-administration; and the judiciary is tainted.[45]

Crucified by the society into which he was born, Balzac's genius was to have put down accurately the artist's plight 'when the terrible forces of production were coming into being'.[46] Balzac both reflected and was a victim of that world: his life, which was the very symbol of work, epitomizes the futility of Western life with its emphasis on doing rather than being; it epitomizes the sterility of even the highest efforts when characterized, as they are in our world, by the divorce between action and belief.[47]

The essay is read here not for the accuracy of Miller's comments on Balzac, which a complementary reading might dispute, but for the way the comments illustrate Miller's vision of the contemplative life over the active life in a grand, 'Spenglerian' narrative of a declining Western culture. Miller's comprehensive view of the 'spiritual life' – which included the radicalism of Blake's contraries as well as invoking Dante's circles of hell – was set against the crass materialism of the West with its emphasis on work, money, materialism and success. Like Thoreau, Miller asked what men lived for. In so doing, however, he left unanswered the question of ethics and the mystic's relation to the earthly temporalities of history. Nonetheless the offered relation of subjectivity and inner life to that of the social and collective world, articulated through and limited by a kind of a utopian vision of the secular sainthood of the artist, deftly and cogently demonstrated its searing ironic values. The democratic hope was that the search of and for the self might resonate at the profoundest level with others: the democratic danger was that the self would disappear into a world of its own.

The Colossus of Maroussi was published in 1942. An indispensable book for its context in terms of the historical moment and the circle of Greek and expatriate writers Miller found himself associated with, is Edmund Keeley's *Inventing Paradise: The Greek Journey 1837–1947* (1999). The work's chief merit is the way it matches text to historical moment, though that necessarily means losing, by paraphrase, the wholeness and some of the complexity of Miller's writing, even if it gains from the historian's point of view by critically readjusting some of Miller's thematic judgements. Its value is to demonstrate different perspectives on the interactions of the players in the historical moment. In parallel invocations of Lawrence Durrell and Patrick Leigh Fermor among other expatriate writers in Greece, a sense builds up of a double past: the world of the ancient Greeks and of a more contemporary pre-industrialized Greece with both simultaneously available to imaginative evocation. There is the pathos too in the last chapters, of the break-up of the circle, of the coming Nazi destruction and the scattering of a world.[48]

In *The Colossus of Maroussi*, the question of temporality is crucial, and especially so given that the timeless world of meditation invoked in Miller's invention of an apparently a-temporal Greek 'paradise', in contradistinction to the post-Balzacian American 'inferno', would seem to rule out considerations of actual historical contingency. Miller's emphasis on the unities of period, time and place in the alert presence and present of the self might seem to favour a horizontal postmodern approach to the text. That would ignore a set of historical conflicts within the text: between the air-conditioned nightmare and an imagined quasi-pastoral past; between European ways of life and the 'modern life' of the United States; between contemplation and action across temporal landscapes; between dream and nightmare; between historical security and insecurity; between official and unofficial life; between characterizations of national identity in the tourist gaze and friendship; and, most important of all, between the theorizing and imagining of difference and historically contingent (and therefore unanticipated) human reciprocity and trust.

The invocation of a critical utopian site imagined in existing landscape is signalled right at the beginning in a brief allusion to the Dordogne valley in France:

> To me this river, this country, belong to Rainer Maria Rilke. It is not French, not Austrian, not European even: it is the country of enchantment which the poets have staked out and which they alone may lay claim to. It is the nearest thing to Paradise this side of Greece. [49]

Miller reverses the future-oriented American dream of the 'city on the hill'. His utopia is an anti-modern past, almost Claude-like, suspended in Pascalian time: 'I believe that this great peaceful region of France will always be a sacred spot for man and that when the cities have killed off the poets this will be the refuge and cradle of the poets to come.'[50]

However, in real terms, the insertion of the tourist-stranger into a traditional society immediately, by sheer presence, alters the 'authenticity' of the milieu of the 'untouched'. Now the 'Englished' Dordogne or the Mexican town serving as a North American retirement belt, turns the tourist-retiree into an unconscious wrecker of any dream of an anterior alternate time and space. It is not a simple question of purity and contamination though that is how the proposition is often offered – that polarity is flawed in any case – but of a complex ongoing and reciprocal theatre of changing definitions of identity on both sides. The 'peasant' or local worker, also relocated, in turn dreams of authenticity, whether using the new boss's money to ('post-modernly') make the site more 'authentic' or in muted antagonism. Of course, in flat political terms, it is always a question of the economics of mobility, not to mention the class-restricted dream that promotes the relocation. The choice is between economic imperialism and the realization that the stranger, however sympathetic, remains a stranger especially if relative socio-economic and class status is uneven. The resultant exchange is various in terms of the alien's (the tourist's or retiree's) desired depth of encounter with the chosen place. In practice, the desire for that depth varies from the non-existent to the intelligent, engaged and imaginative. The desire itself may be articulated with arrogance or humility in relation to the other who suffers the alien presence, if not economically then in the disturbance of slow-moving cultural practices of space, time and memory.

With these necessary preliminaries out of the way, however, Miller's brief 'tourist' book on Greece can be recuperated as a poetic vision, the passing gesture of the stranger that has its own discursive terms and authenticity quite as much as the historian, archeologist, or social anthropologist. Miller is more aware than most of the complex possibilities of this first person autobiographical narrative. Where and, even more important, when is Greece? The answer to both questions may depend on the gaze of those who love it. It is a Claudian landscape of nostalgia and the roots of the word nostalgia make it immediately more complex. Nostalgia means the emotion of the memory of a distant land. The first half of the twentieth century produced many travel books devoted to lands where time seemed to have stood still or seemed to be inflected by the 'primitive'. Following in the footsteps of a genre from Marco Polo to Doughty, even a cursory 'modernist' list would include James and Wharton on France, Thesiger and T.E. Lawrence on Arabia, Stein on France and Spain, Gide in the Congo, Lawrence on Italy, Mexico and Etruscan civilization, Patrick Leigh Fermor on Central Europe and Greece, Paul Bowles on North Africa and so on.

Miller's 'Greece', like all utopias, defines itself against the contemporary moment in both time and space. In this book the contemporary moment acts as a bracket operating at either end of a deliberate suspension of time:

> I had promised myself not to do a stroke of work for a year. It was my first real vacation in twenty years and I was ready for it. Everything seemed right to me. There was no time any more, just me drifting along in a slow boat [...] Out of the sea, as if Homer himself had arranged it for me the islands bobbed up, lonely, deserted, mysterious in the fading light. I couldn't ask for more, nor did I want anything more. I had everything a man could desire, and I knew it. I felt I knew too that I might never have it again. I felt the war coming on – it was getting closer and closer every day. For a little while yet there would be peace and men might still behave like human beings.[51]

Miller hence sets limits to his utopian time and space: it is wrung from commercial time where the clock rules, it moves to the golden age of the Homeric lands, at once a Renaissance and classical semi-mythical and semi-historical space that in turn refers to a Victorian foundational point of temporal origin for privileging 'Western' civilization. It rests finally in uncertainty in the historical present of 1939 with Europe on the edge of war in which closure threatens to be permanent for the teller, if not biblically and apocalyptically for civilization as a whole. It is time borrowed or negotiated out of emergency. It is a classic tale in which the eschatological parameters are clear, for death and apocalypse are suspended in the telling. Nor is Miller without a political and social sense of that impending doom. He knew he could escape the impending war, the peasants could not: 'Money again. Those who have money escape; those who have not are massacred.'[52] There is the recall of historical time in the present moment of unease. This is not a utopia detached from history: 'the atmosphere was charged with memories of Byron. Sitting there, with Missolonghi so near, it was almost impossible to think sanely about war.'[53]

Hence the need for the local good and for transcendent human companionship becomes urgent. Miller built an international community of writers and poets, always with a critical gaze on America and indeed himself: 'Like most educated Europeans they knew more about American literature than I ever will.'[54] The sense of an America ignoring its own best achievements was something the unknown Henry Miller was sensitive about, though he did manage to tell his Greek friends about Sherwood Anderson: 'In my worst days in America he was the man who comforted me, by his writings.'[55]

Like René Char, Miller plays a kind of Lucretian and Nietzschean vision of the world off against the inwardly anguished, self-protecting fear of the self which he ascribes to Christianity and perhaps specifically to Weber's 'protestant ethic', particularly as exemplified in the United States: that psychology of the driven and prudent individual whose fear of the world bolsters a kind of terrible commitment to progress and, above all, to endless work. Offering an alternative, Miller signals the poetry of George Seferis, who 'caught the spirit of externality', an acceptance, almost Buddhist-like, of a world which renders the present vivid in a way those driven by crippling neuroses and distant progressive goals never experience. The sense of the everyday, in which in every moment is unique, flows from this concrete externality, far from materialist positivism and a naive empiricism: an everyday in which appearance is seized ultimately in a poetic gesture. The psychological experience of the sense of time is crucial here. Seferis becomes the ideal man for Miller and his value is judged in its psychological distance from the nationalism of the American Dream:

> He asks innumerable questions in a polyglot language; he is interested in all forms of cultural expression, and seeks to abstract and assimilate what is genuine and

> fecundating in all epochs. He is passionate about his own country, his own people, not in a hidebound chauvinistic way but as a result of patient discovery following upon years of absence abroad. This passion for one's country is a special peculiarity of the intellectual Greek who has lived abroad.[56]

Paradoxically, there are echoes of Whitman here: 'you shall listen to all sides and filter them from yourself'.[57] Whitman's prescriptions for the poet structure this reading of the presence of the Greek poets, the emphasis on the particulars of appearance, the refusal of institutional truth, the anti-materialism of a soul attuned to a mythic sense of reality, the emphasis on friendship, the sense of the eternal in the temporal, the love of the natural world, the interdependence of body and soul, and the unique role of poetic discourse above and alongside philosophy, religion and scientific explanations of the world. In terms of temporality, eternity is immanent, not part of a post-eschatological future: 'Men, women and the earth and all upon it are simply to be taken as they are, and the investigation of their past and present and future shall be unintermitted and shall be done with perfect candor. Upon this basis philosophy speculates ever looking toward the poet'.[58] Like Miller, Whitman spoke of the 'melancholy prudence' that committed so many to 'the toss and pallor of years in moneymaking with all their scorching days and icy nights and all their stifling deceits and underhand dodgings, or infinitesimals of parlors, or shameless stuffing while other starve [...] and all the loss of the bloom and odor of the earth and of the flowers and atmosphere'.[59]

Miller speaks and reminds us of the silent, suffering of those exploited by capitalism, unknown and at a distance: 'the successful American businessman is murdering thousands of innocent men, woman and children in his sleep every day of his life. Here nobody can have a clear conscience: we are all part of a vast interlocking murdering machine.'[60] Though Miller ignores the right-wing politics of the Seferis group, he uses the conservative turn to articulate an uncompromising vision of capitalist damage.

Miller's poetic narrative is both concretely and abstractly directed. Anti-American though he appears to be, he is in fact centrally located in that unifying vision of 'humanity' at the core of the American transcendentalist tradition stemming from the great writers of the nineteenth century. He also provides a link with the Beat generation a decade later. One can easily relineate the prose into Beat poetry sentences, indicating the cadences that Kerouac and Ginsberg at least partially picked up from Whitman:

> At Mycenae I walked over the incandescent dead –
> At Pidaurus I felt a stillness so intense that for a fraction of a second I heard the great heart of the world beat and I understood the meaning of pain and sorrow;

> At Tiryns I stood in the shadow of the Cyclopean man and felt the blaze of that inner eye which has now become a sickly gland
>
> At Argus the whole plain was a fiery mist in which I saw the ghosts of our own American Indians and greeted them in silence.[61]

The 'cosmological eye/I' is concretely indebted to psalmic repetition, parallelism, prophetic vision and even thematic tropes of Biblical lamentation – the sense of person, place and cadence is not far from 'By the rivers of Babylon, there we sat down, yea, we wept, when we remembered Zion.'[62] The names recall a fusion of myth and history in ancient times. The dead speak as to Odysseus in order to tell their stories. In the nineteenth century, Melville's mockery was never far from such breathless lists: 'I walk a world that is mine; and enter many nations, as Mungo Park rested in African cots; I am served like Bajazet: Bacchus my butler, Virgil my minstrel, Phillip Sidney my page. My memory is a life beyond birth.'[63] Miller, however, takes the edge off the potential nationalist arrogance of composite American 'man as heir of the ages' by seeing the inheritance not as an automatic memory beyond birth, set in motion by some impersonal destiny, but one needing to be found in contradistinction to that mindless evolution, the end product of which for Miller was the one dimensional figure of American modernity, an isolated utilitarian, floundering in electronic hyper-reality.

In terms of the telling, Miller continued, any narrative spoken to others sends the recipient into his or her own narrative even before the other speaker has finished. It is suggestive not dogmatic: 'I have always felt that the art of telling a story consists in so stimulating the listener's imagination that he drowns himself in his own reveries long before the end.'[64] In short, it is the opposite of the egotistical sublime of the Ancient Mariner and off to the side of the need for the mortal distraction of a Scheherazade. Listening to his friend Katsimbalis, he notes they are chained to each other, but not like the victims of Coleridge's tale: 'he the teller and I the listener, and that we will go to the end of the world this way, not as prisoners but as willing bondsmen.'[65] Here, narrative stimulates that reverie which prepares other narratives, in which the other as listener is reciprocally bound and free at the same time.

In the stories of Katsimbalis, a man 'crucial to the development of the best writing in Greece in the first half of this century', there was, noted Miller, 'a complete disregard for the element of time.'[66] Complementing the individual fact, Miller characterized cosmic time in very much the same terms as a Shelley or Whitman: 'the World is both young and old: like the individual, it renews itself in death and ages through infinite births. At any stage there is the possibility of fulfilment.'[67] Here ethics involves a recognition of temporal fatality and the presence of the past. At Epidaurus, Greek culture though faded stands as 'a miracle wrought by the human spirit [...] a pure distilled heritage of a past which is not altogether lost.'[68] Along the line of chronological history, like Mumford, Miller distinguished between historical cultural moments in terms of an ethical judgement directed towards life or death, renewal or destruction:

> Tiryns is no more like Knossus, for example, than New York is like Rome or Paris. Tiryns represents a relapse, just as America represents Europe in its most degenerate aspects. Crete of the Minoan epoch stands for a culture based upon peace: Tiryns smells of cruelty, barbarism, suspicion, isolation. It is like an H.G. Wells setting for a prehistoric drama, for a thousand years' war between one-eyed giants and blunder-footed dinosaurs.[69]

Miller's Manichean distinctions of course are part of a satiric project relying on hyperbole rather than a philosophy of time or a historical social anthropology. Paradoxically, this type of thinking is quintessentially American. Its propositions are quasi-ethical cultural judgements and can constitute a double-edged sword. On the one hand there is a real sense in which judgements about civilizations can be made in quasi-ethical terms: Greek, Egyptian, Roman, Medieval European, Mayan, American. For Mumford the lineaments of the way power was dispersed in a culture would be crucial. Gigantism, one-dimensional science, technology, and monumentality are the first enemies given his own situation in 'megalopolis'. Medieval scale on the other hand was 'human'. For Miller it is more an Enlightenment vision that structures his ethical judgements, one that would not have been strange to Tom Paine or Mary Godwin: 'Warrior, jailer, priest – the eternal trinity which symbolizes our fear of life. I don't like Nauplia. I don't like provincial towns. I don't like jails, churches, fortresses, palaces, libraries, museums, or public statues to the dead.'[70] That 'fear of life' gives it a modernist psychological tone, but the rest is a traditional literary anarchism that emphasizes the importance of emotional life that in America goes back to Thoreau, in England to Shelley: 'I have heard, indeed, an ignorant collegian adduce, in favour of Christianity, its hostility to every worldly feeling'.[71]

Fuelling Miller's own satire is a horror of modernity. In a world that advocates managerial consensual adjustment as the highest virtue, it is hard to take on board the absolute disgust of Miller and the absolute contempt he had for inhuman authority, which underlies his absolute insistence on the value of ecstatic and joyful experience, erotic or otherwise:

> Now we are passing over the little bridge above the sundered vault of Clytemnestra's resting place. The earth is flamy with spirit as if it were an invisible compass we are treading and only the needle quivering luminously as it catches a flash of solar radiance. We are veering towards Agamemnon's tomb over the vault of which only the thinnest patch of earth now rests like a quilt of down. The nudity of this divine cache is magnificent. Stop before the heart glows through. Stoop to pick a flower.

> Shards everywhere and sheep droppings. The clock has stopped. The earth sways for a fraction of a second, waiting to resume its eternal beat. [72]

In this general temporal 'suspension', life and death, earth and spirit, the betrayals and revenge of the ancient drama, fragments of archeological and natural waste, are brought together, opaque to clock time, in a moment of reverie. Its tone is in the spirit of 'consider the lilies how they grow, they toil not nor they spin' but without the Christian post-temporal treasure in heaven. [73] The treasure is immanent in the living moment, and brings to itself a concrete past transformed through poetry into a true and healing nostalgia in the face of contemporary war and devastation. In Pascalian terms, cosmic time is also separated from numerical awe:

> Their astronomical figures and calculations, intended to impress and overawe us, only caused us to smile indulgently or to very impolitely laugh outright at them [...] A light year is no more impressive to me than a second, or a split second. This is a game for the feeble-minded which can go on ad nauseam backwards and forwards without taking us anywhere.'[74]

In a satirical adoption of pre-scientific astrology, by contrast, the gloom of Saturn is real and humanly disquieting. Its manifestation is very earthly as Miller puts together one of his most comic lists. Saturn includes: 'sterility, anaemia, indecision, defeatism, constipation, anti-toxins, feeble novels, hernia, meningitis, dead-letter laws, red tape, working-class conditions, sweat shops, Y.M.C.A.s, Christian endeavour meetings, spiritist séances, poets like T.S. Eliot, zealots like Alexander Dowie, healers like Mary Baker Eddy, statesmen like Chamberlain'.[75] The gloom of Saturn is a modernist version of Pope's *The Dunciad* where a universal darkness buries all. What connects T.S. Eliot and Neville Chamberlain, working class-conditions and constipation, is in ethical psychological terms what Matthew Arnold once called the strange disease of modern life. Here, a kind of neurosis, a blocking of desire, has diverted energy inwards in self-hatred and outwards in a destructive rage for order. In this universalist and vitalistic satiric thesis, a betrayal or despair of life manifests itself in an abuse of ethical, spiritual and political truth. One consequence is that mind and body have been reduced to half speed. In contrast the idealized Greek is 'alive to the finger-tips; he oozes vitality, he's effervescent, he's ubiquitous in spirit. The Englishman is lymphatic, made for the arm-chair, the fireside, the dingy tavern, the didactic treadmill.'[76] It is a love of the world and vitality that inspires Miller's dualistic satire against all bad faith. The ancient man of Knossus was 'religious in the only way which is becoming to man, by making the most of everything that comes to hand, by extracting the utmost of life from every passing minute'.[77] This wayward essentializing of national types is part of a satiric strategy and not to be taken too seriously. In 1942 many people obviously loved the book since, as Miller was the first to note, they bought out the British edition of the book in record time.

Miller's rage against modernity makes him as suspicious of the 'atomized individual' as the Marxists and also as suspicious as them of the total absence of anything approaching 'a communal existence'.[78] The stultified life of 'telephone, radio, automobile, tractor et cetera, the meaning of the word communal becomes so fantastically distorted that one begins to wonder what is meant by the phrase "human society"'.[79] The world of the aeroplane, too, is fundamentally the world of the capitalist on the look-out for product:

> [It] lifts you by the seat of the pants, and spits you down in Baghdad, Samarkand, Beluchistan, Fez, Timbuctoo, as far as your money will take you. All these once marvellous places whose very names cast a spell over you are now floating islets in the stormy sea of civilization. They mean homely commodities like rubber, tin, pepper, coffee, carborundum and so forth. The natives are derelicts exploited by the octopus whose tentacles stretch from London, Paris, Berlin, Tokyo, New York, Chicago to the icy tips of Iceland and the wild reaches of Patagonia.[80]

The passage could have been lifted from *Das Kapital*, located somewhere in a discussion of the ultimately violent abstractions of exchange value and late capitalism's imperialist predations. It is still an exact description of the assumptions behind current American foreign policy.

For one apparently so indifferent to politics and to the Spanish Civil War, Miller's recall of the 1922 'Smyrna Affair' in which the Turks burnt the city forcing 1.5 million Greeks and four hundred thousand Armenians back to their original countries, is passionately presented together with the 'disgraceful, supine acquiescence of the big powers'.[81] Reading Miller's anger from a post-Second World War perspective, his main ethical point about the studied indifference of others to this massacre of the innocents was premonitory: 'So long as human beings can sit and watch with hands folded while their fellowmen are tortured and butchered so long will civilization be a hollow mockery, a wordy phantom suspended like a mirage above a swelling sea of murdered carcasses.'[82] There is no need to belabour the point given the allied discoveries of the camps 1944 and 1945, and numerous hushed-up massacres and ethnic cleansings since.

Finally the immediate moment of war caught up with Miller. In 1940, the American Consulate invalidated his passport and told him to clear out. A last minute excursion to Delphi forced him to the long view of history and a final prophetic denunciation on the eve of the most terrible war in history:

> The world which passed away with Delphi passed away as in a sleep. It is the same now. Victory and defeat are meaningless in the light of the wheel which relentlessly revolves. We are moving into a new latitude of the soul, and a thousand years hence

> men will wonder at our blindness, our torpor, our supine acquiescence in an order which was doomed.
>
> [...] We move in clock time amidst the debris of vanished worlds, inventing the instruments of our own destruction, oblivious of fate or destiny, knowing never a moment of peace, possessing not an ounce of faith, a prey to the blackest superstitions, functioning neither in the body nor in the spirit, active not as individuals but as microbes in the organism of the disease.[83]

For Miller writing after the beginning of hostilities, the war has meant the scattering of friends: 'some are in concentration camps in France and Germany, one is rotting away in Siberia, another is in China, another in Mexico, another in Australia. When we meet again some will be blind, some legless, some old and white-haired, some demented, some bitter and cynical [...] the next time we meet, any of us, it will be on the ashes of all that we once cherished.'[84] Back in New York, 'I was among the go-getters again, among the restless souls, who not knowing how to live their own life, wish to change the world for everybody.'[85]

If Miller's book has the limits of its ethical-psychological utopian fable, an interior monologue grafted onto an actual external site, it also has the strengths of its wonder at the strangeness of world that seemed quite other than his own, and remains prophetically accurate about the blindness that still drives the materialist 'soul' of an increasingly imperial America besotted by the immediate. The temporal shifts in the last pages are to a degree classic. The story becomes suddenly old and unreachable: ancient Delphi and contemporary New York occupy different planets of consciousness, and the unsparing honesty of the spiritual exercise is contrasted with the banality of a brainwashed Greek back from America expatiating on the efficiency of the American railways and the delights of the American Dream.

Time is the real subject of this book and redefining it as against 'American' time, that is, against capitalist utilitarian equations of money and clock time, becomes part of a critique of modernity. Miller's friend Katsimbalis becomes, in this respect, the litmus paper against which the entire civilization is judged wanting:

> He spoke of little things and of great with equal reverence; he was never too busy to pause and dwell on the things which moved him; he had endless time on his hands, which in itself is the mark of a great soul.[86]

Miller's sense of temporality is in the end poetic. It would be easy enough to criticize Miller's 'fictionalization' of Greece: the hypostacization of character; the inauthentic brevity of encounter; the absence of self-analysis; a Greece confined to the poets and writers; the rhapsodical memory of 'the glory that was Greece'; the mockery of the encounter with tourists and other expatriates who knew not and hardly cared where they were in time or space; the elision of contemporary Greek politics; the 'absence' of extensive cultural knowledge, language and 'disregard' of the war. But Miller did not set out to write a book that would engage these frameworks. In that sense he is the historian's *bête noire*. Miller wrote poetic narrative not fiction, not cultural, historical or anthropological analysis. For him the present reality leaked in enough in a visceral response to the people and landscape, haunted by memory and the memory of himself in reverie to other places and to other times. 'We work as poets', said Robert Duncan, 'and take seriously what seems to most men the one ground surely not to be taken seriously – the play-reality of imagined religions, philosophies, sciences' (and I would add history). Duncan goes on: 'We have been converted by and have now taken our faith in a truth that is patently made-up.'[87]

Yet the questions persist of what is meant by poetic narrative and they are insistent in Miller's book. The poetic claim is bolstered by the thematic encounter with contemporary poets whose speech is endorsed and co-opted as a legitimating parallel, and adopted as a prosecuting discourse against modernity. Edgar Allan Poe's 'To Helen', a poem that invoked the trans-historical sacred power of Psyche and in which the phrase 'the glory that was Greece' is found, signals a dreamed link between present and past that is present also in Miller's poetic narrative. The psychological eternity revealed in the meditation is practised but concealed in historical discourse, whose strategy is to wrench them apart in order to create history itself as vital difference. As Ricoeur points out, this has many levels of meaning and tone.

Even figuring eternity as a circle has different affective results: for example in fatal return and creative renewal. The 'moving image of eternity' is also not just a collective singular but also belongs to a philosophic story: 'it is only within the philosophical retrieval of a myth that the genesis of time can be brought to language.'[88] Citing Vernant on the great genres of Greek poetry (theogony, epic and tragedy), Ricoeur speaks of the 'neighboring mythical figures that assimilate time to a circle':

> Sometimes the unity and perenniality attributed to this fundamental time radically negate human time, experienced as a factor of instability, destruction, and death; sometimes this great time expresses the cyclic organization of the cosmos, which harmoniously includes the passing of the seasons, the succession of generations, and the periodic return of festivals; sometimes the divine *aion* gets detached from this image of a circle, which is then connected with the unending round of births and births, as can be seen in much Indian thinking and Buddhism.[89]

All three figurations of eternity can easily be demonstrated at different points in Miller's poetic narrative. Again adopting some of Ricoeur's discussion, it is precisely the charge of Miller that modernity thinks of a present without a future or a past ('We move in clock time amidst the debris of vanished worlds'), though Miller, given his preference for Indian and Buddhist thought over Christianity, emphasizes less the inscrutability of time than 'the polymorphism of figurations and, across them of the evaluations of human time, bound to the representation of something beyond time'.[90]

Certainly Miller manages not to reduce his meditations on eternity to the immutability of a stable present, for any mystic glimpse of immutability is immediately threatened by the fateful arrangement of the incidents within the plot. Miller's lamentations are less a result of the distinction between time and eternity than of the loss of seriousness which is in turn a result of the loss of a sense of the inscrutable as figured dramatically in Greek tragedy: a communal theatre that problematizes the self to the self both in the act of witness and as one who undergoes fate. It is precisely a loss of 'play/ful' seriousness that is Miller's most serious charge against modernity – through, among many other things, its one-dimensional philosophy of time. It is the loss of what Vernant in another discussion called the 'religious festival' present both in the public and private sphere: 'this applies to the instalment of a magistrate, an assembly meeting, or a peace treaty, just as it does to a birth, a meal shared with friends, or setting out on a journey'.[91]

Without it the magistrates are reduced to domination, the politicians to fateful operations of pure power, biology to the banality of cosmic evolution, relations between people to pure self-preservation or calculated exchange and the human journey itself to a utility without meaning or what amounts to the same thing, purely abstract profit. *The Colossus of Maroussi* is at once a recovery of sanity through the power of poetic narrative, inflected but not bound by either historical or purely fictional narrative, and still managing to maintain relevance to the historical human condition. Its first allegiance is to the interior monologue of the autobiographical self but it also engages externality in a lamentation for, and a cry of rage against, a civilization whose values, ineptitudes, betrayals and technological arrogance were about to produce horrors undreamed of, even as late as 1939.

TWICE A YEAR and European Culture

For Norman, for the many reasons already given, there was no question of ignoring the bridge between European and American culture. Some of the American contributors had in any case wide-ranging European connections as well as a sense of history and the rest of the world. Charles Olson, for example, became rector of Black Mountain College, which was originally founded by European refugees from Germany. The links were maintained even through the 'American' period of the college from 1950 onwards, under his direction. Norman herself was a member of the Union for Democratic Action during the war, which was chaired by Reinhold Niebuhr.[92] She also knew many refugees personally. Erwin and Maria Piscator, for example, were close friends of hers. Erwin was a famous German refugee radical theatre director, who not only directed experimental political theatre in New York but also taught Marlon Brando and James Dean to act. During their American period both Piscators were highly active in this synthetic transatlantic moment. In 1948 Maria's Poet's Theatre, for instance, tried to reconnect poetry with music and drama. Her year's programme included Genet's *The Servant Girls* and *Two Noh Plays* by Paul Goodman.[93] The Piscators were only one example among hundreds of transatlantic wartime refugees in all disciplines, from Bertolt Brecht and Fritz Lang to Hannah Arendt and Paul Tillich, who added new vitality to a vibrant American cultural scene. Never before, nor again, would there be such a depth of dialogue between free Europe, in or out of exile, and the United States.

Emphasizing Norman's links with European culture in a time of refugees is therefore to celebrate a sense of reciprocity in a transatlantic community not primarily engaged in competitive distinctions between national cultures. Certainly European interest in the American arts (one excepts Britain apart from D.H. Lawrence), as Miller ruefully reflected, was intense. Norman welcomed the European refugee in ways the State Department and certain arrogant New York intellectuals (as de Beauvoir's encounter with some of them showed, see p. 111) did not. The reception of Sartre, as also noted, demonstrated a certain insularity from and resistance to European thought. In spite of this more typical resistance, Dorothy Norman and Mary Lescaze provided just that deep sense of hospitality to the stranger that Miller found among his friends in Greece. They also shared Miller's curiosity for whatever was unfamiliar and different. Was it because they were women in a society that drove men to compete so relentlessly that their generosity seemed to be so careless of their own egos? Of their relationship Norman remarked: 'We can agree or disagree, but a beautiful spirit always underlies our relationship. Neither of us seeks power.'[94] Norman, it must be added, also amicably shared the editorship of the journal at different times with Richard Wright and Brom Weber. Her thoughtful defence of Wright, including her support for his decision to return to France (read as treachery by left and right), can be read in detail in her memoir.[95]

Among her distinguished European contacts were writers, philosophers, playwrights, journalists and politicians. Giuseppe A. Borghese had been head of the Vittorio Emanuele Orlando government's press and propaganda bureau in the First World War and was influential in getting Italy to accept the League of Nations as well as being a powerful voice in discussions that led to the United Nations (his book *Common Cause* attracted much attention in America in 1943). He left Italy after refusing to take the fascist oath. Norman's letters to him reveal a personally close as well as intellectual relationship. Borghese wrote to her about

Plato, Aristotle and Augustine, as well as his reactions to *TWICE A YEAR* and Yalta. In her memoir, Norman recalls his essay in volume III–IV, which had been his address to the PEN club in 1939, called 'How can Culture survive in Exile?' Its flattering praise of English as 'the most welcoming and unprejudiced of languages' can today be read only with embarrassment at the linguistic, political and cultural levels, but with Germany, Spain and Italy under the heel of dictators in 1939, its rhetorical excesses can, perhaps, be forgiven.

The strongest point of the essay was his extension of a Tolstoyan advocacy of the local traditions and local cultures that were being endlessly challenged by contact with the wider world. For Borghese, a paradox emerges that 'tradition', the very recall of the past and cultural memory can be achieved best in exile: 'Practically all the Middle Ages knew how fixed fidelity to one's past and place hamper the creative spirit, how good and generous exile is.' Exile appears as 'permanence in metamorphosis'.[96] The paradox was clear: that a tradition could only be both preserved and re-invented by a radical break from cultural nationalism, often defining itself as 'classic' and bound to a specific geographical space; a conjuncture that might finally become, as an unchallenged 'canonical' text, a destructive cultural tool in the hands of conservatives.

In fact the *TWICE A YEAR* of 1940 was the key issue for the European 'exiles'. Following Borghese's article was one by Ernst Bloch, the German philosopher and literary critic, who was much more tentative about the positive dialectic described by Borghese. This living between two worlds, ('one dead the other powerless to be born') he noted, roughly paraphrasing Matthew Arnold's famous invocation of Sophocles in 'Stanzas from the Grande Chartreuse', is a temporal not a spatial phenomenon:[97] 'This living between two ages is also a kind of exile, in that it is a departure from tradition. It is not a departure from the country of one's birth, of course, but it is a breaking with the social beliefs of one's parents.' Bloch, with the educated European's sense of the turmoils of the past, could make a parallel between the changes of the late Middle Ages and the early modern period: 'Once more a great exodus from the past is taking place, in economics, in sociology in philosophy', adding that 'in our borderline lives we are thoroughly contemporary'.[98]

Bodo Uhse, a German novelist who was also speaking at the Third American Writers Congress, gave that 'contemporary' a long historical frame in the following speech:

> My friend Gustav Regler wrote a novel on the Peasant War in Germany, the first German revolutionary movement. Equipped with a deceptive title and a mythical author's name, it entered Germany as an apparently historical work. People read it, and the instances cited from the struggle for freedom of four hundred years ago were understood! Some time later we received an illegal magazine printed in Germany, bearing as its title the emblem of the embattled peasant armies.[99]

Here is a rare glimpse of the complete cycle of a book in its full and politicized theatre of reception. A narrative strategy is created of shifting historic temporalities by displacement to a quasi-allegorical level, inviting its meaning to be decoded and recoded as part of a contemporary political struggle.

In the same issue Norman published and republished work in translation by the Hungarian writer Andreas Latzko, the German writer Arthur Schnitzler and the bilingual Alsatian writer René Schickele whose books had been banned by Hitler, an article by Dwight Macdonald's friend Nicola Chiaromonte on Borghese, articles on Italian poetry and work by Ernst Toller as well as excerpts from German classics such as Goethe's *Conversations with Eckermann*, Heinrich Heine's 'A Poet's Prediction' and part of Friedrich Hölderlin's *Hyperion*. The extract from Toller's *I was a German*, responding to the events of 1933 and excoriating republicans, revolutionaries, trade union officials, bureaucrats, socialist writers, professional politicians and economists alike, is particularly moving in its unsparing sense of historical failure and the brutal end of any confidence in human progress: 'Moral and spiritual values laboriously and painfully evolved through centuries of martyrdom have become objects of mockery and perverted hatred.'[100]

The French existentialists appeared in the final issue and Norman's relationship with Camus has already been touched upon (see p. 230). In her memoir it is obvious that Norman, together with other Americans, rather preferred Camus to Sartre and de Beauvoir. Norman had, however, also worked with politicians around de Gaulle and the Free French movement. Chief among these were Henri Bernstein and André Gérade. She was particularly close to the latter, a friend of de Gaulle, journalist and political correspondent. He only gets two sentences in *Encounters* but in fact there is a large correspondence between them of a largely intimate kind (at least on his part), but he also told her about post-war British Labour politics in relation to India, the changed postwar scene in France, the moves to Cold War and general Indian politics.

Other Europeans flicker in and out of the correspondence: Niccolò Tucci (a regular contributor to *politics*), Henri Cartier-Bresson, Stephen Spender, Margaret Sanger, Martin Buber, Arthur Koestler and Gunnar Myrdal. It is noteworthy that a correspondence with Marguerite Caetani, shows Norman attempting to get René Char's work promoted in the United States. Caetani was a New England-born heiress who married an Italian prince to newspaper headlines in New York in 1911, as though a character in a Henry James novel. She had her own twice-yearly review, *Botteghe Oscure* (1948–60), a multi-linguistic review for creative writing. A comprehensive review of Princess Caetani's life and work in a recent *Virginia Quarterly* article cites Archibald MacLeish's introduction to the *Botteghe Oscure Index* to the effect that an astonishing 650 writers of thirty nationalities had passed through the review's pages.[101] Clearly she was a woman after Norman's own heart.

Italian writers were represented by Carlo Levi and Ignazio Silone. Levi had clearly had a brief and intense relation with Norman in 1947 after the success of *Christ Stopped at Eboli* but he does not appear in *Encounters*. In 1947 Levi was very current. Norman printed a radio interview with him by Nancy Craig, a catalogue introduction by him to an exhibition of his paintings and selections from an interview with Harvey Breit, originally published in the *New York Times*. Levi explained the creative isolation of his banishment to Luciana by Mussolini and, like Silone before him, drew (with less scepticism and to a degree less complexity) a contrast between fascist modernity and the profound human values of slow-moving peasant culture. In relation to painting he wrote, while expressing hope for the future: 'The adorable monsters of Picasso, the theophanies of the artists of the generation preceding us, belong, I believe, to the past, a past from which we have been separated by the deep ditch of the last war.' To Harvey Breit he spoke of the work of Cesare Pavese, a man acutely aware of the position of a disgraced Europe between Stalinist Russia and Cold War America and unwilling to sign up to either. Breit described him accurately as 'a poet and prose writer, who translated with brilliance Herman Melville's *Moby-Dick*'.[102]

With Ignazio Silone, Norman had an equally personal and intense relationship. Silone's work *Fontamara*, the first volume of the Abruzzo trilogy, had been an enormous success in the United States. It had appeared in German in 1933 from a small Zurich press and was then translated into English and published by Random House in 1934. It was to sell more than 1.5 million copies in twenty-seven languages. In the United States its publication made a big impact on American intellectuals and writers, notably Alfred Kazin, Edmund Wilson, Malcolm Cowley and Irving Howe. Niccolò Tucci declared that he became an anti-fascist the day he started reading *Fontamara*. The second volume, *Bread and Wine*, was even more successful. During the war, the United States army printed an unauthorized version of the books and distributed them to Italians after the Allied occupation of Italy in 1943.[103]

Norman corresponded with both Ignazio Silone and his wife Darina. Silone's wife was clearly interested in the Indian sub-continent and African-American affairs. Norman lent her, among other books, Albert Schweitzer's *Indian Thought and its Development* (1936), Louis Fischer's *Life of Mahatma Gandhi* (1950) and E. Franklin Frazier's *The Negro Family in the United States* (1948).[104] The two women also shared their thoughts about difficult husbands and Norman talked about her divorce. In her memoir Norman described her own first reactions to *Fontamara*: 'I know Silone has had to escape to Switzerland, but he seems to have transcended the trauma of exile and created a contemporary classic.'[105] She and Mary Lescaze set to work to get in contact with him and, ever practical, inquired whether he needed financial help. They published his reply as the second of three pieces by him in the first issue of *TWICE A YEAR*. The first piece is from *The School for Dictators*, which was to be published later in the year by

Harper. The third piece was an extract – the concluding three or four pages – from *Fontamara* itself.

Silone's essay 'The things I stand for', published by Norman in *TWICE A YEAR* in 1943, is perhaps his most significant in terms of the concerns of this book. The last volume of the trilogy, *The Seed Beneath the Snow*, had been published by Harper the year before and Silone began by answering friends who had accused him of abandoning the class struggle in the narrative. In the novel the hero, Pietro Spina, leaves the Communist Party in disgust, worrying that it was showing signs of the same tactics as fascism. In the *TWICE A YEAR* article Silone defended his concentration on the inner life of his character as against the Nietzschean hero of confidence and action. The true communist, he argued, needed more than justification by exteriorizing praxis, the inner psychological and ethical life desperately needed attention. Richard Wright had drawn similar criticism in *Native Son*. It was precisely the nature of subjectivity that the communist bureaucrats had forgotten: 'their spiritual self-mutilation' had put them outside the boundary of 'normal humanity [...] behind their steely masks they are nothing but little, terrified people who have learned to be extremely prudent'.[106] History was made by men, not by social determinisms. He defended too his concentration on the wretched of the earth, the *cafoni*, or the non-industrialized peasant working at the edge of society for starvation wages. He challenged Marx's knowledge of the peasantry and their timeless ways and called for an integral federalism and an ethical socialism. An examination of Silone's trilogy will bring this section on Dorothy Norman to a fitting conclusion, for it is fundamentally engaged with this book's major themes of time, memory and narrative understanding. As such, it engages an even wider theme relevant to its own moment, a moment that crucially witnessed the collapse of ideological certainty.

Reintegration into Time: Ignazio Silone and The Abruzzo Trilogy

In the trilogy itself, it is clear that Silone was negotiating all the ideological conflicts of fascism and its opponents. We now know that Silone was passing information to the fascists, a fact he quickly regretted and abandoned as soon as he was able. But as a recent excellent introduction to the novel has shown, this betrayal not only keeps the novel from becoming stale like other political novels of the period, but actually increases the complexity and depth of the political meaning because it shows an unanticipated weakness in the most committed and intelligent of human beings. The complexity is increased as Silone uses subtle arguments from both Christianity and Marxism in dialogues whose tones and affective nuances range from the comic to the tragic and in a plot whose complex temporalities employ many genres from melodrama to the naturalist novel, from political satire to romance, from parable to the fable, from social realism to folk tale and hagiography.

Three ideologies structure the argument of the plot: Marxism, Christianity and fascism. These engage three different temporal periods. The first involves the Bolshevik revolution's descent into Stalinism over some twenty years, the second the two thousand years of the failure of Christian ethics together with the immediate historical moment of papist collusion with fascism, the third the decade of the rise of Mussolini. With Marxism and Christianity the argument cuts two ways: both offer the best values of the book and in both the betrayals of principles are heavily criticized and satirized. In Silone's fictional world, to be either a sincere socialist or a sincere Christian is very dangerous. Two further conflicts are crucial for the plot, that of the obliteration of historical practices in state, church and community by the ruthless promotion of Italian style modernity of which futurism was so much the artistic prophet.

In Silone's trilogy, the 'old world' of traditional peasant culture is dying alongside the traditional families and clerisy that both maintained the patterns of power that structured it but whose traditional practices also to a degree sometimes took the edge off the worst excesses of exploitation. The new capitalist/bureaucratic concentration and centralization of power under populist fascism, ruthless in relation to the local and the traditional, is a major theme of the book. It is the violence of the rupture that divorces past from present in a virtual eschatological framework that seeks to restore the glories of Rome in neo-imperialist adventure that legitimates all other violence in the book. Here is not Rukeyser's unanticipated past, but that 'classic' past cut off from its own past and anticipated future, simplified and frozen as an icon of worship, 'canonized' as an object of veneration and used to promote an authoritarian order.

Ideological practices rather than either simple belief systems or hypostacized ideologies themselves therefore become the main focus of the book. Socialist realism itself had declined into a propagandist cliché and the one-dimensional need for an industrialized proletariat as part of the historic narrative of Marxist process in a country of almost *ancien régime* peasants, landowners and a small newly emerging bourgeoisie fitted the immediate historical situation very awkwardly indeed. Silone turned his story into a social-anthropological satire, but one inflected with all the rich resources of multi-dimensional narratives whose multiple temporalities broke free of the twin strait-jackets of propaganda and traditional political protest novels.

The class war is evident everywhere in the book, both in the psychology of the way the different characters think and in the way they act. It occupies both the present of communist consciousness in the industrialized urban centres and the older 'bourgeois' time-frame of a sinking landed gentry. Yet again the lowest orders of the class structure seem to fall outside time, the huge class of the poor who never win, the poor as signalled in the Christian eternal framework that 'ye have always with you', the 'wretched of the earth' of Fanon's compelling account of the absolute victims of imperialist enterprise, or Kerouac's 'fellaheen' whom he designated as a universal class. While Marxism criticizes this universalism as a product of the fatalism of the indifferent rich, Christianity acknowledges its presence in history even if it seems somewhat ruthlessly to claim that its permanent presence would be redeemed in a somewhat nebulous eternity. The poor would inherit the earth. The question was: when?

What happens in Silone's work is that ideological belief is prised from ethical behaviour and praxis. The good action flies in the face of what people believe to be good. Those who believe they are communists or Christians are very different from those who act in a genuinely socialist or Christian way. Simone Weil's position that there are no ethical beliefs, there are only ethical actions, underwrites the entire spirit of Silone's novels. When, in *Bread and Wine*, the novel's atheist and communist hero meets his old teacher priest, Don Benedetto, who is under suspicion by the fascists, he explains that he lost faith many years ago to which the priest replies: 'It would not be the first time that the Lord has been forced to hide himself and make use of an assumed name.'[107] Like Mark Twain's Huckleberry Finn confronting Nigger Jim who decides 'to go to hell' (given Christian endorsement of slavery in America) rather than betray his best friend, Silone's characters are authentic only by their acts. The greatest evils in Silone are hypocrisy and cruelty and the worst political acts are cowardly acquiescence and silence, passive or active, in relation to unbridled authoritarian power. As for Gandhi, for Silone if the means are wrong, the ends are wrong. The argument is seriously anti-pragmatic. In the USSR, Germany or Italy, thousands of murdered citizens and slaughtered peasants could not lead to or legitimate a better future, whatever the offered vision and 'necessary' sacrifice.

It is perhaps only in fiction that the whole range of ideological practices, from custom to religious tradition, from psychology to economics, from the memories of the historical past to the critical stance that envisages a future, can be presented, examined and rehearsed in all their complexity. Included in that complexity is the impartial and eventually equalizing fate that Weil demonstrated so clearly in her essay on the *Iliad*. In the novelist's hands its deployment will either support a willing suspension of disbelief or not; used skilfully it can deepen complexity and credibility; as a satiric weapon it can ruthlessly expose hubris; as an epic factor it can enrich the sense of the mystery of human history; as a tragic theme it opens the door to Aristotelian catharsis, pity and fear. Fate, in short, is the enemy of all closed systems and all simplistic narratives of private or public security. The deployment of the concept in political discourse and narrative alike, however, can both enlighten and obscure.

In the first novel of Silone's trilogy, *Fontamara*, the poor of the village of Pescina lose their access to a traditional water supply owing to the re-engineering of the land by powerful interests. An exceptional local peasant provides opposition but is defeated by communist betrayal and a lack of organization and sophistication. In *Bread and Wine*, the semi-autobiographical hero Pietro Spina, an anti-fascist returns after exile, disguised as a priest, to his native land. In *The Seed Beneath the Snow* Spina remains an exile in his own land, hiding first in a hovel with a deaf-mute (the Christian's 'least of these', named 'Infante') and then at his grandmother's house while she risks life and reputation to help him. He is arrested finally for acting as a Christ-like scapegoat for Infante, the inarticulate child who had just killed his utterly indifferent father who had returned from America and kept him virtually as a slave. This excess of exemplary radical piety defeats a happy ending in which real adult love is a possibility, leaving the hero finally caught up in an unanticipated fate, demonstrating the psychological ambiguity of his Christ-like motivation: his absolute need for the helpless to validate his own existence.

All three of the novel endings have a fateful dimension: the first is a political death, driven by fascists, betrayed by communists, and represented finally as a religious vision of poor man's sacrificial death; in the second there is a closure of a classic naturalist kind where the woman who loves the hero wanders into the forest to be eaten by wolves; the third contains a symbolic death in which the educated and articulate hero dies for the sake of the inarticulate and the poor. The closures work at the level of ethical symbolism, that is, they are not really generated within the narrative argument of the plot. They are justified at the level of the contingent and at the level of the sadness of things themselves. Silone's father died when he was eleven years old and his mother died in an earthquake that levelled his hometown in 1915: 'An earthquake achieves what the law promises but does not in practice maintain – the equality of all men', wrote Silone, very much in the spirit of Simone Weil.[108] An originating earthquake also lies as a purely contingent foundational narrative moment of the more recent history of the village in the novel.

So Silone worked Marx against Marxists and Christian principles against Christians. It is worth examining a few instances of this strategy before seeing how the pattern contributes to a deeper sense of the narrative's various generic temporalities. In *Bread and Wine*, the main character asks himself: 'Have I then, escaped from the opportunism of a decadent Church only to end up in the Machiavellianism of a political sect. If these are dangerous cracks in the revolutionary consciousness, if they are ideas that must be banished from it, how is one to confront in good faith the risks of the conspiratorial struggle?'[109] The solution is to attempt to problematize the interiority of the Christian subject in relation to Marxist praxis. The result is that the two discourses both clash and reaffirm each other. Early in *Fontamara*, for example, one *cafoni* explains a dream in which Jesus Christ and the pope are negotiating a better life for the poor. Jesus proposes an abundant harvest, to which the pope replies: 'O Lord if the *cafoni* have an abundant harvest, the prices of agricultural produce will fall and that will be the ruin of many merchants; they, too, being good Christians, deserve consideration.'[110] Jesus' naïve insistence on use-value for the worker is drummed out of court by the triumph of exchange-value, supported by the pope and benefiting the bourgeoisie.

Advanced industrial capitalism and the 'time is money' ethic are parodied in the *cafoni*'s encounter with the theatrically expressionist figure of the Contractor, whose very profitable excessive activity promotes a world in which the only real sin is not being driven by the clock:

> '... I've got no time to waste,' he answered angrily, 'I like work, not idling.'
>
> 'You've discovered America in our part of the world,' I said clutching my rosary in one hand, 'but you mustn't believe that no one ever worked before you did.'
>
> [...] 'The cement workers don't want to work ten hours a day? They say a ten-hour day is too much? I'm boss and I work twelve hours a day.'[111]

The Contractor and his cronies exemplify the mono-explanations of fascist power legitimated in a management culture in which process, technique, and method are used to rule out contradiction and mask the operations of power. The authorities, in an Orwellian moment of newspeak, explain the situation to the illiterate villagers who have unwittingly signed away their rights:

> 'There's no question of an outrage,' he stammered. 'On my word of honor. Under the new government outrages can no longer occur. Outrages? Never. That is a forbidden word. On the contrary, what is taking place is a perfectly legal act, actually it's a favor that the authorities have decided to confer on Fontamara.'[112]

As Silone, emphasizing the fundamentally detached abstraction of fascist culture, remarked: 'no one at Fontamara yet knew where the new government came from or what nationality it was.'[113] This *faux-naif* voice-over is very effective through all three parts of the trilogy. Sometimes the dialogue carries the same effect. Here, redeployed Christian discourse interprets a fascist demonstration.

> 'Are they the living dead?' asked Baldovino, pointing to the men in black carrying those funereal-looking flags. 'Are they the souls bought by Don Circonstanza?'
>
> 'They're the souls bought by the government,' Berado explained.[114]

When the villagers crowd around as their water supply starts to flow in new channels, Silone's voice-over remarks: 'The whole scene also recalled the ceremony that takes place when a new cross is erected in the open country: the celebration of a calvary.'[115]

Class behaviour is criticized throughout the books. In terms of the older families, family honour is seen as a snare, via Christina, the doomed heroine of *Bread and Wine*, and as a double-edged sword, via the behaviour of Donna Maria Vincenza, the grandmother heroine of *The Seed Beneath the Snow*. The *nouveau riche* in all three novels collaborate quickly with the fascist regime and are unremittingly condemned, while the *cafoni* themselves exhibit all the guile and intuitive insight of a potentially 'conscious' proletariat who remain without capacity for analysis and organization, always outmanoeuvred and intensely quarrelsome among themselves. They are neither quite *Lumpenproletariat* nor potentially revolutionary. Politically, the *cafoni* are used as a basis for an insouciant critical irony whose meaning is only grasped by the reader. Theirs is a proverbial wisdom that has a resistant conserving force but no innovative power. Here, in a wonderfully comic moment in *Bread and Wine*, the local collaborationist teacher attempts to instruct the peasantry in the new ways of the fascists:

> She told the audience to pay careful attention and not to be afraid to ask for explanations of difficult words. Then she started reading *News from Rome* in a loud and piercing voice.
>
> 'We have a leader for whom all the nations of the earth envy us,' she read. 'Who knows what they would be prepared to pay to have him in their country …'
>
> Magascià interrupted. As he disliked generalities, he wanted to know exactly how much other nations would be willing to pay to acquire our leader.
>
> 'It's a manner of speaking,' said the school mistress.
>
> 'There's no such thing as manners of speaking in commercial contracts,' Magascià objected. 'Are they willing to pay for him or not? If they are willing to pay, what are they offering?'[116]

Above all, the truth of the inner life and conscience comes into play. Drawing on ironic parallels with conversion experience narratives, martyrdom narratives and the New Testament narrative of the betrayal of Christ (here inverted as a Christ-like figure betraying his disciples), Pietro Spina leaves the Communist Party and, in anguish over the deed, slips into a church. A nun appears and counsels him not to despair, adding that 'the Lord tries no one beyond his strength'.[117]

This moving moment does not signal within the narrative a reversion to the Catholic faith as such but a statement that the problem of authenticity within a political movement for any individual in compromised times makes demands on the soul which are sometimes overwhelming. The words of the nun come from a discourse that in this instance better understands the complexities of human anguish and human subjectivity. Communism has no discourse for human anguish. The fatality of inauthentic collective behaviour at any one actual historical moment has simply to be endured, and compassion for the experience of the depths of human betrayal here suggests that even the worst can be endured. 'I can't sacrifice for the party's sake the reasons for which I joined it', says Pietro at the end of the episode.[118]

Silone is at his best when he turns radical Christianity and Marxism against their institutionalized versions, often in the mode of comedy. One of the best of these moments occurs in *Bread and Wine*, where the *cafoni* are playing cards in the local bar. It is practically a paraphrase of key issues in Marxism (with a touch of Weber) in the sense that Spina provides a complex allegory of the concrete symbolism of money in relation to power, capitalism and different types of authority. In the card game *settemezzo*, the 'king of coins' is the most important card. In the peasants' pack it is rather dirty and easily recognizable (much used and decadent symbol systems), so they propose to substitute another card for it (replacing the king by an equivalent – the bourgeois revolution) and argue which one might be substituted as an equivalent (the Jacobin period). Finding a consensus for the true equivalent proves difficult, given that authenticity is based on universal acceptance, so they ask a priest, Pietro Spina disguised as Don Paulo (the revolution's turn to a single authority). Pietro argues that it's not a matter of sacred images and raises the question of whether the top card has intrinsic or assigned authority (the difference between use- and exchange-value).

The ex-communist and non-priest seizes the opportunity for a lesson in the fetishism of commodities and asks Socratic questions about fixed and variable value, how the same symbol has different values in different contexts and finally whether the games were invented by the players. The issues of traditional, ideal and charismatic authority lie at the back of the argument. The *cafoni* happily invent the rules as they go along and the 'revolutionary' 'priest' more or less urges a swift move to democratic revolution, a swift 'dethronement of the king of coins':[119] 'If the value of this card varies according to the fantasy of the players and what they agree on, it seems to me that you can do what you like with it.'[120] The fact that the *cafoni* can never agree does not prevent them from seriously discussing the whole episode much to the chagrin of the fascist apologist in the shape of the local school mistress who like most bad teachers believes that the 'ignorant' peasants 'nearly always understand the opposite of what is meant.'[121]

Here, the irony works two ways. First, it exposes the arrogance of those whose knowledge never has to be justified, shared or explained and second it shows that underestimating the 'ignorant' is a foolish game for they may well understand you better than you think. The fact that Pietro is rather pleased with himself after this episode masks (although amusingly) his real impotence in the face of the brutality of the regime. It may also reflect Silone's troubled spirit: that uneasiness of the writer in general in the face of a political evil whose lineaments he or she knows more deeply than others but is seemingly powerless to counteract.

The nature of authority in the trilogy is also bound up with issues of temporality and narrative. Illustrations of Weber's traditional and ideal authority and the narrative temporal justifications they offer are everywhere in the novels. In the last of the trilogy, *The Seed Beneath the Snow*, they chiefly centre on the two old families of the village: the De Dominicis and Spina families. In a Dos Passos like condensed narrative (Silone admired the American author), the last male De Dominicis, the father of one remaining daughter ('Aunt Eufemia'), dreams of the restoration of the King of Naples. After a brief condensed autobiographical narrative he is shown attending the funeral of ex-King Francis II in 1895, having all his life insisted to his friends that divine providence and the righteous with 'behind them the invincible host of angels as their strategic reserve' would restore the status quo. Suddenly he realizes his world and view of history is lost forever. It has literally run out of time:

> But at that funeral ceremony, at the sight of the empty catafalque and the black-clad officiants, when he heard the mournful notes of the *Miserere* and the *Requiem*, he realized that in spite of the preference of the gods the end of the Kingdom of Naples was irremediable, and it suddenly struck him that his whole life had been based on an illusion. He died of grief, not so much at the descent in the social scale and the material losses that the new order imposed on him as at the blow to his faith.[122]

Silone's irony is at its tenderest here. The tone is complex when his obvious political argument against the intransigence of this traditional ideological narrative is couched in terms of a black comedy, also not without its tendernesses. The daughter, Aunt Eufemia, who is manly in appearance, has to have a humiliating medical examination at the hands of the fascists to determine whether or not she is a woman to avoid conscription, a village joke which eventually brings her respect for the dignity with which she bears it. Her frozen classicism is clung to as an increasingly meaningless iconographic narrative, not merely of status but as an intransigent definition of her very soul. Here comedy takes the place of pathos:

> Aunt Eufemia's religion remained southern like that of her forefathers, immune to the inflated piety of modern times; she directed her prayers to ancient, genuine, tried and tested saints born between the Abruzzi and Calabria, and for preference she prayed in dialect, so that even if other saints listened in they would not be able to understand. With similar consistency she had always refused to pray for the usurping Piedmontese dynasty, the House of Savoy; on the contrary, she actually went on praying that its members should be visited by the well-deserved chastisement of God and the exterminating wrath of men.[123]

The question of tradition and family honour, with their legitimating narratives, is a serious one within the book but not because of what these days are called 'traditional values'. Rather the deployment of 'classic' traditions and the values involved are seen in very much more complex terms: of what is remembered, of how it is narrativized, of the variant psychology it engages with, of the genuineness or inauthenticity of the nostalgia invoked, of the degree to which the resultant motives for action can be valued positively or negatively, of the question of principled action and of the nature of the contingent circumstances, including fatefulness, which form their immediate historical context. In short, Silone can play a complex Burke against a simplified Tom Paine for radical effect, and vice versa.

In *The Seed Beneath the Snow*, the radical Christian and communist line on tradition and the family is put to Donna Vincenza by Don Severino, one of the most engaging of the book's characters, whom the entire village thinks (erroneously – a slightly sentimental touch) is living in sin with the woman with whom Pietro Spina eventually falls in love. He is the village organist. At the fascist census he puts down his religion as 'Bach' which the *cafoni* assume is Bacchus. His is the symbolic position of artist and he is thrown out of the church where, of course, he has never been paid for his services. His slight though independent means cause one of the fascists to regret that anyone might be independent of the state for income. Donna Vincenza has put to Don Severino the argument of the pragmatic mother's 'ancient' view that if everyone made the family the moral centre of their lives, if children and their families lived locally, if parents set a good example with family prayers and were good Christians who ensured that the sun never set on anyone's wrath, the world would more or less return to normal. To this the Bach-loving Don Severino replies with musical and numerical precision:

> 'You forget, my dear Maria Vincenza,' he said, 'that every scoundrel, every semi-scoundrel, every demi-semi-scoundrel, invariably justifies his depravity by concern for his family. On the other hand, you also know that families are often put into turmoil, not by the devil, but by Someone Else who Himself declared He had come into the world to divide what blood united, to separate son from father, daughter from mother, daughter-in-law from mother-in-law, and if there were five in a house He would set three against two and two against three.'[124]

So Don Severino paraphrases Matthew 10.32–9 for the twentieth-century family.[125] It was a twentieth century that inherited Marx's declaration that the patriarchal family mirrored the patriarchal state, where Freud had declared the Oedipus Complex to be a universal unhappiness in family life, where women were redefining their role within and without the family, where social anthropologists were showing the historicity of the family and its differing social functions in different societies; where global capitalism and global employment scattered families far and wide and drove many of the world's working and non-working poor to produce huge, unmanageable and hungry families in a desperate attempt merely to survive at all; and where, in rich countries, no opportunity was left unexploited to profit from everything, driving bourgeois couples to late marriages and a single child.

In this last book of the trilogy, Donna Maria Vincenza admits that the call to sainthood is in frank contradiction with family life, and worries whether in attempting to rehabilitate her grandson to family and state, she might be doing him a disservice. In the end, Pietro Spina chooses martyrdom over love and ordinary life but the most interesting exchange on these matters, between grandson and grandmother, engages a view of narrative and time in relation to personal life and above all to a political and personal ethics. The conversation occurs just after Donna Maria Vincenza has had her ill grandson secretly transferred to her house where she keeps him safe from the fascist police. Her aristocratic family values contradict the pseudo-family values of the fascist state, indeed put her in direct opposition to it. Old family honour and the local are in paradoxically in direct contradiction with the pseudo-historical and temporally fake 'blood and soil'.

The temporalities signalled within the narrative are complex. For Pietro, the house itself is a return to childhood and memories of boyhood within the narrative's fictional present. Donna Maria Vincenza embodies the entire history and memory of the village. In her narrative, cosmic time, the time of official history and the time of the state, are banished in a warmly enclosing maternal world of Proustian memory. It is also the world of village and countryside, a world of slowness where communal memory still exists:

> Nothing else existed in this life. She had a prodigious memory for kinships, and she went back with ease through the generations to the most remote marriages, from fathers, uncles, cousins to grandfathers and great-grandfathers, in connection with land, mills, fulling mills, spinning mills, sandpits and quarries, stables and sheepfolds, with the result that the people, the livestock, the land of the region turned out to be united by the same vicissitudes and involved in good and bad fortune. Even hedges and stones ended up assuming a family air, eventually coming to resemble the families to which they belonged.[126]

Pietro, radically alienated from this world, replies, 'But to me these family stories sound like distant tales from a vanished world, the world that was burned in the earthquake.'[127] His grandmother, in return, offers the classic argument of Simone Weil, of the need for roots, for memory, as a condition of the soul:

> my poor boy you talk as if you were a foundling, a person without a past, as if we had collected you from the foundling hospital, as if your father and mother and your forebears had left you nothing. I'm not talking about legacies or real estate, my dear boy, I'm talking about your soul.[128]

Pietro then returns to the dilemma of the radical Christian, saint, artist or revolutionary. In an epiphanic narrative he describes hiding out in a cave with the deaf and mute Infante and a donkey – a scene inflected with symbols of the nativity – in which he experiences a kind of spiritual rebirth, a Tolstoyan moment of insight as to his own condition. Here, the story moves into the genre of the spiritual narrative of the saint's life. He describes his Pascalian moment of suspension from time, almost an emancipation from history itself. The indolent school years, the flight from the family and the sterile years of political exile (the recognizable narrative patterns of the Bildungsroman) suddenly make sense: 'I saw my life as a successive casting off of the crude fictions that make life dear to most people, an emancipation from them.'[129] There follows the classic return to the world and it is expressed in terms of the temporality of the soul:

> my first strong feeling was of being reintegrated into time; and I started distinctly perceiving the passage of time, an extraordinary thing that had never happened to me before. To give you an idea of what I mean, let me explain that I was aware of the passing of time as one is normally aware of the flowing of a river; I don't mean that it passed in the uniform, artificial abstract fashion of a clock, it was not at all like that. No, I was aware of real time passing as one is aware of the flowing of a real stream, that is, in continually varying way, now slowly and now impetuously, depending on the slope and nature of the bed, and the banks and on whether it encounters mills or fulling mills and whether there are women doing their washing and beating it on the bank. I had the distinct feeling that in relation to time the jolting little cart on which I was travelling was like an unsafe little boat on a river in flood flowing down from the mountain to the plain. Another surprise was that, when I peeped at the outside world through the gaping seams of the sacks that hid me, every single detail filled me with astonishment, though there was nothing whatever to the scene that was new to me [...] How extraordinary, I said to myself, what an extraordinary world, what extraordinary conventions, how can such a world continue to exist?[130]

The time of the visionary and the time of his grandmother cannot be resolved. For the grandmother, the links between past, present and future come from a profound sense of oneness with the generations and the earth itself. Identity is historical and social memory. The mystical vision of time for Pietro, on the contrary, emerges from being liberated from the memory of personal life articulated as treacherous fictions obscuring, paradoxically, a more profound, more timeless reality of a new vision of the ordinary world including a precarious, anguish-ridden existential sense of the unpredictability of the wayward passage of time itself. It reveals the nature of the abyss that is always masked in the world of common sense. Only the violent break with the past, common sense and custom, for the hero at least, enables the present to emerge in all its fullness, wonder, sense of fragility and terror.

The competing stories of grandmother and grandson in relation to time, memory and narrative are yet more complex, however, because the significance of the passage turns from the subject of Christian or Marxist sainthood, where the personal is expunged in favour of the greater good, to that of the responsibility of the writer. A running commentary rooted in common sense is kept up by the grandmother who reduces the argument to a mother's problems with difficult children, commenting how the mother of Christ must have felt when he decided to go off to the temple at the age of twelve and argue with learned doctors: 'Either they go in for frivolity and vice, or they imperil their immortal souls for the sake of money, or they are too serious and decide that the world is wrongly organized.'[131] So sure is she of her fictional options that, remembering the Passionist father who told her as a child that wrong ideas were the result of wrong feelings (here a touch of William James's foundation of philosophical difference in human psychology), that when presented with Alessandro Manzoni's famous novel *The Betrothed* (which starts with a nationalist authoritarian exclusion order of *bravi* – unemployed and exiled people in sixteenth-century Milan), she reads the word novel on the cover and 'unhesitatingly consigned it to the flames'.[132]

The relation of fiction to history and to personal life is thus signalled as a theme, and the chapter ends with Pietro playing a fictional Sunday drama with the illiterate maid about catching a train and going somewhere else. Eventually Pietro ends up in the cellar writing names under allegorical figures: 'TRADITION ACCORDING TO VENAZIÒ [the house retainer], THE GIRL WITH THE THINGS, AUNT EUFEMIA'S LEGACY, CHRISTIANITY ACCORDING TO GRANDMOTHERS', thus distancing via a Brechtian alienation and a fictionalizing of writing as a theme within the novel, the illusion of fictional time and inviting the reader to step back and think about the text in a more analytic way. The chapter tries to end lyrically: 'The hours passed silently, the river of time flowed far away and was hardly perceptible, just a vast, weak, distant murmur' but the lyricism is cut short with the unmoved grandmother saying: 'You'll end up catching pneumonia.'[133]

The comic reduction both satirizes the limits of common-sense vision in the grandmother and warns against being overwhelmed by an idealistic vision that might involve the destruction of the self or prove merely hallucinatory. The 'right' of the prophet (and by extension the writer, the political leader, the priest) to invent an emplotment of time, memory and the human condition is foregrounded as a problem of truth, authenticity and responsibility in a much more complex way than that being offered in Silone's historical moment by the congealed and authoritarian nature of Christian, Marxist, fascist and capitalist discourse. From the perspective of the twenty-first century and the postmodern cultural analyses that followed, Silone's achievement was indeed 'the seed beneath the snow'.

Coda

This too was Norman's achievement in *TWICE A YEAR*, for the journal gathered more than fragments shored against the world's ruin. Norman broke many boundaries in her own terms: in actively engaging as a woman in serious politics and international political life, in fights for justice for African-Americans, trade unions and the American poor, not to mention the starving millions of Asia. She did this in defiance of the narrow parameters set for women of her time (and here her husband and his family were increasingly not on her side) and in defiance of what was deemed appropriate for a woman of her class. Her fearless insistence that a society, among many other criteria, might be assessed in terms of an exuberant creativity in the arts and in terms of the credibility of its justice system is exemplary for our own time. In a time of social and political meltdown and ideological chaos, she sought to find a community of writers, artists, photographers, architects, political dissidents, dispossessed African-Americans, international refugees, ordinary soldiers, workers, children and distinguished international political leaders to articulate a 'beloved community' that was perhaps most American in challenging socio-spatial and temporal definitions of an America that thought it knew its defining stories. Perhaps in this respect, above all, it was classically American.

4

Lewis Mumford: Remaining Present in 'the Ringing Grooves of Time'

All work serves for life in that it produces art and gives men the liberated vitality of artists.

— LEWIS MUMFORD[1]

In America its skyscrapers, those mechanical creations of the business mentality, bring together apartments, banks, movie theatres, hospitals, schools, and churches in carefully ordered confusion, all behind the same totally anonymous and undistinguishable facade. Its architects have added practically nothing to the legacy of the past except, for its victims, this scientifically imperfectible hive of crimes, vices, and iniquities.

— VICTOR SERGE[2]

A person who is only an American is only half a man: indeed only half an American.

— LEWIS MUMFORD[3]

I

Sacred and Profane: A Preface

'New York is a beautiful city', wrote Dorothy Norman's friend and architectural counsellor Lewis Mumford in 1924, 'if we are building for pilots and angels'. This remark, as Gyula Kodolányi, the Hungarian poet and scholar, has said, is only surpassed by that of Mumford's mentor Patrick Geddes on being shown a plan of a New York skyscraper with a dome on top: 'It looks as if the devil had farted into St Paul's and raised the dome three hundred feet into the air.'[4] Mumford's long literary career addressed historic culture by way of investigating the earthly and heavenly representatives of the heights and overview: pilots and angels: technocrats and gods; physicists and heavenly hosts. For Mumford, the skyscraper would always represent the over-reach of a Faustian pact with the devil. The critics never quite forgave him. The skyscraper was America. How could an American challenge this ur-icon of American-ness? Any discourse which mentioned pilots and skyscrapers then angels and devils in the same breath seemed irresponsible in a seriously technocratic and seriously religious American century. The questions asked in this chapter will examine a discourse in which not only the sacred and secular will seem to have lost their more obvious polarities, but one in which narrative itself embraces and transcends common-sense categories of modernity and time. Mumford remained unrepentant. Indeed, in a *New Yorker* article of 1940, war in Europe just having broken out, he said of the new tall buildings at La Guardia Airport: 'The innocents who designed them must have been dreaming of a time when airplanes would have the wings of doves, not vultures.'[5]

In one of his last books, Mumford cited the World Trade Center as 'a characteristic example of the purposeless gigantism and technological exhibitionism that are now eviscerating the living tissue of every great city.'[6] Mumford would not live to see a new association of religion and technology in an abstractly temporalized 'event' called *9/11*, which has set fair, within a contested religious framework, to become what Ricoeur might have called the 'foundational event' of a new chronology. Whether it will or not is another matter. As will become clear in the course of the argument, however, Mumford had long pondered the relation of monumentality to power and science and of capitalism to religiosity. Had he lived to experience *9/11*, he would certainly have argued that a faithful Muslim would never have hijacked the planes and that a faithful Christian would never have built the towers in the first place.

Mumford was a friend of Dorothy Norman and Alfred Stieglitz, and also of Muriel Rukeyser. Their worlds complemented each other. Mumford, the great city historian, is central to this work because of his power to synthesize different narratives combining cultural history, ethical analysis, patterns of technological development, political judgement, socio-geographical survey and intellectual history, in a manner that transcended the increasingly structuralist moves of the mid-century by profoundly engaging with historical memory, temporality and the nature of time. Mumford's voluminous writings are all of a piece. Different aspects of what he essentially developed as a field theory of culture received different emphasis at different times through his long career. For the historian of the city, a quasi-natural organism of the City of Man replaced the eschatological closure of history in the City of God as the model of historical change. A humanized biological theme in which the finite human life, bound in time, took precedence over both an abstract secular narrative of human development mapped onto an indifferent cosmos and a religious narrative of apocalyptic closure and a priori human corruption. Among the diversity of intellectual roots that critics have pointed to for Mumford is the liberal-dissenting Victorian tradition of England – the England of Carlyle, Ruskin and Morris together with those utopian critics of industrial and technocratic modernity: Robert Lowell, the Cadburys and that prophet and instigator of the Garden City Movement, Ebenezer Howard. It was a tradition Mumford shared with his most important mentor, the Scottish maverick intellectual Patrick Geddes.

If, according to Engels, the utopian thinkers were merely bourgeois surfers on the superstructure of capitalist productive relations and were but dreamily and dimly aware that all was not well with the world, the tradition claims new attention in our own time with the recovery of the idea of the critical utopia in Ricoeur's work and the expansions of radical critique beyond a debased positivist Marxism.[7] Mumford, though no Marxist, was nonetheless part of that revision of thought in which the towering shadow of Marx still lingered. Behind Mumford was Henry Adams, a self-styled 'conservative Christian anarchist' who, with the richness of the mid-nineteenth-century New England critical and literary tradition behind him, was certainly the most perceptive early critic of the modern, post-modern and globalised world. Mumford, neither modernist nor anti-modernist, would survive as America's most brilliant social, technical, historical, architectural and cultural critic well into the second half of the twentieth century.

Mumford was almost unique in a structuralist and post-structural age in bringing a profound sense of time and history to everything he touched. The nature of Mumford's critical historicity may be questioned at various points – the Rankean order of events and any form of theoretical economic and class analyses are absent – but at the cultural level (and the phrase is multiply textured and inclusive) the nature of temporality and narrative is at the centre of the analysis. Mumford sought not for the great good place of Henry James, that image of a spatial imagination which an earlier generation of American critics felt so crucial to an advocacy of cultural nationalism, but for the great good time and place in a very American ransacking of the historical record for ways of living. It was a profound search for meaning, linked ultimately to an existential question of what to live for in world of terrified citizens, massive powers of destruction in irresponsible hands, and virtually inevitable ecological disaster. It was also a search for the kind of narrative in which different orders of temporality might be juxtaposed and synthesized.

It was Henry Adams who had asked ironically whether the bourgeoisie got as much for their money with the new skyscraper building in early twentieth-century New York as the medieval merchants had in building the cathedrals of Europe.[8] In the terms of Adams's assessment, the superiority of the spirit to the flesh and God to Mammon was not apparent in the emerging global superpower. Mumford, too, would be a master of a narrative that would align historical events and cultures across the centuries for the purpose of ethical judgement.

In a *New Yorker* 'Skyline' article of 1938 Mumford took up the Adamsian contrast. Commenting on the newly opened Museum of the Cloisters in New York City, he observed:

> One doesn't have to be an adept in medieval symbolism to see in the Cloisters the extreme opposite, in position, in sense of life, in feeling, of all that exists architecturally in the insolent towers at the other end of the island. The difference between faith and credit finance, between holy dying and profane living, is written there; likewise the difference between pious monks celebrating the glory of God and the faithful female secretary increasing, like Joseph in Thomas Mann's story, the uneasy self-esteem of the Big Boss. [9]

No one in America could match Mumford's critical style with his combination of *New Yorker* witty insouciance, traces of *New Masses*-style class sarcasm and Old Testament prophetic rhetoric. For Mumford, architecture symbolically articulated a sense of life. The almost Freudian dualism of Eros and Thanatos, hinted at here, governed the essentially ethical nature of his judgements. Early letters show Mumford's keen interest in the new psychology, but he never employed its analytic discourse, just as he refused the discourses of religion and Marxism, though he was sensitive to the insights offered by their respective grand narratives of human destiny.

Mumford's narratives engaged a quadruple thematic of religion, Marxism, psychology and philosophy in a rich, ultimately poetic, critical discourse. In a period of strong ideological barriers, he searched for a style that drew on a multiplicity of analytic approaches. This led to him being attacked from all sides but from none more so than the American left. Before an attempt is made to look at Mumford's synthetic narrativity more closely, however, his political positions and, perhaps even more tellingly, his political work will be examined.

Mumford and Politics

'Karl Marx characterized the class into which I was born as the petty bourgeoisie. He didn't think much of it as a class, and neither do I; but that was the angle from which I saw New York.'[10] So wrote Mumford in 1934 for his sophisticated *New Yorker* audience. In distinguishing himself from his upper-class friend Van Wyck Brooks (a major early commentator on classic American literature), Mumford was at pains to emphasize their differences of class and milieu. Mumford represented himself as a son of the metropolitan scene. He was, he said, of a mixed nature stemming from his lower middle-class family, a rough-and-ready Whitmanesque figure taking a fresh stand against an over-glamorized European culture. In an Emersonian vein, he felt he had to be an active participant in the social and political scene, one for whom books, if not exactly relegated to idle times (the output would deny it), had to be complementary to the active life: 'Unlike Brooks, I was not, even as a lonely child, passionately bookish; and I never shared his exclusive, all-absorbing interest in the literary life alone.'[11] For Mumford, lower middle-class meant Whitmanian 'average'.

For all the irony and humour (he understood in detail the fraught ideological atmosphere of the American literary 1930s), Mumford was a deeply political animal both in writing and political activity, a fact that has not been given its due by the commentators. He was an early advocate for American entry into the Second World War and as such was not only mercilessly pilloried by the left until Hitler's attack on the Soviet Union in 1941, but also by isolationists of the pro-German American right. Part of Mumford's argument derived from a strong attack on what is now called 'American exceptionalism' (the belief that America is some kind of unique and 'chosen' nation), a phenomenon which has fed an isolationist position, as well as the nationalistic cultural arrogance typical of all powerful nations, throughout American history. For Mumford, the rapid development of capitalism and technology had led to a worship of pure power that was common to all countries where unrestrained capitalist practice had taken hold. Mumford's ideological debts to commentators such as Marx and Spengler will be examined later. In a typescript of a lecture given at Columbia University in the early 1940s, across the top of which Mumford afterwards wrote 'I was never asked back', he spoke of the power of the techno-capitalist vision to create universal disorder:

> The same disorder today exists throughout the planet, wherever our common civilization, with its railroads, its airplanes, its radios, and its guns has reached. And we in America [cling] to the illusion of isolation, fancying that we are outside these processes of disintegration and by the exercise of a circumspect and pharisaical virtue will escape the evils of our time [...].[12]

Here Mumford combines Marx and Spengler to create a pan-national vision of technological fatality. Precisely to avoid the dogmatism of the Marxists under Stalin, Mumford chose to emphasize 'technology' rather than 'capitalist productive forces', though he certainly knew that capitalism was a symbiotic interaction of both in the abstract dynamics of the exchange of labour and capital. While Mumford refused an analytic discourse of the class war and the dialectics of capitalist exchange, the Marxists, for their part, were besotted with a kind of scientism in their analysis that simply ignored the effects of unrestrained industrialization on human subjectivity, hence they paid insufficient attention to a huge range of cultural practices within the 'reason' of history.

However, no less than Marx himself, Mumford inveighed against that worship of the abstract human figure caught in a power nexus, for, as he declared:

'[when] capitalism urged men to systematic enterprise, to overseas trade, to thrift and profit seeking, when it sanctified usury and put individual gains above social security, when it emphasized time-keeping, regularity, book-keeping – when it did all this it made power an end in itself [...]'.[13] All these themes were developed in books such as *Technics and Civilization* (1934), but they became increasingly urgent as Mumford, with others, helplessly watched the preparations for war in the Soviet Union, Germany, Japan and Italy, and listened to the propaganda which called for the surrender of the individual to the mechanistic and totalitarian state. Rather than developing a Spenglerian eschatology, however, Mumford's grand narrative of technological development clung to a notion of the possibilities of human agency, assisted by a view of history which was not governed by an absolute linearity. In parallel with the great French historian, Fernand Braudel, Mumford developed a narrative of the *longue durée* which could be used both as an explanation and as a critique of other possible temporal models: Christian, Comtist or Marxist. In any case it provided a route other than that of the reductive dualisms of the positivist Marxist and the critical laziness of the bourgeois nationalist vision of American technocratic capitalism as the world's inevitable future.

By looking at some detailed moments from Mumford's dialogue with the left in the late 1930s, it is possible to make some of these rather abstract claims more concrete. This will be followed by a look at his political activity for, no less than F.O. Matthiessen in the same period and quite unsuspected by certain critics, Mumford was endlessly politically engaged in small and large political advocacy groups both prior to and during the war. In addition to the pursuit of his grand narratives, Mumford was always concerned with the contingent and the immediate. For example in the 1930s he was among the first to speak out against Hitler's treatment of the Jews.

Following a description of his practical politics, Mumford's ideological allegiances will be examined in the context of what he saw as the options historically available to him. This will take us into some of the more profound philosophical and critical issues raised by Mumford's work. The transfer of critical judgement to an ethics, as opposed to the behaviourist-structural critiques of capitalist ideologues and the scientific materialism of the Marxists, enabled Mumford to recover a sense of will and agency on the one hand and an important, even tragic, scepticism as to the nature of rational scientific, in fact scientistic, thought on the other. The nature and make-up of Mumford's 'ethics', including its attitude to religion and other forms of belief, will therefore be looked at closely. A number of critics have already explored some of these issues, but where this analysis extends the argument is to take Mumford's profoundly literary sense of culture seriously. Critics have noted that Mumford 'worked more like an artist than a historian',[14] but have rarely proceeded to analyse his work by giving that assumption full and positive weight. Not all the problems and contradictions can be neatly resolved, but by focusing on the generic nature of the texts, a few can perhaps be seen more clearly and, at the very least, the discussion should open up a space in which to ask some different questions. Certainly this section of the book will not give the 'sober' historian any precedence over the 'intoxicated' artist and vice versa.

Finally, Mumford's most neglected great work, *The Condition of Man*, the major work that falls within the remit of this book, will be examined. It was in fact the concluding volume of a trilogy which had already comprised *Technics and Civilization* (1934) and *The City in History* (1938). These critiques of the role of technology and urbanization in history were more than indirectly responses to both the devastation of the First World War and to the worsening international situation of the 1930s. The concluding volume which drew respectful but pallid praise when it was published in 1944, was in fact an attempt to look at European history in a moment of European chaos in order to rediscover what might be salvaged and recovered in terms of a 'faith for living' (to use Mumford's own later phrase) in the post-war period. As such, it was a very American attempt to make a panoramic scrutiny of European culture and history to see what could be saved and creatively renewed for both a European and a New World future. For Mumford, the flight of Minerva's owl allowed no nation to be permanently 'chosen'.

Against the convictions of most of his own countrymen and the denizens of the American Dream, Mumford argued that the United States was not a guaranteed nesting place for an authentic culture, the more so since the mantle of absolute military and technocratic power was about to fall on her shoulders. Mumford's narratives of time and memory will be contrasted with his famous French contemporary, the historian Fernand Braudel. This will show some useful parallels and distinctions on the subject of temporality, and help to particularize Mumford's own vision.

First, however, the historical moment. Mumford's role in national politics was profoundly signalled, from the mid-1930s onwards, by his attack on the traditional American policy of isolationism. A deep sense of human history stretching back to the Sumerian period made him a *rara avis* in a country whose top industrialist had declared history to be bunk.[15] Mumford had watched with increasing horror as the events in Germany and Italy unfolded on the European stage from 1933 onwards. In his early youth, however, he had been aware of the critique of capitalism that Marxism offered and indeed had numbered among his close friends active American communists such as Mike Gold. Many important urban sections of 1920s and 1930s American literary culture were in active dialogue with Marxism. By the late 1930s, however, under the strains imposed by an increasingly demagogic Stalinism, many writers were registering dissent, even though widely read Marxist papers such as *New Masses* kept open a relatively complex view of literary matters.

Mumford was politically at the opposite end of the liberal scale from papers such as *New Masses*. It was equally true, nonetheless, that he had been sympathetic to many of the ideals of communism and socialism. His fundamentally dialectical analysis of technological process in *Technics and Civilization* (1934) is a case in point, and in 1945 he wrote to the British town planner Frederick J. Osborn: 'As to the tactical matter, of achieving socialism without using the word or waving all the banners that go with it, I am entirely at one with you. In any particular situation I am not merely ready to go as far as a socialist or a communist, but possible a little further; but I do my level best to avoid prejudicing the issue by using the current catchwords.'[16]

Mumford was among the first Americans to signal the dangerous developments in Europe and he was direct and unsparing in his advocacy of intervention. In the winter of 1939–40 he was in close contact with the theologian Reinhold Niebuhr, together with their mutual friend Waldo Frank. They were particularly concerned about the isolationism of *The New Republic* (one of whose editors was Malcolm Cowley, who was reluctant to abandon isolationism) and to which they had been contributing editors since the 1920s. [17] On 10 June 1940 Frank and Mumford resigned from *The New Republic* and Mumford wrote:

> In the last two years you published two articles written by me: 'Call to Arms' and 'The Corruption of Liberalism.' The first (written in March, 1938) [published 18 May 1938] was a plea for immediate measures by the United States to resist the plain menace of fascism. The second was an attempt to analyze the curious paralysis that has made the 'liberals' incapable of facing promptly and manfully the ugly realities of the present world. In the case of both articles, your editorial comment showed that you regarded them as attacks upon your own position. You were right.[18]

Mumford switched to Daniel Bell's *New Leader*, which was described by Dwight Macdonald to Victor Serge in 1943 as 'rightwing socialist', 'honest and liberal', 'at times even militant'.[19] An editorial commenting on the resignation said only too perceptively: 'The incident reveals the forces on the left which have obscured all attempts to outline for the American people the tragic error of not aiding the defence of those between us and the Axis.'[20]

In 1939 Mumford expanded the *The New Republic* article into a book, *Men Must Act* (1939), which infuriated the left with its frank ethical and psychological analysis. The ideological merits and demerits of Mumford's synthetic discourse will be examined later but it is noteworthy that in this work his attack on fascism recognized 'subjective' factors which the 'scientific' methodology of the Marxists was unable to recognize. In fact Mumford damned the appeasing Chamberlains and the High Tory and English aristocratic Hitler sympathizers, the French bankers, the Comité des Forges, and the Lavals and Daladiers quite as much as he condemned *New Masses*. With the left, he did not think the Soviet Union as much of a strategic international threat as Germany, Spain and Italy, and indeed argued with them that Western intransigence had pushed the fledgling Soviet state further into reaction. Here he particularly blamed the American Catholic church for talking up the threat of communism.[21] It was clear that for Mumford, to promote a threat of generalized global terror in excess of the immediate danger, as was done in the succeeding Cold War and has been done in our own time, was politically disastrous.

As early as 1922, in his correspondence with the Scottish intellectual polymath Patrick Geddes, Mumford had been speculating on the possibility of using psychoanalysis ('the world within') to characterize negatively and positively the crypto-utopian ambition within technologically driven political change ('the world without').[22] These early and quite brilliant speculations made it virtually inevitable that Mumford, like Wilhelm Reich in his 1935 classic *The Mass Psychology of Fascism*, singled out subjective factors in his insistent distinguishing between fascism and capitalist imperialism:

> Whereas under a capitalist oligarchy, it is always safe to interpret political moves in terms of economic interest, in relation to fascism one must treat economics as an expression of a far more subjective politics. The failure to understand this on the part of Marxian theorists has been one of the reasons for their ludicrous errors in interpreting or meeting this new force: an error that helped give Germany to Hitler.[23]

Mumford was earlier than most in understanding how contemporary totalitarian systems (in the Arendtian sense) exploit subjective needs. His theory of 'organicism' at the very least provided a critical utopian base for a devastating conservative and satiric critique of contemporary bread and circuses, an analysis which would become more familiar in the 1950s and 1960s under the influence of the Frankfurt School and others: 'The desire for communion with nature will not be satisfied long by Sportsmen's Shows and by automobile drives on mountain crestlines; the desire for adventure will not be sated by reports of murder and sudden death in the daily newspaper'.[24]

Given the intransigence of the left and their refusal to oppose Nazism and fascism actively, Mumford and Frank resigned from the left-leaning *New Republic* in letters published on 10 June 1940. Mumford, indifferent to public opinion left and right, saw that Hitler and Mussolini had to be stopped and at whatever cost. His long view of history, exceptional intellectual honesty and lack of dogmatism made him committed to the idea that 'principles have a way of enduring'.[25] He pursued his theme on the radio, in the newspapers, in endless committees, in journals, in schools, in universities and in local discussion groups. For Mumford, to create a human history demanded an endless process of renewal against the odds; thinking about history involved a 'process of imagination and memory'.[26]

In 1940 Mumford, like the left, would excoriate the British appeasers but at the same time, and unlike the left, he praised Britain for its lonely courage during the Blitz. He proposed a permanent federal union between Britain and the United States as a 'core of worldwide organization to which all democratic peoples will in time adhere, as partners in a common task, as builders of a common order.'[27] In the early twenty-first century that vision and its image has been severely tarnished as Britain and the United States have waged war illegally in the name of 'democracy', but in 1940 it had much more than merely rhetorical validity.

Mumford was not simply an enthusiast for war and action. Throughout the war he remained constantly critical of Allied tactics, from saturation bombing to the use of the atomic bomb. In Eliot's words, 'unnatural voices/Are fathered by our heroism.'[28] He lost his son on the Italian front at the very moment he was protesting against the sending of young conscripted soldiers into battle because bosses preferred to keep older men's skills and older trade union members their jobs. Assessing the Italian campaign for *The Nation* in November 1944, Eric Severeid noted that journalists on the spot like him were 'impressed by the major miscalculations made in high places.'[29] In the public arena Mumford also attacked the plans for the United Nations, arguing it should be 'detached from the native American area', that is to say, truly international and not dominated by the United States. He added that it should grow slowly, absorbing and adapting to global political change.[30] The advice, as we know, was totally ignored by those who were to dominate the post-war scene.

But politically inactive Mumford was not. Opposing the dogmatisms of both right and left in the 1940s Mumford's forte was the ideologically non-aligned public debate. Up to and during the war he was on the American Committee for Émigré Writers, the American Committee for Chinese War Orphans, the American Council Against Nazi Propaganda, the American Friends of German Freedom and the Medical Bureau of the American Friends of Spanish Democracy; he played an active role in many others. He has been criticized for 'his characteristic lack of interest in politics' and his 'apolitical nature.'[31] This is simply not true and if his basic belief in communitarian activism (family, 'grange', church, theatre, trade union) was primary, it was absolutely not at the expense of engagement in national or international politics. As with F.O. Matthiessen, the greatest literary critic of the period, the sheer list of organizations Mumford supported or signed up to gives it the lie.

Take, for example, Mumford's local and national battle with the notoriously right-wing Hamilton Fish, isolationist, active Hitler sympathizer and Mumford's local senator. In November 1940 Mumford wrote to Brooks that he had underestimated Fish's strength locally and regretted that with another week of campaigning 'we might have taken the election away from him.'[32] Fish was to be dislodged in 1944 but Mumford and his wife Sophia conducted a tireless campaign against him over the issue of America joining the war. From the summer of 1940 the Mumfords formed the Committee to Defend America by Aiding the Allies, on which Sophia, a key activist, took the role of treasurer. The minutes of the meetings show a vigorous and sometimes touching liberal small town American committee at work in the face of local indifference and apathy. In an old Eastern Seaboard tradition the principles were simple and high-minded. On 29 July the secretary noted that 'there was a spirited discussion on the part the individual must play in the working of a democracy, and a general agreement that active participation in the work of the Committee to Defend America by Aiding the Allies would tend to spread the concept of general participation in the work of government.'[33]

On 5 August, after a notorious speech by the Nazi-sympathizing Charles Lindbergh, the pilot hero of the first Atlantic air crossing, the committee resolved to write to the Secretary of State approving General Pershing's recommendation to sell fifty destroyers to the British. They also aimed to alert police to local active Nazi sympathizers. In mid-August there is the first mention of Fish and plans are set afoot to contact the Republican hierarchy and to recommend that someone more sympathetic to the views of the community be chosen as their representative. The committee actively sought local venues to publicize their work. Local radio stations were contacted and the local cinema allowed a three-minute speech between shows on a Saturday evening for a committee member to publicize their activities. Mumford wrote the speeches. There were telephone canvassings and collections of aluminium for defence purposes. Links were cultivated with national members through many American states, and contacts were made with *The Nation* and sympathizers at Yale University, the California Institute of Technology, the University of Chicago, the American Federation of Labour (AFL) and the Union Theological Seminary where Mumford had links with Reinhold Niebuhr. They also contacted individuals such as Mayor La Guardia of New York City and there were strong links with the women's division of the national committee. This exhibits a very odd 'indifference' to politics.

Sophia Mumford began by simply walking down the high street getting signatures from passers by, waiting for trains at the railroad station and getting every visiting tradesman to sign. Only two did not. The first meeting drew eight farmers and shopkeepers. Then it was decided to get the local community leaders involved: town officers, the bigger store keepers, church leaders, freemasons, the Knights of Columbus, the Chamber of Commerce, the literary coterie and so forth. Progress was slow with attendance at meetings varying from twelve to twenty-four. But the public library received donations of books on fascism and democracy and these apparently were soon circulating better than the regular books. With the election of Roosevelt and the narrow victory of Fish in Roosevelt's own county, the committee decided to move towards a larger public meeting. Edward Spingarn, son of Mumford's friend Joel Spingarn, published photographs of Fish in an address to the Nazis surrounded by Swastika decorations and with the former Japanese ambassador. Fish had made a public appearance in Berlin in which he had argued that Germany's claims were just, that he personally favoured the liquidation of the Treaty of Versailles. He further argued that if Hitler was given Danzig and the Polish corridor, everything might settled by arbitration. This pro-Nazi collusive propaganda was given extensive local publicity by Sophia Mumford's committee.

Matters came to a head at 8pm on 30 August 1941, when Lewis Mumford debated with Fish publicly in the local Armenia High School with five hundred people crammed inside and three to four hundred gathered outside listening to the debate through loud speakers. In his speech Mumford argued, as he had already done to a number of groups, about the false feelings of security gained by isolationism and the real threat of Nazism to democracy. The debate was picked up in national, state and local newspapers. Mumford's filing cards for the speech showed how carefully he had prepared, with notes on Fish's speeches in Berlin and Oslo and material drawn from the Congressional Record. As a result, his repeated charge of quisling against Fish was the more compelling. *The New York Times* of Sunday 31 August 1941, observing that Mrs Roosevelt and Mrs Henry Morenthau Jr had motored over from Poughkeepsie to attend, covered the debate generously and with more than a hint of political nostalgia. Mumford had positively evaluated the New England village as *polis* in *The Culture of Cities*.[34] This was a practical demonstration of it. It also showed that the concept of local versus international politics was not adequate to the events themselves.

> In a revival of old fashioned town meeting democracy tonight the dairy farming people of this village attended a debate in which Representative Hamilton Fish declared that America should stay out of the war while continuing aid to Great Britain and Lewis Mumford demanded an immediate declaration of war against Germany.[35]

The meeting was lively with applause, catcalls, boos and hisses. Fish counter attacked with the familiar rhetoric of the right. He claimed his position was supported by 85 per cent of the population, and that a small group of communists, refugees, international bankers and society people in interventionist newspapers were trying to push America against its will into war. He further appealed to the women of America not to sacrifice their sons for undemocratic nations like the Soviet Union. Fish argued that in the First World War 'our troops' were protected by the French and Italian armies, whereas: 'What have we got to today? The British, the Chinese and the Communists!'[36] The British and the communists in the event turned out to be rather useful.

The New Leader, sympathetic to Mumford, observed that Fish was booed when he attributed the war to 'refugees' and 'Jewish bankers'. He responded by shouting back: 'I did not know there were so many Communists in America.'

The paper noted that the booing continued. Fish went on counter-attacking after the debate, attempting to link Mumford with a communist conspiracy by pointing out that he had signed the call for the first 'Congress of American Revolutionary Writers which had launched the League of American Writers', where he noted that according to Eugene Lyons, author of *The Red Decade*, 'messages from Soviet writers threw the audience into spasms of orgiastic enthusiasm'.[37] Given Mumford's drubbing by *New Masses* in 1941 this has all the flavour of black humour.[38]

Mumford did not relax his anti-Nazi attacks and in a petition he wrote against the Vichy government, signed by Van Wyck Brooks and Edna St Vincent Millay among others, he did not mince his words in relation to the State Department:

> The voice of Ambassador Hay is the voice of Pétain, who has bowed to the terror as Hindenburg did in Germany. The voice of Count René de Chambrun is the voice of his father-in-law, Laval, the old accomplice of Mussolini. Their words are French but they are only pathetic wooden manikins mouthing the words of the Nazi ventriloquists.'[39]

So much for the purely local, politically disengaged Mumford. If a refusal to identify with Marxist left politics is to be 'politically uncommitted', as Leo Marx has argued, then Mumford does stand condemned. But there is a problem with reserving political commitment only for an assumed homogeneous narrow left position or for a 'real' proletariat, and especially in the United States. The problem of 'political commitment' in 1940, for those who really knew what was going on in the Soviet Union was complex. It was difficult to criticize the Soviet Union at all given the hysterical anti-Soviet stance of the inevitably media-supported American right which, as much as the Stalinist left, obscured what was going on. And the totalitarian turn in the Soviet Union, though doubtless there in embryo form in Leninist strategic methods from the start, as Victor Serge suspected, was certainly aided and abetted by the sealing-off of the entire country by panic-stricken Western powers. There was in any case no left party in the United States which had effective national influence. Local activity and country-wide trade-union activity (which Mumford invariably supported) was another matter. To be 'committed' to the left politically in *New Masses* terms in 1937 was to turn a blind eye to the purges, the farm collectivizations, the slaughter of the peasants, the slave labour camps and to the dogmatic scientistic Marxism which was its justifying propaganda. Most of the *New Masses* editorial rhetoric, though certainly not all of the commentary, was jejune. It also ignored the literary and cultural banality of official Soviet culture after the mid-1920s, and the general betrayal of democratic socialism, which had deep roots going back as far as the Bolshevik seizure of power, the Kronstadt rebellion and the crushing of the Mensheviks.

To say that the Bolsheviks in 1917 had no option but to act as they did in a moment of extreme danger is a military and strategic judgement more than a political one, though the two are obviously connected. It opens the difficult question of necessity and freedom at a particular historical moment. Like George Orwell, Victor Serge and Dwight Macdonald, Mumford had a strong sense of what was going on without throwing himself into the arms of either decadent European imperialists or born-again American capitalists. Naturally he was, and still is, misunderstood.

It is not a contradiction in this argument also to try sympathetically to understand the intransigence of the left. Any support of the Soviet Union was inevitably seen as leftist propaganda by a globally terrified ruling class. For a generation whose hopes of a change in the inhuman conditions of the European and American working class under industrial capitalism had been so cruelly raised in 1917, Stalin's creation of an autocratic state via a ruthless Terror was a bitter pill to swallow. Not the least of appalling historical ironies is that the creation of this centralized, militaristic, highly industrialized autocracy provided the kind of war machine that would check and then defeat the Nazi totalitarian forces, similarly organized through autocratic terror, though marching under a different ideological banner. In terms of pure extent of the deployment of military power, and the scale and number of battles fought (not to mention losses), it was Soviet military success that, without question, played the major role in making the world safe for European and American democracy. Such is the ineluctable fact, though it is not exactly overly advertised in the relentless rerunning of the 'events' of the Second World War on the television screens of Britain and America. From 1941 'until the end of the war in Europe in May 1945, the majority of the fighting of the whole war took place on the Eastern Front: more people fought and died there than all the other fronts of the war around the globe put together'.[40]

Marxist critique itself had fossilized, reflecting the absence of a socialist democratic process. Unlike Marx himself, who understood that any critique itself must change in the historical process, American Marxists had little capacity for a theoretical development of Marxism. *New Masses*, for example, showed a decline of that historically various and richly textured local socialist American debate in the first fifty years of the twentieth century. That demise was noted by those who took part in it, for example, by the American poet Kenneth Rexroth and by Mumford himself.[41]

For Mumford, practical international politics were, in the late 1930s and 1940s, too urgent to argue the niceties of the dialectic. This was particularly evident in two international political areas he wrote about: fascism and the atomic bomb. In 1939 Mumford published *Men Must Act*. In the British Secker and Warburg edition, the dust-jacket advertised André Gide's *Back from the USSR* and Thomas Mann's *The Coming Victory of Democracy*. The publisher's back-of-jacket 'puffs' for Gide's book included praise from George Bernard Shaw, Geoffrey Grigson,

Kingsley Martin and E.M. Forster. This suggests a reading context of liberal, dissenting, largely literary voices within the strictly drawn ideological battle lines of the 1930s. Mumford opened his work by describing the left in that demarcated battleground, with its air of pacifist hopefulness, as possessed of 'an air of foggy unreality'.[42] Although sympathetic with the desires of decent citizens for peace, Mumford spoke of a 'moral paralysis'[43] that had gripped the United States and Western Europe. For Mumford, heavily influenced by his reading of Melville and Dostoevsky, and his correspondence with Niebuhr, who, like a Calvinist minister of old, directed his attention to ethical and political inertia.

Mumford excoriated Chamberlain's 'maudlin persistence' in his policies of appeasement, and probed with acerbic humour, the psychological roots of acquiescence: 'Plainly, fascism carries into the conduct of adult men and women the infantile illusions of power that the baby feels in its crib when, by bawling loudly, it achieves magical results: the light in its room is turned on or its diaper is changed without further effort on the part of the child.'[44] Mumford concentrated on subjective factors: the cult of the leader, the infantilization of the populace, the extension of the needs of declared 'crisis' (wars against undefined terror) into peace-time coercions of national populations: 'The crisis is the source of fascism's power: the fascists must prolong crisis in order to maintain their power.'[45]

Mumford extended the argument of crisis into the state's use of terror. Even as he wrote Stalin was exterminating hundreds of thousands of Soviet citizens, in the peasantry, the army, the air force, the navy, the old Bolshevik Party, even among those who, on his orders, had defeated the POUM in Spain and among former members of his own secret police. Similar tactics were being used and would intensify under the conditions of war in Italy and in Germany. In other words, Mumford's analysis of fascism was transnational and trans-ideological. Mumford, equally, emphasized the demagogue's need to break the human spirit. Like Simone Weil, Mumford believed that 'Any fool can showily solve the real problems of political power by martial law: but only a fool would mistake that process for government.'[46] Violence has human abjection as a primary goal in which the destruction of the 'soul', to use Weil's terms, is primary. Weil made the politics of this violence to the soul quite clear:

> With guns, aeroplanes, bombs, you can spread death, terror, oppression, but not life and liberty. With gas masks, air-raid shelters and air-raid warnings, you can create wretched masses of panic-stricken human beings, ready to succumb to the most senseless forms of terror and to welcome with gratitude the most humiliating forms of tyranny, but not citizens.[47]

Mumford is also close to Weil in his analysis of the conditions of the industrial worker's life. Her analysis is deeper and more sophisticated than Mumford's because of its examination of power, but Mumford equally sees the appeal of 'barbarism' to the mechanized worker. In her celebrated article 'Factory Work', which appeared for the first time in English in 1946 in Dwight Macdonald's *politics*, Weil emphasized the ethics of psychological temporality: the robbing of the worker in terms of the proposition of the task, the sense of its future, the alliance of mechanization and the boss's arbitrary will and, for our purposes the deprivation of an authentic future in the imagination itself:

> If thought seeks to sidestep that monotony by imagining a change – namely an unexpected order – it can effect its passage from present time to futurity only by way of a new humiliation. Thus, thought draws back from the future. This perpetual recoil upon the present produces a kind of brutish stupor.[48]

In his analysis of fascism Mumford, too, spoke of the dwarfing of the human future when 'automism and compulsion become pervasive' and the mobilization of 'stupor' towards greater stupefaction in terms of the marketed virtual worlds of the sportsman, the celebrity and the leader. Glorifying the sub-human, Mumford argued, fed the need for a collective revenge and a collective victim. The glorification of war, contempt for the physically weak, disdain for scientific inquiry (and one may add the life of the mind in general), a hatred of democracy and of civilization itself grounded on a delight in physical cruelty: these were the key parameters of the phenomenon.

Nor does Mumford neglect the details in the generalizations. It is Jews, Christians and Protestant pastors who, with many others, are in the concentration camps. In Henry Adams's phrase, the 'degradation of the democratic dogma' is clear: 'Fifty thousand hoarse voices shouting *Sieg Heil*; that is fascist music. A parade ground for a hundred thousand goose-steppers, drilled into flat-footedness: that is Nazi civic art.'[49] Fascism's appeal is above all to inertia and to the destroyed human will: 'One has only to let go: to shout when one is angry, hate aggressively when one is frustrated, destroy when one is puzzled.'[50] It is clear that for Mumford the desire for the strong, autocratic ruler is most characteristic of a nation of semi-mechanized, infantilized sheep.

Alongside Weil's critique, Mumford's analysis at certain points also paralleled that of Wilhelm Reich: 'It is the mechanistic mystical character of modern man that produces fascist parties, and not vice versa.'[51] Reich was to confront Marxism more stringently and seriously than Mumford and include a revisionary class analysis in his system, but here their thought coincides. Although the differences are obvious – Weil, with her 'Catholic-Jewish' lament for the extinct extended family, and Reich with his Marxist view that the authoritarian family was the basis of the authoritarian state – both were a good deal more sceptical than Mumford about the authoritarian and inadequate nature of the nuclear family in the production of fascism. In addition, their collective defence of freedom and democracy, though grounded in differing ideological positions, was nonetheless close in their view of the psychological effects of technological industrialization (state or private) on the nature of the person and the family.

Mumford defends democracy at its most basic ethical level: consent, participation, checks on power, negotiation, the rule of law, personal discipline, civic and political education. With the echoes of nineteenth-century democratic nationalism still part of that recovery of American literature in the prewar period, Mumford also sees the character of American freedom marked out in an oscillating, even dialectical, literary dialogues, for example, between Whitman and Melville (plebeian and patrician) Jefferson and Jackson (plantation and frontier) Bronson Alcott and John Dewey (Platonist and Pragmatist). While the 'American mind' here is exclusively white and masculine, and omits a Madison-style capitalism and is thus limited in its literary myth-making, what should not be ignored is a search for a tradition which expresses Weil's need for roots, not only for identity but for a 'home' which is worth defending. If Mumford's view of the 'American mind' lacks a certain range and inclusiveness, it nevertheless began a search for a counter-consensual historical memory that might give plausibility and dignity to a nation at war. That very same impulse also underwrites current studies of gender and race in their struggles to debate historical memory.

Mumford's analysis of fascism is conducted in humanist terms. These humanist terms are neither obvious nor simple. Nonetheless, his argument did lack historical specificity. Whereas Antonio Gramsci, for example, analysed Italian fascism in terms of particular political and economic movements in nineteenth-century Italian history and in the failure of the communist movement in the early twentieth century, Mumford to a degree threw out the baby with the bathwater in his pragmatic setting to one side of certain issues which had engaged the more intelligent left, even in the United States. The gaps in his argument are, in some respects, a little too obvious: the specific politics of the corporatist take-over of American state power in post-Civil War America; the historical class violence directed against attempts to organize labour; racism; the role of employers' organizations and capitalists in the funding of the distractive virtual worlds of sport and celebrities; the hijacking of Christian teaching by the right; the imperialist direction of foreign policy from the destruction of native peoples to the war of 1845 through to the seizure of the Philippines and the ruthless political and economic domination of Latin America; the neglect of education for citizenship in the schools by promoting simplistic, nationalist ideas of democratic freedom.

On the other hand, Mumford could not risk such an analysis which would then, as now, puzzle most Americans by substituting a truer history of its home and foreign affairs for the generally promoted ameliorist view that the United States was becoming in every respect, with a few 'honest' caveats, the last, best hope of mankind, or in the title of a set of narratives and documents currently massively sold for university study and put together with technical competence and scholarly care, 'The Great Republic'. In the latter the general tone is that for all America's faults we are on the right track and the 'Republic' is simply and endlessly progressively 'Great'. Mumford was more than aware of the gap between American nationalist mythology and the historical record and he was at least as good at pointing to it as any of his critics.

What Mumford did have in common with a more acute European political analyst such as Gramsci was the notion of the 'long period', vital to intelligibility and understanding: a keen awareness of the degeneration of the bourgeois citizen into the atomized individual of capitalist post-modernity, an informed knowledge of fascist violence, and a sense of an urgent long-term need for political education. As for Gramsci, this view of history, an imaginative recovery of the past beyond the immediate event, lifted the fatality of the contingent and challenged the propagandist opportunism of those who dominated the public mind, as well as providing a crucial space for the creation of meaning beyond personal survival as the highest goal.[52]

Most crucially Mumford's historical knowledge enabled him to make distinctions between fascism, Nazism, imperialism and the various types of capitalist democratic socialism. These insights led him to float an immediate plan of resistance to the forces that were destroying Europe. While the left was unable to make such distinctions and dreamt of the final victory of the proletariat, imagining that it was happening in the USSR, Mumford in 1938 and 1939 was suggesting that the United States cease trading with Germany, Italy and Japan, withdraw foreign nationals, and liquidate all American short-term investments in those countries.[53] It was a good 'Marxist' economic strategy. Mumford attacked the arguments of the left directly in terms of its abstract shibboleths and economic reductionism. While admitting capitalist productive relations in capitalist countries had to play a major role in any analysis, he argued that fascism must be treated in terms of 'a far more subjective politics'.[54] These arguments strongly anticipated some of the post-war criticism, the Frankfurt School, the radical psychologists and a number of the arguments of the New Left, as well as Catholic critics such as Jacques Ellul.

Mumford thus attacked right and left. On the left the 'supiness and slackness of labour groups in all countries in meeting the situation – one cannot forget that Blum's Popular Front government accepted the outrageous "non-intervention" agreement which crippled the Republican government of Spain'.[55] On the right the American government had 'followed the leadership of pro-Hitler English Tories' and 'lacked foresight, common honesty, or even intelligent self-interest'.[56] It is precisely by not being signed up either to a positivist Stalinist 'Marxism' or to right-wing corporatism that Mumford can analyse the deteriorating events of the 1930s in terms of clear-eyed detail based on 'Enlightenment' democratic values. Nor is Mumford's argument rights-based. Again, like Weil, Mumford also recaptured the ideal of duty from the right in order to argue for immediate American hostile engagement with the fascist powers.

Turning his attention to his own country, Mumford criticized the Nazi-supporting fascist groups in the United States who trained private armies and spread anti-Semitic propaganda and the Catholic Church for its institutionally close alliance with fascism and for 'playing up the factitious threat of communism and by branding plain liberal reform as an active contribution to bolshevism'.[57] Mumford had Father Coughlin in mind. By the outbreak of war Coughlin, the radio priest who broadcasted to millions, had shifted to the extreme right on a populist ticket, becoming anti-Semitic, an extreme isolationist and an aggressive supporter of Franco and Hitler.

Mumford is clear too about the alliance between American big business and fascism. Autocracy in the workplace and the demand for 'unconditional obedience on the worker's part and irresponsibility on their own'[58] needed consistently opposing. Mumford called for the strengthening of the Wagner Labour Act. This act, passed in 1935, safe-guarded workers' rights to form trade unions, undertake collective bargaining and set limits on unfair and aggressive practices by employers. Mumford, it is clear, strongly supported the general liberal intentions of Rooseveltian politics (whatever its many failures in practice) and applauded the implementation and extension of social security coverage and the work of the Work Projects Administration (WPA).

For Mumford trade unionism was a great training school for political and industrial leadership. He saw the thousands of young men and women serving as shop stewards and local union officials as being equipped to play a leading role in the affairs of the nation: 'Their intelligent leadership provides a firm bulwark against the incursion of demagogy of all forms and a guarantee that the democratic process shall endure'.[59] Mumford's analysis also highlighted threats to American democratic practice by groups such as the Ku Klux Klan and the Silver Shirts. Like Roosevelt, he took a dim view of the demagogic practices of Huey Long who, not unlike like Mussolini, had used a populist ticket to concentrate state power in his own hands. Mumford consistently attacked American moves towards the militarization of the state and called for more democratic practices within the army itself.

Most cogently of all, Mumford argued against American exceptionalism: 'A person who is only an American is only half a man: indeed only half an American.'[60] The same might be said of any nationality, but given the endless project of defining what an American is over the last four hundred years, it is perhaps particularly important to say this now of any American, hyphenated or not. Furthermore, while it is easy to smile at Mumford's rhetorical excesses, his book against fascism, makes the point that democracy is neither easy nor uncomplex, nor ever permanently won, nor automatically permanent in any historical state. The sense of strenuous activism in Mumford's politically ethical plea for democracy is, as will be shown further, also based both on an inclusive view of human history and a tragic sense of life.

In purely ideological terms Mumford is hard to pigeonhole. His mentor, Patrick Geddes, was a product of the liberal progressivism of the nineteenth century. Thomas Huxley had been Geddes's teacher, but Darwin, Ruskin, Kropotkin, Comte and Frédéric Le Play were all influential in the make-up of his ideas.[61] Politically, these teachers were extremely various, from Ruskin, who attempted to found a working men's college despite the upper-class intransigence of mid-Victorian Oxford, to Kropotkin, whose work laid the basis with which to critique the fatalisms of the Social Darwinists and stimulated the anarcho-syndicalists in the early modern period. Then there was Le Play, a nineteenth-century imperialist and right-wing Catholic metallurgist, whose ideas somewhat incongruously influenced the Regional Survey Movement and whose politics with their emphasis on happy Catholic feudal families firmly rooted in some traditionalist medieval soil, found favour with Salazar, Defuses and Mussolini. Even the *Catholic Encyclopedia* complained that he seemed to have ignored the church, and to have missed out the New Testament in his narrow-minded advocacy of the Ten Commandments. His ideas of 'Unions for Social Peace' were once described by Proudhon as 'the scientific organization of servitude'.[62]

Linking Mumford's politics as with this extreme right-wing figure, as some have attempted to do, ignores not only not only details (for example Le Play's theoretical classifications based on physics and metallurgy as opposed to Geddes's and Mumford's ubiquitous organicist theories) but also Mumford's considerable differences in politics both from Geddes, through whom the Le Play influence was mediated, and from Le Play himself. As has been shown, Mumford strongly supported the trade union movement for which Le Play and Geddes had little time. Mumford's strong commitment to participatory democracy and his endless attacks on the 'priesthood' of the military industrial bureaucracy hardly mark him out as a successor to Napoleon III's councillor of state. Mumford spent time in the Le Play house in London in 1920 but his decision not to stay there, or indeed in England, was based on his refusal to become an acolyte of either Victor Branford (Geddes's co-worker) or Geddes himself.

Critical commentary on Mumford's ideological positions has generally emphasized his 'perceptive critique of advanced capitalist social relations' which contrasted with the narrow perceptions of 'much of the American left'.[63] This is accurate. Others have stressed his anticipations of 'the current intellectual ferment about the politics of language, culture and symbolic meaning' and the return to a republican idiom of 'community' and the 'common good'.[64] There has been much commentary on his relationship with the work of the philosopher John Dewey, some succinctly arguing that his accusation of the latter's lack of transcendent values was pertinent in the mid-1920s though not later and others that they were closer on 'the importance of symbolic language and communications in providing a cultural foundation for a participatory politics' and that Dewey's philosophy of mind in conscious interaction with society directly paralleled Mumford's own conception of personality developing through experience.'[65] Some critics have argued for Mumford's appreciation of the value of class analysis but that there were problems with his treatment of 'technological objects as the material expression of sub-structural cultural values'.[66] The former claim is possibly just, though difficult to prove except by inference; the latter claim is simply wrong, never mind its mystificatory ur-symbolic claims, because Mumford's analysis of 'technology' is not essentially object-oriented but in fact very close to a sentence in Marx's famous footnote in the first volume of *Das Kapital*. It is worth repeating:

> Technology reveals the active relation of man to nature, the direct process of the production of his life, and thereby it also lays bare the process of the production of the social relations of his life, and of the mental conceptions that flow from those relations.[67]

Given Mumford's extensive reading it is in any case impossible to tie Mumford to any single influence. One may cite Sombart, Feldhous, Beck, the Webbs, Samuel Smiles and Veblen among countless others and yet ignore the fact that literature plays at least as an important a part in his ideological formation as the social and political theorists. For Mumford, as for his contemporary the Cambridge literary critic F.R. Leavis, a criticism of literature was a criticism of life and for Mumford that meant that politics was included in the holistic view of the worlds the greatest literature offered. A letter to David Liebovitz in 1923 shows that for Mumford the poets came before the philosophers and theorists. Poets, he called rather clumsily the 'mentally whole' people, a phrase which at least suggests a view of the world that insists on an examination of all modes of thought in relation to a world whose structures were also complex and systematically variable. Wordsworth, Whitman, Blake and Shelley were Mumford's guides and he observed to Liebovitz: 'Blake by the way, is only just beginning to have a wider influence; I noted that Gide's critique of Dostoevsky relied upon him heavily, a marvelous change to come about in French thought.' [68]

Many commentators have observed Mumford's ideological debt to Marxism. Even so, as has been shown, Mumford never could accept the dogmatism that the Stalinism had shrunk to from the late 1920s onwards. In a letter of 1934 that is rather touching because no one who ever knew him doubted his commitment to literature and the class struggle, the American communist Michael Gold wrote to his old friend, whom he had known since his own involvement with the earlier publications *Masses* and *Liberator* in the 1920s:

> Lewis, you have done much brilliant work in these years and certainly fulfilled every atom of promise in that lanky, big-nosed New York goy who was such a mystery to me at the time.
>
> But you still need the iron of Marxism – with it, your work would be doubly effective and truer. You are still in the Shelley stage I believe, and today that is dangerous. We all need to be as mature as we can become, and dodge not a single factor of reality.
>
> In some curious way, you have always managed to shut your eyes to the class war and all its revolutionary implications.

Gold added, somewhat lugubriously, 'Well, this letter sounds familiar – the same old lecture' and continued: 'I wish you were a Communist. In a few years you could do a John Strachey [*sic*] for us – you have the equipment. Come on in, the water is fine.'[69] Mumford was to comment many years later that Gold was 'one of the most promising literary talents that was ever sacrificed to the petrified dogmas of Russian Communism'.[70]

Mumford never did enter that particular water for reasons which became increasingly clear from the late 1920s to anyone not blinded by Soviet propaganda. *Ouvriérisme* had been attacked by theorists and writers of the calibre of Victor Serge, Simone Weil, Wilhelm Reich and Antonio Gramsci from different perspectives. Critics of Mumford's politics never suggest what party he might have joined in their critiques of his political position. Mumford found the Communist Party lacking in an intelligent programme for America and he distrusted its orthodox scientism, as well 'its emphasis upon abstract power and revenge.' Strategically he thought its promotion in America would 'generate a terrific fascist reaction' (surely correct) which would sabotage any attempt to create a genuine socialist America.[71]

Nonetheless, Mumford's writing and its theoretical directives more than showed the shadow of the American literary world's dialogue with the socialist debate in the 1920s and 1930s. From Geddes and the Victorian liberal-socialists Mumford had already learned that the writer had to be politically engaged with the contemporary world. In a *New Yorker* article of 1937 he recalled his childhood in the New York of socialist Russian and Polish Jews who shook the complacency of his own genteel poor upbringing. A childhood friend called Stamer (whose father was a Greenpoint cigar-maker of the old '48 stock') 'jarred my middle class complacency with his scornful descriptions of what had hitherto seemed a reasonable and well-balanced world'. He added 'I might have lived and died in my part of the upper West Side without realizing that neither the Democratic nor the Republican party had ever recognized the Class Struggle.'[72]

Mumford had grown up in Greenwich Village's golden era where artists, writers, leftists and bohemians of every hue jostled with each other: Max Eastman, Michael Gold, Hugo Gellert, Walter Pach, John Sloan and Thomas Hart Benton were among the dozens of writers and artists who swarmed in its cheap rents, coldwater flats and streets. It was here that Eugene O'Neill struggled between socialism and Nietzsche and the ghosts of Melville and Albert Pinkham Ryder lingered. It was a time, Mumford said, at which it seemed that if you came up with a good idea the world might be saved: 'One day a Spinozaist, now an anarchist, now a socialist, now a Ruskinian Tory, now a Shavian, now a Platonist, now a disciple of Samuel Butler, a Whitmanite, a Geddesian, or a Tolstoian.'[73] As Henry Adams had hurled the worlds of John Quincy Adams, Locke, Jefferson, Washington, Voltaire, Pascal and Tocqueville at the trusts and early modern industrial capitalists, so Mumford was to hurl the worlds of nineteenth-century idealism, of Emerson, Marx, Kropotkin, Geddes, Weber and William Morris at the emerging totalitarian world of America's military industrial complex.

On the theoretical side, Mumford, wrote in the early 1920s that he resented the jargon of the Hegelian dialectic but that he had to acknowledge that 'it was exactly the sort of corrective that Dewey's philosophy ought to have, if all its real advances in educational method are not to be compromised by that amoeboid pragmatism which refuses to undergo the artistic travail of a giving a shape and a form to ultimate values.'[74] There were limits to 'pragmatism'. Williams James's pragmatist philosophy, essentially a theory of truth, had nonetheless also been simplistically drawn on by the Italian fascists in bolstering their view that the means justified the end. It had acquired this sort of reputation also among many Americans. As late as 1932 Mumford noted to Brooks that:

> when Mussolini seized power in Italy he had an interview with an American newspaper correspondent in which he justified his action in terms of the American philosophy of pragmatism. One of the Albany papers, I was informed, printed this with the caption: Home Town Boy provides Slogan for Fascist Dictatorship.[75]

In ideological terms the choices for literature were also simplified in the options available to Mumford. Dorothy Norman wrote to him in 1937, not unironically, that 'On the one hand, one has the Herbert Reads who, with the Breton-Surrealist-Communists, say that Surrealism is the pure, unadulterated expression of the inner man, which must be divorced from politics, but that communism and Surrealism are one; and the Michael Golds who say that unless one writes about the down-trodden "proletariat", there is nothing to say'. In the same letter she praised the 'highly able pamphleteering' of Henry Hart's recently published *Writer in a Changing World*, but added 'when you begin to examine the inner expressions of the various men involved you again come to an impasse.'[76]

Mumford would not have disagreed. Henry Hart's book contained essays by Ernest Hemingway, Malcolm Cowley, Archibald MacLeish, Martha Gellhorn, Donald Ogden Stewart and Granville Hicks among others and reported on the Second American Writers' Congress, giving an excellent snapshot of writers' reactions to the tumultuous political events of the 1930s. Mumford was wary of this type of instant contemporary commentary, preferring the longer, more considered, historical view.

Mumford had a tendency to test ideological positions on the pulses. Reviewing Sorokin's *Social and Industrial Dynamics* in 1937, he wrote: 'No amount of erudition that Paretos, Spenglers and Sorokins may exhibit can atone in this field for their lack of emotional poise. They go through the motions of scholarship in order to establish ulterior claims to a scientific precision and an object insight they do not command.'[77] However Spenglerian some of Mumford's rhetoric sometimes sounds, he was very critical of the 'fantastic' 'Platonism' of Spengler's mono-causal Faustian theme. He noted the over-the-top emotional colour of Spengler's rhetoric which exhibited 'the same neurotic traits that one finds in the more popular expositions of fascism'.[78] Reviewing Walter Lippmann's *An Inquiry into the Principles of the Good Society* he criticized the journalist for the binary simplicities in his analysis of fascism which offered a choice between militarized collectivism and 'a completely plan-less free economy'. He added, with biting sarcasm, that 'One might describe Mr. Lippmann's position as negative totalitarianism'.[79]

Mumford continued his attacks on inept 'liberalism' in *The New Republic*. The liberal was one without stable convictions, someone incapable of facing the blackness and unscrupulousness of the operations of political power, someone who continually scans 'the horizon for signs of dawn'.[80] Liberalism's record in the 1930s was, for Mumford, quite shameful. On Stalin's reign of terror they were silent, elsewhere they 'tearfully acquiesced in the rule of those who, as Blake said, would "forever depress mental and prolong corporeal war"'.[81] In the period of the United Front, they accepted unthinkingly the elite communist leadership, 'fanatical, unscrupulous, deeply contemptuous of essential human values, incredibly stupid in tactics and incredibly arrogant in matters of intellectual belief.' [82] Mumford also noted, however, that the communists alone had firm convictions and the courage to act upon them. The article on 'liberalism' (in the American use of the word which tends to cover all left positions, rather than, as in Europe, defining a centralist position, social-democratic in character) is an essential one for understanding Mumford's ideological position. It involves not only a critique of a decade of disgraceful political behaviour, but a wide-ranging reassessment of European humanist history to set against the fatalities of cultural production offered by Marxist economic determinations.

In fact, Mumford defended the positive values of that western humanistic liberalism which he felt liberals had so betrayed, especially what he calls its 'universal elements'.[83] On closer inspection these are not the 'humanist' shibboleths too quickly understood by some contemporary academic commentators, but a kind of moving historical genealogy of enduring 'human' ethical and cultural achievements which though specific to a historical culture may be transmitted, shared, 'translated', renewed and, equally certainly, *lost* in any subsequent civilization. Here Mumford's reason of history has Hegelian trappings: Minerva's owl may fly in the dusk of declining civilizations: but unlike Hegel Mumford's reason lacks the reductive excess of an abstract spirit. The owl will shift shape and nature in subsequent appearances, identifiable perhaps only as the continuity of the negation of the negation. Sometimes it will fly backwards. Mumford continued to defend his 'universality':

> These universal elements in liberalism, the moralizing elements, are the real objects of the fascist attacks. They were part of the larger human tradition, embodied in the folkways of the Jews, in the experimental philosophy of the Greeks, in the secular practices of the Roman Empire, in the sacred doctrines of the Christian Church, in the philosophies of the great post-medieval humanists. The Marxian notion that ideas are always the shadows of the existing economic institutions runs bluntly against facts precisely at this point. For although a culture forms a related organic whole, a residue is left in each period and place which tends to become part of the general heritage of mankind. This residue is relatively small in amount but infinitely precious; and no single class or people can create it or be its sole keeper.[84]

It is important to note that in Mumford's historicized social anthropology, 'residues' are both ideas and practices. The 'ideas', as will be shown, are no more some kind of disembodied philosophical or intellectual history than the 'practices' are determined by an abstract development of law or religion. 'Practices' will also include art and architecture from Sumerian domestic pottery to a Rembrandt portrait or a design for a city. If, Mumford argues, the American has debts to every nation on earth, by this fact alone, it should be evident that these debts should not only be acknowledged but compel gratitude, humility and a sense of at least partial belonging to the other. This claim will distinguish Mumford even from his acknowledged forebears like Emerson and Whitman. Mumford was part of that discovery and renewal of the traditions of an American national culture in the 1920s and 1930s, but he combined it with a non-progressivist and radically internationalist perspective.

The corruptions of liberalism Mumford saw as oscillating between two extremes: between a materialist rationalism ultimately traceable to Voltaire (pragmatic liberalism) and an 'ideal liberalism' ultimately traceable to Rousseau. This binary division in a quasi-structural analysis linked to a double figure is in the tradition of Henry Adams and William James. Adams used it for an essentially satiric analysis of the historical process, James to mediate a rationalist impasse by shifting the ground of philosophical analysis to a dualistic psychology. For Mumford, materialist rationalism left out the 'role of instinct, tradition, history'. In addition, 'it was unaware of the dark forces of the unconscious; it was suspicious of either the capricious or the incalculable, for the only universe it could rule was a measured one, and the only type of human character it could understand was the utilitarian one.'[85] Such analyses, begun with Henry Adams, are now familiar in work influenced by the Frankfurt School, historians of science after Paul Feyerabend, and in the work of the radical psychologists and feminists. But Mumford was almost unique for his time in attempting to reclaim the messiness of human history and human irrationality for a radical critique. Such areas were normally the province of the right who used them for a call to 'order', to puritanical, rigid and often invented 'traditional values' and to authoritarian politics in general.

'Liberalism' also was vague about its values. Under the caveats of Marxist atheistic and 'scientific' secularism, it had neglected the fields of aesthetics, ethics and religion and consigned them to the dustbin of history. As a result the pragmatic liberal 'has taken the world of personality, the world of values, feelings, emotions, wishes, purposes for granted'.[86] No less than Melville, Dostoevsky or Gide, Mumford attacked the liberal notion of evil as merely the absence of good and often conceived in utilitarian terms. Reich once observed that it was a typical error of the socialists and communists to consider the building of an apartment house, a subway or a school a 'socialistic achievement': 'Apartment buildings, subways and schools have to do with the technical development of a society but do not indicate whether the members of this society are serfs or free workers, rational or irrational human beings.'[87] Most governments now use their statistical propaganda with exactly the same lacunae. Mumford would additionally have asked whether the buildings were any good or not. Of course the fascists made the same error in terms of fascism and so did most of the social democratic nations in terms of social democracy. 'Evil', for Mumford, as for theologians and the great nineteenth-century novelists, was an active force in the world. It was a word and concept long gone from the vocabulary of the secular humanists, Marxists and materialists and rarely confronted by contemporary liberal Christians. Its only current use was in extreme demagogic propaganda, to obliterate the truth of a situation by characterizing your enemy as 'evil'. As a character in Melville's *The Confidence Man* said, the criminal betrayal of trust in the confidence trick was 'more for the love than the lucre'.[88]

Liberalism also did not think hard enough. No less than the intelligent Marxist Mumford was hard on a formless eclecticism of thought which had not undergone a difficult and radical synthesis. His sarcasm is still useful in our present context of the 'horizontal' equi-valuations of our contemporary post-modern 'theorists': 'here a scrap left over from childhood, there a fragment of Kant or Bentham, or again a dash of Machiavelli, pacifist Quakers one moment and quaking Nietzscheans the next.'[89] To get a sense of what it felt like to read Mumford in the 1940s, we might translate: 'Here a touch of Derrida, there a touch of Foucault, gnostic Bloomites one moment and quaking Lacanians the next.'

In the grand sweep of general ethical condemnation, however, Mumford did not neglect the immediate context. In 1940 his 'universalist' values enabled him to praise the left for having being moved by the plight of the Spanish Republicans but witheringly attack their hypocrisy in doing nothing for the 'fate of the humiliated and bullied Czechs, the tortured Jews, the murdered Poles, the basely threatened Finns – or the French and English who may next face extermination'.[90] Employing a telling conceit from classic American literature, and here he has American liberals such as Charles Beard, Stuart Chase and Quincy Howe in mind, Mumford does not mince his words: 'they cling to the monstrous illusion that they can save themselves and their country by cutting themselves off – to use Hawthorne's words in "Ethan Brand" – from the magnetic chain of humanity'.[91]

Mumford ended his attack on the left and 'liberalism' with a prophetic anticipation of a new religion, a new set of beliefs and values that would give coherence from the private to the public realms in a world torn apart in ideological conflict. Such notions are easy to ridicule. Given the current activity of fundamentalists in both the United States and the Islamic world it is fairly obvious that the last thing needed is a new religion. The mere birth of a new idea, radical insight or and cultural or religious practice is as open to historical corruption as are the most traditional of religions and beliefs, which at least have the advantage of a complex, sometimes critical, sustaining tradition and history. Religious and ideological abuse was all too evident to Mumford: Stalin destroyed Marx in the name of Marxism, the popes signed up to fascism, Cromwell scourged Ireland in the name of Protestant reform, and born-again United States presidents and British prime ministers invade Muslim countries to give them the benefit of Christmas pudding, prayer meetings, consumer materialism, McDonald's and 'democracy'.

Victor Serge, too, had prophesied the possibility of a new religion. Mumford's closure, like Serge's, must be seen in context and examined for tone as well as literal content. It was a utopian call for a new comprehensive pattern of belief and critique which might offer some reconciliation between ethics and politics, between affective and rational life, between the actions of finite imperfect human beings and a holistic sense of the world, and between a creative sociality and the conserving inertias of customary practice. Mumford's representation of ethics, religion and, to a more limited extent, psychology and cultural practice, though intimately bound up with his politics and ideological position, must now be looked at separately.

Ethics, Religion and Social Practices

Mumford's position on the interlinking realms of religion, ethics and social practice was complex. Critics use phrases such as 'moral realism', 'culturist radicalism', 'symbolic language', 'cultural form' and 'political function', to take a few phrases from one essay, to attempt to characterize the slippery nature of Mumford's analytic discourse.[92] Of these, the most promising is an emphasis on 'symbolic language', but it is rarely followed up by a detailed analysis of Mumford's synthetic prose style. The phrase really suggests an attempt to create a critical lineage, perhaps from Cassirer to anthropologists such as Claude Lévi-Strauss and Clifford Geertz.

On the psychological front it is not evident that Mumford was closer to Jung than Freud as such, though it is true he seems to have read Freud as a young man and Jung as an older man; nor is it particularly evident that he would prioritize Fromm over Niebuhr. One critic, while noting accurately that Mumford read Jung's *Memoirs, Dreams, Reflections* twice while writing *Technics and Human Development* (1967) and that it underwrote his own ideas on 'the eternal importance of ritual and tradition', also noted that at the same time he was reading Ernest Jones's biography of Freud.[93] Everything has to be taken together and that is the difficulty of positioning Mumford. As one critic succinctly put it: 'He did not suppose that the "personal" and the "political" or the individual and the social, were distinct poles, between which people had to tack. For him all human activity was at once personal and cultural, individual and social.'[94]

On the religious front Mumford's relationship with Reinhold Niebuhr and the effect of Niebuhr's writing on him have generally been characterized as reinforcing Mumford's already tragic sense of life. But it is arguing too strenuous a case to say that it was not until 1940 that Mumford grasped the full implications of Niebuhr's moral realism 'with its insistence on an Augustinian psychology of humans' divided nature'.[95] Mumford published his book on Melville in 1929. He needed neither Augustine nor Niebuhr to convince him of tragedy or of the divided nature of the self. Here I am much more in agreement with Michael Zukerman's thoughtful assessment of the trajectory of Mumford's thought as a deepening, oscillating and perfectly identifiable and characterizable field of themes, ideas and conjectures, rather than a coherent whole that exhibits those mini- or maxi-progressions or regressions, failures and successes that are needed for the more conventional academic narrative and judgement. Augustine and Niebuhr reinforced or challenged whatever it was that Mumford was already engaged with.[96] Other critics have correctly pointed out that Niebuhr was only one of a number of commentators contemporary with Mumford who attacked the nature of 'pragmatic liberalism', and that Mumford was much more reluctant to jettison a valorization of the ('Protestant') person than Niebuhr as part of the critique. Certainly they were in agreement about the need for force at moments of political crisis which of course shocked the pacifist end of the Christian community and the isolationists on the left.

However, they would dramatically split over the question of the atom bomb. Reviewing Mumford's *The Conduct of Life* in the early 1950s, Niebuhr characterized Mumford as essentially a romantic writer and then damned him by arguing that the eschatological truth of the romantic movement was Nietzsche, Hitler and Mussolini. This was not just simplified nonsense, though this specious lineage of causalities from Nietzsche to the dictators was common enough at the time, but it also showed an astonishing misunderstanding of the complexities of the Romantic movement itself. Niebuhr also took Mumford to task at the height of the Cold War for not taking the communist threat seriously enough. Niebuhr ended up on the cover of *Time*; Mumford never did.

Niebuhr's letters to Mumford speak of the misuse of religion by dictators who assign themselves God-like roles, Roosevelt's weakening liberalism in practice, American apathy over the European war, the ethical and historical simplifications of the Buchmanites (Frank Buchman was the founder of the Moral Rearmament Movement) and of the threat to socialism in southern Europe by Catholic fascists. He solicited contributions from Mumford for his journal *Christianity and Crisis* and he wrote to Mumford about various historical Christian thematics which Mumford was to engage with in *The Condition of Man*: 'About your statement that you prefer Aquinas to Luther, I want to have a long talk with you sometime.'[97]

It is precisely here that the two men come closest in dialogue, though certainly not in mutual consensus. On the issue of Aquinas or Luther, Niebuhr is much more theologically complex and views the issue along dialectical lines. He had not read Marx and Hegel in vain. Niebuhr argued that neither Catholicism nor Protestantism had the single way to truth. If grace in Catholicism undoes the imperfections of nature, the Protestant would argue that this attacks the goodness of nature. In a Hegelian move, Niebuhr suggests that grace is both completion and negation. The original perfection is in process of being worked out, hence the possibility of completion; it is continually challenged because historical reality is corrupt. Niebuhr thus takes the binary but linear myth of the fall and converts it to dialectical process which is guaranteed not by the reason of history nor even by an ultimately linear grand narrative of Christian history, but by a psychological theory of truth of action which is instantly applicable to contemporary political reality: 'Thus the ideal political possibility must always be a completion of what is genuine justice in the British empire and a negation of what is imperialistic corruption in the British empire.' He added: 'I try to carry this pattern out in the various problems of philosophy and politics.'[98]

Mumford would have agreed about the relativity of judgement but he would not have employed the same process of thought. Mumford's take on philosophy is a Jamesian one, that is to say he goes for a direct sense of its psychological and ethical meta-narrative rather than engaging in its analytic propositions as such. The pages on Luther in *The Condition of Man*, for example, are a case in point. However Mumford, unlike Niebuhr, was not a Christian, though he was sympathetic to the insights of religious thought. This simple fact is often overlooked by commentators. Niebuhr would not have spoken of the 'vital lies' of Christianity as Mumford did in *The Condition of Man*, nor did he articulate his biblical narrative of tragic finitude in psychological terms. There is a generic difference in the way they wrote and thought. Niebuhr did not talk about the possible dangers of a 'tragic' view of life and a perpetual insistence upon it. Quite understandably in the American context, Niebuhr hurled 'tragedy' against that shallow, progressivist optimism which was and is part of the official ideology of the American Dream. As such, Niebuhr's recall of 'tragedy' was a very useful correction. On the other side of the coin, however, Mumford knew no less than the Marxists, that a 'tragic view of life', the Christian association of sin and death together with an apocalyptic eschatology, could also be narrativized as an extreme right-wing conservative tool playing on people's natural fears and anxieties:

> In the historic experience of the Christian community there lay, moreover, the source of an even more terrible reaction which gave psychological depth and substance to the new manic-depressive visions of Christian theology [...] The Christian fathers summoned all eternity to their aid to work out a revenge [theology of heaven and hell] sufficiently frightful to match the terrors to which the faithful had been subjected [...] There is scarcely a single aspect of this culture which does not become clearer when one interprets it as a neurotic dream phenomenon.[99]

Mumford had not read Hawthorne in vain. Eternity played a lesser role in Jewish than in Christian eschatology. 'Tragedy' was a complex issue. In political discourse it could be a source of quietism. In ethical discourse it was foundational. The links between the two were the problem. Niebuhr as a man was firmly entrenched in the life, work and community of the radical end of the Protestant church, centred around the Union Theological Seminary in New York. To a degree Mumford was at once more isolated, less placed and freer therefore to look at religions other than Christianity though less bound, it must be said, by the practical necessities of the parish. Certainly the range of texts which fed his philosophy extended far beyond those of the Christian tradition.

However, like Mumford, Niebuhr had a vast intellectual range, a taste for polemic, a distrust of wholly rational explanation, a hatred of the abuse of power and of the will to power, and a mistrust of the world produced by scientific materialism. Niebuhr in the 1930s had been much more engaged with Marxism than Mumford. He favoured the collective ownership of the means of production, placed the claims of the worker over the bosses, especially where they were supported by right-wing Christians, tended toward an economic theory of history and distrusted to the point of secularism the notion of the kingdom of heaven as a reward for obedient servants. On the other side of the coin, he could not believe in a 'sinless' proletarian dictatorship any more than Simone Weil could. Niebuhr was quick to perceive Stalin's brutal new 'religion' of totalitarianism and distrusted the ameliorist eschatology of communism with its absolute determinations of class and class action.[100]

Just to take one example: in his work of 1934, *Reflections on the End of an Era*, Niebuhr argued for a more political engagement by the church and a willingness to open a dialogue with Marxism. In addition and in terms to which Mumford could readily respond, he opened a fundamental attack on the nature of 'reason' and what he called the 'mechanical' ideology of commercial and industrial civilization. 'Reason' has various meanings in Niebuhr's account. It can be an ideological justification of certain actions, often operating in a contradictory manner under the same term; a justification at the biological level of the will to survive; a thing of utopian dreamers right or left, of academic utilitarians, and of one-dimensional justifiers of capitalist practices.

In his argument there are two meta-narratives: one is of the contradictory harmonies of nature of ecological balance versus human beings whose consciousness of the processes of life and its terrors lead to a corrupting will to power. The other narrative embodies the structural trope of the cyclical theory of civilization: the declining civilization bolstered here in a naturalist (social Darwinist) discourse: 'Therefore every social system, faced by the peril of death, is bound to make one final and ruthless effort to avert its doom by destroying or suppressing competing forms of life.'[101] Writing such a book in 1933 clearly cast a shadow over the arguments. Niebuhr was convinced that 'western society is obviously in the process of disintegration' living under the peril of new wars.[102] One sympathizes with that judgement, even though 'disintegration' is always a pan-historical prophetic judgement in time of crisis. With Stalinism in the East, economic depression in the West, and Hitler in power in Germany the judgement can be readily forgiven. However, for Niebuhr, 'disintegration' always had a whiff of finality about it; for Mumford it was often, though not always, a moment in natural cycle which prepared for renewal.

Like Mumford, Niebuhr accurately saw an impasse between the desperate need for reciprocity in the dangerous new world created by technology and the competitive demands of capitalism:

> The real tragedy of our contemporary situation is that modern technology has made social mutuality and international reciprocity an absolute imperative, a very law of survival; while our system of economic ownership makes both intra-national justice and international reciprocity impossible.[103]

Niebuhr's argument is troubled by the sermon mode: the need for the simplifying fable and semi-allegorical argument. For example, it is possible to construct (as Niebuhr did) a narrative from Aristotle and Alexander, Seneca and Nero to Rathenau and Hitler which conveys the reality of the endless defeat of the good but then to suggest that this is the fate of the pragmatic 'liberal mind' courts serious difficulty. It is hard to associate Aristotle with pragmatic 'liberalism' in the modern sense. The judgement is also sometimes difficult in terms of contemporary examples. John Maynard Keynes is one of the 'ineffective' liberals smothered in Tory Britain, but Keynes's theory was the best economic truth of its period and underwrote good deal of the little that remains of social democracy in Britain to the present day. Niebuhr here reflects a *New Masses*-style Marxist view that the Stracheys and Keyneses were merely tinkering with the system. He jumps too quickly from the grand narrative to the contingent event and he seems, like the Marxists, to believe that a complete breakdown of the social order will produce some sort of clarifying breakthrough. Here Christian and Marxist views of the necessary absoluteness of revolutionary change coincide. While acknowledging with Marx that the once revolutionary ideology of the bourgeoisie hardened into an aggressively cruel view of 'individualism' and exploitative disregard of collective sociality, Niebuhr seems unable to join Marx in celebrating its 'youthful' exuberance and achievements. If failure marks the wise then presumably Jesus comes into the same category of the ineffective, though perhaps not pragmatic, liberal. The sense of the past is doom-laden *a priori* for Niebuhr.

Niebuhr is on safer ground where he analyses the Hitler regime. Here there are useful insights such as his description of the manipulation of the lower middle classes against their own interests by a sophisticated populist alliance involving military and state capitalist power and the working class together. He is on less sure ground when he states that world war would create a civil war in which the cheap shows of the leadership cult would be exposed and overthrown. For someone so convinced of the active power of evil and irrationality, Niebuhr fails, perhaps to his credit, to imagine the absolute collusions possible through terror, psychological manipulation and propaganda in Germany and Italy.

Mumford's and Niebuhr's views on the city and 'organism' are also worth comparing. More than Mumford, Niebuhr distrusted the city, although oddly enough, and unlike Mumford, he lived in one. Niebuhr argued that the real root of bourgeois individualism was the character of urban life: 'The man of the city may be mechanically more dependent upon his society than the peasant. But he is not in such intimate organic relation to it.'[104] The word organic has to work hard here. Marx had said at least the rural worker had fresh air and variable working hours according to the season, but the implied critical utopia of the countryside over against the city smacks of pastoralism. Somewhat reluctantly it seems Niebuhr allows that 'urban individualism makes a permanent contribution to the history of the race.'[105] However, equating loneliness with bourgeois individualism and urban space is not very convincing. One can be lonely inside a marriage, a family, a country cottage or a village, as virtually every female character in a nineteenth-century novel or play testified to; one need not be lonely having a cup of coffee alone with a good book inside a bustling urban coffee house. Niebuhr made no distinction between solitude and loneliness, a serious mistake, for it is the denial of solitude that makes for loneliness.

What Niebuhr is after is existential loneliness: 'the individual finally faces the eternal mystery of life alone'.[106] Thus, in a typical religious move, the realization of death and inessentialness becomes automatically the ground of truth which turns us to God. The God who depends on anguish and terror for credibility seems to me not a God one should especially admire. It takes very little imagination to understand that everyone else is in the same boat. It is only the supreme egoist who believes that that particular fate is unique even in the interior life. The existentialists simply thought of death as a scandal, and protested to the last, raging like Dylan Thomas against the dying of the light. There are many human attitudes to death, the opportunity for faith in God only being one of them. Unlike Heidegger who made freedom the other side of anguish, Niebuhr simply places the Christian belief of the worth of the individual soul against anguish, that is as a protection against its possibility, and even goes on to suggest that bourgeois society's individualism is moderated by such a belief.

Nonetheless, Niebuhr has a very clear sense of the atomization of the capitalist individual and the banality of the mechanical figure of the communist (though not Marxist) collectivized individual. Certainly also the breakdown of community under 'flexible' capitalist freedoms is well understood:

> The unpolitical, desocialized creature who lives in a modern urban apartment house, in a dwelling full of people but without any neighbors, subsisting upon the proceeds of the labor of others with whom he has not the slightest human contacts, is the pathetic product and spiritual victim of a decadent individualistic culture and civilization. (p. 95)

It was and is decadence, and remains a true scandal in relation to contemporary urban civilization. All Niebuhr is left with, however, is simply to regret that the working class's growing sense of cynicism about middle-class values will make them blind to the real achievements of the middle class. Given social mobility, and the lack of major pan-working-class organization in America, the statement is over simplified. He also does not mention the multiple ways of sociality people work out for themselves in the rich opportunities the great city always offers to those not absolutely at the bottom of the economic order. Unfortunately contemporary megalopolis, to use Mumford's term, has by sheer gigantism and capitalist political brutality changed the experience of what the city once offered into a sprawling living nightmare.[107]

Individualism then, for Niebuhr, ultimately destroys the individual. The extended family's disappearance automatically brings with it the disappearance of a vast range of 'spiritual' values. Niebuhr seems to have forgotten that one of Christianity's and Judaism's most powerful myths made betrayal and fratricide the first crime of the first family and that this was the basis, with a little help from the Greeks, of Freud's stoic vision of the world in which desire and social formation were forever at war with each other in what was essentially a not very liberating nor very creative family melodrama. Spurned by the left, sentimentalized by the right, sanctified by the religious, destroyed by capitalist economics and driven to stoic survivalist stasis by the psychologists under the rubric of normative 'health', the 'family' was everyone's site of contention. Nowhere was there a greater mismatch between theoretical analysis and practice.

The insistence of Protestantism on individualism, Niebuhr argued, had often provided a point of resistance to tyranny, from the Caesars to Hitler and there was a truth in asceticism which acknowledges the finitude of human tragedy. His reduction of the radicalism of the English revolution and European Protestantism to that ascetic resistance, however, completely neglects its historical and political successes and failures. Their saving 'pessimism' as against Manchester school liberalism with its Whig view of history, in Niebuhr's argument reduces historical and theological detail to sermon-like moral and psychological binary exempla.

The source of strength and weakness in Niebuhr's argument is in fact in the notion of universal tragedy. For Niebuhr, the world, given the vision of Christianity, can only be redeemed in the last day. It is the 'only' that is the problem here for no one can look at history without a sense of its seemingly endless inhumanity and violence. Perhaps it was the inevitable effect of the appalling events of the 1930s (or the lingering shadow of *contemptu mundi*) but nowhere at all does Niebuhr celebrate the achievements of history. At most he praises a St Francis or makes a gesture towards a Morris-inspired medieval synthesis. The weakness is most exposed, quite paradoxically, when he discusses Gandhi and Churchill who slip a little too neatly into his Aristotle versus Alexander trope. For Niebuhr, Churchill ('a fiercer beast of prey than the Oriental [*sic*]') represents the forces of *this* world. Gandhi's essentially religious opposition which he declares 'may not avail' is allied to the ineffectual liberal. He is a religious saint which rules him out as a political leader. Here, over-anxious to correct a tendency to mysticism and otherworldliness, Niebuhr is unwilling to grant Gandhi any political authenticity or his strategy of non-violence any credible political power against the Churchillian forces of darkness. Religion and politics were obliged to operate on different planes given *a priori* assumptions of 'tragedy', the non-recognition of which undermined 'liberals'.

History in this particular proved Niebuhr completely wrong. The British Empire in India collapsed in 1947, seriously assisted by Gandhi's strategy of mass non-violent resistance, the political influence of which was felt from the villages to the global audiences of the cinematic newsreel. The British, weary of war and imperialist rhetoric, threw Churchill out, to the astonishment of most Americans, in 1945. Later on, in the United States, Martin Luther King would alter the course of African-American politics, inspired by Gandhi's philosophy of mass non-violent action, as would Lec Walensa in relation to Stalinist hegemony in Poland. In Niebuhr's prosodic vision there is little sense of the mystic's exaltation that can give practical strength to those whose lives are dedicated to the dispossessed. The relationship between belief and practice is not a simple one. Niebuhr's practical assistance to the dispossessed and, in his most exemplary moment, to refugees was to be beyond praise. He lacked, however, Mumford's 'organic' sense of the renewal of life, the Geddesian curiosity about other cultures, religions and civilizations. Mumford's paean to Geddes sums it up: 'A delight in every manifestation of life, a sense of its wonder and mystery, was what issued forth from Geddes's personality, a kind of radiant emanation, with a halo of visible and usable wisdom, not essentially different from what emanated from William Blake.'[108]

As Hannah Arendt argued in her thesis on St Augustine: 'The world consists of those who love it.'[109] Sin and death haunt Niebuhr's view of life's 'limits'. Limit sometimes seems to replace choice in his philosophy. The individual's inessentialness will not, in his view, invite the concept of the human project to give meaning to life (as the existentialist philosophers thought); it only serves as a limitation on pride. In terms of an attack on both the genteel religious tradition masking the violence of the American right and blinkered sentimental American liberals, his work was timely. In political terms, his judgement about Stalin was absolutely accurate, his sense of the cruelties of American capitalism and its obsessive, abstract, technics-orientated state of mind was just and, most crucially, his anti-isolationist position in the 1930s, based on an accurate judgement of German and Italian politics, was exemplary. In these areas he had a strong and fruitful dialogue with Mumford. Their notions of limits and tragedy also, to a degree, coincided. However, Mumford was most crucially to trust literature rather than theology, the poet rather than the philosopher or theologian. There was finally a quite different sense of human life in their respective books and perhaps a rather different inflection in the way they used the word 'tragedy' itself. Mumford's sense of history, the way he approached belief, ideology, religious experience, his eschatological indifference, the way he framed his grand narrative, his awareness of the richness and multiplicity of the human experience including love and sexuality, his sense of temporality and existence, his fundamentally relativistic and more materialist discourse about the human experience: all this marked him off as of a very different sensibility from the Protestant theologian.

Critics have been right to note that Mumford's discourse about religion never (unlike Niebuhr's) 'explored the religious dimensions of a critical ethics', but he certainly provided an ethical criticism of the religious dimension. A careful reading of *The Condition of Man* reveals even the former claim to be only partly true.[110] It would be more accurate to say that he did not explore the religious dimensions of ethics in twentieth-century Christian theological terms. The basis of his criticism was secular. These discriminations help to open up the larger question of a comparative religious approach to ethics and the claims for an ethics from a non-religious viewpoint. Simone Weil drew on a multiplicity of religious teachings for her Jewish–Catholic-oriented ethics, but then so did Mumford. That the correspondence between Niebuhr and Mumford was warm and fruitful would be expected from two civilized men. In fact, Mumford was to transform radically some of Niebuhr's suggestions about the nature and significance of Christian history in his book most influenced by the theologian, *The Condition of Man.*

Mumford's own thoughts on religion are perhaps best summed up in a letter to Van Wyck Brooks in 1947. He acknowledged that religion was important yet he was convinced that 'none of the existing religions is anything but provisional or Ersatz'.[111] In a series of lectures he gave for the Pacific School of Religion in 1947 he argued that the Christian response to existential questions could not be taken over without change. But he argued too that the church fathers were 'our contemporaries', an argument which to a degree modified with a different sense of temporality Toynbee's then very influential view of history as a succession of civilizations, whose success or failure depended on cultural and religious responses to historical conditions.

In his lectures Mumford adapted Toynbee's phrase 'a time of troubles' to that moment of cyclical breakdown in historic 'organic' community. Estimating that after the war '30 million people have met premature death in our time' (in fact it was at least twice that figure), Mumford argued that the present moment was such a 'time of troubles' with human institutions and social pattern were severely disrupted by war and catastrophe. Mumford saw this moment as an opportunity to respond at the ethical level to the question of community, rather than an evangelical individualist return to God as such, by asking that most powerful of Christian questions: who is my neighbour? And while he did not develop it with the same philosophical sophistication of Arendt in her thesis on St Augustine, his conclusion was the same: 'The vice of civilization lies precisely in the failure to answer the question.'[112]

In the same lecture series it becomes clear that, for Mumford, Albert Schweitzer was at least as important a figure as Niebuhr. Drawing on Schweitzer's *The Decay and Restoration of Civilization* (1923), he signalled his agreement that political failure was at root an ethical failure. Mumford's view of Christianity is that it was born as a source of renewal in a disintegrating Roman empire. To a degree it is the reverse of Gibbon (though he agreed that Christianity was partially instrumental in the fall of the Roman Empire) and his emphasis on renewal is different again from Niebuhr's insistence on the centrality of the cross in a radically fallen world. Nonetheless Mumford acknowledged that Christianity 'taught people how to face the worst'.[113]

But Mumford's judgment is more even-handed and dialectical. Christians failed to participate in state public affairs, which they might have transformed and thereby saved something of the remnants of classical civilization. Further, in order to rebuild family life, 'the Christian church was forced to repress the power of sex almost beyond human endurance and to over-magnify the virtues of celibacy'.[114] Doubtless thinking of Schweitzer, Mumford saw the missionaries as alleviating predatory European imperialism in Africa and Wesleyanism 'as the one saving grace left under capitalism amid the poverty and sordor of the new industrial towns'.[115] The Marxist counter-argument, Mumford would have been well aware, was that religion merely colluded with existing conditions and palliated rather than challenged them. Yet at the same time, it is clear that historically the presence of Christian aid work was often the only (though often inadequate) help against the effects of imperialist and capitalist exploitation. The Marxists had no concept of charity, they believed in the state or looked for promising conditions for a revolution which would make everything right, give or take a few famines and wars. Instead of Christian salvation, Mumford argued for a material and this-worldly notion of 'dynamic balance' between the 'sacred and secular, the eternal and the temporal dimensions of man's experience'.[116] As he himself was the first to acknowledge the words are clumsy and inadequate, but they give a clue to the kinds of questions most relevant for the richest reading of his work which are to do with the fugitive nature of memory, temporality and narrative in human experience as they articulate material conditions and the historical process.

Ethics and Literature

Notwithstanding the importance of historical Christianity, Mumford turned for his deepest insights to literature: Melville had been as profoundly aware of the existence of radical evil as Niebuhr. No one, observed Mumford in a review of Sedgwick's *Herman Melville: The Tragedy of Mind*, who had understood that Melville's demonic characters, Jackson, Claggart and Pierre, 'could have attributed the malignance of fascism to merely economic difficulties that might be appeased by bribes or settled by compromise'.[117] In his 1942 Blashfield Address to the American Academy of Arts and Sciences, Mumford argued that the history of the previous twenty-five years would not have surprised Melville or Dostoevsky. Dostoevsky's character Shigalov wrote the script for 'the unqualified use of terrorism, violence and corruption'.[118] (Writing for Niebuhr's *Christianity and Crisis* in 1941, Mumford had praised Dostoevsky's radical insights into political psychology, reactionary ideologue though he was.)

Literature therefore, for Mumford, uniquely transcended the simplifications of the ideologue in providing the basis for a more complex ethics and psychology. It rehearsed the complexity of the inner life's relation to the outer life, the irrational to the rational, the gap between belief and practice, and the dramatic falsifications of any dogma in any contingent historical moment. Dostoevsky's *Brothers Karamazov*, Mumford wrote to Dorothy Norman in 1937, had helped him 'keep hold on another order of reality' while finishing the final stages of *The Culture of Cities*.[119]

If Melville and Dostoevsky supply a tragic vision (and one wonders whether Mumford had read Charles Olson's two essays on these authors in Norman's *TWICE A YEAR* – he did review *Call Me Ishmael* for the journal), Mumford turned, as Dwight Macdonald, to the New England literature of the classic American period and the English writers John Ruskin and William Morris. For Mumford, the study of serious literature was the basis of ethical judgement itself. The loss of a serious critical audience was regretted: 'they treat a contemporary classic, like Borgese's *Goliath* or Frank's *Virgin Spain* with the same insolent half-attentiveness that is due to the historical generalizations of an amiable newspaper correspondent'.[120] In dark times, radical retreat to the classics was necessary to preserve civilization itself.

Mumford continued, in his Blashfield Address:

> Always a few stray poets and philosophers were conscious of our growing predicament, Kierkegaard, an Emily Dickinson, a Peirce, a Rilke, a Kafka. These people guarded their works from the public eye, distrusted the processes of publicity, preferred to give themselves freely in letters to their friends or in even more solitary communion [...].[121]

Mumford's cry 'let us not fear silence for it can be eloquent', with its distinctively Carlylean ring, was a utopian call in an overwhelmingly noisy world.[122]

A year later at Stanford, Mumford amplified his literature and ethics theme to the university's alumni. The naïve, he argued, do not:

> realize that it was precisely this prosperous, luxurious, money-ridden civilization, with the upper class delights and pleasures and rivalries described by Proust, with the scientific improvements for the treatment of disease so felicitously described by Thomas Mann, with the advertisement and publicity slogans parodied by Joyce and regurgitated by his hero, Bloom, it was the very world which through its adoration of the machine and its contempt for man ushered in the present interregnum of terrorism and nihilism.[123]

Mumford here simply asserts the connection between a disengaged ruling class, an abstracting mechanical view of the world and the reproduction of mass commercial propaganda, adding up to pure modernistic negativity. He does not argue for Proust's exemplary insight into the radical complexity and blindness of the interior narrative of personal consciousness, that haunting and terrorized existential space that suggests a universality of human experience beyond class, economic status, historical moment and gender. Nor does he look at the inertia which is as much cultural, psychological and indeed spiritual as it is mechanical in *The Magic Mountain*. The conjunctures of these typical issues became clearer in his essentially literary project *The Condition of Man*.

Mumford's preference for literature did lead him to downgrade other generic discourses; it was the discourse by which others could directly or obliquely be measured. His rage against mass culture was not so much that of a reactionary traditionalist arguing for an untouchable canon of classics, rather it exhibited a profound conviction of the ubiquitous threat to the life of the mind itself. The whole process of reflection, creation, and communication had been defiled by the acceptance of considerations altogether extraneous to the life of the spirit: 'The word has ceased to be sacred, and the writer takes his own function at the same low value that is placed upon it in the market place; if he conceals his self-contempt with flippancy, he deceives no-one, least of all himself'.[124]

Ethics, Private Life and the Irrational

The fight of deadness and inertia versus life and activity, in Blakean terms, were at the heart of Mumford's ethics. As a young man Mumford, doubtless like many men of his generation and our own, had agonized over the problems of desire, personal behaviour and managing the life of work and family. In a letter to Geddes he argued that sexual abstinence was overrated and a simplistic dodge which shelved rather than confronted the nature of desire. He wondered whether life-long marriage should be a permanent legal necessity. Mumford also, and this is most interesting given his later animadversions against homosexuality, as a young man once noted in a letter to Geddes that while finding the 'third alternative' repugnant, he thought it a lot less repugnant than abstinence.[125] His reviews show him wondering whether sexual and emotional failure produced compensatory achievement in the works of Havelock Ellis and T.S. Eliot. At the same time it is true he had in fact deeply reactionary tendencies in terms of his 'Kinder, Kirche, Küche' approach to women, noting approvingly in 1945 that for women undergraduates 'babies and family life have become important again'.[126] Betty Friedan was to analyse that post-war shift in less glowing terms in her classic work *The Feminine Mystique* in 1959.

The critic's charge of mysticism presumably starts here, but there are deeper questions to ask within the simple charge of mysticism and which concern the relation of erotic to religious life. Bataille argued for the profoundly anti-philosophical and anti-rational nature of this conjuncture in both the interior life of the individual and in the more ritualistic aspects of social life. Neither Mumford nor his critics have ventured into these areas. Nonetheless, Mumford's plea for the inclusion of 'babies and family life' in the more religious dimensions of his organicist view of the world was not entirely reactionary. Marxist rationalism, like certain aspects of Christian doctrine and institutional monasticism, downplayed family life. Capitalism had broken up the family in terms of de-localizing employment, making accommodation prohibitively expensive in developed countries, and reducing it to a minimalist or atomized membership.

That Mumford leaned to a 'religious' advocacy of the family is not in doubt. That such a position might invite hypocrisy in practice cannot be challenged. His relationship with his son was, for example, was a great deal more problematic than the touching and moving tribute to their life together in *Green Memories* implied. The text offered a story that selected the incidents for a generous mourning. That in itself was an act of imaginative contrition. Mumford's advocacy of the 'family' was not allied to fascist propaganda or suppression of democracy, advocating 'the American way of life', or repressive sexual ethics and right-wing politics.

What Mumford did understand was the nature of unpredictability and irrationality in both the personal and the public life, and the need to acknowledge that unpredictability. Mumford understood the 'uses of disorder 'as much as a Richard Sennett. Here is Sennett on city planning, Mumford's own field:

> Because the metropolitan planning persuasion is so naïve in its assumptions of what constitutes the good city, because it is an expression of adolescent refusal to deal with the world in all its complexity and pain, the escalation of urban conflict into violence must inevitably result, for the planners are not really concerned with mediating actual human behaviour or providing fields of unpredictable interaction. The essence of the purification mechanism is a fear of losing control.[127]

Dealing with the world in all its 'complexity and pain' and acknowledging that people lose control, for Sennett as for Mumford, is a view of human behaviour that invites a more generous ethics and more imaginative practice. It is why, in a contentious article, Mumford said he understood the Italian crowd's lynching of Mussolini.[128] To understand the nature of human behaviour in all its irrational blackness and endless capacity for revenge and cruelty was, for Mumford, a possible first step for that tragic view of the self, needed in any act of imaginative compassion. Here again literature was more helpful than academic ethics. He cited Whitman (and his Quaker conscience) on the Reign of Terror in France.

> Pale, silent, stern, what could I say to that long accrued retribution?
> Could I wish humanity different?
> Could I wish the people made of wood and Stone?
> Or that there be no justice in destiny or time?[129]

Whatever the crimes of those who seized power in France, leading ultimately to Napoleonic autocracy, there was no question that history should spare the absolutism of the Ancien Régime from responsibility for the historical struggle for power in France, anymore than the Stalinist Terror in turn should not be analysed to some degree in relation to the habits and infrastructure of centuries-old Tsarist violence and corruption. Anti-democratic tradition adapts to most declared ideologies.

Germany, the Allies and the Ethics of War

Turning from irrationality in relation to the private self, it is instructive to look at Mumford's efforts to describe the most burning question of his time: the 'irrational' behaviour of Nazi Germany. Mumford had long had an interest in Germany and he had had a distrust of its political practices and its imperial ambitions from before the period of the Kaiser, through the period of the Weimar Republic to the rise of the Nazi Party. He had had a Guggenheim Fellowship in Munich during 1932, visiting examples of model factories, town planning and contemporary architecture in Berlin and Frankfurt.

Mumford was well read in German literature and he had not only a good knowledge of well-known German writers from Lessing, Herder, Schiller, Goethe and Hegel through to Weber, Sombart, Spengler and Mann, but a wide knowledge of German scholarship in the areas of architecture, city planning, historical development, economics, cultural theory, theories of state, history and social theory. While it was Geddes who had made the camera an indispensable instrument of town planning and the regional survey, Georg Hirth's six-volume *Kulturgeschichtliches Bilderbuch aus drei Jahrhunderten* (1899–1901) was certainly influential in the use of pictorial documentation in Mumford's own work. His meditations in *The Condition of Man* on the representations of women's bodies and fashion were almost certainly encouraged by Paul Schultze-Naumburg's *Die Kultur des weiblichen Körpers als Grundlage der Frauenkleidung* (1901), thus demonstrating that current academic obsessions with 'the body', visual and otherwise, have a long prehistory. From 1925 to 1930 Mumford was American correspondent for *Die Form* and as a lecturer in the Geneva School of International Studies in the 1920s he met many German scholars and students.

Mumford's most extended work on Germany, *The Passage Back*, is an imaginary set of letters to Germans which reflect on German 'character'. Mumford's attempt here to characterize a post-Webernian theory of cultural influence on political behaviour by way of fictional letters is bad to the point of artistic and intellectual embarrassment. Mumford, the sensitive and imaginative critic of literature, was incapable of writing a good fictional text. It is hard to know whether an incapacity to master the form or an almost overwhelming post-Holocaust rage is the chief culprit. Nonetheless, they are worth examining because they show the limitations of Mumford's 'symbolic' technique. 'Personality' is reciprocally linked to essentialist cultural values which then over-determine a kind of political fatality. Mumford, it must be said, was hardly unique in this kind of exercise at the time. Most famously it has been continued, with considerably more irony and flair, in the fiction of Thomas Pynchon whose satiric mode also inevitably invites a fatalistic set of cultural over-determinations, though these are brilliantly deployed for black humour and satire. At times, Mumford's characterization of the Germans resembles Pynchon's reductionist, folksy psychological and cultural essences of Grimm-like fairy-tale characters offering explanations of Nazi psychology.[130] Whereas Pynchon's Spenglerian fatalisms and sense of the technological abyss have the advantage of humour and brilliantly expose the hyperreality of the so-called post-modernist world, Mumford's epistolary stories woefully lack skill and wit.

Thus in the first fictionalized 'letter' to Frau Z., Mumford recalls his 1932 meeting with Herr Z., who had shown him Buxtehude's organ in the Marienkirche in Lübeck:

> our tour became a sort of postscript to *Buddenbrooks* [...] but even that summer it was obvious that your husband lacked any militant faith in democracy, no matter how he still felt about socialism [...] in other words, Herr Z. believed in democracy in the way your great 'liberal' sociologist, Max Weber, believed in, as reported in his interview with Ludendorff: the election of an authoritarian regime.[131]

Quite apart from the *lumpen* style and irritating tone of self-righteousness, not to mention the brutality of the address to a wife whose husband has just presumably disappeared in the war, Mumford's attempt to characterize Buxtehude's organ as an aesthetic fig-leaf for an authoritarian personality runs into more problems than Wagner and the Nazis in terms of logic and causality. Mumford's notes for *The Passage Back* show he had read Wagner's 'Erkenne dich selbst' in the *Bayreuther Blätter* for February and March in 1881. Wagner, who cannot be forgiven for his *Das Judenthum in der Musik* any more than he can be uniquely responsible for Hitler being obsessed with it, had loaded onto the Jews his hatred of modernity, a modernity that was the polar opposite of the world of spiritual 'medieval' values he had dramatized in *Parsifal*. The appalling irony is that while Mumford also revered the medieval synthesis as a critical utopian model against which modernity would be judged, he reversed the charge, loading onto the Germans all the Spenglerian modernity that Wagner had associated with the Jews. In *The Condition of Man* he articulated a common view: 'Wagner's music sounded the *leitmotiv* of his conscious resurrection of barbarism: his written political testament left an estate to future Ludendorffs and Hitlers. In the lion's den of Wagner's youthful disciple, Nietzsche, with his cult of the superman, the stinking hyenas of Nazism already lurked.'[132] The view was commonplace at the time. It was also oversimplified and shoddy.

The pianist Daniel Barenboim has argued that Wagner's anti-Semitism was a way of challenging the less musically intense and more simplistic world of Mendelssohn who, as an assimilated German, had seen Christianity as a religious stage that followed on progressively from Judaism. Many middle-class Jews thought that they had assimilated into a music-loving Christian German culture via religion, music and the arts. Arendt was to give that view short shrift in *The Origins of Totalitarianism*. The arts, like Christian retreat, may enable life to survive in dark times, but they are a precarious refuge from power politics. To disengage the classics from contemporary life is to do precisely what the great classic writers never did. To 'retreat' to a fantasized world of classics is an act of fundamental bad faith. It is to simplify them, to cut off their past and future, for they yield their riches the more the contemporary world is understood and engaged with. The dialogue is both ways in a pattern that interpenetrates the past with the present and the future.

Further characterizing German socialism as inherently authoritarian and of a piece with 'German' politics, Mumford's account lacks any specificity in terms of actual politics (the aftermath of the murder of Rosa Luxemburg for example) or of the specific weaknesses of the ideology and practice of German socialism at the time. He also ignores the effect of the ruthlessness of Hitler's Brownshirts, the Allied economic squeeze on Germany and a host of other factors. Mumford was even to dismiss these factors elsewhere. Placing Weber in the ineffectual liberal camp in terms of his politics is certainly not to be questioned but if he were dealing with 'ideas' and personality then surely Weber's subjectivist and cultural revision of the analysis of capitalism might have served rather than opposed Mumford's own position. In short, Mumford was all over the place with this kind of exercise.

To the decadence of the Weimar Republic Mumford adds, in further letters, French surrealism, Rilke's lyrics and James Joyce. What is interesting here is that Mumford's attack on modernism courts a familiar common-sense anti-Continental literary cultural conservatism which has been deadly in England, and corrupting in the United States. A crude nationalism involving some kind of normative Anglo-American centre is the danger here: 'For all his boasted courage Nietzsche never wrote such an indictment of specifically German weakness as the mild-mannered Matthew Arnold wrote of British weaknesses in *Culture and Anarchy*.'[133] Mumford's own problematic mentor, Henry Adams, was less than enamoured of Arnold's 'mildness'.[134] Mumford continued that without Milton's *The Tenure of Kings and Magistrates* and Paine's *Common Sense*, alongside Thoreau's *Civil Disobedience* and Carlyle's *Past and Present*, Germany had no chance of being civilized. It would have been interesting to know how many of these books had been read by wartime American and British politicians of any stripe. It is curious that in terms of comparative 'civilization', despite all these advantages 'Britain' managed to submit its industrial working class to savage and brutal conditions for more than 150 years, slaughter millions in imperial wars of conquest and go on killing them: two million were about to starve to death in Bengal as Mumford was writing.

To lay the Nazi terror at the feet of Kant's anticlericalism or Fichte's idealism or indeed the failure of German Christians to act, as Mumford does at one point, is to substitute shallow cultural gossip for analysis. His statement in one letter, 'You will seek Bergson rather than Schopenhauer, Emerson rather than Nietzsche, Goethe rather than Spengler, Jesus rather than Wotan', is simply arrogant and silly. Its anti-intellectual binary dogmatisms is the death of any serious thought. One might note Bergson's right-wing proclivities, Melville's satire on Emerson's general neglect of the nature of evil in *Pierre*, Goethe's ambiguous love of the French revolution, and almost two thousand years of state warfare in the name of Christ. Mumford's swift passage from essentialist dogmas of cultural belief and simplistic literary manifestation to political activity is untenable in this attempt at epistolary fiction.

Yet here and there, there are glimpses of more accurate insights or at least questions. Germany had after all disturbed the peace of Europe three times between 1870 and 1945, driving an arms race and the globalization of violence. Everyone, not only the Germans, was desperate for an explanation. Mumford's attack on liberal silence is not altogether off the mark, his relentless exposure of the acquiescence of the German population (as against the thesis that only a few were culpable) in the Nazi terror is accurate. Nor is the influence of Spengler entirely to be neglected as a litmus paper of academic fatalism, at least as it might paralyse more active thought and action.

Mumford's political views on Germany are suggested in two articles for the *Saturday Review* of August 1945 and March 1946. In the first, Mumford reviewed in some political detail the Kaiser's drive for war before 1914 and attacked the apologists who laid the blame on Russia. He favourably invoked Veblen's survey of imperial Germany against Sombart's characterization of German 'herodom' as against 'the grubby merchants' of Britain, adding 'if anyone thinks that the germs of Nazism were incubated in a beer-cellar in Munich, and were a product of the chaos that followed upon the peace of Versailles, he shows that he has not even an elementary knowledge of the German mind'.[135] He doubted that Germany was driven to abandon democracy by the actions of other nations, noting that secret remilitarization had started in 1927. He noted that none of the writers on Germany whose books he was reviewing dwelt on the fact that 'Ossietzky, in 1927, was sentenced to prison for revealing the secret militarization of Germany at a time when Germany, under Stresemann, was pretending to carry out a pacific and conciliatory policy.' Mumford further noted in 1932, the entire burden of reparations was lifted, at a time when the Germans had paid, over a period of fourteen years, two billion dollars less than Keynes, the bitter critic of the financial peace terms, had estimated they were capable of paying.'[136] Mumford's subjective experience in Germany had also not given him much faith in the instinctive love of democracy in the German middle classes.

In the second article, given that the war was then definitively over, he argued the incompatibility between legally judging the single murder and mass extermination, and against Burke's dictum that 'you cannot indict a nation'. Instead he advocated what in fact transpired, 'confinement' for a number of years. Previously he had argued, in a series of lectures in Stanford, that punishment should be according to indictment and should embrace the entire hierarchy of the Nazi Party. He advocated complete disarmament for the foreseeable future and Germany's temporary exclusion from international life. For a period at least that was certainly just.

Mumford's ethical and legal critique at its best, though, also extended to the Allies. In 1947 he reflected on and condemned the copying of the fascist totalitarian theory of warfare, 'terror-bombing civilians and seeking the complete obliteration not of military targets but of whole cities', and continued: 'With ordinary bombs as well as atomic bombs we turned our own war into unrestricted extermination, though but a few short years before we had recoiled with proper horror at the savagery of the German attack on Warsaw, Rotterdam, or Coventry.'[137] He further criticized the establishment of the 'veto' in the new United Nations in the interests of a hypocritical 'sovereignty', the too-soon ending of Lend-Lease aid to America's European allies, the systematic suppression of information and the political irresponsibility of the so-called free press in America in refusing to discuss the more serious questions the war had thrown up.

But as an erstwhile historian of technology it was the question of the atomic bomb that was the key issue for Mumford.[138] It seemed to him the final madness of that abstract mechanical thinking and technical arrogance whose course he had traced in many books and articles from the early medieval period onwards. It was the ultimate negation of everything he had valued and fought for throughout his considerable writing career. Like Dwight Macdonald, Mumford was appalled that the series of acts that led to its production should have secretly engaged of the lives of ordinary working men and women in laboratories, factories and business. The destruction of human civilization was carried through by individuals 'under the solemn conviction that they are normal responsible people, living sane lives, and working for reasonable ends'.[139] As late as 1982 Mumford noted the Nobel Peace Prize winner Alva Myrdal's criticism in the *New York Times* of the effects of the Cold War: 'Our civilization is in the process not only of being militarized, but also being brutalized.' On a clipping of Myrdal's criticism preserved in the archives Mumford in the handwriting of old age, has scrawled across the top: 'Note: I said this 3 weeks after the first atom bomb was used and spent the next five years in full advertisement and articles, trying to awaken my lethargic contemporaries.'[140] He did indeed say, and do, just that.

Mumford understood that the Cold War, dominated by the Soviet Union and the United States, showed that when it came to power politics and technological gigantism the two countries had many things in common, beyond ideology and beyond advertised political difference. Together, in the crucible of the Second World War, they had shaped a new world. That world is best summed up in a remarkable letter from Henry Miller's friend Michael Fraenkel to Victor Serge of 21 March 1945:

> When you cross the Mexican border into the United States, the one fact that impinges itself upon your consciousness more forcibly than any other is the fact of the American world-change; you feel you are in the presence of something that exercises a terrific world effect. *It is the effect not so much of people as of things, the power of things, of the weight, mass, dimension of things.* You feel that it is something that is shaping the destiny of the world, setting, if you like, the tone of the world, from all corners of the earth, is responding to it, responding to it mightily, overwhelmingly. You think at this point of Russia, of the mighty power it stands for, and at once Russia's power merges in your mind with America's power: *the power of things rather than men, things rather than ideas or sentiments; the power of numbers, statistics, etc. Russia meets America in the anonymity of men and the emergence of the statistical thing.* Russia and America meet in setting the world tone. Between the United States and Russia, the shape of the world for the next one hundred or two hundred years is being fixed.[141]

Unable to sign up to the legitimating discourses of communism or capitalist technocracy, or to subscribe to a Whig view of history, Mumford's ideological stance is difficult to state in simple terms. He did not present his arguments in terms of definable concepts. His 'position', for better or worse, depended on the generic nature of his writing. Like William James in *The Principles of Psychology*, Mumford often argued by negating received wisdom rather than by offering solutions. The nearest he ever got to defining a position was through his theories of organicism and 'dynamic balance'. Even here, their deployment in specific arguments were to be more fruitful than the abstract propositions themselves. It is this issue that will be examined next.

II

Organicism and the Dynamic Balance

The words 'organic' and 'organicism' are among the most treacherous in literary and cultural criticism. Nonetheless, the origins of Mumford's terms are there in English romanticism, in the poetry of Coleridge, the philosopher poet, and in the vitalist-mechanist debates of the nineteenth century. One critic has even called Mumford's vision of architecture a 'Coleridgean version of functionalist modernism'.[1] German *Lebensphilosophie* stemming from Goethe is another key tradition for Mumford. Its twentieth-century successors in the English-speaking world are well known: D'Arcy Thompson, Patrick Geddes, Dorothy Emmet and Alfred North Whitehead. Thompson was a one of Geddes's younger colleagues at the University of Dundee. The concept of society as an organism, as critics have shown, came from many directions. Emmet argued in the context of a discussion of Whitehead's organic philosophy which commentators occasionally cite in relation to Mumford, that the origins of the concept probably go back to Locke.[2] The main difficulty is not so much with the word 'organism' as with society. The 'social' theorists from Comte onwards were gathering in the wake (in both senses of the term) of the apparent failure of seventeenth and eighteenth-century political theorists over the terror of the French revolution. Pattern, structure, custom (cooking, games, dress and ritual), race, artefacts, art, the slowly-shifting modes of family life, kinship, human evolution, sexual behaviour and the long patterns of law were now studied by way of this seismic shift of emphasis from an intellectual challenge to established power in the name of theoretical freedoms, defined in relation to the legitimations or not of kingship, to describing the effect of governance in any given historical or social group with an emphasis on stability and security.

Philosophers, pure historians, political philosophers and theologians were being replaced by anthropologists, psychologists, social workers and health experts, all armed with a dazzling array of statistics and quantitative data. The shift in the late nineteenth century was given a boost by the rise of the professionalized university and the slow beginnings of mass education. Philosophical Marxism would struggle in vain to focus the social theorists' attention on the deployment of political power, even though Marx praised Darwin, Engels and Henry Morgan. In an age of imperialism, what endured was more interesting (and more convenient) than what changed, it diverted attention from the breakneck speed of the changes imperialism was effecting on a daily basis in Africa and elsewhere. Spatial patterns of slow temporal developments rather than the immediate times of political activity were the focus of human attention. Two world wars hardly changed the situation.

So 'society as organism' already ruled out attention to certain things. The 'conservative radicalism' of Mumford was tempered by certain political constraints given the discourses from which he emerged. So disengaged were the new disciplines from considerations of ideology or power that 'organicism' as a concept could be used indifferently by left or right. Certainly there was no obvious relation between 'organicism' and any political ideology or position.[3] Without losing sight of these issues, the much-discussed main outlines of the nature of

Mumford's 'organicism' can be easily formalized. From Geddes he derived that loosely boundaried concept of 'wholeness' of the Regional Survey Movement. Mumford himself noted that Geddes converted Le Play's typical nineteenth-century trinity of folk, work and place to organism, function and environment.[4] Politically, Geddes was far to the left of Le Play but his terminological shift abstracted the presence of the person and the place even further.

Few have also noted that there is a contradiction between inclusiveness and region in terms of wholeness. The relationship between regional and national policy and the local activity and the generality of the movement of capital in political terms were certainly obscured in the typical analyses which were highly local and visual. Diagrams and photographs articulated visually the pattern of the effects of the interaction of geography and historical and technological behaviour within a circumscribed area. Historic agency as a narrative was expunged. Given capitalist and industrial development on a world-wide scale, no 'region' could be completely self-governing or 'local' without closing its eyes to the brutal fact of reciprocity between micro- and macro-economics. The worst effect of capitalist development was to be that no local peoples living traditional lives who had the misfortune to live in regions that had abundant resources – from water to minerals to fossil fuels – were safe from the insatiable appetites of corporate capitalism on a global scale. The aggregations of visual effect or 'evidence', combined with the ubiquitous biological analogies of 'development', often obscured if not obliterated the question of agency in the emerging 'ecological' movement. Association, common requirements, environmental conditions, function, structural interactions and interdisciplinarity all became key phrases but few asked who was responsible for what and when.

In attempting to ally Mumford's 'organic' theory with contemporary critical theory Eugene Rochberg-Halton, discussing the ubiquitous thematics of 'the body' in academic work, speaks of it as 'a conceptualized and etherealized body modelled on the text' as if the flesh was made word and dwelt among us. It is against this stark background that Mumford's organic, purposive, bio-semiotic body stands, a human body created out of the rich interplay of ritual action and symbolic communication with biology.' The author then goes on to argue that hence Mumford might be best situated with the philosophical anthropologists Arthur Koestler or Suzanne Langer.[5] Such commentary is at once enlightening and obscuring, though here one is grateful for the wit, rare enough in the contemporary academy. The key problem is 'bio-semiotic'. The hyphen valorizes a conjuncture that, with a magic visual gesture, obliterates at one stroke, all the classic philosophical problems of consciousness, nature and the symbolic order. One hardly needs to invoke Foucault to understand the irrevocable split between language and the world that occurred with the scientific renaissance, not to mention the classic mind–body problem that will hardly be resolved with a hyphen.

Mumford's debt to the Regional Survey Movement has been more than adequately covered by the commentators. They have noted that the early twentieth-century regional vision was not just a plan for a 'fourth migration' out of the city but 'a mode of thinking and method of procedure', a kind of interdisciplinary mental space for considering the synthetic patters of housing, transport, land use, investment, exploitation and natural geography.[6] They have also noted the trace of the New England vernacular tradition in Mumford's own regional vision, his emphasis on localized knowledge and his commitment to decentralization. Mumford's debts to the French regionalist tradition have been diligently traced.[7] They have not so often noted the silliness to which the excesses of the organicist conceit can sometime descend. Here is Mumford sounding like the most rabid of conservative and crass male-chauvinist ideologues: 'He who has dropped a seed into a garden or into a woman's womb is ready to fight for the right of that seed to grow and fulfil itself.'[8] With unconscious humour, Mumford's enthusiasm links cabbages and babies in epic style for his '*culture* of the family', never mind that it is women, at least in the case of babies, who supply the pre-fertilized seeds. (Mumford's friend the British town planner Sir Frederick Osborn, lecturing to a Town and Country Planning Association lunch meeting in 1942, informed his audience that 'motherhood is the most important occupation of all', in full Mumfordian organicist style, but ended the lecture with a paean to the America's greatest gay poet, Walt Whitman, who had of course with perhaps parallel plausibility claimed to have fathered many children.[9])

So Mumford's organicism has to be read on multiple levels. It is there in the very depths of his synthetic imagination and in his insistence on interdisciplinarity. It is a negotiating position between the increasingly Stalinist–Marxist left and the mechanistic optimism of the American right. It is a means of continuing the traditions of British and American romantic thought. It is hence there as part of his ideology and his metaphysics, of his view of the person and the structure of society, of both the radicalism and conservatism of his 'ecological' take on the world and last, but not least, as part of his exuberance and love of life.

In negative terms, Mumford's organicism risks the treachery as well as the creativity of analogy itself. It can risk, in rhetorical comparison, a too easy similitude over a creative difference. At the other end of the scale of course is the poetic act itself, essentially transformatory, operating in radical contradiction and producing new meaning. In another sense, organicism, while insisting on that wholeness of the world and the mutuality of all living organisms, also risks a facile sense of correspondence between natural process and human consciousness and activity. Marxists, like capitalists, saw 'nature' as something to subdued and overcome. The existentialists never ceased their protest against the absurdity of death. Mumford himself never confronted the difficulty of Tennyson's mid-nineteenth-century anguish:

'So careful of the type?' but no.
From scarped cliff and quarried stone
She cries, 'A thousand types are gone:
I care for nothing, all shall go [...]'[10]

At the same time to lose entirely a correspondence theory of nature and human activity was also to lose the important insight that, in Charles Olson's words, we act in nature acting upon ourselves.[11] 'Either', said Murray Bookchin, 'we succumb to a heavy-handed dualism that harshly separates the natural from the social, or fall into a crude reductionism that dissolves the one into the other.'[12]

Mumford's theory of 'dynamic balance' also sits uneasily with his apocalyptic call for a radically renewed person: a secularist version of the Christian obligation to die to the world in order to be born again. Hence although Mumford feels political revolution upsets dynamic balance (the reaction is too severe), it appears it is necessary at the ethical level. Leo Marx is right to suggest that the 'Emersonian' view that nothing can be changed unless all is changed is way of avoiding the real world.[13] On the other hand, the self in the rhetoric of Christian transformation, no less than in the rhetoric of Marxism, the one converted, the other politicized, may conceal a frightening authoritarianism and lead to the anti-democratic apologetics of the 'saved' and 'chosen'. The narrative eschatology of communism and Christianity placed closure conveniently far off in time: whether in the last judgement or in the dictatorship of the proletariat.

Dynamic balance also sits uneasily with the concept of naïve action. The latter is necessary according to Mumford because, in any case, we are so often robbed of the meaning of our actions. Mumford quoted Krishna in tackling just this question to an audience of Harvard students in 1941: 'The only thing that a human being can settle is whether he should fight [...] the issues of our life, the issues of our fighting are not within our own hands.' He continued: 'We must face the fact that success cannot be guaranteed, that the complete fulfilment of our dreams cannot be guaranteed, and yet the necessity for action remains just the same.'[14] This quasi-Calvinist approach to the exercise of free will within fatality lacks the radicalism and sophistication of Sartrean ethics or Marxist praxis. It is particularly difficult to reconcile with a philosophy of organism in the sense that it gives few clues as to how we judge the good within the flux of organically balanced dynamisms. What is missing is any emphasis on the reflective judgement as a moment in praxis.

This raises the question of the relation of dynamic balance to temporality: human, historical and cosmic. In *The Condition of Man*, in terms of the grand narrative, Mumford will only grant it to a precarious moment in the medieval period. Utopian critical modelling in fact suspends the medieval period in time. Mumford has no theory of how the stillness of metaphor might relate to the temporality of its narrative context, but he often suggests that relationship through the poetic nature of his own prose. At this stage of the argument, the most that can be said is that Mumford's 'dynamic balance' resists the banalities of 'homeostasis', the Parsonian metaphysic that was also derived by analogy from the biological world and which, as applied to society, legitimated a perpetually oscillating status quo in which human agency was lost in structure and statistics and in which the grand panoramic balancing moments were largely fictions in the minds of sociology professors. Whatever its failings as a theory and the risk of its attenuation as a rhetoric of uplift, Mumford's phrase took due account of the person in danger in relation both to nature and civil life while like Melville's Catskill eagle it provided encouragement to keep on the wing in both disaster and triumph. Melville's image points to a poetic figure and narrative in which a received ethics or a political ideology are shown to be limited in their power to interpret the world.

Finally there is the question of organicism and causality. The question will lead ultimately to that of temporality and the issue of narrative itself. Here Sartre is exemplary for he invokes and suspends the Marxist judgement in the tentativeness of a query in a comment on Mumford's *Technics and Civilization*:

> In his excellent book Mumford says: 'Since the steam engine *requires* constant care on the part of the stoker and engineer, steam power was more efficient in large units than in small ones [...]. Thus steam power *fostered* the *tendency* toward large industrial plants.' I do not whish to question the soundness of these observations, but simply to note the strange language – language which has been ours since Marx and which we have no difficulty in understanding – in which a single proposition links finality to necessity so indissolubly that it is impossible to tell any longer whether it is man or machine which is a practical project. We all feel that his language is correct but also realize that we cannot explain or justify this feeling.[15]

To open up Sartre's perceptive comments a little, the problem lies precisely with the words he italicizes, for these encapsulate Mumford's philosophy of organicism in all its richness and contradiction. The personification of the inanimate object in 'requires' gives the machine an intentionality it clearly, at first glance, does not possess. And yet, to borrow McLuhan's notion that every extension of the nervous system has a reciprocal action from margin to centre, there is a degree of reactive 'intentionality' which cannot be avoided. What we design has designs on us. Similarly 'tendency', which is used in more personal characterizations in French than it is in English ('*inclination amoureuse*' is the first definition *Le Petit Robert* gives), raises problems of fatality and specified drift with all its attendant teleological problems. At the same time, it describes the inertia of the way things set in motion escape human will; that rule of nobody in the corporate world of industrial capitalism. Finally, with 'foster', so characteristic of Mumford's language of organicism, the problem arises of what or who exactly is doing the fostering since the very word invites the idea of parenthood.

What is concealed in this ultimately fetishized proposition of mechanistic organic change is not only the obvious question of agency but that of the break between consciousness and the world, which offers the possibility of judgement in human praxis. Sartre, in his post-Hegelian revision of Marx, calls it the 'dialectical intelligibility' which offers the possibility of 'the negation of the undertaking.'[16] It is frequently difficult, however, to discover a 'dialectical intelligibility' in Mumford narrative of 'dynamic balance'. In the rest of the discussion these problems will be kept continuously in mind while not *a priori* ruling out what is achieved in spite of, or perhaps because of, the reduction of complexity. In much of Mumford's articulation of his organicist philosophy these difficulties are a continuous and permanent risk to the credibility of the argument. At the same time, the blindness is partly deliberate as Mumford's attempts to skirt round the simplistic materialist causalities of a historically reduced Marxist debate.

If the weakness of Mumford's deployment of his doctrine of organicism can be relatively easily exposed, there is at the same time a richness in its fundamentally analogically driven propositions. For example, the evolutionary thesis integral to Mumford's organicism and so problematic in Social Darwinist hands has its positive sides. Images of growth, renewal and the exuberant creativity of the life process are one example. But others come in more monitory fashion. Mumford's continual diatribe against unrestrained growth and gigantism invokes the analogy of species death through over-specialization, an incapacity for adaptation and the risk of gigantism.

Commenting on the Abercrombie Plan for London in 1945, Mumford observed: 'The uncontrolled growth of the big cities is as much an anti-vital process as the uncontrolled destructions of totalitarian warfare; they are both symptoms of a deeper disorder.'[17] The political analogy is problematic but the rhetoric is very effective. The 'deeper disorder', in almost Marxist terms, collates war- and peace-time behaviour in terms of qualitative cruelty to human beings. It also undervalues human needs in planning and design, insists on purely profit-driven 'efficiency' as the first-order priority and exhibits a mechanistic philosophy of power that underwrites what is ultimately an ethical failure of caring and imagination. Where the political analogy works is in underlining the violence of the failure and the transformation of quantitative gigantism, the limitless quantitative development of the profiteer, into qualitative nightmare.

Organicism and Time

The multiple intellectual practices signalled by Mumford as organicism and 'dynamic balance' also bring with them their own narratives of time, just as the evolutionary theory from which they are derived. Darwin's theory was ultimately a statistical one based on two unknown selective principles, spontaneous variation (the genetic code then suspected but unknown) and natural selection, which Darwin assumed to promote the new and preserve the living process as such, through group adaptation. There was enough of Hutton's open-ended infinity of time and Lyell's cyclical view of time left in it to pose a challenge to the finite linearity of Christian historical and eternal time. The 'life-time' of the human being seemed to shrink into inessentiality. Any sense of metaphysical safety depended on a God-like stance and a larger faith in the 'type' than in the person. Thus Geddes: 'For there is a larger view of Nature and Life, rebuilding of analysis into Synthesis, an integration of many solitary experiences into a large Experience, an exchange of the narrow window of the individual outlook for the open tower which overlooks college and city.'[18] Who actually encounters or feels 'a large Experience', and when, is rather problematic. Geddes of course had a tower in Edinburgh from the lofty heights of which he could survey the city landscape, and teach his students how to unpack the essentially visual structures of the cityscape with its momentarily visually arrested archeological, topographical, and historical evidence of human 'vitality'.

From this high panoramic view-point Geddes hoped 'to read the concrete tide-marks of history, to interpret the strata laid down by each period, which are the books called History, as the natural strata to the books of Geology.'[19] These kinds of observations were common-place in the high Victorian period. 'Tide-marks' and 'strata' are essentially temporal conceits. The grand temporal narrative (deriving from Comte in Geddes's case) tended to operate, like Marxist grand narrative, in threes, as did the more spatial, structuralist, narratives with their virtually static or very slow moving times. The fossil record both slowed down and lengthened the time of species, and brought with it not only a de-centering of the person in the long view of the life process but also memorialized the life processes of the past with a clear, if value-loaded, differentiation between failure and success. A quasi-forensic uncovering of *the layers* of the past could be spatially represented, like a map converting three dimensions into two. Depth and surface were as automatically and brilliantly allied as the cut glass of a Victorian chandelier. As for popular educated thinking: 'Every English curate', remarked Henry Adams sardonically, 'dabbled in geology and hunted for vestiges of Creation.'[20]

Two things were omitted in this imperial surveyor's view of the world. The first was the downgrading of the document in relation to the artefact. For before oral history and the kind of anthropology developed by Boas, in the document lay the struggles of the games of power (legal, religious, political, artistic and social) that the pure visuality of the trace could not immediately give. In the document lay clues to the very nature of the class and the economic and political contingencies behind the neat spatial categories of the regionalist and town planner.

The second omission, which is implied in the first, was the question of human agency. For while Geddes endlessly drew attention to the dynamic nature (spontaneity, purpose, organic change, renewal, loss) of the human drama and its inter-relatedness (in terms of temporal continuity, the operations of memory across time, generalized human co-operation), he failed to draw attention to the irrecoverable, the contingent, the particular and the political struggle, or to any sense of the individual's or the group's experience of social and political success or defeat, or to the absolute particular loss which marks every human life, given its inessentiality in the grand scheme of things.

It was a more complex view of time that was missing in Geddesian organicism. For this very reason Mumford distrusted Geddes's 'charts of life' and, as his later letters to Geddes show, he exhibited an increasing scepticism about his endless graphs. Not only did Mumford reject the view from the tower but he specifically raised the crucial problem of the representation of time in the organicist vision:

> Yet somehow time plays no part in his 'Chart of life': time is presented only in the person of the muse of History, history sporadically recorded, not history as lived, experienced, remembered. I cannot explain this oversight [...] But how impossible it is to express time in such spatial terms! It is only in the symbols of language and music, or – as Henri Bergson saw – in motion pictures that the flow of living experiences through time can be symbolized.[21]

At the heart of Mumford's work there will be always be a story of time. It will not only incorporate the Bergsonian psychological duration and a Braudelian *longue dureé*, but also present a view of history which is essentially a synthetic narrative of human history. In his own work, as Mumford himself said of Geddes in relation to his contemporaries, 'the plot thickens'.[22] He was quite explicit, in his critique of Geddes, that all the intellectual dazzle was useless unless one 'took one's time' for 'all organic activities take time.'[23] In his commentary on Geddes, Mumford summed up the whole of Ricoeur's project in a single crucial sentence: 'Without enlisting the arts of time, symbolized in language, one could not do justice to life itself or express more than a small part of its significance.'[24] For Mumford, 'Time and History, are strangely absent from Geddes's final "Chart of Life"'.[25]

Mumford had struggled with the problem from his first book. The temporalities of the 'organic world' and those of human history would be difficult to reconcile. Writing to Geddes about the structure and pattern of *The Golden Day*, Mumford pondered how the larger rhythms of history coalesced with the minor ones. The larger rhythms of history might be Comtean stages or oscillations between intuitive idealistic and pragmatic thought, historical piety and practicality. How to map oscillation onto linearity was to be one of Mumford's major problems. To the degree that he followed Ruskin and Morris he was to invoke a founding moment of synthesis for a chronology in the 'medieval synthesis'; to the extent he followed Whitehead he saw 'a founding negation' in the scientific revolution; and to the extent he followed the tragic visions of literature, or the religious historical dynamics of Toynbee, he would see a crypto-Hegelian flux of the negation of the negation in the permanent crisis of modernity.

Having difficulty with one of Geddes's diagrams, Mumford complained of the different types of explanation that they mixed up by sleight of hand and eye. Rather like looking at the boxes on a contemporary management chart, it was not at all obvious where a potentially narrativized discourse of power lay. For example, how on the subject of war, Mumford asked Geddes, does the continuity of the anthropological traditions of the hunter spirit rate as an explanation in relation to the habits of mind developed by science and technology? How does a description of time-bound habits square with an analysis of a specific problem? How does a logical analysis combine with a historical one? Mumford was clear: 'In verbal explanation you get the benefit of alternatively using one or the other, as seems more profitable; but in a rational description one cannot slip so easily from one category to another.'[26] Mumford's 'poetic' prose was to be a very serious answer to the aporias and limits of conventional historical narrative discourse, the philosopher's temporal analytics and the abstractions of the sociologist.

Mumford thought very hard about historical narrative. He had read, for example, Gooch's *History and Historians of the Nineteenth Century* (1913), one of those very few academic books that are still worth reading almost one hundred years after they are published. In it Gooch had brilliantly analysed and differentiated the different styles of German historical writing from the romantics to Ranke and his successors. Drawing on the book, for example, Mumford observed: 'Treitschke once dismissed Riehl as a "historian of the salon," and the reason is plain, for with Riehl the place, the people, the work, the home, the industries, the arts, the folk-music, and so forth are in the foreground, and the political organization enters no more into his history than it does in the life of anyone who is not a functionary of the State.'[27] Mumford tentatively suggested to Geddes that Riehl might show a way of combining Le Play and Comte, that is, regionality and long human historical phases.

Unpromising as this sounds, Mumford extracts a moment which does precisely that. He wrote to Geddes that Riehl 'predicted that freedom would be gone in America when the forests were destroyed; and the beginnings of imperialism here do indeed date from the passing of the frontier in 1890, and the exhaustion of the Appalachian forests.' From two right-wing French commentators Mumford insouciantly and 'poetically' extracts a crypto-Marxist explanation of American imperialism. This example has been chosen not to show whether Mumford was right or wrong in detail (clearly American imperialism has multiple causes) but to show how Mumford's writing can bypass received and fixed positions in order to narrate an illuminating chronological conjuncture in which the most heterogeneous ideas are 'yoked by violence together' and which might fail a strictly analytic test.[28]

All Mumford's work must therefore be looked at in terms of its language, the essentially poetic way in which Mumford takes on problems of historical narrative and philosophies of time. In the 1940s the key work is *The Condition of Man*. It is a book written under the emotional pressure of war and extends the issues and concerns of the two preceding works of the 1930s: *Technics and Civilization* and *The Culture of Cities*. The three were conceived as a trilogy. The agonized memory of one appalling war and the premonition and enactment of another splits the world of Geddes from the world of Mumford. Five years after the end of the Great War, Mumford wrote to Geddes: 'There is a real barrier to understanding between us in the fact that you grew to manhood in a period of hope, when people looked forward with confidence to the great world spinning forever down the ringing grooves of time; whereas I spent my whole adolescence with a generation which, in large part, had no future [...].'[29] For Mumford the question of a human future was seriously in doubt even twenty-seven years before the atomic bomb exploded at Hiroshima.

The shadow of an absence of the future will haunt the entire temporality of the trilogy of works. In *Technics and Civilization* Mumford began his great critique of the general effect of science and scientific thought on human civilization. While the book was organized lineally from the mechanized routines of the monastery to the challenge to mechanism he discovered in the nineteenth-century biologists, the argument is non-linear in the sense that each phase is characterized by cyclical sets of analogous problems. Mumford's synchronic and ethical sense of the deep abstract questions of time and space and human value, from organized culture to metaphysics, characterized the shift from wood to iron, the development of transport systems, the growth of the utilitarian mind, the increase of power with its legitimating mindsets, the effects of print and the shift from steam to electricity.

The very opening chapter is a meditation on time: 'The clock, not the steam engine, is the key machine of the modern industrial age.'[30] Mumford's whole concept of organism was pitted against the deleterious effects of this seismic shift in human sensibility:

> The shepherd measures from the time the ewes lambed; the farmer measures back to the day of sowing or forward to the harvest: if growth has its own duration and regularities, behind it are not simply matter and motion but the facts of development: in short, history. And while mechanical time is strung out in a succession of mathematically isolated instants, organic time – what Bergson calls duration – is cumulative in its effects. Though mechanical time can, in a sense, be speeded up or run backward, like the hands of a clock or the images of a moving picture, organic time moves in only one direction – through the cycle of birth, growth, development,

> decay, and death – and the past that is already dead remains present in the future that has still to be born.[31]

'Organic time', cyclic and mapped onto an existential sense of birth and death, is further given an almost Husserlian sense of extension, a remaining present, a longing, lingering intuition of a complex metaphysics of the continuity of time. Throughout *Technics and Civilization* Mumford wrote variations on this theme. The canonical hours synchronized men as well as the individual soul, and hence always involved issues of power. In perspective, the measured space of the picture reinforced the measured time of the clock to present a 'new ideal network of space and time' in which events took place.[32] Its coordinated framework involved a theoretical separation of time and space.

In medieval culture, Mumford argued, there was hardly a difference in reality between the dropping of a ship below the horizon or a demon down a chimney: 'There was no mystery about the past from which they had emerged, no speculation as to the future toward which they were bound.'[33] Safely locked in the world of miracle and mystery, temporality was literally in God's hands. In a similar way Aristotle's *Physics* accounted for all change and involved every aspect of human life and consciousness. In the new network, space and time were essentially separate. A utilitarian sense of using space and using time developed, infecting the workshop, the counting house, the army and the city:

> The tempo became faster: the magnitudes became greater: conceptually, modern culture launched itself into space and gave itself over to movement. What Max Weber called the 'romanticism of numbers' grew naturally out of this interest. In time-keeping, in trading, in fighting men counted numbers; and finally, as the habit grew, only numbers counted.[34]

Mumford here summarizes the whole project of his trilogy and outlines his psycho-ethical metaphysic of historical explanation. The satirical force of 'only numbers counted' has that condensation of meaning that Pound attributed to great poetry.

Mumford was less concerned with presenting a history of statistics than outlining the effects of a psychological change in human values and action. 'Abstraction' became the new god in the machine. It was there in the 'orderly world' of the Christian (little wonder the scientists were so devout and ascetic), it was there in suppression of the various needs of the body and it was there in the compulsive need to manipulate nature in the laboratory and in the workplace. The excessive emphasis on primary qualities was good for science but ruled out art, poetry, dreams, the organic rhythms of nature and the 'inner world of feeling'.[35] The religion of the machine inaugurated a new world of realizable power. In the promise of technology grew the chimeras of infinite technological control and endless domination of space on earth and, if need be, in the entire universe.

Intoxicated by success those responsible were 'clear as to their goal and confident as to their victory'.[36] In his description of mining and in a dazzling series of characterizations based on Agricola's *De re metallica* Mumford saw the visible effects of what was essentially a state of mind: 'The mine is nothing less in fact than the concrete model of the conceptual world which was built up by the physicists of the seventeenth century.'[37] In this abstractly calculated world, the effects are that brutality, matter and men are organized with the ruthlessness of modern warfare. In the mine, day is swapped for night. Weight, number, speed and above all *time* (the 'shift') create a manufactured environment where even the air has to be imported: 'blast: dump: crush: extract: exhaust – there was indeed something devilish about the whole business.'[38] If the mine was war-like, the whole of industrial development tends towards war: 'The army is in fact the ideal form toward which a purely mechanical system of industry must tend.'[39] Twenty years before the appearance of the phrase 'the military-industrial complex', Mumford had identified a theme which was to remain with him until the end of his life.

Still bearing the temporal traces of his Geddesian Comtean promptings, Mumford adopted three phases for his history of technology, the eotechnic, the paleotechnic and the neotechnic, and Mumford cites his mentor in acknowledgement.[40] But what is a great deal more interesting is the fact that Mumford calls them 'overlapping and interpenetrating phases' and insists on a long cultural foreground. The lengthening and overlapping implicitly emphasize Mumford's anti-progressivist view of history. Nonetheless, the organic model of surprise and balance, the lingering dialectical impulse, and a crypto-Husserlian 'extensiveness' in the model of time modified any Spenglerian impulse. Switching to Henry Adams's model of an 'increase of power' as defining scientific and technological change and to Marx's more dialectical model of change, Mumford was able to see industrial development as producing solutions and cures as well as destruction. Glass, for example, made the medieval cathedral a spectacle of colour, changed indoor life, extended the seasons and the working day, put the world in a frame, extended sight, revealed the cosmos and the world of micro-organisms, gave to the laboratory crucial instruments, and developed the 'mirror personality', thus delivering narcissism with realism and a new searching of the soul. Again one may question the logic of Mumford's discourse of causality but not the incisive significance of its richly suggestive conjunctures.

Then there was the issue of the relation of power to time, especially in the nineteenth century. In speeding up production and divorcing power from the individual labourer and the natural environment, the multiplication of power through steam in industrial capitalism accelerated that always latent tendency to regiment time and commodify it. New phrases such as '*killing* time', '*saving* time' and '*using* time' were the order of the day. In an era of time and motion studies, the most grievous sin became '*wasting* time'. Mumford would have read Melville's short story 'Bartleby', which showed the difficulty of an employer trying to maximize his un-mechanized employees' time consistently throughout the day. On the larger scale, mechanical time and accelerated transport divided the entire planet into a series of coordinated 'time belts'.[41]

Time too came into it with the photograph, the phonograph and the moving-picture camera, all of which added to the means by which time could be fixed, a notion that was already there in the building, the monument, the artefact and in the inscribed word. Mumford was clear:

> For history is non-repeatable, and the only thing that can be rescued from history is the note that one takes and preserves at some moment of its evolution. To divorce an object from its integral time-sequence is to rob it of its complete meaning, although it makes it possible to grasp spatial relations which may otherwise defy observation.[42]

Hence the photograph both arrests and makes time, and the poesis of made time includes a simulacrum of lost time while making it a new object of time; the grand view of the 'moment of evolution'. It is also clear that Mumford wants a temporal correction to the ubiquitous structuralist spatial obsessions of the twentieth century.

Taking a photograph reflects an intention to make a future of the past. Is this why nobody takes photographs at funerals (unlike weddings) where the forever of the dead person has been too literally expunged? There is a sense that the historian plays a double game. A snapshot is taken, a representative moment is isolated and then placed in a sequence which gives it temporal meaning. Mumford imagined the historical past and future of his representative cultural moments and artefacts in relation to his awareness of the past and future of his own cultural and historical moment. There are always two correspondent temporalities. Mumford eschews the academic historian's neutral objective gaze. That is to say, he is more honest about his own position's concealed biases. The restored 'integral time sequence' that Mumford captured in narrative form had all the richness of two correspondent sequences of radically different but poetically correspondent pasts, presents and futures.

Mumford also notes the temporal shift in the changing means of mechanical reproduction. There is a sense in which it modifies the very nature of the object. Mumford offers a sequence for the visualization of the self from the mirror, to the portrait, to the photograph, to the moving picture, arguing that the change is from 'an introspective to a behaviorist psychology, from the fulsome sorrows of Werther to the impassive public mask of an Ernest Hemingway'. Mumford's speculations on the changing nature of the technology of the perception of the self are provocative. He cites Hemingway: 'I must have looked good, carrying the big logs on my back in my underwear.' He comments 'Alone, he still thinks of himself as a public character, being watched.'[43] Actually, the narrator in Stephen Crane's *The Red Badge of Courage* would have been an even better example. There is a peculiar American narcissism at work here that accompanies the ideological and power compulsions of competitive individualism.

The visually produced public world becomes a space of surveillance, internalized by the individual in relation to the self. The public and private selves become confused. In a way Mumford anticipates the substantive argument of Riesman's *The Lonely Crowd*, except of course that there, the time frame was minimal by comparison. Mumford even uses, like Dos Passos, the phrase 'the camera eye' to show the inherent fetishism in this mix of body and object. The world of Dos Passos's novel *U.S.A.* was precisely the atomized world of modernism where the dogmatism of the eye of the *flâneur* revealed only the sad narcissism of other selves on display as the modern shifted to the postmodern crowd. One might imagine the change from the intense bourgeois gaze of Ludwig Ravensberg's Ibsenesque Sunday afternoons in Karl Johannesgate in 'Christiania' (Oslo), to the voyeuristic observations in and around Proust's beach at Balbec, to the tourist confronting the eye-contactless gaze of the lycra-clad rollerbladers in New York's Central Park. Mumford, too, writes a contemporary satire on human behaviour with the human being shown within various narrative frames of time and space.[44]

The last point to be made from *Technics and Civilization* relates to Mumford's speculation on the cult of the past. Again it is not necessary to agree with the details. Mumford, to a degree, idealizes the Middle Ages and loathes the Renaissance, thus betraying his post-Morris prejudices. He sees the recovery of the classical tradition and the rise of modern science as leaving a gap somewhere in the middle in which the insights of ethical and religious life disappeared. Yet both the classical past and the scientific revolution challenged the present, creating a critical distance which opened the way for a critique and renewal. In Mumford's narrative of the spiralling oscillations of time, a renewed cult of the past in the Romantic period pitted itself against both the 'arid humanism of the eighteenth century and the equally arid dehumanism of the mechanical age'. Mumford added, 'William Blake with this usual true instinct for fundamental differences, attacked with equal vehemence Sir Joshua Reynolds and Sir Isaac Newton.'[45] What is important is that for Mumford the past was a variable value. People had much the same freedoms in aggregate as now. Within the reconstructed past it was important to be aware of the past's view of its past, its present and its future and the options for choice mediated in and through that temporal perspective.

The same broad themes were continued in *The Culture of Cities*. Here the plot distinctly thickened because the object of linear historical development was already a field with an intense awareness of its own spatiality. Coulanges's great work *The Ancient City* (1864), itself a history of religion and culture employing a field vision of urban civilization, was a precursor to this work. In addition, Mumford's historical recovery engaged a romantic, even Freudian, trope of excavation and depth. Whereas Freud offered and then rejected, in rationalistic preference, his analogy of Rome with the layers of the subconscious at the beginning of *Civilization and its Discontents*, Mumford figuratively embraced it in his *The Culture of Cities*, and mined it as an organizing poetic trope. For both, however, the past was the shadow of a consciousness yet to be found out.

So in his introduction and in his temporal revision of Geddes, Mumford meditated on the nature of temporality itself. Cities were a 'product of time'. In the city 'time becomes visible':

> Through the material fact of preservation, time challenges time, time clashes with time: habits and values carry over beyond the living group, streaking with different strata of time the character of any single generation. Layer upon layer, past times preserve themselves in the city until life itself is finally threatened with suffocation: Then in sheer defence, modern man invents the museum.
>
> By the diversity of time-structures, the city in part escapes the tyranny of a single present, and the monotony of a future that consists in repeating only a single beat heard in the past. Through its complex orchestration of time and space, no less than through the social division of labor, life in the city takes on the character of a symphony: specialized human aptitudes, specialized instruments, give rise of sonorous results which, neither in volume nor in quality, could be achieved by any single piece.[46]

With language, Mumford continued, the city is the greatest human achievement. Both are conscious and unconscious phenomena. 'Mind', says Mumford 'takes form in the city'.[47]

Mumford's story of mind and time explicitly rejects the political philosophies of the nineteenth century: what he calls that combination of legal and 'cultural abstractions', 'like Humanity [Comte], the Nation [spurious romantic nationalism, for example in Germany], the Folk [here Hitler rather than Le Play or Geddes], or economic abstractions like the Capitalist Class or the Proletariat [Marx]'.[48] Drawing on his by now familiar mentors – Le Play, Riehl, Kropotkin, Howard, Grundtvig and Geddes – Mumford offers an 'organic' 'culture of life' in opposition to contemporary tyranny. The phrase is no mere vitalistic gesture, for its generalized rhetoric defines itself politically, indifferent to nationalist claim, in relation to 'the sardonic funeral towers of metropolitan finance,' and the fascists with their 'stale cult of death'.[49] Within an almost Heraclitean flux of time, however, Mumford insists that if life is change, then there is always a possibility of challenging tyranny. Tides not rivers are the more appropriate conceit. Mumford retains enough of Marx, however, to write: 'The economic history of the town is largely a story of the transformation of a group of protected producers living in a state of relative equality, into a small group of privileged merchants for whom the rest of the population ultimately toils.'[50]

Mumford's spiralling narrative of non-progressive oscillating cultural losses and gains produces some notable moments. The cloister is pitched against open-plan, for in throwing open contemporary buildings to light and air we 'forget at our peril, the co-ordinate need for quiet, for darkness, for inner privacy, for retreat [...] the home without such cells is but a barracks; the city that does not possess them is but a camp'.[51] In the contemporary world, observes Mumford sardonically, 'the only place sacred from interruption is the private toilet'.[52] The permanently 'socialized' space of the open-plan house is neither public nor private.

'Reappearances' of a purely formal kind, however, need different temporal narratives. Drawing on the biological distinction between homologous and analogous forms, Mumford observes that the rectangle meant one thing to an Etruscan priest and another to New York city planners: the one indicating cosmic law, the other real estate speculation. The grand narrative of the struggle between God and Mammon, country and city in the medieval order will receive further consideration in *The Condition of Man*. In a Weberian mood, Mumford cited Protestantism as a powerful spur to that silent individualism, which, combined with a personal God, lent credibility to the abstract relations of capitalist enterprise and broke up the tangible relations of custom and with it the spatio-temporal coherence of the medieval city. Later he defended Protestantism's spirituality against the very phenomena its psychology had encouraged.

Mumford combined dialectics with the analogy of the biological cycle of adaptations. Destruction and growth were neither automatic nor avoidable. In Mumford's socio-biological time-frame, dominants and recessives were no more important than survivals and mutations. Although highly abstract, these contradictory and complementary movements gave great subtlety and flexibility to Mumford's representation of temporality. Survivals in magic and superstition temper and inspire the march of modern science: 'Was it not partly through the stimulus of magical dream books, like that of Artemidorus Daldianus, that Dr. Sigmund Freud made his profound psychological discoveries of the function of dreams?'[53] 'Tendencies' reformulate new epistemic patterns, only becoming observable when the paradigm shift is complete. Times vary in the accomplishment of these shifts: 'Centuries were needed to effect a unification even in such extra-personal activities as the regulation of weights and measures';[54] 'For two centuries' the expense of fortifications was an economic and social burden on the towns.[55]

The ethical judgement, however, is extra-temporal: detatched from historical relativism. Its qualitative atemporality of judgement will note, however, a linear increase in the historical technological power of destruction. The medieval despots were limited in their power drives: 'Their totalitarian imitators today, with no smaller delusions but with greater capacities for destruction, now threaten the very existence of world civilization.'[56] Here we glimpse the Mumford of 1938.

Continuing his epic of temporality, Mumford noted that in the baroque period, the clock first appeared in households. From this moment 'life-time' disappeared. It moved from relatively non-mechanical continuity and accumulation to abstract disjuncture. In some of his most brilliant moves Mumford pinned down the notion of 'being out of date' to this new sense of temporality. Whether his details are strictly accurate or not ('newfangled', which he uses, was a word in use by Chaucer, well before the seventeenth century) the mechanization of time altered the pace of time and led to a new assault of quantitative on qualitative values. In modernity, in the emergent newspaper, the temporality of story and explanation were downgraded into 'logically incoherent' events.[57] Even in archaeology, Mumford argued, the mere presence of the recovered artefact was of itself not history.[58]

Mumford's description of the 'age of abstraction' included narratives of the fictional person and the collectivized corporation of legal definition, the rise of capitalist abstract relations, the abstraction and dehumanization of perception of the landscape due to increased travel speed, the significance of military avenues in the heart of the city and the shopping parades of the upper classes where the rich drive, the poor gape and 'insolence battens on servility'.[59] At the heart of these social effects are technological and economic shifts of speed and abstraction dependent on human time divided and recalculated in an entirely new way.

Sometimes Mumford's rhetoric is more suggestive than clear. It is always, nonetheless, imaginatively provocative. For example, he asserts that with the rise of the 'academies', 'formal correctness took precedence over the inner content and the irresistible creativeness of a living art'.[60] Mumford's diatribes against the academy are increasingly relevant in the age of the corporate university but they also led him astray. For a good correction one should here read Frances Yates's magnificent book on the rise of the French academies, a work written with a similar passion during the Nazi take-over of Europe.[61] But Mumford's animadversions were in the tradition of Veblen's assessment of the twentieth-century corporate university and William James's diatribe against the 'PhD Octopus'.[62] Here, he could justly be accused of reading the present back into the past. Nonetheless he is right to raise the question of the academy's relation to the promotion of a view of the past often perpetuated by academies in general. A merely classicizing view of the past, an effort to repeat it in order to index a spurious lineage for self-authenticating status, does lead to an institutional deadness, and Mumford mentions 'the corpse-like classicism of the New York Public Library, the Lincoln Memorial, the Supreme Court Building, or the new government office buildings in the Washington Triangle'.[63] Were he alive now he would doubtless make similar charges against the 'heritage industry' and the implicit political conservatism of the events-oriented 'history' television programme: two significant post-modern methods of declaring history to be hallucinatory sites of a merely vehement ontological fascination, through endlessly repeated iconic images.

The disappearance of the *polis* (in an Arendtian sense) is the underlying theme of *The Culture of Cities*. The book is in fact an elegy to the city. With the *polis* gone politics enters every area of life. With the mass ballot, representative democracy and the propagandizing of platforms, it became possible to collect votes from people who never have a chance to discuss the issues collectively. Mumford does not take up the Arendtian argument that a separation of the private and public realms is needed for good government. He complains of the simplification of platforms in mass society and the invention in political argument by propaganda distributed by the means of mass media. Political power for Mumford is now founded on arguments for generalized issues of public safety: 'A good war, in Afghanistan or the Soudan, might save a bad peace.'[64] Mumford noted that in thumbing through *The London Illustrated News*, 'in the most turbulent years you will look in vain for scenes of strikes and demonstrations: instead, you will be filled with images of the far-flung British armies and the exotic places in which they conducted their missionary and military operations'.[65] Little has changed since then.

Mumford's temporal narratives worked better at some times than others. His assemblage of photographs and illustrations of Coketown is a case in point. For example in four photographs of Preston, Cleveland, Essen and Hanley and in six illustrations of 'the paleotechnic drama', some of the contradictions of Mumford's vision are most clearly exposed. The reproduced photographs are aerial photographs, the drawings are newspaper illustrations closer to earth and filled with people. Mumford's visual contrast is clearly designed to set the quasi-geometrical urban mess of the photograph against the public drama of mechanization and misery it produces, here shown in a more traditional visual form.

The interpretive connections between urban design and public drama are not at all obvious. The visual artefact needs a story. In his commentary on Schinkel's somewhat futurist praise of the Manchester Cotton Factory, Mumford does make a distinction between space and the human need. He is right to challenge whether gas-lighting and elevators are more worthy of note than the conditions of work. However, the artist drawings and graphics of groups or crowds are clearly already highly interpreted and seen in mid-length or long-distance perspective. They therefore raise the question of Mumford's ideological and personal distance from the urban crowd and mass meeting. The picture of a railroad station of the 1840s signals a scene of urban spectacle and celebration, but apart from a grudging remark about its main freight being coal and the quickening tempo of life it promulgates, Mumford remains grumpy. Doré's picture of a London slum is another of the 'human drama' pictures. Doré shows an absolute negation of human value in the drooping shoulders of the adults and a sense of future waste in the children. These effects of capitalism cannot be gainsaid, but nonetheless the picture lacks a narrative of poverty. The working class is diminished in pure victimhood. In the Artful Dodger, Fagin, Bill Sikes and Nancy, Dickens at least recognized human difference within the homogenization of industrial and urban degradation.

In short, Doré's drama lacks narrative beyond bourgeois sentiment, however brilliantly drawn. In the fourth picture a rally of a strike by the Gas Workers Union only leads Mumford to observe that the government placed army barracks in industrial towns like armies of occupation. Again, the point cannot be argued but there is no sense of the person in this spectacle of force against force. A view of the capacity of the oppressed to resist and creatively resist, such as one finds in Thompson's *The Making of the English Working Class*, would have been welcome. The crowd is a symptom not a possibility. There is no exuberance in Mumford's vision of a British working class that at its best founded co-ops, educated itself in mutual-improvement societies, working men's colleges, based its political teaching along Sunday school lines. Nor is there any sense that it developed a coherent sense of solidarity that could sometimes look outwards as well as inwards, fought with an absolute courage for better conditions, medical care, insurance and retirement deals through tough collective bargaining with brutal employers and produced men of the calibre of Keir Hardie and Aneurin Bevan until it effectively took power from 1945 to 1979 when its influence ended as the Labour Party went on to side with the bosses. Even with an embattled National Health Service, Britain is still a better place for the poor to live in than the United States. Nor, even in middle-class terms, is there any sense in Mumford of the civic pride of the industrial inventiveness of Birmingham, Liverpool, Manchester or Leeds, with their art galleries, orchestras, choral societies and town halls, and their flourishing chapel and non-conformist traditions. Elsewhere, as will be seen, Mumford is much more sympathetic and indeed can celebrate this tradition.

Mumford cannot, however, read the illustration of the London Exeter Hall meetings and the strike meetings beyond potential demagoguery. Working-class terrorization is all Mumford can see in the one and pious flannel in the religious meetings of an Exeter Hall on the other. Mumford did not care to mention the concerts of the New Philharmonic Society nor the Berlioz performances at Exeter Hall nor their popular cheap Wednesday afternoon programmes. He would have been unable to 'read' the phenomenon of a Spurgeon whose preaching in homely language at Exeter Hall gave an enriching vision of life to those barely above the poverty line. His instincts are in line here with the queen-and-country *Punch*, whose readers were busy making money out of imperialist conquest, while mocking the Exeter Hall missionary meetings which gave 'devoted crews' sailing orders 'to carry bibles down the Niger'.[66] Such religious meetings were very much more than Mumford's 'pious hopes and unrelieved futility' and the orators (in both strike meeting and chapel) were very much more than 'eloquent verbalists' who flouted the 'different procedures of the artist, scientist, and engineer'. Here Mumford seems to be arguing for a ruling class of bourgeois technocrats, a Leavisite Oxbridge elite and a Du Boisian talented tenth.[67]

Mumford simply 'ignored' the politics of the huge mid-Victorian dissenting culture which inspired and motivated Browning, Faraday, his own admired Ruskin and Morris, and countless engineers. In spite of his down-town upbringing and early radical connections, he had little sense of the different immigrant cultures of the city, of the variety of life, of the way communities interact and survive with grace in sometimes appalling conditions. In spite of his interest in religion, there is no sense here of the highly imaginative political radicalism within the best of the dissenting tradition, of spiritual vision or that the chapel community might develop organizational and political skills which would eventually serve them well in the unions and in public life. There is no sense that the city street, however impoverished, might sustain a sense of community that the New England village might envy.

There is, in short, no countervailing political or even social drama inside Mumford's 'paleotechnic drama'. These are the limits of his vision and they are considerable. Mumford's distrust of the evangelicalism of the Marxist and Christian vision was not always tempered in either case by a dialectical turn of mind. The limits are restated here simply to illustrate the gap between too swift a jump from the surveyor's gaze of the post-regionalist vision to the real class- and economics-structured historical drama of inhabited space. Mumford's vision radicalized the drift to structural analysis, rather than re-engaging with the life of the urban street. His panoramic space–time vision hence had limitations as well as virtues. In the ideological and religious turmoil of the 1930s Mumford struggled to define and precisely relate his own areas of historical interest and above all struggled to place them in any causal relation, the one to the other. Distrustful of the victory of the proletariat and Christian redemption alike Mumford had difficulty in defining the field of attention in the public and private spheres.

At the end of *The Culture of Cities* he made an attempt to restate his position. His conclusion showed that architecture and the city remained for Mumford a symbolic mode which could be deconstructed in terms of sociality and individuality. He retained his distrust of private property as the basis of individual liberty as well as of the corruption of socialism in terms of state capitalism. 'Habitat' and 'environment', however vague the common-sense meaning of the terms, did challenge the monologic narratives of socialism and capitalism alike. His claims for the new American personality (familiar from Crèvecoeur to Emerson and Whitman and beyond) attempted to link the classlessness of the New England transcendental ideal, to the old American Dream of meritocracy operating in a 'free' land.

For Mumford, the 'biological' bias of his work, a bias generated by Goethe as much as by Darwin, inevitably confronted him with the relationship between death and temporality. In fact, an almost stoic acceptance of death lies at the heart of his view of temporality: 'Biologically speaking, death is an episode in life's renewal: the terminus of a radical maladaptation.'[68] Mumford seems sometimes to have Sartre's indifference, though not the French philosopher's sense of scandal, in relation to death. Nonetheless, Mumford calls for a life-oriented attitude towards death, even if he pushes aside the entire human drama of the interior life to make the point.

Norman O. Brown's work is still useful here, especially his discussion of Hegel's grasp of the person as a history-making creature through identification with death and Freud's extroversion of the 'death instinct' as 'a peculiar human solution to a peculiar human problem':

> It is the flight from death that leaves mankind with the problems of what to do with its own innate biological dying, what to do with its own repressed death. Animals let death be a part of life, and use the death instinct to die; man aggressively builds immortal cultures and makes history in order to fight death: [69]

Brown links the Nietzschean will to power with 'building immortal cultures.' Mumford applies Brown's insight only to 'monumentality', complicating and reining in Brown's quietist absolutism. Here perhaps Mumford's love of Shelley assisted him, for his argument is very much conducted in terms of that incomparable poem 'Ozymandius'. 'Time', says Mumford, 'is a bomb that splits the most august temple open, if indeed the wanton savagery of men does not anticipate death's weapon.'[70] Mumford's notion of 'monumentality' is more sophisticated than Brown's, because Brown damns all historical time in terms of the temporality offered by the universality of repetition compulsion, fixation to the infantile past and the denial of death. Mumford discriminates and links the 'denial of death' to a politics and to that aspect of 'making history' involved only in 'monumentality'.

Linked to 'monumentality' are historical cults of death where, to use Weil's words, 'force is given the name of history'.[71] These were cultures where 'the activities of the living were not real until they could be transposed into terms of death'.[72] This insight dominated the revision of *The Culture of Cities* when Mumford came to write *The City in History* some twenty years later. The difference between the books is certainly the effect on Mumford of the war and the explosion of the atomic bomb. In *The Culture of Cities* Mumford asserts that Christian culture (which he calls 'recent') only makes life probational, whereas, 'for us, death is a making way for life, and all the fixed and memorial processes, the written record, the painting, the sculptured stone, the photograph, the recorded voice are offerings to the living – to be accepted, not out of duty to the dead, but out of loyalty to other remoter generations who will also be capable of deriving life from these symbols'.[73] In *The City in History* the vision was blacker, starting in the open chapter with the question: 'Is there still a living choice between Necropolis and Utopia?'[74]

Hence, against Brown, Mumford sees the past as an area for creative renewal. The act of writing history, to extend the argument, becomes part of making history, indeed it becomes part of a political struggle against 'history-making' in the name of 'monumentality'. Mumford's own history writing works in two quite contradictory ways. He needs a sense of lineal progression ('recent' Christianity) for the more preacherly aspects of his rhetoric (the future is ours if we choose). Yet, at the same time, the synthetic act of recovery has a powerful synchronic aspect to it. History is both present and past in an act of imagination which in turn involves ethical decisions and political choice. In Mumford's view we choose the history we need.

Mumford ends his book with a call (metaphorically) to design the American city on a hill in full partnership with the most creative aspects of a living present. It presents at the very least a critical utopian locus to place against the sprawling, graceless, utterly undistinguished unregulated developments engulfing the American landscape and its ecology, and turning its cities into some of the ugliest on earth. That is his best insight. The organic analogy of mutation, while often abandoned to an Emersonian, almost Nietzchean call for absolute innovation as truth, retains the belief that: 'It is sometimes by unexpected combinations in our social inheritance, or unorthodox re-interpretations of past beliefs, that important mutations are made.'[75] It was in that spirit, and doffing the progressivist mask, that he turned to reviewing the whole cultural legacy of a Europe under threat in *The Condition of Man*.

Towards The Condition of Man

A pencilled note by Mumford of 1930 gives a clue as to how one might read *The Condition of Man*:

> Each age has its own peculiar past, as well as its own temporary future. (The past it chooses to live with; the future it chooses to live *for*: book different from actuality.) Neither is the 'true' past & future; at best they have approximations which direct the movement of life, or, as it sometimes turns out, misdirect it.[76]

This crucial note outlines a complex view of temporality. What kind of past did then Mumford himself choose to live with, and what were the approximations that for him directed the very movement of life?

It is illuminating to compare Mumford's view of temporality with that of his French contemporary Fernand Braudel. Like Braudel, Mumford was to claim organic pattern as the key to his historical narrative: 'The long term is made up of a succession of repeated movements, with variations and revivals, periods of decline, adaptation or stagnation – what sociologists would describe as structuration, destructuration and restructuration.'[77] That is to say, in Mumford's terms, organic change, loss and renewal. Both Mumford and Braudel attempted to historicize the structuralist domination of the mid-twentieth century by making narratives out of structural phenomena. All the vitality Mumford ascribed to those non-economic systems that opposed capitalist fatalism, however, Braudel saw as existing within the infinite potentiality of capitalism to maintain its own 'vitality' including its capacity for change. That was a fundamental difference. Yet both understood clearly that historical events and patterns left everything to be interpreted. Braudel refused to explain the present in the light of history, but fortunately he implied such an explanation frequently for example when he said that after Marx 'capitalism' would never regain even the admiration Marx himself had for it. 'After Marx' implies and to a degree explains a future of the past down to the present.[78] Whether the statement is true or not is still an issue.

Braudel cited Mumford a number of times in his work, noting for example with a certain Gallic wink that Mumford's claim for a new privacy with the physical subdivision of the household in the eighteenth century, with the consequence that love went from being a summer activity to an all-year-round activity was somewhat suspect given dates of births in the records.[79] But he clearly half approved of Mumford's claim that capitalism was the cuckoo's egg laid in the confined nests of the medieval towns in terms of his narrative of the subsequent historical developments, though he still felt the towns nonetheless 'ruled the roost'.[80] He confirmed Mumford's general view of the superior cleanliness of the medieval town to what came after.[81] Braudel (and this is not a minor point) also clearly responded to the line-by-line liveliness of Mumford's writing.

Both Mumford and Braudel understood that culture and 'capitalism' had fought and co-operated since the earliest times: 'Culture is both support and challenge, guard dog and rebel.'[82] The mixtures of temporality in Braudel are as poetic as in Mumford. For a man who understood that 'historical time [...] lends itself less easily to the supple double action of synchrony and diachrony; it cannot envisage life as a mechanism that can be stopped at leisure in order to reveal a frozen image',[83] the following sentences of Braudel might give one pause:

> It was already an explosive enterprise to have reintroduced Greece and Rome to Christian civilization; to tear apart the seamless robe of the church was even more earth shaking. Yet in the end the dust settled, everything was absorbed into the existing order and the wounds healed. The Renaissance ended with Machiavelli's *The Prince* and the Counter-Reformation. The Reformation loosed upon the world

> a new dominant Europe, supremely capitalist; in Germany it produced a crew of petty princelings – not a happy result. And did Luther not betray the rebel cause in the Peasant war of 1525?[84]

Yet that typical Mumfordian 'supple double action of synchrony and diachrony' is everywhere evident in this example. The 'frozen' image of *The Prince* is at least partly 'thawed' as it joins the narrative as closure. Here Braudel, admittedly in slightly unbuttoned mood, is sketching out some oscillations within the *longue durée*. He is close even to Mumford's style here, yet the view of temporality in this brief narrative of historical time is to a degree less flexible than that of Mumford. While avoiding the post-Saussurean absolutes of synchrony and diachrony, there is a sense in which *The Prince* and Luther's political behaviour figure less as frozen moments than as conceits through which a dramatic narrative is built. The temporalities leak into each other.

But what of epochal closure? Braudel reaches for the metaphors of the dust settling and the wounds healing – the latter an almost Mumfordian organic trope. The point is, however, it takes a long retrospective gaze to make the assertion of healing. The question arises: who knows the wounds have healed and when? Is it the historian, who thereby closes this particular past with a sense of epochal closure? On what grounds do we know a particular theme has died? Does fate itself have the indifference of a mysterious force of nature while making contingent interventions in the capacity of human beings to survive and flourish? And on what timescale does fate operate? This was a question not tackled by Simone Weil. Fortunately, however, history can only know itself through us and our various senses of time. Even fate is our invention because it is in the last analysis, a story.

And finally, what of the vertical evaluation as well as the horizontal selection of the incidents which make up the narrative? Braudel's contrast here suggests that an instinct for autocracy can be observable in any ideological practice: Catholic or Protestant. But why choose Machiavelli as political representative of the Counter Reformation and Luther's betrayal of the peasants as the typical political behaviour of the Protestant? What about the reforms of Cardinal Cisneros in the brief Regency after Ferdinand or the powerful impetus given to democratic politics by Protestant church government? Braudel's illuminating moments are to a degree ideologically biased. In addition, the shift from the particular to the general always involves an ethical evaluation of the exact correspondence of the small to the large time-scale. At worst it buries meaning in abstract typicality, at best it illuminates in condensed form the larger patterns of time.

The big questions are probably unanswerable, but at least asking them opens up the whole nature of the complexity of the historical discourse within narrativity itself. For Braudel, narrative history was not an objective method but engaged a philosophy of history with multiple levels of time: geographic, social and individual. Yet the layering was only an analytic gesture within a powerful sense of history's holistic character. Writing history was a 'fragile art' and at times Braudel seems closer to a poetics than to a philosophy of history.[85] This is certainly a clue to his greatness, though it is not likely to persuade the academic historian.[86] Braudel knew that narrative history was a philosophy of history and would attempt to recuperate it beyond the nineteenth-century shibboleths of 'exceptional destinies'.[87]

Mumford's narrative in *The Condition of Man*, which was to some extent a Carlylean history of great men, pushed its review of 'exceptional destinies', however, beyond princes to religious prophets, theologians, philosophers, saints, political theorists, painters, scientists, poets and novelists, designers, engineers, utopian philosophers, cultural critics and town planners, and working-class co-operatives. Mumford democratizes the exceptional destiny. Beyond the individual destiny, however, Braudel, like Mumford, believed in that 'history slower still than the history of civilizations, a history which almost stands still, a history of man in his intimate relationship to the earth which bears and feeds him'.[88] A huge vitalistic metaphysic guaranteed the direction of a multi-dimensional historical narrative.

For the European it was a faith in a meaning of life accepted by the human being destined to die; for the American it was the meaning of historical tragedy accepted by human beings choosing to live. Perhaps, as will be shown later, it was the difference between Catholic and Jewish sensibilities. Both had a passionate belief in 'man' being in an intimate relationship with 'his' organic destiny, yet the tone was sharply different. Braudel's was more Faulknerian – history was the backward glance revealing a slow time of a melancholy, almost stoic endurance. Nonetheless it had the quality of infinity. Mumford saw that endless push for survival in Braudel's 'imperious time of the world' as much more endangered, at least as it related to the human species.[89] Yet both believed in a sharply oscillating rhythm of reciprocal historical narratives and both believed that 'there is never any problem, ever, which can be confined within a single framework'.[90] In a world of specializing academic fragmentation, they embraced the grand narrative of history on an equally grand scale.

As the human agent in history seemed to disappear in the neo-imperial cosmic time-keeping of Parsonian homeostasis, both knew that there was a danger of forgetting 'each separate man, grappling with his own life and his own destiny; the danger of forgetting, perhaps even of denying, the inimitable essence of each individual'.[91] Putting the levels of time together was the most fundamental challenge. Both men distrusted the short time span, and acknowledged that history was always in fundamental dialogue with the present. Both retained enough of a dialectical view of life, if not of method, to understand the nature of 'the multiple illumination of discontinuity', those deep rifts which seem to cut one world off from another.[92] They were both indebted to Marx in their attempts to put social and economic–technological explanations together. 'Between ourselves', said Braudel, 'Karl Marx had every right to be intoxicated with his own originality.'[93] But as Braudel noted, referring to Marx's letter of 18 March 1872 to Maurice La Châtre: 'There is no royal road to science.'[94] Above all, Braudel and Mumford knew that the different levels of time required, as Braudel said, on a hint from Lévi-Strauss, 'different languages'.[95] This key insight forms the core of the argument of this book.

They also saw eye to eye on the double meaning of civilization in its unitary and plural forms, that 'orchestra of particular histories: history of language, of literature, history of science, history, art, history of law, of institutions, history of sensibility, of customs, of technology, of superstitions, beliefs, religions (and even religious feelings), history of daily life, not to mention the rarely attempted history of taste and of cooking (recipes)'.[96] Mumford's *The Condition of Man* attempted precisely just such a scale.

In terms of that large scale, both men's attitudes to Spengler are worth considering. Uncomfortably close to him on certain key issues, Mumford rarely resisted an opportunity to denounce him. In *The Condition of Man*, he attempted to prise from an a priori fatalism those insights from Spengler's Faustian narrative of the 'decline' of the 'West' that were close to his own concerns. At the same time, he denounced him (with Spenglerian fury) as the demon inside the German soul. Spengler had given Mumford an example of the grand narrative of the rise and fall of civilizations, a religious sense of the alliance of science and power, and a sense of the impermanence of any culture. Mumford discriminated in a letter to Van Wyck Brooks on 17 August 1931: 'On technics he is very unsound indeed, unsound and careless; but on cities and on their relation to the country, as well as on the contrasts between the organic and the mechanical thought, I find him very satisfactory.'[97] Similarly Braudel, while shrugging off criticisms of the naïve simplifications of the main argument, noted with more than an ironic sympathy that Spengler's bold attempt, like Toynbee's, to write 'a narrative of the flowering of spiritual values into a coherent succession of dynamic phases until they withered away',[98] was quite irrational from any sane historian's point of view. But he added that, fortunately, some historians were more unreasonable than others. Mumford's *The Condition of Man* was actually such a project, or at least an organic fluctuation of spiritual values was one powerful strand in the grand narrative. Braudel noted that Toynbee was a historian who was much more plausible than Spengler on the history and destiny of spiritual values.

Braudel's observations on Toynbee run parallel in some respects to Mumford's bibliographical note in *The Condition of Man*. At the time, Toynbee was famous for his twelve-volume work on the history of civilizations, as well as a certain public capacity for punditry. 'In his company', said Braudel, 'the contemplation of vast historical horizons comes to seem a useful and even a delightful exercise.'[99] Braudel's very funny praise and destruction of Toynbee is a masterpiece of

Gallic sideways-looking at an untidy, common-sense Anglican Englishman with a lofty imperial gaze, a historian who had perhaps a rather convenient sense that God's time was best at the moment of the collapse of the British Empire. Only an Englishman could so nonchalantly and so urbanely, Braudel felt, put away the history of states, together with the whole social and economic basis of history and abandon that history to 'the mediocrity of its fate'.[100] But it is the model of the birth, life, and death of civilizations which interests Braudel and especially their deaths. What rather amuses him is Toynbee's Polonius-type punditry in his abstract notion of 'challenge and response' in a 'civilization's' response to difficulty. This reduces the role of the environment, Braudel remarks, to 'that attributed to the cane in an English public school'.[101] It is a charge that occurs also to the most sympathetic reader of Mumford in one of his more headmasterly moods.

Nonetheless, as with Spengler, what is important is what Braudel salvages and praises. He praises Toynbee's courage to take on the *longue durée* and those social realities that seem to persist for ever, events such as the founding of religions that have effects centuries and sometimes millennia later: Arnold Toynbee's great merit is 'to have handled these great tracts of time even at the risk of losing himself, to have dared to compare things which happened centuries apart, to have sought out these vast, somewhat unreal, but nonetheless important routes'.[102] Toynbee's atemporal and acultural 'spiritual nature of man' is untenable for it is a result merely of a narrative of resemblances not of dissonance and difference.

Mumford thought that the merits outweighed the weaknesses of Toynbee's vast project. As a product of the same conditions that produced Adams and Spengler, Mumford found Toynbee more tentative and more scholarly, though in *The Condition of Man*, he found the clear preference given to Christianity over other prophets and religions a rather 'non-sociological' conclusion.[103] Whatever the limitations, and they were many, of Toynbee's panoramic temporal vision, the question of religion and religious practice, together with ethical judgement in relation to evidence, could not now be erased from history and left to the specialist tender mercies of the anthropologist or sociologist. Mumford was not to be indifferent to the theme. Historical religion, if not the prime reason of history, was now subjected to narrative description in relation to all other aspects of the culture, as well as to the more traditional issues of the historical gaze.

In many ways, Mumford's less ambitious project (at least in terms of scale) shared many of Braudel's and, tangentially, Toynbee's interests. The collectivity of the practices of an entire culture were to be re-narrativized into a form which admitted different points of view, a philosophy of time, ethical judgement and individual agency. It also cast the Braudelian levels of time with their different languages into a poetic discourse that attempted to show the multifarious and sometimes synthetic movements of the patterns of the culture operating together. Like Braudel, Mumford did not shrink from connecting vastly different moments of time for comparative Pascalian judgement.

The Condition of Man

Mumford's narrative temporality in *The Condition of Man* is complex. First, there is that invocation of the present in the address to the reader, a continual paralleling of contemporary issues and concerns, not so much to explain the present as to temper its confidence. Of the entire trilogy he said: 'These books were written during a period of rapid social disintegration.'[104] In the global slump of the 1930s, through the rise of Hitler, Franco, Mussolini and Stalin alongside the collapsing European empires, it was a brave or innocent soul who could ignore the facts of disintegration. In a period where the authoritarian seizure of power had become endemic, it is not surprising that in his review of European civilization the shadows of the Caesars, Machiavelli, Caesar Borgia and Ivan the Terrible would serve as atemporal and analogical reminders that official communism had succumbed to the brutalities of autocratic power, culminating in 'the pact that gave Hitler the green light for launching his attack upon the world'.[105] The large time-scale is important; the average American historian did not think much about Caesar.

He reviewed legitimations of absolute monarchies from the Justinian code to the late Roman law and calendar. Resistance to legitimations of autocracy were noted in the systematic brutalizing of the human spirit under the promulgation of terror. Twentieth-century violence 'was fortified by a deliberate cult of violence',[106] enticing the populace into the virtual realities created by contemporary media where 'the vulgar tabloid newspaper and the illustrated weekly set a level of frothy dullness which is only one step away from a drugged sleep'.[107] At the political level the indifference of a globalized technology was shown in 'the American cartels that connived with the Nazis to suppress patents essential to democracy's preparation for war'.[108]

Against this period of social disintegration Mumford invoked the 'eternity of art'.[109] Mumford is not analytic or consistent in his treatment of this concept for it contradicts his view of the necessary disappearance of art. Mumford's view of temporality in art is contradictory. In other words two times conflict, the need for stability in personal time and the renewing flux of the *longue durée*. 'Man has often made death the center of his most valued effects [...] translating human beauty into everlasting stone, human experience into printed words, and time itself, arrested in art, into a simulacrum of eternity.'[110] Such statements manifestly contradict: 'Even the grandest works of art must be treated as reckless trifles, mere improvisations, to be abandoned or destroyed on a moment's notice as soon as they begin to stifle the spirit – abandoned with the faith that while the spirit remains alive it will produce as good or better as soon as needed.'[111]

This remarkably irresponsible statement also conflicts with Mumford's own notion of limit and tragedy and exhibits that extreme puritanical faith of the historical iconoclasts whose arrogance is only in proportion to their shrunken view of truth. Did Mumford find support for this apocalyptic Nietzschean moment of destruction in Hawthorne's short story 'Earth's Holocaust'? One wonders who, ethically, has permission to destroy and where and when, in this moment of egotistical iconoclastic righteousness. The vital human need for the past as a resource for a re-imagined present and future is fundamentally a collective and democratic one. Mumford almost assumes that some 'eternal' personified greatness is inherent works of art without anyone looking at them. They are beneficent all by their eternally de-temporalized selves. He never considers that the 'human spirit' might be rendered inadequate or too ignorant to regard them as other than 'stifling', especially in a populace whose dumbed-down tastes are created, then endlessly flattered by relentless mass commercial interest. It must, however, be noted that this irritable moment runs counter to the evident value of Mumford's entire life's work in its re-presentation of the past.

As with Toynbee, there is also a psychological grand narrative of what might be called the collective interior life of the nation and 'civilization'. The 'personified' civilization risks a *reductio ad absurdum*. For Mumford, Rome lacked an 'inner go'.[112] Perhaps, to recall Braudel's witticisms about Toynbee, this is rather like Eton just having lost to Harrow at cricket. Chaps in Rome were half asleep. Here Mumford's failure to recognize the inertia of any endlessly perpetuated ruling class in his temporal narrative of oscillating historical fortunes is a weakness of the language of temporality he here assigns to organism. A judgement of the failure of energy is read in symptoms of devitalization and can connect the most bizarrely different phenomena: 'One can tell from the sensual melancholy of the faces in the Byzantine mosaics that one is witnessing an exquisite corruption in which extreme sophistication blends with extreme naiveté' or 'but the great Code of Justinian and the Greek Anthology were monuments of a non-renewing creativity'.[113] An immediately emotive reading of any phenomena should never be ruled out of any response to the artefacts of the past, but these days it is clear that such judgements are conditioned by cultural values and local traditions of interpretation. Mumford's immediate seizure of the relevance of these artefacts is betrayed by the arrogance of that universal 'One': 'One' can tell, somehow.

Or perhaps not. The Christians, too, lacked 'go'. If quietist and eternity-oriented, where did they then find the energy to build cathedrals, monasteries and hospitals, sculpt, paint, make stained glass, compose music, write volumes of theology, develop huge bureaucratic systems, create global missionary systems, stoutly support reactionary regimes or go on crusades and imperial or capitalist adventures, all of which, elsewhere, Mumford said they did? Apparently 'they wanted peace as a sick man driven frantic by the sound of a vacuum cleaner'.[114] The vacuum cleaner presumably stood in for the noise of an all-too-insistent fallen world. The noise of a fallen world by implication drove them into fantasies of an out-of-world future. Here, the language and argument of Mumford's temporality needs something more than a common-sense, homely explanation.

Elsewhere, Mumford's narrative of time and temporality is much more persuasive:

> Time-keeping, spatial measurement, and numerical calculation at length transformed the study of nature. The medieval church, with its concern for Eternity, lengthened the time-perspective and helped to translate mechanical order into time and time into mechanical order: the great clock of the Cathedral Lübeck, which dated from 1405, was equipped with a calendar which reached forward to the year 2000. Even astrology, which professed to correlate earthly events with planetary movements, popularized the art of exact observation and exact calculation; it caused people to record promptly the hour of birth, if only to make the horoscope more accurate. The dramatic regularity of the heavens gave man a sense of an external order that guaranteed and fulfilled his own inner will-to-order. The very fruitfulness of naturalism as developed during the Middle Ages was bound up with its confidence in an all-pervasive determinism: the predestined will of God.[115]

Here Mumford, in a meditation on time, touches a set of contradictory historical moments demonstrating an interpenetration of the secular and sacred, technics and psychology, magic and measure, cosmic time and psychological time, building rhythmically to the final poetic paradox of freedom and necessity. It is in passages like these that Mumford's theories of organicist dynamic balance fruitfully assist his cultural narratives. The chosen images, too, such as the Lübeck clock, give a vertical thickness to the horizontal argument. There is surprise in the juxtaposition of the years 1405 and 2000. To us, paradoxically, the first thing it suggests is that we are beyond the suggested closure. The narrativity here imagines the past's forward projection then unknown but now held in a retrospective gaze by us. This is narrative of the struggle of the mortal with mortality across different senses of the time of the future. To us, barely beyond the year 2000, it gives a sense of retrospective distance, inversely parallel to an original sense of prophecy. What were they like, these clock-smiths of Lübeck in 1405, imagining their clock and calendar striking finally in a far distant future, closed in their unimaginable time but which is now behind us?

Mumford's meditations on Christian time extend the argument. Again, for all his animadversions against Christian quietism, the church's use of the repression of sexuality, its corruption and its refusal to engage with real 'earthly' political order, to be found elsewhere in his book, it is the Christian sense of temporality that lies at the heart of his medieval critical utopian descriptions of dynamic balance:

> The Christian Church now presided over birth and death and all the momentous crises between. For each of these occasions it had a form and a ceremony; to each of them it gave a rational meaning within the larger pattern of being. The church

> fed the hungry traveler; it nursed the ill and the wounded; it solaced the tired and the defeated. It baptized the new-born infant and it crowned the last moments of the dying with awful dignity. At no moment of his life was even the worst sinner outside the circle of fellowship, unless he had drawn upon himself the church's most bitter punishment, excommunication: living death [...]. Once a week, at least, but usually more often, every member of the community had a glimpse of the highest life possible: lord and peasant, master and journeyman, lady and wench, worshiped together in the same buildings, watched and took part in the same processions, heard the same chants, beheld the same icons, listened to the same sermons, followed the same mass; all equal in the sight and presence of God.[116]

This is as close as Mumford gets to Henry Adams's great description of the precariously stable cathedral of the transition, which metaphorically encapsulated the synthetic fragility of Thomian theology.[117] Mumford, almost by sleight of hand, links Christian temporality and ethics with the ritual of an inclusive community aware of the common fate and conscious of an equality before mortality.

Mumford hurled a post-Morris-style evaluation of the Middle Ages against an essentially Burkhardtian, anti-Christian, view of the Renaissance. Like Frobenius, Mumford thought 'the Renaissance movement was an instance of the ethical force of a process directed towards emancipation from ethical shackles.'[118] Mumford saw neo-classicism as a 'retreat' into deadness, not as the usual revival of learning. In his negative view of this epistemological shift of phase, he also assumed that the despotism of nation-states was worse than the despotism of the Holy Roman Empire. But again, Mumford's narrative of the cultural-temporal shift to 'the Renaissance' has some surprising accents.

Against the grain of virtually everyone who had written about the discovery and settlement of the New World, the discovery and exploration of America is, for Mumford, a new twist in the tail of Mephistopheles. In an extreme anti-exceptionalist paradox Mumford argued that the Turneresque frontier spirit was a form of retreat. Taking Melville's Faustian Captain Ahab as his ethical model, Mumford stated 'the ocean itself was an Egyptian desert', just as the wilderness itself was a 'cloister'. Depicting westward expansion as an almost Faustian hallucinatory process, Mumford articulated its inherent contradictions:

> In a few centuries man altered biotic relations on every part of the planet, upset the balance of nature, and transformed the biological possibilities of existence, not merely for himself but for countless species of animals and plants. Out of man's mythic sense of his own self-importance, fostered by his very acts of exploration and conquest, Western man forced himself to feats of courage and derring-do which would have been inconceivable in people who had a more judicious sense of their own limitations or a more critical understanding of their own unworthiness.[119]

So much for the American Dream. Here, the *longue durée* is one of ecological degradation over 'a few centuries'. This quasi-Spenglerian vision was assisted imaginatively by the central tragedy of *Moby-Dick*, the monomaniac quest of a man who had rejected sociality for a goal that was ultimately more neurotically metaphysical than this-worldly, yet one which was promoted through capitalism's productive relations: the division of labour, the industrial despoilation of nature, the reduction of qualitative to quantitative value (and the excess of quantitative value into qualitative value) and religious failure: 'No doubt the ship sailed faster but what dropped off?'[120] *Moby-Dick*, Mumford had said in 1929, 'brings together the two dissevered halves of the modern world and the modern self – its positive, practical, scientific, externalized self, bent on conquest and knowledge, and its imaginative, ideal half, bent on the transposition of conflict into art, and power into humanity'.[121] In a similar spirit, in one of those illuminating quotations which pepper *The Condition of Man*, Mumford damned the entire American Dream, its constitution and its sanctioning of eighteenth-century rationality, including its written constitution, by sarcastically citing Descartes' *Discourse on Method*:

> I fancied that those nations which, starting from a semi-barbarous state and advancing to civilization by slow degrees, have had their laws necessarily determined, as it were, forced upon them simply by the experience of the hurtfulness of particular crimes and disputes, would by this process come to be possessed of less perfect institutions than those which, from the commencement of their association as communities, have followed the appointments of some wise legislator.

Mumford pondered the price of this 'false simplicity, this deceptive neatness'.[122]

He preferred a slightly more Burkean view of political wisdom and social order, which valued custom, collective memory and the slow process of endlessly modified law. In fact, Mumford saw the American constitution as mediating both Burke and Rousseau. But in the American emphasis on the rational designing of institutions, Mumford was with Tocqueville: 'By putting the whole emphasis upon the transformation of institutions instead of giving equal attention to the re-education of men, the revolutionary leaders of the next century and a half turned their promised land into a mirage that perpetually retreated before them.'[123] And surely Mumford has Stalin in mind when he further comments on the American revolutionists: 'Though they sought to cut society loose from its evil heritage, they forgot that they themselves, they and their guiding ideas, were a product of that heritage: so they evaded the most critical questions: Who is to guard the guardian?'[124] It was precisely narrative closure that Mumford questioned, too, in the Marxists: 'In the myth of revolution', said Mumford, 'a fresh beginning was taken as the guarantee of a happy ending.'[125] The bourgeois revolutions of the romantic period, French or American, for Mumford, were bolstered by a treacherous faith in 'the New World of science, capitalism mechanization and colonial expansion'.[126] The closure of revolutionary beginning might resemble hell rather than heaven.

Mumford's revisionist narrative of time implicitly also attacked the overvaluation of the present. The fundamentally short-term and pragmatic recall of the 'past' in the scientific and commercial project set a poor example for the 'life world'. Long before McLuhan, Mumford noted the commercial advantages of 'binding together the scattered fragments of life by the simple mechanical device of putting them all under the same dateline'.[127] 'In the newspaper and the encyclopaedia the external order of the calendar and the alphabet concealed the conflicts and irrationalities of actual existence: the absence of true organic relationships in either life or mind.'[128] For Mumford drawing on the Latin etymology of the Latin root of modern, which means 'just now', spoke of the substitution of the temporality of fashion for the deeper view of the past.

The substituted present in turn becomes outmoded, so there is a continuous cycle of rejection and substitution. The key human value of lingering is obliterated in a hallucinatory devotion to speed.[129] Lingering becomes only malingering in the new dispensation. Generic fashion becomes a rejection not only of the past – for it is possible to extend Mumford's meditation – but a rejection also of the richness of the insight, in Husserlian terms, that the 'no longer' proceeds from the 'was', not vice versa.[130] This emphasis on creative continuity sums up the spirit of Mumford's defence of the past: 'Once present time becomes more important than life's manifold connections between past and future, the mere contemporaneity of events gives them a special value.'[131] Mumford's so-called attack on modernity is therefore not an attack on modernity as such but a modernity that has cut itself off from the past in absolutist terms, and will not contemplate its own future.

So how does Mumford view of temporality in *The Condition of Man* govern his critical gaze and discourse? The first thing is that for Mumford the past is present in both its radical absence and in its traces which offer an at-once-recognizable link with the present but one which the imagination of the present needs literally to 'bring' to life, not 'bring *back*' to life. The second point is that this operation is not value free. For Mumford especially it involves not simply gathering a multiplicity of traces to pulled into the field, but a range of responses to that field which spill out of more inventive epistemological, historical, scholarly discourses.

To finish this section I propose, with sideways glances at Braudel as a point of contrast, to look at two examples from *The Condition of Man* which take up the question of eternity and art and which consider a very human politics in relation to creating a fragile genealogy as an even more fragile simulacrum of eternity. The question of time's relation to eternity is probably best handled in theology but Dante, Melville and Blake were the writers who were undoubtedly the closest to Mumford's oblique consideration of this topic. Mumford's characterization of Dante in *The Condition of Man* is central not only to his concept of ethics and religion, but to his sense of art's relation to life.

> In Dante's supernaturalism there was a place for all nature. This indicates the task that confronts the philosopher and the poet in our own time: for in one sense, our natural order is but Dante's world in reverse; and our task *is to bring a sense of the eternal and the infinite back into common daily life*: to recast our narrow frame of reference so that it will encompass all that remains humanly valid in the medieval conception of the supernatural: not by claiming false knowledge about the unknowable, but by understanding that our life, too, is an allegory, because what man makes of it in the soul is ultimately as important as what is given in the senses. (my italics)[132]

Mumford continued by arguing, like Arendt, that human existence is valuable only as a story and only 'through that part of it which is translated into meaningful symbols and valuable patterns of conduct does man truly come into possession of his kingdom.'[133] Mumford's focus on symbolic language has a dialectical relation with ethics and its complex temporality. It articulates a fundamentally analogical yet very paradoxical relation with biological life, in its creation and transmission of the past-in-presence.

> The movement of life into the ideal realm in which all existence has meaning, form, and value, and the passage of these ideas back again into life is the essential systole and diastol of the human heart. Man's earthly life, in short, involves the existence of another transcendental world; a world of durable meanings and values that in time detach themselves from the flux of history, and lose their narrow ties to time and place. Only a small part of human existence actually goes into this other world; and a still smaller fraction is passed on from generation to generation, from culture to culture, from epoch to epoch.
>
> Religion, art, ethics, philosophy, poetry, science – these are the ultimate agents in man's self-transformations. All man's other acts, deeds, acquisitions, discoveries, masteries, are significant only to the extent that they finally find expression in these realms. This is an old conception; it could hardly be otherwise. With good reason Dante was grateful to his old teacher, Brunetto Latini, whom he encountered in Hell, because he 'taught me how man makes himself eternal.'[134]

Against this, Mumford throws another time-frame. The 'ideal realm' was there in Dante where, in Mumford's view, the poet had clothed the abstractions of the philosopher in flesh and blood. It was Henry Adams who had noted the temporality of unity undone by multiplicity and multiplicity by movements towards unity, as he searched for a theory of history. In the 'organic' biological flux of life things reach maturity and then die, although here Mumford's metaphor is more cosmically dramatic: 'though Dante's verse continued to enchant and discourage the poets of Italy, his vision of life disappeared with the finality of a meteor whose very speed and heat, as it drives through the atmosphere, causes it to leave no mark in the earth where it buries itself. In Dante, the medieval personality had completed its pilgrimage'.[135]

Yet, in some respects, this closure was premature. For Mumford the human experience was dual. The inherent contradictions of temporality between life looked at from an imagined outside in narratives of biological survivalism, and human life looked at from the inside in allegories of human self-consciousness, between a view of radical inessentiality and the memory of valued presence in art are to be negotiated, not to mention practised, at the heart of the human condition. The world of consciousness and life itself was reciprocal and glimpsed in what he called 'symbolic participation'. It is in this sense that Mumford is fundamentally a religious and materialist thinker. As Whitman declared: 'And I have said the soul is no more than the body/And I have said that the body is no more than the soul.'[136]

The problem of closure, however, remained. Since there was no celestial city, the 'pilgrimage' ends in a nihilistic darkness which actually undoes the value of pilgrimage. The problem is with the word 'personality', that is today linked with the cult of the celebrity and is inscribed in a temporality of minimum duration by substituting recognition for fame. Nonetheless, it offered Mumford the opportunity to explore the psychology and ideology of a period through narrative, art and artefact in a way that combined ethical judgement with psychological analysis and an ideological scepticism that were full of dazzling insights as well as generalization and vagueness. The academy certainly prefers the analytic to the idealist mode: a phrase such as 'the expression of a particular cultural moment'[137] seems too fraught with danger – the moment and the expression invite too difficult an imaginative act on both sides. Yet all historians and cultural commentators do just that, though in rather more disguised forms. It is always there in the choice of the example in its relation to the whole.

Moving from the generic personality to the representation of the person, Mumford's recovery of Dante's teacher's remark about time and eternity is of great value. The story cheats time, as Scheherazade knew. Yet Mumford is mixing up, perhaps disingenuously, several eternities. Brunetto Latini's eternity is one which actually cannot be experienced by human beings. The extension of life in writing is neither a human nor cosmic 'eternity' in any precise sense. Nonetheless, it is an enrichment of the sense of mortal time, that is, it extends it beyond mortal boundaries and indeed beyond the local space. This was certainly the thought behind Mumford's statement in *Technics and Civilization* that with clock time, 'eternity ceased gradually to serve as the measure and focus of human actions'.[138]

There is, however, a sense that for Mumford eternity obliterates the possibility of 'the next'. Here, the literal collapse of Dante's *Weltanschauung* is an example. In fact, Dante's world view cannot be separated from his poetry, and is perfectly recoverable for contemporary use with an imaginative and sympathetic reading of its allegory. It can be present and absent at the same time. Mumford has confused Dante's desire for immortality (a classical concept), to use the Arendtian distinction, with the concept of eternity (a Christian trope based on *contemptu mundi*).[139] For Dante, fame and immortality were possible. Yet, in Arendt's terms, Mumford perhaps sensed the obliteration of the concept of immortality which was to be a ground for her sense of the *vita activa*. Mumford wanted to see the 'eternal present' of art in stark contradiction with the eternity that sets limits to time and to simply leave it as a contradiction. Yet Mumford also clearly agreed with Ricoeur that 'narration is possible wherever eternity attracts and elevates time, not where it abolishes it'.[140]

It is the need to get rid of the limits of the 'just now', the modern, that underwrites Mumford's discussion of eternity here. It is because the medieval world did just that, that he is able to say: 'That is why the supernatural theology of the Middle Ages was closer to reality than the crass materialism of an age which fancies the achievement of an "economy of abundance" will automatically ensure a maximum of human felicity.'[141] Here Mumford suggests that modernity has reduced, in Arendt's distinction, the human condition to human nature. The key word 'condition' in Mumford's title gives full expression to this.

Like Marx, Mumford had a profoundly Jewish sense of time and eternity. Arendt's commentary on Marx's concept of labour as 'the understanding of labouring and begetting as two modes of the same fertile life process'[142] is also close to Mumford's dual and interpenetrating concepts of cultural and biological dynamic balance in the flux of time itself. Arendt, like Mumford, saw that 'effort and gratification follow each other as closely as producing and consuming the means of subsistence, so that happiness is a concomitant of the process itself, just as pleasure is a concomitant of the functioning of a healthy body.'[143] The stories of the patriarchs showed 'how unconcerned about death their lives were, how they needed neither an individual, earthly immortality nor an assurance of the eternity of their souls, how death came to them in the familiar shape of night and quiet and eternal rest in good old age and full of years'.[144] For Arendt, as for Mumford the source of life was fertility in every sense of the word. This is what links Mumford's 'organicism' with his sense of time. The elemental happiness of being alive lies in an endless cycle of physical renewal at the biological level. At the cultural level, it lies in the imaginative renewal of artistic and political memory, in which the activity of *poesis* itself guarantees the authenticity of public and personal life. The one serves as a correspondent analogy for the other. It is a profoundly romantic (analogically correspondent) vision.

Whatever opposes this vision is destructive of life, physically and morally. Herein lies the distinction between work (in Morris's or Ruskin's sense) and labour (in the alienated order of the Marxist vision). Mumford's human condition is an almost Manichean flux of such distinctions. A high drama of 'renewal or catastrophe' gives pace and sharpness to the argument in his descriptions of the commodification of sex and leisure in the late Roman period, the monuments of 'non-renewing creativity' in the Justinian code and the Greek anthology,[145] the ambiguities of retreat in the Christian vision, followed by the restoration of the creative maternity in Henry Adams's vision of the Queen of Heaven, the fragility of the medieval 'balance', the betrayals of the corporate church, the contradictions of the scientific revolution, the very misrepresentations of the past present and future in the age of reason and romantic periods. The same sense of drama is there too in the romantic and utilitarian confusions of Robinson Crusoe, in the cultural indicators of the baroque struggle between lust and love, the mercantile vision and its dream of sexual happiness in the representations of women's bodies, and in the partial victories of the bourgeoisie whose 'salvation by locomotion' as they take the train to riverside cafés in the country, as shown in the paintings of Renoir, are dependent on the working-class misery of Van Gogh's *The Potato Eaters*.

Mumford's theory of 'dynamic balance' is an ethical and political call, no less than Marx's vision of the whole person, to place a creative movement of life against its denial in the fatalistic cycles of capitalism. While for the individual, there is no lasting happiness outside the 'prescribed cycle of painful exhaustion and pleasurable regeneration', it is precisely in the denial of an authentic cycle that Arendt suggests the problem lies:

> And whatever throws this cycle out of balance – poverty and misery where exhaustion is followed by wretchedness instead of regeneration, or great riches and an entirely effortless life where boredom takes the place of exhaustion and where the mills of necessity, of consumption and digestion, grind an impotent human body mercilessly and barrenly to death – ruins the elemental happiness that comes from being alive. [146]

Turning from eternity to the question of the lost time of history, of many possible narratives contained within the book, Mumford's brief history of Protestantism makes a useful contrast with his meditations on time and eternity. The Protestant spirit offers a string of cycles of resistance to the cycles of natural and capitalist fatality. Turning Weber on his head, Mumford saw in Protestantism, precisely a challenge to capitalism, a fact now considerably documented by historians in our own time. Of the three early Protestant sects, the Waldensians, the Fraticelli and the Lollards, Mumford highlights the Waldensians. Long before the labours of E.P. Thompson, Christopher Hill and their followers produced a revisionist history of the English seventeenth and eighteenth centuries, Mumford had outlined a potential narrative of Protestant politics and ideology that constantly challenged the historical status quo.

Citing Waldo, 'things cannot go well in England, nor ever will, until all goods are held in common' and 'for what reason have they, whom we call lords, got the best of us?',[147] Mumford writes a cyclical organic narrative:

> This Christian communism did not die out under persecution and political oppression: the English peasants' revolt of 1381 and the German peasants' uprising in 1525 did not finish the story: the protest against both feudal and capitalist exploitation was still alive in the Digger movement in Cromwell's time, and it returned again in various communistic settlements, like those of the Shakers and the original Mormons in the New World.
>
> Nor was this all. Protestantism was essentially a layman's rebellion. The will to apply Christian standards to economic life finally laid the foundations for the great consumers' co-operative movement which was started by the Rochdale weavers in the middle of the nineteenth century. In less than half a century these pious British non-conformists built up a great organization for distribution and manufacture, rivalling the highest capitalist organizations in technical skill and managerial economy. The chief figure in building up this great enterprise, J.T.W. Mitchell, never received more than £150 a year for his services: proof that other incentives were available besides the gross regards capitalism offered. That co-operative movement was perhaps the last embodiment of medieval Protestantism, with its demand for a truly Christian economic order: its further spread in our day awaits a moral and spiritual regeneration at least as deep, as engrossing, as that which created the protestant personality.[148]

In our own time every budding labour historian will have cut his or her teeth on the story of the Rochdale weavers. Mumford, like all good historians, to an extent finds the history he needs. This reading of Protestant history has a distinctively American communitarian twist to it. Its sense of closure ignores the radical Catholic tradition which embodied almost identical theories of the person and, in contemporary form, was on Mumford's door step in Dorothy Day's Catholic Worker Movement. Mumford redeems himself to an extent in this recall of Protestant radical history, though his fault is that he cannot imagine a radical politics beyond the small community.

Mumford's sense of closure in his narrative might be just, though he does not pursue other alternatives in, for example, the endless sons of poor priests who agitated for political and social reform in Russia from 1812 onwards, the Baptist engineers who assisted Trotsky at the beginning of the Russian revolution, the non-conformists who stopped the British slave trade, the Welsh chapels which gave the British Liberals and the early British Labour Party much of its radicalism and the more general non-conformist spirit that pushed the great political reforms of Victorian Britain in the widening of the suffrage, prison reform, the creation of the National Health Service and the movement for Indian independence. Nonetheless, Mumford's narrative strongly encouraged a critique of consensual histories.

Mumford's valorization of the activities of small communities was instinctively right, as power became global and indifferent to the community and the person in his or her time. But what political direction could it give to the possibilities within that megalopolis in which the world's population increasingly lived. Perhaps one should suspend pessimism, for people more than survive even there, courtesy of micro-communities variously based on religion, mutual work, interests, family and ethnic base. Encouraging co-operation between the small groups is the political task of the future. Mumford's narrative of Protestantism, however, usefully brought attention to the continuity of a transcendent principle within specific historical praxis. In the long time-frames of anthropology and sociology, it is important to be reminded that the contingent 'personality' of leaders is not irrelevant in determining the fate of historical narrative. Luther's flogging father and he loss of his close friend in early youth, as Mumford points out, influenced his politics and his theology. If Mao was evasively and demagogically obtuse in his famous quip about the effects of the French revolution (that it was 'too early to tell'), the theories and actions of Danton and Robespierre in fact do still materially affect what used to be called 'the course of history,' and above all our memory of it in present practice. One must not be too quick to judge Mumford, for the political focus of the contemporary academy has frequently failed to link its comprehensive social investigations with the larger political issues in a more temporally comprehensive field of a possible historical narrative and action.

Significant action in the face of overwhelming power while managing to survive remains as potent a problem for the world's peoples as ever. Marx's internationalism while accurately locating the range and abstract indifference of invisible capitalist power simply neglected the conservative pull of human custom in local and personal life that, while often resistant to change, is also a conserving force in moment of crisis. Mumford's narrative of Protestantism which terminates its good phase in the eventually somewhat inward-looking self-protectionism of the Rochdale weavers, is nonetheless a worthwhile tale of resistance. The Rochdale weavers were a remarkable example of the human spirit surviving under the worst of circumstances. In Victorian Rochdale the women stood up to give birth because they had no change of bed linen. As the movement progressed, it produced the first-ever communal housing designed for the industrial poor. Mumford anticipated by years the kinds of attention among labour historians that the Rochdale weavers now regularly attract. In this example, a history of imaginative crypto-socialism, ethically and politically derived from radical Protestantism crossed the larger pattern of technological and cultural shifts and the contingent circumstances of the specialized political narrative in a truly poetic synthesis.

In 1942 Mumford's neighbour and friend, the publisher, scholar-gentleman and community activist Joel Spingarn, wrote two articles in *The Atlantic Monthly* on 'Politics and the Poet', declaring:

> Politics alone [...] will not make poetry. The political novels of Disraeli and Wells show that only too well. But the political sense must be recaptured: the sense of a *civitas*, of a whole, must be embodied in poetry.[149]

This statement also captures Mumford's own idea of the relation of poetry and politics. It is paralleled in Arendt's statements that in the Greek City State, 'to be political, to live in a *polis*, meant that everything was decided through words and persuasion and not through force and violence' and 'finding the right words at the right moment, quite apart from the information or communication they may convey, is action'.[150]

On 11 May 1944, Muriel Rukeyser wrote to Lewis Mumford:

> *The Condition of Man* has reached me very deeply. The test – the one test – of a book of conviction is in its images, and your book is full of that fire and life. It is deeply moving to me in its great accumulation – of love and grace and resistance, and of the opening of a sense of the world that is the mask of the greatness of our time. You confirm one's belief that this is the age when poetry may come, to make its connections again, to praise the whole woman, the whole man [...].[151]

She concluded: 'Your work demands poems. It is one of the things in the world that makes me wish to write wonderful poems and – how can it be said – to have many children.' In the letter Muriel Rukeyser included her poem 'The Antagonists' and wrote at the end 'This is the myth of the Elegies.' The poem was in fact the Ninth Elegy. In it Rukeyser rehearsed a fierce Blakean theme of innocence and experience, creation and destruction as contradictory poles of the historical human spirit. In it she celebrated an American tradition, taking the nationalist spirit of Hart Crane's *The Bridge* into a darker more contradictory American myth. Rukeyser's *Elegies* were to complement Mumford's *The Condition of Man*, through a celebration of 'that grace and resistance' in private and public life, though in somewhat different terms. The terms would celebrate conflict and prophetically long for an end of conflict in love. Close to Mumford's ethics is Rukeyser's call for intensity, not rest, a poetic attempt to reconcile cosmic and worldly time, and a vision of a less Spenglerian America, an 'America of contradictions'[152] where (and here Mumford's panoramic history of cultural beliefs and practices is most pertinent) opposition, enmity, hatred and conflict call forth their countervailing movements and persist in them. In the poem she sent to Mumford, Rukeyser wrote:

> To that far meeting place, call home the enemies
> They keep their oppositions, for the strong
> Ironic joy of old intensities
> Still carries virile music.[153]

It is the long foreground and achievement of Rukeyser's *Elegies* that will be the subject of the last section of this book.

5

The Art of Memory: Muriel Rukeyser and the Turning World[1]

If we're going to set ourselves up as policing the whole world after the war, we've got to start understanding what responsibility will mean. Otherwise our policing will be worse than fascist domination because it won't be so honest although quite as ruthless.

— 'ETHEL'[2]

One need not be a materialist to confront idealism with the crushing reality of the material world. We shall come back to this point [...]

— JEAN-PAUL SARTRE[3]

Poetry creates in us a kind of memory.

— MURIEL RUKEYSER[4]

Praise that the homeless may in their bodies be
A house that time makes, where the future moves
In his dark lake.

— MURIEL RUKEYSER[5]

I

The Search for Muriel Rukeyser

'Forgot to say I liked the Muriel Rukeyser piece too', wrote Henry Miller to Dorothy Norman in 1941.[6] Miller was referring to Rukeyser's recent essay 'The Fear of Poetry', which had just been published in *TWICE A YEAR* and was pointing specifically to her defence of the German poet Hans Carossa. Carossa had read to Hitler's troops and was hence felt by the refugee community to have sold his soul. He had in fact refused the position of presidency of Hitler's National Socialist Akademie der Dichtung in Germany, explained Rukeyser, but his acceptance had been printed in advance and this is what people knew. He was therefore seen as an unwitting apologist for Goebbels's propaganda of normalcy. Rukeyser's defence of the unfortunate German poet was based on what she called his 'quiet voice'. His one authentic way of coping, she argued, was in fact courageous: an insistence on complexity that implicitly challenged the lying simplifications of the Nazi regime. She touched on his personal situation. He was an aging man with an invalid son. If nothing more, she insisted on hesitating before the absolutist judgement. Rukeyser, with Elizabeth Mayer, had translated, one of the poems Carossa had actually read to German troops for *TWICE A YEAR* and she published it in her defence of him. The 1936 poem immediately revealed itself as a powerful attack on the barbarity of war. Hitler himself was clearly figured in the poem's reference to an 'arrogant strange leader'.[7]

Though at this time firmly positioned on the left, defending complexity in an absolutist world was typical of Rukeyser's habitual judgements. Her instincts were always inclusive even if her intelligence was ruthless in the face of political brutality and the cynical use of terror. This is why the academic need to construct a specific genealogy around her has to be treated with caution. A too-exclusive focus, whether socialist, feminist, lesbian or Jewish (and she acknowledged and positively celebrated all of these), will do less than justice to her achievement.

In October 1944, the Mexican poet Octavio Paz wrote to Victor Serge in Mexico from Berkeley, California.[8] It was a long, detailed and affectionate letter: one exceptional voice appealing to another while surveying the wreckage of war and its approaching end. In it Paz outlined his fears for a cynical peace, a world dominated by Stalin, horrifying technological devices and the 'ideological destitution' of the United Nations ('*la penuria ideológica de las Naciones Unidas*'). Above all he bemoaned the ideological confusion: Picasso on the one hand had scurried to the communists, and Auden was 'caught between a betrayed revolution and the "controlled" ["*dirigo*"] world being planned for us [and had] chosen the desperate shelter of the Anglican church' (literally 'the burning nail of the Anglican church', '*se ha acido al clavo ardiente de la Iglesia Anglicana*'). When these people, he noted bitterly, 'renounce the world', they achieve their greatest worldly success.

Paz told Serge that in the case of Ezra Pound and T.S. Eliot, the aesthetically revolutionary poet was allied to the reactionary thinker: though one went to fascism and the other to the church. The younger poets, he continued, while generally influenced by the previous generation, and to a degree by Wallace Stevens, were seeking a freer more direct means of expression, which failed of true art but seemed more alive, not excluding the use of slang, than work by current French or Spanish poets. For Paz, the two best young poets were Karl

Shapiro (a *Partisan Review* favourite, he noted, though alas he too was heading toward Catholicism), the other was Muriel Rukeyser who, 'when she does not fall for eloquence', has 'true energy and poetic density.' Paz noted a 'suspicious cruelty' in the attacks on her in *Partisan Review*.[9]

Dorothy Norman published Rukeyser on six separate occasions in *TWICE A YEAR*, significantly more than any other writer. Yet she did not mention her at all in *Encounters*, her memoir of 1987. The reception of Rukeyser's work is something that is only now, some twenty-five years after her death, being taken up by younger scholars.[10] It has taken twenty-seven years to reissue (a fuller) *Collected Poems*, a volume that sold out almost immediately when first published, though there was an elusive paperback edition in between. It is not the purpose of this book to rehearse her 'reception': reception theory is popular enough in the academy, and, given current interest, the details will doubtless emerge sooner or later. There were, however, many fairly obvious reasons for her comparative neglect. The centrality of her career during the war was itself a fact. People were occupied elsewhere and afterwards desperate to forget both the war and the austerity of the 1930s. 'Comparative', however, is the operative word. She always had readers for her many books, which ranged from poetry to plays to complex critical biographies to books for children. Her own perception of her neglect was wry. 'I write books', she said to me in 1973, 'for one or two people.'

First and foremost, however, she was a poet. But she was a poet who fitted few categories of then-current fashion. She was too 'rhetorical' and too 'subjective' for the followers of the imagist and objectivist schools. She was too ideologically suspect for the New Critics who, in the majority of cases, though not invariably, preferred the traditional lyric form whose content was a little melancholy and mildly ironic about life in general (and preferably in transparently classical forms). She was too 'experimental' and too tainted with a 1930s socialist brush for others. Her 'socialist' credentials, ironically, on the other hand, were not immaculate enough for the fading literary dominance of the Stalinist left and she had hardly written to social-realist type even in the 1930s. She was lost among the new voices of the Beat generation, or the New York critics championing Elizabeth Bishop, Marianne Moore, Robert Lowell, Sylvia Plath or in the academy's general preference for the urbane sophisticated Wallace Stevens (whom she admired), or those who were championing the traditions of Eliot, Pound, Williams and Zukofsky, who were later taken up by the Black Mountain poets and led by Robert Creeley and Charles Olson into other directions. Those in today's dominant L=A=N=G=U=A=G=E school are respectful but equally have problems fitting her into their definite yet never quite defined 'poetics' frameworks. Her status hence remains ambiguous and her poetry falls outside marketable critical frames.

Like some other, until comparatively recently, brilliant and neglected American women poets of her generation (H.D., Mina Loy, Lorine Niedecker), Rukeyser wrote outside fashion, in the wrong modes, at the wrong time. In addition there were extraordinary personal attacks on her: she was too Jewish, too 'communist', too suspect in her sexual orientations, too disgracefully a single mother (in the 1940s this was still significant) and even too 'fat'. The influential critic M.L. Rosenthal, who did serious work on her, doubtless sensed the prevailing mood, as he never published the results of that work, something that might have set the course of her reputation somewhat differently in the post-war period.[11] That Rukeyser was acutely aware of this, can be judged from the English poet and scholar Eric Mottram's characteristically blunt letter to her as late as 1978: 'I take it as axiomatic that we must get rid of the Rosenthals and Trillings of this world by ignoring them into oblivion.'[12] It should also be added that, in the still exclusively nationalist orientation of American literary and cultural studies after the war, all of which the 'myth and symbol' school endorsed and subsequent schools have only just started to challenge, her voice addressed themes which were far too *international* for home consumption. One recalls the words of Chandralekha Pandit on arrival in war-time America: 'Nobody here has ever heard of India except ourselves' (see p. 246).

Nonetheless it will become clear that Rukeyser was by no means outside her own historical space and time. Quite the contrary: she was at the centre of the political and poetic affairs of the period, sharing, even with poets and critics most antipathetic to her, concerns for form and content that mark her out as a woman very much at a precise historical period, engaged in current literary and political debates. Her poetic world and practice simply resolved them in a different way. Rukeyser welcomed, for example, *TWICE A YEAR* as a journal that was needed for its time. She followed Norman's columns for *The New York Post* and advised on possible contributors for *TWICE A YEAR* from the West Coast where she was living and working in the late 1930s and the early 1940s. Like Kenneth Rexroth for Dwight Macdonald, she did not have much success here. East was East and West was West.

Rukeyser was always engaged in her particular moment and active, creatively and politically. She noted, for example, that Norman had used Anna Freud's recent work (with Dorothy Burlingham) *Young Children in Wartime* (1942), or rather the American edition, *War and Children* (1943), in her *New York Post* column, and remarked that she had also found it useful for her Eighth Elegy: 'Children's Elegy'. In the same letter of 1943, she explained to Norman that after she quit working for the Office of War Information she had held an exhibition for the New York Public Library, 'Words at War', sponsored by, among others, Pearl Buck (incidentally a close friend of the Pandit daughters), Wendell Wilkie, H.S. Canby and W.R. Benet. She was also organizing, she explained, poetry readings in the New York Public Library; she commented that the 'library people are ready now to have many more living connections between writers and readers through the library' and wrote that she was thinking of ways in which this new willingness might be used.[13]

She knew about 'words at war'. In spite of working for the office for war propaganda, Rukeyser was very concerned that limits were set to lying. She meditated more generally on the nature of the way in which words and images were used together in an article for the *New Republic* in 1943. The picture is not to be named as such in words but the two were to work together: 'Goya does it, when he calls a scene, through the side of whose frame pierce the rifles of the firing squad, "This is not to be looked at".' She was concerned, even in war, for a certain democratic honesty for posters that 'will explain our allies, not only as a set of flags, but in terms of their armies, their leaders, their people and what they fight for.'[14] Here she is very close to Lewis Mumford's views. Nurtured in the 1930s in which the film documentaries of the New Deal and the murals of the Mexican painters were major new media, visual culture as it is now called, was a very important aspect of her work. *Elegies*, an extraordinary sequence of long poems written during the 1940s would reflect its influence.

Norman left Rukeyser out of her memoir but the two women were very close in the 1940s. Not only were they Jewish New Yorkers of a certain class and economic background, they also shared that new sense of American confidence in the arts, partly focused around Alfred Stieglitz, not to mention Mumford and others. There was some difference in milieu, given Rukeyser's West Coast activities and her connections with the considerable Californian tradition of poets, artists and peace activists, for example, Kenneth Rexroth and Robert Duncan. This was a very different tradition from that of New York and New England, and few worked in both worlds. Rukeyser did. The Beat writers of course also did so famously in the 1950s, but the conjuncture for them was not without its difficulties, and was brief.

Most of all, both Norman and Rukeyser were political internationalists and committed to the fight for justice and civil liberties both at home and abroad. Both had strong mutual interests in religion, psychology, education, children, welfare, architecture and music. Rukeyser was further to the left but her world had the almost unique merit among the left of being complex and open without losing a sense of political commitment. She was sceptical of the dogmatism of the communists in both political and literary terms. Like Mumford (she was a close friend of his wife), she knew what was going on in the Soviet Union and in Germany long before most other people. In her last years she was president of PEN, still protesting, as a prematurely aged woman, against the incarceration of the poet Kim Chi Ha in South Korea. She visited Vietnam with Denise Levertov during the Vietnam War and was briefly imprisoned for her anti-war activities. All this was of a piece and a consistent thread through a life that had begun in the 1930s with an attempt to organize the migrant grape-pickers in California with Ella Winter.[15] For Rukeyser, as for Weil, there were only ethical actions. *Elegies* was certainly one of the most important long American poems of the twentieth century and has been virtually neglected by the critics.

Three of the *Elegies* were published by Norman, suggesting that the world of *TWICE A YEAR*, with its war-oriented international outlook, its concern for civil liberties, its engagement with the world of American labour, women, racial issues and the foundation of the postwar world of the United Nations, the Marshall Plan and the Bretton Woods Agreement is, politically, one of the most vital contexts for understanding the poems. But there are other contexts too, specifically in the poetic traditions to which Rukeyser was heir. The journal's concern with exiled and forgotten voices, its key ambitions of reinventing and bringing forward forgotten pasts to renew usable traditions, its emphasis on narrative and memory are also contextually relevant. In *TWICE A YEAR* there were key poets who gave context to *Elegies*, both living (Kenneth Patchen and Charles Olson among many other new voices) and republished dead poets (Whitman, Rilke, Hart Crane). Norman reprinted the Second Elegy: 'Age of the Magicians' in the second volume (III–IV 1939), the poem had just been published in *A Turning Wind* (1939). The Sixth Elegy: 'The River Elegy', in volume V–VI (1940–1) would be published three years later in *Beast in View* (1944). The Eighth Elegy: 'Children's Elegy', appeared in volume XII–XIII (1945). It had been published the year before, also in *Beast in View*. The precise context of these appearances of the poems can be quite poignant. For example in volume XII–XIII (1945) of *TWICE A YEAR* Norman printed Lewis Mumford's 'Admonition to Those Bereaved in War', a poem attempting to come to terms with his son's recent death on the Italian front. It therefore appeared in the context of Rukeyser's 'Easter Eve 1945' and 'Children's Elegy', both published in the same issue.

Norman also published some of Rukeyser's shorter poems, such as 'The Private Life of the Sphinx' from *The Green Wave* of 1948, as well as poems from *U.S. 1* (1938) and *A Turning Wind* (1939). Also appearing in *TWICE A YEAR* were selections from two of Rukeyser's most significant prose works: in volume VII (1940–1) 'The Fear of Poetry', which would later be variously incorporated into her *The Life of Poetry*, published in 1948,[16] and in volume VIII–IX (1942) 'The Amistad Mutiny', which was Chapter 2 of her remarkable book *Josiah Willard Gibbs: American Genius*. For the 1942 readers of *TWICE A YEAR*, this was a sneak preview of the entire work which was to be published a month later in book form. If Stieglitz was the visual spirit of *TWICE A YEAR* and Randolph Bourne its political spirit, Rukeyser might with justice have laid fair claim to be its poetic soul.

In 1942 Rukeyser was at the height of her reputation. With Stalin on the Allied side, her leftist convictions were tolerated, with her greatest prose work respectfully received if not terribly well understood, with four of her finest books of poems behind her and while she was writing what is arguably her finest long sequence in the great tradition of the American twentieth-century long poem, perhaps it was the moment of war itself that was to obliterate the attention that should have been accorded to her. Her work began to re-emerge again in the late 1960s only to go under again as the political atmosphere shifted once more to the right in the 1970s and 1980s. Literary critical attention and American Studies shifted from US international activity in relation to its ruthless global foreign policy, to highly theoreticized critical discourses about race, gender and personal life.

With a few distinguished exceptions, the feminists missed Rukeyser, partly because her absolutely committed feminist politics were gender implicit rather than explicit and were offered in relation to a more multiply engaged international politics, and partly because a very direct criticism of American politics and culture has always been a minority activity within the American academy, a fact which simply mirrors the broad consensus of a very conservative and inward-looking country. It was politically less dangerous to speak about the dynamics of gender psychology and behaviour (the way the 'individual' is 'constructed' as the not very illuminating jargon has it) and in broadly similar terms about the socio-psychological dynamics of race and identity, than to speak directly about the effects of American global economic and hegemonic power. While this may be an over-reductive binary analysis, the fact is the two critiques need to be made complementary.

Rukeyser's hands-on domestic and international political experience fed her instincts for inclusion, practical teaching, mutual discovery, non-dogmatic stances and spontaneous and collectivist strategies in any given situation. The shrill insistence on difference with its hierarchies of authenticity (political correctness) were anathema to her. Her preference was for intellectual play and intellectual seriousness, for the life of the mind and the life of the body together and direct political action. The rigid category, the axiomatic stance, right or left, was to her all part of the problem, not part of the solution.

In an undated fragment in the archives, for example, she wrote about women and poetry: 'I do not like to separate out a group for the sake of their likenesses; but here – making a group of women who write poems – the likenesses hold only for a moment, and then vanish.'[17] In the same paper, she spoke of her hatred of the fact that women were targeted as both as consumers and as stockholders, and spoke of the needed solidarity of women in the rejection of these influences on their lives. Here the 1930s socialist to a degree played down the pure insistence on a gender perspective. She spoke, too, of the need to harness anger in creativity and the necessity 'to set apart a flight of she-poets in the concentration of great images here', adding: 'What are their myths? What are their sacred objects? Are they objects indeed?'

Rukeyser always attempted to span the gap between 'politics' (addressed to the exterior world) and 'myth' (addressed to the interior world). For her the space between them would always be dynamic, always in very uncertain balance. The apparently exclusive narratives of both would be dramatically synthesized in the way the contradictions played out within her poetry. She spoke in the same fragment of Sappho rather than of Sacco, of Miriam's song, and of Deborah within her own Jewish tradition but, in case the feminists got rather over-excited about that, she also said that it was pre-eminently David and the writers of the Psalms 'who take us into personal poetry'.[18] In a counter-gesture to one of her most famous lines, 'Sacco not Sappho', she wrote that Sappho's songs opened an art 'of secret melody in the soul, creatively echoing the life, so that every stirring of the emotions became a miniature cosmos and formed itself into supreme poetry'.[19] Categories and one-line identifications, and the view created by the too-anthologized poem ('Effort at speech between two people' was what she had in mind), were there for radical unbalancing and destabilizing. She fought any attempt to pigeon-hole her as one who preferred 'reality' in an impossible opposition to 'myth', often using both concepts as moments in a dramatic argument of poetic discourse that could go either way, or indeed, preferably, somewhere else.

At the same time her fierce concern with women's lives led her to ask why brilliant girls failed; why rich women should be limited to lives of good taste, or poor women purely to materialist self-improvement. This is an analysis tied to old socialist convictions but it challenges over-simplified assumptions in class definition. The clichéd (that is, oppressive) parameters of pre-programmed (today's 'constructed') social behaviour were as hateful to her as the academic cliché, the tired fashionable phrase. Like Orwell, she knew that tired phrases were shoddy thinking and probably a symptom of demagogic practices: 'The poet as social critic', she said, 'I know what that is.'[20] As Shelley said long before her: 'Let us not be betrayed from a defence into a critical history of Poetry and its influence on Society.'[21] Like most of the contributors to *TWICE A YEAR*, she insisted on the long view of history as a means of evaluating the present. For Rukeyser, the very nature of the human itself depended upon a creative articulation of memory in writing.

The Inner World of Childhood

Perhaps it was her Jewish inheritance that made Rukeyser link her life as a story with her life as a poet so intimately, in a world of stories, political and otherwise. Arendt spoke of the patriarchs of the Old Testament dying 'in good old age and full of years'.[22] For Rukeyser, the fullness of the years was also the fullness of the story it described: 'Remember they say and Incarnatus Est.'[23] Her diaries, day by day, from the age of ten show just how strong a sense she had of the story she wanted to unfold: an upper-middle-class child with a passionate need for knowledge of the world and with many opportunities to fulfil that need. Music, for example, was a great part of her childhood for it was the sole emotional expression available in a conflicted and very repressive family life. So the visits to the opera from a very early age and her piano practice were points of stability together with ice-creams and horse-riding. Something of her widely tolerant interest in religious life is indicated in the fact that she seemed to go both to Temple and Sunday school without any conflict. Tim Dayton has shown how education at the Fieldston schools, associated with 'Ethical Culture' (a quasi-religious movement founded by Felix Adler), was of crucial importance to Rukeyser. In Adler, Dayton continues, citing Howard Radest, 'the labor question, Kant and Emerson mingle with currents of the Jewish prophetic tradition and reform'.[24]

Her interest in science is foreshadowed in an entry for Monday 7 January 1924: 'Found microscope and how to work it. Wonderful!' A few days later the same exclamation was used for Cecil B. DeMille's first *The Ten Commandments* (1923), with the 'Grand Duke of Hollywood' Theodore Roberts in the title role. Her interest in movies, as for many children of her generation, never wavered. What she later thought of Charlton Heston in DeMille's second version of 1959 is not recorded.

In a typed autobiographical fragment, Rukeyser noted that there was no Judaism in her childhood, there was a silver ceremonial cup, handed down from her great grandfather who had been a cantor. She added there was a legend that her family was directly descended from Akiba, the Jewish second-century martyr to Rome, the poor shepherd who had collected the oral tradition into writing form and tried to match practice with scripture. Legend it probably was, but the key points of his life mentioned here are easy enough to translate into Rukeyser's adopted credo: her alertness to folk and oral poetry, her drive for drawing writing, truth and praxis together. She was less interested in Jewish history than in the Bible, though she said 'I was told never to name Jesus'.[25]

Rukeyser grew up, then, a passive Jew and she worried that her middle-class family wanted a religion of reassurance rather than of suffering. As for the Bible, and here she most coincides with the traditions of radical Protestantism, 'its clash and poetry and nakedness, its fiery vision of a conflict resolved only in God, were closer to what was outside in the city than anything that was going on in the Temple.'[26] Concluding *The Life of Poetry*, she wrote:

> Akiba, who fought to include the Song of Songs in the Bible, who was smuggled out of Jerusalem in a coffin by his disciples, who believed in Bar Cohba's revolution, who was tortured to death by his Roman friend, the general Rufus until he said smiling: 'The commandment says: Thou shalt love the lord thy God with all thy heart, with all thy soul, and with all thy might. I have always loved Him with all my heart and with all my soul; now I know that I love Him with all my life.' And he died.[27]

More than half a dozen years later, she recorded in her diary moments of her reading and writing with her early political experiences and reactions. Short plot outlines for stories mirror the emotional triangle between mother, father and aunt and her sense of rebellion within the family circle. In her literary notes there is an essay on Lewis Carroll and James Joyce with particular comments about the nature of dreams and 'telescoping words, multiplication in place of addition – overtones – (over words)';[28] all of which show the burgeoning poet engaged in the nature of dream, sound and diction. And as for *Alice in Wonderland*, there is one pregnant phrase given her later attempts to think of the world of science and the inner life together as correspondent intelligibilities: 'Dodgson a mathematician – application to dream, to life.' She also expressed admiration for Proust's great work, and for what she called the danger of language becoming too strict, of the need for it to be 'allegory enriched by multiple meanings' and she added 'realism ditto Alice as Allegory!'

On the usual adolescent promptings she had a wry self-reflection and above all a very healthy sense of humour: 'Virgin birth all right, if a poem comes out of this Masturbation! [...] sleep well Muriel.' However, while she thought they were 'good', she did not like Luis Buñuel's and Salvador Dalí's *L'Age d'Or*, finding the surrealist sexual symbolism 'sterile': 'lubricious always, never priapic, never lusty.' This is when she is writing *U.S. 1* and the degree to which she insisted on joining worlds, the world of emotion and dreams with that of politics, is further instanced in the comedy of an entry: 'To bed with Trotsky (how would that have been?).' In the atmosphere of the 1930s, that ever-ready ability to puncture male sententiousness was refreshing.

By 1933 there is a sense that her childhood is over: 'God those old days – poor kid, lost utterly, except for the Oxford Book [of Poetry]. And Bach. And the Pavane [Fauré?] And the "Jeune fille aux cheveux de lin" [Debussy, *Preludes*].' The intellectual and emotional complexity of music was to carry over in many ways into her poetry. The fragmentary diary also reveals a critical self-examination as strong as any Puritan: for those with Jewish or strong Protestant non-conformist backgrounds, it came with the territory. The entry for 18 March 1933 records her enthusiasm for being engaged in covering the Scottsboro trial[29] and between 28 March and 7 April there is a breathless list of travel and cities visited. Besides catching typhoid fever she worked for the International Labor Defence, which dealt with Scottsboro defendants' appeals. On 14 April, some twenty-six days before the burning of 20,000 books in the Opernplatz, Berlin on 10 May, she notes that 'Hitler and Nazi students are burning all Jewish and Marxist books.' In April she attends T.S. Eliot's lectures on Milton, commenting:

> Eliot on Milton and imagination emotion recollected in tranquillity, right relationship and not precise words, significance of length of lives, Samson Agonistes, Dante, when he spoke of Ant[ony] and Cleo[patra], he quoted 'of many thousand kisses, the poor last [I lay upon thy lips]'[30]

The war years were to be a time of personal trial and also of astonishing creativity. These are the years, in terms of the poetry, that are most relevant to this book. They were followed, however, by years of even more personal difficulty which tested to the limit her faith that the moment of failure was also a moment of potential renewal through faith in herself and her work. The years 1945 and 1946 were spent in recovery from her marriage. After a lunch with Mrs Salinger at which the latter had remarked that Wilhelm Reich had said to her 'You must make habit in your life. Nobody will make it for you', Rukeyser noted: 'It hit me very hard.' These were years of self-recrimination, a struggle to move back out of self-preoccupation, 'to cut down to joy, where the next cycle begins again.'[31] On 3 November 1946, she finds a palpable release:

> Flying again! [...] the feeling of stick and controls, yielding with the tilt (look at wing angle) and suddenly it's all yours [...] The ability to turn and do the first things [...] The air excitement continued all day.[32]

It was not simply an emotional release. The skill needed in these still relatively early days of flying where sensuous contact with the elements required crucial personal physical reactions and instant judgements had a serious parallel for her in negotiating a poem in the unpredictable appearance of diction, rhythm, image, and intelligibility in the act of creation itself. 'The ability to turn' was foundational in poetry and in life.

Turning was turning away and turning into. Rukeyser always attempted to exteriorize her strong interest in her own inner life by her life-long interest in children and their development. No less than Olson and in very different terms the movement between inner and outer was at the heart of and incorporated in her 'project'. Her books for children, for example, are exemplary in their invention and pedagogic sense of what the child needs in terms of encouragement to curiosity, serious thinking and learning, exhibiting a balance between needful care and liberty.[33]

In this respect her life-long friendship with Frances Wickes, the child psychologist, whose literary executor she became, was important. In an undated letter Wickes wrote to Rukeyser: 'I want to do an inner diary of my own inner life as it touches the highly lighted memories that have been beacons lighting the way from childhood to old age. What is your feeling about that?'[34] They shared thoughts about dreams and the theories of Jung, who had written the introduction to Wickes's first book, *The Inner Life of Childhood* (1927). He noted that: 'It is no wonder that most nervous disorders of children start from a troubled psychic atmosphere of the parents.' He added: 'This book gives a number of remarkable instances of parental influence fatal for the child.'[35] Most important of all, Jung made a distinction between the 'soul' and the 'psyche':

> Apart from the problem of the environmental influence the book lays stress on psychic factors that have to do with the child's soul rather than with his psyche. The latter can be the subject of scientific research, but the spiritual values, the appurtenances of the soul escape a merely intellectual treatment. It does not help to have sceptical views about them – nature does not care for your opinions – when you have to deal with man's soul, you can meet it only on its grounds. And you have to do it when you are confronted with the real and overwhelming problems of life.[36]

The British educational radical A.S. Neill, who was sceptical of most psychoanalysts, made the same point when he said, 'I grant the great value of books dealing with clinical features, but a book on – say – cases of anal-eroticism in children does not assist the parent much in the fundamentals of child nature.'[37] Jung of course was anathema to the left, and not taken seriously by most Freudians, who were as sceptical of the 'soul' as any Marxist convinced that it was a mystical and cynically manipulated illusion of bourgeois subjectivity. Something of these old ideological tensions between politics and psychology, and the left's preference for Freud over Jung in relation not only to politics but to child development, were submitted to the blandishments of black humour in Pynchon's *The Crying of Lot 49*, where an ex-Nazi psychiatrist, who has gone mad, locks himself in his office with a Gewehr 43 rifle. Negotiating with the heroine, the mad psychiatrist explains:

> If I'd been a real Nazi I'd have chosen Jung, nicht wahr? But I chose Freud instead, the Jew. Freud's vision of the world had no Buchenwalds in it. Buchenwald, according to Freud, once the light was let in, would become a soccer field, fat children would learn flower-arranging and solfeggio in the strangling rooms.[38]

However, in a note Rukeyser copied down from Norman O. Brown's *Life Against Death* (which she happily mis-transcribed as *Love Against Death*), the absoluteness of the divide of the 1930s was given a revisionary reading by one of the post-war 'radical Freudians'. Rukeyser's own note read: 'Modern poetry, like psychoanalysis and Protestant Theology, faces the problem of the Resurrection of the Body – Whitehead – Blake.'[39] The context of that sentence was Brown's revisionary reading of Freud's Death Instinct. Resurrection is not about the literal resurrection of the body, but a coming to terms with the fact that it dies, thus producing a life-oriented attitude to death and the body that hence, through a Blakean sense of rhythm and exuberance, produces the true 'risen body'. The 'immortal soul' of the Christians, according to Brown, in fact only confused the issue. The only theologian worth considering in this sense was 'the cobbler of Görlitz, Jacob Boehme'.[40] That philosopher–mystic was as important for Rukeyser as he was for Brown and indeed Rilke. Against the eschatological speculations of modern theologians such as Paul Tillich and Karl Barth, stood Boehme's *theologia ex idea vitae deducta*.

Boehme was a central thinker for Rukeyser. In Brown's words: 'backward he is linked, through Parcelsus and alchemy, to the tradition of Christian gnosticism and Jewish cabalism, forward he is linked, through his influence on the romantics, Blake, Novalis, and Hegel, with Freud.' Brown was at pains to distinguish Boehme's 'mystical' sense of a joy in the vitality of the earth and a sense of connectedness with it from the 'sublimation mysticism' of Evelyn Underhill and Aldous Huxley: a representation of experience rightly problematic for Marxists, scientists, Freudians and indeed, it has to be said, a number of theologians. This important distinction, properly maintained, explains Sartre's refusal to endorse the materialist/idealist divide that bedevilled bad socialist thinking. With all Boehme's faults (his paradisiacal body is too ambiguous and immaterial and he refused to accept the brutal physical death of the body), for Brown he arrives at much the same point as Joseph Needham's study of Taoism or Eliade's study of yoga. These thinkers, argued Brown, also refuse to accept death as part of the body and the same is implicit in Whitehead's philosophy of nature, which was much admired by Needham. Brown's discussion touches on many of the important influences on Rukeyser's own world. The heirs of Boehme are William Blake, Novalis, Hegel and Goethe: those whom Freud credited with being the real discoverers of the unconscious. But Brown refused to grant psychoanalysis a monopoly on interpretations and ways to a healthy life: 'anyone who *loves art* knows that psychoanalysis has no monopoly on the power to heal.'[41]

Brown finally comes back down on the side of Freud, believing that Jung ultimately was in 'flight from the problem of the body'. Brown, like Rukeyser, was engaged with a spectrum of concerns from the repression of the child to a Goethe-like sense of a holistic and ecological self acting in complex interaction with the world of nature. Brown also noted that Marxism did not have exclusive use of dialectics. Using Trilling's connection between dream logic and poetic logic (symbolism, condensation of meaning, displacement of accent), Brown touched on the connection between poetry and dream: 'Dreams are certainly an activity of the mind struggling to circumvent the formal-logical law of contradiction.'[42]

Brown's visionary concluding exegesis at the end of *Life Against Death* provides an illuminating summary of many parameters of the field of Rukeyser's poetic world in the early to late 1950s. Rukeyser must have read it with attention, given the number of writers and thinkers evoked in Brown's work with whom she herself had already been engaged. Nonetheless, certain cautionary notes must be sounded. In Brown the poetic world is too easily recuperated within the worlds of religion, psychoanalysis and to a lesser extent Marxism. Marcuse's later critique of Brown's *Love's Body* showed that while Brown, as Richard King has pointed out, had correctly pointed to the symbolic nature of human history, he had failed to address the question 'symbolic of what?'.[43] The intentionality of the symbol faces a real world. Rukeyser herself, whatever her later appreciation of Jung, never went down this road, any more than she finally joined the Anglican Church (though here she was very tempted). Rukeyser refused the 'cosmic melodrama' because she wrote poetry not psychoanalysis, theology or socialist theory. The cosmic drama was something else: always in contention and contact with the immediate world that you could stub your toe against, to be fought as much as embraced. Marxism was just as much prone to the cosmic melodrama as capitalism, theology and Jungian psychology. Rukeyser's world was too Heraclitean, much too much in flux, with the self always active, however battered. It was a world in which poetry rehearsed the very movement of mind and body together in real time and concrete history. And it was very specific: 'I am an old she-poet of the Village', she said to me at the artist's co-operative Westbeth, below 14th Street, New York, in 1973. For Rukeyser, quietism and transcendental mysticism, particularly of the bourgeois kind, were never options. There was something very earthly in the great contraries her poetic world revealed.

The strength of Brown's insight, at least in 1959, was that there was a distinction to made between 'sublimation mysticism' and what might be positively gained for poetry from the rich discourses of ethical, philosophical, and religious writing and practice: from mystics, theologians, dreamers, philosophers, the belief systems of non-western peoples, and the writings of psychoanalysts. The range for Rukeyser was from Chinese philosophers and German theologians to Hopi Indians; from the Native Americans of Boas and his students, whom she studied from the early years of the century onwards, to Jung and D'Arcy Thompson. For Rukeyser, many of the canonical discourses of metaphysics, social and cultural practice, Marxism and science, not to mention the church, had failed precisely because they had taken an exclusivist approach to their particular discourse and failed to relate their respective visions to the human, unpredictable and suffering world.

So there was to be a difference then between the 'soul' of a child and its 'psyche' in Frances's Wickes judgement as there was also a difference between the visionary world of a Blake and 'sublimation mysticism'. The relationship between the visionary and the mystic could be complex and the distinction is fought out in every discourse of human beings engaged in the turmoil of history. Innocence and experience in Blake's *Songs of Innocence and Experience* were, after all, often perilously close to each other, the one often appearing in the guise of the other. Poetry offered powerful ways of both identifying the conjuncture and specifying the difference, as Wickes herself noted:

> We must, even in our dealing with young children, keep clear the distinction between the phantasy which is creative and has the value that we find in poetry and works of imagination, and the phantasy which is used as a retreat from reality.[44]

Under the influence of both Freud and Jung, Wickes combined the notion of dream with unconscious content relating to neurosis and its potential origins in infant memories and sexual repression. In relation to creative work, she noted that Freud was often reductive and she was favourably disposed to Adler's theory of the neurosis of the self-aggrandizing male 'roused by his failure to impress himself on others.'[45] She preferred the multiple causality of Jung's symbolic interpretations, which went beyond a unique reference to neurosis. Again she made a distinction between the malign use of cosmic symbols ('when the whole world is withdrawn from outer reality') as in 'elemental hates, fears, or religious ecstasies – embodiments of racial experiences', and their benign use as 'treasures of the unconscious' in 'images of compelling beauty or terror, symbols of the spiritual experiences through which man has developed mythological and cosmic images [that] rise to the conscious and become the material of the poet, the artist, or the spiritual prophet.'[46] Rukeyser's *Elegies* develop a quasi-dramatic dialectical relation between the two. For her, the 'Prophet' is the 'seer' in Blake's sense, here usefully paraphrased by Northrop Frye: 'It is the superior clarity and accuracy of the prophet's vision that makes him an artist, and that makes the great artist prophetic.'[47] In *Elegies*, the 'Magician' is the figure of sublimation mysticism, the malign distorted twin of the 'Prophet', the Blakean poet.

Throughout her life, Frances Wickes, pupil of Jung and child pyschotherapist, was a close friend of Rukeyser's. They shared a passionate concern with the nature of the inner life of both children and adults and with the ways in which that might be articulated in speech and language. Silence between people, the refusal to speak, for both of them was innately cruel and destructive. Wickes's work, however, was much closer to a purely religious sensibility than Rukeyser's. Both, however, from rather different perspectives, were seriously engaged with the meaning of mythology and the possibility of its continuing usefulness in both psychology and poetry.

In a somewhat Victorian tradition, Wickes felt that the inner world of the child was close to the mythological world, a closeness that in turn expressed the truths of the collective unconscious. While 'universal', it had different symbolic expressions in historically different races. Above all, Wickes was concerned with the growth of the child, and the need for the inner life, or 'soul' to develop with some degree of freedom in a world that only valued exterior and pragmatic experience, never mind danger and violence. A political dimension was, a necessary part of this: 'This does not mean a rebellion against the collective, for true individuation accepts the responsibility of the individual as part of the social order.'[48] Further, the responsibility for recognizing that inner world of the child was part of a dialectical gaze: 'We must know our own inner life if we would know the child.'[49]

This imaginative need for a deep sense of the other, a recognition that is finally imaginative on the basis of an absence of fear, was a major theme in all

Rukeyser's poetry. Rukeyser saw hostility to poetry as the fear of complex words allied to deep and powerful feeling that had been suppressed in the pragmatic world of common-sense language. In Wickes's words: 'The other side is our growth in deeper life through making conscious those forces which lie buried within us all.'[50] To accept the story of the child without ridiculing it is a first step in this dialogue of mutual recognition. After all, the child has a way of gathering from us 'the atmosphere of all that we most carefully ignore in ourselves'.[51] In the reciprocity of the exchange, the parents, the bringers of the story of the past and themselves, bear a heavy responsibility. Like A.S. Neill, she believed the problem child reflected the 'problem parent'.[52] So she details a number of case studies of the relationships between husbands and wives, their relationships with their own parents, not to mention relationships between parents and institutional personnel (nurses, doctors and so forth). These relationships are described in detail for their effect on the child. En route, a number of criticisms are made of the inadequacy of social consensus, promoted through various authorities from the medical profession to the church, in relation to any individual case.

There are many influences that accelerated this attack on the still significantly repressive Victorian world. These include examples from Ibsen plays to the anthropologist Paul Radin on the fear of ridicule in 'primitive' peoples.[53] Wickes, however, did not have Rukeyser's open attitudes to masturbation and gay sex and the book's designation of these as 'distortions' is, from the present perspective, a serious fault. Rukeyser also never went as far as Wickes, close though the two women were, in relation to the more transcendental aspects of Jung's discourse. Nonetheless, the sense of authoritarian behaviour in relation to the child is clearly condemned by both: 'We have no more right to a personal will-to-power attitude with our child than in any other human relation.'[54] This was most manifest in what she called 'the struggle of modern youth'.[55] In words that were drawn upon in Rukeyser's *Elegies*, Wickes argued that young people ought to decide for themselves questions of sexuality. Largely concerned with middle-class young people, she argued that increasing social, professional and educational demands (examinations, strict social rules and conventions) created a situation where key issues of personal development were postponed or never addressed. Wickes took seriously the dreams, invented stories (including the familiar 'imagined companion', occasionally displaying a Jekyll-and-Hyde ambiguity), and self-revelations of her children-patients. Getting the balance right between the inner and outer worlds, was her aim: in the dualistic terminology of the period, to create a rhythm between 'introspection' and 'extroversion', so that the self and the world was in a kind of moving equilibrium.

The chapter on 'fear' was one that Rukeyser must have found particularly absorbing. Perhaps she noted particularly that moment when a patient reveals a permanent terror 'because of the sound of her mother's voice when quarrelling with her father'.[56] However limiting some of the discussion of sexuality seems from this distance in time, the power of desire as it is structured via the mediations of social consensus and approved habit is given full credit, especially in relation to self-repression and children suffering the effects of unfulfilled adults: 'It is this that makes the unsatisfied older person such a dangerous guide and companion for the young.'[57] Certainly Wickes felt that the child had a right to a private space in which dreams were also private: 'It is, therefore, a true instinct which bids the child to guard these secrets', and she compared this refusal with the made-up stories tribal peoples told to missionaries to guard their own privacy. Her conclusion was frank: 'Unless some provision is made for the acceptance of the irrational and of the instinctive, and the forces of the unconscious are accepted there is danger of a split between these two sides which may result in destroying the supposedly impregnable fortress of the conscious structure.'[58]

The other book of crucial importance to Rukeyser's view of the child in *Elegies* was Anna Freud and Dorothy T. Burlingham's *War and Children* of 1943. Anna Freud was the daughter of Sigmund and, like the Jung-influenced Wickes, presented a series of case studies of children disturbed not just by the London Blitz but also by the very difficult British policy of evacuation which traumatized many children forcibly separated from their parents. It is a difficult book to characterize, part diary, part mini-biography, part documentary, part descriptive psychology, part anecdotal narrative and part war propaganda. With the American market in mind, war and above all, the separation of 'the mother and child' had the same explosive propagandistic effect as Harriet Beecher Stowe's *Uncle Tom's Cabin* a century earlier. The American edition was subtitled 'A message to American parents.'

Today the book still moves one. The voices of Anna Freud and her co-worker are remarkable in their refusal to use jargonized or theoretical language. The volume is exemplary in its child-centeredness, in its frank acknowledgement of their own many failures, in its pragmatism, in its admission of 'luck' in certain cases, in its admission too of the huge problems of the policy of evacuation on children's states of mind and the variable care that the children actually got. It admitted immediately that no female nurse with her need for time off and weekends is going to have the serious and in-depth involvement with the child that the mother can bring. Foster families outside London involved huge problems of readjustment, especially in a very class-conscious society. Children billeted above their status resented the *modus vivendi* as a criticism of their parents, those billeted below their class status thought they were being punished in some way. As Wickes would have said, the very soul of the child was in peril.

Occasionally one senses a certain chilliness in the slightly unnerving unambiguous authority of the daughter of Freud, a little frostiness in the decisiveness of an oddly English tone of judgement from the maternalist heights of wealthy Hampstead. One misses the warmth of a Wickes. Anna Freud makes no distinction between the soul and the psyche. By way of compensation the point of view is much more collective and there is a strenuous effort to avoid prejudice and typecasting in terms of class behaviour, whether in relation to mother or child. The newspapers were not without blame in this respect, given some of the right-wing class snobbery of tabloid reactions to the evacuations. Anna Freud, in defiance of the tabloids, found poorly educated working-class mothers both imaginatively caring and intelligent in relation to the situation. They were emphatically not, as the papers trumpeted, articulating middle-class anxieties in relation to the working classes: 'only too glad to dump their children on us and forget all about them'.[59]

Anna Freud's practical recognition of the need for personal attachments, small groups for identification, emotional stability and continuing educational training after the traumatic break-up of family life was exemplary. So too was the breaking of all the strict English hospital visiting hour rules, so parents had access to their children at any time, indifferent to the convenience of staff, a practice continued in the Great Ormond Street children's hospital to this day. The sheer narrative skill of the case histories was also exemplary and the second half of the book gives the 'raw' material of the notes for the reader to check the conclusions of the earlier and more reflective case histories. In practice, of course, these were both 'constructed' narratives but it enabled two styles of rhetoric to narrate the 'medical' story, complicating it in favour of what is heard, and hence opening a critical space in relation to the pragmatic professional judgement.

The questions of safety versus trauma for the child in war are left as ambiguous but ways of palliating the situation are imaginatively and sympathetically addressed: 'War above everything else, signifies the period of time for which children have to be separated from their parents.'[60] Some unfortunate and disturbed children wandered back and forth from out of town back to London in intense psychological crisis. The choice between two evils was overwhelming for some, depriving the child of any sort of security. Perhaps the most devastating quotation in the entire book comes from a child at the Hampstead Nurseries as they were then called. Ivan, who was five years old, declared from the depths of existential anguish: 'I am nobody's nothing.'[61] In 'Children's Elegy', Rukeyser coalesced this moment with another 'case history' of a child named Iris, who coughed like her father who had died of lung disease after the family had been bombed out, and declared her lost father to be her mother. In the poem, as will be demonstrated, this 'transference' becomes a moment in a larger argument about those 'who were broken off from love'.[62] The cough becomes a sign of pure absence variously transferred:

> Mother is gone away, my cat sits here coughing,
> I cough and sit. I am nobody's nothing.[63]

Anna Freud also reported: 'In observing the little girls, one often feels that the doll does not represent the baby which the child can "mother" but rather that the doll represents the absent mother herself.'[64] Rukeyser was to give this observation a rather different inflection:

> You will not know, you have a sister and a brother;
> My doll is not my child, my doll is my mother.
>
> However strong we are, it is not strong enough.
> I want to grow up. To come back to love.[65]

Rukeyser seems here to reject the compulsions of family love, especially in its denial and to reverse the natural order, so that, expressed in subtly altered gender terms here (and surely she knew exactly what she was doing), the child becomes mother/father of the woman/man and, beyond even that, needs to recreate the person in love outside the determinations of biology or the trauma-ridden oedipal psyche. The doll is rejected as representing a future maternal role (a symbol of normative peacetime conditions) and reinterpreted as mother to palliate the temporarily erased past. Rukeyser suggests both are traps and actions of weakness. Love and growing up are ways out of the archetypal cycle of psychological fatalism. The case history will be rescued as a human story with a free future.

Indeed, Anna Freud noted how the child reacting to the separation of evacuation often produced surprising and unpredictable results. Children had mercifully (and unmercifully) short memories after all. Often the unfortunate parents found that out of sight was out of mind. The intensity and longevity of trauma depended a great deal on the parents' own state of mind and whether both parent and child could face and articulate the difficulties. The sense of reality and unreality in child and parent produced quite different states of anxiety which deflected, reinforced or slowed the normal adjustments of the growing child: the short attention spans, ordinary aggressive behaviour, the development of a sense of guilt and prohibition. Anna Freud had only respect for the 'quiet manner in which the London population on the whole met the air raids' which reduced the number of 'shocked children'.[66]

More than the actual violence of war, it was the evacuation itself, though obviously a result of that violence, that produced the most trauma. Anna Freud adopted her father's Manichean conflict between desire and the reality principle to structure her description of the first five years of the child's development. How evacuation effected this transition from 'savagery' to 'civilization',[67] however simplistic a proposition, produced some complicated effects. Hate for the parent and guilt about that hate were intensified in war. Fantasies of love and hate, alternating between the imagined absent parent and real present one on the visits to the nursery produced a series of complicated and detailed stories with huge variations in behaviour.

Rukeyser would particularly have been struck by the need for imaginative speech. Finding the words for the very young child was difficult enough, but when the experiences were frightening, it was almost impossible: 'Under the conditions of nursery life the children do not talk about their frightening experiences immediately after they have happened.'[68] Often they deflected it in play and made-up stories. For Rukeyser, finding the imaginative words for intense emotional experience began in childhood and the same task continued into adulthood was the task of poetry.

As for the representation of the subjective self in poetry, Rukeyser was quite ruthless in cutting out the direct reference. Her 'I' is multiple, although unlike the Pound-influenced poets, she does use it. But it is not for the mode of immediate concrete self-revelation any more than Wordsworth's 'I' in 'I wandered lonely as a cloud'. In *The Green Wave*, for example, in the poem 'Foghorn in Horror' the last line reads: 'Thirty years, and my full strength, and all I touch has failed/I sit and see/ the black clothes on the line are beautiful, the sky drifting away.'[69] In an earlier draft these lines read: 'Thirty years, and my full strength, and all I touch has failed/love gone, my work rejected, my marriage annulled/I sit and see'. The immediate 'realistic' context for the presentation of the ego in the final version is taken out in order to banish self-absorption, and self-pity: 'I'd rather be Muriel', she once said, 'than dead and Ariel.'[70] Confessional poetry was to be resisted as much as social-realist poetry. For Rukeyser, both claimed authenticity too easily.

A Story of Spain

It was a very brief moment in Spain that became the defining political and personal experience for Rukeyser. The Spanish Civil War was of course a *cause célèbre* for radicals in the 1930s, and with justice. In 1936 Franco, with the help of German and Italian arms and Moroccan troops, moved in against the democratically elected government in Spain. It was the bloodiest civil war in Western Europe since the French revolution and the Armenian massacres, a curtain raiser for the Second World War. For Rukeyser it was an extraordinarily brief but very intense experience of international politics and personal love.

Rukeyser went to Spain in 1936, initially at the request of the London magazine *Life and Letters Today*, to cover the first 'People's Olympiad'. The games were organized as a political and sporting challenge to the 1936 Berlin Olympics, which Goebbels had used as occasion for Nazi propaganda, and where Hitler had refused to hang a gold medal around the neck of the great African-American athlete Jesse Owens. While she was in Spain the Spanish Civil War broke out and Rukeyser was evacuated. She wrote up some of the experience in 'Mediterranean', a four-page poem first published as a pamphlet by the New York Writers and Artists Committee Medical Bureau to Aid Spanish Democracy in 1937. She prefaced the poem with a brief note:

> On the evening of July 25, 1936, five days after the outbreak of the Spanish Civil War, Americans with the Anti-Fascist Olympic Games were evacuated from Barcelona at the order of the Catalonian Government. In a small Spanish boat, the *Cuidad di Ibiz*, which the Belgians had chartered, they and a group of five hundred, including the Hungarian and Belgian teams as well as the American, sailed overnight to Sète, the first port in France. The only men who remained were those who had volunteered on the Loyalist forces: the core of the future International Column.[71]

Rukeyser had left New York (heading for Spain) in a hired Ford car on 10 June 1936 to sail from Quebec to London on the *Duchess of Richmond*. Passing Troy, New York, she remembered the revolutionary battle of Saratoga. On board ship, sailing by Saquenay fjord, she wrote 'Leica in sheets of shadow, river glazed sepia, single lights, strong calm ripples & I was flower & advice thrown on the water – write *U.S. 1* now.'[72] With the 'end of America', as she phrased it in the diary notes, passing Labrador and Belle Isle, she felt her twenty-three-year-old self different, moving into strange and new territory. She wrote it up a short while later in a poem called 'Outpost' published in *U.S. 1*:

> End of America! The ocean opening,
> Lighthouse and iceberg, vestige of vegetable green
> The sad face everywhere sinking backward last:
> Not rock, not ice, but here lost civilized man,
> Outpost survivor [...][73]

The last phrase was to describe herself and feelings about her work and the lost civilized man was about to become grotesquely apparent in Spain: in both the personal and the political sense. But at first the mood was outwards and adventurous. The Western Isles of Scotland with Ailsa Craig filled her, the poet of islands, with wonder. Disembarking at Liverpool she followed the classic route of the nineteenth-century literary visitors to England: Liverpool to London, via Chester, Leominster, Shropshire, the Cotswolds: 'England green and winding and dug in, hedged, cloistered, lovely.' In London she walked down Piccadilly, turned into St James Park towards Buckingham Palace and noted the house of John Murray (the publisher of Byron and Darwin). In Shaftesbury Avenue she exclaimed to herself 'everyone tries to pick me up I must look so happy.' She saw Edith Evans, John Gielgud and Peggy Ashcroft in Chekhov's *The Seagull*. An assiduous tourist on this first occasion, she never lost her affection for England.

But she was meeting poets, too: H.D., T.S. Eliot and people from the *Left Review*, not to mention Otto van der Sprenkel, whose name she thought amusing. He was part of the Fabian circle at the LSE, a Workers' Educational Association (WEA) organizer and later a distinguished sinologist in Australia. She went to the ballet with H.D. and Robert Herring to see *Swan Lake, Don Juan* and *Petroushka*. Herring was the man whom H.D.'s companion, Bryher, the Cunard heiress, set up to edit the ill-fated magazine *Life and Letters*. It was under the auspices of this journal that Rukeyser went to Barcelona. On 16 July she wrote with a touch of irony, in her diary notes, 'To Barcelona for *Life and Letters*!' In less literal terms it proved truer than she would ever imagine. According to H.D.'s biographer, both the poet and her companion Bryher had rather fallen for Rukeyser but then pulled back, sensing early 'Auden-like' 'left wing tendencies': 'H.D.'s final comment on her was that it was difficult to concentrate on the trial of the Scottsboro boys during a Mozart ballet [*sic*].'[74] Rukeyser whose knowledge and love of music was unimpeachable, would emphatically not have thought about it during the ballet but she saw no difficulty participating in the worlds of both music and politics.

That other world of war and politics was becoming increasingly shrill and insistent. Rukeyser left Victoria station for Dover, Calais and Paris on 18 July, the day the Spanish Civil War broke out. The rest of the story can be read in her moving retrospective article for *Esquire Magazine* of 1974: 'We came for games'.[75] In this article, the sixty-year-old Rukeyser, having been to Vietnam with Senator Hart and Denise Levertov as part of a war protest and peace mission, reflects, in the middle of another terrible war, on the beginning of the Spanish Civil War. It was true, as she said: 'I lived in the first century of world wars'.[76] She began the article in real fictional time. 'We could see very little from the train.' The Afterword begins 'Now, a lifetime later, I think of all that followed', and then switches back to fictional real time, taking up the story. The break, which would be timeless in her memory, is the journey from Barcelona to Sète, a refugee voyage from Spain to France that was the reverse of that undertaken by Victor Serge and his companions from Marseille in 1941, five years later and in another war.

Rukeyser's memoir spoke of her meetings in London with 'people who afterward would be the Labour Government [...] poets and refugees'. Then later she observed 'the Spanish frontier at Port-Bou, and then this train, going slowly, with a flash of the Mediterranean, and the shoulders of olive hills, and a Catalan family in the wooden compartment with me'. The Catalan people particularly caught her attention. A few months later George Orwell observed:

> But I defy anyone to be thrown as I was among the Spanish working class – I ought perhaps to say the Catalan working class, for apart from the Aragonese and the Andalusians I mixed only with Catalans – and not be struck by their essential decency; above all their straightforwardness and generosity.[77]

Orwell's lengthy defence of the Catalan-based POUM in *Homage to Catalonia* is well known. It squares well with the accounts by Serge and indeed Camus. It was Mary McCarthy, writing for Nancy Macdonald's moving book of 1987, *Homage to the Spanish Exiles*, who spoke effectively of Orwell's work as being much more evocative 'than such respected "objective" histories as Hugh Thomas's'.[78] The terrible plight of the Spanish refugees in France after both the Civil War and the Second World War was taken up by Nancy Macdonald, Sonia Orwell and others and continued the practical work of the journal *politics* into the next two decades. Rukeyser's brief judgements were accurate, and in any case her acute political sense helped her make the distinctions early on.[79]

As the train conveying Rukeyser to Barcelona stopped in the declaration of the general strike and the tourists panicked, Rukeyser noted how the Catalans left the train to find immediate shelter locally leaving her with the Hungarian and Swiss water-polo teams. There was also a man named Otto Boch with whom she fell very much in love and who had come to run in the Games, a cabinet maker from Paris, 'Bavarian, with a broad strong face like a man in Breughel picture – or a Käthe Kollwitz'. He joined the fighting after the evacuation and died on the banks of the Segre river. Rukeyser never forgot this moment of passionate brief encounter. There were sundry other passengers whom she meticulously notes. Stuck on the train, they listen to the radio for the news of the battle in Barcelona: 'Beethoven's fifth, government bulletins, tangos, *You're driving me crazy*, sardanas, Catalan songs.' She notes who gives money to help the wounded and who does not: 'not the German family, not the Italian business man, not the Cockney shoe salesman; not the six platinum blondes, the Rodney Hudson Young Ladies, who were supposed to open tonight in Barcelona'. A League of Nations observer helps to write a letter to the mayor of the local town.

The one moment of her experience recorded in official histories of the war concerns a professor on the train who refused to hide a priest whose church had stored ammunition for the officers: 'The train had become famous for the story of the priest and the professor of philosophy.' In the words of a thoughtful left republican at the time: 'In the name of fatherland and religion, the Spanish right was prepared to commit any crime to save its privileges [...] the Spanish right was rooted in clericalism [...] a religion that had nothing to do with Christianity.'[80] The desecration of churches, nonetheless, was to trouble many on the left also in this war of unremitting violence. Rukeyser noted in her *Esquire* article that in Barcelona two contrasting spirals: 'Coils and spires of smoke rising from burning churches. The coils of color climbing the architectural heart of the city, Gaudi's marvelous church, untouched by harm.' As she writes, Rukeyser interprets the historical moment in terms of that discrimination a so-called 'mob' can often exhibit in its acts of revenge.

Using her multilingual phrase book, each language on a separately coloured set of pages, Rukeyser and Boch made an effort at speech between two people:

'With our language of many colors, we make a beginning.' Speech and colour would denote any authentic moment encountered in her poetry from that point onwards. They were finally rescued by 'Communists' (actually the Catalonian United Front of Socialists, Communists and Anarchists) and hence, to the chagrin of some of the Americans, they passed through the machine gun nests, the dead horses and dead mules to Barcelona where the shooting was still going on. Preparations are begun for the evacuation immediately, although the American and British athletes tried to stay. Rukeyser notes with disgust that 'our three Hollywood men' who have managed to get back to France have already lied to reporters of 'wild scenes of looting from the train, that they suffered deprivations and saw horrors.' But she herself experienced that first elation of Barcelona that Orwell talked about as she walked about with the British athletes always 'wonderful, brave, droll' in any crisis. Orwell wrote a few months later:

> Churches here and there were being systematically demolished by gangs of workmen. Every shop and café had an inscription saying that it had been collectivized; even the bootblacks had been collectivized and their boxes painted red and black. Waiters and shop-walkers looked you in the face and treated you as an equal. Servile and even ceremonial forms of speech had temporarily disappeared. Nobody said '*Senor*' or '*Don*' or even '*Usted*'; everyone called everyone else 'Comrade' and 'Thou', and said '*Salud!*' instead of 'Buenos días'.[81]

Rukeyser's account was that of a poet, it was certainly not factual in a documentary way. It was already rich with her familiar themes and images: colours, speech, language, spirals, sharp political judgements; the contingent moment was always infused with interpretation. In her Afterword in the *Esquire* reprint of the 1970s she spoke how she left because she did not have sufficient skills to nurse or to do child-care, the two skills the Catalan government needed. Otto stayed to join the militia: 'He had been waiting to fight fascism since Hitler came to power.'

She finished the narrative for *Esquire* in short strokes: the Hungarian printer asking about the place for poetry in time of war; the arrival at the Cap d'Agde and Sète; Hitler refusing to recognize the victory of Jesse Owens; the letters from Otto; a visit in New York from Ernst Toller to say the Republicans had been driven far into the north; Joseph Kennedy's argument to Roosevelt that Spain was the place to stop communism; *Time*, with the rabid anti-communist Henry Luce refusing her story on the refugees and buffer zone. She concluded her mid-1970s recollection with a contemporary vision of Spain: 'the high-rise apartments, the tourist industry, the American naval bases'; this last revision of the event was still two years before the death of Franco.

It was, as she said ironically, 'nearer our own time'. She ended her article in Pascalian mood: historical times connected by the recurrent need for ethical judgement and discrimination. She recalled the troubled 1968 Olympics in Mexico where 'the black athletes made their protest'. She might also have spoken of the students who had been killed ten days before, demonstrating for democracy and justice. Even closer were the Munich Olympics of 1972 where eleven Jewish athletes had been killed. In 1972, she also went to Vietnam with the Harts and Denise Levertov. They were meeting American Vietcong prisoners. Senator Hart's wife Jane told the soldiers the exact number of athletes killed; they promised to phone the families on their release. In a dream-like shift Rukeyser cuts back to Otto's death, which she learned of via Germans in Mexico: a flash-back to 1936. It was for her a defining and eternal moment, a moment standing outside the normal forgetting of the passing of time itself.

> 'Why do you care about Spain so much?' a friend asks me, a curious look in her green eyes, the question real on her fine face. She is watching the Derby on TV with passionate interest. During the time before starting, there are film clips of human runners. 'It was so long ago,' she said.

The reply was simple, the film and the athlete, the sport and the politics could not be separated. It was as alive now as then: 'Going on now. Running, running, today.' Writing the past was an act of recreation and intentionality, especially needed in a world prone to a perilous forgetting. In Pound's words, it was what made literature itself, and perhaps poetry in particular, the 'news that STAYS news'.[82]

As for Lawrence, Hemingway and Gertrude Stein before her, Spain and Spanish culture would hold a privileged place in Rukeyser's world, even apart from her first intense political entry into the country. It was an ancient land whose roots stretched back to early Mediterranean culture. She exoticized it slightly, placing it against the coldness of Anglo-Saxon culture. Hence, in a set of typed notes on Lorca's theatre, Rukeyser recognized the roots of the Spanish playwright in the Mediterranean culture of Greek tragedy. The plays, she said, had the purity and violence of the early theatre in which denial and repression undercut the rigidity of law and control. Death here had the active vehemence of a passionate life. Yet the plays had all the warmth too of the South 'the red capes, the balconies, the saffron and cloves'.[83] It is perhaps a fitting footnote to an experience that would haunt her for the rest of her life.

Time and the Fear of Poetry

Rukeyser thought very hard about the nature of poetry itself: from details of its techniques to its history, themes and place in the world's attention. It was the inclusive literary genre that could rehearse and celebrate the hope and anguish of the human condition itself. For her, as for Shelley, translating the Augustinian conception of the divine into more earthly but still transcendental terms, it was also 'at once the centre and circumference of all knowledge'.[84] The achievement of Rukeyser and her ability to remain politically and psychologically honest in a conflicted ideological world, not only in politics but in poetry was recognized early by James R. Caldwell in a perceptive review of *The Life of Poetry*, *Elegies* and 'Orpheus' in 1950:

> In a generation of artists all angry rejectors of this murderous world she rejects only arty rejection [...] The dialectical process is a third major key, seen not as a tight and easy rationale of class struggle but in a poetic vision of the eternal counterpoise and reconcilement of forces, and pervading the whole is the ideal for poetry and for life of full consciousness, free of inhibition, contempt and neurotic coldness.[85]

The way Rukeyser thought about poetry, its nature, its role in the world, its techniques, and its relation to the art of memory, can be found scattered throughout her entire work. However, on three occasions she attempted to codify her practice. One of these is in print, *The Life of Poetry*, first published in 1949.

The others exist as lectures she gave to college students. The first of these is five talks she gave to Vassar College, under the title of 'The Usable Truth' between 19 October and 1 November in 1940. Here she initially rehearsed some of the material that went into *The Life of Poetry*. With a few alterations 'The Fear of Poetry' in Norman's *TWICE A YEAR* was the first of the five lectures. The third description of her practice, still unpublished, is an undated transcript of a tape of a talk she gave to students at MIT in the late 1960s. This last talk is important for the subject of this book and will be dealt with after the others. It was entitled 'Poetry and Time'.

The early Vassar lectures had the immediacy of the crisis of war. She spoke of Nazism and fascism and of

> poetry as the kind of weapon that can best meet these enemies, the outer cloud, the stealthy inner silence of fear. Now we invoke memory, we search all the days we had forgotten for a tradition that can support our arms in this moment; we invoke a rigorous positive that will enable us to make our choices; we invoke poetry as the attitude that can clear us and make whole the spirit to face life.[86]

She spoke to the students of the inadequacy of the education process and, like Simone Weil, of the corruption of the story of the past: 'But tradition is not repetition, that is, a blasphemy against tradition.'[87] Like Pound she alluded to the dullness of the educators. Pound's comments on professors of English are always worth repeating. Those with 'some natural aptitude for comprehending their authors' communicated 'a general sense of comfort in the presence of literary masterworks'.[88] In a similar spirit Rukeyser wrote 'The middle pitch of life is not where we are going to live.'[89] For the academy, she noted, Caesar's Gallic Wars seemed to be there to teach grammar. Everyone spoke of civilization as a sequence, 'a mounting curve of incident whose heights came as a dramatic relief'. In life, however, 'shock seemed to follow shock'.[90] Like Henry Adams, Rukeyser was to search for a different way to articulate the temporality of historical narrative. Also like Adams, she was concerned for education: there had been a breakdown between what had been learned and communicated and what had happened.

Here Rukeyser registers the effect of two world wars, and the Spanish Civil War on the Victorian consensual 'progressive' narrative of history. What numbs us, she continued, on the outbreak of the Second World War is the scale of disaster: 'who can imagine the Chinese people flooded and starved and broken by earthquake and bombing. Who can imagine the people of France, refugees at home, going mad on the roads, starving and betrayed and lost at home?'[91] This moment of the invasion of France and suffering of the Chinese people, is, then, after the Spanish Civil War, the spur to writing what would become her major credo, *The Life of Poetry*.

The continued political and personal need pushed her to think of the techniques of communication in poetry. There was an urgency about finding out what really mattered. Cutting and reassembling material led her to think of film. In her second lecture, analysing a moment from Hitchcock's *39 Steps* (the moment where the woman opens her mouth to scream having seen the knife sticking from the corpse and then cutting before the anticipated scream to the train roaring out of the tunnel), she writes: 'The cutting of film is a parable in the ethics of communication.' The 'train's scream' had 'severed the moment before'.[92] Time, causality, narrative speed and condensation, the terror of psychological shock and of the break between worlds it engendered in every sense, articulated the parameters of that complex phrase: 'a parable in the ethics of communication'. In *The Life of Poetry*, she revised the lecture and added a temporal dimension to the argument: 'The cutting of films is a parable in the motion of any art that lives in time [...] as well as a parable in the ethics of communication.'[93] And in the revised work she also noted that there was war inside the United States as well as outside. Referring to the Hayes Code, she objected to the adjustment of stories and ideas, and also what she would refer to in *Elegies* as the 'sexually witty', the 'attractive bodies and the green lights of custom, the drinks and the music and the money'.[94] The economic and social conditions of Hollywood also came under fire and in the witch hunts of the late 1940s, she attacked

> the political-hunting, the technicians who never meet the 'artists', the laid-off and rejected who live in the place, ready to be drawn on during a labor crisis of any kind: and the few working artists, dancing their razor-edge, pouring their energies into various fights: the fight to insist on their work's getting through, the fight to resist corruption of consciousness, the fight to organize the others.[95]

If ethics were to use the parable form, then ethics had to have deep links with telling a story: one in which the truth of the imagination in emplotment was paramount. In the Vassar lecture, Rukeyser reviewed further moments from Hitchcock's *Woman Alone* (1936) and *Foreign Correspondent* (1940). In the latter, the way a plane is filmed falling from the sky (the camera moves in through the aircraft window and the rest of the crash is experienced from within), given her own pilot experience and the key image of flight in her discursive world, is particularly significant. She outlined each momentary image: 'fragments arbitrarily – and ethically – assembled'.[96] Totally convincing in its melodrama, the sequence is completely 'successful within its own definition.' Rukeyser continued: 'These examples all have their parallels in poetry.' [97] Reassembling and cutting fragments together inevitably recalled for her Eliot's *The Waste Land*, and indeed Rukeyser calls it a 'masterpiece of collision':

> and yet at its close, the cry for belief and the cry of despair that whatever belief arrives will have arrived too late is clear, and the reader realizes that these cries have provided a constant as pronounced as the sound track in *Foreign Correspondent's* airplane sequence.[98]

In 'fragment' and in 'collision' there was a 'deep wish for structure'.[99]

One senses that whereas for Eliot the new imagist-based technique of *The Waste Land* was intended to show 'fragments shored against my ruin' precisely in the sense of shoring up attempts to preserve a structure that is absent in them, that is derelict beyond repair. In Rukeyser a stronger narrative element and a different sense of collision and indeed of the fragment-image would indicate an elusive order of a recreated world that ranged from nature to the person's interior life. Eliot is overwhelmed by despair, Rukeyser searches, a woman among the dead and the ruins, looking for the wounded to heal and for whatever might be useful to start again. Both have their own truths. A dialogue with, not to say a serious challenge, to the thematics of *The Waste Land* became a major aspect of *Elegies*.

In these series of lectures, Rukeyser also stressed technical issues. Drawing attention to refrains and parallels (surely techniques suggested to her by the Psalms of David), she provided a visual image of the New York skyline. The skyscrapers rose vertically and repetitively, but not one was the same shape. This kind of visually oriented explanation was strong in all her more self-reflective commentary. That had already been evident, for example, in her review of MacLeish's *Land of the Free* for *New Masses*. She felt that while MacLeish had acknowledged the 'stubborn inward life' of the photographs by Dorothea Lange and Walker Evans, among others, and subordinated text to the position of the photographs, arranging the sequence dramatically, nonetheless there was a great lack of balance not helped by the looseness and sentimentalities of the poem itself. In other words, the poem did not rise precisely to that arbitrarily assembled detail here caught within the frame in its instant of time (rather than in the collision of the cut) that marked the imaginative particularity of the photographs such as Walker Evans's 'brilliant view of Bethlehem, Pa., its darkened chimneys and poles and pillars crossed out by the white granite cemetery in front of you'.[100]

In *The Life of Poetry*, she mentioned James Agee's and Walker Evans's collaboration in *Let Us Now Praise Famous Men* (1940), hoping that more of the photographs would be restored so that 'a milestone in our literature of meeting places may be fully seen'.[101] It was the 'lost periodless quality' of MacLeish's poetic portraits of human beings that was at fault in ruling out the imaginatively unique historical moment in which the person dwelt, transient and lost in the particularity of specific appearance. [102]

The New Deal's Farm Administration photographs threw up the question of visual reality, and of truth to the real at further stages of abstraction. In a remarkable sentence Rukeyser affirmed that: 'The passage from the map to the symbol and all we can say of both of them is that the structure, in each case, is another structure.' [103] There were simply different orders of representations of the world. The Babylonians, she said, had used Ptolemy, the post-Renaissance world, Kepler and Newton, and contemporary astronomers, Einstein. Yet along with the structures of material world discoverable in science was an equally intense concern with the inner world.

In her lecture 'The Speed of the Image', given on Wednesday 30 October 1940, she referred to Einstein, Dostoevsky, the Bible, Eliot and Kierkegaard, finishing by reading 'In Praise of Abraham' from Kierkegaard's *Fear and Trembling*. Undoubtedly this was a corrective to Marxism's indifference to the uniqueness of the suffering person in time. What, as Sartre said, Kierkegaard complained of in Hegel (and in a sense the legacy was passed to Marxism if not exactly to Marx) was that the Hegelian view of history 'neglected the *unsurpassable uniqueness* of the lived experience'.[104] Resistant to ideas, Kierkegaard affirmed the 'irreducibility and specificity of what is lived'. [105] That lived experience could not be made the object of knowledge as such, for its inwardness was always transcendent: 'It is the action of Christian romanticism against the rationalist humanization of faith.' While deeply antipathetic to Christianity as such, Sartre acknowledged that 'grief, need, passion, the pain of men, are brute realities which can be neither surpassed nor changed by knowledge'.[106] It was passion and existential crisis that changed people. At the end of 1940, Rukeyser, faced with the hardening of positions on the left, the intransigence of Stalinist cultural and political propaganda and the positivism of social realism, reacted as fiercely against them as Kierkegaard had done with Hegel's reason of history. She knew that 'a work of art is a thing in the world, not just a text or commentary *on* the world'.[107] She found herself isolated and without an immediate audience.

In her third lecture, entitled 'Poetry and Peace', she turned her attention directly to poetry. She praised the poets 'outside any group': H.D., Wallace Stevens and Robinson Jeffers. It was a position in which she increasingly found herself. She praised Stevens's stand against chaos in the form of his 'eye for the fantastic, for the painted quality of life, the wrenched forms in everyday occurrence' and Jeffers 'since he has seen all history as a plunge toward catastrophe echoed in all the forms of nature and love and death – a catastrophe which must have a cleansing effect.' She had problems with any self-promoting group in art, even the imagists with their 'very civilized wish not to give into ritual impotence'.[108] A country in which everyone was advertising themselves as noisily and visibly as possible had a very real difficulty in distinguishing the true from the known. The poets were, of course, no exception but at least here and there advancement by group identity, she argued, had been strongly broken, for example by H.D., 'the purest of the imagists'.[109] She cited H.D.'s note to that effect, in the then current *Oxford Book of American Literature*.[110]

In these lectures of 1940, she also argued that the worst thing possible for poetry would be for it 'to become the occasional poetry of war'. Social realism and the instant commentary on the known event was a 'display of wounds, a rotten sort of begging for literary attention'.[111] Her practical attitude to the war was, like Lewis Mumford's, simply to call for action. Recalling the vacillations and irresponsibility of Britain and France in relation to Germany and Spain, she nonetheless was sympathetic to the plight of Britain, very much fighting alone at this moment in 1940. She noted, in very Mumfordian tones, that 'conference tables will not make peace here, and the shrewd hidden reason of statesmen will not make very much happen. There will need to be live acts.'[112]

There remained the problem of time and memory, of the way poetry occupied its own time and of how to think of history in terms of time. In a note scribbled on the back of her fourth Vassar lecture, 'Communication and Poetry', given on 1 November, she wrote: '1860 – 1900 – 1940. Emergence of Henry Adams into twentieth century most conscious entrance, possibly in history. Nearer year 1 or 1900 question.'[113] That last enigmatic phrase referred to Adams's description of himself in *The Education* as 'an elderly American in 1900' who 'knew neither the formula nor the forces [of history]' and as a 'traveller in the highways of history' noting that 'two thousand-years failure of Christianity roared upward from Broadway, and no Constantine the Great was in sight.'[114] The year 1860 of course refers to the onset of the American Civil War. For Adams, the moment initiated a major change of phase in his own personal adult life. Behind Rukeyser and Mumford there is always the shadow of the Henry Adams who had fought for the human story against the structuralist patterns of the new social scientists and the ethnologists, against their too confident temporalities, their different reasons of history assigned categorically to authentic history, and from right and left of the political spectrum.[115]

In her critical biography of Willard Gibbs (1942) Rukeyser had cited Adams's meditation on the Yale mathematician in his own late work, *The Rule of Phase Applied to History* (1909). The rule of phase was a mathematical description of the way a chemically homogenous substance took different form in different conditions, like ice, water and vapour. Rukeyser saw Gibbs as an embodiment of a defining moment in historical discourse that precipitated what today one would call a paradigm shift. As with Adams or Mumford this might be a major scientific theory or, citing Adams, 'the discoveries of printing, the telescope and America'. It was also whatever left 'the deepest impression on men's memory'.[116] But like Rukeyser, Adams was concerned not only with the difficulty of describing and making sense of time and change but its political implication for democracy and the mark left on the human soul. Having invoked the New Haven scientist, Willard Gibbs, Adams wrote in *The Rule of Phase*:

> No phase compares in wonder with the mere fact of our own existence, and this wonder has so completely exhausted the powers of Thought that mankind, except in a few laboratories, has ceased to wonder, or even to think. The Egyptians had infinite reason to bow down before a beetle; we have as much reason as our beetle phase and to recognize that everything, animate or inanimate, spiritual or material, exists in phase; that all is equilibrium more or less unstable, and that our whole vision is limited to the bare possibility of calculating in mathematical form the degree of a given instability.[117]

Rukeyser was to turn Adams's sophisticated and ironic vision into something warmer, yet retain in her poetry a parallel ensemble of wide-ranging cultural thematics, felt on the pulses. Her narrative world would be less statically dual and hence less satiric, but they both shared, of course also with Mumford, a sense of the temporality of history as unstable fields with precarious moments of equilibrium.

For Adams, it was part of a tragic (and conservative) vision in which modernity, in spite of its compelling fascination, was truly terrifying. Rukeyser's sense of dynamic equilibrium was closer to Melville's vision of the Catskill eagle in *Moby-Dick*:

> And there is a Catskill eagle in some souls that can alike dive down into the blackest gorges, and soar out of them again and become invisible in the sunny space. And even if he for ever flies within the gorge, that gorge is in the mountains; so that even in his lowest swoop the mountain eagle is still higher than other birds upon the plain, even though they soar.[118]

Rukeyser's ability to keep on the wing, to find equilibrium within instability marked her off from Adams's 'Tory' gloom and placed her closer to Melville's romantic deployment of wisdom literature, yet with a much greater love of the world.[119] As she wrote in her poem 'The Outer Banks', citing Wilbur Wright: 'No bird soars in a calm.'[120] The thought is at least as old as Pascal's 'Our Nature consists in movement, absolute rest is death' and is crucial to Rukeyser's world.[121]

What Rukeyser shared with Adams was a Pascalian need to recover a sense of wonder at human existence itself, and perhaps especially in relation to the problematic of our being in time:

> Time comes into it
> Say it Say it
>
> The universe is made of stories
> Not of atoms[122]

Rukeyser concluded her Vassar lectures with a final meditation on time. She wanted a 'non-axiomatic' tradition, which was an idea she was using in *Willard Gibbs*. Against the perceived atemporality of the still Euclidian universe and its cultural redeployment to authenticate an objective mechanical cast of thought, and with technics invading all aspects of human life and organization, she promoted the necessity of the break, the paradigm shift, the revolutionary gesture – whether describing the seventeenth-century regicides hiding out in New Haven or Whitman's revolutionary new programme for poetry in 1855 or Gibbs's *Rule of Phase*. The life of the imagination included a Husserlian sense of temporality in terms of the way the past leaked into the present and the present into the future, and a powerful Heideggerian, or even Sartrean, sense of the future as grounding the project in its creative seizure of the world. Here Rukeyser defines it with a keen sense of its absence:

> And there would be a fortifying, a sense of the past and a continuous present that would defy the paralysis which is seizing so many here, and which must have been creeping across Europe in an epidemic before the war itself broke; the paralysis of anticipation which is likely to prey on the creative mind.[123]

Finally, there were the practical difficulties. How in fact do you deal with what she called 'time-material' in a poem? Prose as such has 'more time' but the problem is there for the longer poem. In the fluidity of representing the evanescence of time, an intense preparation must be made to capture the moment as 'it goes past in full intensity'. That intensity would include choosing the past that was needed for creative survival, as well as understanding the nature of dream, the patterns of music and science, the political and social moments of war and the personal story of the private self in a public sphere.

That public sphere was breaking up in war. Current chaos and human anguish was a result of the devastating legacies of science and technology and the failure of education to set limits to it. Like Brecht and Mumford, two men of very different ideological persuasions, Rukeyser understood that the war was one of industrial productivity, a war of attrition between rival industrial technological systems on a gigantic scale.[124] Industrial production, as Marx had noted, was a system of separations: workers from the means of production, the vicarious life of capital from sensuous life and the holistic task from the nature of the production line's specialized task. Poetry was a way of offering a vision of wholeness in complexity.

> But what poetry can do that many of the other forms cannot, or can do less directly, is to focus that complexity – to throw it into an order, to lead its traced development, as subtly as the developments of music, and explicitly – and, in showing us focus after focus of complexity, strengthen that area of attention that so urgently needs to be strengthened now.[125]

Her essay 'The Fear of Poetry', published in *TWICE A YEAR*, had all the urgency of 1940 during the destruction of Europe. Its second appearance in *The Life of Poetry* (1949) rearranged and expanded the materials from the Vassar lectures to book length, and is very much a creature of the late 1940s with Cold War pressures beginning to elicit responses from Rukeyser to new hegemonic controls of media and popular culture. Her last expository gesture, 'Poetry and Time' (c. 1967–8), was a series of lectures at MIT. These were given in the context of American superpower military action in Vietnam.

Continuity of themes suggests that Rukeyser's broad concerns do not fundamentally change but they deepen and take on new life as they return to build further and more nuanced arguments. In 'Time and Poetry', moments of *The Life of Poetry* reappear: the work of D'Arcy Thompson, her interests in film and the poets Whitman and Eliot among others, but Needham and Frazer are added. Rilke and Proust, however, return, a 'recollection' in the late 1960s perhaps, of their appearance in the long-ago and by then forgotten world of *TWICE A YEAR*.

The Life of Poetry missed a little of the immediate urgency of the 1940 lectures. In the introduction some of the specific references – to the Civil War, the flight from Barcelona, the Battle of Britain, the French refugees of the Nazi invasion, Carossa – are left out or rather referred to obliquely.[126] What comes in are the new materials she has been working on in relation to Willard Gibbs, and the reading she has been doing, and thinking about for *Elegies*. But the central question that the Hungarian printer put to her as she left on the boat from Barcelona that is instanced in her *TWICE A YEAR* essay. 'The fear of poetry' is cited in both works: 'And poetry – among all this – where is there a place for poetry?' Parts of the initial argument are expanded and reflect on the range of topics Rukeyser was so engaged with before the Second World War but with a different atmosphere surrounding them: the symbolic structures and patterns of religion; the psychological development of the child and what psychology itself does and does not reveal; the passion for the achievements of American writers, artists and poets put back into circulation by writers and scholars of Mumford's and Stieglitz's generation; jazz; the particular claims to describe the world of film and documentary, European and Hollywood cinema, dance, theatre, radio, and the American musical. She shared with Dwight Macdonald a deep interest in popular culture. The political debates as structured in the 1930s have gone, but there is a new awareness of the politicized cultural debates that would be pioneered after the war by the Frankfurt School among others. The shadow of the 1930s nonetheless still haunts *The Life of Poetry*:

> Looking back from what I learnt in Spain. I must remember the silent storms of puberty, the unleashed marvel of power that could only wreck what I knew, a world of constriction and fear, a materialist world that exposed the American danger, in materialism, to be mystical about material values.
>
> The real estate crash and the stock market crash ripped open the veils of that world [...] in art of course the mysticism of success and failure will not hold. The world of business is open warfare, cold iron through every throat, and the battle-shriek, 'success!'[127]

Against Eliot, Pound, Zukofsky, Oppen and the objectivists, Rukeyser insisted that poetry could directly address, in an artfully constructed, quasi-personal voice, what Wilhelm Reich called the 'emotional plague', and counter it through an imaginative poetry of feeling. The thesis was psychological with a strong political inflection. It was the authoritarian nature of leaders (politicians, parents, teachers, clergy, psychologists) who were at the root of both public and private ills. In that sense Rukeyser was also closer to the radical Freudians (from Fromm through to Marcuse and Norman O. Brown), what Richard King has called the 'party of Eros'.[128] In general, however, she had an old socialist's scepticism about the reductive nature of a lot of psychoanalytic explanation, though it did crucially focus for her the nature of the quasi-narratives of emotional life and development.

The 'fear of poetry', for example, was a symptom of the strongest and subtlest of authoritarian repressions, a direct consequence of the dominance of Freud's reality principle over forms of conscious and unconscious life. It was fed by many cultural aspects of modernity itself: specialized education that, as for Mumford, destroyed a holistic sense of the person; technical specialization in general; the repressive codes of gender behaviour passed on by equally terrorized or religiously orthodox parents; the refusal to speak of sexuality or politics in general during adolescence; the reliance on positivistic knowledge where an inadequate 'empirical practice' promised an order through method, and a certainty it could never deliver; forms of neurotic and repressive behaviour and the way rituals of public order, from the state to the family, codified and drew on that fear.

Against these multiple authoritarian cultural practices, Rukeyser called for 'the security of the imagination' that called for 'more liberty, more rebellion, more belief'.[129] To have life more abundantly was Rukeyser's answer to Freud's locked stasis of desire and the reality principle that inevitably produced that neurosis which provided an open field for exploitation.[130] The authoritarian rage for order denied the fact that, as Rukeyser cited Clerk Maxwell, 'crises in systems of high rank' occurred in all experiences of system and outer inherited order. But Rukeyser was also concerned with the inner self. The interiority of the human subject, as with Pascal, is experienced in timeless ethical terms: 'Time in culture is capable of many arrangements.'[131] Dante's system may be outmoded but the truth of the personal voyage, 'of the skull-grinding horror, the white chance, leopard, star and belief, are present'.[132] Indeed it was Shelley before her who spoke of the poetry of Dante as being 'the bridge thrown over the stream of time'.[133] She spoke of the 'multiple time-sense in poetry, that is the ever new, which is recognized as something already in ourselves, but not discovered'.[134] This is again Pascalian, we find what we discover and discover what we find.

Rukeyser sought a poetic figure that could at once describe the interior life and the external world in what is ultimately a correspondence theory, a sacramental universe in which, however, the sacraments had to be re-invented in artistic terms (a project in English poetry that begins with Wordsworth and Coleridge). In Donald A. Mackenzie's *The Migration of Symbols* (1927), Rukeyser was to find the figure of the spiral. In this work, Mackenzie had argued against the reduction of key visual cultural symbols to a pure aesthetics of the folk and for their profound relation to magico-religious beliefs and practices. More controversially, he argued that their repetition in diverse cultures, while clearly serving quite different interpretative functions, as the anthropologists are never weary of reminding us, retain some trace of a transcendent fundamental meaning in their temporal transmission across cultures. Here he is close to D'Arcy Thompson's notion of a certain shapes of mathematical order produced in the living world as a result of the evolutionary development of forms through time and the spatial field-force patterns in which they occur across the changes of chronological time.

These fundamental orders of nature, as described in Mackenzie's meditation on the 'spiral', inspired Rukeyser's later poem 'Spirals and Fugues' (1968). The first line runs: 'Spirals and fugues, the power most like music/Turneth all worlds to meaning.'[135] For Mackenzie, the shell of the snail, coiled wire, the external part of the ear, spiralling ivy, the constellation of Ursa Major, the whirlwind, the spiral form of the ancient gods, Dante's spiral shaped Inferno, Democritus's 'vortex of atoms' are imaginative 'primitive' ways of conferring meaning on a chaotic sense of the world as pure appearance. The recognition of the form in early historic anticipations of contemporary scientific modelling were not to be scorned. Mackenzie gave both sides of the post-Darwin debate about 'diffusion' or 'separate origins' for the appearance of the 'spiral' in diverse cultures, and reviewed the available literature. He further argued, somewhat platonically, that they were less imitative of natural forms, or suggested empirically for example, by Egyptian craftsmen winding gold wire, than an 'expression of ideas regarding natural phenomena, natural processes'.[136]

Mackenzie pursued his theme through various ancient cultures, suggesting that in Western Europe in the 'Upper Paleolithic' period as the people 'made a magico-religious use of shells and inaugurated in their art the use of the spiral, it may be that the shell spiral came first.'[137] In Indian culture the figure of the 'whirlpool of the primordial deep contained the embryo' and further:

> In the *Rigveda* (x, 92, 5) the god Rudra is referred to 'as putting the waters in motion', and it is significant to find references to his 'spirally-braided hair' – braided in shell-spiral form. Rudra was a story god – a whirlwind-riding god.[138]

The spiral, in its whirlpool form of air and water, he argued, was associated with birth, creation, destruction, an image of creative powers in various early forms of human culture and from Hesiod's *Theogony* to the God who speaks out of the whirlwind in the Book of Job. This mixture of wind and water in swirling motion at the heart of so many magico-religious stories was bound to catch Rukeyser's attention. With Amy Johnson as a role model, she was a middle-class independent woman of the 1930s who loved flying planes and knew intimately the turbulence of the wind and rising spirals of air.

Mackenzie concluded his chapter on whirlpools and whirlwinds with a reference to the image in Chinese culture, citing Dutch authorities on the dragon festivals with their accompanying large, spiral-shaped ball representing the moon, or 'moon pearl', always connected with water in contrast with the fiery spiral of the dragon. If the spiral is a symbol of natural energy then it was, they argued, also connected with the dual world of Yin and Yang.[139] The spiral as a mediator of dualistic forces is a crucial image for Rukeyser's poetic world. A further chapter in Mackenzie's book, however, considers *The Egyptian Book of the Dead* in the same thematic context, which was a favourite book for writers and intellectuals of the 1920s and 1930s. Rukeyser, for example, took it up directly in her poem on the Gauley Mine disaster. Simone Weil was to read it in the New York Public Library on her brief visit to New York during the war, and it was a key text for the Beat generation. Kerouac read it because it was a set text for Raymond Weaver's classes at Columbia.[140]

Citing various authorities alongside it, Mackenzie spoke of the fact that Osiris had a strange double identification as both sky god and as a water-encircling being who represents the coils of the nether world around the earth itself. Later, Osiris becomes 'god of the Nether world or underworld (Dewat)'. Mackenzie noted that Plato in the *Phaedo* 'made Socrates describe the Greek "Dewat", Tartarus with its whirling and panting winds and central "whirlpool lake" and its rivers forming spirals as they ascend from and descend to the central lake in the chasm.' In the conclusion to this chapter Mackenzie makes a move, crucial for Rukeyser, from myth to describing early Greek science. Leucippus 'originated the atomic theory which he combined with the theory of the whirlpool in space'. His pupil Democritus continued the idea of 'the vortex of atoms'. Attacked by Epicurus and ignored by Lucretius, the idea, suggests Mackenzie, has come alive again in astronomical discoveries of spiral nebulae. He cites Holden's observations with the Lick telescope: 'it is difficult to resist the convictions that these are arranged in space in the form of a true helix.' Mackenzie was of course too early for the double helix, but his modest and tentative conclusion connects the two worlds of mythology and science as imaginative acts that will be crucial for Rukeyser:[141]

> The early thinkers and observers of natural forms and process, who introduced the spiral symbol, beginning with the snail-shell and ultimately including climbing plants, whirlpools and whirlwinds, and those who ultimately transferred these to their 'sky world', have after all, some claim to be mentioned in the history of science as well as that of religion.[142]

Mackenzie's speculations were less directed to establishing Jungian style archetypes or seeking some kind of unitary explanation out of a religious impulse, than to giving a sense of moving connections between mind and nature within a sense of the wholeness and interconnectedness of the world. And this is precisely how Rukeyser read him even though she was very much engaged with Jung's theories of dreams. She summed up her reading in *The Life of Poetry*:

> The spiral, which began by being imitative – the form, is of course, found countlessly in nature (in ivy, in water, in hair, in shells, ears, whirlwinds) and went on to be associated with the process. The symbol then asked the question, or declared the existence of the problem of the relationship of movement with life.[143]

This was not the asynchronic archetypal universe of Jung. She cited D'Arcy Thompson: 'in the equiangular spiral the time element always enters in'. She wanted the history of the symbol and the 'history of human passion for a relationship – in this instance between growth and form.'[144] The growth and development of any individual was historical and political. The ethical world, however, was achronological. The body-mind equilibrium of the 'primitive' society, for example, is offered as a timeless critical utopian site for the disorder of modernity, characterized in *The Life of Poetry* as follows:

> Our education molds us toward conduct, the outward and ethical are given lip-service, the outward and predatory are glorified by business society, and the young are brought up in conduct leading toward aggression surrounded by strict tabus. We know from the movies, the radio, and from every ad in the morning, what behaviour is expected.[145]

At the heart of this was the misuse of words, above all the lack of words driven into silence by fear and by a prompoted terror of exterior chaos turned into neurotic behaviour: what she called in *Elegies* 'the inmost frenzy and the outer doom' (p. 250).

Rukeyser's political world in *The Life of Poetry* began at the personal level, in the question of consciousness itself. For the Marxists, consciousness had been about the intelligibility of class consciousness, for Rukeyser, citing R.G. Collingwood, consciousness had to be freed from that repression which 'turned toward others as projection, massed in experience as dissociation, and in a selective structure (which is claimed) as fantasy'.[146] 'Imagination' for her would work against the power of fantasy, a battle that in Reichean terms the left had lost against the mass persuasion techniques of the Third Reich and fascism and were to lose again in the post-modern world of American commercial exploitation of desire. The common brutality had been both achieved and legitimated in the fantasies created by their propaganda machines. Poetry was one countervailing force. In her own words, it was an imaginative act combining the experience of time and memory and was at the heart of all human activity

> The imagination is a function of belief and experience: that is, of course, why the realization of a poem is an event of belief and experience. This event takes place in a time-sequence involving the reverberation of images and sounds. The reaction is one in which discovery and memory are sealed together for you; and the relationship that seals them is what we call beautiful.[147]

Between art and neurosis there was no common ground, any more than between liberty and tyranny. The truth of the imagination (a phrase that helped to negotiate and get round the Marxist and psychoanalytic discourses of her time) was as important for society as an economically just democratic political system.

That imaginative life itself was fitfully there in traditional popular culture and in some of the mass commercial arts. For Rukeyser, the blues had a particularly important place, not just for 'its minor thirds, and subdominant modulations, its tragic despair and its edge of sharpened humor' but for the inventiveness of its words: that 'amazing mixture of keen poetry and vulgarization has never come into our texts, either for what it is or for its influence on our poetry'.[148] Rukeyser claimed that the tradition of Lead Belly, Blind Lemon Jefferson, Jelly Roll Morton and Bessie Smith, the devotional songs, the slave songs and the cowboy songs had a variety of imaginative verbal and syntactical invention the imagists and the *transition* crowd might have envied. With her detailed knowledge of music, Rukeyser speculated on the syllabic singing of scat and bop and noted there were similar 'syllable songs' to be found in the notes of medieval students: 'I am sure we are on the road back to incantation – or, full circle, to the game-songs of children, used to set a rhythm in motion.'[149] Traces of these traditions in her poetry doubtless sometimes caused her more tone-deaf critics to call her poetry 'rhetorical'. Noting that music, mathematics, rhetoric and theology were the core-syllabus of the medieval world and all interlinked, Rukeyser shifts swiftly from bop to Helmholtz's great study of tone: 'Water in motion has an effect similar to that of music; the motion of waves, rhythmic and varied in detail, produces the feeling of repose or weariness – and [...] reminds us of order and power and the fine links of life.'[150] She concluded that memory, poetry and rhythm were deeply interconnected.

Rukeyser was concerned with taking down the barriers among the arts. She cited Martha Graham working with Emily Dickinson's poetry or Fred Astaire 'beginning to tap, to the religious dance and chant of the Indian rituals'.[151] No less than the image of the spiral, pulse, rhythm, tonal patterns, scale structures were to be sought figuratively and literally through all the arts. But rhythm carried with it intelligible meaning and not all benign. Noting the commercialization of early New Deal experiments in documentary, Rukeyser cited Paul Rotha's *Documentary Film* on the filming for purely aesthetic visual effect, of mechanical movement such as a rotary-press or 'the parade of a milk bottling machine': 'They did not, for a moment, realize that these repetitive rhythms, beautiful to watch in themselves, raised important materialist issues of the men at the machine, of the social and economic problems lying behind modern machinery and transport.'[152] Technological 'beauty' might be one thing to the bosses, another to the workers. Perhaps Rukeyser here needed a further distinction between beautiful and fascinating.

Nothing escaped her attention. She praised what was to become the new European cinema, the 'art' films of the New Wave whose greatest period was yet to emerge. It is the flow of images with which Rukeyser is concerned. These also connect the world of Hitchcock improbably to that of Buddhist painter-monks at Ajanta. Unlike the western painters who are invited to look through the canvas to the object, the monks emphasis with colour the crystals and prisms of the cave walls: 'it is said have the energy of a locomotive on the screen [...] the Western idea of still life is unknown.'[153] Rukeyser returned to the question she had raised in *Willard Gibbs*, about how a particular kind of imaginative effort underwrote the best practice of science and poetry. Adapting Charles Pierce's idea of semiosis (sign, object, interpretant) to the triad poet, poem and witness, she insisted again that none of them was static.

The same went for the writing of a poem. Towards the end of *The Life of Poetry*, Rukeyser described the creative process itself like the successive risings of the whirlpool, showing that for her the various drafts of the poem succeeded each other as series of surfacings. The Ninth Elegy: 'The Antagonists' (1944) and *Orpheus* (1949) are the poems chosen as examples. She noted how, for *Orpheus*, the process began for her with a poem about Eurydice after a long hospitalization for typhoid fever at the age of nineteen, 'contracted in an Alabama station-house during the second Scottsboro trial'.[154] The poem also touched on a 'brilliant' performance of Gluck's *Orpheus* (with Tchelitchew designs), embodied a sense of 42 Street with its 'pieces of people', and a reading of Thomson, and Mumford's mentor, Patrick Geddes. Collectively these inspired a new an interest in morphology, and a reading of the Orphic hymns in the New York Public Library 'six years after the night on Forty-Second Street'.[155] In *Orpheus*, memories of artistic and cultural encounter, political memory, different kinds of rhythm and all at encountered different times come together to make a poem which has its own 'life in time' running parallel to her own autobiographical moments in the poem's long composition.[156]

In the final pages, bits and pieces of Rukeyser's own life are revealed. In short, almost diary-entry paragraphs, the life of a poet appears, almost Joycean in the brief gestures. The narrative of the poet as well as that of the person are entwined like a double temporal spiral of tentative meanings circulating through the tormented and conflicted child but moving toward the poet: 'Every year since my childhood has been better, in spite of the losses and mistakes.'[157] The 'life of poetry' is entwined with a portrait of the artist as a young girl among nurses, maids, chauffeurs, through family conflict, and war. There is a Dos Passos-like moment as she adds a remembered headline from her childhood in the Great War: 'ALLIES ADVANCE SIX MILES SOUTH TO SOISSONS'.[158] There are glimpses of her father's business, trials of adolescence, the discovery of books, the defining moment in Spain and always New York itself punctuating the intensity of experience with a very American modernity: the Woolworth Building, the bored nurses on Riverside Drive, the rise of the skyscrapers, the news of the execution of Sacco and Vanzetti, music and painting, socialism, the crash on Wall Street. Rukeyser feels an urgent need to review and mediate the entire legacy of the world of a bourgeois urban childhood in order to move towards a deeper responsibility in both politics and in poetry.

The Life of Poetry is also the story of a woman and a Jewish American poet of her time. One cannot image Pound or Eliot disclosing the growth of intellectual and artistic life with such an engaged, personal and warm love of the world, in spite of a historical world in which the private life was at the mercy of every repressive class, social and religious order, and in which the public world entered on the worst war in history: a veritable Spenglerian orgy of technological ferocity in which among tens of millions of deaths, six million Jews would be slaughtered with cold-blooded bureaucratic precision. That world was confronted without self-pity: 'In our weakness and limitation, in ignorance and several poverties and doubt and disgust, we thought of possibility.'[159]

Rukeyser concluded *The Life of Poetry* by culling moments of the 1940 lectures at Vassar: calling for serious poetry to find a way of rehearsing a holistic response to a world in which psychological damage, war, dog-eat-dog capitalism and sold-out socialism had reduced the meaning of the human to pure survival and traduced every generous motive. She repeated her conviction that 'one of the worst things that could happen to our poetry at this time would be for it to become an occasional poetry of war': that claim to a spurious authenticity via a self-validating immediacy that can be the curse of a contemporary poetry at any time. Such poetry rarely rises above the second rate. In a terse conflation of her best religious and socialist insights she wrote: 'We hear the saints saying: Our brother the world. We hear the revolutionary: Dare we win?'[160] This oratorical appeal was part of the Jewish and radical Protestant traditions, but was consistently condemned as rhetoric by her critics. In romantic and post-romantic poetry this style can be found in Blake and Hugh MacDiarmid, in Whitman and in Rilke. As for later poets of Rukeyser's own time, one might cite Ginsberg, Rexroth and Robert Duncan. For Rukeyser, against the tide of the fastidious ironic academy, the prophetic appeal was part of a properly rhetorical gesture relating to the public speaking of poetry itself.

'Poetry and Time'

The question of poetic discourse was uniquely bound up with the question of time and narrative. In a transcript of an undated taped talk given at MIT entitled 'Poetry and Time' (c.1967), Rukeyser explored different patterns of time within different human discourses from science to poetry. The talk gathered and summarized many of the issues that had occupied her in the 1940s. Internal evidence shows this to be a talk given in the late 1960s, and it is taken here as a heuristic means of interrogating the range of her meditations on the subject.[161] It may also be seen as a summary of her mature thoughts on the problematics of history, poetry and time.

In considering time, Rukeyser began: 'I think we will want to talk about many things.'[162] A philosophical exegesis is not what follows, rather a series of invocations of issues to do with the question of time. These become creative gestures or strokes, attempts to capture fully the question that haunts human existence more than any other. The essay also shows just how much Rukeyser had thought about this question. Her range of authorities include D'Arcy Thompson, Proust,

W.E.B. Du Bois, Pasolini, Norbert Wiener, T.S. Eliot, Whitman, Rilke, Keats and Benjamin Whorf. Of these the two given most attention are Proust and Keats, but the generic areas drawn on are roughly as follows. First is the range of human experience of time and the nature of the concrete event within the continuity of time. Second is the key concept of growth. Third is a meditation on Proust's *À la recherche du temps perdu*. Fourth there is a review of time in poetry with a final comment on its relation to history.

In relation to the human experience of time (linear time), the time equated abstractly with space, is immediately rejected. The equally unmoving time of the painting, the stillest of times, is not ruled out. The poem, too, represents the fullness of the present moment. For Rukeyser, it was the 'curious system within the poem' that creates (and here she is close to the phenomenologists) the time of 'the world of the poem'.[163] Chance and the intensity of the dramatic inflect the human experience of time. The 'moment of the real' is included within a temporal system. It is as far from the random and eclectic as it is possible to be: 'One hundred diverse instances do not construct a poem, which is a time of growth and like a figure in time.'[164] In narrative the event emerges endowed with temporality. Growth and figure might seem contradictory, the first prefigured, the second belonging to some symbolic order in which nature is intuited by setting limits which grasp a definable order, a spatio-temporal figure of the natural order.

Rukeyser characterizes the poem as a 'grasping' of shapes of data at once intentional and as escaping intention in the surprise of their juxtaposition and intuitive selection. The temporality of Darwin's species evolution was a strong theme in the work of Alfred North Whitehead, a model of space–time without closure. His view, however, of the person as a 'society of occasions', while it does not sufficiently demarcate the private from the public, nor invoke a judgement as to the prehending limits of those occasions, at least suggests a transcendence of the immediate present of the psyche: 'Care for the future of personal existence, respect and pride in its past, are alike feelings which leap beyond the bounds of the sheer actuality of the present.' Rukeyser wanted to put back some individual human agency into Whitehead's social generality of 'how the past perishes the future becomes'. [165] At the same time, she was concerned to find a link between the patterns of the natural world and a notion of 'form' that would link, almost in a modern ecological sense, the choice of a reciprocity of rhythm between mind and nature, human and natural order.

Rukeyser was fortunate that, in her own time, biology was on its way to divesting itself of the rigid divisions that had grown up between itself and the hard sciences. After 1945, with the discovery of DNA, the movement gathered pace. Discussing Arthur Kornberg's mixing together of the four molecular subunits of DNA and noting the result that DNA 'multiplied in an almost alchemical way', the historians of science Stephen Toulmin and June Goodfield concluded:

'At last we can begin to dismantle the barriers which, after the discovery of microorganisms and the formulation of the classical cell-theory, still seemed to divide chemistry from biology.'[166] For the terms of that new scientific synthesis in an earlier moment, Rukeyser, like Charles Olson, turned to the work of the Scottish biologist D'Arcy Thompson. Thompson based his work on physics, mathematics and chemistry but he had a philosophical turn of mind. His notions of growth (the interior development of the organism) and force (the contextual force field of that growth) led him to say 'it may or may not be that these phenomena will yield in time to the methods of physical investigation' and 'whether they do or no, it is plain that we have no clear rule or guidance as to what is "vital" and what is not; the whole assemblage of so-called vital phenomena, or properties of the organism, cannot be clearly classified into those that are physical origin and those that are *sui generis* and peculiar to living things.'[167] This extraordinary classical scholar, who saw the organism as a locus of forces interacting with its environment, was a gift for Rukeyser who had been working, as it were, in parallel, on Gibbs's rule of phase – a law that described chemical structures changing form under certain conditions. Thompson is not mentioned in *Willard Gibbs*, so it is possible that Rukeyser read him in 1942 when Oxford University Press reprinted *On Growth and Form*. It had first appeared in 1917.

Thompson was a beautiful prose stylist and part of that beauty was his ability to include philosophical speculation in a description of formal patterns. In his chapter 'The Equiangular Spiral', for example, he distinguished the simple screw or cylindrical helix from the spiral whose radius of curvature continually increased and for which there was a distinct point of origin. The screw, mathematically, 'neither starts from a definite origin nor changes its curvature as it proceeds'.[168] In short, the difference is the presence of temporality in the one but not in the other. This theme (in short-hand, Euclid versus Darwin) is developed within the chapter. In his conclusion Thompson noted that the physicist can speak of the properties of matter and mathematically classify them only provided they are inanimate things:

> But when such forms, such conformation and configurations, occur among *living* things, then at once the biologist introduces his concepts of heredity, of historical evolution, of succession in time, of recapitulation of remote ancestry in individual growth, of common origin (unless contradicted by direct evidence) of similar forms remotely separated by geographic space or geologic time, of fitness for a function, of adaptation to an environment, of higher and lower, of 'better' and 'worse'. This is the fundamental difference between the 'explanations' of the physicist and those of the biologist.[169]

Thompson himself queried whether evolution was in fact progressive, such as indeed the both the temporal systems of both Aristotle and Hegel had claimed.

He wondered whether the 'pterodactyl flew no less well than does an albatross'.[170] The forces remained atemporally in complex balance but the shape changed in time. Thompson summarized the issue in a quotation from Henry Bergson: 'The evolutionist theory, as Bergson puts it, "consists above all in establishing relations of idea kinship, and in maintaining that wherever there is this relation of, so to speak, logical affiliation between forms, *there is also a relation of chronological succession between the species in which these forms are materialized.*"'[171]

What these meditations gave Rukeyser was a grand analogical narrative of growth, change and form that enabled her to adhere to Pascalian stillness while endorsing the concrete temporal finiteness of the process of change within a multiple field of forces. She commented directly on *Growth and Form*: 'If this is so, we have come down, so to speak, *on* a principle of continuity *to* a principle of discontinuity, and are face to face with what we might call quanta of growth' (my italics).[172] Rukeyser knew the dangers of scientific analogies as such, but the search for the similar, which is only one moment of the metaphoric act, was for her less a matter of discovering an enduring or completed poeisis than a quasi-mystical sense of how movement and rhythm were shared by both animate and inanimate nature, a sharing which brought the irreducible other of the contingent world closer to human experience. If there was caution to be expressed in relation to scientific analogy, nonetheless the vision included a Blake-like sense of the body's reciprocal movement in relation to the inanimate world:

> The rhythmic quality of growth, along with the rhythmic quality of everything we do, the counting, the most subtle rhythm in a poem has in it only the subtlety of your heart beat, your breathing, your body rhythms thrown against each other as fronts of crystals against each other [...].[173]

Moving from science to literature in her meditation of time, Rukeyser inevitably turned to the work of Proust. Dorothy Norman had reprinted passages from Proust in the first volumes of *TWICE A YEAR*, with one short story translated into English for the first time. Proust, at first seen as decadent by the Marxists, was gradually being recuperated into a more radical critique much as Henry James was to be from the 1970s onwards. As well as 'La Mort de Baldassare Silvande Victomte de Sylvania' (see p. 220), Norman had also reprinted 'A Young Girl's Confession', translated by Louise Varèse (published for the first time in the United States) in the same issue (Fall–Winter 1941) as Rukeyser's 'The Fear of Poetry'. Proust's early story, in complex supra-Freudian style, tells of young girl whose mother dies after catching a glimpse (or did she?) of post-orgasmic bliss in her daughter's face virtually *in flagrante delicto*, a few months before her wedding: a neat reversal of the primal scene.

Doubtless in Hayes Code America, the story threw down its own challenges to the censorship, but as well as fitting in well with Rukeyser's concern with the repressive sexual hypocrisies endemic in the ideological practices of the normative family, its moment of tragic rite of passage introduced the question of time, a subject with which Rukeyser was equally concerned: 'Proust, in a great book, has taken that long, the minimal of time, really, in that huge book, to deal with one instant in time, with everything it rouses and evokes and he speaks of the end of the sight of man as a creature of time.'[174] The emotional intensity of the detail, the moment that transcends all experience of chronology and haunts memory and the sensitivities of the interior life were germane to Rukeyser's keen concern for the emotional life of the child.

But there were also the politics: 'in Proust you have the time of the First World War, the acute consciousness of the Dreyfus case.'[175] Like Proust, Rukeyser was concerned that under the conditions of modernity, human beings would cease to be creatures of time in any profound way and lose a sense of the way narrative might deploy complex temporalities to register the depths and complexities of human experience. Rukeyser illustrated the predations of modernity with a joke about the travelling salesman who came to New York: 'I came to sell space, and I've stopped to buy time.'[176] She recalled a conversation with W.E.B. Du Bois, at the Rockefeller Institute: 'We could all of us at the Institute, at the University now, make a life work out of the problem which Proust has set.'[177] Proust's memory-haunted stories were offered against the number-haunted hyper-realities of the capitalist world.

As in her earlier lectures, Rukeyser also thought about the narrative temporalities involved in editing a film. Here too, the subject is raised again: 'And the more skilfully you cut film, you edit film, the more you work at the way the sequences evoke meaning, evoke experience and the question of trust of experience comes in and that trust is related to growth itself.'[178] Meaning came about in the way the sequence was handled, the juxtaposed moments presented a synthetic experience not made of the sum of the parts. The truth of the world of the film so presented, by virtue of its imaginative excellence, or by the viciousness of its imaginative mediocrity, would either encourage the growth of, or deaden, the mind. The advantage of this proposition was that theme and formal aesthetic were inseparable, the one from the other.

Turning finally to poetry, Rukeyser cited the opening lines of *The Waste Land*. She linked the notion of desire to the experience of time and here specifically to the structure of Western languages, which we 'think of as present and future, that is sensation and whatever desire moves from the present into the future, with memory, standing for the past, you get the ways in which this art works.'[179] This statement is fairly elusive, but in a sense she is challenging the breaking of the links between past and present expressed in Eliot's sense of rupture and psychological haunting, a result of the violent effect the Great War had on traditional certainties that extended from class to religion. Like many others of her generation she felt that there was something in the way Indo-European syntax worked that spatially separated the self from the world and was too divisive or too categorical in its implicit temporal propositions.

Altering the language would somehow solve all this. Its most positive results were manifest in the poets from the imagists to the objectivists, and in writers such as Gertrude Stein. Its worst aspects manifested themselves in the scientistic faith of the less gifted logical positivists and in the tyrannical scientism of the eugenicists of language. Rukeyser hence also mentioned Benjamin Lee Whorf's 'Essay on Time, Space and Language', which dealt with non-Western experience of space and time, here in relation to the Hopi Indians. As well as the issues it raised in this context, it is useful as a reminder that Rukeyser's poetic world extended to include non-Western poetries: Navaho and Eskimo songs among others. Whorf emphasized linguistic meaning as produced from the patterns in which they occurred, arguing that the truly creative scientists, poets and lovers 'are alike in being "flights" above and away from the slave world of literal reference.'[180] In Rukeyser's reading, it was another piece of supporting evidence to challenge the ontological vehemence of a treacherous common-sense and positivist view of time, space and 'language'.

Rukeyser would have agreed with Simone Weil that what was remembered might be mediocre both in theme and imaginative presentation, the two of course being inextricably linked. There was an ethical intelligence of memory as well as a psychology. In T.S. Eliot, the telling of the past was perhaps too certain in its sense of loss: of what, exactly, was the ruin and for whom, and with what intensity did it appear as ruin, and were the fragments, with which people needed to shore themselves up against that ruin, to any degree obvious or indeed the same in every case from the *déraciné* aristocrat to the worker in the London pub? Rukeyser's *Elegies* were to be a reply to *The Waste Land* on many levels: socially, thematically, politically and in terms of their poetics.

Although alluding to *The Waste Land*, in this lecture Rukeyser's most detailed analysis was reserved for a reading of Keats's 'Ode to the Nightingale'. Making the point that it was written by someone who had been to a medical school hospital ('Here, where men sit and hear each other groan'), Rukeyser noted that it was a profound meditation on the nature of time and death. It is impossible to give a full account here but the way the poem is approached is very interesting for Rukeyser's general poetic practice. She skilfully combined both the local site of the poem's production with large philosophical and poetic issues. In addition to Keats's medical school experience, she noted that there was the 'Nightingale' letter that described how Keats 'met Mr Curan my demonstrator from Guys, with Coleridge', together with the list of things they talked about, and his feelings about his brother's death. Side by side with this, however, Rukeyser also cited Rilke: 'You thought because you were used to another standard it was only for a while, but now you are caught in time and time is long and time goes on and time mounts up and time is like a long illness.'[181] Here the sense of time is multiple: entrapment, extension, remorseless in its addition; experienced as a psychological haunting to the point of illness and that time between now and an anticipated point so clearly understood by Heidegger.

She then turned again to Proust, equating the Biblical poetic technique of parallelism with his sense of multiple times. The most obvious example might be 'The Lord *is* my shepherd, I *shall* not want': the one synchronic, the other diachronic, yet joined in a parallel and simultaneous moment. But the Jewish poetic comparison with Proust was also paralleled with the Hindu sense of time. She suggested the richness of the Hindu term 'long body':

> in which you consider your own life in the world with the infant body [...] with all the change of the body as Marcel Marceau indicated in a miming of this, but in which none of the sequence is forgotten, – history which is something chosen by each one, – none of us sees history alike, our sense of history differs. The sense of the present with everything in it, no matter how irrelevant it looks, no matter how random it looks or funny, and the sense of potential which can be faulty, – all of this.[182]

History becomes, therefore, a series of the unique performances of the memory-invested body in time. It is general and particular at the same time, conscious and unconscious, a development that is at once given and chosen. There is an exuberance of memory and desire in Rukeyser that is the opposite of Eliot's painful fatality. Developing her theme, Rukeyser referred to Julius Thomas Frazer's anthology of essays *Voices of Time* (1923), and to Joseph Needham's commentary on *The Book of Changes* (presumably the discussion of the *I Ching* in the second volume of *Science and Civilization in China*). The latter particularly would have reinforced Rukeyser's sense of the rhythmic ebb and flow of the changes in time and space, the restless Heraclitean world as a series of momentary balances, in a Chinese cosmology that mapped the cosmos onto the body. Here, she commented, 'time is seen as cyclical and in which, according to the psychologist, the circle can be broken to make the spiral as one makes consciousness out of experience.'[183] The idea of breaking the circle of repression and normalcy to engender a spiral that signalled creativity and resistance, as well as a cooperation with desire and the imaginative life, had already been used and generated from other earlier and parallel sources and was a key governing image of *Elegies*. The spiral image not only captured the movement of nature itself but also the dialectical vision of the best in Marxism and the appearance of the known in the unknown for which the triple movement of time presented an interlinked yet unpredictable temporality.

In the late twentieth century, the double helix emerged and, with its twisted ladders and complementary pairings, was also of course a spiral-like form, but spirals were something that Rukeyser had thought about for a long time. Rukeyser, as always, wanted to present a multi-disciplinary context for the reading of Keats's

'Ode to the Nightingale'. She recalled a moment in Keats's correspondence, where Keats, walking from Hampstead to Highgate in London meets his anatomy demonstrator, Dr Green from Guy's Hospital, with Coleridge. It is one moment in the famous long letter to his brother and sister-in-law George and Georgiana Keats in America, written from February to May 1819. Rukeyser insisted on the totality of the list of topics Coleridge, as observed by Keats, covered:

> In these two miles he broached a thousand things – let me see if I can give you a list – Nightingales, Poetry – on Poetical sensation – Metaphysics – Different genera and species of Dreams – Nightmare – a dream accompanied by a sense of touch – single and double touch – a dream related – First and second consciousness – the difference explained between will and Volition [...].[184]

For Rukeyser, Keats's poem had to be approached in at least as many ways. Her commentary shows how deeply she was indebted to the English Romantic poets, how, in parallel with Robert Duncan in California, she immersed herself in them at a time when 'Romanticism' was still under a cloud, and the imagists and post-imagists preferred the medieval, Elizabethan and Metaphysical poets. Keats's pre-occupation with the 'soul' in his American letter was Rukeyser's also, but in a way that broke up its atemporal identity. The first stanza of Keats's poem, she said, was 'the taking hold of identification and the letting go of it'.[185] This was followed by the letting go of ordinary sight and finally of death itself. One after the other Keats abandoned the visibly spatial and personal aspects of reality and understanding the world. Time in the poem was multiple: the time of the garden (the time of fantasy – perhaps Blake's Beulah); with the time of wine (Bacchus, the time of intoxication); the time of Emperor and Clown (the time of history), and finally the time of Ruth 'who stood in tears amid the alien corn' (the time of myth and Pascalian ethics). These plural times, she argued analogously, are like Gibbs's phases of substances taking their places against and with death in hidden but deeply structurally temporal transformation.[186]

'Ode to the Nightingale' is seen as an invocation and abandonment of the ordinary sense of life moving toward death, accompanied too much perhaps by the fear of death. It was the denial of death, Rukeyser argued, that made for those 'generations' 'that tread down the song'. 'Generation' is here used in Blake's sense: the world of getting and spending, pragmatic materialism, the struggles of power, all of which are contrary to the world of the imagination. It is above all a state of denial, an 'epiphany of Satan' as Northrop Frye called Blake's concept of 'generation' in his 1947 masterpiece *Fearful Symmetry: A Study of William Blake*. It was a state which made tyrants 'revengeful and victims terrified, this mutual interaction of revenge and terror being the basis of fallen society'.[187] But for Rukeyser, Keats's poem is the song of poetry moving in and through successive actual generations: 'of nightingale, of bird carrying as it were song viewed through time simply in many birds, and you get the quality of recurrence, because of course, there is no true repetition here.'[188] This is the sense that the pianist Daniel Barenboim meant when he described the re-entry of the theme in a Beethoven sonata as 'recollection'. Recollection is already prepared for by the memory of the first announcement of the musical subject, hence in its 'repetition' of that theme, which at its first appearance only has a future, sings alongside the founding event, transforming its memory.[189] Here Rukeyser's figure of the spiral comes back into play, that of a circle without repetition: 'we are moving and the recurrence comes through with an increment, each time, it becomes, I think *romantic recurrence* in life, because it has that echo, that resonance which to me is a romantic thing which is the increment of life' (my italics).[190]

Rukeyser, perhaps scandalously given the predispositions of historian and philosopher alike, brings Keats's deepest intuition back to history itself. And it is worthwhile remembering the intuitive political radicalism of Keats's own passion for justice. There is, for example, his objection to the use of the failed French revolution by English reactionaries to stifle all movement towards greater justice: 'they have made a handle of this event in every way to undermine our freedom.'[191] That handle is an impoverished and brutalized memory.

Rukeyser ended her lecture 'Poetry and Time' by thinking again about the sense of history

> not along as a series of past events but as a world of ideas that one carries in the present, and how, in accepting the structure of resonance that one accepts in a poem, I need then to develop this for you, but I offer it to you as a figure in time, as Valéry says a poem is [...] as the true description of the growth of perception.[192]

The key phrase, the 'structure of resonance', is perhaps best glossed by René Char's famous statement that a 'poet must leave traces of his passage not proof'; the word 'trace' was something Rukeyser was to pick up again in her poetic reconstruction of the life of a Renaissance explorer in *The Traces of Thomas Hariot*.[193] The word trace, too, is linked to the deployment of memory and the narrativization of memory in *Elegies*. Taken together, these comments take us back to the famous statement in Aristotle's *Poetics* that as a result of the sense of the future operating on human psychology, that is the disposition that opens up a critical difference with the status quo: 'the thing that might happen': 'Poetry is something more philosophic and of graver import than history, since its statements are of the nature rather of universals, whereas those of history are singulars.'[194]

Aristotle linked probability to universality, an issue that inevitably raises the question of ethics. What is further needed is a sense of the past and here Char's distinction between proof and trace is of first importance. The one validates itself by known legal processes (testimony, judgement, consensus, precedent), all of which slow down the present in terms of the past and in terms of that pre-organized memory directed by the needs of established power. The other imaginatively opens the past in terms of the analysis of present need, the lacunae of which are filled by the 'what might be' and freed from, indeed often working against, the always insistent powerful consensus around the past's image. What is needed is a 'poetic anticipation of a renaissance of human values', in Payne's words. Of course the distinction is not absolute in terms of any one practice. When one sees what a historian such as E.P. Thompson can do with the historical 'trace', the writing of history glimpses a dim kinship with poetry, its traditional far-flung and sworn enemy. All of this contributes a more analytical understanding of what Rukeyser meant by the 'elation of poetry'.[195]

Keys for the Music of Time

In and beyond time there was and is, always music. The last poem in Rukeyser's third volume of poems, *A Turning Wind* (1939), was a poem on the American composer Charles Ives. In the notes that served as a preface to the volume, she acknowledged that the poem was helped by conversations with Aaron Copland.[196] Rukeyser's early training in music cannot be over-estimated in considering her work as a poet.[197] Many of her later ideas find their birth here in complex analogies with the world of music. Music was for her fundamentally poetic, an act of making. She wrote that music was 'emotion, ideas, synthesized by intellectual activity into design'.[198]

Pound's three criteria for poetry, *Melopoeia*, *Phanopoeia* and *Logopoeia*, were not remote from such a formulation.[199] Formulating the relations within design became a life-long search for Rukeyser. But there was a problem: there was no symbolism as such in music and Rukeyser wondered whether this was the ultimate barrier between poetry and music. She also wondered whether 'there was ever a communistic musician'.[200] The affective, intellectual and subjective life fully expressed in music looked perhaps in vain for an ally in dialectical materialism, as many Soviet musicians were to find to their cost. The one moment perhaps where they did meet was in the singing of Paul Robeson. She knew the great singer personally; he was scandalously mistreated during the Cold War and still has no street in the United States named after him because of his communist sympathies.

Throughout her undergraduate notes on music there is an emphasis on the emotional life and its relation to intellectual life. Above all, it was the perception of 'time' relations that occupied her, the 'flow of [the] musical past [in] through time'. A curt note to herself admonishes: 'Avoid over-emphasis on any one function.' Before she began a more precise chronological examination of music history, it is clear that she was fascinated by the necessary abstraction of musical thought and its relation to the emotions: 'Melody', she either copied down or chose to emphasize, 'a coordination of time – and pitch relations [...] Motion in a compound curve.' What is important here is that the idea of movement, a structured curve within given heterogeneous relations, the temporary coherence and evanescence of music itself, prompted questions not only about poetry but also of the scientific orders of nature and the very psychology of the human world. It is as if she were searching for a synthesis last experienced in the late medieval or early Renaissance world, before Eliot's dissociation of sensibility. It was that temporary synthesis of art and life that her friend Lewis Mumford (and before him Henry Adams) had so celebrated in his Ruskin-like vision of the Middle Ages, a gesture that, in critical utopian terms, stood in stark contrast with the fractured world of modernity.

It was a persistent thought of the times. As late as 1945 in Hermann Broch's *The Death of Virgil*, for example, the medieval world in its totality remained a dream to which the poet alone had access. Nietzsche's statement in *The Birth of Tragedy*, 'Art is not an imitation of nature but its metaphysical supplement, raised up beside it in order to overcome it', also begins to approach Rukeyser's way of thinking.[201] Rather, however, than 'overcome it' she would have felt it was more accurate 'to illumine it'; the self, remaining distinct and yet related, in an irresistible totality.

In medieval music, Rukeyser observed the conflict between the secular music of the folk and that of the church, noting both the sophistication of the former and the tensions in the parallel motions of the extensions of plainchant. It is almost as if she is reading the world of music in terms of Thompson's *Growth and Form*. And again it is the emerging idea of a doubly structured contradictory world achieving temporary coherence that made her notice the necessary presence of both consonance and dissonance in counterpoint. To cite just a few examples: in Purcell's *Dido and Aeneas* she found declamation based on words and melody, folk-source, a bit melodramatic but with a 'formal design balanced by deep emotional quality.' She made very long notes on Handel and Bach, emphasizing the dissonance within the polyphonic tonality of Bach, the independent voices, the strong accentuated rhythms, but perhaps above all, the haunting quality of his 'endless drift in time'. There is a further note on Bach that anticipates her emphasis on the buried life of the culture in figures such as Gibbs and Hariot. Bach was 'unencumbered by public opinion', almost unknown, and his local fame dependent on his ability simply to do things well. Her notes show her also analysing the music in detail. On 1 December 1932 she examined in detail Bach's C minor fugue from Book II of *The Well-Tempered Clavier*. The sense of the longer work and the short piece are equally valued. Schubert's piano works were 'divinely long' though she thought the shorter works better structured.

The modern world of music claimed her attention equally. There are detailed notes on Chopin's *Études* (not surprising for someone who had analysed Bach),

Berlioz, Liszt and Wagner. The obviously demanding and extraordinarily thorough course at Vassar, which had begun with the Greeks, ended with Sibelius, Grieg, Debussy, Satie, Ravel, Dukas, Scriabin, Berg's *Wozzeck* and Les Six. At the end of her notebook she wrote a single phrase: 'The ineluctable modality of all things heard'.

By way of exemplifying that ineluctable modality, one might cite three versions of three lines of Ninth Elegy: 'The Antagonists' that were tried out simply for the sake of the sound. The manuscript has a note 'Bring the sounds very close in all of these.'[202] One of the versions of the opening lines read:

> Pieces of animals, pieces of all my friends
> You meet in me and I live, I do not die
> I reach my America of contradictions.

In the final version it became:

> Pieces of animals, pieces of all my friends
> Prepare assassinations while I sleep.[203]

Not only is the thought changed and concentrated, but, in these words which open the Ninth Elegy, she has indeed brought the sounds very close together, both in the alliteration at the beginning and in the middle of words where a memory of internal sound is built up.

A sense of the ordered, yet wayward, world of music, included also both a mystical and scientific sense of a mathematical order inherent in nature itself. For example, at one point in a draft of the Ninth Elegy, she writes in a way that shows how her music analysis serves a general principle of creativity:

> You, like the
>   Men of mind [music] who contain all contradiction
>   do not move through the world. It moves through them
>   They make quartets
> Men of mind whom I can love[204]

Here that Olson-like sense of we act in nature acting upon ourselves moves one step further into rehearsing a condition in which skilled receptivity receives something not proposed but given as a grace of revelation: made and discovered at the same time.

In a later poem, the use of music as a paradigm of all knowledge, once the heart of medieval learning, becomes a clue again to contemporary knowledge, here certainly with echoes of Blake. It re-echoes the themes of the 1939 *A Turning Wind* and it will serve here as a summary of the issues in this section:

Spirals and fugues, the power most like music
Turneth all worlds to meaning
And meaning to matter, all continually,
And sweeps in the sacred motion,
Spirals and fugues its lifetime,
To move my life to yours.
And all women and men and the children in their light
The little stone in the middle of the road, its veins and patience,
Moving the constellations of all things.[205]

Politics and the Soul: Visions of the American Left

As early as 1935 a *Time* magazine review of *Theory of Flight* noted that Muriel Rukeyser is 'a left winger and a revolutionary', but also that 'her poetry contains no direct appeals to the proletariat and her symbols of revolt are imaginative'.[206] Hostile reviews from left-wing and, in literary terms, reactionary critics began to appear with *A Turning Wind* (1939). Most of the poems, they argued, bore scarcely any relation to the announced theme, there was a total lack of concreteness, everything was disconnected; there was little 'logical' resolution, too many compositional mannerisms, and indiscriminate scramblings of terms. Formerly, she had written clearly enough in her poem 'The Book of the Dead'. There, 'working with a subject of vital human significance that carried in itself a natural sequence of development, Miss Rukeyser proved she could write clearly and simply, with genuine emotional conviction.' A wrong turning and been taken: 'I should like', argued the reviewer, 'to see her go back again to the solid highway of *U.S. 1*'.[207]

There are critics, then as now, interested in both politics and poetry who find it very hard to abandon touchstones of social realism, 'clarity' and direct political reference in poetic discourse. There is probably not much to be done about that. Nevertheless, recent books that place Rukeyser within a left tradition in the United States are to be welcomed because it is impossible to understand Rukeyser without realizing just how deeply she worked practically and intellectually within a broad socialist tradition. In that respect the work of two recent critics, Alan Wald and Tim Dayton, is exemplary. Wald has traced the trajectory of Rukeyser's political allegiances: how her publication of 'Scottsboro' in April 1933 and 'The Trial' in the *Student Review* in January 1934 led to the editor Harry Magdoff introducing her to Joseph Freeman of *New Masses*, thus beginning her subsequent contributions to that journal.[208] He also mentions her work in left-wing theatre groups and her tenuous alliance with communist circles. Wald's comparison of Rukeyser, however, with her friend Ella Winter showed her 'far less active and prominent than Winter', and certainly (as her attraction to the

Catalan anarchists has also shown above) having an allegiance with dissident groups including Trotskyites. In California in the late 1930s, she was active with Harry Bridges, president of the International Longshoremen's Warehousemen's Union (ILWU) and participated in communist-led activities. She was also close to the Oppenheimers (Robert Oppenheimer had been a few years ahead of her at high school).[209] In the 1940s she taught at the communist-led Californian Labor School but then returned in the 1950s to teach at Sarah Lawrence College. Surviving the McCarthy era with some difficulty, her original misgivings about communism were confirmed by the revelations about Stalin in the Khrushchev era. Wald aptly quotes Benjamin's phrase 'profane illumination' to characterize her technique of blending the visionary with the documentary: 'the term refers to art capable of vivifying the common experiences of humankind with a religious glow, through the use of images from the non-sacred material world.'[210] As we have seen, it is a good deal more complicated than that but it makes a very good place indeed to start.

Wald was mainly referring to 'The Book of Dead', the poem on the Gauley Bridge Mine disaster of the early 1930s. Union Carbide, in digging a tunnel to divert a West Virginia river for a power station without sufficient safety precautions, caused the deaths of hundreds of workers who breathed in silica from the tunnel. The circumstances of this massacre for quick capitalist profit, and the poem 'The Book of the Dead' that followed, is examined in great detail by Tim Dayton in his *Muriel Rukeyser's The Book of the Dead*. He reviews the politics minutely.[211] His argument in relation to the poetry negotiates her use of the generic triad lyric, epic, dramatic and a series of dualisms: subjective meaning versus objective values; poetic versus non-poetic; lyric monologue versus mythic text. The aim is to show how a more complex poetics does not endanger the truth value of the historical fact.[212] Discussing Rukeyser's use of the 'Egyptian Book of Dead', he argues that she uses its elements of 'geography', the moral status of the dead and the idea of resurrection to articulate a life–death dualism, and an ethical stance in which divine judgement is directed to earth-bound values and resurrection as a collective resurrection in presumably socialist terms. All this is very suggestive and to the point. The argument for a base in a Marxist theory of history is rather deflected by Dayton's illustration of the Whitmanian 'American' 'spiritual' individual journey as a basis for her separation of the objective and subjective worlds. Dayton's key point is that 'Rukeyser's documentary, or social, poems do not negate her lyric, subjective poems, and vice versa. Rather, these different poetic modes reveal at the level of form, different, interdependent aspects of human reality.'[213]

Rukeyser's poetry in fact dramatizes that interdependence with different emphases and different intensities. In interpreting her poems, it is not possible to neglect Jung and the psycho-mythic aspects of her poetry or Marx and the social commentators. In a chapter of her second book, *The Inner World of Choice*, called the 'Journey Toward Wholeness', Frances Wickes, citing Underhill, Nietzsche, Jung, Meister Eckhart, Martin Buber's *Tales of the Hasidim* and *The Tibetan Book of the Dead*, concluded with an examination of Rukeyser's 'Orpheus'. Here the argument engages not the contradictions of modernist poetics but the psychological experience of modernity whose lineaments of anxiety turn out, nonetheless, not to be historically exclusive to it. In the following passage, the 'newly transformed creature' and the poem are part and parcel of the same thing:

> Our dismemberment is our journey through the hell of our refusals, the violations of our intended wholeness by our own conflicting elements. Yet in the essential element of the Self, if it has been chosen and developed as it was destined to become manifest, lies the power to reassemble the split-off parts into a newly transformed creature in whom:
>
> [...] the exile of our music
> and the dividing airs are gathered home.[214]

That 'gathered home' of 'dividing airs' was a fundamental part of Rukeyser's vision, and it filled the huge lacunae in the materialist's vision.

As in a great deal of American literature, from the Puritans to the transcendentalists and beyond, physical geography is read as symbolic and vice versa and the space between borrows authenticity from either pole in a complex and often ironic set of quasi-blasphemous dramatizations and propositions. The classic mid-nineteenth-century literature of the United States demonstrates this in many ways. Rukeyser's theory of history, insofar as she has one, is an almost Carlylean notion of key figures who resist the increasing corruption of the American Dream. Unlike Carlyle, and here the socialist convictions do kick in, the 'heroes' are likely to be radically unofficial.

The most fruitful path for examining Rukeyser's 'monologues' is along the line of the narrative and temporal moves of 'testimony'. A useful contrast is Resnikov's poetry. Here, direct personal testimony is placed so that it becomes emblematic of a general condition. It is not a question of subject versus objective judgements, the diseased lungs of the worker simply are emblematic of, as well as the literal consequences of, the wastage of capitalism. They are the intrinsic earthly meaning of a diabolical plot and accurately recognized as such.

Years later, in an undated manuscript note written while flying, Rukeyser wrote.

> Turbulence of air now
> The movement of life – to live fully in the present – consists partly of the work of bringing this history to 'light' and understanding. The 'unconscious' of the race, and its trace in art and social structure and 'invention' are our inheritance. In facing

> history, we look at our inheritance and in facing our entire personal life. The events and meanings, and forgettings of one lifetime.

In *Breaking Open* (1973), she transformed the note to:

> The movement of life: to live more fully in the present. This movement includes the work of bring this history to 'light' and understanding. The 'unconscious' of the race, and its traces in art in social structure and 'inventions' – these are our inheritance. In facing history, we look at each other, and in facing our entire personal life, we look at each other.[215]

As Hannah Arendt pointed out, citing Maurice Merleau-Ponty, there is no subjectivity in any case. That goes for objectivity as well. There is no absolute 'formal realization' of 'the capitalist subject', lyrical or otherwise. Here, Rukeyser understands more complexly that 'perceptual faith': 'Our certainty that what we perceive has an existence independent of the act of perceiving, depends entirely on the object's also appearing as such to others and being acknowledged by them.'[216] And in this poem of the Vietnam War, nothing is neglected, not the imprisonment of herself for protesting, not Auschwitz, nor the arbitrary contingent moment of the three-year-old and what she did to her kitten.

Dayton was absolutely right to note that in *U.S. 1*, Rukeyser had 'a foot in both camps' in relation to the Poundian and other poetic traditions, although actually she had a foot in many camps. His judgement about the emphasis on class and poverty (by implication), rather than race, in the poem is also excellent, even though Rukeyser will not use the terms to aim for a broader ('Popular Front') consensus. After Scottsboro, Rukeyser could hardly be accused of avoiding race issues. Although Dayton's argument works consistently in analytic dualisms (lyric versus documentary mode for example) its urge is toward attempting to define the synthetic inclusive practice that was always Rukeyser's aim and goal.

The drive for an abstract aesthetics or poetics theory as guide can be illuminating; it would have been simpler to explore Rukeyser's own view of the structure of 'The Book of the Dead' in the interview with Samuel Sillen that Dayton produces in his appendix: 'I have tried to write a series of poems which are linked together as the sequences of a movie are linked together [...] so that during the sequence the reader has built up for him the story and the picture.'[217] To analyse frame by frame, cut by cut, is harder work than finding similitude with a general proposition.

Sometimes Dayton materializes Rukeyser's 'mythical side' too readily and too crudely. Nor is Rukeyser's vision simply forward-looking in contradistinction to Benjamin. The figure of the spiral immediately complicates this too-ready opposition. Nonetheless, in a superb conclusion, Dayton understands that the mythical elements, although not much used in this particular 'political' poem, emerge from and acknowledge

> the multidimensionality of human subjectivity and the inexorable demand to consider moral questions in order to address the inescapable problem of meaning. It is after all a profound moral problem to try to comprehend the meaning of such events as the Gauley Tunnel tragedy, as it is to try to comprehend the meaning of a history in which such events are hardly uncommon.[218]

How that meaning related to a politics could never be simple in any case. It is the problem this book also wrestles with, and for Rukeyser in her own time it was particularly fraught given the ideological legacies of the first part of the century.

II

Time, Poetry and Truth: European Critical Philosophers

To place Rukeyser exclusively within a left tradition is also to tell much less than half the story, even at the time of her maximum involvement with it. To a degree, her fidelity to the truth of poetry inevitably brought her into conflict with the increasingly Stalinist world offered by the communists. By the end of the 1930s the literature debates in *New Masses*, for example, were a good deal more tolerant of difference than the political polemics in the same journal. Replying to Granville Hicks at one point, Rukeyser wrote:

> Granville Hicks in his review of *New Letters in America*, speaks of his 'tolerating' the conversion story in his search for hope in literature. It seems to me that the time for such tolerance gives way now; that application of a rigid standard of the (moral) happy ending is useless and has been proved so every time it has been applied to left-wing literature. A great many people feel now that whatever excellence the left-wing writers have depends more on their sensitive straight facing of present scenes and values than on the happy posturing of their theses. Whatever is inert is hopeless, now as always; whatever is living and aware contains its base of hope. And that's no discovery or denial.
>
> [...] the hope in this book is not the familiar one, for the next strike to be better than this last; or the survivor of calamity to be not so much alone, now that he has found his group; but another, profounder one, by which writers can touch their time

> and their country and find not the sweetness and light here called for, but its life and a steadier, less blatant hope than Mr. Hicks demands—a hope to be worked for continually, not shouted before its time.[1]

Here she explicitly criticizes a Marxist view of history in the simplicity of its narrative. She disputed the evangelical story, the impoverishment of narrative in naïve simplification. Sentimentality was the refusal to give the whole story. In her own time, the political and literary debates were fierce. The fact that simplistic post-Voltairean atheism linked with Marxist scientism to claim exclusive rights to a description of the human world presented the poet with a severe problem of possible worlds of discourse on which to draw. The metaphysical jump that insisted this linkage was the basis for 'realism' was more a belief than a working hypothesis. For the most part, for Marxists and logical positivists alike, to claim any kind of truth in poetry or religion was retrograde. Rukeyser was also trying to find a way to authenticate the poetic project itself, given the intellectual arrogance of scientific modernity.

The most famous example is to be found in Rudolf Carnap's philosophy. Here poetry and metaphysics were simply 'meaningless' and science itself was only meaningful by connecting formal logic with the principle of verifiability. In language the meaning of a sentence was purely determined by truth conditions. To express something metaphysical was what artists and theologians did and with artists in general, it was assumed, truth and falsehood were not at stake. They were capable only of vague expressions of an affective world, in themselves to a degree real but not very important. Even Wittgenstein was a bit too 'literary', a word that along with 'poetic' was a key term of abuse. In general terms, the debate set in motion between Heidegger and Carnap continues to this day, though commentators now like to stress the similarity of the origins of their thought, a mutual debt to Nietzsche, and a less than absolute polarity between neo-Kantianism and life-philosophy (*Lebensfuhl*) in their thought. Between cognition and feeling, 'logical syntax' and poetry, however, there appeared for a while to be no bridges. [2]

The debate was conducted in many ways – was it possible to heal the rift between poetic metaphor and logical analysis, between feeling and cognition, assuming somewhat dubiously that the mutually exclusive polarities of the proposition actually squared off in the first place? Rukeyser, in her rejection of the proposition that axiomatic logic was the highest form of truth, was to be closer to Heidegger's reaction to Carnap in the epilogue to *What is Metaphysics?*: 'Exact thinking is never the strictest thinking.'[3] As Keats once noted, 'in Poetry I have few Axioms and you will see how far I am from their centre'.[4]

From a different direction Jean-Paul Sartre, for example, also famously rejected poetry. He connected it with the reverse of the project, a passive pursuit of being, tossed endlessly between unity and disintegration as though the event were a thought of the one spirit, a false universalization in which the poet purely lost him or herself: 'the curse stemming from poetry, which is to say, the love of failure. Love of the impossible.' Interestingly enough, Sartre connected this idealistic duality with that type of generalizing temporality in history where the event becomes average, losing uniqueness, and where the subject as a result historicizes itself. It is an obvious reference to the familiar narrative of positivist Marxist eschatology, not to mention Social Darwinism. Death is at the centre of this process, unlike Heidegger's *Sein-zum-Tode* (being towards death).[5]

Its literary name was naturalism: determinism plus chance (psychology and social narrative predicated on models of nature). An absolute scepticism paves the way for the tyrants of 'history' whose realism is inflected with this fatalistic anonymity. Sartre's commentary on Mallarmé, where he spoke of the anger of the French poet when faced with the death of God and the turning of that anger into a disgust at the human condition and into hatred of others, shows Sartre nonetheless praising Mallarmé's honesty while doubting his motives: 'From 1850 onwards, faith is a negation of the negation. Nothing can prevent us from being in a world that God had abandoned.'[6]

Again and again Sartre emphasized the negative work of the poet:

> In Hegelian terms one could say that the meditation on the pure act turned Mallarmé from Stoicism, a pure formal affirmation of thought in the face of being-there, to Scepticism which 'is the materialization of which stoicism is only the concept [...] [In scepticism] thought becomes pure thought annihilating the being of the world in the multiple variety of its determinations, and the negativity of the knowledge of the self becomes an actual negativity.[7]

Hence Mallarmé's world represents for Sartre a somewhat inert and paradoxical materialization of a solipsistic gesture in which the world, rather than disappearing with the gaze that consumes it, confers a strangely universal but recognizable bleakness on it as a result of two distinct passivities (gaze and world as object) to which a concealed metaphysics of realism returns.

In Sartre's famous distinction between poetry and prose in *What is Literature?*, the language of poetry emerges, again as a purely reflective thing of the external world. It becomes almost an extension of the poet's body: 'not knowing how to use them as a *sign* of an aspect of the world, he sees in the word the *image* of one of these aspects.'[8] The insistence of Sartre's distinction is tendentious and ultimately, as with all either-ors, absolutist. One remembers Shelley: 'The distinction between poets and prose writers is a vulgar error.'[9] The problem is that the language of poetry is untidy and wilful. If the poem should not mean but be, which is basically Sartre's argument in more familiar words, and if he turns this into a negative rather than a positive affirmation, (the being of the poet's world hopelessly contending with the contingent other), he is simply turning 'meaning' into an absolute negation of the 'aesthetic' (magical associations of fitness and incongruity, like colours and sounds) and vice versa, thus providing both camps with a fundamentalist faith. Sartre accused poetics of pure revelling in linguistic technique which represents rather than expresses meaning.

This denial of the signification of poetry is amusing and outrageous. Even if Sartre were right, then his changed role for poetic language (the 'crisis'), which was actually very specific to the aesthetic movements at the turn of the century, would in itself be significant purely in terms of a historical change, a dialectically interpretable response to certain precise historical moments of the onset of 'modernity' in life and art. Sartre stops the movement at the negation of the negation. Even as he seeks a psychoanalytical explanation for the poetic practice and world of Mallarmé's or Rimbaud's, the sign, to keep his terminological opposition, overcomes and wilfully infects the pure image. The language of poetry in its argument is also perfectly capable of showing, prosaically a distance that opens a critical space between language and the world, even though it bears at the same time a greater memory of its oneness with the world from before the time of the dissociation of sensibility and the Foucaultian split. The passion of Heidegger for Höderlin or Sartre for Mallarmé perhaps tell us more about poetry than any argument they might offer, but to use a particular poet's practice as a synecdoche for 'poetry' (even assuming it is correctly described) and its relation to 'reality' had its obvious limitations.

Possessing a keen grasp of the general problems of critical philosophy, not to mention sharing a teacher (they were both taught by 'Alain' – Émile Chartier), Simone Weil and Sartre developed absolutely opposing views over a range of shared issues. Nonetheless they would have agreed on the nature of the pure aesthetic. For Weil it was 'sacrilegious': 'It consists in amusing oneself with beauty by handling it and looking at it. Beauty is something to be eaten; it is a food.'[10] On the other hand, Sartre's explanation of the magical fitness of sounds and colours in poetry, would for Weil have been too analytical, indeed too aesthetic in tendency. The listing of effects, or the celebration of technical effects detached from significance, did not add up to beauty or inspiration.[11] Sartre assumed an absolute idealism in the poet's relation to language, the kind then current in, for example, the work of Cassirer. 'Men do not see in the word a product of their own creation, but find an objective real that exists and finds its significance in itself.'[12] The problem is that this self-signifying, objective verbal real needs the mind of God or a Platonic archetype to ensure its significance in the first place.

This less-than-innocent return to the sixteenth century where, in Foucault's words, 'the sign provided a mark exactly in so far as it was "almost the same thing"', which together with 'what was marked and that which did the marking' provided a more complex sense of representing than that of Port Royal grammarians who simply believed the sign enclosed two ideas, 'one of the thing representing, the other of thing represented, the first being excited by means of the second'. [13] Cassirer's return to 'being' over the 'work' of representing is not regression but perhaps an ironic contesting of the 'general science of order', the 'system of positivities', the abstractions of a system of equivalents, including money and value theory. As Guy Debord noted: 'This stage in the economy's life entailed an obvious downgrading of being into having.'[14] The 'being' (not obviously a strictly ontological appearance) that poetry calls up, has therefore at least a possible dialectical and hence critical relationship to Sartre's prose project.

The philosophers aside, to mark the real political difference between Sartre and Weil only the following is needed:

> Workers need poetry more than bread. They need that their life should be a poem. They need some light from eternity. Religion alone can be the source of such poetry. It is not religion but revolution which is the opium of the people.[15]

Weil placed the Biblical truth that put the life of the spirit above necessity ('Man doth not live by bread alone'[16]) against that pure materialism that the more positivist Marxists announced with all the concealed metaphysics of its proposed essentiality, not to mention the determinist eschatology of its view of history. The work of history was not to be purely a chronology of variant productive relations determined in the last analysis by scarcity.

Yet Christianity had failed poetry too. For Weil, in the ancient world, in China, India and Greece, 'the love of the beauty of the world had had a very important place in men's thoughts and surrounded the whole of life with marvellous poetry'. From the Christian tradition, she asserted, 'beauty is almost absent'.[17] For Weil, art imitates the beauty of the world; for Sartre, art is to be classed somehow with the reality of the world. In Weil's more complex 'imitation' is a space for a creativity that both transcends the world and remains firmly attached to the world. Here, the place of nostalgia and utopian dreaming is far from being negative. Further, politics and art share an affinity, especially the arts of poetry, music and architecture, in that they involved simultaneous composition on several planes at once. Beauty itself meant that the unity of the work of art must be in constant peril, it could not be seized by abstract concepts, it was characterized by identity in variety, it had to grasped in its own instant, a moment held between passion and rhythm.[18]

Quite unlike Sartre, Weil regarded Mallarmé (whom she felt was to be admired 'no less as a saint than as a poet') as a true poet.[19] For Weil, there was very little passivity, very little negativity and nothing approaching scepticism in the operations of this double role. For Sartre, Mallarmé experienced the death of God more than Nietzsche. His suicide was a desperate attempt to make that 'no' the cause of nothingness, to proclaim the triumph of a non-material cause.[20] On a scrap of paper in the archives, Rukeyser wrote also on the suicide of F.O. Matthiessen, a Harvard professor who was the greatest critic of American literature of the time. He was hounded for his radical activities and he felt threatened, in a homophobic society, for simply being a gay man:

> Angel of suicides, gather him in now
> Who threw himself away,
> Defend us from doing what he had to do[21]

Rukeyser acknowledged the necessity of the act with compassion and marked her distance also from that necessity.

For Weil, as it was to be for Rukeyser, it was certainly not passive contemplation but an active love of the world that the greatest poetry embodied. As for the Marxists: 'No poetry concerning the people is authentic if fatigue does not figure in it, and the hunger and thirst which come from fatigue.'[22] The love of necessity was the supreme good for Weil; for Sartre it was the supreme evil. There seems to be no possibility of reconciling these two positions. At the deepest levels of the consciousness of existence perhaps the individual finds him- or herself constantly thrown, striving for balance, between the two positions, needing to find strength to confront and endure necessity and the contingent yet by an effort of will assert that only in a transcendent act is the human possible. Is it even possible to love the nature that destroys us in that terrible beauty where destruction and creation lie so close together? The Marxists had no discourse for helplessness, for defeat, for anguish, no discourse for the rites of passage: birth, marriage and death. For them, nature embodied only a grim necessity to be fought and conquered. In Marx's writings, however, it is possible to find a more multiple sense of the reproduction of the self and society within nature, but that part of his thought was never fully developed either by himself or others and certainly not in terms of ethics or ecological philosophy.

With very different attitudes taken towards the fact, however, both Weil and Sartre depended on a recognition that God had abandoned the world. For Weil, it was the deepest meaning of the crucifixion, a meaning that paradoxically transcended time, a unique moment within an essentially linear Christian history. For Sartre, it had been named, in Nietzsche's proclamation as a definitive historical watershed: a foundational moment that ended Christian truth and announced a new era. In that sense (a founding moment for a chronology), it was also, paradoxically, 'religious' and 'mythical'. For Sartre, the death of God in the nineteenth century was an opportunity to reinstate human responsibility; for Weil, in the transcendent moment of the first-century crucifixion, it was a call to recognize the anguish of the human condition. In neither case, however, did it lead to nihilism. For both writers, this abandonment by God made duty to others mandatory. Hence, they arrived at the same result by different routes. In neither Weil nor Sartre is there any hint of a personal God or a theory of the end of time. Weil's God is like that of Plotinus. While he looks down, we cannot look back.

In relation to poetry, however, Sartre had perhaps confused passivity with attention and disengagement with, to use the Heideggerian term, 'dwelling' (*Wohnung*). 'Dwelling' for Heidegger demonstrated the basic capacity for the poetic. While its connotations in English suggest a certain archaic passivity, the way Heidegger developed the concept demonstrated quite the opposite. Two of the most important aspects of 'dwelling' relate to 'taking measure' and to a sense of where the human being is in relation to an awareness of the self in the world. Taking measure and dwelling are the opposite of techniques of utility and 'occupying a lodging'.[23] Where Heidegger most connects with both Weil and Sartre, or rather they with him, is in relation to the nature of temporality offered by dwelling, that is, an existence that may be judged authentic, above all in relation to the future. For to resume an argument rehearsed earlier (see pp. 14–15), like Ricoeur, Heidegger cites Augustine in a discussion of clock time to wonder whether the spirit itself is time, a disposition that remains after things have passed: 'My very finding myself disposed, I repeat, is what I measure when I measure time.'[24]

Heidegger writes that clock time 'makes the event itself explicit, but more with respect to its unfolding in the now than with respect to the how-much of its duration'.[25] This consciousness structures the depredations of a modernity that is only conscious of clock time, both in work and in play. It occupies the heart of the sense of the self. It is the ubiquitous presence of the every-day; it is ultimately a calculation of the time before death. In contrast:

> Maintaining myself alongside my past in running ahead I have time. All idle talk, that in which such idle talk maintains itself, all restlessness, all busyness, all noise and all racing around breaks down. To have no time means to cast time into the bad present of the everyday. Being futural gives time, cultivates the present and allows the past to be repeated in how it is lived.
>
> With regard to time, this means that the fundamental phenomenon of time is the future.[26]

'Maintaining' and 'running ahead' to recapture time for the human world is a major key to understanding Rukeyser's poetry. In Weil, maintaining included the vital need of a past that had to be chosen to prepare for, to leak into, a prospective time, and for the following reasons:

> The transmission of a spurious greatness down the centuries is not peculiar to history. It is a general law, and governs equally well, for example, literature and the other arts. There is a certain domination of literary talent over the centuries which

> corresponds to the domination of political talent in space; they are forms of domination of a like kind, equally temporal, equally attached to the realm of matter and force, equally base. They can, furthermore, form the subject of sale or exchange in the open market.[27]

For Weil, the market's strenuous cult of mediocrity was the death of the culturally authentic. Hence, as distinct from Heidegger, the linkage of past to future would not be repetitious, rather a radical renewal, a fight for the very meaning of history itself within contemporary forms of domination and transmission. Sartre was closer to her here in terms of a sense of responsibility, and, like Rukeyser, felt that to advocate an active choice was central: 'Of course the dead choose us but it is necessary first that we have chosen them. We find here again the original relation which binds facticity to freedom: we choose our own attitude toward the dead, but it is not the possible for us not to choose an attitude.'[28]

For Sartre, the Heideggerian insights meant that the future had to be chosen both in the present and in terms of the memory of the past:

> But while freedom is the choice of an end in terms of the past, conversely the past is what it is only in relation to the end chosen. There is an unchangeable element in the past, (e.g., I had whooping cough when I was five years old) and an element which is eminently variable (the meaning of the brute fact in relation to the totality of my being).[29]

And further, 'by the choice which it makes of its end, freedom causes the datum to be revealed in this or that way, in this or that light in connection with the revelation of the world itself'.[30] Equally: 'Precisely because I am free I always have the possibility of positing my immediate past as an object.'[31] In Rukeyser the flowing of time in story mediated by the poetics of dwelling would politicize the erasure of the 'what' into the 'how'. All three would sign up to that collectivization of the self in relation to anguish, to the uniqueness of that individuation and self-consciousness, that primacy of the interior life, first offered by Augustine. In '"running ahead" "Dasein" becomes visible as this one singular uniqueness of its singular fate in the possibility of its singular past'. However:

> In being together with death *everyone* is brought into the 'how' that each can be in equal measure; into a possibility with respect to which no one is distinguished; into the 'how' in which all 'what' dissolves into dust. (my italics)[32]

Time remains an open question. In what way then are we our time?

As much as any philosopher in the modern era, Rukeyser negotiated these contradictions in her poetry. What view of science might overturn the logical positivism of Carnap, intent on saving the soul from the discourse of metaphysical unreality? Was there a view of nature that was not automatically linked with necessity and fatalistic order? How did politics square with the question of nature and the science that addressed it? In the chaos of contingent orders, in the inessentiality of the human and in the anguish that accompanied the realization, would poetry be able to distinguish itself enough from science's faith in the progressive revelation of order? The latter appeared not to need contradictory human subjects in their complex relation with others, or religion's faith in a God who offered comfort at the price of evading every difficult intellectual question, including the demands of scientific logic and its methods of verification.

And what was then left over to articulate the role of the subject, including the inner life faced with the problem of meaning in the face of the existential imponderables and severe psychological damage (the 'remembered' story of the past haunting the present) and the difficulty in motivating ethical action? What was the relation between these absences and the way people participated in and made history? In what sense might poetry and science be seen as part of complementary articulation of the life of the mind? How might the demands of bread and poetry be reconciled and beauty reclaimed both for the worldly project and the daily necessity? To grasp multiple levels of meaning at once in imaginative composition was at least a start in rehearsing the ways in which politics and poetry might survive the grasp of the monologic narratives of authoritarian violence.

Rukeyser in a sense picked up the pieces of the world abandoned, not so much by science or God, but by the Gradgrind-like utilitarianism of a world of opportunistic survival legitimated by a scepticism that endorsed the fatality of technological and capitalist drift. In a stray typescript Rukeyser wrote:

> Poetry declares, in a terms of the movement of
> Meaning, the possibility [existence] of a brief and
> [perfect] *fertile* equilibrium [touch] between the
> person and the world

Then, thinking again, she wrote:

> poetry declaring
> in terms of the movement of meaning
> sometimes the existence
> sometimes the possibility[33]

In the two drafts, in the choices and rejections, and in the argument itself, a moving tension is set up between possibility and existence, fertility and perfection, the invisible orders of the world and touch, that is, between completion and incompletion, stasis and movement, and between appearance and being there. Rukeyser was as concerned as Sartre about the atrophy of a desired future.

The problem of nature (scientific and philosophical) and the problem of consciousness and agency were fundamental to Rukeyser's poetic thinking. Was it possible to reconcile the scientific experience of nature with the idea of 'dwelling'? Was it possible to heal Eliot's dissociation of sensibility, to find a way of overcoming the split in consciousness and human activity and thinking, which Mumford had recognized as splitting Western Civilization? Was it possible to dream of the wholeness of the human world again? Must science change or poetry, or both? The problem was signalled in a note Rukeyser copied out from Alfred North Whitehead: 'We are now so used to the materialistic way of looking at things, which has been in our literature by the genius of the seventeenth century, that it is with some difficulty that we understand the possibility of another mode of approach to the problem of nature.'[34]

Rukeyser's capacity to see the worlds of prose and poetry as linked through dissimilar and analogous moves, bypassing the Sartrean distinction, is nowhere better signalled than in a letter she wrote to a potential publisher, Curtis Brown, with a proposal for her critical and cultural biography of the American scientist Willard Gibbs:

> I have written about Gibbs already in the poem, GIBBS, in *A Turning Wind* (Viking, 1939), which has enlisted the support of the Rockerfeller Institute. The poem is a highly compressed biographical sketch, I should like to include a great deal of documentary evidence in the proposed book in the same, or in a closely similar, manner to that used in the books *A Turning Wind*, *U.S.1.*, and *Theory of Flight*.[35]

At its simplest it was a matter of compression (Pound's *dichten = condensare*),[36] as well of categorizable generic differences. The 'documentary' involved all the filmic complexities of the metaphorical process. Poor people, 'primitive' people, foreign people and working people had to face other people behind the camera in a complex relation that chose its own temporal unfolding and engaged a more generalized ethical and political gaze whose objectivity was less than axiomatic, and might engage with or reject certain kinds of reciprocity. Poetry, even in Rukeyser's 'The Book of the Dead' with its spliced and cut reported speech and brief connective narratives, would not deliver a narrative history with an automatic sense of authentic reality. That was to its credit, for had it done so it would precisely have made suffering people an object of organized pity rather than invoking a shared outrage for reflection. There were sufficient modes of estrangement in the poem to guarantee critical distance. The techniques of documentary might overlap analogously with the techniques of poetry, but they delivered different truths because mediated by their generic differences. First among those differences was the different ways of presenting material visually and in verbal terms. As Rukeyser wrote in a proposal to a different editor in 1951:

> There is hardly any adequate writing for picture stories. I hope for a quick, fluent copy and memorable pictures. The words would not 'describe' the pictures; the pictures would not 'illustrate' the words. Together they would carry a stamp and tell a story. I believe a definite recognizable quality would be offered with this approach.[37]

In the end Rukeyser wrote *Willard Gibbs* in nothing like the manner of *U.S. 1*. That ambition was attempted years later in the *Traces of Thomas Hariot*, her 'biography' of the mathematician who sailed with Raleigh to the New World. That is another story but given the extraordinary achievement of American modernist poetry, from the 1900s to the late 1960s, including Rukeyser's, the very premises assumed by analytic philosophers, of what poetry was or could do, would need seriously revising. The fundamental questions posed by the philosophers, friendly or unfriendly to poetry, however, would still have to be addressed in different terms and in different times.

The Strong Ironic Joy of Old Intensities: Elegies

There is evidence in her archive that Rukeyser first considered giving *Elegies* a different title: *A Turning Wind*, *The Refugees* or *The Fear of Poetry*.[38] *A Turning Wind* was the 1939 volume in which the first five 'Elegies' first appeared together. Any of the titles would have been to some degree appropriate, some emphasizing the socio-political themes, others the psychological ones. 'A Turning Wind' was possibly a phrase derived from the German mystic Boehme, a citation from whose work headed the first two printings of the complete *Elegies*:

> [...] for the forms of nature are awakened,
> and are as a turning wheel, and so they carry their spirit the wind.[39]

The effect of the simile is to make the human artefact emerge from nature and create a consciousness of form, which in turn becomes a second nature within human awareness. Wayward and organized movement, order and disorder, the Apollonian and Dionysian fit into a larger intuited framework.

In terms of the trans-Atlanticist theme of this book, it is fitting to note that it was an Englishman living in America, Robert Payne, who first gave *Elegies* a decent review. This extraordinary, and largely forgotten man, whose first book had been published by Virginia and Leonard Woolf's Hogarth Press, wrote over 110 books: biographies of Chaplin, Garbo, Hitler, Lenin, Gandhi, Stalin, Trotsky, Schweitzer, Dostoevsky, Chiang Kai-shek, Mao, Malraux, Shakespeare and Alexander the Great, among others. He wrote historical works on Christianity, Islam, China, Israel, the Spanish Civil War and the Crusades. He translated from Chinese, Danish, French, Greek, Italian, German, Polish, Spanish and Russian. He was the first person to translate Kierkegaard's *Fear and Trembling* into English. Persuaded by no less a figure than Joseph Needham he taught poetry and naval architecture in China. With Chinese scholars, he compiled *The White Pony* which Rukeyser described in *The Life of Poetry* as a 'rich anthology of Chinese poetry'.[40]

For Rukeyser, alongside Yeats's translation of the Upanishads, Isherwood's *Bhagavadgita*, and E. Powys Mathers's *Black Marigolds*, Payne had been a means of bringing down the barriers between national arts. He wrote novellas, screenplays, librettos, novels, plays, philosophy and poetry. He covered the Spanish Civil War as war correspondent for the London *News Chronicle* and the battle of Changsha for *The Times* in 1942. Moving to the United States in 1946 he was the founding editor of *Montevallo Review* in which he published the work of both Muriel Rukeyser and Charles Olson. He died in 1983.[41] As another incomparable poet (whose work took thirty-three years after her death to be properly edited and published) Lorine Niedecker wrote to Louis Zukofsky in reference to Payne: 'There must be one who sleeps less than you.'[42]

When such a man reviews a work of poetry he is to be taken seriously. And his review of *Elegies* seems to be exemplary, though the 'humanist' language would not appeal to the current academy. This early champion of both Rukeyser and Olson complained of the blankness of most current poetry. He spoke forthrightly, much as Orwell had done on the known English poets, of the magnificent precision yet bloodlessness of W.H. Auden, Marianne Moore and T.S. Eliot. A few poets, however, stood out for Payne. Rukeyser was exemplary for her fearlessness and passion, for presenting a poetic world where the values remained human and where sensitivities were not deadened by fear. Of course, Payne's reference points were not those of American or English literary interest groups. Rukeyser was the kind of poet who 'live[d] within the landscape which André Malraux has called *espoir* which is not hope so much as the poetic anticipation of a renaissance of human values in a revolutionary age'.[43] The poems, he said, had all the appearance of being spoken, not by a poet but 'by an age we live in'. Their sense of the lament, ode and psalm was not in any sense elegiac but conferred a 'grace on the haunted multitudes of our time'. Above all, Rukeyser had launched into a 'new and serious mythology, a mythology in which the tormented people of the world assume heroic and even divine stature.'[44]

We are uncomfortable with such language at the present time. Yet the notion of the age speaking through a great gesture of the poet would have been familiar to the European romantic poets in the Blakean or Shelleyan sense of the prophet engaging in radical political activities, delimiting the interior life and articulately resisting the neurotic human psychology that produced reactionary and authoritarian activity. Payne's sense of the ambition of Rukeyser's poetry's attempt to claim a radical political ground through a recovery of the mythical and his sense of her transnational vision of unting diverse peoples in the most imaginative way were on target. The recall here of Blake and Shelley and Payne's reference to Malraux is a needful context to assist removing Rukeyser from the petty squabbles of a nationalist poetry scene. While, however, the great traditions of European poetry were fundamental to her work, Melville, Whitman, Dickinson and Hart Crane were perhaps her closest teachers. In a sense, she took up the variant creative syntheses they had already made of the European tradition. Politically and transnationally, like Thoreau, she simply asked what it was that people lived for in relation to what was generally thought to constitute real value in any culture. The problem with most current poetry and criticism then as now was that there seemed to be nothing at stake. In Rukeyser, everything was at stake.

The 'mythical' for Rukeyser can perhaps best be approached in a short undated note she wrote on a plane: 'the conviction that what is meant by the unconscious is the same as what is meant by history'.[45] The first thing that this registers is to doubt an obvious polarity between the mythical and the historic. The second is that 'history' was like a collective unconscious waiting for the work of the historian to produce history, much as the unconscious waited for the work of the analyst to produce a diagnosis. To recall Weil, the actual story as handed down might well be mediocre. History might be the work of the victors, a retrospective self-justifying propaganda. It might be the work of a self-promoting school of historians with a consensus of methodology or an object of attention and ideology mapped out. In psychological terms it might be the kind of common-sense story that buried the trauma. History and psychology were both subject to the complexity of narrative itself, ideology and temporality.

The poet's view of history differed from that of the historian in the sense that its aim was to give a sense of a personal encounter with history, though such an encounter might not be articulated in a personal story. The recall of that past could be articulated consciously to articulate the very subjectivity of the inner life of people in all their complexity, especially in relation to specific times and general memory. The outer world and the events of history, in all the particularities of the cultural legacies, public and personal, presented moments of freedom of articulation in which the self might operate with or without good faith. Paradoxically, the greater the complexity and the greater the consciousness, the more the self was impelled outwards, back into the world in renewed radical encounter. But above all, and here socialism came back into play, that drama was played out with others: 'In facing history, we look at each other, and in facing our entire personal life, we look at each other.'[46] What Rukeyser called the 'meanings and forgettings of one life time' were always a negotiation and articulation of both the public and private world, which in Arendtian terms had lost their radical separateness in the triumph of new totalitarian order. As Reich had so clearly demonstrated in his *Mass Psychology of Fascism* (1935), the inner world was being manipulated and invaded by the evangelical state, just as much as the outer public world had been under the traditional tyranny of the now decaying imperialist powers.

It is proposed to give a brief overview of the movement and scope of the entire work of the *Elegies*, in terms of moments from the narrative given above of the world of Rukeyser's thought and practice, and then to look in detail at a few selected moments in relation to a more exclusively poetic practice. It is hoped that closer, though necessarily brief, readings will throw light on the entire project of the work. The first five *Elegies* also have a place with the whole context of other poems in *A Turning Wind* (1939), the next four with the other poems of *Beast in View* (1944) and the Tenth Elegy similarly with the poems in *The Green Wave* (1948). But given the publication of all the Elegies together in 1949 in a special boxed and signed edition of three hundred copies printed in Stuttgart-Bad Cannstatt by Walter Cantz, it is clear that they were meant to form a whole on their own.

Elegies share many aspects of Mumford's vision in *The Condition of Man*, which was written through the same period: first there was the essentially ethical and psychological approach to the human condition; second the ethical inflection was informed by a spatio-cultural view of history which was not resolvable in classical circularity, nor in Hegelian–Marxist reason, nor in Christian extra-temporal closure; third there was a Blakean movement of contraries that played out poetically rather than in terms of a post-Hegelian materialist dialectic; fourth a standing in and out of history in which Pascalian atemporality was in dialogue with the anguish of the contingent and irrecoverable event. Mumford's theory of renewal was close to Rukeyser's own spirit in which the human will choose to challenge the almost immobile circularity of the structures of slow-moving social pattern and inherited historical violence.

As we have seen, it was Mumford's neighbour Joel Spingarn who argued that 'the sense of a *civitas*, of a whole, must be embodied in poetry'.[47] This statement is a permanent reminder that poetry that addresses politics with an immediate assumption of the realism or truth of a contemporary reference (a direct reference to a Christian or Islamic demagogue, the condition of women, or oil-wells is treacherous indeed). More relevantly here, Spingarn also captures Mumford's own idea of the relationship between poetry and politics and, parenthetically, Charles Olson's idea of the *polis*. It can be paralleled in Arendt's statement that in the Greek City State 'To be political, to live in a *polis*, meant that everything was decided through words and persuasion and not through force and violence', and that 'finding the right words at the right moment, quite apart from the information or communication they may convey, is action.'[48] For Rukeyser, as for Mumford, poetry had an important role in that 'persuasion'.

In her letter to Lewis Mumford of 11 May 1944 on *The Condition of Man* (see p. 377), Rukeyser included her poem 'The Antagonists' and wrote at the end: 'This is the myth of the Elegies.'[49] The poem was in fact the Ninth Elegy. In it, Rukeyser rehearsed a fierce Blakean theme of innocence and experience, creation and destruction as contradictory poles of the historical human experience in time. There, too, she celebrated an American tradition, taking the nationalist spirit of Hart Crane's *The Bridge* into a darker more contradictory, less exceptionalist myth. In this respect, Rukeyser's *Elegies* were to complement Mumford's *The Condition of Man*, through a celebration of 'that grace and resistance' in private and public life that marks positive achievement in any historical moment. The terms would celebrate the moving contradictions of human society and personal life, and prophetically long for an end to conflict in love. Close to Mumford's ethics was the call for intensity, not rest, a poetic attempt to reconcile cosmic and worldly time, and a vision of an 'America of contradictions'[50] where (and here Mumford's panoramic history of cultural beliefs and practices is most pertinent) opposition, enmity, hatred and conflict call forth their countervailing movements and persist through them. In the poem she sent to Mumford, Rukeyser quoted:

> To that far meeting place, call home the enemies
> They keep their oppositions, for the strong
> Ironic joy of old intensities
> Still carries virile music.[51]

The *Elegies*, taken together, move through the whole world of Rukeyser's concerns: the nature of dream and myth; children and growth; the nature of desire in relation to politics and the person; socialism and ethics; the correspondence between the imagined worlds of science, nature and the arts; the inadequacy of the one-dimensional vision in technics and modernity; the crisis of war; the meaning of 'America' in relation to these issues; and her particular personal memory of the intense time in Spain. In addition, there is the creation of a world made in direct response to Eliot's concept and use of 'tradition' and the melancholy of his high Tory and high Anglican vision. Over it all brood the great existential questions, a narrative of the dark night of the soul moving if not to illumination then to overcoming the crisis in a determination to recover some authentic version of the self and finally a poet's approach to the issues of time, memory and story in a period which saw the most violent and destructive human war the world had ever known.

The first five elegies begin with a quasi-allegorical journey, a descent, like a Miltonic fallen angel, to a lake of hell, a voyage of the soul which is articulated through a quasi-autobiographical recall of the numbed emotions of childhood, the slow movement to adulthood: the movement out of America to the intensity of the days in Spain when the war broke out. Spain becomes a generic site of war and human failure and of the emotional plague that makes people consent to war. Glimpses of a half-real, half dream landscape, like Hemingway's protagonist in 'Big Two Hearted River', structure topographically an attempt to put the self back together after severe trauma. It is as if she had adapted Grosz-like city figures for a more dream-like interior landscape which registered in the soul the effect of the crippled lives of the hungry and destitute, students, the unemployed, and the half-responses of official love. The personal voice moves in and out of dream, structured by a neurosis driven by loss, the power-games of intimacy: lying, revenge and betrayal. The interior war intersects with and indeed structures the outer war. Finding a way, then, between what she later called the 'inner frenzy and the outer doom' is what the poem is about and, in spite of the initial vision of hell, the First Elegy ends with a vision of the phoenix rising from the ashes.

This is not a collective vision, rather it obliquely conveys a sense of the failure of both capitalism and socialism: the one to care for others, the other to care for the one. At that historical moment both were under the heel of fascism and Nazism, the only recourse was to Gramsci's 'optimism of the will'.

> now I begin again the private rising
> the ride to survival of that consuming bird
> beating up from dead lakes, ascents of fire.[52]

The Second Elegy, 'The Age of the Magicians', introduces the binary world, patterned around the almost white magic of the 'prophets' and the Spenglerian, Faustian black magic of the magicians. The latter have contemporary and mythical form.

> The children grow in authority and become
> Molitor, Dr. Passavant, powerful Dr. Falcon.[53]

Molitor is almost certainly the writer's pseudonym for the prolific ultramontane Catholic writer and jurist Benno Bronner (d. 1880), who was an advisor to the Vatican Council of Pius IX, whose children's works were republished as exemplary texts for the Hitler Youth.[54] Passavant, by contrast, was a highly influential extreme evangelical Lutheran from West Pennsylvania, famous for his orphanage and other social services. 'Dr. Falcon', however, might well simply be the mythical Horus, the predatory flying hawk, image of divine kingship: the god of order and justice who united upper and lower Egypt by destroying Seth the god of disorder. The point is that the binary simplification is always the basis of authoritarian order and the legitimation of absolute power in any iconography, incorporating a modern version of divine right is intrinsically malignant. A socialist, Rukeyser had done her homework on the clear and present dangers of 'order', populist ideology, evangelical simplification and 'help'. Binaries, for example Catholic–Protestant at their extremes, created a fertile ground for political demagoguery. Neither Germany nor America (while thinking itself religiously tolerant) was immune. The poem cites the authorizing icons of cosmic discourse, here spelt out like a rhyming, alliterative children's chant 'the zone, the zodiac, the King on his throne'.[55] Against them ranged the 'prophets' with 'the dragon, the ecliptic and the heart'.[56] The dragon bore all the connotations of her reading of Mackenzie, the spiral form (air, water and fire) signifying birth, awakening at spring, the birth of the year, associated with the turning of the constellation of the Great Bear and so on. The ecliptic is the appearance of the sun's path from the non-circular plane of the earth's orbit, and the heart is simply the human heart. There are, in other words, autocratic and non-autocratic ways of using powerful political and religious icons. Inevitably in many rituals of power there are topographical abstractions of the cosmos and powerful psychological images and symbols. Rukeyser's point is that there are good and bad ways of using the instruments of Weberian 'charismatic' authority.

The Third Elegy addresses itself to tyrannies of method which include the 'museumification' of culture. In contrast, the Catalan communists, briefly cited, have a direct relation to cultural achievement. They honk '1–2–3 on the horn' as they speed in their cars past a surrealist house, ('a spiral in Catalonia') reminding us that these enlightened 'anarcho-syndicalists' were not dogged by social realism and that surrealism had a radical political dimension often overlooked in our own more 'museumified' time. This type of contrast is maintained throughout, with fastidious distinctions maintained: 'Children's art is not asylum art.'[57] As Foucault declared in *Madness and Civilization*: 'Where there is a work of art, there is no madness; and yet madness is contemporary with the work of art, since it inaugurates the time of its truth.'[58] That is a virtually an exact description of the thematic contradictions dramatized in *Elegies*.

The theme of children and the future also dominates the next elegy, 'The Refugees'. Here, existential anguish combines with a terrible historical sense of defeat and homelessness. Like Arendt, Rukeyser sensed the beginning of a new post-industrial, post-imperialist, post-democratic world in which anonymity and atomization rush into the vacuum left by decayed belief and once-genuine socialist dreams.

> They saw the cute, the intelligible world
> So wild become, it fell, a hairy apparent star
> This time with not a public saint in sight
> To record miracle. The age of the masked and the alone begins[59]

The refugee children fleeing the burning cities of the world become a sign not only of the dispossessed, but of the future. But it is also the child inside the adult that is at stake, the paradoxical child confronting a diminishing future. Whitman's too-confident 'born here of parents the same and their parents the same', receives an anguished twist and then a recovery from Rukeyser:

> It is yourself
> Walks down this street at five-year intervals,
> seeing yourself diminishing ahead,
> Five years younger, and five years younger, and young,
> until the farthest infant has a face
> ready to grow into any child in the world.[60]

The vision is further of shipwrecked people of the world figured as children born in their new power but fighting all the old enemies. Here it is the fear of death confronted and resisted in imagined stories:

> They dream the relaxed heart, coming again to power
> The struggle, the Milk-Tree of Children's Paradise.
>
> They are the real creation of a fictional character
> They fuse a dead world straight.[61]

If a free people are fiction at this moment, nonetheless it is a saving fiction, occupying the suspended time of a story that the imagination offers against mortality. It is possible Rukeyser may have read about the 'Milk-Tree' in Alexander F. Chamberlain's classic *The Child and Childhood in Folk-Thought* (1896) where he cites the ancient peoples of Venezuela. Infants who died a few days after their birth were seated around the Tree of Milk, or Celestial Tree, that distilled milk from the ends of its branches. He notes also that there are similar beliefs elsewhere.[62] This 'fictional' refreshing of the dead, also prepares a ceremonial acknowledgement of the nearness of life and death, and of a present robbed of the future but which becomes a living memory. Thus palliated, death more positively haunts the future of the life of memory.

Poetry was always, for Rukeyser, a link with the customs and ceremonies of non-Western peoples (she proposed and half wrote a book on Franz Boas) – it is indeed a kind of memory. Much of her attitude to these issues can be summed up by recalling here the French philosopher Gaston Bachelard's own attempt, in 1938, to make a distinction between 'primitive' and modern scientific thought in relation to dream and psychoanalysis:

> These scientific explanations originate in an arid and cursory rationalism which claims to be profiting by recurring factual evidence; but which is, however, quite unrelated to the *psychological* conditions of the primitive discoveries. There is then a place, we feel, for an indirect and secondary psychoanalysis which would constantly seek the unconscious under the conscious, the subjective value under the objective evidence, the reverie beneath the experiment. One can study only what one has first dreamed about. [...] For primitive man thought is a centralized reverie; for the educated modern man reverie is a loose form of thought. The dynamic meaning is completely different.[63]

As this section moves to a close, the world at war is again recalled. With the destruction of cities where hunger and thirst close down on children and human imagination together, amid the torrent of lies that have destroyed the peace, the injunction is to 'to say and to remember and avenge.' And all this comes together in an outrageous conjunction: 'A lullaby for a believing child'.[64]

The final elegy of the first group of five has a more visionary cast to it with the figure of the moving person in a moving world. It begins with an invocation of migrant America: fanatical, obsessive, moving with the daylight across the face of the country whose very topography moulds both the shape of that movement and the shape of the psyche. Here is an ironic touch that alludes not only to Frederick Jackson Turner's famous frontier thesis but, more profoundly, Braudel's and Mumford's psychological sense of the structure of a region. Europe is invoked, classically and antiphonally, in the American myth as stasis and barrier, but the population movement from one to the other becomes only a small part of a larger narrative of human migration in global topographical terms, with a hint of a complex geometry of people and space that governs its growth and form as much as the spirals of D'Arcy Thompson. Within that movement and to a degree more significantly, the more local cultural and ethical terms of the polarities of the myth fail before the purer and the more abstract 'axis of symmetry' – of brutal capitalist geometric calculation:

> Torn off from sympathy with the past and planted,
> A primitive streak prefiguring the west, *an idea*
> *Which had to be modified for stability,*
> *To make it work.*[65]

That torn-off sympathy with the past (the condition, classically, of American slavery and its consequences) was to be as crucial for the American as any over-simplified story of a progressive movement across the continent in terms of an imagined and blissfully 'anti-European' gesture: a pure antithesis that would automatically guarantee a democratic future of egalitarian splendour. To ignore fundamental links with history, Rukeyser suggested, would produce a 'ritualized'

America, blinded by the 'glass eye of unreal ambition', whose materialist goals were already producing a kind of malignant folk lore about those who failed:

> These are the ritual years, whose lore is names of shapes.
> Grabtown, Cockade Alley, Skid Row where jobless live,
> Their emblem a hitch-hiker with lips basted together,
> And marvel rivers.[66]

The workless hobo rather than the Beats' saintly wanderer is signalled here. His silence before fantasy rivers is a complex image of stasis and impotence, as the poor confronted capitalism's ruthless use of unrealizable dream images to render the failure even more impotent. America is also 'a nation of refugees that will not learn its name' alongside the thousands of men roaming across the continent looking for work after 1929. Depression America had exposed the reality of the dispossessed. Its naked cruelty and its abandoned industrial army betrayed a darker side to its relentlessly upbeat vision. Less mythically and politically disingenuous than Hart Crane (the great myths contend in their public and private theatres in a contradictory play of light and dark), Rukeyser nonetheless preserves through it all a wonder of the American landscape and a sense of the moving structure of nature itself: a nature with which the human activity must align, not fight and destroy. The elegy ends with a critical–utopian prophecy that the place of America is yet to be found and to be re-imagined in psychological and erotic terms:

> The shape is organized in traveling space,
> This hope of travel, to find the place again,
> Rest in the triumph of the reconceived,
> Lie down again together face to face.[67]

The Sixth Elegy, 'River Elegy', is possibly the most anguished of all the elegies, the most Biblical, the closest to Old Testament prophetic lamentation, the most compelling in its use of the great abstract words, for which, seeking a counterpart in American literature, one would have to go to the quasi-Shakespearean soliloquies of Ahab in *Moby-Dick* or to the great meditations on time, eternity and wasted human effort in Faulkner's *Sound and Fury* or indeed to Thomas Wolfe's looping rhetorical sentences in *Look Homeward, Angel* or *Of Time and the River* that so inspired Kerouac and the Beat generation. To be sure, this is 'rhetoric' but it has rhetoric's chief aim in mind which is the power of persuasion and its capacity to overwhelm. Poetry has always drawn on 'rhetoric' in the simple sense. One cannot imagine the Old Testament Jewish poets, Shakespeare, Spenser, Milton, Blake, Wordsworth, Byron, Shelley, Whitman or the Beat poets and writers without it. It is easy to see why the ironic, and fastidious academy with its minimalist emotions and its middle-class aesthetic, toying with unengaging simplified technical 'poetics', could not easily come to terms with the following:

> World without form. Chaos beaten and beaten
> raging and suffering and hoping to take shape.
> I saw your summer. I saw your river low.
> I being wasted everywhere saw waste.
> Hell's entropy at work and torment general.
> Friend against most-known friend, love fighting off love.
> They asked for an end to emptiness; their sick throats filled with foam,
> Prayed to be solved, and rose to deal betrayal.
> And I falling through hell passed many friends, and love,
> And a haunted woman warned me as I fell.
> Downward through currents, the horrors with little hands.[68]

Yet there is plenty to analyse. These lines more than anticipate Ginsberg's 'I have seen the best minds of my generation destroyed by madness', where the combination of long line and condensed image work so well together.[69] They have the visionary quality and passion of the 1930s socialist jeremiad and more than a passing link with the poetic tradition of the infernos of Dante and Milton. An analysis of rhythm here shows variation within the iambic pentameter in a contrast with the four syllabically stressed lines. There would be a place to explain why it is traditional for 'elegies' to engage with that particular metre, citing precedents, and there is plenty to talk about in terms of the conceits, the contrast between image and abstract statement: why the downward movement, the classical nudge towards the shadowy Cassandra figure, the other of the self, the role of psalmic repetition, the use of the controlling theme of the river, the scientific references to chaos, form and entropy, and the surrealist, dream-touch at the finish.

There is later more than a touch of Whitman, that other poet of war and erotic lyricist of death:

> Water will hold my shadows, the kiss of darkness,
> Maternal death's tender and delicate promises
> seethe at the lips, release and the full sleep.[70]

To call any of this 'rhetoric' would be to make a sloppy misreading of the nature of the kind of poetry this is, in all the richness of its traditions. It accurately and skilfully thematizes its immediate context: the worst moments of the worst war in history, a war in which sixty-six million people died, and in which human beings wiped out civilian cities as a tactic of pure terror, in which people were reprocessed like artefacts on a conveyor belt, and in which 'objective' scientists created the first possibility of destroying all life on earth

This elegy, simply acknowledges and faces that humanly driven chaos, the moment, in Serge's words, 'when it is Midnight in the Century'.[71] The pre-modernist poetic diction is compelling, and moves with an extraordinary sure pace to the final defiant and moving two stanzas, in which anguish, loss, doubt and despair become a turning point where the very music of poetry begins its work of healing. It is also a turning point in the dramatic structure of the *Elegies*:

> a broken crying for seasonal change until
> Oh God my love in time the waste become
> the sure magnificent music of the defeated heart[72]

The rhythmic control here of what is effectively an almost singly breathed line conceals its own complexities and ultimately a hidden meaning. The first pentameter interrupts the iambic stress twice before descending to five completely regular ones in the second line and the ritual beat continues only to break the pentameter in the last line with six stresses. Here Rukeyser deftly breaks the pentameter so that the theme of music and the rhythmic break endorse each other. Hence the season in hell is at once pitilessly described, and redeemed, in this poem. Dorothy Norman, who first printed this elegy in *TWICE A YEAR*, said to Rukeyser: 'Don't you mean *undefeated* heart?' There were some limitations to the great editor and photographer's understanding of the depths of this poetry.[73]

The lines also of course suggest a complex temporality. There is ambiguity in the phrase 'my love in time'. It at once suggests mortality and hope for the future. The change of season opens up more possibilities than in Eliot's ironic and dogmatic 'April' of the beginning of *The Waste Land* and is more defiant and less objective in relation to nature than William Carlos Williams's 'Against the Weather'. It is at once a point of emotional and ethical courage and a political refusal to despair. It is precisely that refusal of suicide that she had so gently turned away from in her poem on Matthiessen. In fact, the declaration of faith is also contained in the same poem, and is uttered just before the bleakness of its betrayal:

> Let me tell you what I have meant all along:
> meaning of poetry and personal love,
> A world of peace and freedom, man's need recognized,
> and all the agonies that will begin that world.[74]

This 'confession' is at once personal and public, its voice is intimate yet it directs its speech away from the self. It is not a 'hope shouted before its time' as she had noted, criticizing the naïve socialist eschatological narrative of the previous decade. It defends the experience of agonized disorder that takes a quasi-spiritual courage to make creative. Without the defeated heart and a facing up to the tragic cruelty of history, the world cannot be seen with any degree of truthfulness.

As Pascal said, there are many 'diversions' for those who refuse to face themselves or political reality: they are hardly a creation of post-modernity. The sentimentalities of the powerful Rukeyser located both in the social-realist propaganda of the Stalinists, in the vision of the ultramontane Molitor, in the evangelical Passavant, in the market truths of the capitalists, and in any ruler who thought he or she was ordained by God. The poet, in this serious reappraisal of what is essentially a revolutionary romantic vision, as well as a powerful spiritual vision, takes the monologic of the propagandist's determinist 'tragedies', sanctioning 'myths', 'authorized' versions of history and eschatological narratives (such as the future as a victory of one religion, the victory of the proletariat, the laissez-faire capitalist paradise of 'trickle-down' benefits and charity) and turns them into a poetic story of creative and resistant anguish.

> Carrying counter agony into the world,
> Dream-singing, river-madness, the tragic fugal love
> Of a theme balancing another theme.[75]

The last four elegies slowly rise from this point of anguish in the Sixth Elegy, for Rukeyser shared with Mumford a serious belief in renewal and rare and precarious rhythmic balance. The first of these, the Seventh Elegy, 'Dream-Singing Elegy', dreams with and against the haunting of birth and death. At the same time, the theme moves between confidence and utter scepticism about the nature of dreaming itself. Neither is offered as a final resolution. The defeat in Spain has to be gone through, the actual failure faced. Standing with the Spanish refugees she speaks of the 'black water far before us, a glitter of time on the sea'.[76] The poem's dreaming shows different times. Not least is the real time of the historical moment of the Spanish Civil War, the post-factum dreams of the memory of defeat and its treacherous post-factum dreaming and bad nostalgia are mercilessly exposed by the appraisal: 'We did not plan enough'. There is also, however, a 'dream-singing' of an almost Odysseus-like experience, of hearing again the stories of those slain in war. The point is that it is poetry that can put together unsparingly the 'telling' or 'singing' of dreams in which the re-visionary political judgement plays its part as much the acknowledgement of the power of unconscious involuntary images.

The Eighth Elegy is the 'Children's Elegy'. Here, as has been shown, the separation of London children from parental care and love, as the consequence of adult, political and ideological war, becomes a dramatic moment that has consequences for the Proustian memory of childhood in the adult as well for as the child's relationship with the parent in a moment of crisis. The Ninth Elegy:

'The Antagonists' is the one she sent to Lewis Mumford. Its spirit is close to *The Condition of Man*, and perhaps even closer to her making of an American tradition in her biography of Willard Gibbs.

It begins with an image of the poet torn apart by friends. This tearing apart of the poet-god is of course the ancient myth that Eliot used in his deployment of the myth of the hanged god of the researches of Frazer and Jane Harrison for *The Waste Land.* It is the fate the autocratic Pentheus, who has stepped outside the order of custom, with its balancing of wisdom, skill, craft and cunning, meets at the hands of the Bacchae, all in the context of a world of desire which is neither moral nor immoral. It is simplistic interpretations, negative or positive, of the waywardness of the power of sexuality and death, that authenticates the logic of the demagogue and the mindless violence of human irrationality.[77] Not feeling the need, however, to lament the specific decline of Christianity or the hierarchical kingship that Pound and Eliot felt to be the sole enabling traditions in which art itself might flourish, Rukeyser goes once more to the writers of antiquity to prepare her theme: this time Ovid's 'The Death of Orpheus'.

Her own poem, 'Orpheus', was in fact a kind of companion piece to 'The Antagonists'. The theme of the drama of disintegration and wholeness has already been touched on via Caldwell's review where he recognized a poetic dialectic against the pseudo-dialectics of the Stalinists in Rukeyser's work: 'The dialectical process is a third major key, seen not as a tight and easy rationale of class struggle but in a poetic vision of the eternal counterpoise and reconcilement of forces.'[78] This was precisely the subject of Euripides' *The Bacchae.* The play of contrary motions has already been shown in Frances Wickes's meditation on Rukeyser's Orpheus poem. Rukeyser's own account of the genesis of the poem showed that it was many years in the making. Not least in importance and probably inspired by Rilke was her reading of *The Orphic Hymns* in the New York Public Library. Among many other things, *The Orphic Hymns* would have given a sense of a vitally and intelligibly animated universe in perpetual contradictory motion in which God was at once present and invisible, whole and scattered in pieces, everywhere and nowhere.

Its world, as she says in the Ninth Elegy, is 'not of rest but of intensity'[79] and there follows a narrative of American contraries, American forms of the *dejecta membra* of the polis, what she called 'the forms of incompleteness in our land'.[80] The poet's vision is that of wholeness in brokenness, of the necessity of the fragment without which the whole cannot be known. This is the opposite of Eliot's notion of the fragment. For Eliot, the fragment embodied nostalgia, an index of the lost exiled place, a damaged sign that points back to an original wholeness rather than the immediate presence of vital life linked to other fragments and indexing a usable past for future synthesis. Shelley's dome of many-coloured glass, for Rukeyser, does not stain the white radiance of eternity, rather it is lit by eternity.

However, as always in Rukeyser, the contraries are exhibited in an immediate social and historical moment:

> [...] our ancestors, all antagonists:
> Slave and Conquistador, dead hand-to hand,
> Scented fastidious Tory with his whore,
> distinguished rebel and woman at the plow.
> The fiery embryo umbilical
> always to failure, and form developing
> American out of conflict.[81]

The touch of dualistic typological satire here shows the eternal recurrence of power in different forms: slave and conquistador, Tory and whore, and the 'distinguished rebel and woman at the plow' are forms of polarized exclusions, an endless master-slave couple of which, perhaps, the latter is as clichéd in its Stalinist iconography as the dualism can make it. But the hope is that the forms of these 'doubled phantoms', to borrow a phrase further on, can be made a 'meeting place' where in a prophetic vision the 'agonies/lie down at last together face to face'.[82] Conflict is invoked to prophesy an end to conflict: a distant possibility of Orphic music.

The last elegy, Tenth Elegy: 'Elegy in Joy', appeared in *The Green Wave* published in 1948. The main themes of the foregoing are still present but there is a new sense of poetry and the nature of time. Possibly the birth of her child at this time meant a certain reorientation of her own sense of time, the images of fire and the green world, the phoenix and the tree of life and growing things, bring a new visionary sense of a resolution, perhaps, of certain personal conflicts. One is reminded a little of the first poem of Hugh MacDiarmid's first book, *Annals of the Five Senses* (1923), that perfectly captured the spirit of the Orphic Hymns:

> I was a multitude of leaves
> Receiving and reflecting light,
> A burning bush,
> Blazing for ever unconsumed,
> Nay, ceaselessly,
> Multiplying in leaves and light
> And instantly
> Burgeoning in buds of brightness
> – freeing like golden breaths
> upon the cordial air
> A thousand new delightrs
> – translucent leaves
> Green with the goodness of Eternity,
> Golden in the Heavenly light [...][83]

Rukeyser knew of MacDiarmid's work, both Marxist and visionary, from early on. In 1963, for example, she wrote to Lewis Mumford that she had taken a break from her work on Hariot at Alnwick Castle and had been to see the great Scottish poet in Scotland.[84] Two decades earlier, Rukeyser's opening lines turned the visionary tradition into a prophecy of peace in what she called in the poem 'the old same war'.

> Now green, now burning, I make a way for peace
> After the green and long beyond my lake
> Among these fields of people, on these illumined
> Hills, gold, burnt gold, spilled gold and shadowed blue,
> The light of enormous flame, the flowing light of the sea,
> Where all the lights and nights are reconciled.
> The sea at last, where all the waters lead.
> And all the wars to this peace.[85]

MacDiarmid's image of the romantic, inspired poet, burning yet unconsumed, claiming the consuming green out of which God spoke to Moses, uttering breath infused with golden light, hence eternal, is given a more temporal goal by Rukeyser. The images indicate not just a prophetic role, but prepare a direction, a 'way' of peace. It was time and eternity as noticed in a very earthly vision that occupied Rukeyser: 'Years of our time *this* heart!',[86] and the demonstrative pronoun takes the same accentual weight as 'heart'.

This thematic run-through of the ten elegies has perhaps somewhat treacherously suggested the linear nature of Rukeyser's private/public journey. The progression is far from certain, however, and there are contrary motions within any one of the *Elegies*. Even the prophetic vision just cited gains its force from a terrible awareness of its opposite. It is more a declaration of courage than an anticipation of resolution. Also, the dozen or so themes the poem presents – the nature of dream, myth, science, the inner life, children, Spain, technocracy, the sociality of emotional plague, American identity, and its cultural traditions are like shifting pieces of glass in a kaleidoscope swirling round each other in different relations at any point in a given poem.

The theme of time and narrative, though fragmented, is persistent throughout. Just to take the First Elegy, there is the ethical time of the quasi-allegorical spiritual quest, needed for all historical and personal judgement, but radically unconnected with the linear times of change, progress or regression: 'As I went down to Rotten Lake I remembered/the wrecked season.' The ethical effort needed to combat anguish occupies a strange space outside time. Anguish traps and roots us in memory, demands a revisionary narrative, and presents the future as pure terror because it is refused. The season is wrecked not only because it was the personal experience of that season but because historical contingency can find the person wrecked in any season. In other words April both is, and is not, necessarily the cruellest month. The opening also inevitably recalls Rimbaud's opening of 'Le bateau ivre: 'As I came down to impassive rivers'. However, that nightmare of exotic landsca}pe inflected with brief imagistic touches of imperial mercantile capitalism is only remotely parallel with Rukeyser's vision, except perhaps in the Coleridgean nightmare seascapes and remotely in the penultimate stanza:

> If I want a water of Europe, it is the black
> Cold puddle where in the sweet-smelling twilight
> A squatting child full of sadness releases
> A boat as fragile as a May butterfly.[87]

Rukeyser moves from inner psychological time, with its memories, scars, involuntary recall, and anxiety, to a sense of time that is ethically cyclical in its call for renewal. Any moment recalled in the poems present a familiar and recurrent place of choice, a call for imaginative effort and courage, likely to be defeated except for a determined movement out again:

> When you have left the river you are a little way
> nearer the lake; but I leave many times.

Out of sequence and as in a moment of involuntary recall Rukeyser brings in actual personal history, its factuality parodied by the alliteration and generalization:

> Parents parried my past; the present was poverty,
> The future depended on my unfinished spirit.[88]

It is of course a very singular thought that parents, who are in common-sense terms thought to be the past of any child, here ward off a re-narrativized past needed for the child's own authentic identity. The parents offer the inadequate past of the bruised intimate relation, now to be set aside for the wider issues of renewed selfhood and the public issues of history itself.

For Rukeyser, as for Pascal, it was probably the cowardice, the slovenly imaginative mediocrity and sheer cruelty of a person's silence that was most distressing. Here, the sense of lostness and devastation of human silence depended on personal courage to turn the psyche from depression and intimations of mortality to the open opportunity of the 'unfinished'. In short, it is finding courage to begin speaking again. Completion is feared less than the vacuity of the space from here to there. To die full of days is not to be feared, only the banality of days structured by terror, whether of early psychological wounding or in the involuntary and persistent scars of human betrayal or in the memory of, and threat of, actual illness, death and war.

From atemporal psychological and ethical memory, Rukeyser turns from childhood to Spain. After a moment where the sexual and intellectual needs of the person are presented as rarely in balance, too physically gross or too mentally feeble, the historical moment of Spain is recalled.

> But the poet
> and his wife, those who say Survive, remain;
> and those two who were with me on the ship
> leading me to the sum of the years, in Spain.[89]

Here the present is at once presented as contingent experience and as an interpreted or narrativized present. The 'sum of years' has multiple temporal significance: it is at once a climax, the highest moment, pure aggregate, totality (which is slightly different), summary, and ultimate goal.[90] In fact, the variant possibilities work against pure aggregate through the will of the poet to make it a kind of epiphanic moment, directing that unfinished spirit between the lingering of the past (summary), towards a totalizing present that the future leaks back towards in terms of the proposed goal or Sartrean project.

The historical child is then taken back from the personally remembered childhood to the general human condition of children. Here is an achronic ethical need for which no calculation has been made in historical adult politics: 'the sad frightened child, continual minor'.[91] Then, too, there is the ethics of the choice of narrative, and above all what is chosen to be remembered: 'what must be crossed and cut out of your heart/what must be stood beside and straightly seen'.[92] In a sense here, Rukeyser is finding ways in poetry to combine the discussion of story and temporality together with a philosophical analysis and an ethical project. Here, Ricoeur's words are again timely:

> If it is true that one of the functions of fiction bound up with history is to free retrospectively, certain possibilities that were not actualized in the historical past, it is owing to its quasi-historical character that fiction itself is able, after the fact, to perform its liberating function. The quasi-past of fiction in this way becomes the detector of possibilities buried in the actual past.[93]

The detection of possibilities needs not only imaginative empathy and doubtless an intuition to look where no one has looked before, but also an ethical and ideological decision. Yet another type of temporality is offered in this elegy and that is not only the shorter timeframe of modernity but a precisely politicized 'modernism'. Here the Marxist base line of necessity recalls an immediate historical past, the past from the crash of 1929 onwards:

As I went down to Rotten Lake I remembered
how the one crime is need. The man lifting the loaf
with hunger as motive can offer no alibi, is
always condemned

These are the long lines at the employment bureau
And the tense students at their examinations;
Needing makes clumsy and robs them of their wish
In one fast gesture

Plants on them failure of the imagination [...][94]

The first 'time' here recalls the historical crash of 1929 and the capitalist incorporation and bureaucratic professionalization of education from 1880 onwards in America; the second 'time' concerns the achronic psychological effects of the practices of authoritarian power on the young: a judgement that stands in and out of history because of its disregard for nurture. In this 'documentary list', cutting filmically from one scene to the next, the move is from bread to the imagination. Need is not however narrativized as pure scarcity. A more extreme example of this can be found in some notes in Rukeyser's papers on rushes from a malaria documentary:

Lines of people being vaccinated
        Wary woman
        Woman laughing
        Woman and child
    Market place (pan)
    Leaves and jungle, burro train
    Hills and two crosses.[95]

Even in this 'pure documentary' list, the women, private and intimate here, are already imaginatively generalized in terms of their overcoming of prejudice and in terms of their vitality. The governing contrast is special public space, moving in a pan shot, of the market place. The means of transportation of goods to be sold are offered under the sign of death and crucifixion, aligning the lines of people being vaccinated both against and with Christian symbols of anguish and death.

If it is Marx on the one hand, it is the gospels on the other. Rukeyser knew that man could not live by bread alone, but she insisted that the one hand saw what the other was doing. Bread and imagination were not alternatives, they were cut into each other and were hence indissolubly linked as vital human needs. The First Elegy ends with a visionary section that redefines the nature of desire itself. The 'black beast', her dream or alter ego's 'double' that she describes running alongside her in the poem's opening lines, is desire itself, anarchic, amoral, creative and destructive. The need is to use 'the beast' imaginatively for a world of human values and sane wishes not for Faustian egotism and power. 'Seest thou that black dog', Goethe's Faust said to the terrified apprentice Wagner. For Rukeyser the need was to 'be beside herself' in multiple senses.

But this doubling has a more subtle function. It has that sense of being alongside oneself, a way of accompanying oneself (if the musical pun may be allowed) that Heidegger talked of in his *Concept of Time*. In everyday experience there is little reflection on the self, and yet this sense of 'being there' (*Dasein*) '*finds* itself *disposed* alongside itself. [*Es befindet sich bei sich selbst*] It comes across itself there in whatever it is generally dealing with.'[96] In her disposal of temporal moves in *Elegies*, Rukeyser finds incomparable ways of aligning the inner life with the outer, the private with the public, and reflecting on both as an accompaniment to historical and personal description. She is both outside herself while aware of her inner self. The poem rehearses ways of being both alongside oneself and alongside history, indicating a barely perceptible gap but one directed to the utopian possibility of critically examining the meaning of human completeness and intelligibility. That in itself, fully understood, initiates the critical project.

The poems have been read both for themselves and as part of Rukeyser's poetic and imaginative world, as well as one particular response to a particular historical and personal moment in the 1940s. But the final word must rest with the poem itself. It is important to understand that Rukeyser was a poet among poets. She is not finally to be defended simply against the poetic practice of her time: offering a reply to Eliot's *The Waste Land*, or dissenting from the Pound tradition or rebelling against the literary orthodoxies of the *Partisan Review* and the New Critics or modifying the socialist jeremiad. Through her love of the ways and cultures of non-Western peoples and her sheer openness to all poetries, her range of reference was vast. Some of these must at least be touched on.

As we have seen, the range of influences on her poetry extended from the Psalms of David and the Old Testament prophets to Sappho, the Orphic Hymns, Shakespeare, Blake and Shelley. There was also a deep involvement with the whole range of poetry of England and Scotland. Keats was as important as MacDiarmid. In terms of southern Europe her notes show her making translations from Paul K. Masson's collection *Chants de Carnaval Florentines de l'époque de Laurent le Magnifique* and Jacques Ibert's *Deux Chants de Carnaval de Machiavelli*. The Russian dissident poets too were part of her poetic map, including Mayakovsky, Pasternak, Yevtushenko and Akhmatova. In terms of her more immediate contemporaries her reading and active translation included the Swedish poet Gunnar Ekelőf and the Mexican poet Octavio Paz.

Rilke's own famous *Duino Elegies* were a point of both reference and dissent. Her very choice of the genre of elegy and the Orpheus poem, the theme recurrent throughout her life, is germane to this. Her comments on Rilke's sense of time, 'the long illness', has already been cited in relation to Proust and her meditation on poetry and time, but there were other sources here not least the 'rhetorical' line. We do not accuse of rhetoric: 'Who, if I cried out, might hear me – among the ranked angels?'[97] Its anguished power is enough, as indeed are the lines that conclude Rukeyser's Sixth Elegy. The tree of life was as threatened for her as for Rilke. Her poetry exhibits also the necessity for praise and the recognition that 'Nothing stays still'.[98] Music, too, for her invaded the desolate wilderness. As with Rilke, space was never pure space; it was always a world, and 'things' lived in reciprocity with the person. But the ecstasy of being for her was always directed outwards into the world it revealed; the existential anguish had human and political roots and sources, as well as bearing the terror of pure contingency.

She seems less vulnerable than Rilke to the transitoriness of sexual passion as an analogy for the weakening of human energy toward death. For Rilke, the configuration of pure biological desire seems in danger of becoming its opposite – an idealistic metaphysic, a closed determinist narrative whose eschatological absolutism wipes out all human value in overwhelming anguish. In *Sonnets to Orpheus*, Rilke fought back, not for a complete victory but a sense of value in defiance. It is in the following lines that Rilke is closest to Rukeyser:

> Ah the earth! Who knows what the years erase?
> Only one who sings loud praise will feel the cost
> And sing the heart being born into the whole.[99]

This review of poets has a single purpose: to show the range of Rukeyser's own sense of poetry as a transnational art of many traditions and open to be thought of as such whether or not any particular ideological or poetics-specific American group 'liked' or 'disliked' her work. Facilitator of local contacts and the local collective spirit as she was, for her the true poet was on her own and indeed, given the general state of the culture of poetry in any contemporary society, whether in or out of the academy or in or out of the dominant metropolitan literary journals, she was even likely to be ignored.

During December 1944, Rukeyser was also occupied with a play: 'Anne: A Play: The Middle of the Air', a sort of Yeatsian poetic drama. Notes in the margin again indicate the range of her thinking: Mayakovsky, Strindberg, Sophocles, Sappho, Congreve, Yeats. A principal male protagonist is a Jewish psychologist called Walter Ensor. Her note on his character might almost be a description of herself:

> he talks about chess, music, burlesque, disease, women, politics, poetry, dreams: he exchanges many of the terms among these. But his mind is not a jumble; he is a kind of pantheist Jew, that is he believes that everything is a name for God, and he is deeply concerned with the problem of evil.

The open field of Rukeyser's poetic world was also not a 'jumble'. Diffuse, with asyntactical linkages, with a line as much indebted to ancient Jewish poetry as to the imagists, while employing and rejecting many 'traditional' verse forms, her poetry, read without prejudice, shows a remarkable skill and complexity in all domains and perhaps especially in that of rhythm and musicality. The opening few stanzas of the *Elegies*, a kind of prologue to the entire series, will provide a short concluding example:

> As I went down to Rotten Lake I remembered
> The wrecked season, haunted by plans of salvage,
> Snow, the closed door, footsteps and resurrections,
> machinery of sorrow.
>
> The warm grass gave to the feet and the stilltide water
> Was floor of evening and magnetic light and
> Reflection of wish, the black-haired beast with my eyes
> walking beside me.
>
> The green and yellow lights, the street of water standing
> point to the image of that house whose destruction
> I weep when I weep you. My door (no), poems, rest,
> (Don't say it!) untamable need.[100]

The opening pentameter in fact is subverted by the natural break of the caesura in the following line turning it almost casually into one seven beat line. The effect is musing, almost dreamy yet interrupted by the strength of thematic revelation and authority. In fact the first really strong stress in natural speech is 'wrecked', giving it appropriate emphasis, though in fact in English poetry 'stresses' cannot be simply divided into *either* strong *or* weak. The old Victorian classificatory systems, based on Greek and Latin scansion, with all those off-putting Greek names, are not very helpful, though some are reluctantly used here. For example, the tetrasyllabic opening foot followed by a trisyllablic (amphibrach) – 'to Rotten' – is stopped in a single strong stress – 'Lake' – next to the single strong stress 'I', that is in turn relieved again by another 'amphibrach' – 'remembered'. It gives an effect of musing, things coming forward and dying away. The opening 'pentameter' is followed by an iam and troche back to back, or one could simply hear it as an 'antipast' (short-long-long-short) – 'the wrecked season'. The end of the second line scans a trochee, then is reversed into an iam, followed again by the trisyllabic amphibrach, that, following the two very strong stresses in the unit, seems to let the voice trail off a little, perhaps emphasising the paradox of passivity and strength in the semantics of 'haunted' and 'plans'. The third line breaks the mould: a single strong stress, followed by the again now familiar amphibrach, then an iam, followed by a tetrasyllabic foot with the stress on the second syllable. The last line of the quatrain, in tonal summary of the list, repeats the last tetrasyllabic foot with the second syllable accent, working by repetition against the line-break, coming to rest in a last trisyllabic amphibrach – 'of sorrow' – now bearing a rhythmic memory by repetition, with its a hint of meditation and melancholy, of 'remembered', 'of savage', 'the closed door'.

These observations are made not somehow to 'go technical' on the unsuspecting reader, but to illustrate the fact that Rukeyser's skill in building rhythmic complexity (with which she was as concerned as William Carlos Williams with his 'variable foot') was of a very high order. It is very difficult to write a line with so many rhythmic shifts. She does indeed show an acute awareness of the strong accented rhythms of the 'endless drift in time' she had noted in her studies of Bach and Handel as an undergraduate. It is not proposed to look at the other two stanzas in such detail, but the second quatrain has a long looping rhythm to it which shows her master of the extended line, and the third quatrain breaks it all up again in doubt, uncertainty, musically carrying the thematic intermittent challenges and exhortations to the self: the self *alongside* the self.

As Charles Olson said: 'he who possesses rhythm possesses the universe'.[101] Nothing renders the drift in time more palpable and concrete in immediate presence than the play of rhythm whether in dance, music or in poetry itself. Here we reach the mysterious heart of our perception of human time. If my reflections on rhythm appear over-technical or remote from the subject of this argument, might they not also perhaps serve the purpose of reminding us of the difficulty not only of rhythmic complexity, but the long training needed to do it well. This is of course commonplace knowledge to the professional dancer or musician. Time and the nature of temporality have been discussed and analysed in this book from many perspectives. Perhaps the very nature of rhythm in dance, music and poetry should have the penultimate word. Nothing expresses more palpably, and beyond words, the very soul of the human being in time.

If the opening line has more than a hint of the self-declaring romantic 'I' (and there are many voices of that 'I' in the poem), with the contrary motion of a hint of a story to come as it reveals its own past, then there is strong imagist influence in the third line, where conventional organizing syntax is removed and the images are left on their own to offer a silent heuristic space between the units: 'Snow, the closed door, footsteps and resurrections/machinery of sorrow.' Unlike the Poundian ideogram, whose meaning is formally resonant and condensed within a squared-off rather static space, this set of images has a forward movement: a paradox of quasi-narrative within isolated fragments. Is the closed door set against the snow, or is it parallel figure of enclosing and shutting in? Are the footsteps a threat or a comfort and does the sudden abstract concept 'resurrection' in its otherworldliness suggest a quasi-narrative of burial, rescue, and deliverance, a reassurance of the cyclical quality of nature, or of belief equally? They are mysterious as Debussy's *Des pas sur la neige* which surely she must have noticed alongside her note on *Jeune fille aux cheveux de lin* in 1933. If that is so, they are abruptly dismissed in the last phrase making the images seem treacherous in their very lyricism.

In the second stanza, the poet makes her own intervention in the existential drama. She robs the cyclical movement of its motion in a moment of inspired peace, sensual and still at the same time, one in which the world, as in a picture by Blake, is seen as indivisible. Here are no footsteps, frozen, immobile, indicators of gone movement, but the feet in warm grass. Even 'gave to the feet' is ambiguous, the human touch at once active in nature and passively receiving. The water and the sky, and the 'magnetic light', with its hint of the physical unity of energy – light and electricity and magnetism structuring a scientifically perceived abstract world of forces, here come into union with human desire itself. One is reminded in the 'stilltide water' here of the 'inland murmur' of the Wye just past the effects of the tides in Wordsworth's 'Lines written a few mile above Tintern Abbey'.

In counter movement, however, the shift in the third quatrain is to the ruined city, here water stands immobile (quite different from 'still') on the street, a dream of destruction of the house and the person together in a her memory of Spain, here standing for all ruined cities. The issue of the door, closed or open, of the spirit of the past and future becomes crucial, as desire reasserts itself as 'untamable' and the pull back into the world begins.

Rukeyser's emphasis on movement, the 'turning wind' was crucial to her work. It had all the restlessness of the pre-Socratic vision of a Heraclitus, a vision which Hegel took up and passed to Marx, and which inspired the contrary movement of dialectical thinking itself, opening an honest recognition of necessary changes of the self in reciprocity with others, and in history and nature, including 'productive relations' – the holistic 'technology' (grammar) of ourselves acting in nature. It was this maintenance of integrity in facing the actual world that the 'bourgoisie' or any demagogue with neurotic security drives, in an always terrifying historical world, was at pains to deny and, when necessary, to act with the utmost cruelty to defend that denial and assert the 'traditional' status quo.

However, Rukeyser's ethical and 'existentialist' perspectives, endowed that movement with a less aggressive distrust of nature, and a warmer more visionary sense of the natural order than science reveals. As with Wordsworth and Coleridge, it was 'Poetry and geometric Truth' together, 'the knowledge that endures upon these two/And their high privilege of lasting life' that concerned her.[102] Unlike them, however, she did not see 'whatever else the heart holds dear' as constituting necessarily their absolute alternative.[103] For she was a woman in both poetry and science, with a child and a consuming interest in children.

Coda

Muriel Rukeyser's life and work served, hence, as a critical bridge between the 'modernist' (industrialized/imperialist) and 'postmodern' (totalitarian/globalized) worlds. In both worlds and in the transition, she would remain politically clear-eyed and actively critical of injustice and in her poetry take up with consuming passion and skill the defence of the vulnerable, the commitment to collective action, and the precious and irreplaceable nature of the individual human soul in its unique moment in nature. But to do so was not a simple matter. Radical politics and a language and discourse that might truthfully articulate it are in any case extremely rare. The practice of poetry was as hard as the practice of politics, and as hard as the practice of personal life. In her vision, at least, all these were directed towards make a change in existing conditions and encouraging a love of the world. The alternative was not negotiable for her and, like another neglected American writer and political activist, Emma Goldman, she centred her critique in the denial of love itself:

> In our present pygmy state love is indeed a stranger to most people. Misunderstood and shunned, it rarely takes root; or if it does, it soon withers and dies. Its delicate fibre cannot endure the stress and strain of daily grind. Its soul is too complex to adjust itself to the shiny social fabric. It weeps and moans and suffers with those who have need of it, yet lacks the capacity to rise to love's summit.[104]

Rukeyser's poetry was strenuously directed, in the end, to raising the human capacity for courage, whether for social change or personal love. The very meaning of poetry itself, however honest in its despair, had to terminate finally in love of the world.

Epilogue: Rare Calendars of Feeling[1]

> LEAR: Take heed, sirrah; the whip.
> FOOL: Truth's a dog must to kennel; he must be whipp'd out when the lady's Brach may stand by th' fire and stink. [...]
>
> — WILLIAM SHAKESPEARE

> [...] the Men who for their desperate ends
> Had plucked up mercy by the roots were glad
> Of this new enemy. Tyrants, strong before
> In devilish pleas, were ten times stronger now,
> And thus beset with foes on every side,
> The goaded Land waxed mad; the crimes of few
> Spread into madness of the many, blasts
> From hell came sanctified, like airs from heaven;
>
> — WILLIAM WORDSWORTH[2]

> Language itself became a currency debased and corrupt; token sentences rubbed clear of message, like worn coins.
>
> — JAMES CAMERON[3]

> I am a prisoner who owns nothing but the stories he makes up about his freedom [...]
>
> — ELIAS KHOURY[4]

It must have been towards the end of 1980 or the beginning of 1981, just under a decade before the official ending of the Cold War, when I attended lectures on modernist architecture by the art historian Vincent Scully in the Law School of Yale University, on one of my many privileged visits to the libraries of that university. A crisp rhetorical style, lucid explanations, an always engaging argument, combined with detailed expert knowledge derived from a life of writing many superb books, ensured that the lectures were always packed out with the élite, hard-working, well-heeled young of America who had given the speaker the ultimate compliment of their attendance and time.[5] How many of them, I thought, would commission the great architects of the future? Was it not satisfying that they were being so engagingly and so well informed?

In one such lecture on early twentieth-century Vienna, Professor Scully turned his attention to the Viennese *Gemeindebauten* (municipal tenement complexes) and, inevitably, to the most famous one designed by Karl Ehn. He spoke of Ehn's relation with Otto Wagner, issues of city clearance and refurbishment, and the problems relating to mass public housing, transport and design that this remarkable tenement attempted to resolve architecturally. With the slide of the building projected onto a large screen, he paused (half-theatrically I thought though I could have been mistaken) and announced the name of the building: The Karl-Marx-Hof. There was momentary silence from the audience followed by a deafening gale of spontaneous laughter.

Perhaps for anyone who had been educated in Western Europe, the spontaneity and volume of the laughter would have been a strange experience, irrespective of ideological position. It was a Cold War laughter of imperial confidence, ringing with certainty. Of course, I knew that the United States was very far to the right of the always-threatened and today fast-disappearing European social-democratic consensus. I knew about the century-and-more-old tradition of red-baiting, the Haymarket riots, 1919, the Dies committee, McCarthy, the manipulated as well as actual 'Red terror' during the Cold War and the ingrained distrust of any political collective responsibility in the name of a culture of freedom and individualism.

However, among intelligent, well-educated undergraduates at one of the very greatest universities in the world, it still came as something of a surprise. Could they not distinguish Stalin from Marx? Did they not know it was here, in the building under discussion, the workers had barricaded themselves in during the Österreichischer Bürgerkrieg of 1934, forced to surrender to the fascists who later, as Austria disappeared into the maw of the Nazis, obliterated the name of Marx from the building (as they now obliterated it with their laughter) and substituted the local name of Heiligenstädter Hof? Well clearly they did not, nor did Scully mention it. It was a good instance, in all its emotional spontaneity, of young people as unwitting victims of years of disinformation and lying by omission, with poor knowledge of cultures other than their own.

This is not a scholarly gripe against the ignorance of the young: that last banal refuge of the despairing and aging professor. The Yale undergraduates had simply never had the opportunity of knowing about the Marx who had covered their own American Civil War, Marx the theatre critic, Marx the great Victorian who, like Dickens, excoriated the cynical indifference of the men who sent children down mines or brutally employed them for more than fourteen hours a day in sweat-shops. They didn't know about Marx the greatest critic of abstraction in relation to the qualities of sensuous human life as it is actually lived, Marx whose early (and later) writings enunciated enough theories and problems to keep sociologists, anthropologists and psychologists (not to mention critical theorists at universities) busy to this day; Marx whose redeployment of Hegel produced a whole theory of capital, labour and technology and set in motion theoretical problems of 'exchange': that is, who wins and who loses beneath the plutocratic rhetoric of trickle down, freedom and individual choice. Marx described with flair and satire a world in which things submitted to labour and capital in circulation become magical fleeting sacraments, with lives and values of their own. It was Marx who, before anyone else, accurately predicted 'globalization', virtual 'post-modernist' reality, the break-up of traditional values and the family, the assault on local identity and historical memory, and the migration of workers (including slaves) who risked losing culture and identity in the process. It was Marx whose inflexible loyalty to the poor and exploited put the majority of Christians, Jews and Muslims to shame; Marx who, contrary to universal assumption, described religion as a 'heart in a heartless world'; Marx whose first emphasis was on the necessity of difference in the quality of the individual lives that industrial capitalism so ruthlessly and abstractly homogenized. Now of course even bears and bulls, and weather have gone and 'stuff' merely 'happens'. However wrong the bases of his analyses have proved to be, to ignore this intellectual giant of the Victorian era and perhaps greatest analyst of the Industrial Revolution is at best a case of intellectual shallowness.

Yet the laughter of the young Yale undergraduates would have been appreciated by many Eastern European dissidents who, having had the Stalinist state version of Marx thrust down their throats for decades and having suffered intolerable repression, would, with some justice, have merrily joined in. For of course there was also the demagogic Marx whose tone and behaviour would lend some of its qualities to the inflexible, sometimes scarcely human single-mindedness of Lenin, the increasingly hollow rhetoric of Stalin and Mao, the Marx whose belief in progress and 'scientific method' as a natural handmaiden of social reform now seems to us misplaced, the apocalyptic and millennial Marx whose advocacy of revolution and the linear stages of human progress, along with virtually every other Victorian historian, matched that of the narrative of Christ's Second Coming with about as much literal plausibility – that evanescent promise of utopian Paradise germane to most evangelical religions, the Marx who could be as easily used as Christ or Allah by the vilest of human beings.

Notwithstanding all this, for these Americans, the name Marx had coalesced into a homogenous site of an iconic joke, obliterating all historical complexity: the post-Marxist debate from Lenin through to Trotsky, Alexandra Kollontai, Rosa Luxemburg and Gramsci to the American Emma Goldman, to European social democrats such as Hilferding and Keynes, to theorists of the calibre of

Arendt, Benjamin and the Frankfurt school, Sartre and de Beauvoir, to name but a very few. A history of the modern world without a serious knowledge of Marx and the many other socialist traditions seriously courted half-truths: an omission that amounted to lies and censorship. A little more respect for the history of socialism in all of its varieties, not simply Marxist, including its more than symbolic history in their own country, would not come amiss in America and in the amnesic West in general, even though its dream appears as dead as the dodo. With this disinformation by omission, the new conservatism of the 1980s, its aftermath accelerated by 1989 and continuing into our own day, and ignorance tempered by arrogance, these unwitting undergraduates (and I certainly do not judge them harshly personally) were set fair to be a long and enduring cultural triumph of the Cold War.

In American Studies, with its always lingering nationalism, the few remaining shreds of radical thought took on a not altogether satisfactory renaissance in identity politics with its ambiguous and contradictory radicalisms. It turned its face away from real power conflicts, issues of class, the real events of history, the silent work of American capital in the global economy, the numerous persistent little wars far away in which hundreds of thousands of real people got silently killed by force of arms in countries where legitimate governments were destabilized by American covert activity and bribes, and the millions more who died through globally financed debt recovery ('restructuring') and disease. The successors of the public intellectual assumed far too readily that the personal was political. At best a litmus paper of social and psychological oppression, an indicator of the social violence of normative rhetoric, disinformation and Reichian psychological oppression; at worst, identity politics turned real politics inwards, spreading out into competing micro-analyses among specific groups of people. In a country composed of peoples from virtually every country in the world and with huge illegal immigrant populations, the competition for status and power is inevitable and academics took to their word-processors to advocate 'empowerment' for the excluded as the new righteous goal of scholarship. Empowerment for whom was obvious (the excluded and wretched of America), empowerment for 'what' exactly was rarely spelt out. It was seldom expressed in anything but individualist terms. Generally it was taken to mean a power to have an equal share in the American Dream, and the dream was, as usual, to be 'successful', that is, largely to make money, as a result of which all political contradiction would happily melt away. Yet that dream translated into libertarian economics and materialist individualism, promoting competition as the most reliable basis of freedom, also promoted a culture in which millions failed, and that failure was writ large in the mal-distribution of wealth and disempowerment for the majority. Similarly, to be 'empowered' as a woman, as an African American, as gay or lesbian, while useful for bases of solidarity, still left the question open as to exactly how that 'empowerment' related to economic, political and social relations with others outside the group, and further that group's relation to a more general politics. Otherwise identity politics risked degenerating into the choir singing to the choir, driven by essentialist misapprehension. Liberally bespattered with academic slogans and arcane postmodernist phrases, identity politics has pleaded for the individual freedom of its 'constructed' gendered and group ethnic life-styles while incorporating a hard-won new freedom for middle-class women into selected aspects of a still virtually untouched power structure that continues to exhibit ruthless plutocratic behaviour, daily devaluing law and democracy itself. In the more liberal sections of the universities a quasi-anthropological and psychological emphasis on behaviour, gender psychology, belief systems and personal lifestyles has pushed political and economic analysis into the distance.

Of course the picture is not quite as simple as that. The banality of right wing critics, in their favourite phrase 'political correctness,' reduces any serious attack on the status quo to a stereotypical 'behaviour'. This behaviour is apparently characterized by a few examples of deranged 'evangelicals' (itself a more complex term than is commonly considered) who mysteriously represent everyone who takes a critical attitude to the power structure, as if the right did not have its own maniacs. Those accused of this behaviour are thus reduced to a caricaturing simplicity as much those on the left who simplify types of 'natural behaviour' and believe they know, for example, contrary to the evidence of the world's greatest literature, what a woman or an African American definitively is.

Any level of real thinking and analysis is always to be welcomed and, at least theoretically, any examination of a personal condition in ethnicity and gender should lead to greater political awareness. At best those concerned with identity politics are aware of how their specific oppression relates to the general picture; many are in fact engaged in some of the larger issues from politics to the environment, in spite of the appalling general manufacturing of consent by global media bosses. Viewed as a nexus of power relations, as a political and social theatre of interaction with others not of the group and properly emplotted in variable temporal narratives both personal and social, analysing identity can be powerful tool, especially in the multinational city. As a figure of essentialist truth used to dominate others (and this is always a risk) it is worse than useless.

Contemporary democracy is ever more threatened as the means of distributing news and information falls into fewer and fewer hands. This censorship by omission and diversion is quite as ruthless as Russia's current rather old-fashioned shooting of journalists or poisoning of dissidents abroad, for 'omission is the most virulent form of censorship'.[6] In spite of all this, where local knowledge prevails and among many Americans, there is still an openness and willingness to criticize and to take action which might well provide a model for other western countries and the world in general.

In foreign policy, however, which is directed towards the globalized scramble for resources (water, oil, coal, gas, minerals) American power and its corporate international allies are the scourge of the luckless peoples who happen to live in proximity to those resources. In that respect the United States is equally matched by Russia, both true heirs to the hegemonic greed of the European empires. To live in Iraq, Chechnya, Afghanistan, or the Delta region of Nigeria, or on mineral-rich traditional land, as for some of the indigenous peoples in India, or Gambia, to name but a few, is to bear witness to suppression of local culture, ruthless economic and violent exploitation producing perpetual mass poverty directed by local corporate Quislings of any colour.

Opposition where it exists is often, though not always, dominated by mafia-style groups of angry and brainwashed young men who are politically, psychologically or religiously super-charged with an intense sense of life and purpose.[7] We do not understand enough the sheer pleasure of the unambiguous world of war for young men, with its lurid lights of risk, daring, male companionship, the fetishism of guns, arms and uniforms, the narcotic of perpetual adventure. Simplistic religious narratives authorize tales of heroism, survival and the sexual domination of women. From these perspectives the more complex and much more difficult life of peace, traditional stabilizing patterns, a sense of a future on earth and a peaceable culture seem impossible. Through economic, educational and social deprivation they have no access to even the ordinary pleasures that make the anguish at the heart of mortal life endurable. They are as much addicted to the excitement of righteousness as the rich and powerful who understand only too well how to exploit them. The American right needs Bin Laden as much as he needs them.

It would, however, be quite wrong to think that the United States is historically exceptional in economic predatory behaviour and certainly no historian or cultural commentator in Western Europe after the last century's disgraceful wars can assume any *a priori* position of national, political or ethical superiority. A thorough glance at Paul N. Hehn's book *A Low Dishonest Decade* (the title-phrase is from Auden's poem 'September 1, 1939') will make the point simply and briefly, and will also show continuities between the 1930s–1940s and the present time. For the present argument his work has the advantage of bringing back a much-needed economic perspective to the way the story of history is told. It provides an additional context for the period of events covered in this book. The comparisons readily suggest themselves for Hehn's account is persuasive in the way he shows how the rawness of the decade's economic competition supported and subverted declared official allegiances, and ideological practices. If the German foreign office telegram to its minister in Belgrade in 1939 declared 'Copper is a life and death matter', it takes little imagination to substitute word 'oil' to understand the same thinking in the US State Department, the British Foreign Office or in their equivalents in Russia or China. Happily, Hehn is in favour of the 'narrative descriptive form' which makes his work useful for this book.[8] While the following account of his argument will stress the economic factors, his warning that these cannot be taken in isolation must be kept in mind: 'Ideology as the meeting point between social theory, economics and politics [...] plays a special role in the articulation of real, material interests.'[9]

To begin with Hehn takes issue with A.J.P. Taylor downplaying economic factors in the Third Reich (the idea that Hitler was no worse than many another international statesman, only his 'acts' were more wicked) and criticizes the German Marxist historians who, as with the left in general, as we have seen in Mumford's attack on them in the 1940s, were too fond of the all-embracing causality of 'militaristic imperialism'. For British and German historians, the politics of appeasement and the burden of guilt, he suggests, have somewhat distorted the range of causal assumptions. No one can dismiss any of these non-economic factors, but Hehn's examination of the 'economic rivalries of the Great Powers on the international market and the war – particularly over the raw materials of Eastern Europe',[10] is an excellent and crucial addition to the narrative, especially since 'economic factors' have been under a cloud since the death of the old Marxist materialist history and since the rise of social and cultural critical discourses post-Weber and Freud. Today, however, billions of the world's people suffer 'a fate worse than debt', as Susan George's classic and pioneering work reminds us.[11] It is time to look again at some of the assumptions of capitalist triumphalism, then and now.

As for the 1930s, a cool appraisal of the material interests of nations tells a sobering story. Somehow America's entry into the war in 1941 has been seen as that of an aloof bystander, a reluctant innocent who saved the world, at that point driven by the fate of Pearl Harbor. American entry into the war certainly gave Churchill his first peaceful night's sleep and saved the necks of the British, but Hehn awkwardly reminds us that throughout the 1930s, 'American trade rivalry with Britain and Germany provided the global avatar within which seethed the political ideological conflicts'.[12] Germany's drive for raw materials in Eastern Europe, Hehn's argument goes, underwrote, in a neo-colonial power-drive, its attempt to recover its lost financial and industrial supremacy. Brecht noted in his diary on 14 June 1940 that Germany had arrived a bit too late 'for the imperialist carve-up of world markets'.[13]

In our own time the drive for raw materials in the Middle East, Asia (the Stans), and beyond the Urals in Russia (not to mention the scramble for the Arctic[14]) is also seriously imperiling world peace with the cost in lives already running into the hundreds of thousands. This does not suggest the current powers are 'Nazis' but that the raising of the economic and political stakes risks the same temptations of unchecked power: the same lying and the same bloodshed. It is difficult to see where the human, let alone democratic, restraints on this global scramble will come from.

War, however ideologically dressed, has nearly always been about booty. Hehn continues his story after the Nazis had taken over Austria: 'The Reichsbank absorbed the Austrian State Bank while the Deutsche Bank took over the majority share of the Austrian Credit-Anstadt and the Dresdner Bank swallowed the Mercurbank.'[15] What used to be called 'material interests' remain a powerful force, even the life blood of the theatre of power. In 1914 the British newspaper *The Daily Telegraph* declared: 'There is no reason why we should not permanently seize for this country a large proportion of Germany's export trade.'[16] In the time leading up to the main period that this book covers, the war, viewed from an economic perspective, was as much internal as external in any given country. Indeed the two were linked. After the First World War, as the investments and exports of Britain declined, 'unemployment never fell below 10% [...] as British capital fought a class battle with labor to offset falling profits and remain competitive on the world market'.[17]

In the 1930s, before the so-called 'managed' capitalism of the later twentieth century, an intense war for trade and world markets divided the world into economic blocs: the British imperial bloc, French franc bloc, the American dollar bloc and the German 'clearing countries'. The latter included Austria and Hungary and formed the basis of a German dream to be the centre of a European trading region 'encompassing Eastern and Southern eastern Europe', largely to supply man-power and cheap raw materials.[18] This was no more than the British and French habitually had done elsewhere.[19] Looked at coldly, German nationalist thought took 'its cue from the United States and began to cultivate ideas of *Grossraumordnung* (system of large areas) based upon a German adaptation of the Monroe Doctrine as well as 'Manifest Destiny'.[20] The psycho-religiosity of Manifest Destiny still haunts American foreign policy, while historically, of course, it justified the ethnic cleansing of native races. Hehn makes a powerful case that war was a necessity for Hitler, driven by the dire economic situation of an almost bankrupt Germany just prior to 1939.[21]

Trade battles developed throughout the 1930s and one of the most intense was between Britain and America, the latter buying British gold in large quantities to uphold the pound and make American goods more competitive against British exports. A long trade rivalry with the British Empire was a serious impediment to America ending its isolationist policies during the early part of the war.[22] After the war, under the banner of anti-imperialism, the United States would set unsentimental terms to dismantle what fragments remained of British economic power, not to mention the 'socialism' of the new Labour government, as John Maynard Keynes found to his cost, trying to broker American post-war loans just before he died.

As for Britain before the war, there were agreements with Germany to trade and defer debt 'which enabled Hitler to carry out its rearmament programme'.[23] The deals were made supra-nationally to protect the interests of British shareholders and renewed right up to weeks before Munich: 'from the advent of the National Socialist regime, a steady stream of British upper class visitors arrived in Germany to find out whether it would be possible to do business with Hitler, starting with Lloyd George and ending with Neville Chamberlain', in spite of astute military commentators such as Brigadier Arthur Temperly, military representative at the League of Nations, who in 1933 argued that Germany was a mad dog that should be destroyed or quarantined while there was still time.[24] In fact the dire effects of an economic collapse in trade with Germany were exaggerated given that Germany only accounted for 4.4 per cent of British trade. It was more a psychological fear that turned out to be a useful piece of economic propaganda in a general policy of appeasement.[25] Far-right pressure groups that preferred Hitler to Soviets, Jews and Americans were not without influence on Chamberlain and his Tory henchmen. Of them, Hehn uses the phrase, 'historically besmirched'.[26] Certainly, as a result, Hitler did not think Britain would go to war over Poland.[27]

Before the FBI padlocked its offices after Pearl Harbor, American loans in the 1930s to restore Germany, its industry and armaments had been channelled through Otto Wildenfeld (a former Krupp director and German Ambassador to the United States) directly to the Krupp-Nirosta Company operating under Delaware's licensing laws.[28] The roles of Farben, Krupp and Germany industry's collaboration with Hitler are well known.[29] Even the normally cool prose of the economic historian can rise a degree or two: 'In hindsight, the crass, purposive behavior of these higher commercial interests during Hitler's drive to seize the Czech provinces still leaves an unrelievedly cynical impression six decades later.'[30]

In a postscript to his work, Hehn cites a 1936 article by Rudolf Hilferding, the Austrian social democrat and economic theorist who was with Serge (who admired his theories) and the surrealists in Marseille in 1941, where in spite of the best efforts of Varian Fry, he was recaptured by the Nazis and taken to Paris where he probably died under torture.[31] In the article Hilferding noted a shift from the old 'finance capital' of the liberal state, used to develop underdeveloped areas, to a new kind of total state that used its power 'to cyclically expand and consolidate, a plunder economy, which can only be maintained by constant expansion'.[32] Hehn describes Hilferding's analysis of Nazi Germany as astonishingly accurate. The relation between state military power and economic interest remains a serious problem in our own time; in the much-quoted words of the recently retired chairman of the Federal Reserve Bank about the Iraq war: 'I am saddened that it is politically inconvenient to acknowledge what everyone knows: the Iraq war is about oil.'[33] It has also been generally politically inconvenient for many cultural commentators to take on board economic factors in discussing the foreign policy of the United States, and for a long time now.

During the 1930s, the United States refused to support Britain and France in their demands for sanctions against Mussolini and, 'Pilate-like, allowed the oil companies to ignore Hull's "moral embargo" on oil and sell oil to Italy despite the League's sanctions'.[34] 'Isolationism' was not merely 'traditional' and 'characteristic' in American foreign policy – the way it is commonly taught by consensual historians – it was also very economically convenient, not to say aggressive in its refusal to acknowledge its political responsibilities in relation to demagogic, undemocratic regimes. Hehn goes even further, matching in hindsight Mumford's foresight: 'The critical absence of the United States in the political equation, and America's refusal to become involved in a European war, which Roosevelt's minister Bullitt repeatedly reiterated to Delbos and to the distraught former premier Chautemps, contributed greatly to sealing the fate of Czechoslovakia.'[35] (Roosevelt did however for a long time consider sending US troops into Brazil to combat German commercial activity there.[36])

We are increasingly aware these days that it was not just a few marginalized extremists who were impressed by Hitler in the United States. As recently noted by Michael Lowy and Eleni Varikas, Henry Ford has always been presented as a figure of benign technological modernity and American know-how, who gave the car, an aristocratic preserve, to the ordinary people. His role in the culture of Nazism, including his virulent anti-Semitism, has understandably been overlooked. They state:

> The long embarrassed silence is understandable. The case of Ford raises difficult issues about the role of racism in US culture and the relationship between 'western civilisation' and the Third Reich, between modernity and anti-Semitism, and between economic progress and social regression.[37]

Following what he calls a 'serious historical interpretation' first suggested by a British historian Tim Mason, Hehn notes that in its turn Germany embarked on an actual and economic neo-colonialism to feed its rearmament programme. It was labour-short, and set out on a 'plunder of peoples'. A by-no-means-uninteresting gender footnote was that German working-class men were not keen on having their women work, thus assisting the drive for foreign workers. At the other end of the scale of class behaviour, there was Chamberlain's terror that a war would promote a global workers' revolution; as Oliver Harvey, private secretary to both Eden and Halifax, dryly remarked: it 'would destroy the rich and idle classes'.[38]

General suspicion of other countries' economic behaviour was rife as economic nationalism grew. Germany, Japan and Italy were defined as dangers to the United States' economic interests even before the war broke out, and Hehn cites William Appleman Williams's well-known *The Tragedy of American Diplomacy* to the effect that America's leaders had accepted the necessity of military action to defend their trade empires long before the attack on Pearl Harbor.[39] Certainly Williams's withering book on American foreign policy has been further validated by events in the forty or so years since its publication.

However, brutality and greed are hardly American prerogatives. The shocking politics around the Great War, the less than pragmatic punishment of Germany, dying European colonialism and rising American and Stalinist Soviet power were all in varying degrees to blame for the worst war in history. Operating behind the scenes in the abstract world of economic rivalry, the leaders fought for economic supremacy. Conservative British economic policies towards France in the mid-1930s led to London's refusal to support the franc and, crucially, French rearmament, dragging it into appeasement, and slowing Blum's social reforms: 'It was the "wall of capital" and the spiteful strike against the social and economic reforms by the Patronat class, which feared Bolshevism first and Hitler only second or not at all, that contributed to France's defeat, and not the CGT and the working class as is sometimes mistakenly claimed.'[40] The role of the old-fashioned French military elite, its outmoded military strategies and incompetent leadership were, of course the other cause. Today these events are hardly remembered in carefully massaged memories of the period's visible politics and events put out by heritage television series and blockbuster movies. From the British to the Japanese, from the Americans to the Germans, from the Soviets to the French and Italians, as Hehn so cogently reminds us, no one escapes censure.

Unless one takes a pacifist position, distinctions on relative moral grounds, as Mumford argued correctly, had to be made. Nazism, fascism and a crazed imperialist Japan would have to be fought outright, but it is perhaps worth reminding ourselves that when it came to war and the pure game of power, the West was also happy to side with Stalin's USSR, which fought the majority of its battles for it. In addition, the United States after the first and so far only use of atomic power against civilian cities, would dominate the ensuing 'peace' to a large extent in its own economic interests, destabilizing and reducing to chaos country after country, using punitive violence and terror where necessary. The current disaster in Iraq where four billion dollars per month cannot ensure regular water and electricity supplies in the single city of Baghdad is merely the latest in a long line of what seem to be inevitable state military-economic adventures since 1945. The more serious issues of the political ethics of war-mongering and the irresponsibility of brutal or ignorant political leaders are then to be considered.[41]

Anyone who scratches beneath the surface of omission and disinformation is powerfully tempted to an absolute cynicism, to a sense that Fussell's wartime in multiple peace-time disguises, with its temporal abolition of past and future, is now a universal permanent condition, impervious to temporal change. We even have a quasi-religious sense of apocalypse, backed by powerful scientific evidence, of a threat to life on earth by human-driven climate change. Our best and most courageous journalists and the few remaining intellectuals who speak directly and politically in the service of the oppressed, paint a devastating picture of the world in those few places they are allowed to speak. They follow bravely in the traditions of Serge, Macdonald, Mumford, Norman and Rukeyser.

For there are major links to and consequences of the events of the 1930s and 1940s still operating in our own time. In Russia, journalists and dissidents are still feared enough to be murdered or poisoned abroad by the state, as the descendents of the KGB clamber back into power, determined to revenge themselves on the triumphalist West. They are supported we are told (and can we actually believe the absoluteness of this claim without considering State intimidation?) by a population too cynical, too weary of scarcity, or too removed from any credible historic democratic experience to resist.

In the United States and in the rest of the developed world, television, newspaper and radio networks fall into fewer and fewer hands, and 'diversions', as Pascal long ago called them, sophisticatedly marketed, now occupy what remaining time people have from the necessities of work and family life. The American people are deprived of information of what happens outside their own country. As well as the indirect means of omission, occasionally there will be a direct attempt at ruining the career of a dissident academic attempting to speak the truth, as the recent case of Norman Finkelstein so powerfully and disgracefully shows. Finkelstein had the temerity to describe accurately the daily atrocities committed by the Israeli Zionists against the Palestinians, and suggest that the Israel Defense Force's justification for killing large numbers of civilians as a 'deterrent' was only 'a flea's hop' away from the Nazi justification for killing Jewish children to prevent a generation of avengers from growing up.[42] As Weil noted long ago, you can control people for long periods with violence and terror, but you cannot finally control the soul of a people by refusing them citizenship. Historically fate will turn its wheel, which is not to suggest stoicism in Benjamin's classic argument, but rather that fate has no relation to innocence.[43]

The brutal foundation of Israel in the 1940s, in the last few years much more widely known in the West, is the ur-narrative. Again it is a story in parallel time to this events of this book, and one of low dishonesty, robbery, murder and rape, as a guilty world overlooked what is now a well-established incident of 'ethnic cleansing'. Ilan Pappe's celebrated and thoughtful analysis of the period that carefully considers the highly emotive phrase, however, did not get him dismissed from the University of Haifa, a thought which American Zionists might ponder. [44] As George Soros has pointed out, 'the debate in Israel about Israeli policy is much more open and vigorous than in the United States', where public opinion has been unscrupulously manipulated by the American Israel Public Affairs Committee in alliance with the neocons: a grave and serious threat to the stability of global peace efforts.[45]

Pappe is engaged, with almost Gandhi-like tactics, in a quiet persistent effort at reconciliation on the basis of a non-self-serving appraisal of the past, together with annual pilgrimages of remembrance with the few Israeli Jews 'who go against the grain', to some of the five hundred and more destroyed villages of the Palestinians.[46] I shall return to the politics of narrative and testimony, so clearly the driving force, as we have seen, in the work of Victor Serge. The honest facing up to the persistent memory of an atrocious historical past and the acknowledgement of its continuing links with the present, whether the British in Africa and India, the Germans disturbing the peace of Europe and the world three times within a hundred years, the Japanese in Burma and China, the Chinese in Tibet, the Turks in Armenia, the Russians in Chechnya, the French in Algeria, the Americans in Latin America, the Philippines and the Middle East, or the Indonesians in East Timor, has to be the first step in negotiating reconciliation and giving a justice an even chance. Any state or academic power which suppresses or distorts (by commission or omission) open debate on any historical narrative serving public memory is an enemy of humanity itself.

The general reputation of the United States in the world has never been so low as currently. This is shocking, but it is because of a mismatch between its rhetoric of democracy and freedom and, since 1945, its perceived activity in the world, legitimized by talked-up threats of 'communism' or 'the war against terror', which have been far in excess of any actual international security situation. In its own interests it has destabilized governments, whether autocratic or democratically elected, and the sheer wastage of blood and money in the interests of a few who believe they have right to help themselves to the resources of the globe has been staggering.[47] It is what Muriel Rukeyser, in her book on Willard Gibbs in the 1940s, called 'the loose translations of democracy into any kind of can-do brutality'.[48] These are the true meanings of that intellectually shoddy concept of 'globalization'.

What has changed since 1945 are the means of organizing what goes on in people's minds and consciousness. John Pilger has referred to the 'eternal present' which characterizes this phenomenon and his observations can serve as an introduction as to why this book, and its recall of the world of half a century ago, might serve as a way of challenging that 'eternal present' favoured by the powerful and based upon the suppression of more complex temporal narratives. It is important to insist on a continuing story, to oppose a 'postmodern virtual present' that consistently undermines a sense of the past. An abstract 'relevance' is mystically attached to the contemporary moment which is apparently transparently clear. In fact it is often underwritten by an anti-intellectual cultural populism, the running mate of its political shadow. If the young themselves demand the present, is it because they have lost faith in the future, which desperately needs the historical past in order both to choose their future options and distinguish themselves from it. In the eternal present, any judgment of worth and values disappears altogether. The aim here is to give a more political meaning to the insights of Ricoeur. First Pilger:

> Central to the growth of this 'business state' are the media conglomerates, which have unprecedented power, owning press and television, book publishing, film production and databases. They provide a virtual world of the 'eternal present'. As *Time* magazine called it: politics by media, war by media, justice by media, even grief by media (Princess Diana).[49]

Any recall of history, and an understanding of what in this book has been insisted on as the way we plot it, attacks this hegemony of the eternal present, with its relentless 'reality' shows. Historical memory in its story makes every politician and demagogue uncomfortable because the very contrast between then and now invites a judgment. A week is a conveniently long time in politics.

At the beginning of this book certain questions were opened up about memory, and time, and their articulation in and creation through the writing of history, fiction and poetry. Behind it was a sense that nothing was more vital in a world where the speed of change, driven by war and technology disrupts memory, community, and any stable, let alone homogenous, society. After the neo-con American era of the late twentieth and early twenty-first centuries, with its 'economic liberalism' apparently triumphant, its dream lies in tatters, its political disasters in foreign policy are plain to see and its ability, as Tom Nairn put it, with its '57 + varieties of managed capitalism', to address the important problems of worsening world poverty and climate change appear far from adequate. 'If ever there was a time when the sovereignty of the market posed a mortal danger, it is surely now.'[50] It will be interesting to see how its now-fracturing consensus regroups, whether any of them will formulate a serious response to pressing global problems, and whether the Democratic Party is capable of moving beyond a merciless pragmatism accompanied by liberal sentiment.

As for the left, the social democratic consensus not to mention anything approaching socialism, is severely under pressure in Britain, Germany and France, and is challenged in many other European states. In heroic attempts to save something, the remnants speak of diverse second nature communities, shifting reciprocal boundaries, 'imagined communities', a re-appraisal of local value, and a regrouping of people of good will around issues of vital ecological importance, gender and race. They cling quite rightly to 'fraternity', equality having failed and liberty having been traduced by the neo-cons.[51] With some distinguished exceptions it is short on hard economic facts and long on abstraction. But this book is a contribution nonetheless to their concept of 'imagined communities', an idea, as we have seen, which predated by centuries the American Studies version of it.

Who are the Serges, Macdonalds, Normans, Mumfords and Rukeysers of our own time? They are not hard to find. We need not match them precisely but indicate those of similar spirit. In terms of political truth telling one only has to go to Anna Politkovskaya, John Pilger, Noam Chomsky, Mike Davies,

Naomi Klein or Robert Fisk. There are of course many others. Politkovskaya, has been murdered, as have many other journalists in Russia, whether by the state or by its conveniently distanced cronies remains uncertain. Pilger, though relegated in the UK to the occasional late night television show, has produced a series of remarkable documentaries and books. He is regularly denounced by English right-wing literateurs. Davies is very American (Mumford-like) in his apocalyptic statistical fervour and global perspectives: we need to know, as Gertrude Stein said, the exact number of everything. But the result is a wake-up call to planners, economists, politicians and concerned citizens alike. He is less good on the way real life is lived at the level of the deprived city street and on the many imaginative and determined ways people survive. Here, a politicized social-anthropologist could add a richer detail to his impressive work.

Clearly help from every direction is needed. Chomsky has harried the State Department as ferociously as Balzac or Galdós harried the nineteenth-century bourgeoisie. In the Western world's most right-wing and evangelical country, he has paid the price of abuse and minimum publicity, drowned out by the white noise of the media networks he has so unsparingly and so truthfully criticized. America is as much at risk as Russia in closing down independent media voices, though the methods work through laws favouring private capital. Under Clinton the deregulation of the media market according to Eric Klinenberg means that 'the government did not so much deregulate the market as re-regulate it', allowing a single media company to own eight or more radio stations in a community.[52] As in Russia, independent radio stations have been swallowed up. Naomi Klein's *The Shock Doctrine* (2007) mercilessly exposes the global political and economic devastation of American neo-liberal economic ideology in our own time. Fisk, a refugee from the Murdoch empire, once of *The Times* and now bravely supported by the English newspaper *The Independent* has managed in a life-time of journalism consistently to thrust awkward and particular facts and truths in the face of the bland consensual half-truths of prime ministers and presidents, Foreign Office and State Department lackeys, and relentlessly challenged the crimes of omission of the global media barons.

The world needs its impassioned reporters. Many hundreds of others, less well known, have followed in the steps of Macdonald, Mumford, Serge and Norman, and many have paid the ultimate price.[53] We need perhaps a Serge-like book of short creative obituaries of them from around the world to show us the true heroes of our time. Yet we might also ask of contemporary commentators what clues their narratives give us in order to understand our own unstable times. The question is both formal and political for this book has argued that the two are inseparable. Two brief glances at the work of Anna Politkovskaya and Robert Fisk will help at least begin an argument, which is all that is attempted here, and present this book with an open-ended conclusion.

Politikovskaya's face on the cover of *Russian Diary* is that of a woman whose anguished eyes reveal something of what she has witnessed, endured and told the world. Her stories are of a re-Stalinizing Russia where the hopes of *glasnost* and *perestroika* have been crushed and where freedom of speech has become, in the immediate past, virtually non-existent. Unlike with Serge, there is no tragic memory to sustain her dissenting activity, but the terror and anguish remain. As Alexei Simonov, head of the Glasnost Defence Foundation, said on her death: 'Every journalist will now practice self-censorship, think thrice, before you write.'[54] The present state of internal censorship and terror in Russia are best summed up in the words of Perry Anderson: 'Politikovskaya was killed with scarcely a ripple in public opinion.'[55] His account of Russia's 'managed democracy' tells a grim tale. As he points out that while all state leaders deny their crimes, in Western democracies (and this is the luck we inherit from our stalwart forebears) they are still subject to public opinion: Blair quit with an approval rating of 30 per cent, Bush fell to between 27 per cent and 37 per cent.[56] Anderson has spoken eloquently of the recent background to Russian state oppression, of the wave of criminality and corruption let loose by Yeltsin and the subsequent disintegration of the economy struggling to convert to some form of free market.

Then there was the good fortune for Putin in the rise in oil prices; the consequent relative stability has apparently made him a hero of the Russian people against memories of the 'abyss of Yeltsin'. Anderson accounts for the charisma of Putin in his command of the language, with the precise drops into slang, the austere self-discipline, the photo opportunities with his judo – a union of fist and mind capturing the public imagination. The attack on the 'oligarchs', the looters of the state systems, was popular and presented to the public with aplomb, notwithstanding the return to what the old Trotskyists used to call state capitalism: 'The new regime is dominated by a web of Kremlin staffers and ministers with "security profile", who also head the largest state companies quoted on the stock market.'[57]

The conduct of the second Chechnyan war was as cynical as the Bush–Blair escapade in Iraq. In February 2000, Putin announced that the 'counter-terrorism' operation was over and flew down to celebrate victory. Clinton hailed the 'liberation of Grozny'. Blair sped to St Petersburg to embrace the liberator and two weeks later Putin was elected by a landslide.[58] The leaders of the world joined hands in 'the war against terror'. With a few well-paid (and occasionally corrupt) academics massaging the story the consensual view is that we must 'criticize without animosity and making the right allowances for peculiarities of history and culture'. This view, as cited by Anderson, from *The Financial Times*, leaves one to muse on the force of the word 'peculiarities'.[59]

For our purposes of examining political narrative, we can reread Anderson's account by questioning the assumed temporalities of the 'occasional blemish' in the 'normal courses of development', or in Anderson's own words, 'the indurated vices of the longue durée' of Western apologists.[60] The first envisages an absurd offer of progress, the second is the voice of the stoic. Both are corrupt; the one in abstraction, the other in terms of a responsible ethics.

The conditions in Russia are serious. University budgets are down to a twelfth of what they were in Soviet times, bribes to pass examinations are commonplace, the free press is close to extinction, television programmes descend to 'levels of crassness of deepest America'.[61] Russia also rivals the West's heritage culture in its 'mass culture fixated on pastiche version of the dynastic past'.[62] This Disneyfication of culture makes for a spurious history: 'No living memory connects with this past – it is too different, and too remote, from the present serve as more than vicarious pap.'[63] The Stalinist era and forwards from it is too close to think about intelligently: 'In the culture at large, the tensions in social memory have produced patchy amnesia.' Anderson has always had an interest in literature and while I do not have the qualifications to confirm or deny the evidence he provides of contemporary Russian literature, his assertion that it is a formalist 'combination of provocation and dépaysement' has a depressingly familiar ring, rather like the brilliant but somehow all-knowing tours de force of a Thomas Pynchon in the West, whose historical tales keep dozens of academics employed in their postmodernist theorizing, while reducing anything historically serious to ultimately politically insulting aesthetic fairy tales. It is only saved by a dazzlingly satiric, aristocratic black humour of which there are many pleasurable examples.[64]

Anderson confirms what is everywhere apparent in Politkovskaya's own writing that, while private opposition to Putin is widespread, a crypto-Stalinist terror has crushed all public expression of it. He furthers argues that the second Chechnyan war broke the fragile opposition of the intelligentsia, as all countries in the world moved to reaction, especially when later, *9/11* unleashed right-wing forces across America. The demagogues on both sides of the old Cold War could now find common cause against the 'Islamic tide'. Their ludicrous simplicities were pushed with all the fervour that the invasive technology of mass-media information channels could provide for those whom Pilger has called 'the new rulers of the world'.

In the following account I wish neither to aestheticize the writings of Politkovskaya, nor to descend to the level of vicarious academic breast-beating about the horrors of the contemporary world. Rather the aim here is to note continuities and differences in engaged writing from the world of the 1930s and 1940s to the present time. For such writing has not died in our time and, in more than a few cases, it continues to provide those Weilian moments of goodness which do sparkle, albeit at long intervals, in dark times. Indeed, in spite of differences of culture and task, it is Weil that most often comes to mind in reading Politkovskaya. The Russian's outrage at the reduction of human beings to things never falters:

> It is the eve of the summer of 2002. We are in the thirty-third month of the second Chechen war. The end of this hopeless war is nowhere to be seen. The 'purges' never stop: they resemble mass autos-da-fé. Torture is the norm. Executions without a trial are routine. Maurauding is commonplace. The kidnapping of people by Federal soldiers in order to conduct slave trading (with the living) or corpse trading (with the dead) is the stuff of everyday Chechen life.
>
> 'Human substance' disappears overnight, without a trace, à la 1937.[65]

Politically, this is the new global politics of national state armies fighting 'group terrorism', that is ethnically and/or religious based indigenous resistance fighters reduced by official state terror to mafia-style thugs who mirror the activities of their oppressors. In concocting this state of affairs, Russia is certainly not unique. The British and Americans are creating and enabling these conditions in both Iraq and Afghanistan. Simplicities of the *either-or* fill the pockets of the leaders on both sides at the price of the terrorization of entire populations and the disappearance of credible social and political life.

Temporal and narrative indicators in the passage cited show the Pascalian ethical judgment outside time while invoking the actual events of history as comparative irony. History is without change, without progression, without hope, without a past, without unique present, without a future. It has been reduced to homogenous 'history-time'. Auto-da-fé represents the organized anarchy of cruel and irresponsible power from the medieval Inquisition to Stalin – the differences of historical time strangely and uncannily absent in the timeless repetitions of human cruelty. The result is of course irony and outrage at the reduction. The precision of 'it is the eve of the summer of 2002' takes it to the full. Indeed the phrase might mark the beginning of a narrative, a pleasurable jolt into a pastoral scene, or even the possibility of something precisely unique and different, unexpected even. A possibility is raised of an unpredictable human story, but it turns out to be something strangely repetitious, underwriting what Arendt famously called 'the banality of evil'.

Putin's return of Russia via this war to Stalinist terror is the public message. The private message is the destruction of the human soul itself. Interrogated by the FSS (old KGB) Politkovskaya notes that her interrogator has 'the nasty smile of his professional predecessors of 1937'.[66] At the level of the real suffering human being trying to preserve a sense of the interlocking continuities of the time of personal life, there is the remark of Raisa Amtayeva, now with two mute teenage daughters as a result of bombardments: 'I don't have a single photo left of our past.'[67]

This image of silence and emptiness, the deprivation of the last visible *aide-mémoire* of personal life, indicates a pure desolation of soul, a reduction to pure existence. It is another version of the moment before the sword of Achilles, the terror that backs the deprivation of memory. To reduce a person to a thing you have to obliterate memory and sociality. To erase the village or city from the earth, according to Weil is the worst imaginable human crime in its destruction of the memory and soul of a people. The anguish of a brutal silence lies at its heart. As Politkovskaya remarked in a life-threatening moment under bombardment: 'Death is the one situation where you can never find companionship.'[68] Racked by death, hunger and tuberculosis in the huge refugee camps of Ingushetia, the Chechyans 'are rapidly losing their soul as a people,' they become 'beasts, even to each other'.[69]

Under the conditions of lawlessness and military indiscipline, soldier and victim become sharers in an anarchy of survival and profiteering. All political, social, religious and ethnic distinction disappear as allegiances shift in 'barbaric order': 'We have all reached the depths [...] and there's no order for rescue.'[70] Even in strictly religious terms, the unique local versions of Islam, with conflicting Sufist virds and 'individual interpretations of Islam' have disappeared into a cosmopolitan 'Saudi Wahhabism' breaking apart even family consensus and setting son against father.[71] The homogenous story, the authorized version, is the heart of religious and political propaganda. In Fisk's words Wahhabism's interpretation of sharia law with its 'head-chopping, hand-chopping and a totally misogynist perspective were easy to associate with the Taliban's hostility towards all forms of enjoyment.'[72]

The disappearance of extended time with its variable stories, is therefore one consequence of the nihilistic ruthlessness of those who have permitted this to happen. There is no existential reassurance here that the most minimal future is still an ethical opportunity for a choice that confers the dignity of a human reality: 'No one expects to live until morning. So they don't spare any emotion. What if there is no tomorrow? For you or the other person?'[73]

Politkovskaya was one of the best and most sophisticated political journalists of her time. The story was at the heart of her writing. And she worked from the ground up, not from any abstract theoretical or academic set of counters for the 'postmodern condition', though her writing shows by indirection a highly educated and sophisticated mind. For her, globalization *is* NATO, it *is* the UN with its VIP clubs of the 'coalition against terror', in which all criticism of Russia is stifled in the charade of 'historic [*sic*] visits' of former Cold War opponents, and in the interest of carving up the world's material resources. It produces the 'sluggish sessions' at the UN Commission on Human Rights in Geneva;[74] the ignoring of the evidence of the 'Red Cross, Doctors of the World, the Salvation Army, human rights advocates';[75] the 1941 Marseille-like bureaucratic restriction of internal movement through IDs and passports, with its slave-trading of arrested people;[76] and the FEDS returning to Stalinist tactics of divide and rule by making people pay for the deaths of their neighbours, a genocidal tactic.[77] As for the UN, Politkovskaya quickly learns in relation to human rights in Chechnya, what has long been known in the West, that the 'office loving' Secretary General, is in thrall to the State Department.[78] As a leader in the British newspaper *The Independent* noted: 'It is ludicrous that this crucial decision-making forum is still dominated by the major powers of the 1945 era.'[79] Mumford's old plea for the UN not to be built on American soil and to have seven centres to reflect impartial international debate, has, in critical utopian terms, the intuition of prophetic judgment. The failure of the UN to challenge Russia over Chechnya smells of positive collusion. Just as in the West, the substitution of 'cult figures' (we call them political celebrities), with highly networked media recognition profiles, to divert attention away from political complexity and analysis, begins a process of lying which ultimately betrays a contempt for law and democracy. These are the vicarious narratives of propaganda and in the absence of any press freedom they are lethal.

In Russia, the founding of the FSS (the KGB's successor) returns Russia to 'increased power of the national secret services [which has] taken root in all government nooks and crannies of the country just like in the Soviet era.'[80] Politkovskaya, like any good journalist, dots her general narrative with vivid personal instances. Of course, in this conscienceless war the Soviet raw recruit is at least as much in danger as those he supposed to be fighting. Many disappear without trace. After nineteen months of searching for his grandson, one Russian grandfather, doubtless still with some expectations of the heroics of the war-time Soviet era, finally gets sent the wrong body (no explanation of what happened). Naively he asks for at least a military farewell salute: 'They explained to me that cartridges and a band were allowed only for officers. Not for privates.'[81] So much for the memory of socialism in Russia.

And it is with Marxist irony also that Politkovskaya describes the Russian way of business success as its ability to 'suck money from the budget.'[82] Milo Minderbinder, the profiteer of *Catch-22* seems a greenhorn compared with the neo-Stalinists. In government projects, Italian toilets and Spanish ceramics turn out to have been made locally, 'only the price is Italian.'[83] It is here that the US and Russian material interests in oil coincide in their respective wars, and Politkovskaya adopts a Dickensian tone: 'His Royal Majesty the Chechen Pipe and Their Royal Majesties the Chechen Wells have been the unquestioned rulers of hundreds of thousands of people for the past ten years.'[84] 'The Pipe' fosters an anarchist culture of criminal groups, which even profit twice from a *pas de deux* between oil arsonists and the fire-brigades, with their mutual protection rackets. If the fire brigade turn up it simply means the oil resource has changed hands.[85]

Even in pure business terms, none of this makes sense. It is hardly particularly efficient, let alone productive of public wealth. What it also means is that no one seriously wants peace or order given the profitable nature of sub-legal power plays. In a world of terrorizing spin, the impassioned muck-raking eloquence of Politkovskaya is the surest sign that the Russian soul may be gagged but is far from extinct. The power of the narrative confronts one of the major issues this book has addressed, the disposal of temporality in the plot of the story. Against the temporalities of the narratives of power are those of the suffering individual. We can read the following passage alongside moments from both Serge's and Silone's fiction, Mumford's view of clock-time, Braudel's variable plots times.

> I believe less that ever in the usual way of measuring time. More and more, it seems to me that each of us has his or her own personal calendar, and that we all live by these calendars – and not from January to February to March – depending on the circumstances that we find ourselves in. Or perhaps we choose them ourselves.
>
> I have a calendar like this, for the 2002 *Nord-Ost* [her newspaper] year which has passed so quickly, and for the beginning of 2003. This calendar has no chronology and no external logic. It has nothing but images tied together by the logic of feelings surrounding this tragedy […]
>
> I am not very good at prognosticating. Besides, we live in the time of Putin, when it is once again permissible to sacrifice thousands of lives 'in the name of a bright nonterrorist future.' There are people who can analyze this, but few who can sympathize. And since feelings are so rare now, they are the most important thing in my calendar.[86]

No knowledge, as Sartre once said, can mitigate the brute realities of existence. But Politkovskaya's realities are not those of biological existence, they are realities made by real men in real history. She registers the terrible effect of ruthless power on the very sense of human worth that is deeply entwined with the temporalities of human story. The 'bright nonterrorist future' is of course not a uniquely Russian phenomenon. Like a plague, it has infected a huge number of world leaders. To be robbed of an extending and extensive sense of time in which past, present and future are linked in the work of memory (which will inevitably complicate any political question) is to be robbed of human life itself, from a public sense of history to a private sense of dwelling.

Politkovskaya tragically lacked Serge's experience of dissenting comrades, the memory of glorious days of hope, the faith in possibilities of the future that his love of history and his experience of revolution was able to encourage to the end. She remained in a darker world of atomized emotions. An occasional flicker of love can produce a Hemingwayesque exchange of dialogue – the unadorned, unsentimental short exchange, with its shadowy indications of the effect of war and the premonition of war on human feeling in all its denials and edgy panic:

> 'You know I can't get upset by things like not having any money anymore.'
>
> 'Neither can I. Or that my husband left me.'

'Your husband left you?'
'Yes.'
'That's nothing.'
'True.'[87]

In a sense she chose spiritually to be homeless with the homeless. Her brief portraits are of women, children, families torn apart, soldiers corrupted and destroyed, honest men undercut by far-away authority. She wrote of the anguish of people never engaged in politics who just wanted to live in peace in their own terms.

Her concern for children and the corruption of the young people who have only known the terrifying present of brute survival was persistent. In that sense she is close to Muriel Rukeyser. Rukeyser's words remain pertinent, for they offer the hope that in its denial had so clearly fed not just the courage and the anguish of Politkovskya, but the persistent and clear-eyed work for the wretched of the earth:

Praise that the homeless may in their bodies be
A house that time makes, where the future moves
In his dark lake.[88]

The same sense of outrage at the unmitigated cruelty and brutality of unrelenting power against the dispossessed also characterizes the work of Robert Fisk: 'one wondered how brutalised the Palestinians must become before they inherit a state'.[89] His capacity for telling the stories those in authority do not want to hear, or from a perspective they refuse to countenance, is in the same heroic vein as Politkovskaya. Even as this is being written, a typical *New York Times* reporting of another nine dead in Gaza through Israeli air-strikes, emphasizes a drearily predictable sequence of events: the certainty and pride with which 'militant commanders' with Palestinian Authority Services and Islamic Jihad military credentials have been eliminated; a mild regret that a whole civilian family has also been wiped out – it was the gunmen's fault in operating from civilian areas; the fact that a recently fired missile into Israel had a range of 13.7 miles; an observation that an Israeli woman is in a state of shock, one such missile having landed in a nearby field; the difficulty of persuading Egypt to refuse returnees from the hajj to go through other than Israeli-controlled checkpoints; an outbreak of bird flu; the fact that Ariel Sharon in a coma has 'showed some responses to the sound of voices of his close family'.[90] It is blackly comic in demonstrating the way strategic apologetics become "linked" historical facts sugared in sentimentality.

The reporting world of Robert Fisk tells a very different kind of story. Like Politkovskaya, Fisk is a highly self-conscious story teller. Like her he is aware of the limitations of his task. Like her he digs beneath the official story, and notes

We recognize the mid-century male character's stance from Chandler's Marlow through countless imitators, the world-weary, rootless, isolated man of integrity, up against the double corruption of both the lawful and unlawful who somehow understand each other perfectly in a fatalistically locked and permanently self-confirming plot. It is the world of Genet's *Thief's Diary* with its static rituals of power and dispossession that reduces any ethical action to another move in the game. Yet Cameron could also drop the mask and come out straight: 'I still do not see how a reporter attempting to define a situation involving some sort of ethical conflict can do it with a sufficient demonstrable neutrality to fulfil some arbitrary concept of "objectivity".'[97]

Fisk is nothing but self-reflexive and engaged, and unlike Hitchcock's foreign correspondent, highly educated in relation to his job. In terms of the stories he offers he joins the linear continuities of a personal life of memory to the disjointed fractured and alienated worlds endlessly presented to the international journalist. Like Cameron he is very fond of his own ultimately distant father, wrapped in otherness, needing to understand the linkages between the parental historical moment (at once public and personal) and that of his own. The temporality of a somehow connected, remote but recognizably recent history provides a tenuous substitute for personal rootedness, the fragile thread of a story that might constitute a fleeting and concrete grasp of the soul:

> My father was born in the century before last. I was born in the first half of the last century. Here I am, I tell myself in 1980, watching the Soviet army invade Afghanistan, in 1982 covering the Iranian front line opposite Saddam's legions, in 2003 observing the first American soldiers of the 3rd Infantry Division cross the great bridge over the Tigris river. And yet the Battle of the Somme opened just thirty years before I was born. Bill Fisk was in the trenches of France three years after the Armenian genocide, but only twenty-eight years before my birth. I would be born within six years of the Battle of Britain, just over year after Hitler's suicide.[98]

How do we read a passage like this, this designation of the personal identity in relation to the events of history? An air of fatalistic mortality hangs over it, an almost pure fascination with number which is hard to drag into any significance except that of fascination. One situates oneself alongside the concrete moment of time, which seems to confer an authenticity of 'placing' the subject within a specific historical time, but it seems also wholly arbitrary, any other event might have been aligned to the appropriate date. A Hamlet like mournfulness hangs over it: 'The time is out of joint; – O cursed spite! That ever I was born to set it right!'

The risk is of temporal voyeurism. Does he not risk, as Sartre's brilliant review of the strengths and weakness of John Dos Passos suggests to us, making a fiction of history in which the event is a nameless presence, in which the facts emerge *a priori* to be thought about, in which the jerking unreeling of uneven memory sums up arbitrary lengths of time in a few words, mimicking and gaining credence from the operations of our real memories with their miniatures and frescoes, but here somehow disposed with a certain cunning in scattering them at random. Does finally the past remain irreducible and randomized, so it becomes somehow seeped in a flavour of the present? Does he merely want to show us the world, does the perfect tense exist on the surface only, a mad sort of historical time without the sensibility of fiction or humanizing narrative resource? Is there some sort of causality in chronological order? Who is he talking to: himself, us, the politicians? Are death and war for Fisk a behind-the-looking-glass death and war in which the fine appearance of nothingness emerges?[99]

Fisk's work risks all this and occasionally succumbs. It is saved, however, by an ever-present sense of disgust at his own fascination, and a troubled sense of impotence, in relation to what he calls, somewhat journalistically but accurately, the 'porno-market of death'. Looking at photographs of atrocities in Algeria in 1994, he notes: 'after a few minutes it dawns on me that the attention I pay to this horror, the detail I find in the photographs, makes me complicit in these crimes'.[100] However, unlike Fisk, Dos Passos never questioned the parameters of his vision of reality except with fatalistic irony: American capitalist atomization, rootlessness, the narcissistic sense of the self in competitive community (the social presentation of the self as a consumable image) nor the metaphysics of a life conceived in the social Darwinist mode of success and failure. At best there is a kind of hip journalist irony and stoicism.

Fisk's world is a lot more desperate, there is no refuge in blind energy or mere fascination, and it is lot more emotionally and historically sophisticated, the horrors are beyond irony. There is also a compassionate warmth one seeks for in vain in Dos Passos's fictional worlds. In Fisk the countervailing strengths more than outweigh the dangers. His work exploits the temporalities of historical and fictional narrative and employs the uneasy resources of autobiography with its ambiguous relation between confession and the assembling and arranging of the public incidents.

And of course there is the difference of medium and genre. The newspaper story with its electronic resources of instant communication is suspended in a kind of global space and now in ubiquitous cyberspace. It is well known that modern to postmodern fiction was born in the field of journalism, with its field organization of information. More cynically, we know that news is always bad news, because it plays into security fears from sex to social and political order in order that advertising, which is always good news, appears the more credible in its relentless and sophisticated offers of paradise.[101]

Nonetheless, the existence of a Cameron or Fisk, whose works also appear in book form, gives the lie to post-McLuhan theorists who would reduce the real world to sequences of 'constructed' and interiorized electronic fantasy. Everyone knows the television war involves real blood and suffering; it is the massification of instantly transmitted global horror that numbs the soul into feelings of impotence and denial. The elision of the line of reality is the province of those who, with lesser or greater efficiency and credibility, have to deal with consequences of mental confusion and psychological 'sickness', which may well have other and more complex roots.

In addition, there is Fisk's respect for journalists of integrity before him, including Cameron, 'whose iconic 1946 report from the Bikini atom tests was perhaps the most literary and philosophical article ever published in a newspaper'.[102] Fisk's outrage at media lying is as strong as Politkovskaya's or Cameron's and, before either, Orwell's:

> Soldier and civilian, they died in their tens of thousands because death had been concocted for them, morality hitched like a halter round the warhorse so that we could talk about 'target-rich environments' and 'collateral damage,' that most infantile of attempts to shake off the crime of killing – and report the victory parades, the tearing down of statues and the importance of peace.'[103]

The justifiable anger extends to himself as he bitterly quotes a Palestinian while prisoners from Gaza are being taken away, and the heavily wounded are being assessed in hospital: 'You've just come here to watch us dance.'[104]

One extended passage illustrates how Fisk evokes and negotiates the treacherous shoals of his genre and chosen work. Here is a narrative from the 1980s detailing his journey to Pakistan from Afghanistan where he had been reporting on the Russian–Afghan conflict:

> I admired the great plumes on the headdress of the soldiers of the Khyber Rifles on the Pakistani side of the border, the first symbol of the old British raj, a regiment formed 101 years before, still ensconced at Fort Shagi with old English silver and visitor's book that went back to the viceroys.
>
> But of course it was an illusion. President General Mohamed Zia ul-Haq ran an increasingly Islamic dictatorship in which maiming and whipping had become official state punishments. He ruled by martial law and had hanged his only rival, the former president Zulfikar Ali Bhutto, less than a year earlier, in April 1970. And of course, responded to the Soviet invasion of Afghanistan with publicly expressed fears that the Russian army planned to drive on into Pakistan. The United States immediately sent millions of dollars of weapons to the Pakistani dictator, who suddenly became a vital American 'asset' in the war again communism.
>
> But in Ali's wooden bus, it seemed like freedom. And as we descended the splendour of the Kyber Pass, there around me were the relics of the old British regiments who had fought on this ground for more than a century and a half, often against the Pathan ghazi fighters with their primitive jezail rifles. 'A weird, uncanny place

> ... a deadly valley,' a British writer called it in 1897, and there on the great rocks that slid past Ali's bus were the regimental crests of the 40th foot, the Leicestershires, the Dorsetshires, the Cheshires – Bill Fisk's regiment before he was sent to France in 1918 – and the 54th Sikh Frontier Force, each with its motto and dates of service. The paint was flaking off the ornamental crest of the 2nd Battalion, the Baluch Regiment, and the South Lancs and the Prince of Wales' Volunteers had long ago lost their colours. Pathan tribesmen, Muslims to a man of course, had smashed part of the insignia of a Hindi regiment whose crest included a proud peacock. Graffiti covered the plaque of the 17th Leicestershires (1878–9). The only refurbished memorial belong to Queen Victoria's Own Corps of Guides, a mainly Pathan unit whose eccentric commander insisted that they be clothed in khaki rather than scarlet and one of whose Indian members probably inspired Rudyard Kipling's 'Gunga Din'. The lettering had been newly painted, the stone washed clean of graffiti.[105]

What first strikes one on a common sense level is how this piece is directed towards a British audience with its shadowy nostalgia of empire. The chapter ends with Kipling's 'Arithmetic on the Frontier': 'Two-thousand pounds of education/drops to a ten-rupee jezail',[106] which captures perfectly the nation of shopkeepers' view of human worth, not to mention the cash nexus basis of its imperialist public school ethos into which, of course, the irony plays. Yet like Serge finding a battered copy of the writings of Lenin in Stalinist Siberian exile, or finding himself in the Museum of Guadalajara, it also represents more generally the fascination of modernism and even postmodernism with the detritus of a past, the signs of which have lost any current concept of the object they once represented. Restoring them critically is the work of both historical narrative and a transcendent ethics.

In this book's earlier discussion of Serge, Walter Benjamin's *Theses on the Philosophy of History* was briefly recalled to illuminate some aspects of the way Serge deployed narrative temporalities in his semi-fictional, semi-historical work. It is also useful to recall it here to unpack the fluent but complex aspects of Fisk's work. Other moments of Benjamin's essay can be used, beginning with the question of happiness. Looked at in a rather strange way, Fisk's work is about the nature of happiness in a world that the sensitive can only experience as anguish: 'Reflection shows us that our image of happiness is thoroughly coloured by the time to which the course of our own existence has assigned us.'[107] The colour of the time that Fisk represents is presented in term of narrative that is an exchange between personal and public memory located very precisely in concretely recalled moments of time. Anguish is real and perhaps foundational to the sense of ourselves as human beings in the world, as Heidegger argued. It also, however, robs us of the capacity to act. Happiness therefore remains attached to a creative recall of the events of personal life and public life, serving a capacity to act and resist being overwhelmed by a one-dimensional story whose ethical dimension is bad faith.

In the passage cited, there is a keen sense of historical colour close to personal time, that moment of history *where one comes in* via one's immediate parentage, though 'illusionary' is clearly pleasurable. It is declared illusionary, because of the risk of sentiment and by implication because of its vivid contrast with the present political opportunism in Pakistan and the United States, which seems at least as bad as the British Raj. But the plumes on the headdress of the soldiers of the Khyber Rifles will not quite go away, not for imperialist nostalgia, but as an indicator of a time, different from ours but in which real and unrepeatable people lived their specific historical moment. It combats the twentieth-century historian's, and statistician's 'horror of the event'.[108] The image also links two historical moments, inviting a contrast that throws the activities of the present centres of power into a more lurid light. It is an act of remembrance for the men of forgotten wars. Their stories never make the transition between military and more general history. It is as if wars, by some magical break in political connection, were detached from other forms of human history rather than being integral with them, even profoundly representing them. We have difficulty in thinking of them this way.

The names of regiments representing English counties from Dorset to South Lancashire indicate that violent disruption of time and space that is a soldier's lot and also invokes but does not quite endorse Fussell's perpetual war time. Something escapes the fatalism of temporal homogeneity. For it is precisely this moment, this precise colour in Benjamin's sense, that is unrepeatable in its human uniqueness: this narrative of a journalist in 1980 thinking back and rescuing the unique feel of the century-old visitor's book (a record in writing, the ashes of story waiting to be breathed into life) and the timeless and time-filled old English silver. Here we have all the representational theatre that takes place, in Ricoeur's words, 'between the image's referring back to the absent thing and its self-assertion in terms of its own visibility'.[109]

The illusion is the momentary presence of the past offering the possibility of a story that is recalled by indirection and suggestion. Its illusory character might have suggested the indulgence of a romantic view of the Raj, and in that sense it both connects and forms a break with the operations of present power: the Islamic dictatorship of Mohamed Zia ul-Haq and his successful manipulation of the Americans in their own cynical opportunism involving gaining far-flung influence in fighting the good fight against the 'communist' plot.

Cleverly Fisk reclaims what he has just rejected: 'But in Ali's bus, it seemed like freedom.' The personal moment not only registers the immediate escape from danger, but throws the correspondent into a pleasurable sense of the luxury of concentrating on an immediacy, an image released from the past though debarred a future. The 'freedom' transforms into a new search for lost time. It is the pleasure, albeit a melancholy one, of recalling times that the present extends backwards into, prompted by an experience (detached by its transitory escape between moments of work) of a geographical space with its arbitrary human relics, a space that is a monument to past history, though indifferent to it, and rapidly gaining other intelligibilities brought about through the remorseless changes from old to new imperialists.

The pleasure is there also in the personal linkages. The Cheshires were his father Bill Fisk's regiment 'before he was sent France in 1918'. These interjections give the prose the haunting lingering of reverie, complete with images that symbolically thicken, slow down and endorse the inevitable passage of time: 'the paint was flaking off the ornamental crest of the 2nd Battalion'.

Fisk chooses his past. As Benjamin noted: 'Only a redeemed mankind has its past citable in all its moments.'[110] Fisk's work needs and is denied redemption because fragment remains just that, lifted only with difficulty into a narrative where it is somehow both abandoned and central. Fisk's forgotten moments become melancholy gestures towards an impossible *citation à l'ordre du jour* that might make a complete narrative of history, and they carry with them a sense of the impossibility of impartial universal judgement. Benjamin saw the key 'spiritual' side of the materialist class struggle not in the spoils of the victor but in the theatre of an essentially ethical struggle involving, and Serge was exemplary here, courage, humour, cunning and fortitude, which always question every victory of rulers. Like Serge, Fisk has that ability to grasp the image that rises up in an instance never to be seen again, to seize hold of a memory as it flashes up at a moment of danger. He understands, too, that the dead, or perhaps we should say the stories of the dead, are not safe in the victor's hands.

In the spring of 1940, Benjamin was questioning the traditional historian's sense of empathy with the past, 'whose origin is the indolence of the heart, *acedia*, that despairs of grasping and holding the genuine historical image as it flares up briefly'.[111] In the debates of the time he saw historical materialism as challenging that rather comfortable despair. He further noted, like Weil, that 'history' itself had to recognise the permanent state of emergency for the oppressed that is its rule not its exception: 'The current amazement that the things we are experiencing are "still" possible in the twentieth century is *not* philosophical.'[112] He speaks of an image by Paul Klee which he sees as the angel of history, face turned toward the past as a single catastrophe of wreckage upon wreckage, a storm which propels him backwards into the future, while the pile of debris grows skyward – the storm's name is progress – the chimera of politicians.[113] It has to be added also, that for Benjamin, the same illusion was manifest in vulgar Marxism with its devastating rhetoric of the mastery of nature (identical to that of capitalists) and displays of technocratic control (identical to that of the fascists): 'The new conception of labor amounts to the exploitation of nature, which with naïve complacency is contrasted with the exploitation of the proletariat.'[114]

Fisk does not engage with this particular argument, which is so rich in truths for the contemporary radical ecologist, but he understands that 'history is the subject of a structure whose site is not homogenous, empty time, but time filled by the presence of the now [Jetzeit – *nunc stans*, not Gegenwart].'[115] This is to say that there is something mystical about it, but that the very fact can be a double edged sword. The ruling class turns to the past for a fashionable confirmation of similitude, not to engage in an argument, dialectical or otherwise, with it. When Fisk invokes military history, in melancholy pseudo-achronological similitude, it is an ironic gesture designed to rob the ruling class of both its stoic fashionability and its melancholy in a domain that has traditionally been its preferred territory: in Nietzsche's words, that version of history offered by 'the spoiled loafer in the garden of knowledge'.[116]

Theatrically, however, Fisk sometimes offers himself as a spoiled loafer, rather like the brilliant and witty James Cameron before him, but he also has something of the revolutionary's desire to fight for the 'oppressed past'.[117] He does attempt, in very detailed ways, to 'blast a *specific* era' out of not simply the homogenous course of history, but out of the versions offered by the powerful who do not on the whole travel in 'Ali's bus'. Each of the dates offered in the passage (1980, 1880, 1979, 1918, 1897, 1878–9) not only challenges fateful abstract chronology but become constellated images rich with specific meaning: geographical, military, ideological, religious, all with their specific auras that invite both critical and emotional appraisal, turning empathy into an intellectual work for ethical and political engagement.

These specific judgements contextualize and set off the 1980 moment of Soviet imperial invasion, State Department paranoia-fed power drives and Pakistani opportunism and demagoguery, thus providing a warning that as far as the centres of power are concerned it is business as usual. The paragraph leaves us with the difficult question of whether the graffiti-covered memorials of gone regiments are more authentic than the refurbished memorial of the Pathan unit with its lettering 'newly painted, the stone washed clean of graffiti'.

The thousand and more pages of Fisk's accumulated life's work provide an inoculation against that manufacturing of consent which is the curse of a developed world struggling to ensure in its own generation that those who have fought for authentic democratic principles in the past, have not fought in vain. Current lying is colossal, spin is ubiquitous (describing Bill Clinton as 'centre-left').[118] Fisk gives a terrible account of twentieth-century history: from the contemporary moment of the aristocratic Bin Laden and his Taliban fighters around which he struggles to maintain some kind of complex narrative, to the disastrous Russian invasion of Afghanistan to the terrible Iran–Iraq war, to his tracing of his father's role in the Great War, which is contextualized by the shoddy behaviour of the Great Powers in those 'low dishonest' decades we have already examined, to the Armenian massacres, to the foundation of Israel and the destruction and brutalization of Palestine, to imperialist and post-imperialist Algeria and its horrors, and the first and second wars in Iraq.

For the world's oppressed are forced, in words Fisk uses about the Palestinians, to live their past history (that is the history of oppression), 'again and again, every day'.[119] This coalescing into a perpetual present has its own tyrannies of not allowing the past to die which is not the same as ignoring it. The only poem he concludes that moves him to tears is Christina Rossetti's poem: 'Better by far you should forget and smile/Than that you should remember and be sad.' The affective tone of the poem, of course entirely contradicts its rational injunction.

The most cogent and articulate contemporary parallel to Hehn's examination of the economic politics of the 1930s is John Pilger's short but incisive *The New Rulers of the World*. Here, in much briefer outline, is a readily acknowledged Orwell-inspired vision of our own condition. For Pilger, 'global economy' is an Orwellian term where beneath 'the gloss of instant financial trading, mobile phones, McDonald's, Starbucks, holidays booked on the net' is a 'globalisation of poverty, a world where most human beings never make a phone call and live on less than two dollars a day, where 6,000 children die every day from diarrhoea because most have no access to clean water'.[120] Far from making the state obsolescent, in the words of the Russian dissident economist, Boris Kagarlitsky: 'Globalisation does not mean the impotence of the state, but the rejection by the state of its social functions, in favour of repressive ones, and the ending of democratic freedoms.'[121]

Pilger has been regularly been vilified for simple truths that are indisputable but no one cares to acknowledge, citing, for example a UN report in 2001 that American and British obstruction of 4 billion dollars of aid to Iraq was the largest cause of suffering in that country, responsible, according to a further Unicef report, the deaths of 6,000 children a month.[122] And this was before the recent disastrous war. His recall of Henry Luce's 1941 *American Century* announces a tradition of a *Reader's Digest* view of the world (though such demagogic simplification in the United States goes much further back than this) and accuses the United States of undermining 'the greatest western achievement, that of secular, redistributive politics'.[123]

Democracy is to a degree, nonetheless, alive and well in the United States. It is deeply flawed in many aspects, by money, chicanery, gerrymandering, indifference, apathy, inward-looking and provincial suburban life, scepticism, media distraction and censorship by omission, religious extremism, racism and so on, but it is still very much there. Furthermore the vitality and generosity of the American people are not illusions and it must be remembered they have often been their own best and most unsparing critics. The problem has been extreme American imperialist activity outside its own borders, in virtually every country of the world, from Britain after 1945, laying out loan conditions for the democratically elected Labour government, to more ruthless activity in Colombia and elsewhere in Latin America, the Middle East and Afghanistan in more recent years: simplistically justifying its violent actions with a pseudo-democratic propaganda and anti-communist, or anti-terrorist rhetoric. At this moment it is more aware than ever of the bridges it must rebuild with the rest of the world, and of its pressing need to exchange brute force for dialogue and respect for cultures other than its own. Pragmatically, of course, America is under pressure to do this given that its unique superpower status now has a foreseeable end, given the rising wealth of countries such as China and India. This book provides ample evidence for the efforts of the best Americans, but it hardly palliates the current horrors, which produce a suffocating and daily sense of shame shared by many people of good will on both sides of the Atlantic.

Pilger's book is a litany of inconvenient facts. For example, as with Weil's great essay on factory work, Pilger reports on Nike factories in Indonesia in one telling example and notes the Dickensian conditions of the workers (worse than Engels's Manchester) as a result of the carve up of Indonesia's economy by global corporate giants in 1967. All this took place in agreement with Suharto, who was eventually 'retired' on a 15 billion dollar 'pension': American multinational companies got the copper and gold, nickel and bauxite; a group of American, Japanese and French companies got the tropical forests.[124]

Where oil is the goal we have already noted that the former Cold War enemies exhibit identical behaviour. The 'war on terror' – a phrase which speedily identifies anyone who uses it as collusive with the worst of international criminals – provides new equations of exploitative justification: '"Economic growth" (rich elite, poor majority) equals anti-terrorism.' This equation prompted Christian Aid's head of policy, Mark Curtis, who attended Doha (a World Trade Organization meeting) in 2001 to say: 'It was utterly outrageous [...] the issue of multinational corporations as a cause of poverty was not even on the agenda; it was like a conference on malaria that does not even discuss the mosquito.'[125] An African delegate said 'if I speak out too strongly, the US will phone my minister. They will say I am embarrassing the United States.'[126] Pilger concludes also that 'America's economic wars are now backed by the perpetual threat of military attack on any country, without legal pretence.'[127] Roosevelt had at least hesitated to send troops into Brazil in the 1930s.

Pilger is rough, too, on the academics, the supineness of Western humanities departments driven by a system (introduced into Britain from the United States by New Labour) of competitive conformity and quantitative assessment: to ensure success and credibility in an academic hierarchy, 'academics are more eager to credit ethical intent to government policy makers than the policy makers themselves.'[128] And as for politics departments, 'liberal realists' 'ensure that western imperialism is interpreted as crisis management, rather than the cause of the crisis and its escalation. By never recognising western state terrorism, their complicity is assured.'[129] There are always a few brave souls, of course, who are the exceptions to this rule and I count myself extremely fortunate to have known a number of them, but in forty years of academic life I have sadly little serious evidence to counter Pilger's assessment.

But the few, as this book shows and celebrates, are always worth cherishing. Serge's world, born of the debris of the nineteenth-century socialist dream and extending into a world of refugees still throws a long shadow of courage, sharp political judgement, and commitment. It speaks to today's Russia and its politics in the trans-Caucuses as well as its more European cities. Serge's ability to keep on the wing with a deeply personal sense of himself, fractured in time and space, is astonishing. So too is his perpetual curiosity about the real world and its actual conditions, his ability to read what he encounters both historically and in terms of the contingencies of the present moment. He has a sense of himself in many times and many places, yet never loses faith in intelligent energetic goodness, even when every original ideological crutch has been snatched away. His is the true humanism in which a deep knowledge of literature, philosophy, the history of politics, religion and psychology becomes a sustaining force in dark times. His faith in the human story is the foundation of his resistance to nihilism.

Macdonald, though his life was nothing like as politically engaged nor historically symbolic of great shifts in world history, in a sense had perhaps the more difficult task of surviving with conscience intact in an already postmodernist culture which thought that in political terms it had definitively solved the problem of government two centuries earlier. The rest was managing the anomalies. Macdonald reached for the only traditional radical American resource available to him, that of relatively un-theorised democratic communitarian ethical action. From this slender but tough thread, he freed himself from an increasingly Stalinist American left (though as we have seen the story was not uncomplicated), and made a serious attempt to draw together in the pages of *politics* the best fragments of an international intelligentsia and dissident writers to continue a serious critique of a world at war, not to mention, with his wife Nancy, engaging in very practical and organized campaigns on behalf of refugees and aid to a starving Europe. His work in the best sense encouraged an interdisciplinary approach to analysing culture: from political philosophy to literature to cinema to a rare journalistic ability to write about current affairs. From his swift radical response to Hiroshima to his courage in surviving personal breakdown and returning to be a major critic of the Vietnamese war later in his life, he was, not withstanding some of the limitations discussed above, a shining example of the best of American dissident intellectuals.

With Dorothy Norman we find a different, though equally interdisciplinary mix in her promotion of European and American modernism, shot through with a civil rights ethic whose relationship with politics would play out, initially at any rate, perhaps more so in the United States than in other countries. She side-stepped the classical political analyses of Europe from communism and fascism to social democracy, in favour of testing the strengths of an America radical tradition which would lead from John Quincy Adams, through Bourne to Richard Wright. Nonetheless in the pages of *TWICE A YEAR* a number of Europeans more familiar with the European ideological debates, such as Silone, Sartre and de Beauvoir, would also find a home. Untrammelled freedom of debate was in itself no mean achievement. The fact that Norman's work is still almost unknown is a scandal. If issues of class and economics were not central to her vision, her concern with personal life, children, the analyses of modernity implicit in Proust's work, her faith in the temporality of the long past and her concern with key ethical questions addressed by the essentially critical world of modern art, photography and writing opened up a terrain of unsuspected personal and political issues. Her encouragement of writers such as Wright and Henry Miller, among many others, the first criticized by Marxists of having broken faith and the later self-confessedly contemptuous of all politics, paradoxically provided a seriously political vision of postmodernity in the sphere of race and in the conditions of life of the 'air-conditioned' nightmare, all unsuspected by most Marxist social realists. Her political work with influential women in international politics, the unflinching integrity of her democratic convictions, not to mention the compelling quality of her own photographic work, made her one of the most outstanding American women of the century.

Mumford's long view of history was fundamentally critical of the claims of the American century. The depth of the historical comparison was a powerful weapon with which to counter Pilger's 'eternal present'. He was very early and publicly unrelenting in his warnings about Nazism and fascism. His insistence on capitalist technology as a driving force of history is still ignored by most historians to this day (as with military history, they bracket it off). His attempts at multidisciplinary history were pioneering and brilliant in the gracefulness of the writing that articulated them. His endorsement of centres of goodness and cultural achievement through every century of recorded and unrecorded history was executed with passionate engagement and a sense of contemporary relevance. He resisted the abstractions of twentieth-century academic structuralism as much as those of the positivist Marxists. If he occasionally got it badly wrong, nonetheless, something was always at stake in Mumford's writing. The range of fields and output was Victorian, or perhaps we should say American, in its commitment and unflagging energy. His criticism of megalopolis, gigantism, monumentality, displays of power as numbing political spectacle and the banalities of globalization were relentless. His roots were in the best of English and American culture. He was a pioneer of sustainable development, the small is beautiful movement, ecological responsibility, the drive for renewable sources of power, of conservation and the need to preserve and respect the achievements of the past as a creative resource, whether in architecture, photography, literature, art, or in honest writing of the story of history itself.

His work is crucial to us now if believable democratic practice is ever going to have a chance to survive.

Rukeyser's work, too, was both inclusive and interdisciplinary, and directed to political justice. 'I lived', she said 'in the first century of world wars,' and if that seems too all embracing, she also said: 'To be a Jew in the twentieth century/Is to be offered a gift.' [130] It was to be a tormented gift as events presaged in early 1940s poem were fulfilled in tragedy. Starting in active politics as a socialist/communist, though her vocation was always more intensely that of a poet, her work speaks to us now because she refused to maintain artificial barriers between politics and affective life, between culture and scientific issues, between nationalist pride (and she fought to define American identity in its best traditions) and the concerns of the wider international world. In a time of positivist Marxism and consensual history, she insisted on the importance of psychology and the history of science; in a time where poets were supposed to write as 'objectively' as scientists, she used the personal voice; in a time when academic history insisted on a political event-oriented summary with a nationalist or materialist flavour and never touched on science, technology or cultural issues, she was the exception, writing a poetic prose that articulated a world of Blakean contradiction.

As a woman, women and children were subjects for her poetry, a subject virtually untouched by better-known poets. Everything she wrote had a direct political value, though it steered clear of the kind of subjects too easily read as 'political', and though earlier she made her own contribution to the American jeremiad. In a time when psychology either had its ready-made stories in psychoanalysis, or in mechanistic behavioural abstraction, she explored the complexities of the human soul in poetry, redeploying discourses retranslated from science, ethnic culture, anthropology, cinema, photography, the recently discovered and celebrated beginnings of an American cultural tradition, noticing, using and reacting to English, European and Latin American poets with their different worlds and different vocabularies.

She too began as a journalist, as a 'foreign correspondent', and a sense of international responsibility never left her. In spite of vilification on all fronts (even now her work will not fit academic categories and some of the old prejudices remain), her poetic vision and sense of her vocation never left her. From the long poem to the intense lyric her craft was exact with a visionary quality and emotional intensity which very few contemporary poets, so academically and technically chiselled, dare go near. The achievements of the past were as important to her as Mumford. She knew, in René Char's words, that the past comes to us by no will and testament, that it had to be worked for, discovered and recreated against powerful, simplistic versions of history that amounted to lying: For her, as for Serge, the human story was supreme: 'Time comes into it/Say it Say it/ The world is made of stories/not of atoms.'[131] Yet no one took the discoveries of science more seriously and tried to connect a way of thinking about them with the human story and the deepest impulses of the human heart. She knew, in the words of the title of John Berger's most recent and most moving book, that we have to 'hold everything dear'. [132]

Perhaps in this work about the nature of time and story, we should close with a thought about the nature of the eternal. In *Willard Gibbs* (1942) Rukeyser wrote:

> Death, which biologically is merely the terminus of a natural process, acquires significance for man because he anticipates it, and modifies his activities so as to circumvent it: by memory and foresight, by choosing his ends, dreaming of immortality, erecting monuments and statues and museums, and above all, by transmitting the written word, man creates a destiny beyond his life's physical span. It is just because the worms lie in wait that man defies the gods, cherishes the images he has created and the relations he has solidified in custom and thought, and centres his efforts on those things which are least given to meaningless change.[133]

Those 'things least given to change' are one aspect of human eternity. There are also other ways of thinking about it. Berger notes that 'in [Emily] Dickinson's poetry the presence of the eternal is attendant in every pause'.[134] The eternal, he notes, according to Spinoza is now: 'It is not something awaiting us, but something we encounter during those brief yet timeless moments when everything accommodates everything and no exchange is inadequate.'[135] He cites as an example the moment when the Somoza dictatorship in Nicaragua was overthrown: 'The fact that the US and its mercenaries later destroyed the Sandinistas in no way diminishes that moment existing in the past, present and future.'[136] Orwell experienced such a moment briefly in Catalonia, as have many others throughout history when for a moment the crushing veil of reality has been lifted. We have, said Ricoeur, 'nothing better than testimony in the final analysis to assure ourselves that something did happen in the past'.[137] Such moments live in parallel with the supporting experience of great art, the sudden understanding of a scientific problem, intense religious experience, or in more accessible and ordinary ways, in selfless and generous love, in steadfast friendship, or in those profoundly-moving moments when one experiences true and undeserved human kindness. The moments may be rare, but they enable us, to cite Berger one last time, to 'break out of the prison of modern time [...]'.[138]

Notes

Introduction: Lighting the Circle

1 ‘You put a match to your lamp and what flares up does not bring illumination. It is far away, very far away from you, that the circle lights up.’ René Char, ‘Fureur et mystère’ from *Feuillets d’Hypnos* in *René Char: Œuvres complètes*, intr. Jean Roudaut (Paris: Gallimard, 1983), p. 203. My translation.

2 John Keats to George and Georgiana Keats, 14 February–3 May in *The Letters of John Keats*, ed. Maurice Buxton Forman (London: Oxford University Press, 1948), p. 336.

3 *Radio Times*, 2–8 July 2005.

4 Paul Fussell, *Wartime: Understanding and Behaviour in the Second World War* (New York and Oxford: Oxford University Press, 1989).

5 Herman Melville, *Moby-Dick, or The Whale* (New York: Library of America, 1983), p. 798.

6 Jean-Paul Sartre, *Notebooks for an Ethics*, trans. David Pellauer (Chicago, IL and London: University of Chicago Press, 1992), p. 35.

7 Email from Ela Kotkowska to author, 8 July 2005.

8 Simone Weil, *The Need for Roots: Prelude to a Declaration of Duties towards Mankind*, preface by T.S. Eliot (London and New York: Routledge, 1996), p. 222.

9 Ibid.

10 Ibid.

11 While I have not for the most part employed specialized vocabulary, Heidegger’s great work *Being and Time* is a starting point for a way of thinking more about the problem. Along with Sartre’s *Being and Nothingness*, which was strongly influenced by Heidegger, notwithstanding his political weakness and failure, these are two works of the mid-twentieth century that have influenced the heuristic development of this book’s discursive argument as well as some of its content.

12 Primo Levi, *If Not Now, When?*, trans. William Weaver (Harmondsworth: Penguin, 2000), p. 75.

13 Norman O. Brown, *Life Against Death: The Psychoanalytical Meaning of History* (New York: Vintage, 1959), p. xi.

14 Muriel Rukeyser, *Willard Gibbs: American Genius* (Garden City, NY: Doubleday, Doran & Co., 1942) and *The Traces of Thomas Hariot* (London: Victor Gollancz, 1972).

15 See Clive Bush, *Muriel Rukeyser: The Poet as Scientific Biographer* (London: Spanner Press, 1977),

reprinted in Clive Bush, *Holding the Line: Selected Essays in American Literature and Culture* (Bern: Peter Lang, 2009), pp. 213–38.

16 Paul Ricoeur, *Time and Narrative*, 3 vols, trans. Kathleen Blamery (vol. 3), Katherine McLaughlin, and David Pellauer (Chicago, IL: University of Chicago Press, 1984).

17 Ricoeur, *Time and Narrative*, vol. 1, p. 38.

18 Ibid., p. 80.

19 Ibid.

20 Ricoeur, *Time and Narrative*, vol. 3, p. 75.

21 Ibid., p. 131.

22 Ricoeur, *Time and Narrative*, vol. 2, p. 151.

23 Ricoeur, *Time and Narrative*, vol. 1, p. 86.

24 Joseph Conrad, 'Henry James' in *Notes on Life and Letters* (London and Toronto: J.M. Dent, 1921), p. 23.

25 Lewis Mumford, 'From Revolt to Renewal,' Benjamin Franklin Lecture, University of Pennsylvania, 1950, reprinted in *Lewis Mumford at 100* (Philadelphia, PA: Graduate School of Fine Arts and Van Pelt Library, University of Pennsylvania, 1995), p. 40.

26 Conrad, 'Henry James', p. 15.

27 Hannah Arendt, *Men in Dark Times* (San Diego et al.: Harcourt Brace, 1955), p. 21. My italics.

28 Charles Darwin, *The Origin of Species* (1859; Harmondsworth: Penguin, 1968), p. 458.

29 Blaise Pascal, *Pensées*, trans. A.J. Krailsheimer (Harmondsworth: Penguin, 1966), p. 125.

30 Patrick Leigh Fermor, *A Time of Gifts* (Harmondsworth: Penguin, 1979), p. 172.

31 Albert Schweitzer, *Quest of the Historical Jesus*, 3rd edn, trans. W. Montgomery (London: Adam and Charles Black, 1954), p. 2.

32 Victor Serge, 'Adieu à Gramsci', *La Wallonie*, 8–9 May 1937. Victor Serge Papers. My translation.

33 Paul Ricoeur, *The Reality of the Historical Past* (1984; Milwaukee, WI: Marquette University Press, 1998), p. 36.

34 Ricoeur, *The Reality of the Historical Past*, p. 36.

35 Conrad, 'Henry James', p. 20.

36 Serge, 'Adieu à Gramsci', n.p.

37 René Char, *Hypnos Waking: Poetry and Prose by René Char*, trans. Jackson Mathews et al. (New York: Random House, c.1956), p. 167.

38 George Orwell, *Nineteen Eighty-Four* (1949; Harmondsworth: Penguin, 1987), p. 162.

39 Muriel Rukeyser, 'Poetry and Time', typescript, n.d. (probably c.1967–8), tape transcription of a talk given at MIT, Muriel Rukeyser Papers, p. 34.

40 Arendt, *Men in Dark Times*, p. 97.

Part 1: 'It is Dead and it is Not Dead': Time and Testimony in Victor Serge

Section I

1 The title is taken from George Oppen's poem 'Of being numerous' in *The Collected Poems of George Oppen* (New York: New Directions, 1975), p. 147.

2 Joseph Conrad, 'Youth' in *Great Short Works of Joseph Conrad* (New York: Harper and Row, 1966), p. 166.

3 John Berger, *Ways of Seeing* (Harmondsworth: Penguin, 1972), p. 10.

4 Jean-Paul Sartre, *Notebooks for an Ethics*, trans. David Pellauer (Chicago, IL and London: University of Chicago Press, 1992), p. 35.

5 Boris Pilniak, 'Mahognany' in *Chinese Story and Other Tales*, trans. and intr. Vera T. Reck and Michael Green (Norman, OK and London: University of Oklahoma Press, 1988), p. 107.

6 Michel Foucault, *The Order of Things: An Archaeology of the Human Sciences* (London: Tavistock, 1974), pp. 63–4.

7 Respectively these refer to Henry James's *The Golden Bowl*, Proust's *À la recherche du temps perdu*, Woolf's *The Waves*, Joyce's *A Portrait of the Artist as a Young Man*, Faulkner's *The Sound and the Fury*.

8 This brief outline is partly based on Greeman's chronology provided at the end of Victor Serge, *Men in Prison*, trans. Richard Greeman (London: Writers and Readers Publishing Cooperative, 1977), pp. 255–7.

9 Boris Pilniak, *The Naked Year*, trans. Alexander R. Tulloch (Ann Arbor, MI: Ardis, 1975), p. 92.

10 Vera T. Reck: *Boris Pil'niak: A Soviet Writer in Conflict with the State* (Montreal and London: McGill-Queen's University Press, 1975), p. 77.

11 Victor Serge, *Memoirs of a Revolutionary*, trans. Peter Sedgwick (1951; Oxford: Oxford University Press, 1963), p. 365. This is the only English edition and is cut by an eighth. The best (magnificently scholarly) edition is Jean Rière and Jil Silberstein (eds), *Mémoires d'un révolutionnaire et autres écrits politiques* (Paris: Robert Lafont, 2001).

12 Clive Bush, 'Escape from Marseille: An American story? Writing Victor Serge's, Laurette Séjourné's, Dwight and Nancy Macdonald's Balzacian book' in *Prospects: An Annual of American Cultural Studies* (New York: Cambridge University Press, 2003), pp. 311–40.

13 Mexico, after the revolution, under Cárdenas was welcoming to radical political refugees, especially from Franco's Spain. On 24 August 1940 the Mexican minister to Germany, Azcárate, offered to relieve Vichy of the economic burden of ten to fifteen thousand Spanish political refugees. The Germans at first insisted on selecting the refugees, then in November rescinded the unsatisfactory agreement, and began deporting Spanish refugees to concentration camps in Germany. See Friedrich E. Schuler, *Mexico Between Hitler and Roosevelt: Mexican Foreign Relations in the Age of Lázaro Cárdenas* (Albuquerque, NM: University of New Mexico Press, 1998), pp. 193–5.

14 For the best and fullest account of this remarkable man see Andy Marino, *A Quiet American: The Secret Life of Varian Fry* (New York: St Martin's Press, 1999).

15 Victor Serge to Dwight Macdonald, 21 January 1939. This letter and all subsequent ones are to be found in the Dwight Macdonald Papers. All translations are my own.

16 G.L.K. Morris had been a classmate of Macdonald, was an abstract expressionist and a financial backer for *Partisan Review*. Presumably Macdonald had asked him for assistance in Laurette Séjourné's case. See *A Moral Temper: The Letters of Dwight Macdonald*, ed. Michael Wreszin (Chicago, IL: Ivan R. Dee, 2001), p. 100.

17 Laurette Séjourné to Nancy and Dwight Macdonald, 3 May 1941.

18 Victor Serge to Dwight Macdonald, 7 July 1941.

19 Miriam Davenport Ebel, *An Unsentimental Education* (posted at www.chambon.org, with permission of Dr Charles Ebel, © Miriam Davenport Ebel, 1999), p. 8.
20 Davenport Ebel, *An Unsentimental Education*, p. 21. See also Varian Fry, *Surrender on Demand* (New York: Random House, 1945), pp. 222f.
21 Timothy P. Maga, *America, France and the Refugee Problem, 1933–1947* (New York and London: Garland Publishing, 1985), p. 205.
22 Victor Serge to Dwight Macdonald, 26 June 1941.
23 Victor Serge to Nancy and Dwight Macdonald, 2 November 1941.
24 Serge, *Memoirs of a Revolutionary*, p. 361.
25 Ibid., p. 362.
26 Ibid., p. 363. Serge in fact attended Bergson's lectures at the Collège de France in 1909–10. Bill Marshall, *Victor Serge: The Uses of Dissent* (New York and Oxford: Berg, 1992), p. 36.
27 Serge, *Memoirs of a Revolutionary*, p. 364.
28 See Eric Mottram, 'Out of Sight but Never Out of Mind: Fears of Invasion in American Culture' in *Blood on the Nash Ambassador: Investigations in American Culture* (London: Hutchinson/Radius, c.1993), pp. 138–80.
29 Fry, *Surrender on Demand*, p. 29.
30 William Burroughs, *Cities of the Red Night* (1981; London: Picador, 1982), p. 145.
31 Serge, *Memoirs of a Revolutionary*, p. 263.
32 Ibid., p. 379.
33 Ricoeur, *Time and Narrative*, I, p. 79.
34 Serge, *Memoirs of a Revolutionary*, p. 382.
35 Job 1.16: 'The fire of God is fallen from heaven, and hath burned up the sheep, and the servants, and consumed them; and I only am escaped alone to tell thee.'
36 Paul Ricoeur, *History and Truth*, trans. Charles A. Kelby (Evanston, IL: Northwestern University Press, 1965), p. 301.
37 Ricoeur, *Time and Narrative*, I, p. 99.
38 Lawrence L. Langer, *Holocaust Testimonies: The Ruin of Memory* (New Haven, CT and London: Yale University Press, 1991), p. 2.
39 James Baldwin, *Tell Me How Long the Train's Been Gone* (London: Corgi, 1968), p. 62.
40 Langer, *Holocaust Testimonies*, p. 204.
41 Victor Serge, *Conquered City*, trans. Richard Greeman (London: Victor Gollancz, 1976), p. xii.
42 Victor Serge, 'La tyrannie des fictions', *l'anarchie*, (9 novembre 1911); reprinted in Yves Pagès (ed.), *Le Rétif: articles parus dans 'l'anarchie', 1909–1912* (Paris: Librairie Monnier, 1989), p. 54.
43 Claude Lévi-Strauss, *Tristes Tropiques*, trans. Doreen and John Weightman (Harmondsworth: Penguin, 1973), p. 26. Thanks to Maria Kostaridou for drawing my attention to this reference.
44 Serge, 'La tyrannie des fictions', p. 55.
45 Ibid.
46 Bill Marshall writes, 'But it is most of all the *Lebensphilosophie*, or philosophy of life, of Nietzsche that pours forth from the pages of *L'Anarchie*.' *Victor Serge: The Uses of Dissent* (New York and Oxford: Berg, 1992), p. 34.
47 Victor Serge, 'Noels des russies' (1941), Victor Serge Papers.

48 Victor Serge, 'Réflexion sur la morale', in *l'anarchie* (6 décembre 1911); reprinted in Pagès (ed.), *Le Rétif*, pp. 74–8.
49 Victor Serge, 'Ouvrièrisme' in *l'anarchie* (24 mars 1910); reprinted in Pagès (ed.), *Le Rétif*, pp. 103–6.
50 Ignace Lepp to Victor Serge, 27 August 1940, Victor Serge Papers.
51 Victor Serge, 'Socialisme' [1942], Victor Serge Papers.
52 Ibid.
53 Victor Serge, 'Socialisme et psychologie March 1947', Victor Serge Papers.
54 Ibid.
55 Victor Serge, 'Wilhelm Reich, *The Function of the Orgasm*', holograph, n.d., Victor Serge Papers.
56 Ibid.
57 Ibid.
58 Alain Badiou, *Deleuze: The Clamor of Being*, trans. Louise Burchill (Minneapolis, MN and London: University of Minnesota Press, 1999), p. 97.
59 Marshall, *Victor Serge*, pp. 1–30.
60 E.F. Schumacher, *Small Is Beautiful: A Study of Economics as if People Mattered* (London: Blond and Briggs, 1973).
61 George Lichtheim, *A Short History of Socialism* (London: Flamingo, 1975), p. 78. I am indebted to this account for some of the narrative here. It is an excellent introduction to the subject but, as David McLellan points out in his preface, he's hard on anarchists and simplistic on Lenin's theoretical analyses.
62 Ibid., p. 224.
63 Hannah Arendt, 'Karl Jaspers: A Laudatio' in *Men in Dark Times* (San Diego, CA: Harcourt Brace, 1968), pp. 79–80.
64 George Orwell, *Nineteen Eighty-Four* (1949; Harmondsworth: Penguin, 1989), p. 55.
65 Victor Serge, 'La conscience de l'écrivain', holograph notes [May 1946], n.p., Victor Serge Papers.
66 Serge, *Memoirs of a Revolutionary*, p. 195.
67 Ibid., p. 199.
68 Marshall, *Victor Serge*, pp. 90–5.
69 Serge, 'La conscience de l'écrivain', n.p., Victor Serge Papers.
70 Tom Conner, introduction to André Gide's *Politics: Rebellion and Ambivalence* (New York: Palgrave, 2000), p. 3.
71 Serge, *Memoirs of a Revolutionary*, p. 2.
72 Ibid., p. 4.
73 Ibid., p. 10.
74 Ibid., p. 37.
75 Ibid.
76 Ibid., p. 89.
77 Ibid., p. 93.
78 Ibid., p. 140.
79 Ibid., p. 159.
80 Ibid., p. 61.
81 Ibid., p. 177.
82 The Executive Committee of the Communist International.
83 Serge, *Memoirs of a Revolutionary*, p. 227.
84 Ibid., p. 178.
85 Ibid., p. 181.
86 Ibid., p. 182.
87 Thomas Pynchon, *Mason & Dixon* (London: Jonathan Cape, 1997), p. 170.
88 Serge, *Memoirs of a Revolutionary*, p. 286.
89 Ibid.
90 Ibid., p. 302.
91 Ibid., p. 316.
92 Ibid., p. 320.
93 Ibid., p. 321.
94 Ibid., p. 357.

95 Ibid.
96 See Bush, 'Escape from Marseille'.
97 Serge, *Memoirs of a Revolutionary*, p. 357.
98 Ibid., p. 360.
99 Ibid., p. 381.
100 Ibid., p. 382.
101 Serge, *Memoirs of a Revolutionary*, p. 32.
102 Ibid., p. 64.
103 Ibid., p. 77.
104 Ibid., p. 101.
105 Ibid., p. 111.
106 Ibid., p. 123.
107 Ibid., p. 249.
108 Victor Serge, *Year One of the Revolution*, intr. and trans. Peter Sedgwick (Chicago, IL: Holt Reinhardt and Winston, 1972), p. 11.
109 Serge, *Memoirs of a Revolutionary*, p. 367. My italics.
110 Ibid.
111 Matthew 19.29.
112 Matthew 20.16.
113 Serge, *Memoirs of a Revolutionary*, p. 123.
114 Ibid., p. 132.
115 Ibid., p. 134.
116 Ibid.
117 Ibid.
118 Ibid.
119 Ibid., p. 163.
120 Ibid., p. 191.
121 Ibid., p. 174.
122 Ibid., p. 348.
123 Ibid., p. 349.
124 Ibid., p. 381.
125 Ibid.
126 Ibid., p. 148.
127 Ibid., p. 201.
128 Ibid., p. 52.
129 Ibid., p. 44.
130 Ibid., p. 68.
131 Ibid., p. 169.
132 Ibid., p. 193.
133 This is the subject of part four of *Being and Nothingness*. Jean-Paul Sartre, *Being and Nothingness: An Essay on Phenomenological Ontology*, trans. and intr. Hazel E. Barnes (New York: Philosophical Library, 1956), pp. 433–5.
134 Jean-Paul Sartre, *Notebooks for an Ethics*, trans. David Pellauer (Chicago, IL and London, 1992), p. 17.
135 Sartre, *Notebooks*, p. 21.
136 Ibid., p. 24.
137 Ibid., p. 33.
138 Ibid.
139 Ibid., p. 84.
140 Serge, *Memoirs of a Revolutionary*, p. 228.
141 Ibid., p. 229.
142 Ibid.
143 Ibid., p. 85.
144 Ibid., p. 229.
145 Ibid., p. 5.
146 George Oppen, *Collected Poems* (New York: New Directions, 1975), p. 147.
147 Sartre, *Notebooks*, p. 554.
148 Ibid., p. 431.
149 Serge, *Memoirs of a Revolutionary*, p. 299.
150 Ibid., p. 334.
151 Ibid.
152 Ibid., p. 373.
153 Ibid.
154 Arendt, *Men in Dark Times*, p. 14.
155 Serge, *Memoirs of a Revolutionary*, p. 373.
156 Ibid., p. 374.
157 Acts 18.26–8: 'For he hath made of one blood all nations of men for to dwell on all the face of the earth, and hath determined the times before appointed, and the bounds of their habitation. That they should seek the Lord, if haply they might feel after him, and find him, though he be

not far from every one of us: For in him we live, and move, and have our being: as certain also of your own poets have said, For we are also his offspring.'

158 Serge, *Memoirs of a Revolutionary*, p. 339.

159 Ibid.

160 George Orwell, *Homage to Catalonia* (Harmondsworth: Penguin, 1966), p. 15.

161 Orwell, *Homage to Catalonia*, p. 29.

162 Ibid., pp. 62–3.

163 Ibid., p. 67.

164 There is a pertinent sentence or two by Mary McCarthy in her preface to Nancy Macdonald's book on the Spanish exiles, *Homage to the Spanish Exiles* (New York: Insight Books, 1987), who speaks of the greater evocativeness of the testimonies in this work over the standard 'objective' histories, useful as they are, such as Hugh Thomas's *The Spanish Civil War* (New York: Harpers, 1961).

165 Orwell, *Homage to Catalonia*, p. 111.

166 Ibid., p. 102.

167 George Orwell to Dwight MacDonald, 4 April 1945, Dwight Macdonald Papers.

168 George Orwell to Dwight MacDonald, 5 December 1946, Dwight Macdonald Papers.

Section II

1 Victor Serge to Dwight Macdonald, 11 October 1941.

2 Ibid.

3 Victor Serge, 'Ernst Toller s'est tué dans une chambre d'hôtel de New York ...', Victor Serge Papers.

4 Victor Serge to Dwight Macdonald, 6 March 1941, Victor Serge Papers.

5 Review of the work of Henry Poulaille, Victor Serge Papers.

6 Victor Serge, 'Musée du Soir', *La Wallonie*, n.d. on clipping but c.1939, Victor Serge Papers.

7 Walter Benjamin, 'Unpacking my Library' in *Illuminations*, intr. Hannah Arendt (London: Fontana, 1973), p. 61.

8 Victor Serge, 'Le Musée de Guadalajara', Victor Serge Papers. The typescript is much scribbled over and is dated 16 January 1945. No further references are given.

9 T.A. Bernshtam, 'Russian Folk Culture and Folk Religion' in Marie Mandelstam Balzer (ed.), *Russian Traditional Culture* (Armonk, NY and London: M.E. Sharpe, 1992), p. 43.

10 Serge, *Memoirs of a Revolutionary*, p. 201.

11 Ibid., p. 262.

12 Ibid.

13 Ibid.

14 Ibid.

15 Ibid., pp. 263, 717.

16 'Testimony', *Shorter Oxford English Dictionary*; 'Témoinage', *Le Petit Robert*.

17 Serge, *Memoirs of a Revolutionary*, p. 264.

18 Ibid., p. 265.

19 Ibid.

20 Ibid., p. 266.

21 Ibid.

22 Ibid., p. 267.

23 Ibid.

24 Ibid., p. 268.

25 Ibid., p. 272.

26 January 1925 saw the First All-Union Conference of Proletarian Writers which demanded 'the recognition of the principle of hegemony' of proletarian literature. Herman Ermolaev, *Soviet Literary Theories, 1917–1934:*

The Genesis of Socialist Realism (Berkeley and Los Angeles, CA: University of California Press, 1963), p. 35.

27 Roger Shattuck, 'Having Congress: The Shame of the Thirties' in Tom Conner (ed.), *André Gide's Politics: Rebellion and Ambivalence* (Houndsmill: Palgrave, 2000), pp. 139–59.

28 Frances Stonar Saunders, 'The Meetings of Minds: Writers for the Defence of Freedom Conference, Paris, 1935'. BBC Radio 3, 1 September, 2005, producer: Matthew Dodd.

29 Serge, *Memoirs of a Revolutionary*, p. 263.

30 Jean-Paul Sartre, 'John Dos Passos and "1919"' in *Literary and Philosophical Essays*, trans. Annette Michelson (London: Radius / Hutchinson, 1968).

31 Simone de Beauvoir to Jean-Paul Sartre, 21 December 1939, in *Letters to Sartre*, trans. Quintin Hoare (London: Radius, 1991), p. 223.

32 Sartre, 'John Dos Passos and "1919"', p. 93.

33 Ibid.

34 Ibid., p. 94.

35 Ibid., p. 95.

36 Ibid., p. 91.

37 Ibid., p. 89.

38 Ibid., p. 90.

39 Ibid.

40 John Dos Passos, *Nineteen Nineteen, U.S.A.* (1932; Harmondsworth: Penguin, 1966), p. 617.

41 Ibid., p. 616.

42 Serge, *Memoirs of a Revolutionary*, p. 144.

43 Jean-Paul Sartre, 'Myth and Reality in the Theatre' in *Politics and Literature*, trans. J.A. Underwood (London: Calder and Boyars, 1973), p. 27.

44 Walter Benjamin, 'Theses on the Philosophy of History' in *Illuminations*, ed. Arendt, p. 257.

45 George Orwell, *Nineteen Eighty-Four* (1949; Harmondsworth: Penguin, 1987), p. 184.

46 Benjamin, 'Theses on the Philosophy of History', pp. 255–6.

47 Raymond Aron, *Introduction to the Philosophy of History*, trans. George J. Irwin (London: Weidenfeld and Nicolson, 1961), p. 36.

48 Benjamin, 'Theses on the Philosophy of History', p. 257.

49 Ibid., p. 262.

50 Ibid., p. 264.

51 Ibid., p. 265.

52 Ibid., p. 257.

53 Ibid., pp. 255–6.

54 Ricoeur, *Time and Narrative*, I, p. 92.

55 Serge, *Men in Prison*, p. xxv.

56 Ibid., p. xxv.

57 Ibid., p. 1.

58 Ibid., p. 10.

59 Ibid., p. 20.

60 Ibid., p. 160.

61 Arendt, *Men in Dark Times*, p. 97.

62 Serge, *Men in Prison*, p. 28.

63 Arthur Rimbaud, *A Season in Hell and The Drunken Boat*, trans Louise Varèse (New York: New Directions, 1961), p. 93. Serge, *Men in Prison*, p. 100.

64 Ibid.

65 Ibid., pp. 100–1.

66 Ibid., p. 20.

67 Ibid., p. 18.

68 Ibid., p. 226.

69 Ibid., p. 124.

70 Ibid., p. 246.

71 Ibid., p. 247.

72 Ibid.

73 Ibid.

74 Victor Serge, *Conquered City*, trans. and intr. Richard Greeman (London: Victor Gollancz, 1976), p. xii.
75 Serge, *Conquered City*, p. 1.
76 Ibid.
77 Ibid., p. 2.
78 Ibid., p. 4.
79 Jean-Paul Sartre, *Critique of Dialectical Reason*, trans. Alan Sheridan-Smith (London: New Left Books, 1976), p. 233.
80 Serge, *Conquered City*, p. 19.
81 See 'Arthur Arnould', *The Anarchist Encyclopaedia: a Gallery of Saints and Sinners*, http://recollectionbooks.com/bleed/Encyclopedia/ArnouldArthur.htm.
82 Susan Sontag, 'Cases of the Comrades: Why Victor Serge Should be as Famous as Koestler and Orwell', *Times Literary Supplement*, 9 April 2004, p. 15.
83 Serge, *The Case of Comrade Tulayev*, p. 321.
84 Ibid., p. 322.
85 Ibid., p. 197.
86 Ibid., p. 198.
87 Ibid., p. 200.
88 Ibid., p. 201.
89 Lewis Mumford, *Technics and Civilization* (1934; New York and London: Harcourt Brace Jovanovich, 1963), p. 14.
90 Ibid., p. 17.
91 Serge, *The Case of Comrade Tulayev*, p. 200.
92 Mumford, *Technics and Civilization*, p. 17.
93 Martin Heidegger, *The Concept of Time*, trans. William McNeill (Oxford: Blackwell, 1992), p. 17E.
94 Karl Marx, *Capital*, vol. I, trans. Ben Fowkes (Harmondsworth: Penguin, 1976), p. 376.
95 Heidegger, *The Concept of Time*, pp. 18E–19E.
96 Pilniak, *The Naked Year*, p. 137.
97 Mumford, *Technics and Civilization*, p. 22.
98 Ibid., p. 14.
99 Victor Serge, 'Sur les Routes du Caucases' (1942), Victor Serge Papers.
100 John Donne, 'A nocturnall upon S. Lucies day, Being the shortest day', in *The Poems of John Donne*, ed. Sir Herbert Grierson (London: Oxford University Press, 1933), p. 39.
101 Jean-Paul Sartre 'On *The Sound and the Fury*' in Jean-Paul Sartre, *Literary and Philosophical Essays*, trans. Annette Michelson (London: Radius/Hutchinson, 1968), p. 87.
102 Jean-Paul Sartre, *Search for a Method*, trans. Hazel E. Barnes (New York: Vintage, 1968), p. 10.
103 Paul Ricoeur, *History and Truth* (Evanston, IL: Northwestern University Press, 1965), p. 299.
104 Arpad Kadarkay, *Georg Lukács: Life, Thought and Politics* (Oxford: Blackwell, 1991), p. 305.
105 Victor Serge, *Midnight in the Century*, trans. Richard Greeman (London: Writers and Readers Publishing Cooperative, 1982), p. 79.
106 Jason Wehling: 'Anarchism and the History of the Black Flag', http://www.anarchy-movement.com/topic.php?ID=47. The discussion of blackness is indebted to this article.
107 Serge, *Midnight in the Century*, p. 95.
108 Ibid., p. 55.
109 Ibid.
110 Ibid., p. 56.
111 Ibid.
112 Ibid.
113 Ibid., p. 57.
114 Ibid., p. 65.
115 Ibid., p. 56.
116 Ibid., p. 60.

117 Ibid., p. 57.
118 Ibid., p. 242 (Greeman's afterword).
119 Ricoeur, *Time and Narrative*, II, p. 131.
120 Ibid., pp. 131–2.
121 Ricoeur, *Time and Narrative*, III, p. 133.
122 Ibid., p. 134.
123 Ricoeur, *Time and Narrative*, II, p. 144.
124 Ibid., p. 49.
125 Ibid., p. 151.
126 Cited in Edward Thompson, *William Morris: Romantic to Revolutionary* (London: Merlin Press, 1977), p. 722.

Part 2: Posts of the Good: Dwight Macdonald's politics

Section I

1 Victor Gollancz, *My Dear Timothy: An Autobiographical Letter to his Grandson* (Harmondsworth: Penguin, 1952), p. 333.
2 Samuel Taylor Coleridge, 'The Rime of the Ancient Mariner' in *The Poems of Samuel Taylor Coleridge* (1912; London: Oxford University Press, 1960), p. 202.
3 Victor Serge, *Memoirs of a Revolutionary*, trans. Peter Sedgwick (1951; Oxford: Oxford University Press, 1963), p. 360.
4 Paul Fussell, *Wartime: Understanding and Behaviour in the Second World War* (Oxford and New York: Oxford University Press), p. 219.
5 George Orwell, *Nineteen Eighty-Four* (1949; London: Penguin, 1989), p. 92.
6 Gregory D. Sumner, *Dwight Macdonald and the* politics *Circle* (Ithaca, NY: Cornell University Press, 1996), p. 127.
7 Hazel Rowley, *Richard Wright: The Life and Times* (New York: Henry Holt, 2001), p. 288.
8 Ibid., pp. 288–90.
9 Note also the delightful extravagance of Richard King's comment in relation to Marx's and Dewey's insistence that philosophy realize itself in action, in his still important book of 1972: 'John Dewey was America's Karl Marx.' Richard King, *The Party of Eros: Radical Social Thought and the Realm of Freedom* (Chapel Hill, NC: University of North Carolina Press, 1972), p. 28.
10 Simone de Beauvoir to Dwight Macdonald, 12 February 1947 in Michael Wreszin (ed.), *A Moral Temper: The Letters of Dwight Macdonald* (Chicago, IL: Ivan R. Dee, 2001), p. 136.
11 See Christopher Hill's commentary on Milton's *Paradise Lost* (X: 312–13, 348) in Christopher Hill, *Milton and the English Revolution*, (London: Faber and Faber, 1977), p. 391.
12 Dwight Macdonald, *politics* (September 1945), pp. 285–6.
13 Simone de Beauvoir to Jean-Paul Sartre, 7 February 1947, in Simone de Beauvoir, *Letters to Sartre*, trans. and ed. Quintin Hoare (London: Radius, 1991), p. 422.
14 Sumner, *Dwight Macdonald and the* politics *Circle*, p. ix.
15 Ibid., p. 16.
16 Ibid., p. 65.
17 Ibid., pp. 71–3.
18 Caffi is not dealt with here given the more than adequate commentaries in the works by Sumner and Wrezsin.
19 Sumner, *Dwight Macdonald and the* politics *Circle*, p. 77.
20 Ibid., p. 87.

21 I am here indebted to papers given by Timothy Gray ('Pacific Pacifism: Morris Graves and the New American Poets'), Paul Merchant ('"Justice will take us millions of intricate moves": William Stafford and the Commitment to Pacifism') and Philip Metres ('From Utopian Hopes to a Chronicle of Division: William Everson, the Fine Arts Camp, and Pacifist Poetry During World War II'), which were all given at the excellent conference 'Poetries of the 1940s: American and International', given by the National Poetry Foundation at the University of Maine, Orono, June 2004.

22 Sumner accurately talks of his insensitivity to the 'religious left'. See Sumner, *Dwight Macdonald and the* politics *Circle*, pp. 113–14.

23 Ibid., p. 113.

24 Kenneth Rexroth to Dwight Macdonald, 29 October 1945. Those referred to are T.S. Eliot, Etienne Gilson and Jacques Maritain. In a letter of 22 November 1946 Rexroth suggested reviews of books by Henry Miller, Patchen, Goodman, Comfort, Woodcock, Savage, Everson and himself.

25 Karl Marx, 'Manifesto of the Communist Party' in *The Revolutions of 1848: Political Writings: A Critical Note: Volume 1*, ed. and intr. David Fernback (Harmondsworth: Penguin in association with New Left Review, 1973), p. 89.

26 Dr Reinhold Niebuhr was Chair of the American Friends of German Freedom and founded the Emergency Rescue Committee that enabled the activity of Varian Fry. See the prologue to Mary Jayne Gold, *Crossroads Marseille, 1940* (New York: Doubleday, 1980).

27 Karl Marx, *Capital Vol. I*, trans. Ben Fowkes (Harmondsworth: Penguin, 1976), p. 740.

28 Karl Marx, *Economic and Philosophic Manuscripts of 1844*, ed. Dirk J. Struik (London: Lawrence and Wishart, 1970), p. 148.

29 Sumner joins the current fashion for picking over Myrdal, and cites Ellison on Myrdal's sometimes less than politically correct articulation of black culture (p. 105). Whatever *An American Dilemma*'s current limitations are seen to be it is worth noting that Ellison's Cold War politics were also less than immaculate – especially given his appalling caricature of communists and West Indians in the second section of *Invisible Man*, and the defeatist fatalisms of its navel-gazing protagonist in its concluding pages – music though all this was to McCarthyite ears. The West Indian population was certainly more politically radicalized than African-Americans at the time, given their struggles with the British Empire. Richard Wright was also surely right to say that no one in the United States apart from Myrdal and his team had made such a serious or sustained effort to understand white American racism.

30 Sumner, *Dwight Macdonald and the* politics *Circle*, p. 112.

31 Muriel Rukeyser, *Theory of Flight* (New Haven, CT: Yale University Press, 1935), p. 37.

32 As an example of the contradictions of 'gigantism' for good and evil see Mike Davis, *City of Quartz* (New York: Vintage, 1992).

33 Sumner, *Dwight Macdonald and the* politics *Circle*, p. 167.

34 Kenneth Rexroth to Dwight Macdonald, 12 October 1939.

35 29 September 1945. Dewey's emphasis on infant-oriented educational liberalism was a common-place charge against him from the left at the time. Richard King endeavours to defend Dewey from this charge in *The Party of Eros*, p. 29.

36 Rexroth to Macdonald, 3 Jan. 1946.

37 Rexroth to Macdonald, 17 Mar. 194?.

38 Kenneth Rexroth to Dwight Macdonald, n.d. but probably 1946.

39 Ibid.

40 Kenneth Rexroth to Dwight Macdonald, n.d. but probably 1946.

41 Rexroth to Macdonald, 22 Nov. 1946.

42 Leon Trotsky, 'The USSR in War', *The New International* (November 1939).

43 Cited in Dwight Macdonald, 'The Root is Man, I', *politics* (June 1946), p. 98.

44 Ibid.

45 Ibid.

46 Ibid.

47 Ibid.

48 Ibid., p. 101.

49 Alexis de Tocqueville, *Œuvres complètes* (Paris: La nouvelle revue française, 1961), I, vol. 2, p. 271. See also my discussion in Clive Bush, *The Dream of Reason: American Consciousness and Cultural Achievement from Independence to the Civil War* (London: Edward Arnold, 1977), p. 126.

50 Macdonald, 'The Root is Man, I', p. 103.

51 Lewis Carroll, *Alice Through the Looking Glass* in *The Works of Lewis Carroll* (London: Spring Books, 1965), p. 174.

52 *Macbeth*, Act 5, Scene 5, lines 21–2.

53 A detailed review of the changing position relating to Macdonald is given in Sumner, *Dwight Macdonald*, pp. 87–99.

54 Simone Weil, *The Need for Roots*, trans. A.S. Willis (London and New York: Routledge, 1978), pp. 151–3.

55 Macdonald, 'The Root is Man, I', p. 105.

56 Ibid., p. 109.

57 Ibid., p. 113.

58 Ibid. Cf. Luke 6.44: 'For every tree is known by its fruit. For of thorns men do not gather figs, nor of a bramble bush gather grapes.'

59 Macdonald, 'The Root is Man, I', p. 113.

60 Lewis Mumford, *The Pentagon of Power* (London: Secker and Warburg, 1970), p. 39.

61 Bertolt Brecht, *Journals 1834–1955*, trans. Hugh Rorrison, ed. John Willet (New York: Routledge, 1996), p. 139.

62 Ibid., p. 276.

63 Ibid., p. 229. In Hungary during the Cold War Soviet authorities originally banned 'decadent' western popular music, until they realized that its paralysing volume was a useful weapon against free discussion in public places.

64 Macdonald, 'The Root is Man, I', p. 197.

65 Ibid., p. 198. Weil, *The Need for Roots*, pp. 245–6.

66 Macdonald, 'The Root is Man, I', p. 199.

67 Ibid.

68 Ibid., p. 200.

69 Ibid.

70 George Santayana, *The Life of Reason: Or, The Phases of Human Progress* (New York: Scribner's, 1905–6), p. 284.

71 Macdonald, 'The Root is Man, I', p. 203.

72 Ibid., p. 204.

73 Ibid., p. 206.
74 Ibid.
75 Mumford, *The Pentagon of Power*, p. 115.
76 Macdonald, 'The Root is Man, I', p. 206.
77 Ibid.
78 Ibid.
79 'A Life of Dissent: Remembering E.P. Thompson', Channel 4 Rear Window series, broadcast 18 September 1994, produced by Tariq Ali, directed by Alexandra Anderson.
80 Theodore Roszak, 'Introduction' to E.F. Schumacher, *Small is Beautiful: Economics as if People Mattered* (New York: Harper and Row, 1973), pp. 3–4.
81 Sumner, *Dwight Macdonald and the* politics *Circle*, p. 171.
82 Kenneth Rexroth to Dwight Macdonald, n.d. (1946).
83 Wreszin, *A Moral Temper*, p. 195.
84 Ibid., p. 134.
85 Sumner, *Dwight Macdonald and the* politics *Circle*, p. 172.
86 Ibid., p. 173.
87 Ibid., p. 174.
88 Ibid., p. 175.
89 Daniel Bell to Dwight Macdonald, 19 July 1944. Macdonald's view of Bell soured later in their relationship. He felt Bell had sold his soul for a mess of academic potage, shifting with political winds and critical fashion. Worse still, he thought that his writing had become abstract and jargonized in the worst academic manner. Dwight Macdonald to Daniel Bell, 11 December 1961 and 18 January 1965.
90 Hannah Arendt to Dwight Macdonald, 21 February 1945.
91 Hannah Arendt to Dwight Macdonald, 24 December 1946, 16 August 1951.
92 Hannah Arendt to Dwight Macdonald, 23 April 1965.
93 Hannah Arendt to Dwight Macdonald, 'Sunday' (n.d.), 1945.
94 Hannah Arendt to Dwight Macdonald, 16 August 1951.
95 Hannah Arendt, *The Origins of Totalitarianism* (1958; Cleveland, OH and New York: Meridan, 1967), p. 67.
96 Joanna Vecchiarelli Scott and Judith Chelius Stark, 'Rediscovering Hannah Arendt', in *Love and Saint Augustine: Hannah Arendt* (Chicago, IL and London: University of Chicago Press, 1996), p. 178.
97 That is the pretence that your nature or constructed identity does not allow you freedom to act.
98 Hannah Arendt, *The Human Condition* (New York: Doubleday Anchor, 1959), p. 13.
99 Ibid., p. 19.
100 Arendt, *The Origins of Totalitarianism*, p. 11.
101 Arendt, *The Human Condition*, p. 158.
102 Ibid., pp. 222–3.
103 Arendt, *The Origins of Totalitarianism*, pp. 389–459.
104 Arendt is quoting Karl Jaspers here. Hannah Arendt, 'Karl Jaspers: Citizen of the World' in *Men in Dark Times* (San Diego, CA: Harcourt Brace, 1968), p. 89.
105 Ibid., pp. 92–3.
106 Ibid., p. 92.
107 Hannah Arendt, 'Isak Dinesen' in *Men in Dark Times*, p. 98.
108 Ibid., p. 97.
109 Hannah Arendt, *The Life of the Mind* (San Diego, CA: Harcourt Brace, 1971), p. 78.
110 Ibid., p. 12.
111 Ibid., p. 21.
112 Ibid., p. 35.
113 Ibid., p. 106.

114 Ibid., p. 205.
115 Ibid.
116 1 Kings 19.12.
117 Arendt, *The Life of the Mind*, pp. 209–10.
118 Arendt, *The Origins of Totalitarianism*, p. 381n.
119 Ibid., p. 393n.
120 Ibid., p. 420.
121 Ibid.
122 Wreszin does not refer to him at all and Sumner mentions him factually in passing three times.
123 *Le grand mensonge* was followed in 1950 by *Sibérie, terre de l'exile et de l'industrialisation*, the title of which was more literally translated in its English version.
124 Sumner, *Dwight Macdonald and the* politics *Circle*, p. 25. Together, Sumner argues, they 'provided readers a detailed and authoritative history of the early development of the Stalinist dictatorship'.
125 Dwight Macdonald to Victor Serge, 15 June 1941.
126 Dwight Macdonald to Albert Camus, 3 September 1948.
127 Anton Ciliga, *The Russian Enigma* and *Siberia: Land of Exile and Industrialisation*, part I trans. Fernand G. Fernier and Anne Cliff, part II trans. Margaret and Hugo Dewar (London: Ink Links, 1979), pp. 81, 197.
128 Ibid., p. ix.
129 Jacques Ellul, *Propaganda: The Formation of Men's Attitudes*, trans. Konrad Kellen and Jean Lerner (New York: Vintage, 1973).
130 Ibid., pp. 294–302.
131 Ciliga, *The Russian Enigma*, p. 11.
132 The author remembers with some amusement his first visit to Budapest in 1975 where it was easy to observe important Communist Party members driving Mercedes, frequenting the best restaurants and dining at the Hilton hotel.
133 Ciliga, *The Russian Enigma*, p. 13.
134 Ibid., p. 65.
135 Ibid., p. 67.
136 Ibid., p. 69.
137 Ibid., p. 83.
138 Ibid., p. 83.
139 Ibid., p. 170.
140 Ibid., p. 200.
141 Ibid., p. 203.
142 Ibid., p. 312.
143 Ellul, *Propaganda*, p. 56.
144 Ciliga, *The Russian Enigma*, p. 298.
145 Ibid., p. 39.
146 Ecclesiastes 3.16.
147 Many later migrated to Los Angeles. They are distinguished by the retention of folkways and community singing of the ancient hymns, their instinct with Russian folk melodies, and recitations of prayers which retain old Slavonic words.
148 Mumford, *The Pentagon of Power*, pp. 390–1.
149 N.N. Veletskaia, 'Forms of Transformation of Pagan Symbolism in the Old Believer Tradition' in Marjorie Mandelstam Balzer (ed.), *Russian Traditional Culture: Religion, Gender, and Customary Law* (Armonk, NY and London: M.E. Sharpe, 1992), p. 48.
150 Ciliga, *The Russian Enigma*, p. 162.
151 Ibid.
152 Ibid., p. 210.
153 Ibid., p. 245.
154 Ibid., p. 92.
155 Ibid., p. 107.
156 Ibid., p. 145.
157 Franco Venturi, *Roots of Revolution: A History of the Populist and Socialist Movements in 19th Century Russia*, rev. edn, intr. Isaiah Berlin (London: Phoenix Press, 1971), p. xii.

158 Ciliga, *The Russian Enigma*, p. 246.
159 Ibid., p. 247.
160 Ibid., p. 282.
161 Ibid., p. 263.
162 Ibid., p. 271.
163 Ibid., p. 68.
164 Ibid., pp. 19, 43, 68, 70.
165 Ibid., p. 2.
166 Ibid., p. 24.
167 Ibid., p. 54.
168 Ibid., p. 192.
169 Leo Tolstoy, *War and Peace*, trans. Rosemary Edmonds (London: Penguin, 1982), pp. 1370–1.
170 Venturi, *Roots of Revolution*, pp. lxi–lxiii.
171 Ciliga, *The Russian Enigma*, p. 27.
172 Ibid., pp. 27–8.
173 Ibid., p. 58.
174 Ibid., p. 76.
175 Ibid.
176 Ibid.
177 Ibid., p. 176.
178 Mumford, *The Pentagon of Power*, commentaries to illustrations 8 and 9, between pp. 181–2.
179 Ciliga, *Siberia*, p. 452.
180 Ibid.
181 Adapted from email to author from Ela Kotkowska, 5 November 2004.
182 Herbert Marcuse, *One Dimensional Man: Studies in the Ideology of Advanced Industrial Society* (Boston, MA: Beacon Press, 1964), p. 5.
183 Ciliga, *Siberia*, p. 318.

Section II

1 Sumner, *Dwight Macdonald and the* politics *Circle*, p. 165.
2 Francine du Plessix Gray, *Simone Weil* (London: Weidenfeld and Nicolson, 2001), pp. 67, 69.
3 Simone Weil, 'The Iliad, or the Poem of Force', *politics* (November 1945), pp. 321–31. In the *Simone Weil Reader* (1977) 'force' is replaced with the word 'might'. See George A. Pachinas (ed.), *The Simone Weil Reader* (Mount Kisco, NY: Moyer Bell, 1977). Page references here are to the Mary McCarthy translation in *politics*.
4 Dwight Macdonald, *politics* (January 1946), p. 29.
5 Plessix Gray, *Simone Weil*, p. 142.
6 Dwight Macdonald, *politics* (January 1946), p. 29.
7 Simone Weil, *La condition ouvrière* (Paris: Gallimard, 1951), p. 186. My translation.
8 Ibid., p. 100. My translation.
9 Ibid., p. 103. My translation.
10 Simone Weil, *Lectures on Philosophy*, trans. Hugh Price (Cambridge: Cambridge University Press: 1978), pp. 198–9.
11 Simone Weil, 'Factory Work' in *The Simone Weil Reader*, p. 55.
12 Ibid., p. 56.
13 Ibid., p. 57.
14 Ibid.
15 Ibid., p. 58.
16 Jean Paul Sartre, *Nausea*, trans. Robert Baldick (1938; Harmondsworth: Penguin, 1965), p. 84. With the disappearance of Sunday as a day of rest, the workers' sense of time is even bleaker.
17 Weil, 'Factory Work', p. 64.
18 Ibid., p. 66.
19 Ibid., p. 69.
20 Ibid.
21 Weil, 'The Iliad, or the Poem of Force', p. 323.
22 Weil, 'Factory Work', p. 70.
23 Simone Weil, 'Analysis of Oppression' in *The Simone Weil Reader*, p. 136.
24 Simone Weil 'Reflections on War' in *politics* (February 1945), p. 52.
25 Ibid.

26 Ibid., p. 53.
27 Ibid.
28 Fussell, *Wartime*, p. 240. Fussell offers the parenthetical comment 'too bloody and ironic?'
29 Weil, 'The Iliad, or the Poem of Force', p. 326.
30 Ibid.
31 G.W.F. Hegel, *The Phenomenology of Mind*, trans. J.B. Baillie (London: Allen and Unwin, 1977), p. 207.
32 Ibid., p. 233.
33 Ibid., pp. 232–3.
34 Ibid., p. 325.
35 Ibid., p. 322.
36 Ibid., p. 323.
37 Ibid.
38 Henry David Thoreau, 'On the Duty of Civil Disobedience' in *Walden and Other Writings of David Henry Thoreau*, ed. Brooks Atkinson (New York: Modern Library, 1937), p. 637.
39 Hegel, *The Phenomenology of Mind*, p. 328.
40 Ibid., p. 325.
41 Ibid., p. 327.
42 Ibid., p. 323.
43 Ibid., p. 327.
44 Ibid., p. 329.
45 Ibid.
46 Simone Weil, *The Need for Roots* (1949; London and New York: Routledge, 1952), p. 42.
47 Ibid., pp. 48–9.
48 Ibid., p. 52.
49 Ibid., p. 57.
50 Ibid., p. 68.
51 Simone Weil, *Gravity and Grace*, trans. Arthur Wills, intr. Gustave Thibon (Lincoln, NE: University of Nebraska Press, 1997), p. 143.
52 Plessix Gray, *Simone Weil*, p. 169.
53 Pachnias (ed.), *The Simone Weil Reader*, p. 207.
54 Simone Weil, 'Decreation' in *The Simone Weil Reader*, p. 356.
55 See Pachinas (ed.), *The Simone Weil Reader*: 'The Responsibility of Writers'; 'Morality and Literature'; 'Human Personality'; and 'Friendship'.
56 Weil, *Gravity and Grace*, p. 206.
57 Kenneth Rexroth to Dwight Macdonald, 3 January 1946.
58 Possibly 'Reflections on War'.
59 Kenneth Rexroth to Dwight Macdonald, n.d. (1946?).
60 Weil, 'The Iliad, or the Poem of Force', p. 331.
61 James Baldwin, *Tell Me How Long the Train's Been Gone* (London: Corgi, 1970), p. 62.
62 Ann Fulton, *Apostles of Sartre: Existentialism in America, 1945–1963* (Evanston, IL: Northwestern University Press, 1999). I am largely indebted to this excellent book for the whole of the section on Sartre which follows here.
63 I remember, as a graduate student in 1965, an exciting and heady seminar with John Smith on just that subject, a seminar which ended with the distinguished Yale professor on the platform of a London bus, still passionately articulating the links and differences over the head of the bemused bus conductor as the sound of his voice disappeared along with the bus from the exit of King's College in the Strand towards Trafalgar Square. Smith, was, however, something of an exception.
64 Fulton, *Apostles of Sartre*, p. 10.
65 Ibid., p. 60.
66 Simone de Beauvoir, 'Eye for an Eye', trans. Mary McCarthy, *politics* (August 1947), p. 134.
67 Ibid., p. 135.
68 Ibid.
69 Ibid., p. 136.
70 Ibid.

71 Ibid., p. 138.
72 Ibid.
73 Ibid.
74 Ibid.
75 Ibid., p. 139. Cf. John 8.7: 'Let him that is without sin cast the first stone.'
76 De Beauvoir, 'Eye for an Eye', p. 139.
77 Nathaniel Hawthorne, *The Scarlet Letter* in *Collected Novels* (New York: Library of America, 1983), p. 286.
78 De Beauvoir, 'Eye for an Eye', p. 139.
79 Ibid., p. 139.
80 Ibid., p. 140.
81 Albert Camus, 'Neither Victims nor Executioners', *politics* (August 1947), p. 141.
82 Ibid.
83 Ibid., p. 142.
84 Ibid., p. 141.
85 Ibid., p. 143.
86 Ibid.
87 Ibid.
88 Ibid.
89 Ibid., p. 144.
90 Ibid., p. 146.
91 Ibid., p. 162.
92 Ibid., p. 163.
93 Ibid.
94 Jean-Paul Sartre, *Search for a Method*, trans. Hazel Barnes (1963; New York: Vintage, 1968), p. 28.
95 Ibid., p. 48.
96 Ibid.
97 Jean-Paul Sartre, 'Materialism and Revolution', *politics* (August 1947), p. 165.
98 Ibid., p. 166.
99 Ibid., p. 167.
100 Ibid., p. 170.
101 Ibid., p. 172.
102 Sartre, *Search for a Method*, pp. 32–3n.
103 Maurice Merleau-Ponty, 'Marxism and Philosophy', *politics* (August 1947), p. 173.
104 Ibid.
105 Ibid.
106 Ibid.
107 Ibid., p. 174.
108 Ibid.
109 Ibid.
110 Ibid.
111 Ibid., p. 175.
112 Kai Bird and Lawrence Lifshultz (eds), *Hiroshima's Shadow: Writings on the Denial of History and the Smithsonian Controversy* (Stony Creek, CT: Pamphleteer's Press, 1998).
113 James Cameron, *Point of Departure: Experiment in Biography by James Cameron* (London: Arthur Barker, 1967), p. 285.
114 Brecht, *Journals 1834–1955*, p. 246.
115 Georges Bataille, 'On Hiroshima', *politics* (August 1947), p. 147.
116 Ibid.
117 Ibid., p. 148.
118 Ibid., p. 149.
119 The phrase is borrowed from Bataille's *Eroticism* where he discusses the inadequacy of the statistical modes of truth in the Kinsey Report. See Georges Bataille, *Eroticism*, trans. Mary Dalwood (London and New York: Marion Boyars, 1987), p. 154.
120 Georges Bataille, 'A Story of Rats' in *The Impossible*, trans. Robert Hurley, (San Francisco: City Lights, 1991), p. 17.
121 Georges Bataille, 'The Love of Truth and Justice and Marcel Proust's Socialism' in *Literature and Evil*, trans. Alistair Hamilton (London and New York, Marion Boyars, 1985), p. 144.
122 Brecht, *Journals 1834–1955*, p. 167.
123 Ibid., pp. 167, 229.
124 Kenneth Rexroth to Dwight Macdonald, 4 October 1945.

125 John Hersey, 'Hiroshima' in *Reporting World War II: Part Two American Journalism 1944–1946* (New York: Library of America, 1995), p. 811.
126 Ibid., p. 821. My italics.
127 Ibid., p. 831.
128 Ibid., p. 782.
129 Jean-Paul Sartre, *Literary and Philosophical Essays* (London: Hutchinson/Radius, 1968), pp. 90, 92. My italics.
130 Hersey, 'Hiroshima', p. 784.
131 Ibid.
132 Ibid., p. 785.
133 Ibid., p. 787.
134 Ibid., p. 855.
135 Ibid., p. 896.
136 Ibid., p. 789.
137 Ibid., p. 791.
138 Ibid., p. 801.
139 Ibid., p. 799.
140 One of the many plausible reasons argued in Kai Bird and Lawrence Lifschultz, 'The Legend of Hiroshima' in *Hiroshima's Shadow*, pp. xxxi–lxxvii.
141 Dwight Macdonald, 'The Bomb', *politics* (September 1945), pp. 258–9. See Bird and Lifschultz, 'The Legend of Hiroshima', pp. xxxi–lxxvii.
142 Macdonald, 'The Bomb', p. 259.
143 Ibid., p. 259.
144 Ibid., p. 260.

Part 3: 'My Dear Plutocratic but Lovely Friend': Dorothy Norman and TWICE A YEAR

Section I

1 The leading phrase is taken from a letter by J.J. Singh (president of the India League of America) to Dorothy Norman, 26 September 1951.
2 R.S. Pandit (ed., trans., intr.), *Ritusamhara* (Bombay: National Information and Publications, 1947), pp. 4–10. Cited in Vijaya Lakshmi Pandit, *The Scope of Happiness: A Personal Memoir* (1979; New Delhi: HarperCollins India, 2000), p. 399.
3 Henry Miller, *The Colossus of Maroussi* (1941; Harmondsworth: Penguin, 1967), pp. 200–1.
4 George Bernard Shaw, *Saint Joan* (1924).
5 William Carlos Williams to Dorothy Norman, 5 May 1941. Stieglitz's biographer notes his 'silence on both Hiroshima and Nagasaki as puzzling'. This wayward note indicates his position quite clearly. As for silence, the juxtaposition of the two *TWICE A YEAR* photographs speaks volumes. Sue Davidson Lowe, *Stieglitz: The Founding Father of Modern Photography* (London: Quartet Books, 1983), p. 375. Following Stieglitz's death, Mumford frequently mentioned his own essay on the bomb and matters relating to it in his letters to Dorothy Norman.
6 William Carlos Williams to Dorothy Norman, 17 October 1946.
7 Dorothy Norman to William Carlos Williams, 22 January 1947.
8 William Carlos Williams, 'What of Alfred Stieglitz?', Alfred Stieglitz Papers.
9 Dorothy Norman, 'Writing and Conversations of Alfred Stieglitz' in *TWICE A YEAR* (Fall–Winter 1938), p. 78.
10 William Carlos Williams to Dorothy Norman, 13 May 1941: 'Mrs Williams gave me a talking to when she read it [...]'.
11 Robert Lowell, 'For the Union Dead' in *Selected Poems* (London: Faber and Faber, 1965), p. 64.
12 Henry Miller to Dorothy Norman, 7 February 1940.

13 Pamphlets by and about Alfred Stieglitz, Alfred Stieglitz Papers.

14 Dorothy Norman, *Alfred Stieglitz: Introduction to an American Seer* (New York: Duell, Sloan and Pearce, 1960), p. 40.

15 Waldo Frank to Alfred Stieglitz, 9 August 1931.

16 Marcel Proust, *Pleasures and Days*, trans. Andrew Brown (London: Hesperus, 2004), p. 127.

17 Robert Jermaine Cole 'Scandinavian Arts and Crafts on view at Nordic Studio/Stieglitz Gives Feeling of Strong Power in Prints' (unidentified newspaper cutting), 21 March 1925. Pamphlets by and about Alfred Stieglitz, Alfred Stieglitz Papers.

18 Sue Davidson Lowe, *Stieglitz: The Founding Father of Modern Photography: A Memoir/Biography* (London: Quartet, 1983), p. 73.

19 Stephen Toulmin and June Goodfield, *The Architecture of Matter* (London: Hutchinson, 1962), pp. 248–9.

20 David Campany, 'Art, Science and Speculation: August Strindberg's Photographics' in Olle Granath, *August Strindberg: Painter, Photographer, Writer* (London: Tate Publishing, 2005).

21 Samuel Taylor Coleridge, 'The Eolian Harp' in *The Poems of Coleridge* (London: Oxford University Press, 1912), p. 102.

22 Ibid., pp. 102–4.

23 Herman Melville, *Redburn, White Jacket, Moby-Dick* (New York: Library of America, 1983), p. 1127.

24 Norman, *Introduction to an American Seer*, p. 36.

25 Ibid.

26 Ibid.

27 Dorothy Norman, 'Writing and Conversations of Alfred Stieglitz', *TWICE A YEAR* (Fall–Winter 1938), p. 109.

28 Jean Toomer to Alfred Stieglitz, 21 January 1924. Alfred Stieglitz Papers.

29 Lewis Mumford. 'The Metropolitan Motion' in Lewis Mumford, Waldo Frank, Dorothy Norman, Paul Rosenfeld and Harold Rugg (eds), *America and Alfred Stieglitz: A Collective Portrait* (Garden City, NY: Doubleday, Doran & Co., 1934), p. 47.

30 Mumford. 'The Metropolitan Motion', p. 47.

31 Gaston Bachelard, *The Poetics of Reverie*, trans. Daniel Russell (Boston, MA: Beacon Press, 1971), p. 158.

32 Alfred Stieglitz to Marsden Harley, 27 October 1923. Alfred Stieglitz Papers.

33 Lewis Mumford to Alfred Stieglitz, 3 July 1933. Alfred Stieglitz Papers.

34 Lewis Mumford to Alfred Stieglitz, 15 November 1943. Alfred Stieglitz Papers.

35 Robert Flint, 'Post-Impressionism' in Mumford et al. (eds), *America and Alfred Stieglitz*, p. 138.

36 Kathleen Raine, *Blake and Tradition* (1968; London: Routledge, 2002).

37 Daniel V. Erdman, *Blake, Prophet against Empire: A Poet's Interpretation of the History of his Own Times* (Princeton, NJ: Princeton University Press, 1954).

38 Marsden Hartley to Alfred Stieglitz, 1917. Alfred Stieglitz Papers.

39 Charles Henry Caffin, 'Whistler', *Camera Work* 12 (1905).

40 Marsden Hartley to Alfred Stieglitz, ? July 1911, 1 February 1913, 28 September 1913, 19 November 1929, 12 March 1929. Alfred Stieglitz Papers.

41 Hart Crane to Alfred Stieglitz, 15 April 1923. Alfred Stieglitz Papers.
42 Cited by Eric Mottram, from Robbe-Grillet's *Future of the Novel* in Faith Pullin (ed.), *New Perspectives on Melville* (Edinburgh: Edinburgh University Press, 1978), p. 230.
43 Alfred Stieglitz to Lewis Mumford, 28 August 1929. Lewis Mumford Papers.
44 Mumford, 'The Metropolitan Motion', p. 49.
45 Dorothy Norman, 'From the Writings and Conversations of Alfred Stieglitz', *TWICE A YEAR* (Fall–Winter 1938), p. 94.
46 Norman, *Alfred Stieglitz*, p. 36.
47 Robin Tanner, *The Etcher's Craft* (Bristol: Friends of Bristol Art Gallery, 1980), p. 21.
48 Ibid., p. 18.
49 Charles Olson, 'Lear and Moby-Dick', *TWICE A YEAR*, vol. I (Fall–Winter 1938), pp. 175–6.
50 Sadakichi Hartman, *Camera Work* 36 (1911), pp. 19–20.
51 Olson, 'Lear and Moby-Dick', p. 176.
52 Olson noted that Melville checked in the margin of *Antony and Cleopatra*, 'That truth should be silent I had almost forgot.' Olson, 'Lear and Moby-Dick', p. 167.
53 Alfred Stieglitz to Lewis Mumford, 7 July 1928. Lewis Mumford Papers.
54 Alfred Stieglitz to Marie Boursault, 19 July 1917. Alfred Stieglitz Papers.
55 D.H. Lawrence to Alfred Stieglitz 12 September 1928. Alfred Stieglitz Papers.
56 Dorothy Brett to Dorothy Norman, 23 November 1954.
57 Randolph Bourne, 'The Puritan's Will to Power', in *The Radical Will Randolph Bourne, Selected Writings 1911–1918*, ed. Olaf Hansen, preface Christopher Lasch (New York: Urizen Books, 1977), p. 300.
58 Alfred Stieglitz to Marie Boursault, 26 August 1916 and 3 September 1916. Alfred Stieglitz Papers.
59 Alfred Stieglitz to Marie Boursault, 26 August 1917. Alfred Stieglitz Papers.
60 Alfred Stieglitz to Waldo Frank, 6 July 1935. Alfred Stieglitz Papers.
61 Adolff Wolff to Alfred Stieglitz, 1 October 1914. Alfred Stieglitz Papers.
62 Marsden Hartley to Alfred Stieglitz, 2 August 1917. Alfred Stieglitz Papers.
63 Isidore Schneider, 'Paul Rosenfeld', *New Masses* (27 August 1946), p. 20.
64 Alfred Stieglitz to Seligman, 18 July 1932 and 16 July 1933. Alfred Stieglitz Papers.
65 For a detailed assessment of the subject in contemporary gender study terms, see Vivien Green Fryd, *Art and the Crisis of Marriage: Edward Hopper and Georgia O'Keeffe* (Chicago, IL: University of Chicago Press, 2002).
66 Dorothy Norman, *Encounters: A Memoir* (San Diego, CA: Harcourt Brace, 1987).
67 Lewis Mumford, *Sidewalk Critic: Lewis Mumford Writings on New York*, ed. Robert Wojtowicz (New York: Princeton Architectural Press, 1998), pp. 112, 115–16.
68 Mary Lescaze to Dorothy Norman, 28 November 1951. Dorothy Norman Papers.
69 Dorothy Norman to Anaïs Nin, 24 November 1942. Dorothy Norman Papers.
70 Dorothy Norman to William Carlos Williams, 29 June 1937. Dorothy Norman Papers.

71 Edward Dahlberg to William Carlos Williams, 27 October 1937. Dorothy Norman Papers.
72 Edward Dahlberg to William Carlos Williams, 5 November 1937.
73 Norman, *Encounters*, p. 126.
74 Dorothy Norman to Lewis Mumford, November [?] 1938. Mumford Papers, University of Pennsylvania.
75 Norman, *Encounters*, p. 40.
76 Ibid., p. 44.
77 Ibid., p. 62.
78 Ibid., p. 47.
79 Dorothy Norman to Edward Dahlberg, 5 November 1937.
80 Edward Dahlberg to William Carlos Williams, 9 December 1937. William Carlos Williams to Edward Dahlberg, 13 December 1937.
81 Dorothy Norman to Paul Rosenfeld, 15 September 1938.
82 Henry Miller to Dorothy Norman, (Friday) February? 1940.
83 Muriel Rukeyser, 'The Fear of Poetry', in *TWICE A YEAR*, vol. VII (Fall–Winter, 1941), pp. 20–1.
84 Marcel Proust, 'La mort de Baldassare Silvande Vicompte de Sylvania', trans. Emilie Amram, *TWICE A YEAR*, vol. II (Spring–Summer, 1939), pp. 155–75.
85 Nicholas Calas, 'Transforming the Past', *TWICE A YEAR*, vol. VII (Fall–Winter, 1941), p. 127.
86 See Norman, *Encounters*, pp. 157–9.
87 Victor Serge to Dorothy Norman, 13 January 1947. Victor Serge Papers.
88 Dwight Macdonald to Dorothy Norman, 30 March 1943. Dorothy Norman Papers.
89 Dorothy Norman to Lewis Mumford, November 1938. Lewis Mumford Papers.
90 Lewis Mumford 'Memorandum on the United Nations Organization Headquarters and Community', typescript, c.1946. Parts of the typescript were published in *The Journal of the AIA* (December 1946) and in *Progressive Architecture* (April 1946). Lewis Mumford Papers.
91 Lewis Mumford, 'A Chronology of Events 1945–1949', n.d. Lewis Mumford Papers.
92 Lewis Mumford to Dorothy Norman, 30 September 1960.
93 Lewis Mumford to Dorothy Norman, 16 July 1960.
94 Roger N. Baldwin, 'Should the Dies Committee Die?', *TWICE A YEAR*, vol. II (Spring–Summer 1939), p. 232.
95 Roi Otley to Dorothy Norman, 27 August 1944.
96 Victor Riesel, 'June–December – 1941', *TWICE A YEAR*, vols VIII–IX (Fall–Winter 1942), p. 295.
97 Ibid., p. 297.
98 Gallman Gottesman (president of Pan-American Films), 'Petition for Review to The Board of Regents of the State of New York' (appeal against the refusal to license *The Forgotten Village*), *TWICE A YEAR*, vols VIII–IX (Fall–Winter 1942), pp. 321–41.
99 *TWICE A YEAR*, vol. IX (Fall–Winter 1942), pp. 321–42.
100 Horace M. Kallen, 'Behind the Bertrand Russell Case', *TWICE A YEAR*, vols V–VI (Fall–Winter 1940), pp. 441–66.
101 *New York Times* obituary, 25 July 1951, Albert Barnes file, Dorothy Norman Papers.
102 Norman, *Encounters*, p. 20.
103 Arthur Koestler, 'Scum of the Earth – 1942', *TWICE A YEAR*, vols X–XI (Spring–Summer, Fall–Winter 1943), pp. 81–90.
104 Max Nomad, 'Civil and Cultural Liberties in Russia', *TWICE A YEAR*,

vols V–VI (Fall–Winter 1940), pp. 499–500.

105 Alfred Kazin, 'War, Education and People (Britain)', *TWICE A YEAR*, vols XIV–XV (Fall–Winter 1946–7), pp. 120–43.

106 David Riesman, 'Selections from Writings on Civil Liberties', *TWICE A YEAR*, vols X–XI (Spring–Summer, Fall–Winter 1943), p. 289.

107 Ibid., p. 290.

108 [Selected] 'Committee Hearings on Un-American Activities', Eighteenth Congress: 20–31 October 1947, reprinted in *TWICE A YEAR* (tenth anniversary issue) (New York: Twice a Year Press, 1947), p. 474.

109 Interview with Alo Altripp, single typed page of an interview, n.d. Dorothy Norman Papers.

110 Harold Clurman 'Soviet Diary', 6 May 1934, typescript. Dorothy Norman Papers.

111 V.L. Pandit to Dorothy Norman, 13 June 1948.

112 'Lippmann was not anti-Franco and believed Hitler's statements way back in 1933.' Louis Fischer to Dorothy Norman, 23 October 1943.

113 Waldo Frank to Dorothy Norman, n.d.

114 Hannah Arendt to Dorothy Norman, 28 July 1947.

115 Albert Camus, 'The Human Crisis', *TWICE A YEAR*, vols XIV–XV (Fall–Winter 1946–7), p. 23.

116 Ibid., p. 26.

117 Ibid., p. 27.

118 Lewis Mumford to Dorothy Norman, 23 February 1946, 14 March 1946, 23 May 1948, 22 June 1948.

119 Lewis Mumford to Dorothy Norman, 28 July 1948.

120 Lewis Mumford to Dorothy Norman, 26 May 1950, 17 July 1952.

121 Norman wanted Mary Beard to write on women's history for *TWICE A YEAR*. Unfortunately she was too involved in writing history with her husband to oblige. Norman, *Encounters*, p. 130.

122 Eleanor Roosevelt, 'On My Own', *New York Post* (8 March 1958), p. 72.

123 Eleanor Roosevelt to Dorothy Norman, 3 March 1961.

124 Dorothy Norman to Eleanor Roosevelt, 12 January 1952, 18 May 1959.

125 Eleanor Roosevelt, 'I Learn about the Communists', *Saturday Evening Post* (22 February 1958), p. 59.

126 Isaiah Berlin, review of John Carswell, *The Exile: A Life of Ivy Litvinov*, *Sunday Times* (8 May 1984), p. 41.

127 Victor Serge, 'La renvoie de Litvinov', *La Wallonie*, 13–14 May 1939.

128 See Arthur Upham Pope, *Maxim Litvinoff* (New York: L.B. Fisher, 1943), pp. 319f. This wartime biography glosses over the purges and collectivisation, and indicts Trotsky for lack of pragmatic realism in the building of the Soviet State making much of his globally scattered 'fanatical' followers. Ivy Litvinov made corrections to some factual errors in a copy in the Dorothy Norman Papers. She wrote in the margin for example when Pope asserted Litvinov as a young man, was thought by people with eligible daughters to be a good catch (p. 97): 'Rubbish he didn't know any people like that!'

129 Ivy Litvinov to Dorothy Norman, 6 April 1943. Cited in Norman, *Encounters*, p. 165.

130 Dorothy Norman 'Editor's Introduction', *TWICE A YEAR*, vol. VII (Fall–Winter 1941), p. 13.

131 Norman must have given her vols VII and XIII–IX because the children's poems are in volume VII and the Agnes Enters diary excerpts, 'Hollywood horrors', are in the double volume XIII–IX, pp. 112–24.
132 Ivy Litvinov to Dorothy Norman, 6 April 1943.
133 Ivy Litvinov to Dorothy Norman, 26 April 1943. Cited in Norman, *Encounters*, p. 164.
134 Ivy Litvinov to Dorothy Norman, 30 April 1943.
135 It had originally been published by Heinemann in 1930 and had been called *His Master's Voice*.
136 Ivy Litvinov, *Moscow Mystery* (New York: Coward-McGann, c.1943), flyleaf.
137 Ibid., introduction, n.p.
138 Ibid., pp. 18–19.
139 Ibid., p. 76.
140 Ibid., p. 242.
141 Ibid., p. 82.
142 Ibid., p. 35.
143 Ibid., p. 258.
144 Carswell, *The Exile*, p. 115. The biographical details selected here rely on this work.
145 Ibid., p. 151.
146 Anaïs Nin, 'Birth', *TWICE A YEAR* (Fall–Winter 1938), p. 137.
147 Ibid., p. 135.
148 Simone de Beauvoir, *The Second Sex*, trans. and ed. H.M. Parshley (London: Picador, 1988), p. 245.
149 Ibid., p. 180.
150 Anaïs Nin, *The Diary of Anaïs Nin, 1934–1939* (New York: Harcourt Brace Jovanovich, 1969), p. 267.
151 Ibid., p. 12.
152 Ibid., p. 14.
153 Ibid., p. 45.
154 Ibid., pp. 53, 67.
155 Ibid., p. 76.
156 Ibid., p. 144.
157 Ibid., p. 157.
158 Ibid., p. 231.
159 Ibid., p. 118.
160 Dorothy Norman to Anaïs Nin, n.d.
161 Anaïs Nin to Dorothy Norman, n.d.
162 Dorothy Norman to Anaïs Nin, 24 November 1942.
163 Her memoir shows Norman extremely sensitive about her privileged background and about her husband's wealth. See Norman, *Encounters*, p. 86: 'Edward and I are living on money gained in a system he is trying to fight. I am disturbed both about not earning my own living and about my father's difficulties. I even feel guilty about wanting to help more and more causes.'
164 Dorothy Norman to Anaïs Nin, 15 June 1944.
165 Lewis Mumford to Dorothy Norman, 18 March 1931.
166 Norman for example, in her edition of her correspondence with Indira Gandhi, p. 25, noted that in 1954 she planned to visit the hill towns of northern Italy and attend the Jungian Eranos Conference in Ascona, Switzerland. The conference was to include Mircea Eliade, Henry Corbin, Suzuki, Gershom Scholem among others.
167 'Gandhi's and Viceroy's Letters', *TWICE A YEAR*, vol. X (Spring–Summer 1943), pp. 60–3. George Bernard Shaw, 'From a Message to the Tagore Society', *TWICE A YEAR*, vol. X (Spring–Summer 1943), p. 64.
168 The four participants in the broadcast were Louis Fischer, John Goette, Lt Col. W. Stewart-Robbie and Fred F. Clark.
169 'Freedom for India', sponsored by the Blue Network and the American Economic Foundation. Broadcast in

the *Wake Up America* series over the Blue Network, 29 November 1942, *TWICE A YEAR*, vol. X (Spring–Summer 1943), pp. 46–59.

170 See Anne Guthrie, *Madame Ambassador: The Life of Vijaya Lakshmi Pandit* (New York: Harcourt Brace, 1962), pp. 128–32.

171 Dorothy Norman, *Nehru: The First Sixty Years*, 2 vols (New York: John Day Company, 1965).

172 These biographical details are from Guthrie, *Madame Ambassador*.

173 Nayantara Sahgal, *Prison and Chocolate Cake* (London: Victor Gollancz, 1954), p. 19. I am thinking, of course, of Conrad's famous short story 'Youth'.

174 Sahgal, *Prison and Chocolate Cake*, p. 28.

175 Ibid., p. 29.

176 Ibid., p. 34.

177 Guthrie, *Madame Ambassador*, p. 64.

178 Sahgal, *Prison and Chocolate Cake*, p. 30.

179 Ibid., p. 124.

180 Ibid., p. 126.

181 Ibid.

182 Ibid., p. 133.

183 Ibid., p. 138.

184 Ibid., p. 158.

185 Ibid., pp. 154–6.

186 See Pandit, *The Scope of Happiness*.

187 Chandalekha Pandit, 'The Infanticide' and 'The Garden' in *TWICE A YEAR* (Fall–Winter 1945), pp. 342–8.

188 Dorothy Norman to Vijaya Lakshmi Pandit, 26 September 1945.

189 There is an exchange between Norman Thomas and Norman in 1954 over India. Thomas complains that Norman is too uncritical of Nehru to which she replied that while she appreciated his criticism, her view was that India was so misunderstood by the United States that she preferred to err on the positive side: 'heaven knows we make enough mistakes ourselves'. Norman Thomas to Dorothy Norman, 5 February 1954; Dorothy Norman to Norman Thomas, 20 February 1954. Norman's own account of Nehru and American hostility to the non-alignment policy can be found in Norman, *Encounters*, p. 231.

190 Rita Pandit to Dorothy Norman, 13 August 1946. Pandit, *The Scope of Happiness*, pp. 225f.

191 The narrative of the foregoing paragraphs is distilled largely from the following letters: Dorothy Norman to Vijaya Lakshmi Pandit, 26 September 1945; Rita Pandit to Dorothy Norman, 13 August 1946; Tara Pandit to Dorothy Norman, 3 June 1947; Dorothy Norman to Vijaya Lakshmi Pandit, 3 July 1947; Tara Pandit to Dorothy Norman, 21 November 1947; Rita Pandit to Dorothy Norman, 5 February 1948; Vijaya Lakshmi Pandit to Dorothy Norman, 13 June 1948; Dr Krishna Lal Nehru to Dorothy Norman, 7 April 1951. Dorothy Norman Papers.

192 It was Coomaraswamy who, with John Lodge, had persuaded the Boston Museum of Fine Arts to buy some of Stieglitz's prints in 1924. Norman, *Encounters*, p. 77.

193 Ibid., p. 142.

194 Ibid., p. 206.

195 Bhicoo Batlivala, 'Civil Liberties in India', *TWICE A YEAR*, vols V–VI (Spring–Summer 1941), p. 518.

196 Indira Gandhi to Dorothy Norman, 2 December 1983, in Dorothy Norman, *Indira Gandhi: Letters to an American Friend 1950–1984* (San Diego, CA: Harcourt Brace, 1985),

p. 168. The foregoing paragraph is based on this book.

197 Judith M. Brown, *Nehru: A Political Life* (New Haven, CT and London: Yale University Press, 2003), p. 340.

Section II

1 Paul Rosenfeld, 'We want Varèse', *TWICE A YEAR*, vols V–VII (Fall–Winter 1941), pp. 252–8; Dorothy Norman, 'Edgar Varèse: Ionisation-Espace', *TWICE A YEAR*, vols V–VI (Fall–Winter 1941), pp. 259–60.

2 Norman and her husband developed a very close personal relationship with the Varèses. Norman, *Encounters*, p. 69.

3 Edgar Varèse to Dorothy Norman, 24 July 1946.

4 Harry Dunham to Dorothy Norman, 8 November 1936.

5 John Kirkpatrick to Dorothy Norman, 13 January 1940.

6 Obituary in *New York Times*, 25 July 1951, clipped in Dorothy Norman Papers.

7 Isa Kapp, 'Civilization and Steinberg', *The Reporter* (20 June 1950), p. 34.

8 Saul Steinberg to Dorothy Norman, 23 September 1950.

9 John Marin, *The Selected Writings of John Marin*, ed. and intr. Dorothy Norman (New York: Pellegrini & Cudahy, 1949), p. xii.

10 William Carlos Williams, tribute to Marin in *John Marin: Tributes by William Carlos Williams, Duncan Phillips, Dorothy Norman* (Berkeley and Los Angeles, CA: University of California Press, 1958), n.p.

11 Alfred Stieglitz, *Stieglitz Memorial Portfolio* (New York: Twice a Year Press, 1947).

12 Muriel Rukeyser, *Willard Gibbs: American Genius* (New York: Doubleday, Doran & Co., 1942), pp. 41–2.

13 Alfred Kazin, 'A Note on John Quincy Adams', *TWICE A YEAR*, vols X–XI (1943), p. 138; John Quincy Adams, 'Diary', *TWICE A YEAR*, vols X–XI, (1943), pp. 140–1.

14 Ibid., p. 145.

15 Ibid., pp. 145–6.

16 John Quincy Adams, 'From his Diary 1826–1844', *TWICE A YEAR*, vols XII–XIII (Fall–Winter 1945), p. 281.

17 Dorothy Norman, *Encounters*, p. 74.

18 Adams, 'From his Diary 1826–1844', p. 481.

19 Rainer Maria Rilke, 'Some War-Time Letters', trans. M.D. Herter Norton, *TWICE A YEAR*, vol. I (Fall–Winter 1938), p. 25.

20 Henry David Thoreau, 'From: A Plea for John Brown', *TWICE A YEAR*, vol. I (Fall–Winter 1938), pp. 70, 71.

21 Rilke, 'Some War-Time Letters', p. 12.

22 James Oppenheim, 'From the Foreword to Randolph Bourne's *Untimely Papers*', *TWICE A YEAR*, vol. I (Fall–Winter 1938), p. 37.

23 Randolph Bourne, 'The War and the Intellectuals', *TWICE A YEAR*, vol. I (Fall–Winter 1938), p. 46.

24 Ibid., p. 44.

25 Ibid., pp. 45, 46, 48.

26 Ibid., p. 48.

27 Randolph Bourne, 'The Doctrine of the Rights of Man as formulated by Tom Paine' in *The Radical Will: Selected Writings 1911–1918* (New York: Urizen Books, 1977), p. 236.

28 Norman, *Encounters*, p. 176.

29 'Elected Mayors of New York City' http://www.nyc.gov/html/nyc100/

html/classroom/hist_info/mayors.html#o'dwyer

30 Bourne, 'The War and the Intellectuals', p. 48.

31 Clive Bush, *Halfway to Revolution: Investigation and Crisis in the Work of Henry Adams, William James and Gertrude Stein* (New Haven, CT and London: Yale University Press, 1991), pp. 266–8.

32 Allen Ginsberg, 'Howl' in *Collected Poems: 1947–1980* (New York: Viking, 1985), p. 130.

33 Henry Miller to Norman, 24 November 1941.

34 Henry Miller to Dorothy Norman, 17 March, no year.

35 Henry Miller to Dorothy Norman, n.d.

36 Henry Miller to Dorothy Norman, 5 August 1937. Dorothy Norman to Henry Miller, 12 October 1937. Dorothy Norman Papers.

37 Henry Miller to Dorothy Norman, 8 November 1937.

38 Henry Miller to Dorothy Norman, 23 November 1937. Henry Miller to Dorothy Norman, 21 April 1939.

39 Henry Miller to Dorothy Norman, 23 November 1938.

40 Henry Miller to Dorothy Norman, 8 September 1938.

41 Henry Miller to Dorothy Norman, 9 April 1942.

42 Henry Miller, 'Balzac and his Double', *TWICE A YEAR*, vols V–VI (1940–1), p. 250.

43 Ibid., p. 258.

44 Ibid., p. 262.

45 Ibid., p. 263.

46 Ibid., p. 268.

47 Ibid.

48 Edmund Keeley, *Inventing Paradise: The Greek Journey, 1937–1947* (New York: Farrar, Straus, and Giroux, 1999).

49 Henry Miller, *The Colossus of Maroussi* (1941; Harmondsworth: Penguin, 1967), p. 6.

50 Ibid., p. 7.

51 Ibid., p. 15.

52 Ibid., p. 26.

53 Ibid., p. 28.

54 Ibid., p. 36.

55 Ibid., p. 37.

56 Ibid., p. 49.

57 Walt Whitman, 'Leaves of Grass' (1855), *Collected Poetry and Collected Prose* (New York: Library of America, 1982), p. 28.

58 Ibid., p. 16.

59 Ibid., pp. 20–1.

60 Miller, *The Colossus of Maroussi*, p. 54.

61 Ibid., p. 60.

62 Psalm 137, v. 1.

63 Herman Melville, *Typee, Omoo, Mardi* (New York: Library of America, 1982), p. 1022.

64 Miller, *The Colossus of Maroussi*, p. 75.

65 Ibid., p. 79.

66 Ibid., p. 76. Keeley, *Inventing Paradise*, p. 53.

67 Miller, *The Colossus of Maroussi*, p. 84. See Percy Bysshe Shelley, 'Worlds on worlds are rolling ever/ From creation to decay', Percy Bysshe Shelley, 'Hellas' in *Collected Poems*, ed. Thomas Hutchinson (Oxford: Oxford University Press, 1927), p. 452, and Whitman, 'Not a day passes [...] not a minute or second without an accouchement;/ Not a day passes [...] not a minute or second without a corpse.' Walt Whitman, 'Leaves of Grass' in *Collected Poetry and Collected Prose*, p. 100.

68 Miller, *The Colossus of Maroussi*, p. 89.

69 Ibid.

70 Ibid., p. 79.
71 Percy Bysshe Shelley, 'Notes on Queen Mab' in Thomas Hutchinson (ed.), *The Complete Poetical Works of Percy Bysshe Shelley* (London: Oxford University Press, 1927), p. 797.
72 Miller, *The Colossus of Maroussi*, p. 97.
73 Luke 12.27.
74 Miller, *The Colossus of Maroussi*, p. 105.
75 Ibid., p. 106.
76 Ibid., p. 110.
77 Ibid., p. 124.
78 Ibid., p. 125.
79 Ibid.
80 Ibid., p. 130.
81 Ibid., p. 175.
82 Ibid., p. 177.
83 Ibid., pp. 197, 199.
84 Ibid., pp. 228–9.
85 Ibid., p. 237.
86 Ibid., p. 242.
87 Robert Duncan, *The Truth and Life of Myth* (Fremont, MI: Sumac Press, 1968), p. 71.
88 Paul Ricoeur, *Time and Narrative*, vol. III (Chicago, IL: University of Chicago Press, 1988), p. 262.
89 Ricoeur, *Time and Narrative*, III, pp. 263–4.
90 Ricoeur, *Time and Narrative*, III, p. 264.
91 Jean-Pierre Vernant, *Myth and Tragedy in Ancient Greece*, trans. Janet Lloyd (New York: Zone Books, 1990), pp. 186–7.
92 Norman, *Encounters*, pp. 153–4.
93 Maria Piscator to Dorothy Norman, 12 April 1948 ('Manifesto of the Poet's Theatre').
94 Norman, *Encounters*, p. 131.
95 Ibid., pp. 189–201.
96 G.A. Borghese, 'Culture in Exile', *TWICE A YEAR*, vols III–IV (1940), p. 142.
97 'Wandering between two worlds, one dead,/The other powerless to be born.' Matthew Arnold, 'Stanzas from the Grande Chartreuse' in *Matthew Arnold: Poetry and Prose*, ed. John Bryson (London: Rupert Hart-Davis, 1954), p. 203.
98 Ernst Bloch, 'Writers in Exile?', *TWICE A YEAR*, vols III–IV (1940), pp. 143, 144.
99 Bodo Uhse, 'Writers in Exile', *TWICE A YEAR*, vols III–IV (1940), p. 147. The novel was *Söldner und Soldat* (Paris: Editions du Carrefour, 1935).
100 Ernst Toller '1933 – from *I was a German*', *TWICE A YEAR*, vols III–IV (1940), p. 156.
101 Helen Barolini, 'The Shadowy Lady of the Street of Dark Shops', *The Virginia Quarterly Review* (1998), pp. 297–313.
102 Carlo Levi, Radio Interview, *Catalogue for Exhibition of Paintings* (Winterthur Gallery, NY, May 1947), 'From 'An Interview with Carlo Levi by Harvey Breit', in *TWICE A YEAR* (tenth anniversary issue, 1948), pp. 190–4.
103 Alexander Stille, 'Foreword' to Ignazio Silone, *The Abruzzo Trilogy: Fontamara, Bread and Wine, The Seed Beneath the Snow*, trans. Eric Mosbacher, rev. Darina Silone (South Royalton, VT: Steerforth Italia, 2000), pp. vii–viii.
104 Darina Silone to Dorothy Norman, filing card, n.d.
105 Norman, *Encounters*, p. 127.
106 Ignazio Silone, 'The things I stand for', *TWICE A YEAR*, vols X–XI (1943), pp. 93–4.
107 Silone, *The Abruzzo Trilogy*, p. 412.
108 Stille, 'Foreword', p. ix.
109 Silone, *The Abruzzo Trilogy*, p. 273.

110 Ibid., p. 24.
111 Ibid., p. 46.
112 Ibid., p. 53.
113 Ibid., p. 81.
114 Ibid., p. 86.
115 Ibid., p. 124.
116 Ibid., p. 312.
117 Ibid., p. 353.
118 Ibid., p. 365.
119 Ibid., p. 311.
120 Ibid., p. 310.
121 Ibid., p. 311.
122 Ibid., p. 557.
123 Ibid., p. 555.
124 Ibid., p. 591.
125 Matthew 10.35–6: 'For I am come to set a man at variance against his father, and the daughter against her mother, and the daughter in law against her mother in law. And a man's foes shall be they of his own household.'
126 Silone, *The Abruzzo Trilogy*, pp. 519–20.
127 Ibid., p. 522.
128 Ibid., p. 522.
129 Ibid., p. 524.
130 Ibid., p. 525.
131 Ibid., p. 526.
132 Ibid., p. 527.
133 Ibid., p. 543.

Part 4: Lewis Mumford: Remaining Present in 'the Ringing Grooves of Time'

Section I

1 Lewis Mumford, *The Condition of Man* (London: Secker and Warburg, 1944), p. 385.
2 Victor Serge, *Men in Prison*, trans. Richard Greeman (London: Writers and Readers Publishing Cooperative, 1977), p. 28.
3 Lewis Mumford, *Men Must Act* (London: Secker and Warburg, 1939), p. 207.
4 Gyula Kodolanyi, 'Lewis Mumford and the Metaphor of the Open System', *Annales Universitatis Scientiarum Budapestiensis* XVI (1985), p. 7.
5 Lewis Mumford, *Sidewalk Critic: Lewis Mumford's Writings on New York*, ed. Robert Wojtowitz (New York: Princeton Architectural Press, 1998), p. 254.
6 Lewis Mumford, *The Pentagon of Power* (London: Secker and Warburg, 1971), plate 20.
7 See Frederick Engels, *Socialism: Utopian and Scientific* (New York: International Publishers, 1935) and Paul Ricoeur, *Lectures on Ideology and Utopia* (New York: Columbia University Press, 1986).
8 Henry Adams, *Mont-Saint-Michel and Chartres* (New York: Gordon Press, 1974), p. 54. See also Clive Bush, *Halfway to Revolution: Investigation and Crisis in the Work of Henry Adams, William James and Gertrude Stein* (New Haven, CT, and London: Yale University Press, 1991), pp. 90–1.
9 Mumford, *Sidewalk Critic*, p. 79.
10 Ibid., p. 32.
11 Lewis Mumford, Introduction to *The Van Wyck Brooks Lewis Mumford Letters: The Record of a Literary Friendship, 1921–1963*, ed. Robert Spiller (New York: E.P. Dutton, 1970), p. 4.
12 Lewis Mumford, 'A Brief Outline of Hell' [typescript], public lecture at Columbia University, given at MacMillan Theatre, n.d. [early 1940s], p. 2. Lewis Mumford Papers.
13 Ibid., p. 20.
14 Donald L. Miller, 'The Myth of the Machine I: Technics and Human Development', in Thomas P. Hughes and Agatha C. Hughes (eds), *Lewis*

Mumford: Public Intellectual (New York: Oxford University Press, 1990), p. 155.

15 'History is more or less bunk. It's tradition. We don't want tradition.' Henry Ford, in the *Chicago Tribune* (25 May 1916).

16 Lewis Mumford to Frederick J. Osborn, 19 September 1945, in Michael Hughes (ed.), *The Letters of Lewis Mumford and Frederic J. Osborn: A Transatlantic Dialogue 1938–1970* (New York and Washington, DC: Praeger, 1972), pp. 105–6.

17 Donald L. Miller, *Lewis Mumford: A Life* (New York: Weidenfeld and Nicolson, 1989), p. 394.

18 Lewis Mumford, Letter to the Editors, *The New Republic* (10 June 1940), p. 795.

19 Dwight Macdonald to Victor Serge, 22 February 1943. Dwight Macdonald Papers.

20 Editorial, *The New Leader* (13 July 1940), p. 5.

21 Lewis Mumford, *Men Must Act* (London: Secker and Warburg, 1939), p. 173. Mumford of course did distinguish between the Father Coughlins and George Shuster, Monsignor Ryan and the liberalism of the Catholic Welfare Council.

22 Lewis Mumford to Patrick Geddes, 29 March 1922, in Frank G. Novak (ed.), *Lewis Mumford and Patrick Geddes: The Correspondence* (London and New York: Routledge, 1995), p. 124.

23 Mumford, *Men Must Act*, p. 102.

24 Ibid., p. 48. There is a thoughtful and intelligent commentary on Mumford's much discussed 'organicism' by Gyula Kodolányi who extends the concept in relation to the idea of open systems of Bertalanffy and others. See Gyula Kodolányi, 'Lewis Mumford and the Metaphor of the Open System', *Annals Universitatis Scientiarum Budapestinensis de Rolando Eövös Nominataei* XVI (1985), pp. 1–19.

25 Christopher Hitchens, *Orwell's Victory* (London: Allen Lane, 2002), p. 150.

26 From an additional typescript not used by Spingarn for his article, 'Politics and the Poet: A Prophecy by J.E. Spingarn', *The Atlantic Monthly* (19 November 1942). Lewis Mumford Papers.

27 Typescript of radio address made by Lewis Mumford for the 'Hour for Union Now Series', transcribed 31 October 1940, p. 2. Lewis Mumford Papers.

28 T.S. Eliot, 'Gerontion' in *The Waste Land and Other Poems* (1972; London: Faber and Faber, 1990), p. 16.

29 Eric Severeid, 'The Price We Pay in Italy' [*The Nation*, 9 December 1944] in *Reporting World War Two: Part II: American Journalism 1944–1946* (New York: Library of America, 1995), p. 567.

30 Lewis Mumford, 'A Centre for the United Nations', *Journal of the A.I.A.* (December 1946), pp. 254, 256, 258.

31 Stanislaus von Moos, 'The Visualized Machine Age or: Mumford and the European Avant-Garde', in Hughes and Hughes (eds), *Lewis Mumford: Public Intellectual*, pp. 235, 238.

32 Lewis Mumford to Van Wyck Brooks, 14 September 1940. *The Brooks Mumford Letters*, ed. Spiller, p. 193.

33 Minutes of the Committee to Defend America by Aiding the Allies (Amenia local branch),

19 July 1940. Lewis Mumford Papers. Much of the subsequent discussion is based on these minutes and on the material relating to the Committee to Defend America by Aiding the Allies in the Mumford Papers.

34 Lewis Mumford, *The Culture of Cities* (London: Secker and Warburg, 1938), p. 140.

35 *New York Times* (Sunday 31 August 1941).

36 Ibid.

37 Lewis Mumford, 'Shall the United States Declare War Against the Axis Powers?', typescript of speech given at the Amenia High School, Amenia, New York, 30 August 1941. Lewis Mumford Papers.

38 See Clive Bush, 'Left-wing Isolationism, Literature and Ideology in America during the Run-up to World War II', *Comparative American Studies* 1.1 (2003), pp. 131–52.

39 Typescript of a petition against the Vichy government deputation in America signed by, among others, Elmer Rice, Edna St Vincent Millay, Christian Gauss, Van Wyck Brooks, Maxwell Anderson and Herbert Agar, n.d. Lewis Mumford Papers.

40 Gerhardt L. Weinberg, *A World at Arms: A Global History of World War II* (Cambridge: Cambridge University Press, 1994), p. 264.

41 See Kenneth Rexroth on the decline of pluralistic socialism in *An Autobiographical Novel* (Weybridge: Wittet Books, 1977), pp. 204–8, and Lewis Mumford, on the same subject in *Findings & Keepings: Analects for an Autobiography* (London: Secker and Warburg, 1976), pp. 204–5.

42 Mumford, *Men Must Act*, p. 21.

43 Ibid., p. 25.

44 Ibid., p. 30.

45 Ibid., p. 35.

46 Ibid., p. 39.

47 Simone Weil, 'Sketch of Contemporary Life', from *Reflections Concerning the Causes of Liberty and Social Oppression* (1934), reprinted in *The Simone Weil Reader*, ed. George A. Pachinas (Mount Kisco, NY: Moyer Bell, 1977), p. 38.

48 Weil, 'Factory Work'. Part of this article first appeared in French as 'Expérience de la vie d'usine', *Economie et Humanisme* 2 (1942), pp. 187–204, under the name Emile Novis, an anagram of Simone Weil. Translated by Felix Giovanelli, a full version appeared in *politics* 3.11 (December 1946). The text used here is from *The Simone Weil Reader*, ed. Pachinas, p. 57.

49 Ibid.

50 Ibid., p. 58.

51 Wilhelm Reich, *The Mass Psychology of Fascism*, trans. Vincent R. Carfagno (New York: Farrar, Straus, and Giroux, 1970), p. xiii.

52 For these general remarks I have relied on Antonio Gramsci, *Pre-Prison Writings*, ed. Richard Bellamy (Cambridge: Cambridge University Press, 1994).

53 Mumford, *Men Must Act*, p. 143.

54 Ibid., p. 102.

55 Ibid., p. 106.

56 Ibid., p. 107.

57 Ibid., p. 173.

58 Ibid., p. 179.

59 Lewis Mumford, 'Plea for Collective Bargaining between Labor and Management', *The New Republic* (8 November 1939), p. 64. Mumford attacks Christian Frontists and Father Coughlin in the same article.

60 Mumford, *Men Must Act*, p. 207.

61 Duncan Macmillan, 'A Single-minded Polymath: Patrick Geddes

and the Spatial Form of Social Thought', *Edinburgh Review* 88 (Summer 1992), p. 79.

62 I am indebted here to Georges Goyau, 'Pierre-Guillaume-Frédéric Le Play', transcribed by Douglas J. Potter, *The Catholic Encyclopedia*, Volume XII (New York: Robert Appleton, online edition, 2003) and to D.T.F. Evans, 'Le Play House and the Regional Survey Movement in British Sociology, 1920–1955', unpublished MPhil thesis, City of Birmingham Polytechnic, 1986, http://www.dfte.co.uk/ios.

63 Richard Wightman Fox, 'Tragedy, Responsibility, and the American Intellectual, 1925–1950' in Hughes and Hughes (eds), *Lewis Mumford: Public Intellectual* (New York: Oxford University Press, 1990), p. 327.

64 Casey Blake, 'The Perils of Personality: Lewis Mumford and Politics After Liberalism' in Hughes and Hughes (eds), *Lewis Mumford: Public Intellectual*, p. 283.

65 Charles Molesworth, 'Inner and Outer: The Axology of Lewis Mumford' in Hughes and Hughes (eds), *Lewis Mumford: Public Intellectual*, p. 249. Blake, 'The Perils of Personality: Lewis Mumford and Politics After Liberalism', p. 287.

66 Rosalind Williams, 'Lewis Mumford as a Historian of Technology', in Hughes and Hughes (eds), *Lewis Mumford: Public Intellectual*, pp. 56, 63.

67 Karl Marx, *Capital: A Critique of Political Economy*, trans. Ben Fowkes (Harmondsworth: Penguin, 1976), vol. I, p. 493, n. 4.

68 Lewis Mumford to Daniel Liebowitz, 4 July 1926. *The Lewis Mumford, Daniel Liebovitz Letters, 1923–1968*, ed. Bettina Liebowitz Knapp (Troy, NY: Whitston, 1983), p. 18.

69 Mike Gold [Irwin Cranich] to Lewis Mumford, 2 September 1934. See also John Pyros, *Mike Gold: Dean of American Proletarian Writers* (New York: Dramatika Press, 1979), p. 3.

70 Lewis Mumford, *Sketches from Life* (New York: Dial Press, 1982), p. 19.

71 Daniel Aaron to Lewis Mumford, 19 July 1961. These quotations are from Mumford's letters to Malcolm Cowley and Edmund Wilson, August 1932, which Daniel Aaron wanted permission to publish for his book, *Writers on the Left* and which appeared four months later in November 1961.

72 Lewis Mumford, 'A New York Adolescence: Tennis, Quadratic Equations, and Love' first appeared in *The New Yorker* dated 4 December 1937. It was reprinted in *The Human Prospect* (London: Secker and Warburg: 1956) and in *Sidewalk Critic* from which this quotation is taken, p. 42.

73 Lewis Mumford, *Findings and Keepings* (London: Secker and Warburg, 1976), p. 45.

74 Lewis Mumford to Van Wyck Brooks. 17 June 1922. Van Wyck Brooks and Lewis Mumford, *Brooks Mumford Letters*, ed. Spiller, p. 13.

75 Lewis Mumford to Van Wyck Brooks. 14 January 1932. *Mumford Brooks Letters*, ed. Spiller, pp. 76–7.

76 Dorothy Norman to Lewis Mumford, 20 December 1937. Lewis Mumford Papers. See Henry Hart (ed.), *Writer in a Changing World* (New York: Equinox Cooperative Press, 1937).

77 Lewis Mumford, review of Pitirim A. Sorokin, *Social and Industrial Dynamics. New Republic* (14 July 1937), p. 284.
78 Lewis Mumford, 'Books that Changed our Minds: Spengler's "The Decline of the West"', *New Republic* (11 January 1939), p. 278.
79 Lewis Mumford, review of Walter Lippman, *An Inquiry into the Principles of the Good Society, New Republic* (29 September 1937), p. 219.
80 Lewis Mumford, 'The Corruption of Liberalism', *The New Republic* (29 April 1940) [Mumford wrote in red on proof 13 January], p. 568.
81 Ibid.
82 Ibid.
83 Ibid., p. 569.
84 Ibid.
85 Ibid.
86 Ibid.
87 Wilhelm Reich, *The Mass Psychology of Fascism*, trans. Vincent R. Carfagno (New York: Farrar, Straus, and Giroux, 1970), pp. 183–4.
88 Herman Melville, *The Confidence Man* (New York: Library of America, 1984), p. 979.
89 Mumford, 'The Corruption of Liberalism', p. 569.
90 Ibid., p. 573.
91 Ibid.
92 Blake, 'The Perils of Personality', pp. 283–300.
93 Donald L. Miller, 'The Myth of the Machine: I. Technics and Human Development', in Hughes and Hughes (eds), *Lewis Mumford: Public Intellectual*, p. 160.
94 Richard Wightman Fox, 'Tragedy, Responsibility, and the American Intellectual, 1925–1950', in Hughes and Hughes (eds), *Lewis Mumford: Public Intellectual*, p. 327.
95 Blake, 'The Perils of Personality', p. 297.
96 Michale Zukerman, 'Faith, Hope, Not Much Charity: The Optimistic Epistemology of Lewis Mumford', in Hughes and Hughes (eds), *Lewis Mumford: Public Intellectual*, pp. 361–8.
97 The reader is invited to find these references by reading Pynchon's novels.
98 Reinhold Niebuhr to Lewis Mumford, 23 March 1941. Lewis Mumford Papers.
99 Lewis Mumford, *The Condition of Man* (London: Secker and Warburg, 1944), pp. 105, 107.
100 June Bingham, *Courage to Change: An Introduction to the Life and Thought of Reinhold Niebuhr* (New York: Scribner's, 1961), pp. 158–9.
101 Reinhold Niebuhr, *Reflections on the End of an Era* (New York and London: Scribner's, 1934), p. 18.
102 Ibid., p. 23.
103 Ibid., p. 29.
104 Ibid., p. 91.
105 Ibid., p. 92.
106 Ibid.
107 I am thinking of the appalling world described by Mike Davis in his book *Planet of Slums* (London: Verso, 2005).
108 Lewis Mumford, 'The Geddesian Gambit', in Frank G. Novak (ed.), *Lewis Mumford and Patrick Geddes: The Correspondence* (London and New York: Routledge, 1995), p. 372.
109 Hannah Arendt, *Love and Saint Augustine*, ed. Joanna Vecchiarelli Scott and Judith Chelius Stark (Chicago, IL, and London: University of Chicago Press, 1996), p. 66.
110 Blake, 'The Perils of Personality', p. 298.

111 Lewis Mumford to Van Wyck Brooks, 10 August 1949. *Brooks Mumford Letters*, ed. Spiller, p. 344.
112 Lewis Mumford, 'The Christian Transformation', p. 8. There are various drafts of this lecture in typescript. I have used what seems to be the third draft, given on 13 January 1947 to the Pacific School of Religion. Lewis Mumford Papers.
113 Ibid., p. 15.
114 Ibid., p. 14.
115 Ibid., p. 27.
116 Ibid., p. 23.
117 Lewis Mumford, 'The Tragic Mind of Herman Melville' (review of W.E. Sedgwick, *Herman Melville: The Tragedy of Mind*), *New York Times Book Review* (21 January 1945).
118 Lewis Mumford, 'Blashfield Address to the American Academy of Arts and Sciences', typescript, 1942, p. 2.
119 Lewis Mumford to Dorothy Norman, 12 December 1937. Dorothy Norman Papers.
120 Mumford, 'Blashfield Address', p. 12.
121 Ibid., p. 17.
122 Ibid., p. 21.
123 Mumford, 'Speech at Stanford Alumni Conference', typescript, February 1943, p. 7.
124 Mumford, 'Blashfield Address', p. 10.
125 Novak (ed.), *Lewis Mumford and Patrick Geddes: The Correspondence*, p. 76.
126 Lewis Mumford, 'Lewis Mumford on the Future of London', *The Architectural Review* XLVII.577 (January 1945), p. 9.
127 Richard Sennett, *The Uses of Disorder: Personal Identity and City Life* (New York: Knopf, 1970), pp. 97–8.
128 Donald Miller, *Lewis Mumford: A Life* (New York: Weidenfeld and Nicolson, 1989), p. 240.
129 Walt Whitman, 'France, the 18th Year of these States', in *Leaves of Grass (1891–92)* in *Whitman: Poetry and Prose*, ed. Justin Kaplan (New York: Library of America, 1982), p. 376.
130 I am thinking of moments in Pynchon's *Gravity's Rainbow* and *Mason & Dixon*.
131 Lewis Mumford, 'The Passage Back', typescript, n.p. Lewis Mumford Papers.
132 Mumford, *The Condition of Man*, p. 366.
133 Lewis Mumford, 'Letter to Alfons F., a German writer in Austria' in 'The Passage Back' (unpublished typescript, c.1945). Lewis Mumford Papers.
134 See Bush, *Halfway to Revolution*, p. 121.
135 Lewis Mumford, 'German Apologists and the German Record', *The Saturday Review of Literature* (11 August 1945), p. 5.
136 Ibid., p. 6.
137 Lewis Mumford, 'Lecture II: The Trial', typescript. Draft among a number of lectures Mumford called 'The Christian Transformation'. Last draft is dated 1947.
138 For a good summary of the issues see Everett Mendelsohn, 'Prophet of Our Discontent: Lewis Mumford Confronts the Bomb', in Hughes and Hughes (eds), *Lewis Mumford: Public Intellectual*, pp. 343–60.
139 Lewis Mumford, 'Gentlemen, You are Mad!', *The Saturday Review* XXIX.9 (2 March 1946), p. 6.
140 Written across the top of clipping from the *New York Times* (12 December 1982) reporting Alva Myrdal's Nobel Peace Prize speech. Lewis Mumford Papers.

141 Michael Fraenkel to Victor Serge, 21 March 1945. Victor Serge Papers. My italics.

Section II

1 Leo Marx, 'Lewis Mumford: Prophet of Organicism' in Hughes and Hughes (eds), *Lewis Mumford: Public Intellectual*, p. 169.
2 Dorothy Emmet, *Whitehead's Philosophy of Organism* (London: Macmillan, 1932), p. 100.
3 See Greta Jones, *Social Darwinism and English Thought: The Interaction between Biology and Social Theory* (Brighton: Harvester Press, 1980), and Bush, *Halfway to Revolution*, especially the chapter 'Philosophising a Social Pathology', pp. 183–207.
4 Lewis Mumford, 'The Geddesian Gambit', appendix 3 of *Lewis Mumford and Patrick Geddes: The Correspondence*, p. 359.
5 Eugene Rochberg-Halton, 'The Transformation of Social Theory', in Hughes and Hughes (eds), *Lewis Mumford: Public Intellectual*, p. 144.
6 John L. Thomas, 'Lewis Mumford, Benton McKaye and the Regional Vision', in Hughes and Hughes (eds), *Lewis Mumford: Public Intellectual*, pp. 67, 74–5. See also Justin Kaplan, *Walt Whitman: A Life* (New York: Simon and Schuster, 1980), p. 48.
7 Howard P. Segal, 'Mumford's Alteration to the Megamachine: Critical Utopianism, Regionalism, and Decentralization', in Hughes and Hughes (eds), *Lewis Mumford: Public Intellectual*, pp. 105, 119.
8 Lewis Mumford 'The Culture of the Family', in *The Human Prospect* (London: Secker and Warburg, 1956), p. 278.
9 Sir Frederick Osborn, 'Planning for the Family', typescript, talk given to the Town and Country Planning Association Lunch meeting, 16 April, 1942, p. 5. Osborn Papers, Welwyn Garden City Library.
10 Alfred Tennyson, 'In Memoriam', in *The Poems and Plays of Tennyson* (London: Oxford University Press, 1953), p. 243.
11 Charles Olson, *The Human Universe and Other Essays* (New York: Grove Press, 1967), pp. 4–11. Olson contrasts the contemporary Mayan way of life with Western dominance of profiteering from nature offering a 'dynamic' sense of interaction close to Mumford's 'organicism' in this respect only.
12 Murray Bookchin, *The Ecology of Freedom: the Emergence and Dissolution of hierarchy* (Palo Alto, CA: Cheshire Books, 1982), p. 27.
13 Marx, 'Lewis Mumford: Prophet of Organicism', p. 174.
14 Lewis Mumford, typescript, talk given to the Harvard Student Defense Group, 20 May 1941, p. 10. Lewis Mumford Papers.
15 Jean-Paul Sartre, *Critique of Dialectical Reason*, trans. Alan Sheridan-Smith, ed. Jonathan Rée (London: New Left Books, 1980), pp. 159–60.
16 Sartre, *Critique of Dialectical Reason*, p. 160.
17 Mumford, 'Lewis Mumford on the Future of London', p. 5.
18 Patrick Geddes, 'Life and its Science' [*The Evergreen*, Spring 1895], reprinted in *Edinburgh Review* (Summer 1992), p. 28.
19 Patrick Geddes, 'The Scots Renaissance', [*The Evergreen*, Spring 1895], reprinted in *Edinburgh Review* (Summer 1992), p. 22.

20 Henry Adams, *The Education of Henry Adams: An Autobiography* (1918; Boston, MA: Houghton Mifflin, 1961), p. 225.
21 Mumford, 'The Geddesian Gambit', p. 363.
22 Ibid., p. 360.
23 Ibid., p. 367.
24 Ibid., p. 367.
25 Ibid., p. 259.
26 Ibid., p. 199.
27 Lewis Mumford to Patrick Geddes, 25 January 1934, *Lewis Mumford and Patrick Geddes: The Correspondence*, ed. Novak, p. 198.
28 The well-known phrase is from Samuel Johnson, *The Lives of the Poets*, Vol. II, 'Abraham Cowley' (London: J.M. Dent, 1925), p. 11.
29 Mumford to Geddes, 6 July 1923 in *Mumford and Geddes: The Correspondence*, p. 177.
30 Lewis Mumford, *Technics and Civilization* (1934; London: Routledge, 1946), p. 14.
31 Ibid., p. 16.
32 Ibid., p. 20.
33 Ibid., p. 19.
34 Ibid., p. 22.
35 Ibid., p. 49.
36 Ibid., p. 59.
37 Ibid., p. 70.
38 Ibid., p. 74.
39 Ibid., p. 89.
40 Ibid., p. 109.
41 Ibid., p. 198.
42 Ibid., p. 242.
43 Ibid., p. 243.
44 Casey Blake, while justly and fluently praising this remarkable sequence, to a degree missed its tone and came to the strange conclusion that Mumford thereby inferred a 'technological' solution to the crisis of bourgeois individualism while not really doing so because elsewhere he did emphasize culture, ethics, and politics! It also shows the manifest dangers of attempting to turn a 'poetic' argument into an 'analytical' one too quickly. I am also not sure that the relativistic, fragmented self is so wonderfully celebrated in 'postmodern' art; it is also a site of nightmare. That it is more truthful to view the self this way is not in doubt, but that is quite a different matter. Mumford's comments on visualization are swift brush strokes intended to open not finalize debate. One always disagrees with more or less 50 per cent of anything that Mumford says, but he pushes us to places to which we had not thought of going. As for postmodernism, it hasn't on the whole noticed that choosing to be any number of selves and having to be this number of selves are somewhat different, and it is here that the key political and social issues, not to mention the nature of power to dispose of people's lives, lie. This is an historic crisis of a phase of key economic aspects of capitalism (I am reluctant to call it 'late' given that this temporality is too, perhaps understandably given the contemporary mess, uncomplexly and apocalyptically assigned), not simply the crisis of 'modernity' or 'postmodernity', those epochal baggy monsters. Unity and multiplicity also depend on each other, the different needs the same (even postmodern 'virtuality' needs a sense of what is not virtual), as Henry Adams knew. See Blake, 'Mumford and Politics', p. 296.
45 Mumford, *Technics and Civilization*, p. 288.

46 Lewis Mumford, *The Culture of Cities* (London: Secker and Warburg, 1938), p. 4.
47 Ibid., p. 5.
48 Ibid., p. 9.
49 Ibid., p. 11.
50 Ibid., p. 22.
51 Ibid., p. 29.
52 Ibid.
53 Ibid., p. 75.
54 Ibid., p. 80.
55 Ibid., p. 84.
56 Ibid., p. 88.
57 Ibid., p. 92.
58 Ibid., p. 93.
59 Ibid., p. 97.
60 Ibid., p. 131.
61 Frances. A. Yates, *French Academies of the Sixteenth Century* (London: University of London Press, 1947).
62 William James, 'The PhD Octopus', *The Harvard Monthly* 36 (March 1903), pp. 1–9.
63 Mumford, *The Culture of Cities*, p. 131.
64 Ibid., p. 181.
65 Ibid., p. 182.
66 *Punch* (January–June 1842). Cited in 'Victorian London: Buildings, Monuments and Museums – Exeter Hall', www.victorianlondon.org.
67 209 See George P. Landow, 'Charles Haddon Spurgeon at Exeter Hall', *The Victorian Web: Literature, History & Culture in the Age of Victoria*, http://65.107.211.206/religion/sermons/exeter.html. 'Berlioz in London', The Berlioz Website, http://www.hberlioz.com/London/BerliozLondon.html 'Victorian London-buildings, Monuments and Museums: Exeter Hall.' http://www.victorianlondon.org/buildings/exeterhall.html
68 Mumford, *The Culture of Cities*, p. 435.
69 Norman O. Brown, *Life Against Death: The Psychoanalytical Meaning of History* (New York: Vintage, 1959), p. 101.
70 Mumford, *The Culture of Cities*, p. 438.
71 Simone Weil, *The Need for Roots: Prelude to a Declaration of Duties for Mankind* (London and New York: Routledge, 1952), p. 231.
72 Mumford, *The Culture of Cities*, p. 439.
73 Ibid.
74 Lewis Mumford, *The City in History* (1961; London: Pelican Books, 1966), p. 11.
75 Mumford, *The Culture of Cities*, p. 457.
76 Lewis Mumford, pencilled note dated 16 January 1930. Lewis Mumford Papers.
77 Fernand Braudel, *The Perspective of the World*, trans. Siân Reynolds (London: Collins/Fontana Press, 1984), p. 621.
78 Braudel, *The Perspective of the World*, p. 626.
79 Fernand Braudel, *The Structures of Everyday Life: The Limits of the Possible*, rev. trans. Siân Reynolds (London: Collins, 1981), p. 308.
80 Ibid., p. 514.
81 Ibid., p. 556.
82 Braudel, *The Perspective of the World*, p. 624.
83 Fernand Braudel, *On History*, trans. Sarah Matthews (Chicago, IL: University of Chicago Press, 1980), p. 48.
84 Braudel, *The Perspective of the World*, p. 626.
85 Braudel, *On History*, p. 6.
86 At a recent conference at which the author was present, where a passage from Braudel's *The Mediterranean*

was discussed, a well-known, distinguished historian remarked that if any contemporary undergraduate wrote like that, the essay would fail!

87 Braudel, *On History*, p. 11.
88 Ibid., p. 12.
89 Ibid., p. 48.
90 Ibid., p. 15.
91 Ibid., p. 20.
92 Ibid., p. 89.
93 Ibid., p. 160.
94 Ibid.
95 Ibid., p. 43.
96 Ibid., p. 178.
97 *Brooks Mumford Letters*, p. 117.
98 Braudel, *On History*, p. 189.
99 Ibid., p. 190.
100 Ibid., p. 192.
101 Ibid., p. 194.
102 Ibid., p. 196.
103 Ibid., p. 445.
104 Ibid., p. 2.
105 Ibid., p. 341.
106 Ibid., p. 170.
107 Ibid., p. 198.
108 Ibid., p. 397.
109 Ibid., p. 3.
110 Ibid., p. 3.
111 Ibid., p. 122.
112 Ibid., p. 34.
113 Ibid., p. 82.
114 Ibid., p. 88.
115 Ibid., p. 143.
116 Ibid., pp. 150–1.
117 Bush, *Halfway to Revolution*, pp. 108–11.
118 Leo Frobenius, *The Childhood of Man: A Popular Account of the Lives, Customs and Thoughts of the Primitive Races*, trans. A.H. Keane (London: Seeley, 1909), p. 488.
119 Mumford, *The Condition of Man*, p. 232.
120 Ibid., p. 260.
121 Lewis Mumford, *Herman Melville* (London: Jonathan Cape, 1929), p. 193.
122 Mumford, *The Condition of Man*, p. 261.
123 Ibid., p. 322.
124 Ibid.
125 Ibid.
126 Ibid.
127 Ibid., p. 261.
128 Ibid., p. 262.
129 I am indebted to the work of the Scottish poet Thomas A. Clark for this rich concept of 'lingering'.
130 Ricoeur, *Time and Narrative*, vol. 3, p. 31.
131 Mumford, *The Condition of Man*, p. 261.
132 Ibid., p. 147.
133 Ibid.
134 Ibid.
135 Ibid., pp. 148–9.
136 Walt Whitman, 'Song of Myself', *Leaves of Grass*, in *Whitman Poetry and Prose*, p. 244.
137 Mumford, *The Condition of Man*, p. 148.
138 Mumford, *Technics and Civilization*, p. 14.
139 Hannah Arendt, *The Human Condition* (New York: Doubleday Anchor, 1959), pp. 18f.
140 Ricoeur, *Time and Narrative* I, p. 236.
141 Mumford, *The Condition of Man*, p. 148.
142 Arendt, *The Human Condition*, p. 92.
143 Ibid., p. 93.
144 Ibid., p. 93.
145 Mumford, *The Condition of Man*, p. 82.
146 Arendt, *The Human Condition*, pp. 93–4.
147 Mumford, *The Condition of Man*, p. 183.

148 Ibid., p. 184.
149 J.E. Spingarn, 'Politics and the Poet: A Prophecy by J.E. Spingarn', *The Atlantic Monthly* (19 November 1942), p. 78.
150 Arendt, *The Human Condition*, pp. 25, 26.
151 Muriel Rukeyser to Lewis Mumford, 11 May 1944. Lewis Mumford Papers.
152 Muriel Rukeyser, 'Ninth Elegy: The Antagonists' in *The Collected Poems of Muriel Rukeyser* (New York: McGraw-Hill, 1978), p. 259.
153 Ibid., p. 260.

Part 5: The Art of Memory: Muriel Rukeyser and the Turning World

Section I

1 One of my first conversations with Rukeyser was about Frances Yates's *Giordano Bruno and the Hermetic Tradition*. As a result, I lent her my copy of Yates's *The Art of Memory*, which she 'forgot' to give back. Perhaps forgetting is an art of memory too, and I hope this chapter will show that Frances Yates's book could not have been in better hands.
2 Ethel ? to Muriel Rukeyser, n.d. This unidentified correspondent, also complaining in the same letter of the sentimentality and inaccuracy of much of the war propaganda, writes in the context of Rukeyser's work at the Ministry of Information in the early 1940s.
3 Jean-Paul Sartre, 'Materialism and Revolution', trans. Ralph Manheim, *politics* (July–August 1947), p. 166.
4 Muriel Rukeyser, handwritten note, n.d.
5 Muriel Rukeyser, 'Nine Poems for the Unborn Child' in *Collected Poems* (New York: McGraw-Hill, 1978), p. 287.
6 Henry Miller to Dorothy Norman, 15 November 1941. Dorothy Norman Papers.
7 Muriel Rukeyser, 'The Fear of Poetry', *TWICE A YEAR* (Fall–Winter 1941), pp. 27–9.
8 Octavio Paz to Victor Serge, October, 1944. Victor Serge Papers. I am grateful to Dr Pedro Garcia-Caro for helping me to translate this letter.
9 Ibid.
10 While I was working in the Muriel Rukeyser Papers at the Library of Congress in the summer of 2004, the librarians informed me that there had been 'a great deal of activity' with young scholars in relation to the papers. This is surely to be welcomed.
11 In conversations with Rukeyser in the late 1960s and early 1970s, I had some inkling of the difficulties, but I was then largely ignorant of the period and the context of her earlier life. I had no idea of just how fierce the hostility had been until I heard an excellent paper given by Jenny Goodman (Colorado State University) 'Dear Miss Rukeyser: The Relationship between M.L. Rosenthal and Muriel Rukeyser', together with the subsequent discussion, at the conference 'Poetries of the 1940s: American and International', University of Maine, Orono, 23–7 June 2004. Louise Kertesz's early brave book is much too accommodating to the 'centrality' (the canonical consensus) of the point of view of the dominant poetic voices of the 1940s and 1950s, really to strike out confidently for the unique world of Rukeyser's poetics and voice.

12 Eric Mottram to Muriel Rukeyser, 29 September 1978. Muriel Rukeyser Papers.

13 Muriel Rukeyser to Dorothy Norman, 6 October 1943. Dorothy Norman Papers.

14 Muriel Rukeyser, 'Words and Images', *New Republic* (2 August 1943), pp. 140, 141.

15 Ella Winters, herself very politically active on the left, was first married to Lincoln Steffens the muck-raking journalist of the Progressive Era, and second to Donald Ogden Stewart, the author of the screen-play (from Philip Barry's play – a Broadway hit) for that incomparable movie *The Philadelphia Story* (1940). Ogden Stewart won an Academy Award for the screen play. I was fortunate enough to spend a most instructive afternoon with Donald Ogden Stewart, Winters and Rukeyser in 1975 in their Hampstead home in London.

16 'I'll be back in two or three months with a prose book going on from *The Fear of Poetry* that you printed', Muriel Rukeyser to Dorothy Norman, 25 October 1942 (?).

17 'Many Keys', n.d. Muriel Rukeyser Papers.

18 Ibid.

19 Ibid.

20 'Searching/Not Searching' in *Breaking Open* (1973). *The Collected Poems of Muriel Rukeyser* (New York: McGraw-Hill, 1978), p. 502.

21 Percy Bysshe Shelley, 'A Defence of Poetry', in *The Complete Works of Shelley* (New York: Gordian Press, 1965), p. 131.

22 Hannah Arendt, *The Human Condition: A Study of the Central Dilemmas Facing Modern Man* (Garden City, NY: Doubleday & Co., 1959), p. 93.

23 Muriel Rukeyser, 'Fields Where We Slept', in Rukeyser, *Collected Poems*, p. 343.

24 Tim Dayton, *Muriel Rukeyser: The Book of the Dead* (Columbia, MO: University of Missouri Press, 2003), p. 14.

25 Muriel Rukeyser, typed autobiographical fragment. Muriel Rukeyser Papers.

26 Ibid.

27 Muriel Rukeyser, *The Life of Poetry* (New York: A.A. Wyn, 1949), p. 206.

28 Muriel Rukeyser, diaries and appointment books, 1923–36. Muriel Rukeyser Papers. The following quotes can also be found here.

29 The trial of the 'Scottsboro boys' was one of the most celebrated law cases in the history of the United States' struggle to overcome historic racism in the South. In 1939 nine black men were indicted in a rape case. Fuelled by a racist mob and a racist court, eight of the defendants were sentenced to be hanged. After huge public attention, the sentences were commuted by the Supreme Court to various terms of imprisonment. Rukeyser covered the case as a journalist and in her poems.

30 William Shakespeare, *Antony and Cleopatra*, Act 4, Scene 15.

31 I hope to have made all very brief biographical references strictly subordinate to the critique of the work, and they are mentioned only insofar as they relate to techniques or thematics of Rukeyser's prose or poetry.

32 Muriel Rukeyser, diaries and appointment books, 1923–36. Muriel Rukeyser Papers.

33 These sadly lie outside the remit of the present chapter.

34 Frances Wickes to Muriel Rukeyser, n.d..
35 Carl G. Jung, *The Inner Life of Childhood: A Study in the Analytical Psychology*, intr. Frances G. Wickes (New York and London: D. Appleton, 1929), p. xiii.
36 Jung, *The Inner Life of Childhood*, p. xiv.
37 A.S. Neill, *The Problem Parent* (London: Herbert Jenkins, 1932), pp. 236–7.
38 Thomas Pynchon, *The Crying of Lot 49* (1967; Harmondsworth: Penguin, 1974), p. 104.
39 In the papers this quotation from Norman O. Brown's *Life Against Death: The Psychoanalytical Meaning of History* (New York: Vintage, 1959), p. 312, which she calls 'Love Against Death' is placed with the 1946 diary as 15 September. This is clearly impossible since *Life Against Death* was not begun until 1953 and not published until 1959.
40 Brown's *Life Against Death*, p. 309.
41 Ibid., p. 312.
42 The summary and citations are from Brown, 'The Resurrection of the Body', Chapter 16 of *Life Against Death*, pp. 307–72. My italics.
43 Richard King, *The Party of Eros: Radical Social Thought and the Realm of Freedom* (Chapel Hill, NC: University of North Carolina Press, 1972), pp. 170–1.
44 Jung, *The Inner Life of Childhood*, intr. Wickes, p. 243.
45 Ibid., p. 4.
46 Ibid., p. 6.
47 Northrop Frye, *Fearful Symmetry: A Study of William Blake* (Boston: Beacon Press, 1947), p. 59.
48 Jung, *The Inner Life of Childhood*, intr. Wickes, p. 14.
49 Ibid.
50 Ibid., p. 16.
51 Ibid., p. 22)
52 The *locus classicus* is, as already cited, Neill, *The Problem Parent*.
53 Jung, *The Inner Life of Childhood*, intr. Wickes, p. 227.
54 Ibid., p. 77.
55 Ibid., p. 86.
56 Ibid., p. 253.
57 Ibid., p. 304.
58 Ibid., p. 371.
59 Ibid., p. 95.
60 Anna Freud and Dorothy T. Burlingham, *War and Children: A Message to American Parents* (New York: Medical War Books, 1943), p. 19.
61 Ibid., p. 85.
62 Rukeyser, *Collected Poems*, p. 255.
63 Ibid.
64 Freud and Burlingham, *War and Children*, p. 70.
65 Rukeyser, *Collected Poems*, p. 255.
66 Freud and Burlingham, *War and Children*, p. 33.
67 Ibid., p. 56.
68 Ibid., p. 65.
69 Rukeyser, *Collected Poems*, p. 274.
70 Rukeyser, 'NOT TO BE PRINTED/ NOT TO BE SAID/NOT TO BE THOUGHT', in *Collected Poems*, p. 558.
71 Muriel Rukeyser, *MEDITERRANEAN* (New York, NY: Writers and Artists Committee, Medical Bureau to Aid Spanish Democracy, n.d., c.1936–9).
72 Muriel Rukeyser, unidentified diary, 12 June 1936. Muriel Rukeyser Papers.
73 Rukeyser, *Collected Poems*, p. 126.
74 Barbara Guest, *Herself Defined: The Poet and her World* (New York: Quill, 1984), p. 235.
75 Muriel Rukeyser, 'We Came for Games', *Esquire* 82 (October 1974),

pp. 192–4, 368–70. It was previously published in *Life and Letters* ('Barcelona, 1936') and in *New Masses* ('Death in Spain: Barcelona on the Barricades', 1936). I use the *Esquire* version here because of the additional temporal dimension offered by the retrospective Afterword. Owing to compression of the double columned piece, page numbers are not given.

76 Rukeyser, *Collected Poems*, p. 450.

77 George Orwell, *Homage to Catalonia* (1938; Harmondsworth: Penguin, 1962), p. 15.

78 Nancy Macdonald, *Homage to the Spanish Exiles: Voices from the Spanish Civil War*, preface by Mary McCarthy (New York: Insight Books, 1987), p. 22.

79 This is backed up by two recent scholars, Alan Wald and Tim Dayton. See Dayton, *Muriel Rukeyser: The Book of the Dead*, pp. 10–11. Dayton quotes from a letter of Rukeyser's letter to Wald, expressing disappointment that that she could not be close to the Communist Party, but found her desired and imagined 'United Front' in Catalonia where socialists, anarchists, communists, trade unions and gypsies all co-operated.

80 Ronald Fraser, *Blood of Spain: An Oral History of the Spanish Civil War* (New York: Pantheon, 1979), p. 80.

81 George Orwell, *Homage to Catalonia* (1938; Harmondsworth: Penguin, 1966), p. 8.

82 Ezra Pound, *ABC of Reading* (1951; London: Faber and Faber, 1961), p. 29.

83 Muriel Rukeyser, 'Notes on Lorca's theatre written for Katrina Paximan to speak at Lorca evening, Feb. 1951 in Paximan's absence spken by M.R.', typescript. Muriel Rukeyser Papers.

84 Shelley, *A Defence of Poetry*, p. 135.

85 James R. Caldwell, 'Imagination and a Brilliant Hope' (review of *The Life of* Poetry, *Elegies, Orpheus*), *The Saturday Review* (11 March 1950), p. 26.

86 Muriel Rukeyser, 'The Usable Truth: Five Talks on Communication and Poetry', typescript, given at Vassar College, 29 October to 1 November 1940. Lecture I: 'The Fear of Poetry' (29 October 1940), p. 1a. Only four talks seem to be in the papers (Tuesday to Friday) and there is note at the end that states they were also given as a series of lectures at the California Labour School and Columbia University.

87 Rukeyser, 'The Fear of Poetry, p. 6.

88 Ezra Pound, 'How to Read' in *Literary Essays of Ezra Pound* (New York: New Directions, 1968), p. 16.

89 Rukeyser, 'The Fear of Poetry', p. 9.

90 Ibid., p. 1b.

91 Ibid., p. 5.

92 Rukeyser, 'The Speed of the Image', p. 4.

93 Rukeyser, *The Life of Poetry*, p. 151.

94 Ibid., p. 156.

95 Ibid., p. 157.

96 Rukeyser, 'The Speed of the Image', p. 5.

97 Ibid., p. 5. Interestingly Hitchcock discusses this moment in detail and how the effects were technically done in a conversation with Truffaut. See François Truffaut, *Hitchcock*, trans. François Truffaut (New York: Simon and Schuster, 1967), pp. 97–8.

98 Muriel Rukeyser, 'The Speed of the Image', p. 26. Muriel Rukeyser Papers.

99 Ibid.

100 Muriel Rukeyser, review of Archibald MacLeish's *Land of the Free* in *New Masses* (19 April 1938), pp. 26–9.
101 Rukeyser, *The Life of Poetry*, p. 148.
102 Rukeyser, review of MacLeish, *Land of the Free*, p. 26.
103 Rukeyser, 'The Speed of the Image', p. 33.
104 Jean-Paul Sartre, *Search for a Method*, trans. Hazel E. Barnes (New York: Vintage Books, 1968), p. 9, n. 6.
105 Sartre, *Search for a Method*, p. 10.
106 Ibid., p. 12.
107 Susan Sontag, 'On Style', in *A Susan Sontag Reader*, intr. Elizabeth Hardwick (New York: Farrar, Straus, and Giroux, 1982), p. 142.
108 Muriel Rukeyser, 'Poetry and Peace', p. 46.
109 Ibid., p. 46.
110 Ibid., pp. 45–6.
111 Ibid., p. 52.
112 Ibid., pp. 52–3.
113 Muriel Rukeyser, 'Communication and Poetry', written on the back of p. 46.
114 Henry Adams, *The Education of Henry Adams*, intr. D.W. Brogan (Boston, MA: Houghton Mifflin, 1961), pp. 379, 499–500.
115 This is an issue I discussed at length in *Halfway to Revolution: Investigation and Crisis in the Work of Henry Adams, William James and Gertrude Stein* (New Haven, CT, and London: Yale University Press, 1991).
116 Muriel Rukeyser, *Willard Gibbs* (Garden City, NY: Doubleday, Doran & Co., 1942), p. 410.
117 Ibid., p. 410. See Henry Adams, 'The Rule of Phase' (1909), in Henry Adams, *The Degradation of the Democratic Dogma*, intr. Brooks Adams (New York: Macmillan, 1919), pp. 267–311.
118 Herman Melville, *Moby-Dick* (New York: Library of America, 1983), p. 1248. Melville's reference is to Proverbs 21.16.
119 The issue is perhaps not so easily resolved as here indicated. For today's thoughtful young, the world seems overwhelmingly terrifying. Teaching *Elegies* to an exceptionally gifted undergraduate class in 2003, a young woman asked: 'how can she be so optimistic?'
120 Rukeyser, *Collected Poems*, p. 469.
121 I am grateful to Patricia Kückelmann for reminding me of this moment from the *Pensées*. Blaise Pascal, *Pensées*, trans. A.J. Krailsheimer (Harmondsworth: Penguin, 1966), p. 238.
122 Rukeyser, 'The Speed of Darkness' in *Collected Poems*, p. 486.
123 Rukeyser, 'Communication and Poetry', p. 62.
124 Brecht, *Journals 1934–1955*, pp. 129–30. In his entry for January 1941, Brecht in fact makes an early characterisation of the 'military industrial complex'. Thirty years later there is a touching letter in the Muriel Rukeyser Papers from Ella Winter to Muriel Rukeyser on a friendship with the Brechts of more than thirty years. Helli Brecht had died just a month earlier. Ella Winter to Muriel Rukeyser, 22–3 October 1971.
125 Rukeyser, 'Poetry and Communication', p. 65.
126 Carossa is referred to but not mentioned by name. Rukeyser, *The Life of Poetry*, p. 35.
127 Rukeyser, *The Life of Poetry*, p. 222.
128 See Richard King, *The Party of Eros: Radical Social Thought and the Realm of Freedom* (Chapel Hill, NC:

University of North Carolina Press, 1972).
129 Rukeyser, *The Life of Poetry*, pp. 28–9.
130 John 10.10.
131 Rukeyser, *The Life of Poetry*, p. 29.
132 Ibid.
133 Shelley, 'A Defence of Poetry', p. 128.
134 Rukeyser, *The Life of Poetry*, p. 30.
135 Rukeyser, 'Spirals and Fugues', in *Collected Poems*, p. 448.
136 Donald A. Mackenzie, *The Migration of Symbols* (New York: Alfred Knopf, 1926), p. 66.
137 Ibid., p. 66.
138 Ibid., p. 66.
139 Ibid., p. 83.
140 See below for Tim Dayton's extended discussion in relation to Rukeyser's poem. See also Gerald Nicosia, *Memory Babe: A Critical Biography of Jack Kerouac* (Harmondsworth: Penguin, 1986), p. 139 and Francine du Plessix Grey, *Simone Weil* (London: Weidenfeld and Nicholson, 2001), pp. 153–4.
141 Mackenzie, *The Migration of Symbols*, pp. 102–8.
142 Ibid., p. 107.
143 Rukeyser, *The Life of Poetry*, p. 37.
144 D'Arcy Wentworth Thompson, *On Growth and Form* (1917; Cambridge: Cambridge University Press, 1968), p. 38.
145 Rukeyser, *The Life of Poetry*, p. 42.
146 Ibid., p. 51.
147 Ibid.
148 Ibid., p. 115.
149 Ibid., p. 121.
150 Ibid.
151 Ibid., p. 138.
152 Ibid., p. 158.
153 Ibid., p. 165.
154 Ibid., p. 196.
155 Ibid., p. 198.
156 Ibid., p. 201.
157 Ibid., p. 204.
158 Ibid., p. 206.
159 Ibid., p. 223.
160 Ibid., p. 229.
161 This is suggested by references to Marcel Marceau, the great French mime artist who first toured the United States in 1955–6 and then became popular on American television, to Pasolini's *Gospel According to St Matthew* (1965), and to J.T. Frazer's *Voices of Time: A Co-operative Survey of Man's Views of Time as Expressed by the Sciences and the Humanities* (New York: G. Braziller, 1966).
162 Muriel Rukeyser, 'Poetry and Time'. typescript, n.d. (probably c.1967–8), tape transcription of a talk given at MIT, p. 4. Page references are to the typescript.
163 Ibid., p. 5.
164 Ibid., p. 7.
165 See my discussion in Bush, *Halfway to Revolution*, pp. 282–91. This quotation (from *Adventures in Ideas*) is cited on p. 288.
166 Stephen Toulmin and June Goodfield, *The Architecture of Matter* (London: Hutchinson & Co., 1962), p. 170.
167 Thompson, *On Growth and Form*, p. 13.
168 Ibid., p. 172.
169 Ibid., pp. 200–1.
170 Ibid., p. 201.
171 Ibid., p. 201n.
172 Rukeyser, 'Poetry and Time', p. 9.
173 Ibid., p. 15,
174 Ibid., p. 11.
175 Ibid., p. 13.
176 Ibid., p. 13.
177 Ibid., p. 10.
178 Ibid., p. 17.
179 Ibid., p. 21.

180 Benjamin Lee Whorf, *Language, Thought and Reality: Selected Writings of Benjamin Lee Whorf*, ed. and intr. John B. Carroll (Cambridge, MA: MIT Press, 1956), p. 158. See Bush, *Halfway to Revolution*, pp. 292–318, for an extended discussion of these issues.
181 Rukeyser, 'Poetry and Time', pp. 26f.
182 Ibid., p. 24. She was to use the phrase for a section of the title poem in *Waterlily Fire* (1962).
183 Ibid., p. 24.
184 John Keats to George and Georgiana Keats, 14 February to 3 May 1819 in *The Letters of John Keats*, ed. Maurice Buxton Forman (London: Oxford University Press, 1948), p. 324.
185 Rukeyser, 'Poetry and Time', p. 27.
186 Ibid., pp. 32–3.
187 Northrop Frye, *Fearful Symmetry: A Study of William Blake* (Boston: Beacon Press, 1947), p. 135.
188 Rukeyser, 'Poetry and Time', p. 33.
189 Daniel Barenboim, Master class with Lang Lang and others, Television Programme, BBC 4, 30 May, 2005.
190 Rukeyser, 'Poetry and Time', p. 33. My italics.
191 John Keats to George and Georgiana Keats, 17–27 September 1819 in *Letters*, p. 407.
192 Rukeyser, 'Poetry and Time', p. 34.
193 'Un poète doit laisser des traces de son passage, non des preuves. Seules les traces font rêver.' René Char, 'La bibliotèque est en feu' in *La Parole en archipel*, René Char, *Œuvres complètes*, intr. Jean Roudaut (Paris: Gallimard, 1983), p. 382.
194 Aristotle, *The Art of Poetry*, trans. Ingram Bywater (Oxford: Clarendon Press, 1920), ch. 9, p. 43.
195 Rukeyser, 'Poetry and Time', p. 34.
196 Muriel Rukeyser, *A Turning Wind* (New York: Viking, 1939).
197 Fortunately, her college notes on a major music course have been preserved. These notes were a result of her classes and at least three assigned books: Paul Becker, *The Story of Music*; L'Andoming, *History of Music*; and Mason, *Beethoven and his forerunners.* The college notes are the most detailed and meticulous among all her papers.
198 Muriel Rukeyser, 'School Music Notes' (1932). The course was called 'Music 140'. There are no page numbers. No further references to this text will be given. Muriel Rukeyser Papers.
199 Ezra Pound. 'How to Read', in *Literary Essays of Ezra Pound* (New York: New Directions, 1968), p. 25.
200 Muriel Rukeyser, 'Music 140' (1932), in Notes 1934–57, n.p. Muriel Rukeyser Papers.
201 Cited in Susan Sontag, 'On Style' in *A Sontag Reader*, intr. Elizabeth Hardwick (New York: Farrar, Strauss, and Giroux, 1982), p. 150.
202 Rukeyser, 'The Antagonists', typescript.
203 Muriel Rukeyser, 'Ninth Elegy: The Antagonists' in *Complete Poems*, p. 257.
204 Muriel Rukeyser, typescript draft of 'The Antagonists', in Notes 1934–57. Muriel Rukeyser Papers.
205 Rukeyser, *Collected Poems*, p. 448.
206 Review of *Theory of Flight* in *Time* (16 December 1935).
207 Ruth Lechlitner, review of Muriel Rukeyser, *A Turning Wind*, *New York Herald Tribune* (7 January 1940), p. 10.
208 For all the subsequent information see Alan M. Wald, *Exiles from a Future Time: The Forging of the Mid-Twentieth-Century Literary Left* (Chapel Hill, NC, and London:

University of North Carolina Press, 2002), pp. 299f.

209 According to Wald she 'had a favourite routine with Robert Oppenheimer, who was a few years ahead of her in school; they would sneak up to the roofs of her father's nearly completed buildings on cold winter days. Lying on top of the water towers to feel the ambient hear from the water stored below, young Robert delivered mini-lectures on physics to her.' Wald, *Exiles from a Future Time*, p. 399.

210 Ibid., p. 305.

211 Dayton, *Muriel Rukeyser: The Book of the Dead.*

212 The argument is excellent on identifying the polarities, slightly less good on showing by close reading the way the options actually work, since the emphasis is on the nature of the possibility of extracting a historical discourse from the poetry rather than realizing it within the world of poetry itself.

213 Dayton, *Muriel Rukeyser: The Book of the Dead*, p. 61.

214 Frances G. Wickes, *The Inner World of Choice* (Boston, MA: Sigo Press, 1963), p. 289.

215 Muriel Rukeyser, 'Breaking Open', in *Collected Poems*, p. 529.

216 Hannah Arendt, *The Life of the Mind* (San Diego, CA: Harcourt Brace, 1978), p. 46.

217 Dayton, *Muriel Rukeyser: The Book of the Dead*, p. 147.

218 Ibid., p. 135.

Section II

1 Muriel Rukeyser, in an extended discussion with various authors, 'Trends in American Literature' *New Masses* (12 October 1938), p. 18.

2 See Michael Friedman, *A Parting of the Ways, Carnap, Cassirer, Heidegger* (Chicago, IL: Open Court, 2000). Also Gottfried Gabriel, trans. Andrew Inkpin, 'Carnap's 'Elimination of Metaphysics Through Logical Analysis of Language'. A Retrospective Consideration of the Relationship between Continental and Analytic Philosophy.' www.phil.cmu.edu/projects/carnap/jena/GabrielJena.rtf

3 Cited by Gabriel in 'Carnap's 'Elimination of Metaphysics Through Logical Analysis of Language'. Martin Heidegger, Afterword to: Was ist Metaphysik? In *Wegmarken (Gesamtausgabe*, vol. 9), (Frankfurt am Main: Klostermann, 1976).

4 John Keats to John Taylor, 27 February 1818 in *Letters*, p. 107.

5 Jean-Paul Sartre, *Notebooks for an Ethics*, trans. David Pellauer (Chicago, IL: University of Chicago Press, 1992), pp. 37–9.

6 Jean-Paul Sartre, *Mallarmé: la lucidité et sa face d'ombre* (Paris: Gallimard, 1986), pp. 18–19. My translation.

7 Ibid., p. 156. My translation.

8 Jean-Paul Sartre, *What is Literature?*, trans. Bernard Frechtman (London: Methuen, 1967), p. 6.

9 Shelley, *A Defence of Poetry*, p. 114.

10 Weil, *The Need for Roots*, p. 89.

11 *The Simone Weil Reader*, p. 438.

12 Ernst Cassirer, *Langage et mythe*, trans. Ole Hansen-Love (Paris: Minuit, 1973), pp. 52–3. Cited in Anne-Marie Smith DiBasio, '"The Ebb and Flow Of Conversation": A Metaphorics of Maternal Presence', *Études britanniques contemporaines* (Automne 2004), p. 84. My translation.

13 Michel Foucault, *The Order of Things: An Archaeology of the Human Sciences* (London: Tavistock, 1974), pp. 64 and 62.
14 Guy Debord, *The Society of the Spectacle*, trans. Donal Nicholson-Smith, 2nd edn (New York: Zone, 1995), p. 16.
15 Simone Weil, *The Simone Weil Reader*, ed. George A. Panichas (Mount Kisco, NY: Moyer Bell, 1977), p. 120.
16 Deuteronomy 8.2–3.
17 Weil, 'Forms of the Implicit Love of God', in *The Simone Weil Reader*, p. 471.
18 Simone Weil, *Lectures on Philosophy*, trans. Hugh Price, intr. Peter Winch (Cambridge: Cambridge University Press, 1978), pp. 186–9.
19 Weil, *The Need for Roots*, p. 225.
20 Jean-Paul Sartre, 'Mallarmé: The Poetry of Suicide', in *Between Existentialism and Marxism*, trans. John Mathews (New York: Morrow Quill Paperbacks, 1970), p. 173.
21 Muriel Rukeyser, 'F.O.M. died today April 1 1950', note added to the obituary notice.
22 Simone Weil, *Gravity and Grace*, trans. Arthur Wills, intr. Gustav Thibon (Lincoln, NE: University of Nebraska Press, 1997), p. 263.
23 Martin Heidegger, *Poetry, Language, Thought*, trans. Albert Hofstadter (New York: Harper and Row, 1975), pp. 213–29.
24 Martin Heidegger, *The Concept of Time*, trans. William McNeill (Oxford: Blackwell, 1989), p. 6E.
25 Heidegger, *The Concept of Time*, p. 5E.
26 Ibid., p. 14E.
27 Weil, *The Need for Roots*, p. 222.
28 Jean-Paul Sartre, *Being and Nothingness: An Essay on Phenomenological Ontology*, trans. Hazel E. Barnes (New York: Philosophical Library, 1956), p. 542.
29 Ibid., p. 467.
30 Ibid., p. 487.
31 Ibid., p. 467,
32 Heidegger, *The Concept of Time*, p. 21E.
33 Muriel Rukeyser, notes 1934–57. Muriel Rukeyser Papers
34 Muriel Rukeyser, notes 1934–57, 1963–78. n.d. On Sarah Lawrence College headed paper. Muriel Rukeyser Papers.
35 This is proposal to Curtis Brown is undated.
36 Ira Bruce Nadel, *The Cambridge Companion to Ezra Pound* (Cambridge: Cambridge University Press, 1999), p. 34.
37 Muriel Rukeyser to Ted Patrick, May 2 1951.
38 Muriel Rukeyser Papers. 1.28. File, *A Turning Wind.*
39 Rukeyser, *Collected Poems*, p. 146.
40 Ibid., p. 139.
41 This information is culled from an excellent on-line biographical note to the Payne Papers in the Stony Brook Manuscript Collection (no. 293). http//www.sunysb.edu/libspecial/collections/manuscripts/payne/bio.
42 Lorine Niedecker to Louis Zukofsky, 4 December 1952, in *Niedecker and the Correspondence with Zukofsky, 1931–1970*, ed. Jenny Penberthy (Cambridge: Cambridge University Press, 1993), pp. 199–200. In a letter to Zukofsky of 26 June 1957 (p. 236), Niedecker said she had just bought a copy of Payne's translations of Chinese poetry: *The White Pony.*
43 Robert Payne, review of Muriel Rukeyer's *Ten Elegies*, no journal/paper details. Muriel Rukeyser Papers.

44 Ibid.
45 Muriel Rukeyser, ms note, n.d. Reproduced in 'Breaking Open', *The Collected Poems*, p. 529.
46 Ibid.
47 J.E. Spingarn, 'Politics and the Poet: A Prophecy by J.E. Spingarn', *The Atlantic Monthly* (19 November 1942), p. 78.
48 Arendt, *The Human Condition*, pp. 25, 26.
49 Muriel Rukeyser to Lewis Mumford, 11 May 1944. Lewis Mumford Papers.
50 Muriel Rukeyser, 'Ninth Elegy: The Antagonists', in *Collected Poems*, p. 259.
51 Ibid., p. 260.
52 Ibid., p. 148.
53 Ibid., p. 150.
54 See Herbert Preuss and Wilhelm Molitor, *Seefahrt-Fibel des deutschen Jungen* (Munich and Berlin: Lehmann, 1941).
55 Rukeyser, *Collected Poems*, p. 151.
56 Ibid.
57 Ibid., p. 152.
58 Michel Foucault, *Madness and Civilization: A History of Insanity in the Age of Reason* (London: Tavistock, 1967), p. 289.
59 Rukeyser, *Collected Poems*, p. 154.
60 Ibid., p. 156.
61 Ibid., p. 157.
62 Alexander F. Chamberlain, *The Child and Childhood in Folk-Thought* (New York: Macmillan, 1896), pp. 150–1.
63 Gaston Bachelard, *Psychoanalysis and Fire*, trans. Alan C.M. Ross, preface by Northrop Frye (Boston, MA: Beacon Press: 1968), pp. 21–2.
64 Rukeyser, *Collected Poems*, p. 157.
65 Ibid., p. 158. My italics.
66 Ibid., p. 159.
67 Ibid., p. 161.
68 Ibid., p. 248.
69 Allen Ginsberg, 'Howl', in *Collected Poems*, p. 126. See also Clive Bush, 'Holding the Line: Allen Ginsberg between Past and Future' in *Holding the Line: Selected Essays in American Literature and Culture* (Bern: Peter Lang, 2009), pp. 163–78.
70 Rukeyser, *Collected Poems*, p. 249.
71 See Victor Serge, *S'il est minuit dans le siècle* (Paris: Grasset, 1939). This work translated into English as *Midnight in the Century* is the provenance of the title of this book.
72 Rukeyser, *Collected Poems*, p. 250.
73 Rukeyser to author in conversation, Westbeth, New York City, c.1973.
74 Rukeyser, *Collected Poems*, p. 248.
75 Ibid., p. 249.
76 Ibid., p. 251.
77 I have drawn here on William Arrowsmith's excellent introduction to Euripides' *The Bacchae* in *The Complete Greek Tragedies: Euripides V* (Chicago, IL, and London: University of Chicago Press, 1968), pp. 142–53.
78 James R. Caldwell, 'Imagination and a Brilliant Hope', review of Muriel Rukeyser, *The Life of Poetry, Elegies, Orpheus*, in *Saturday Review* (11 March 1950), p. 26.
79 Rukeyser, *Collected Poems*, p. 257.
80 Ibid.
81 Ibid., p. 258.
82 Ibid.
83 Hugh MacDiarmid [Murray Grieve], 'A Moment in Eternity' in *Hugh MacDiarmid: The Complete Poems, 1920–1976*, ed. Michael Grieve and W.R. Aitken (London: Martin Brian & O'Keefe, 1978), pp. 1, 3.
84 Muriel Rukeyser to Lewis Mumford, 3 September 1963. Lewis Mumford Papers.
85 Rukeyser, *Collected Poems*, p. 281.
86 Ibid. My italics.

87 Jean-Nicolas-Arthur Rimbaud, *Rimbaud: Complete Works, Selected Letters*, trans. Wallace Fowlie (Chicago, IL, and London: University of Chicago Press, 1966), p. 121.
88 Rukeyser, *Collected Poems*, p. 147.
89 Ibid.
90 'Sum', *Shorter Oxford Dictionary*, 3rd edn.
91 Rukeyser, *Collected Poems*, p. 147.
92 Ibid., p. 148.
93 Ricoeur, *Time and Narrative, Vol. 3*, p. 191.
94 Rukeyser, *Collected Poems*, p. 148.
95 Muriel Rukeyser, small black notebook (1942), n.p. Muriel Rukeyser Papers.
96 Martin Heidegger, *The Concept of Time*, trans. William McNeill (Oxford and Cambridge, MA: Blackwell, 1989), pp. 9, 9E.
97 Rainer Maria Rilke, *Rilke: Duino Elegies*, trans. Stephen Cohn (Manchester: Carcanet, 1989), p. 21.
98 'Denn Bleiben ist nirgends.' Rilke, 'The First Elegy' in Rilke, *Elegies*, p. 23.
99 Rainer Maria Rilke, *Sonnets to Orpheus*, Part II, no. 2, trans. Willis Barnstone (Boston, MA and London: Shambhala, 2004), p. 159.
100 Rukeyser, *Collected Poems*, p. 147.
101 Charles Olson, *Human Universe and Other Essays* (New York: Grove Press, 1967), p. 10.
102 William Wordsworth, *The Prelude, Book Five* in *Wordsworth: Poetry and Prose*, ed. W.M. Merchant (London: Rupert Hart-Davis, 1955), p. 344.
103 Wordsworth, *The Prelude, Book Five*, p. 346.
104 Emma Goldman, *Anarchism and Other Essays*, 2nd rev. edn (New York and London: Mother Earth, 1911), p. 245.

Epilogue: Rare Calendars of Feeling

1 The title is derived from Anna Politkovskaya's conclusion to *A Small Corner of Hell: Dispatches from Chechnya*, trans. Alexander Burry and Tatiana Tuchinsky, intr. Georgi Derluguian (Chicago, IL, and London: University of Chicago Press, 2003), p. 216: 'since feelings are so rare now, they are the most important thing in my calendar'.
2 William Wordsworth, *Book X of the Prelude* (1805). Cited in Robert Fisk, *The Great War for Civilisation: The Conquest of the Middle East* (London: Harper Perennial, 2006), p. 112.
3 James Cameron, *Point of Departure: Experiment in Biography by James Cameron* (London: Arthur Barker, 1967), p. 240.
4 Elias Khoury, *Gate of the Sun* [*Babi El Shams*], trans. Humphrey Davies (London: Harvill Secker, 2005), p. 222.
5 It has to be said that in recent years Yale has made a great effort to raise money for bursaries. Nonetheless these highly commendable efforts are overwhelmed by the uneven quality of high school education.
6 John Pilger, *The New Rulers of the World* (London and New York: Verso, 2002), p. 148.
7 See for a recent example the fate of the Adivisi peoples, now caught between State Militias and Maoists in India: Cédric Gouverneur, 'India's undeclared war,' *Le Monde diplomatique* (December 2007), 4–5.
8 Paul N. Hehn, *A Low Dishonest Decade: The Great Powers, Eastern Europe, and the Economic Origins of World War II, 1930–1941* (New York and London: Continuum, 2002),

pp. ix, x. It appears that Professor Hehn had difficulty in publishing this 'oversized and involved work', and especially thanked the courage and imagination of his publishers at Continuum: 'the longer the better.' One can only be grateful to the publishers.

9 Ibid., p. 118.

10 Ibid., p. 3.

11 Susan George, *A Fate Worse than Debt* (London: Grove Weidenfeld, 1990).

12 Hehn, *A Low Dishonest Decade*, p. 3.

13 Bertolt Brecht, *Journals 1935–1955*, eds John Willett and Ralph Manheim (New York: Routledge, 1996), p. 59.

14 See Dominique Kopp, 'Russia the polar grab' in *Le Monde Diplomatique*, September 2007, 8–9.

15 Hehn, *A Low Dishonest Decade*, p. 38.

16 Ibid., p. 12. A recent comment in a personal memoir by Alan Greenspan, 'I am saddened that it is politically inconvenient to acknowledge what everyone knows, the Iraq war is largely about oil', has received wide publicity. In a tongue-in-cheek article in the *London Review of Books*, Jim Holt has argued in that economic realpolitik a controllable though unstable Iraq will enable the United States to access the trillions of dollars of Iraqi oil for the foreseeable future thus offsetting the trillion dollars worth of denominated debts (including four hundred billion in US treasury bonds) held by China. In that sense the war in Iraq might be said to have been an economic success. However, the neo-cons ambitious plans for this particular economic future, as Weil said of fate, will probably, as Holt also concludes, be undermined by the unpredictable future itself. Jim Holt, 'It's the Oil', *The London Review of Books* 29.20 (18 October 2007), pp. 3–4.

17 Hehn, *A Low Dishonest Decade*, p. 12.

18 Ibid., p. 15.

19 Ibid., p. 99.

20 Ibid., p. 121.

21 See Chapter 4 of Hehn's *The Economic Origins of World War II*.

22 Hehn, *A Low Dishonest Decade*, p. 168.

23 Ibid., p. 19.

24 Ibid., pp. 124, 129.

25 Ibid., p. 164.

26 Ibid., p. 202.

27 Ibid., p. 220.

28 Ibid., p. 37.

29 Ibid., p. 117.

30 Ibid., p. 19.

31 Serge wrote to Macdonald on 9 October 1941: 'Le cerveau du marxisme-rev. détruit à Coyoacan et à Moscou (Boukharine, Preobrjenski) par Guepeou, le cerveau du marxism libéral-reformiste détruit dans un sordide prison par la Gestapo, cela montre bien quelle lutte se poursuite à travers cette guerre de réaction mondiale contre les formes supérieures de la conscience sociale. — Le sort de Hilferding devrait aussi permettre de reposer la question des réfugiés [...] en France [...]'.

32 Hehn, *A Low Dishonest Decade*, p. 405.

33 See Holt, 'It's the Oil.

34 Hehn, *A Low Dishonest Decade*, p. 20.

35 Ibid., p. 23.

36 Ibid., p. 36.

37 See Stefan Kühl, *The Nazi Connection: Eugenics, American Racism and German National Socialism* (Oxford and New York:

Oxford University Press, 1994) and Max Wallace, *The American Axis: Henry Ford, Charles Lindbergh and the Rise of the Third Reich* (New York: St Martin's Press, 2003). These works are cited by Michael Lowy and Eleni Varikas in 'Hitler's Hero: Heinrich Ford', *Le Monde Diplomatique* (May 2007), pp. 12–13. The article details the virulent anti-Semitism of Henry Ford and notes that in 1922 Ford had Hitler's portrait hanging on the wall behind his desk.

38 Hehn, *A Low Dishonest Decade*, p. 25.

39 Ibid., p. 27.

40 Ibid., p. 84.

41 For recent report on the continuing mayhem, corruption and violence in Baghdad, see Ed Harriman, 'Burn Rate', *London Review of Books* (6 September 2007), pp. 15–17.

42 Norman G. Finkelstein, *Image and Reality of the Israel-Palestine Conflict* (1995; London: Verso, 2003), p. xxv. Finkelstein has recently been denied tenure at Depaul University under pressure from the American academic Zionist Right. His 'tone' is regarded as being immoderate. My own view is that his facts are hard to dispute, and that his entirely appropriate anger is that of the engaged intellectual whose absence, elsewhere, American academics are lamenting. See Christopher Brown, 'A Question of Scholarship: On the Tenure Controversy of Prof. Norman G. Finkelstein', *The [CUNY Center] Advocate* (4 May 2007).

43 Walter Benjamin, 'Fate and Character', in *One Way Street and other Writings*, trans. Edmund Jephcott and Kingsley Shorter (London: New Left Books, 1979), p. 126.

44 Ilan Pappe, *The Ethnic Cleansing of Palestine* (Oxford: Oneworld, 2006). Alan Dershowitz, the Harvard law professor who has led the campaign against Finkelstein came to prominence after 9/11 when the then Republican administration felt free to 'promote punishments for Israel's opponents that came close to the advocacy of war crimes'. Dershowitz favours the limited use of torture to extract information. Fisk, *The Great War for Civilization*, p. 603.

45 George Soros, *New York Review of Books* 54.6 (12 April 2007).

46 Pappe, *The Ethnic Cleansing of Palestine*, p. 259.

47 Hernando Calvo Ospina, 'The CIA's Successors and Collaborators. US: Overt and Covert Destabilisation', *Le Monde Diplomatique* (August 2007), p. 4. Ospina reviews the activities of the National Endowment for Democracy (NED), a new organisation formed after the CIA's activities against figures such as Lumumba, Allende and Castro were investigated by a Senate Committee in 1975.

48 Rukeyser, *Willard Gibbs*, p. 8.

49 Pilger, *The New Rulers of the World*, p. 2.

50 Jonathan Freedland, 'When it Comes to Global Warming, Market Rule Poses a Mortal Danger', *The Guardian* (25 October 2006).

51 Tom Nairn, 'The Enabling Boundary', review article of: Roberto Magabeira Unger, *What Should the Left Propose?* and *The Self Awakened*; Jacques Attali, *Une brève histoire de l'avenir*, *London Review of Books* 29.20 (18 October 2007), pp. 5–7.

52 Cited in Danielle Folet and Thoms Boothe, with the assistance of David Ramm, 'The Show that Challenges Presidents', *Le Monde diplomatique* (January 2008), pp. 11–12. See, for a fuller picture, Eric Klinenberg, *Fighting for Air: The Battle to Control America's Media* (New York: Metropolitan Books, 2007). The *Le Monde* article charts the encouraging rise and progress of the independent radio station *Democracy Now*.

53 The publicity surrounding the recent death of Politkovskaya should not obscure the fact that many other Russian journalists have been killed. Free-speaking opposition journalists the world over are in danger. For example, the exiled Uzbek opposition activist Alisher Saipov was shot dead in 2007 in Kyrgyzstan, across the border from Uzbekistan, where the brutal illiberal regime of President Islam Karimov has been in power for eighteen years. Leila Saralayeva, 'Dissident Uzbek Reporter Shot Dead', *The Independent* (26 October 2007). The latest incident as this conclusion is being written is the exile of the twenty-four-year-old Natalya Morar, *The Independent* (19 January 2008).

54 Report by Tom Parfitt, *The Guardian* (10 October 2006).

55 Perry Anderson, 'Russia's Managed Democracy' *The London Review of Books* 29.2 (25 January 2007), pp. 3–7. The following account is based on this article.

56 http://www.hist.umn.edu/~ruggles/Approval.htm at the end of 2007.

57 Anderson, 'Russia's Managed Democracy', p. 7.

58 Ibid., p. 6.

59 Ibid., p. 7.

60 Ibid.

61 Ibid., p. 8.

62 Ibid.

63 Ibid.

64 If this seems grumpy, let me be the first to admit that I see the opening paragraphs of *Gravity's Rainbow* as a magnificent tour de force. Perhaps it is the limits of the satiric genre in dealing with historical narrative and the limits of black humour dealing in endlessly marketed virtual cultural stereotypes that is the problem. The difficulty is an unselfconscious lack of awareness of the limits of satire that in the end reduce history to an endless joke, backed somehow by a too obvious universalist fetishistic psychology and all accompanied with a fatalistic aristocratic weariness. In this genre I much prefer William Burroughs, also from the American upper classes, but who carries with him some of the real political intelligence of the mid-century.

65 Anna Politkovskaya, *A Small Corner of Hell: Dispatches from Chechnya*, trans. Alexander Burry and Tatiana Tulchinsky, intr. George Derluguian (Chicago, IL, and London: University of Chicago Press, 2007), p. 27.

66 Ibid., p. 47.

67 Ibid., p. 46.

68 Ibid., p. 32.

69 Ibid., p. 41.

70 Ibid., pp. 87, 136.

71 Ibid., p. 140.

72 Fisk, *The Great War for Civilisation*, p. 31.

73 Politkovskaya, *A Small Corner of Hell*, p. 71.

74 Ibid., p. 29.

75 Ibid., p. 43.

76 Ibid., pp. 56, 67.

77 Ibid., p. 60.
78 Ibid., p. 187.
79 Leading Article on the UN. *The Independent*: 13 Nov. 2007.
80 Politkovskaya, *A Small Corner of Hell*, p. 119.
81 Ibid., p. 153.
82 Ibid., p. 164.
83 Ibid.
84 Ibid., p. 166.
85 Ibid., pp. 168–72.
86 Ibid., p. 216.
87 Ibid., p. 199.
88 Muriel Rukeyser, 'Nine Poems for the Unborn Child' in *Collected Poems* (New York: McGraw-Hill, 1978), p. 287.
89 Fisk, *The Great War for Civilization*, p. 607.
90 Steven Erlanger, 'Israeli Forces Kill 9 in Gaza', *New York Times* (4 January 2008). James Cameron called the *New York Times* 'the best and worst newspaper on earth, a daily monument to the sloppy and extravagant simplification of the overdone'. Cameron, *Point of Departure*, p. 71.
91 Fisk, *The Great War for Civilization*, p. 671.
92 Ibid., p. 673.
93 Ibid., p. 557.
94 Ibid., p. 558.
95 Ibid., p. xxi.
96 Cameron, *Point of Departure*, pp. 87–8.
97 Ibid., p. 72.
98 Fisk, *The Great War for Civilization*, p. xxii.
99 Jean-Paul Sartre, 'John Dos Passos and "1919" in *Literary and Philosophical Essays*, trans. Annette Michelson (London: Radius/Hutchinson, 1968), pp. 88–96. It is amusing that most American commentators always emphasise Sartre's closing words with a degree of nationalist pride: 'I regard Dos Passos as the greatest writer of our time', without observing its insouciant Parisian irony. Sartre's devastating critique of Dos Passos in the essay should be clear, notwithstanding his accurate recognition of the American writer's ability to capture and delineate the nightmarish modernist world that Dos Passos so chillingly, yet at the same time so unconsciously, discloses.
100 Fisk, *The Great War for Civilization*, p. 675.
101 The *locus classicus* of these observations is Marshall McLuhan, *Understanding Media* (London: Routledge and Kegan Paul, 1964), p. 210.
102 Fisk, *The Great War for Civilization*, p. xxi.
103 Ibid., p. xix.
104 Ibid., p. 480.
105 Ibid., p. 83.
106 Ibid., p. 84.
107 Walter Benjamin, 'Theses on the Philosophy of Time', in *Illuminations*, ed. and intr. Hannah Arendt, trans Harry Zohn (London: Fontana/Collins, 1982), pp. 255–6.
108 Paul Ricoeur, *Memory, History, Forgetting*, trans. Kathleen Blamey and David Pellauer (Chicago, IL: University of Chicago Press, 2004), p. 240. Further page references follow in the text.
109 Benjamin, 'Theses on the Philosophy of Time', p. 237.
110 Ibid., p. 256.
111 Ibid., p. 258.
112 Ibid., p. 259.
113 Ibid., pp. 259–60.
114 Ibid., p. 261.
115 Ibid., p. 263. And 263n.
116 Ibid., p. 264.
117 Ibid., p. 265.

118 See John Pilger, "Good 'ole Bill the liberal hero". http://www.johnpilger.com/page.asp?partid=449
119 Fisk, *The Great War for Civilization*, p. 1286.
120 Pilger, *The New Rulers of the World*, p. 2.
121 Ibid., p. 5.
122 Ibid., p. 8.
123 Ibid., p. 11.
124 Ibid., p. 4.
125 Ibid., p. 120. See also Dan Hind's useful book *The Threat to Reason* (London and New York: Verso, 2007), p. 60: 'No element of the rhetoric surrounding the War on Terror can survive careful, actually enlightened inquiry. As a description of reality it amounts to well-organised fraud, a piece of enchantment. It is as an attempt to reconcile the world to permanent war.'
126 Pilger, *The New Rulers of the World*, p. 120.
127 Ibid., p. 121.
128 Ibid., p. 156.
129 Ibid.
130 Muriel Rukeyser, 'Poem' and 'Letter to the Front', in *The Collected Poems*, pp. 450 and 239. In the second poem Rukeyser accepts that 'the gift is torment', but in a familiar move asserts that this deep contradiction is an opportunity for imaginative resistance, and the rejection of bad faith.
131 Rukeyser, 'The Speed of Darkness' in *The Collected Poems*, p. 486.
132 John Berger, *Hold Everything Dear: Dispatches on Survival and Resistance* (London and New York: Verso, 2007).
133 Rukeyser, *Willard Gibbs*, p. 362.
134 Berger, *Hold Everything Dear*, p. 119.
135 Ibid.
136 Ibid.
137 Ibid., p. 147.
138 Ibid., p. 140.

Bibliography

ARCHIVES

Victor Serge

Otherwise unreferenced articles by Serge are typescripts (dated or undated) in the Victor Serge Papers, Beinecke Manuscript and Rare Book Library, Yale University, New Haven.

Dwight Macdonald

Unpublished letters to and from Macdonald are located in Manuscripts and Archives, Sterling Memorial Library, Yale University, New Haven.

Dorothy Norman

Unpublished letters to and from Norman are located in Beinecke Rare Book and Manuscript Library, Yale University, New Haven.

Alfred Stieglitz

The relevant papers can be found in the Stieglitz Papers, Beinecke Rare Book and Manuscript Library, Yale University, New Haven.

Lewis Mumford

Unpublished letters to and from Mumford are located in the Mumford Papers, Special Collections, University of Pennsylvania, Philadelphia.

Muriel Rukeyser

All unpublished letters to and from Rukeyser, together with other cited unpublished material are in the Muriel Rukeyser Papers, Library of Congress, Washington DC.

PUBLISHED WORKS

Adams, Henry, *The Education of Henry Adams: An Autobiography* (1918; Boston, MA: Houghton Mifflin, 1961).

Adams, Henry, *Mont Saint Michel and Chartres* (1904/1913; New York: Gordon Press, 1974).

Adams, Henry, *The Degradation of the Democratic Dogma*, intr. Brooks Adams (New York: Macmillan, 1919).

Adams, John Quincy, 'From his Diary 1826–1844', *TWICE A YEAR*, vols XII–XIII (Fall–Winter 1945), pp. 453–96.

Anderson, Perry, 'Russia's Managed Democracy', *The London Review of Books* 29.2 (25 January 2007), pp. 3–7.

Arendt, Hannah, *The Human Condition* (New York: Doubleday Anchor, 1959).

Arendt, Hannah, *The Life of the Mind* (San Diego, CA: Harcourt Brace, 1971).

Arendt, Hannah, *Love and Saint Augustine: Hannah Arendt*, ed. Joanna Vecchiarelli Scott and Judith Chelius Stark (Chicago, IL and London: University of Chicago Press, 1996).

Arendt, Hannah, *Men in Dark Times* (San Diego, CA: Harcourt Brace, 1955).

Arendt, Hannah, *The Origins of Totalitarianism* (1958; Cleveland and New York: Meridian Books, The World Publishing Company, 1967).

Aristotle, *The Art of Poetry*, trans. Ingram Bywater (Oxford: Clarendon Press, 1920).

Arnold, Matthew, *Matthew Arnold: Poetry and Prose*, ed. John Bryson (London: Rupert Hart-Davis, 1954).

Aron, Raymond, *Introduction to the Philosophy of History*, trans. George J. Irwin (London: Weidenfeld and Nicholson, 1961).

Bachelard, Gaston, *Psychoanalysis and Fire*, trans. Alan C.M. Ross, preface by Northrop Frye (Boston, MA: Beacon Press, 1968).

Badiou, Alain, *Deleuze: The Clamor of Being*, trans. Louise Burchill (Minneapolis, MN and London: University of Minnesota Press, 1999).

Baldwin, James, *Tell Me How Long the Train's Been Gone* (London: Corgi, 1968).

Baldwin, Roger N., 'Should the Dies Committee Die?', *TWICE A YEAR*, vol. II (Spring–Summer 1939), pp. 226–33.

Balzer, Marie Mandelstam, *Russian Traditional Culture* (Armonk, NY and London: M.E. Sharpe, 1992).

Bataille, Georges, *Eroticism*, trans. Mary Dalwood (London and New York: Marion Boyars, 1987).

Bataille, Georges, *Literature and Evil*, trans. Alistair Hamilton (London and New York, Marion Boyars, 1985).

Bataille, Georges, *The Impossible*, trans. Robert Hurley (San Francisco, CA: City Lights, 1991).

Batlivala, Bhicoo, 'Civil Liberties in India', *TWICE A YEAR*, vols V–VI (Spring–Summer 1941), pp. 512–18.

Beauvoir, Simone de, 'Eye for an Eye', trans. Mary McCarthy, *politics* (August 1947), pp. 34–6.

Beauvoir, Simone de, *Letters to Sartre*, trans. and ed. Quintin Hoare (London: Radius, 1991).

Beauvoir, Simone de, *The Second Sex*, trans. and ed. H.M. Parshley (London: Picador, 1988).

Benjamin, Walter, *Illuminations*, intr. Hannah Arendt (London: Fontana, 1973).

Benjamin, Walter, *One Way Street and Other Writings*, trans. Edmund Jephcott and Kingsley Shorter (London: New Left Books, 1979).

Berger, John, *Hold Everything Dear: Dispatches on Survival and Resistance* (London and New York: Verso, 2007).

Berger, John, *Ways of Seeing* (Harmondsworth: Penguin, 1972).

Berlin, Isaiah, review of John Carswell, *The Exile: A Life of Ivy Litvinov*, *Sunday Times* (8 May 1984), p. 41.

Bingham, June, *Courage to Change: An Introduction to the Life and Thought of Reinhold Niebuhr* (New York: Scribner's, 1961).

Bird, Kai, and Lifshultz, Lawrence (eds), *Hiroshima's Shadow: Writings on the Denial of History and the Smithsonian Controversy* (Stony Creek, CT: Pamphleteer's Press, 1998).

Blake, Casey, 'The Perils of Personality: Lewis Mumford and Politics After Liberalism' in *Lewis Mumford: Public Intellectual* (New York: Oxford University Press, 1990), pp. 283–300.

Bloch, Ernst, 'Writers in Exile', *TWICE A YEAR*, vols III–IV (1940), pp. 143–5.

Bookchin, Murray, *The Ecology of Freedom: The Emergence and Dissolution of Hierarchy* (Palo Alto, CA: Cheshire Books, 1982).

Borghese, G.A., 'Culture in Exile', *TWICE A YEAR*, vols III–IV (1940), pp. 138–43.

Bourne, Randolph, *The Radical Will: Randolph Bourne, Selected Writings 1911–1918*, ed. Olaf Hansen, preface by Christopher Lasch (New York: Urizen Books, 1977).

Bourne, Randolph, 'The War and the Intellectuals', *TWICE A YEAR*, vol. I (1938), pp. 38–49.

Braudel, Fernand, *On History*, trans. Sarah Matthews (Chicago, IL: University of Chicago Press, c.1980).

Braudel, Fernand, *The Perspective of the World*, trans. Siân Reynolds (London: Collins/Fontana Press, 1984).

Braudel, Fernand, *The Structures of Everyday Life: The Limits of the Possible*, rev. and trans. Siân Reynolds (London: Collins, 1981).

Brecht, Bertolt, *Journals 1834–1955*, trans. Hugh Rorrison, ed. John Willet (New York: Routledge, 1996).

Brown, Christopher, 'A Question of Scholarship: On the Tenure Controversy of Prof. Norman G. Finkelstein', *The CUNY Center Advocate* (4 May 2007).

Brown, Judith M., *Nehru: A Political Life* (New Haven, CT and London: Yale University Press, 2003).

Brown, Norman O., *Life Against Death: The Psychoanalytical Meaning of History* (New York: Vintage Books, 1959).

Bush, Clive, *The Dream of Reason: American Consciousness and Cultural Achievement from Independence to the Civil War* (London: Edward Arnold, 1977).

Bush, Clive, 'Escape from Marseille: An American Story? Writing Victor Serge's, Laurette Séjourné's, Dwight and Nancy Macdonald's Balzacian book' in *Prospects:*

An Annual of American Cultural Studies (New York: Cambridge University Press, 2003), pp. 311–40.

Bush, Clive, *Halfway to Revolution: Investigation and Crisis in the Work of Henry Adams, William James and Gertrude Stein* (New Haven, CT and London: Yale University Press, 1991).

Bush, Clive, 'Holding the Line: Allen Ginsberg between Past and Future' in *Holding the Line: Selected Essays in American Literature and Culture* (Bern: Peter Lang, 2009), pp. 163–78.

Bush, Clive, *Holding the Line: Selected Essays in American Literature and Culture* (Bern: Peter Lang, 2009).

Bush, Clive, 'Left-wing Isolationism, Literature and Ideology in America during the Run-up to World War II', *Comparative American Studies* 1.1 (2003), pp. 131–52.

Bush, Clive, *Muriel Rukeyser: The Poet as Scientific Biographer* (London: Spanner Press, 1977),

Caffin, Charles Henry, 'Whistler', *Camera Work* 12 (1905).

Calas, Nicholas, 'Transforming the Past', *TWICE A YEAR*, vol. VII (Fall–Winter 1941), pp. 25–9.

Caldwell, James R., 'Imagination and a Brilliant Hope' (review of Muriel Rukeyser, *The Life of Poetry, Elegies, Orpheus*), *The Saturday Review* (11 March 1950), p. 26.

Cameron, James, *Point of Departure: Experiment in Biography by James Cameron* (London: Arthur Barker, 1967).

Camus, Albert, 'The Human Crisis', trans. Lionel Abel, *TWICE A YEAR*, vols XIV–XV (Fall–Winter 1946–7), pp. 19–33.

Carroll, Lewis, *Alice Through the Looking Glass* in *The Works of Lewis Carroll* (London: Spring Books, 1965).

Carswell, John, *The Exile: A Life of Ivy Litvinov* (London: Faber and Faber, 1983).

Chamberlain, Alexander F., *The Child and Childhood in Folk-Thought* (New York: Macmillan, 1896).

Char, René, *Feuillets d'Hypnos* in *Œuvres complètes*, intr. Jean Roudaut (Paris: Gallimard, 1983).

Char, René, *Hypnos Waking: Poetry and Prose by René Char*, trans. Jackson Mathews et al. (New York: Random House, c.1956).

Ciliga, Anton, *The Russian Enigma and Siberia: Land of Exile and Industrialisation*, trans. Fernand G. Fernier, Anne Cliff and Margaret and Hugo Dewar (London: Ink Links, 1979).

Coleridge, Samuel Taylor, *The Poems of Samuel Taylor Coleridge* (1912; London: Oxford University Press, 1960).

Conner, Tom, *André Gide's Politics: Rebellion and Ambivalence* (New York: Palgrave, 2000).

Conrad, Joseph, *Notes on Life and Letters* (London and Toronto: J.M. Dent, 1921).

Conrad, Joseph, *Youth* in *Great Short Works of Joseph Conrad* (New York: Harper and Row, 1966).

Darwin, Charles, *The Origin of Species* (1859; Harmondsworth: Penguin, 1968).

Davis, Mike, *City of Quartz* (New York: Vintage, 1992).

Davis, Mike, *Planet of Slums* (London: Verso, 2005).

Dayton, Tim, *Muriel Rukeyser: The Book of the Dead* (Columbia, MO: University of Missouri Press, 2003).

Debord, Guy, *The Society of the Spectacle*, 2nd edn, trans. Donal Nicholson-Smith (New York: Zone, 1995).

Donne, John, *The Poems of John Donne*, ed. Sir Herbert Grierson (London: Oxford University Press, 1933).

Dos Passos, John, *Nineteen Nineteen, U.S.A.* (1932; Harmondsworth: Penguin, 1966).

Duncan, Robert, *The Truth and Life of Myth* (Fremont, MI: Sumac Press, 1968).

Ellul, Jacques, *Propaganda: The Formation of Men's Attitudes*, trans. Konrad Kellen and Jean Lerner (New York: Vintage, 1973).

Emmet, Dorothy, *Whitehead's Philosophy of Organism* (London: Macmillan, 1932).

Engels, Frederick, *Socialism: Utopian and Scientific* (New York: International Publishers, 1935).

Ermolaev, Herman, *Soviet Literary Theories, 1917–1934: The Genesis of Socialist Realism* (Berkeley and Los Angeles, CA: University of California Press, 1963).

Euripides, *The Complete Greek Tragedies: Euripides V*, intr. William Arrowsmith (Chicago, IL and London: University of Chicago Press, 1968).

Finkelstein, Norman G., *Image and Reality of the Israel-Palestine Conflict* (1995; Verso: London, 2003).

Fisk, Robert, *The Great War for Civilisation: The Conquest of the Middle East* (London: Harper Perennial, 2006).

Flint, Robert, 'Post-Impressionism' in Dorothy Norman, *Alfred Stieglitz: Introduction to an American Seer* (New York: Duell, Sloan, and Pearce, 1960), p. 138.

Folet, Danielle, and Thomas Boothe (with the assistance of David Ramm), 'The Show that Challenges Presidents', *Le Monde Diplomatique* (January 2008), pp. 11–12.

Foucault, Michel, *Madness and Civilization: A History of Insanity in the Age of Reason* (London: Tavistock, 1967).

Foucault, Michel, *The Order of Things: An Archaeology of the Human Sciences* (London: Tavistock, 1974).

Fox, Richard Wightman, 'Tragedy, Responsibility, and the American Intellectual, 1925–1950' in Thomas P. Hughes and Agatha C. Hughes (eds), *Lewis Mumford: Public Intellectual* (New York: Oxford University Press, 1990), pp. 323–38.

Fraser, Ronald, *Blood of Spain: An Oral History of the Spanish Civil War* (New York: Pantheon Books, 1979).

Frazer. J.T. (ed.), *Voices of Time: A Co-operative Survey of Man's Views of Time as Expressed by the Sciences and the Humanities* (New York: G. Braziller, 1966).

Freud, Anna, and Dorothy T. Burlingham, *War and Children: A Message to American Parents* (New York: Medical War Books, 1943).

Friedman, Michael, *A Parting of the Ways: Carnap, Cassirer, Heidegger* (Chicago, IL: Open Court, 2000).

Frobenius, Leo, *The Childhood of Man, A Popular Account of the Lives, Customs and Thoughts of the Primitive Races*, trans. A.H. Keane (London: Seeley & Co., 1909).

Fryd, Vivien Green, *Art and the Crisis of Marriage: Edward Hopper and Georgia O'Keeffe* (Chicago, IL: University of Chicago Press, 2002).

Frye, Northrop, *Fearful Symmetry: A Study of William Blake* (Boston, MA: Beacon Press, 1947).

Fulton, Ann, *Apostles of Sartre: Existentialism in America, 1945–1963* (Evanston, IL: Northwestern University Press, 1999).

Fussell, Paul, *Wartime: Understanding and Behaviour in the Second World War* (New York and Oxford: Oxford University Press, 1989).

Geddes, Patrick, 'Life and its Science', *The Evergreen* (Spring 1895), reprinted in *Edinburgh Review* (Summer 1992).

Geddes, Patrick, 'The Scots Renaissance', *The Evergreen* (Spring 1895), reprinted in *Edinburgh Review* (Summer 1992).

George, Susan, *A Fate Worse than Debt* (London: Grove Weidenfeld, 1990).

Ginsberg, Allen, *Collected Poems: 1947–1980* (New York: Viking, 1985).

Gold, Mary Jayne, *Crossroads Marseille, 1940* (New York: Doubleday, 1980).

Goldman, Emma, *Anarchism and Other Essays*, 2nd rev. edn (New York and London: Mother Earth, 1911).

Gollancz, Victor, *My Dear Timothy: An Autobiographical Letter to his Grandson* (Harmondsworth: Penguin, 1952).

Gottesman, Callman, 'Petition for Review to The Board of Regents of the State of New York', *TWICE A YEAR*, vols VIII–IX (Fall–Winter 1942), pp. 321–42.

Gouverneur, Cédric, 'India's Undeclared War', *Le Monde Diplomatique* (December 2007), pp. 4–5.

Gramsci, Antonio, *Pre-Prison Writings*, ed. Richard Bellamy (Cambridge: Cambridge University Press, 1994).

Granath, Olle (ed.), *August Strindberg: Painter, Photographer, Writer* (London: Tate Publishing, 2005).

Gray, Francine du Plessix, *Simone Weil* (London: Weidenfeld and Nicholson, 2001).

Guest, Barbara, *Herself Defined: The Poet H.D. and her World* (New York: Quill, 1984).

Guthrie, Anne, *Madame Ambassador: The Life of Vijaya Lakshmi Pandit* (New York: Harcourt Brace, 1962).

Harriman, Ed, 'Burn Rate', *London Review of Books* (6 September 2007), pp. 15–17.

Hart, Henry (ed.), *Writer in a Changing World* (New York: Equinox Cooperative Press, 1937).

Hawthorne, Nathaniel, *The Scarlet Letter* in *Collected Novels* (New York: Library of America, 1983).

Hegel, G.W.F., *The Phenomenology of Mind*, trans. J.B. Baillie (London: Allen and Unwin, 1977).

Hehn, Paul H., *A Low Dishonest Decade: The Great Powers, Eastern Europe, and the Economic Origins of World War II, 1930–1941* (New York and London: Continuum, 2002).

Heidegger, Martin, *Being and Time*, trans. John Macquarrie and Edward Robinson (1962; Oxford and Cambridge, MA: Blackwell, 2000).

Heidegger, Martin, *The Concept of Time*, trans. William McNeill (Oxford: Blackwell, 1992).

Heidegger, Martin, *Poetry, Language, Thought*, trans. Albert Hofstadter (New York: Harper and Row, 1975).

Hersey, John, 'Hiroshima' in *Reporting World War II: Part Two: American Journalism 1944–1946* (New York: Library of America, 1995).

Hill, Christopher, *Milton and the English Revolution* (London: Faber and Faber, 1977).

Hind, Dan, *The Threat to Reason* (London and New York: Verso, 2007).
Hitchens, Christopher, *Orwell's Victory* (London: Allen Lane, 2002).
Holt, Jim, 'It's the Oil', *London Review of Books* 29.20 (18 October 2007), pp. 3–4.
Hughes, Michael (ed.), *The Letters of Lewis Mumford and Frederic J. Osborn: A Transatlantic Dialogue 1938–70* (New York and Washington DC: Praeger, 1972).
Hughes, Thomas P. and Agatha C. Hughes (eds), *Lewis Mumford: Public Intellectual* (New York: Oxford University Press, 1990).
Johnson, Samuel, *The Lives of the Poets* (London: J.M. Dent, 1925).
Jones, Greta, *Social Darwinism and English Thought: The Interaction between Biology and Social Theory* (Brighton: Harvester Press, 1980).
Jung, Carl G., *The Inner Life of Childhood: A Study in the Analytical Psychology*, intr. Frances G. Wickes (New York and London: D. Appleton, 1929).
Kadarkay, Arpad, *Georg Lukács: Life, Thought and Politics* (Oxford: Blackwell, 1991).
Kallen, Horace M., 'Behind the Bertrand Russell Case', *TWICE A YEAR*, vols V–VI (Fall–Winter 1940), pp. 441–66.
Kaplan, Justin, *Walt Whitman: A Life* (New York: Simon and Schuster, 1980).
Kapp, Isa, 'Civilization and Steinberg', *The Reporter* (20 June 1950), p. 34.
Kazin, Alfred, 'A Note on John Quincy Adams', *TWICE A YEAR*, vols X–XI (1943), pp. 163–8.
Kazin, Alfred, 'John Quincy Adams, *Diary*', *TWICE A YEAR*, vols X–XI (1943), pp. 139–73.
Kazin, Alfred, 'War, Education and People (Britain)', *TWICE A YEAR*, vols XIV–XV (Fall–Winter 1946–7), pp. 120–43.
Keats, John, *The Letters of John Keats*, ed. Maurice Buxton Forman (London: Oxford University Press, 1948).
Keeley, Edmund, *Inventing Paradise: The Greek Journey, 1937–47* (New York: Farrar, Straus, and Giroux, 1999).
Kertesz, Louise, *The Poetic Vision of Muriel Rukeyser*, foreword by Kenneth Rexroth (Baton Rouge, LA: Louisiana State University Press, c.1980).
Khoury, Elias, *Gate of the Sun*, trans. Humphrey Davies (London: Harvill Secker, 2005).
King, Richard, *The Party of Eros: Radical Social Thought and the Realm of Freedom* (Chapel Hill, NC: University of North Carolina Press, 1972).
Klinenberg, Eric, *Fighting for Air: The Battle to Control America's Media* (New York: Metropolitan Books, 2007).
Kodolányi, Gyula, 'Lewis Mumford and the Metaphor of the Open System', *Annales Universitatis Scientiarum Budapestiensis* XVI (Budapest, 1985).
Koestler, Arthur, 'Scum of the Earth – 1942', *TWICE A YEAR*, vols X–XI (Spring–Summer, Fall–Winter 1943), pp. 81–90.
Kopp, Dominique, 'Russia the Polar Grab', *Le Monde Diplomatique* (September 2007), pp. 8–9.
Kühl, Stefan, *The Nazi Connection: Eugenics, American Racism and German National Socialism* (Oxford and New York: Oxford University Press, 1994).
Langer, Lawrence L., *Holocaust Testimonies: The Ruin of Memory* (New Haven, CT and London: Yale University Press, 1991).

Lechlitner, Ruth, review of Muriel Rukeyser, *A Turning Wind*, *New York Herald Tribune* (7 January 1940), p. 10.

Leigh Fermor, Patrick, *A Time of Gifts* (Harmondsworth: Penguin, 1979).

Levi, Carlo, 'From An Interview with Carlo Levi by Harvey Breit', *TWICE A YEAR* (tenth anniversary issue, 1948), pp. 190–4.

Levi, Primo, *If Not Now, When?*, trans. William Weaver (Harmondsworth: Penguin, 2000).

Lévi-Strauss, Claude, *Tristes Tropiques*, trans. John and Doreen Weightman (Harmondsworth: Penguin, 1973).

Library of America, *Reporting World War II* (New York: Library of America, 1995).

Lichtheim, George, *A Short History of Socialism* (London: Flamingo, 1975).

Litvinov, Ivy, *Moscow Mystery* (New York: Coward-McGann, c.1943).

Lowe, Sue Davidson, *Stieglitz: The Founding Father of Modern Photography* (London: Quartet Books, 1983).

Lowell, Robert, *Selected Poems* (London: Faber and Faber, 1965).

MacDiarmid, Hugh [Murray Grieve], *Hugh MacDiarmid: The Complete Poems, 1920–1976*, ed. Michael Grieve and W.R. Aitken (London: Brian & O'Keefe, 1978).

Macdonald, Dwight, 'The Bomb', *politics* (September 1945), pp. 258–9.

Macdonald, Dwight, *A Moral Temper: The Letters of Dwight Macdonald*, ed. Michael Wreszin (Chicago, IL: Ivan R. Dee, 2001).

Macdonald, Dwight, 'The Root is Man, I', *politics* (June 1946).

Macdonald, Nancy, *Homage to the Spanish Exiles: Voices from the Spanish Civil War*, preface by Mary McCarthy (New York: Insight Books, 1987).

Mackenzie, Donald A., *The Migration of Symbols* (New York: Alfred Knopf, 1926).

McLuhan, Marshall, *Understanding Media* (London: Routledge and Kegan Paul, 1964).

Macmillan, Duncan, 'A Single-Minded Polymath: Patrick Geddes and the Spatial Form of Social Thought', *Edinburgh Review* 88 (Summer 1992), p. 79.

Maga, Timothy P., *America, France and the Refugee Problem, 1933–1947* (New York and London: Garland, 1985).

Marcuse, Herbert, *One Dimensional Man: Studies in the Ideology of Advanced Industrial Society* (Boston, MA: Beacon Press, 1964).

Marin, John, *John Marin: Tributes by William Carlos Williams, Duncan Phillips, Dorothy Norman* (Berkeley and Los Angeles, CA: University of California Press, 1958).

Marin, John, *The Selected Writings of John Marin*, ed. and intr. Dorothy Norman (New York: Pellegrini & Cudahy, 1949).

Marino, Andy, *A Quiet American: The Secret Life of Varian Fry* (New York: St Martin's Press, 1999).

Marshall, Bill, *Victor Serge: The Uses of Dissent* (New York and Oxford, 1992).

Marx, Karl, *Capital Vol. I*, trans. Ben Fowkes (Harmondsworth: Penguin, 1976).

Marx, Karl, *Economic and Philosophic Manuscripts of 1844*, ed. Dirk J. Struik (London: Lawrence & Wishart, 1970).

Marx, Karl, *The Revolutions of 1848: Political Writings: Volume 1*, ed. and intr. David Fernback (Harmondsworth: Penguin with New Left Review, 1973).

Marx, Leo, 'Lewis Mumford: Prophet of Organicism' in Thomas P. Hughes and Agatha C. Hughes (eds), *Lewis Mumford: Public Intellectual* (New York: Oxford University Press, 1990), pp. 164–80.

Melville, Herman, *Moby-Dick, or The Whale* (New York: Library of America, 1983).
Melville, Herman, *Pierre, Israel Potter, The Confidence Man, Uncollected Prose, Billy Budd* (New York: Library of America, 1984).
Melville, Herman, *Typee, Omoo, Mardi* (New York: Library of America, 1982).
Mendelsohn, Everett, 'Prophet of Our Discontent: Lewis Mumford Confronts the Bomb' in Thomas P. Hughes and Agatha C. Hughes (eds), *Lewis Mumford: Public Intellectual* (New York: Oxford University Press, 1990), pp. 343–60.
Merleau-Ponty, Maurice, 'Marxism and Philosophy', *politics* (August 1947), pp. 173–5.
Miller, Donald L., *Lewis Mumford: A Life* (New York: Weidenfeld and Nicolson, 1989).
Miller, Donald L., 'The Myth of the Machine: I. Technics and Human Development' in Thomas P. Hughes and Agatha C. Hughes (eds), *Lewis Mumford: Public Intellectual* (New York: Oxford University Press, 1990), pp. 152–63.
Miller, Henry, 'Balzac and his Double', *TWICE A YEAR*, vols V–VI (1940–1), pp. 247–69.
Miller, Henry, *The Colossus of Maroussi* (1941; Harmondsworth: Penguin, 1967).
Mottram, Eric, *Blood on the Nash Ambassador: Investigations in American Culture* (London Hutchinson Radius, c.1993).
Mumford, Lewis, 'A Centre for the United Nations', *Journal of the AIA* (December 1946), pp. 254, 256, 258.
Mumford, Lewis, *The Condition of Man* (London: Secker & Warburg, 1944).
Mumford, Lewis, 'The Corruption of Liberalism', *The New Republic* (29 April 1940), p. 568.
Mumford, Lewis, *The Culture of Cities* (London: Secker and Warburg, 1938).
Mumford, Lewis, *Findings and Keepings: Analects for an Autobiography* (London: Secker and Warburg, 1976).
Mumford, Lewis, 'From Revolt to Renewal', Benjamin Franklin Lecture, University of Pennsylvania, 1950, reprinted in *Lewis Mumford at 100* (Philadelphia, PA: Graduate School of Fine Arts and Van Pelt Library, University of Pennsylvania, 1995).
Mumford, Lewis, 'Gentlemen, You are Mad!' *The Saturday Review*, XXI (2 March 194?), p. 6.
Mumford, Lewis, 'German Apologists and the German Record', *The Saturday Review of Literature* (11 August 1945), p. 6.
Mumford, Lewis, *The Human Prospect* (London: Secker and Warburg, 1956).
Mumford, Lewis, *Lewis Mumford and Patrick Geddes: The* Correspondence, ed. Frank G. Novak (London and New York: Routledge, 1995).
Mumford, Lewis, *The Lewis Mumford, Daniel Liebovitz Letters, 1923–1968*, ed. Bettina Liebowitz Knapp (Troy, NY: Whitston, 1983).
Mumford, Lewis, 'Lewis Mumford on the Future of London', *The Architectural Review*, XLVII.577 (January 1945), p. 9.
Mumford, Lewis, *Men Must Act* (London: Secker and Warburg, 1939).
Mumford, Lewis, *The Pentagon of Power* (London: Secker & Warburg, 1970).
Mumford, Lewis, 'Plea for Collective Bargaining between Labor and Management', *The New Republic* (8 November 1939), p. 64.
Mumford, Lewis, Review of Pitirim A. Sorokin, *Social and Industrial Dynamics*, *New Republic* (14 July 1937), p. 284.

Mumford, Lewis, Review of Walter Lippmann, *An Inquiry into the Principles of the Good Society, New Republic* (29 September 1937), p. 219.

Mumford, Lewis, *Sidewalk Critic: Lewis Mumford Writings on New York*, ed. Robert Wojtowicz (New York: Princeton Architectural Press, 1998).

Mumford, Lewis, *Sketches from Life* (New York: Dial Press, 1982).

Mumford, Lewis, *Technics and Civilization* (1934; London: Routledge, 1946).

Mumford, Lewis, *The Van Wyck Brooks, Lewis Mumford Letters: The Record of a Literary Friendship, 1921–1963*, ed. Robert Spiller (New York: E.P. Dutton & Co., 1970).

Mumford, Lewis, Waldo Frank, Dorothy Norman, Paul Rosenfeld and Harold Rugg (eds), *America and Alfred Stieglitz: A Collective Portrait* (Garden City, NY: Doubleday, Doran & Co., 1934).

Nairn, Tom, 'The Enabling Boundary', review article of Roberto Magabeira Unger, *What Should the Left Propose?* and *The Self Awakened* and Jacques Attali, *Une brève histoire de l'avenir, London Review of Books*, 29.20 (18 October 2007), pp. 5–7.

Neill, A.S., *The Problem Parent* (London: Herbert Jenkins, 1932).

Niebuhr, Reinhold, *Reflections on the End of an Era* (New York and London: Scribner's, 1934).

Niedecker, Lorine, *Niedecker and the Correspondence with Zukofsky, 1931–1970*, ed. Jenny Penberthy (Cambridge: Cambridge University Press, 1993).

Nicosia, Gerald, *Memory Babe: A Critical Biography of Jack Kerouac* (Harmondsworth: Penguin, 1986).

Nin, Anaïs, 'Birth', *TWICE A YEAR*, vol. I (Fall–Winter 1938), pp. 132–7.

Nin, Anaïs, *The Diary of Anaïs Nin, 1934–1939* (New York and London: Harcourt Brace Jovanovich, 1969).

Norman, Dorothy, *Alfred Stieglitz: Introduction to an American Seer* (New York: Duell, Sloan and Pearce, 1960).

Norman, Dorothy, 'Edgar Varèse: Ionisation-Espace', *TWICE A YEAR*, vol. VII (Fall–Winter 1941), pp. 259–60.

Norman, Dorothy, *Encounters: A Memoir* (San Diego, CA: Harcourt Brace, 1987).

Norman, Dorothy, *Indira Gandhi: Letters to an American Friend 1950–1984* (San Diego, CA: Harcourt Brace, 1985).

Norman, Dorothy, *Nehru: The First Sixty Years*, 2 vols (New York: John Day Company, 1965).

Norman, Dorothy, 'Writing and Conversations of Alfred Stieglitz', *TWICE A YEAR*, vol. I (Fall–Winter 1938), pp. 75–110.

Olson, Charles, 'Lear and Moby-Dick', *TWICE A YEAR*, vol. I (Fall–Winter 1938), pp. 165–89.

Olson, Charles, *The Human Universe and Other Essays* (New York: Grove Press, 1967).

Oppen, George, *The Collected Poems of George Oppen* (New York: New Directions, 1975).

Oppenheim, James, 'From the Foreword to Randolph Bourne's *Untimely Paper* (1919)', *TWICE A YEAR*, vol. I (Fall–Winter 1938), p. 37.

Orwell, George, *Homage to Catalonia* (Harmondsworth: Penguin, 1966).

Orwell, George, *Nineteen Eighty-Four* (1949; Harmondsworth: Penguin, 1987).

Pandit, Chandalekha, 'The Infanticide' and 'The Garden', *TWICE A YEAR* (Fall–Winter 1945), pp. 342–8.

Pandit, R.S. (ed., trans., intr.), *Ritusamhara* (Bombay: National Information and Publications, 1947).

Pandit, Vijaya Lakshmi, *The Scope of Happiness: A Personal Memoir* (1979; New Delhi: HarperCollins India, 2000).

Pappe, Ilan, *The Ethnic Cleansing of Palestine* (Oxford: Oneworld, 2006).

Pascal, Blaise, *Pensées*, trans. A.J. Krailsheimer (Harmondsworth: Penguin, 1966).

Pilger, John, *The New Rulers of the World* (London and New York: Verso, 2002).

Pilniak, Boris, 'Mahognany' in *Chinese Story and Other Tales*, trans. and intr. Vera T. Reck and Michael Green (Norman, OK and London: University of Oklahoma Press, 1988).

Pilniak, Boris, *The Naked Year*, trans. Alexander R. Tulloch (Ann Arbor, MI: Ardis, 1975).

Politkovskaya, Anna, *A Small Corner of Hell: Dispatches from Chechnya*, trans. Alexander Burry and Tatiana Tuchinsky, intr. Georgi Derluguian (Chicago, IL and London: University of Chicago Press, 2003).

Pope, Arthur Upham, *Maxim Litvinoff* (New York: L.B. Fisher, 1943).

Pound, Ezra, *ABC of Reading* (1951; London: Faber and Faber, 1961).

Pound, Ezra, *Literary Essays of Ezra Pound* (New York: New Directions, 1968).

Preuss, Herbert and Wilhelm Molitor, *Seefahrt-Fibel des deutschen Jungen* (Munich and Berlin: Lehmann, 1941).

Proust, Marcel, 'La mort de Baldassare Silvande Vicompte de Sylvania', trans. Emilie Amram, *TWICE A YEAR*, vol. II (Spring–Summer 1939), pp. 155–75.

Proust, Marcel, *Pleasures and Days*, trans. Andrew Brown (London: Hesperus, 2004).

Pullin, Faith (ed.), *New Perspectives on Melville* (Edinburgh: Edinburgh University Press, 1978).

Pynchon, Thomas, *The Crying of Lot 49* (1967; Harmondsworth: Penguin, 1974).

Pynchon, Thomas, *Mason & Dixon* (London: Jonathan Cape, 1997).

Pyros, John, *Mike Gold: Dean of American Proletarian Writers* (New York: Dramatika Press, 1979).

Reck, Vera T., *Boris Pil'niak: A Soviet Writer in Conflict with the State* (Montreal and London: McGill-Queen's University Press, 1975).

Reich, Wilhelm, *The Mass Psychology of Fascism*, trans. Vincent R. Carfagno (New York: Farrar, Straus, and Giroux, 1970).

Rexroth, Kenneth, *An Autobiographical Novel* (Weybridge: Wittet Books, 1977).

Ricoeur, Paul, *History and Truth*, trans. Charles A. Kelby (Evanston, IL: Northwestern University Press, 1965).

Ricoeur, Paul, *Lectures on Ideology and Utopia* (New York: Columbia University Press, 1986).

Ricoeur, Paul, *Memory, History, Forgetting*, trans. Kathleen Blamey and David Pellauer (Chicago, IL: University of Chicago Press, 2004).

Ricoeur, Paul, *The Reality of the Historical Past* (1984; Milwaukee, WI: Marquette University Press, 1998).

Ricoeur, Paul, *Time and Narrative*, 3 vols, trans. Kathleen Blamery, Katherine McLaughlin and David Pellauer (Chicago, IL: University of Chicago Press, 1984).

Riesel, Victor, 'June–December – 1941', *TWICE A YEAR*, vols VIII–IX (Fall–Winter 1942).

Riesman, David, 'Selections from writings on civil liberties', *TWICE A YEAR*, vols X–XI (Spring–Summer, Fall–Winter 1943), pp. 285–303.
Rilke, Rainer Maria, 'Some War-Time Letters', trans. M.D. Herter Norton, *TWICE A YEAR*, vol. I (Fall–Winter, 1938), pp. 11–36.
Rilke, Rainer Maria, *Rilke: Duino Elegies*, trans. Stephen Cohn (Manchester: Carcanet, 1989).
Rimbaud, Arthur, *Rimbaud, Complete Works, Selected Letters*, trans. Wallace Fowlie (Chicago, IL and London: University of Chicago Press, 1966).
Rimbaud, Arthur, *A Season in Hell and The Drunken Boat*, trans. Louise Varèse (New York: New Directions, 1961).
Rochberg-Halton, Eugene, 'The Transformation of Social Theory' in Thomas P. Hughes and Agatha C. Hughes (eds), *Lewis Mumford, Public Intellectual* (New York: Oxford University Press, 1990), pp. 127–51.
Roosevelt, Eleanor, 'I Learn about the Communists', *Saturday Evening Post* (22 February 1958), p. 59.
Rosenfeld, Paul. 'We want Varèse', *TWICE A YEAR*, vols V–VI (Fall–Winter, 1941), pp. 352–60.
Rowley, Hazel, *Richard Wright: The Life and Times* (New York: Henry Holt, 2001).
Rukeyser, Muriel, *The Collected Poems of Muriel Rukeyser* (New York: McGraw-Hill, 1978).
Rukeyser, Muriel, 'The Fear of Poetry', *TWICE A YEAR*, vol. VII (Fall–Winter 1941), pp. 15–31.
Rukeyser, Muriel, *The Life of Poetry* (New York: A.A. Wyn, 1949).
Rukeyser, Muriel, *MEDITERRANEAN* (New York: Writers and Artists Committee, Medical Bureau to Aid Spanish Democracy, n.d., c.1936–9).
Rukeyser, Muriel, 'Poetry and Time', typescript, n.d. (c.1967–8), transcript of a talk given at MIT, Muriel Rukeyser Papers.
Rukeyser, Muriel, Review of Archibald MacLeish, *Land of the Free*, *New Masses* (19 April 1938), p. 26.
Rukeyser, Muriel, *Theory of Flight* (New Haven, CT: Yale University Press, 1935).
Rukeyser, Muriel, *A Turning Wind* (New York: Viking, 1939).
Rukeyser, Muriel, 'We Came for Games', *Esquire* 82 (October 1974), pp. 192–4, 368–70.
Rukeyser, Muriel, *Willard Gibbs, American Genius* (New York: Doubleday, Doran & Co., 1942).
Rukeyser, Muriel, 'Words and Images', *New Republic* (2 August 1943), pp. 140–1.
Sahgal, Nayantara, *Prison and Chocolate Cake* (London: Victor Gollancz, 1954).
Santayana, George, *The Life of Reason: Or, The Phases of Human Progress* (New York: Scribner's, 1905–6).
Sartre, Jean-Paul, *Being and Nothingness: An Essay on Phenomenological Ontology*, trans. Hazel E. Barnes (New York: Philosophical Library, 1956).
Sartre, Jean-Paul, *Between Existentialism and Marxism*, trans. John Mathews (New York: Morrow Quill Paperbacks, 1970).
Sartre, Jean-Paul, *Critique of Dialectical Reason*, trans. Alan Sheridan-Smith (London: New Left Books, 1976).
Sartre, Jean-Paul, *Literary and Philosophical Essays*, trans. Annette Michelson (London: Radius /Hutchinson, 1968).

Sartre, Jean-Paul, *Mallarmé: la lucidité et sa face d'ombre* (Paris: Gallimard, 1986).
Sartre, Jean-Paul, 'Materialism and Revolution', trans. Ralph Manheim. *politics* (July–August 1947), p. 166.
Sartre, Jean-Paul, *Nausea*, trans. Robert Baldick (1938; Harmondsworth: Penguin, 1965).
Sartre, Jean-Paul, *Notebooks for an Ethics*, trans. David Pellauer (Chicago, IL and London: University of Chicago Press, 1992).
Sartre, Jean-Paul, *Politics and Literature*, trans. J.A. Underwood (London: Calder & Boyars, 1973).
Sartre, Jean-Paul, *Search for a Method*, trans. Hazel E. Barnes (New York: Vintage Books, 1968).
Schuler, Friedrich E., *Mexico between Hitler and Roosevelt: Mexican Foreign Relations in the Age of Lázaro Cárdenas* (Albuquerque, NM: University of New Mexico Press, 1998).
Schumacher, E.F., *Small is Beautiful: Economics as if People Mattered* (New York: Harper & Row, 1973).
Schweitzer, Albert, *Quest of the Historical Jesus*, 3rd edn, trans. W. Montgomery (London: Adam and Charles Black, 1954).
Segal, Howard P., 'Mumford's Alternatives to the Megamachine: Critical Utopianism, Regionalism, and Decentralization' in Thomas P. Hughes and Agatha C. Hughes (eds), *Lewis Mumford: Public Intellectual* (New York: Oxford University Press, 1990), pp. 100–9.
Sennett, Richard, *The Uses of Disorder: Personal Identity and City Life* (New York: Knopf, 1970).
Serge, Victor, 'Adieu à Gramsci', *La Wallonie* (8–9 May 1937).
Serge, Victor, *Conquered City*, trans. Richard Greeman (London: Victor Gollancz, 1976).
Serge, Victor, *Memoirs of a Revolutionary* (1951; Oxford: Oxford University Press, 1963).
Serge, Victor, *Mémoires d'un Révolutionnaire et autres écrits politiques*, ed. Jean Rière and Jil Silberstein (Paris: Robert Lafont, 2001).
Serge, Victor, *Men in Prison*, trans. Richard Greeman (London: Writers and Readers Publishing Cooperative, 1977).
Serge, Victor, *Midnight in the Century*, trans. Richard Greeman (London: Writers and Readers, 1982).
Serge, Victor, 'La tyrannie des fictions', *l'anarchie* (3 November 1911), reprinted in Victor Serge, *Le Rétif: articles parus dans 'l'anarchie', 1909–1912*, ed. Yves Pagès (Paris: Librairie Monnier, 1989).
Serge, Victor, *Year One of the Revolution*, intr. and trans. Peter Sedgewick (Chicago, IL: Holt Reinhardt and Winston, 1972).
Serge, Victor, 'Musée du Soir', *La Wallonie* (c.1939).
Shaw, George Bernard, 'From a Message to the Tagore Society', *TWICE A YEAR*, vols X–XI (Spring–Summer 1943), p. 64.
Shelley, Percy Bysshe, *Collected Poems*, ed. Thomas Hutchinson (Oxford: Oxford University Press, 1927).
Shelley, Percy Bysshe, *The Complete Works of Shelley* (New York: Gordian Press, 1965).

Silone, Ignazio, *The Abruzzo Trilogy: Fontamara, Bread and Wine, The Seed Beneath the Snow*, trans. Eric Mosbacher, rev. Darina Silone (South Royalton, VT: Steerforth Italia, 2000).

Silone, Ignazio, 'The things I stand for', *TWICE A YEAR*, vols X–XI (1943), pp. 91–5.

Smith DiBasio, Anne-Marie, '"The Ebb and Flow Of Conversation": A Metaphorics of Maternal Presence', *Études britanniques contemporaines* (Autumn 2004), p. 84.

Sontag, Susan, 'Cases of the Comrades: Why Victor Serge should be as Famous as Koestler and Orwell', *Times Literary Supplement* (9 April 2004), p. 15.

Sontag, Susan, *A Susan Sontag Reader*, intr. Elizabeth Hardwick (New York: Farrar, Straus, and Giroux, 1982).

Soros, George, *New York Review of Books* 54.6 (12 April 2007), http://www.nybooks.com/articles/20030.

Spingarn, J.E., 'Politics and the Poet: A Prophecy by J.E. Spingarn', *The Atlantic Monthly* 19 (November 1942).

Stieglitz, Alfred, *Stieglitz Memorial Portfolio* (eighteen photographs by Alfred Stieglitz) (New York: Twice a Year Press, 1947).

Sumner, Gregory D., *Dwight Macdonald and the* politics *Circle* (Ithaca, NY and London: Cornell University Press, 1996).

Tanner, Robin, *The Etcher's Craft* (Bristol: Friends of Bristol Art Gallery, 1980).

Tennyson, Alfred, *The Poems and Plays of Tennyson* (London: Oxford University Press, 1953).

Thomas, Hugh, *The Spanish Civil War* (New York: Harpers, 1961).

Thomas, John L., 'Lewis Mumford, Benton McKaye and the Regional Vision' in Thomas P. Hughes and Agatha C. Hughes (eds), *Lewis Mumford, Public Intellectual* (New York: Oxford University Press, 1990), pp. 66–99.

Thompson, D'Arcy Wentworth, *On Growth and Form* (Cambridge: Cambridge University Press, 1968).

Thompson, Edward, *William Morris: Romantic to Revolutionary* (London: Merlin Press, 1977).

Thoreau, Henry David, 'From: A Plea for John Brown', *TWICE A YEAR*, vol. I (Fall–Winter 1938), pp. 61–75.

Thoreau, Henry David, *Walden and Other Writings of David Henry Thoreau*, ed. Brooks Atkinson (New York: The Modern Library, 1937).

Tocqueville, Alexis de, *Œuvres complètes* (Paris: La nouvelle revue française, 1961).

Toller, Ernst, '"1933" from *I was a German*', *TWICE A YEAR*, vols III–IV (1940), pp. 155–8.

Toulmin, Stephen and June Goodfield, *The Architecture of Matter* (London: Hutchinson, 1962).

Trotsky, Leon, 'The USSR in War', *The New International* (November 1939).

Truffaut, François, *Hitchcock*, trans. François Truffaut (New York: Simon and Schuster, 1967).

Varikas, Eleni, 'Hitler's Hero: Heinrich Ford', *Le Monde Diplomatique* (May 2007), pp. 12–13.

Venturi, Franco, *Roots of Revolution: A History of the Populist and Socialist Movements in 19th Century Russia*, rev., ed. and intr. Isaiah Berlin (London: Phoenix Press, 1971).

Vernant, Jean-Pierre, *Myth and Tragedy in Ancient Greece*, trans. Janet Lloyd (New York: Zone Books, 1990).

Wald, Alan M., *Exiles from a Future Time: The Forging of the Mid-Twentieth-Century Literary Left* (Chapel Hill, NC and London: University of North Carolina Press, 2002).

Wallace, Max, *The American Axis: Henry Ford, Charles Lindbergh and the Rise of the Third Reich* (New York: St Martin's Press, 2003).

Weil, Simone, *La condition ouvrière* (Paris: Gallimard, 1951).

Weil, Simone, *Gravity and Grace*, trans. Arthur Wills, intr. Gustav Thibon (Lincoln, NE: University of Nebraska Press, 1997).

Weil, Simone, 'The Iliad, or the Poem of Force', trans. Mary McCarthy, *politics* (November 1945), pp. 321–31.

Weil, Simone, *Lectures on Philosophy*, trans. Hugh Price (Cambridge: Cambridge University Press, 1978).

Weil, Simone, *The Need for Roots: Prelude to a Declaration of Duties towards Mankind*, preface by T.S. Eliot, trans. A.S. Willis (1952; London and New York: Routledge, 1978).

Weil, Simone, 'Reflections on War', *politics* (February 1945), p. 52.

Weil, Simone, *The Simone Weil Reader*, ed. George A. Pachinas (Mount Kisco, NY: Moyer Bell, 1977).

Weinberg, Gerhardt L., *A World at Arms: A Global History of World War II* (Cambridge: Cambridge University Press, 1994).

Westbrook, Robert B., *John Dewey and American Democracy* (Ithaca, NY and London: Cornell University Press, 1991).

Whitman, Walt, *Collected Poetry and Collected Prose*, ed. Justin Kaplan (New York: Library of America, 1982).

Whorf, Benjamin Lee, *Language, Thought and Reality: Selected Writings of Benjamin Lee Whorf*, ed. and intr. John B. Carroll (Cambridge, MA: MIT Press, 1956).

Wickes, Frances G., *The Inner World of Childhood: A Study in Analytic Psychology*, intr. Carl G. Jung (New York and London: D. Appleton & Co., 1927).

Wickes, Frances G., *The Inner World of Choice* (Boston, MA: Sigo Press, 1963).

Williams, Rosalind, 'Lewis Mumford as a Historian of Technology in *Technics and Civilization*' in Thomas P. Hughes and Agatha C. Hughes (eds), *Lewis Mumford: Public Intellectual* (New York: Oxford University Press, 1990), pp. 42–65.

Williams, William Carlos, 'What of Alfred Stieglitz?', Alfred Stieglitz Papers.

Wordsworth, William, *Wordsworth: Poetry and Prose*, ed. W.M. Merchant (London: Rupert Hart-Davis, 1955).

Wreszin, Michael, *A Moral Temper: The Letters of Dwight Macdonald* (Chicago, IL: Ivan R. Dee, 2001).

Yates, Frances. A., *French Academies of the Sixteenth Century* (London: University of London Press, 1947).

Zukerman, Michael, 'Faith, Hope, Not Much Charity: The Optimistic Epistemology of Lewis Mumford' in Thomas P. Hughes and Agatha C. Hughes (eds), *Lewis Mumford: Public Intellectual* (New York: Oxford University Press, 1990), pp. 361–76.

INTERNET AND MEDIA RESOURCES

Anderson, Alexandra (dir.), 'A Life of Dissent: Remembering E.P. Thompson'. Channel 4 Rear Window series, 18 September 1994, produced by Tariq Ali.

'Arnould', 'Arthur', *The Anarchist Encyclopaedia: A Gallery of Saints and Sinners*, http://recollectionbooks.com/bleed/Encyclopedia/ArnouldArthur.htm.

Barenboim, Daniel, 'Masterclass with Lang Lang and Others', BBC 4, 30 May 2005.

Berlioz website, 'Berlioz in London', http://www.hberlioz.com/London/BerliozLondon.html.

Ebel, Miriam Davenport, *An Unsentimental Education*, posted at www.chambon.org, with permission of Dr Charles Ebel, © Miriam Davenport Ebel, 1999.

Evans, D.T.F., 'Le Play House and the Regional Survey Movement in British Sociology, 1920–1955', unpublished MPhil thesis, City of Birmingham Polytechnic, 1986, http://www.dfte.co.uk/ios

Goyau, Georges, 'Pierre-Guillaume-Frédéric Le Play', transcribed by Douglas J. Potter, *The Catholic Encyclopedia*, Volume XII, online edition, 2003 by K. Knight.

Gabriel, Gottfried, 'Carnap's "Elimination of Metaphysics Through Logical Analysis of Language": A Retrospective Consideration of the Relationship between Continental and Analytic Philosophy', trans. Andrew Inkpin, www.phil.cmu.edu/projects/carnap/jena/GabrielJena.rtf.

Landow, George P., 'Charles Haddon Spurgeon at Exeter Hall', *The Victorian Web: Literature, History & Culture in the age of Victoria*, http://65.107.211.206/religion/sermons/exeter.html.

Molokan website: http://gecko.gc.maricopa.edu/clubs/russian/molokan/.

Nupen, Christopher (dir.), 'We Want the Light: the Jews and German Music', written and directed by Christopher Nupen, executive producer Peter Maniura, BBC DVD, 2004.

Payne Papers in the Stony Brook Manuscript Collection (no. 293), http//www.sunysb.edu/libspecial/collections/manuscripts/payne/bio.

Saunders, Frances Stonar, 'The Meetings of Minds: Writers for the Defence of Freedom Conference, Paris, 1935', BBC Radio 3, 1 September 2005, produced by Matthew Dodd.

Wehling, Jason, 'Anarchism and the History of the Black Flag', http://www.anarchy-movement.com/topic.php?ID=47.

Victorian London website, 'Victorian London-buildings, Monuments and Museums – Exeter Hall', http://www.victorianlondon.org/buildings/exeterhall.html.

Index